In Final Defense of the Reich

AN ASSOCIATION OF THE U.S. ARMY BOOK

In Final Defense of the Reich

The Destruction of the 6th SS Mountain Division "Nord"

Stephen M. Rusiecki

NAVAL INSTITUTE PRESS
Annapolis, Maryland

Naval Institute Press
291 Wood Road
Annapolis, MD 21402

© 2010 by Stephen M. Rusiecki
All rights reserved. No part of this book may be reproduced or utilized in any form or by any means, electronic or mechanical, including photocopying and recording, or by any information storage and retrieval system, without permission in writing from the publisher.

First Naval Institute Press paperback edition published in 2021.
ISBN: 978-1-68247-678-9 (paperback)
ISBN: 978-1-61251-001-9 (eBook)

The Library of Congress has cataloged the hardcover edition as follows:
Rusiecki, Stephen M.
  In final defense of the Reich : the destruction of the 6th SS Mountain Division "Nord" / Stephen M. Rusiecki.
    p. cm.
  Includes bibliographical references and index.
  ISBN 978-1-59114-744-2
  1. Waffen-SS. SS-Gebirgs-Division Nord, 6. 2. World War, 1939-1945–Regimental histories–Germany. 3. World War, 1939-1945–Campaigns–Europe, Northern. I. Title.
  D757.85.R87 2010
  940.54'1343–dc22

2010021999

♾ Print editions meet the requirements of ANSI/NISO z39.48-1992 (Permanence of Paper).
Printed in the United States of America.

9 8 7 6 5 4 3 2 1

For Angie and JB, my everlasting inspirations
and
For my nephew, Evan, who showed me the true meaning of courage
and
For my parents, Mary and Ron, the first heroes I ever knew

Contents

List of Maps and Figures		viii
Foreword		ix
Preface		xi
Prologue		xvii
Chapter 1	Birth of the Nord Division	1
Chapter 2	Operation Nordwind and Beyond	23
Chapter 3	The Saar-Palatinate Falls	46
Chapter 4	Convergence	77
Chapter 5	Nord Falls Behind, 31 March 1945	91
Chapter 6	The First Day: Assenheim and Altenstadt, 1 April 1945	108
Chapter 7	The Second Day: Waldensberg, 2 April 1945	172
Chapter 8	The Second Day: Leisenwald, 2 April 1945	234
Chapter 9	The Third Day: Dissolution, 3 April 1945	284
Chapter 10	Completing the Record	323
Appendix A	Table of Comparative Ranks	356
Appendix B	Glossary of Terms and Equipment	358
Appendix C	Select Order of Battle	363
Notes		371
Selected Bibliography		415
Index		425

Maps and Figures

Maps

Map 1.1	Operation Birke, September–October 1944	13
Map 2.1	Operation Nordwind: Low Vosges Mountains, 4 January 1945	31
Map 3.1	6th SS-Gebirgs Division in the Saar-Palatinate, 7–30 March 1945	50
Map 3.2	71st Infantry Division in the Saar-Palatinate, 10–31 March 1945	66
Map 5.1	6th SS-Gebirgs Division's advance to the Büdingen forest, 31 March–1 April 1945	94
Map 6.1	6th SS-Gebirgs Division at Assenheim and Altenstadt, 1 April 1945	112
Map 6.2	2nd Battalion, 14th Infantry's attack north of Rodenbach, 1 April 1945, drawn by Lt. Col. Philip D. Brant, from Brant's scrapbook of his war experiences	143
Map 6.3	6th SS-Gebirgs Division in the Büdingen forest, 1–2 April 1945	170
Map 7.1	6th SS-Gebirgs Division east of Altenstadt, 2 April 1945	207
Map 8.1	6th SS-Gebirgs Division in the Büdingen forest, 2 April 1945	236
Map 9.1	6th SS-Gebirgs Division in the Büdingen forest, 3 April 1945	296

Figures

Figure 3.1	U.S. propaganda leaflet directed at the 6th SS-Gebirgs Division	69

Foreword

If in January 1945 one of my comrades had prophesied that sixty-one years later an American military historian would ask me to write a foreword for a book on the last battle of my division, I would have declared him insane. First, I would have expressed my doubts that I would live to see my twentieth birthday; second, the idea of my division being destroyed by the U.S. Army was still remote in those days; third, the Americans, or Amis as we called them, were our bitter adversaries, after all.

AND YET, BY THE WONDROUS WAYS OF FATE, a good many of us, if not many of the frontline troops, survived. We then built up our dreadfully destroyed country, and we met with our former adversaries to pay our respects and to share our remembrance with the former soldiers in the foxholes on the other side. Many a friendship sprang from these postwar gatherings.

To me this book is a rare example of a thoroughly researched and unbiased account in which a Waffen-SS division is the main subject. The sober and extraordinarily impartial presentation is what makes this book an outstanding work of World War II military history. Beside that fact, as a veteran of SS-Gebirgsjäger Regiment 11, I followed with growing fascination portraits of the two adversarial divisions emerge from the author's narration. And pursuing the final and deadly blows to the remnants of our once-proud unit was, once again, a shocking experience. Behind the sober description of leadership, tactics, persons, and events, all the images of our comrades lost in that final battle and before reappeared in my memory, together with the remembrance of our triumphs and defeats, of our hopes and frustrations, and of our endeavors to live up to our ideals—even when hope was lost.

Today, the surviving European age group that saw active service during World War II looks back on the remarkable course history has taken during the past sixty years. This war generation quickly transformed Europe from a war-torn stage of national rivalries into a prospering community of nations bound together by a common law and mutual economic dependencies that all but rule out future European wars. All this would not have happened without America's support. And the last great achievement, the overcoming of the Yalta postwar partition of the world along with the German unification, was also in great part due to America's determined course of action. A united Europe in freedom, now extending from the Atlantic coast to the Russian border, is, in my opinion, the true and final outcome of our bitter war of the 1940s.

Dr. Jochen Seeliger
Essen, Germany
30 August 2006

Preface

Spring 1945. Newspapers belched forth banner headlines of the Allies' battlefield progress in Germany: "First Armor Breaks Loose; Seventh Army over Rhine." "1st and 9th Armies Join, Cutting Off Ruhr, Germany Loses Last Great Industrial Area." "3 Allied Armies Cross Lower Rhine."[1]

THESE EXCITING HEADLINES graced the front pages of newspapers such as *The Stars and Stripes*, *The New York Herald Tribune*, and *The Evening Bulletin* of Philadelphia in the spring of 1945. The race for Germany's heartland was on, and the Allied armies in the west and their Russian allies in the east were rapidly crushing Germany in an iron vise. The atmosphere of excitement among the fast-moving American GIs in particular was electric with anticipation. An Allied victory was clearly in the cards—but no one seemed to have told the German armed forces.

Many historians have chronicled the events of March and April 1945 in Germany as a blur of pursuit operations with Allied forces in the west rolling almost effortlessly through Germany as scores of dispirited Wehrmacht troops surrendered without a fight. This general perception is clearly misguided. The last six weeks of the war in Europe represented some of the fiercest fighting on record. The German Army and the civilian populace were trapped between two converging Allied forces that demanded unconditional surrender, the mere thought of which stiffened their resolve and prompted them to fight to the last.

Scores of small, fierce, bitterly fought actions soon occurred throughout central Germany. Some of these smaller actions have warranted a mere footnote in history books about the last days of the war in Germany. For many soldiers on both sides, these violent, intense clashes were more than a simple footnote. One of these fierce, last-ditch battles—a battle that destroyed the remnants of a well-trained, experienced, and well-led Waffen-SS mountain division—occurred in the backyard of the town of Gelnhausen, Germany. From 1983 to 1987 Gelnhausen was my home—and my own backyard.[2]

As a young infantry lieutenant in Germany from 1983 to 1987, I spent my free time interviewing German World War II veterans about their combat experiences. My lifelong passion up to that point had been to write detailed combat histories of specific battles from the individual soldier's perspective. War is won at the level of the individual soldier; as a young, combat-inexperienced infantry officer I wanted to learn as much as possible about war's effects on the average soldier—but from "both sides of the hill."

While preparing a World War II history of our small *kaserne* (military installation or garrison) near Gelnhausen for one of our monthly Officer Professional Development sessions, I interviewed several older German men—former members of the Wehrmacht—who worked in the *kaserne*'s facilities engineer office. As these former German soldiers related the *kaserne*'s history to me, they mentioned that I should look into the "great battle" that had taken place in the forest to the north—the Büdingen forest. As part of our infantry training, our battalion often conducted numerous rucksack marches along the complex network of logging trails that ran throughout this dark, mystical forest.

Ever-curious about the mysterious Büdingen forest and intrigued by the suggestion of a "great battle" in my own *kaserne*'s backyard, I began seeking information about what had happened there during the war. At the time, my interest revolved around the Battle of the Bulge in December 1944 (the subject of my first book). Despite other interests, though, I decided to gather as much information about this Büdingen forest battle as possible.

During one of our battalion social functions, I met a German civilian who had been a longtime friend of the battalion—Günter Hengstmann of nearby Linsengericht. He told me he had been an officer cadet in the Waffen-SS and that his father's division, the 6th SS-Gebirgs Division Nord, had been the unit destroyed by the Americans in the Büdingen forest on Easter weekend in 1945. He invited me to his home the following weekend so we could talk in greater detail. I was hooked.

After dinner at the Hengstmanns's home, Günter told me about the battle with the 6th SS-Gebirgs Division. Hengstmann's father, Friedrich Hengstmann, had been a forty-three-year-old *SS-Sturmbannführer* with the division during its final battle in a small town named Leisenwald on the eastern fringe of the Büdingen forest. Günter warned me that the battle had severely affected the local townspeople—leaving wounds that had not healed after forty years. He mentioned a cemetery at a place called the Weiherhof that had particular significance. At the time I was not aware that he was alluding to a possible massacre, and he never told me what had happened to his father. I dared not ask.

In the coming weeks Günter provided me with copies of numerous fascinating but unpublished wartime accounts by the local populace. I visited Leisenwald and the surrounding towns and gathered as much information as possible. Then I let my research efforts rest until after my return to the United States.

Between 1987 and 1993 I was preoccupied with my Army career and my first book, on the Battle of the Bulge. While teaching English at West Point, I submitted my first book for publication in 1994 and began searching for the topic of my next project. The battle in the Büdingen forest on Easter weekend 1945 had long remained in the back of my mind, so I began researching the battle in earnest.

Since the American 71st Infantry Division was the Nord Division's chief adversary, I contacted the division's veterans association and obtained a roster of its members. Luck was with me: several battalion commanders and other senior officers were still alive. I was extremely fortunate to receive help from the 71st Division's historian, the prolific and gifted Gerald F. "Mac" McMahon. His assistance, generosity, and friendship proved invaluable. Unfortunately, he did not live to see this book in print. I truly miss him.

Next, I contacted the Nord Division's veterans association and received a letter from the editor of the association's publication, Dr. Jochen Seeliger. Seeliger, a brilliant veteran of the division and retired corporate and international lawyer, speaks perfect English; he became my link to the German veterans of the battle.

Details of the battle began to take shape. However, little information on this three-day event existed anywhere. Assembling the pieces to this puzzle had become my greatest research challenge.

In 1996 the Army (to my surprise and delight) sent me back to Germany for four more years. Armed with a plethora of first hand accounts from the 71st Infantry Division veterans (and some of the 5th Infantry Division veterans who had a supporting role in the battle), I began expanding my research from the German perspective.

Jochen Seeliger sponsored me at two Nord Division reunions in Bad Windsheim. The veterans welcomed me with open arms, and participants in the division's final battle in Leisenwald such as Georg Stöwe, Egon Krüger, and others readily shared their experiences with me.

In July 2000 I returned to the United States and was assigned to the Army's Inspector General Agency at the Pentagon in Washington, DC. I gathered additional research material from the National Archives in nearby College Park, Maryland, and, in the spring of 2001, I began the first chapter of what would be my greatest historical challenge—a detailed, blow-by-blow analysis of a battle during the last days of the war in Europe about which little information existed. I was breaking new ground.

The terrorist attacks of September 11, 2001, delayed my writing for several months as the U.S. Army geared up for the Global War on Terrorism. This delay proved uniquely fortuitous. I received a call from Philip Brant of Texas a month or two after the attack. Phil was the son of the late Lt. Col. Philip D. Brant whose battalion, the 2nd Battalion, 14th Infantry, had been the first to encounter the Nord Division. He had heard about my book project and offered to loan me a scrapbook his father had assembled in the weeks following war's end in Germany. I readily accepted.

When the scrapbook arrived, I was astonished. Lieutenant Colonel Brant had chronicled a day-by-day, first-person account of the war with original messages, orders, photographs, and sketches of specific battles. The scrapbook provided information I never imagined existed. Phil allowed me to keep the scrapbook for more than five years as I painstakingly wrote the history of this battle. I am eternally grateful to him, his sister Virginia, and the entire Brant family for the privilege of using the scrapbook—a true family heirloom—as a source for this book. With this final, one-of-a-kind source document in hand, I began piecing together the events that led to the destruction of the 6th SS-Gebirgs Division Nord.

My focus has always been on telling the stories of soldiers from both sides—the human aspect of battle. I judge no one, and I tell the story as it is, warts and all. I do not concern myself with anyone's political beliefs except as they have an impact on the battle itself. What these men endured in a war that changed the face of the second half of the twentieth century should give us pause and teach us to respect their individual sacrifices.

In an effort to insert as much realism as possible into the text, I used as many German and American terms as possible. German unit designations such as SS-Gebirgsjäger Regiment 11 for the 11th SS-Mountain Troop Regiment or *SS-Standartenführer* instead of *SS-Colonel* appear as they did during the war. Throughout the book I often use the phrase "SS man" to describe a member of the Waffen-SS. During the Third Reich, the term "SS-Mann" connoted a member of the Allgemeine (or General) SS who wore black uniforms and usually belonged to a politically oriented organization such as the secret state police. My use of the phrase "SS man" should not confuse the two: I am referring directly to members of the Waffen-SS.

I would further like to recognize the contributions of a few exceptional individuals whose assistance and guidance proved essential to the successful completion of this book. I am grateful to the late Ruth Zoepf, who kindly permitted me to use part of her late husband Wolf Zoepf's superb book *Seven Days in January* (Aberjona Press, 2001). W. P. "Pete" Sims readily provided me with a copy of his great wartime memoir *Blue Mike: The Story of Company M, 14th Infantry in World War II*, as well as a plethora of other information. Col. (Ret.) Edward W. Samuell Jr. offered numerous details about the battle and great insight into how a division cavalry reconnaissance troop operated during the war. The late Dr. David Ichelson shared with me his remarkably detailed memoirs of the 71st Infantry Division. The late Col. (Ret.) Bryce F. Denno sent me an invaluable, handwritten account of his battalion's actions in Leisenwald. My good friend Charles Graul helped me gain easy access to the National Archives in College Park, Maryland. I am grateful for the help and support of these and other individuals who provided me with their encouragement, time, and experiences—both German and American. Thank you one and all.

Last, I owe thanks to my wonderful wife, Angie, and my son, J. B., for their never-ending support of everything I have ever done or set out to do. Without them, nothing I do means anything.

I alone am responsible for any errors in interpretation or fact that appear in this book.

Prologue

SS-Gruppenführer *Karl Brenner stepped from outside the barn that housed his division command post and onto the rain-soaked cobblestone street. Although darkness filled the neighboring countryside, the town of Leisenwald was bathed in brilliant, flickering light. Scores of homes and farm buildings burned brightly. American mortar rounds whistled through the air and burst on rooftops or between houses. SS men from Brenner's command, the 6th SS-Gebirgs Division Nord, rushed about shouting for more ammunition and for more troops to move to the edge of town.*

THE SPEARHEAD OF Lt. Gen. George S. Patton Jr.'s Third Army had long since bypassed Leisenwald on its fast-paced, eastward drive into the heart of Germany. But the remnants of Brenner's combat-worthy division, bypassed by the Americans as well, had become a thorn in the backside of Patton's vanguard, the XII Corps. On Easter weekend April 1945, the Americans were about to put an end to that threat in their rear area once and for all.

On the eastern edge of Leisenwald, an American infantry company, supported by several tanks, was assaulting the town in an effort to eradicate the remnants of Brenner's once-powerful command. Shouts and curses in German and English filled the town as the two sides clashed in a final struggle that, for Brenner, would be his Waterloo. Small-arms and machine-gun fire echoed throughout the streets. Screams of "Medic!" and "*Sani!*" (short for *sanitäter*, or medic) seemed to follow each burst of fire.

Brenner looked wistfully back inside the cow barn at his staff officers bent low over maps and other documents as lanterns and hand-held flashlights flickered about them. Staff orderlies rushed to and fro across the hay-strewn floor handing messages to one another. *SS-Unterscharführer* Georg Stöwe and his team of radiomen (*funkers*) sat inside a nearby cattle stall and spoke steadily into radio handsets asking for reports or trying to contact other German units outside Leisenwald. A few division staff officers slept fitfully in the befouled hay, trying to capture for themselves a few brief moments of peace in the besieged cauldron of Leisenwald.

On a stool in the corner, nearly outside the glow of the numerous lanterns flickering inside the barn, sat the one officer on whom Brenner had relied greatly to get the Nord Division out from behind American lines and eastward to the German lines. This officer, *SS-Standartenführer* Helmuth Raithel, sat incapacitated with a large, bloodied bandage covering most of his head. He had recently been wounded in the eye fighting alongside the few remaining men from his SS-Gebirgsjäger Regiment 11. The medics had brought him directly to the division command post. Barely conscious, Raithel sat with his shoulders slumped, leaning against the wall. A medic tried to comfort him by gingerly adjusting his bandage.

The tableau both inside the barn and outside in Leisenwald seemed eerily like the last act of a Wagnerian opera. Chaos was in command, not Brenner. He could only rely on the leadership of his junior officers and sergeants to hold the Americans at bay. An American battalion blocked the division's escape route to the south; two infantry companies blocked the woods to the north. Standing and fighting was the only option—or was it?

As Brenner reentered the barn, he saw a young soldier, *SS-Sturmmann* Egon Krüger, standing in the doorway. The man looked forlorn and exhausted. Krüger had been separated from his 3rd Battalion, SS-Gebirgsjäger Regiment 11, during the fighting and was looking for someplace to go—or someplace to belong. Krüger quickly detected the chaos and uncertainty that consumed his division's command center. He looked apprehensively at Brenner. His eyes sought leadership and direction, but Brenner only feigned a smile and walked away. He could offer Krüger none of those things at the moment.

As Brenner sat down on a stool inside the command post, orderlies began handing him numerous messages. The communiqués were vague and unclear. The situation was deteriorating. Brenner could only reflect on a division that once boasted 22,000 troops but that had fewer than 2,000 remaining—and this group was fighting for its life on Easter weekend in a small cow town named Leisenwald in central Germany. How had this turn of events come to pass? How could such a storied, powerful SS mountain division that once held the Russians at bay in Finland become a mere shadow of its former self in the heart of the very country its men had sworn to defend?

CHAPTER 1

Birth of the Nord Division

The 6th SS-Gebirgs Division Nord began as SS-Kampfgruppe (Battle Group) Nord on 24 February 1941 when the Waffen-SS Headquarters in Berlin ordered SS-Infanterie Regiment 6 and SS-Infanterie Regiment 7 to form a battle group— or kampfgruppe—*around which the Waffen-SS could eventually build a division. These two regiments were already located in German-occupied southern Norway and would serve as one of the Wehrmacht's northern assault forces in the coming invasion of Russia in June 1941: Operation Barbarossa. Both hailed from Czechoslovakia— the 6th from Prague and the 7th from Brno—and, as early Allgemeine (or General) SS formations, had performed police-type duties only in the occupied Sudetenland. As a newly formed* kampfgruppe, *Kampfgruppe Nord lacked the type of combined-arms, multiechelon training that would make them a significant force in the coming war against Bolshevism. The SS men had had paramilitary training and could fire a rifle, but they could not yet employ effectively—as a unified force—the artillery, antitank, and other capabilities at their disposal.*[1]

By 15 March 1941 the nucleus of what would eventually become the 6th SS-Gebirgs Division Nord began to grow. The *kampfgruppe* received a full complement of staff personnel, a cartographic section, two Pionier (combat engineer) companies, a reconnaissance battalion, and a variety of service and support elements. *SS-Brigadeführer* Richard Herrmann soon arrived and assumed command. This hastily assembled hodgepodge of troops moved in April and May to northern Norway above the Arctic Circle in preparation for the coming offensive. While assembling in the Kirkenes region of northern Norway, another infantry regiment arrived, SS Infanterie Regiment 9, bringing the battle group closer to full strength.

As SS Kampfgruppe Nord sprang to life in Norway, Germany's diplomatic machinery moved into high gear. Germany wanted to exploit Finland's hatred for the Soviet Union, which stemmed from the three-and-half-month Russo-Finnish Winter War of 1939 and 1940. The Russians had invaded Finland on 30 November 1939, but the Finns held their own against a better-equipped and larger Red Army force. Embarrassed by poor battlefield results against a weaker enemy and with world opinion against them, the Soviets cut their losses and signed an armistice with Finland. Unfortunately for the beleaguered Finns, the peace settlement ceded to the Russians a large portion of territory known as the Karelian Isthmus. This bitter pill fueled an even greater hatred within the Finnish people for Russia, and a scheming Adolf Hitler hoped to use this pent-up rage to his—and Germany's—advantage.

Finland readily agreed to Germany's overtures for an ally in the upcoming invasion of Russia. The Finns saw an opportunity to regain their national honor and the territory they lost—all as part of what the Finns termed a Continuation War. The Finnish–German agreement allowed the newly motorized SS-Kampfgruppe Nord to move south into Finland and take up positions along the frontier territory between Russia and Finland. On 17 June *SS-Brigadeführer* Karl-Maria Demelhuber replaced Herrmann as Berlin upgraded the battle group to a motorized infantry division. The newly designated division moved once more on 18 June to final pre-invasion positions for Operation Barbarossa west of Russian-occupied Salla, in Finland.

Immediately after closing on their final assembly area west of Salla, the men of SS-Gebirgs Division Nord quickly prepared for combat. What Demelhuber found disturbed him greatly: Few commanders at the regimental and battalion level claimed even moderate experience with the ways of modern warfare. The antitank gunners had never fired their guns. The mixed bag of vehicle makes and models in the motorized fleet created severe maintenance problems. The division was not ready for combat, despite the men's high morale. Demelhuber reported his findings in writing to the XXXVI Korps commander, *General der Kavallerie* (Cavalry) Hans Feige, but his entreaties fell on deaf ears.[2]

❖

Germany invaded Russia on 22 June 1941, but offensive operations in the north did not begin until a week later. Finland was ready to attack but would not do anything to provoke the Russians—it would not even conduct reconnaissance. Russia would have to act first, and Finland's German partners in the north respected this decision.

Planning and preparation continued for the eventual attack that would seize the greatest prize in the north: the railway system running from the port of Murmansk on the Barents Sea to the heart of the Soviet Union in the south. Interdicting this railway and cutting the Russians off from a key international supply line was the ultimate objective.

The Finnish front was split into two separate operational areas. The Germans operated under Armee Oberkommando Norwegen (AOK Norwegen; Army High Command Norway) from Petsamo in the north to Uhtua in the middle of Finland; the Finnish armed forces under Field Marshal Baron Carl Gustav Mannerheim operated south of the German right flank.

On the day that Operation Barbarossa began, 22 June, Russian aircraft crossed the Finnish–Soviet frontier and bombed several small towns. Premier Johann Wilhelm Rangell convened the Finnish Parliament and, after a unanimous vote of confidence, on 28 June rescinded the ban on reconnaissance patrols and offensive operations. The next day *Generalleutnant* Eduard Dietl's Gebirgskorps Norwegen (Mountain Corps Norway) in the far north attacked to seize Murmansk. Feige's XXXVI Korps (with SS-Gebirgs Division Nord) and the Finnish III Corps followed and attacked on 1 July. Farther south the Finns under Field Marshal Mannerheim swept across the territory occupied by the Soviets in March 1940 and reclaimed much of the land in short order. The northern front did not give way as easily, however.

With the year-round "midnight" sun shining at their backs, the men of Feige's XXXVI Korps swept into the Salla wilderness. SS-Division Nord attacked with two regiments (SS-Infanterie Regiment 9 was with Dietl's corps in the north) directly through Salla's evergreen forests. The combination of no reconnaissance and poor infantry training resulted in disaster for SS-Infanterie Regiment 6 and SS-Infanterie Regiment 7. Nearly 20 percent of the officer and enlisted strength of both regiments became casualties in the first week of combat. This horrific first battle severely damaged the SS division's reputation in the eyes of the senior German leadership, and a full year would pass before the division could regain the confidence of the Wehrmacht's leaders.

SS-Division Nord's nightmare ended on 8 July when Kampfgruppe Schack of the 169th Infanterie Division encircled the Russian positions from the north. At the same time the Finnish 6th Infantry Division broke through in the south and threatened the Russians by nearly cutting off Salla from the rear. Unnerved by the coming double-envelopment, the Russian corps commander withdrew and handed Feige and his troops a respectable first victory.

The crisis in confidence created by SS-Division Nord's poor performance in the forest compelled Feige to disband the division temporarily. He sent SS-Infanterie Regiment 6 and the division's artillery regiment to the Finnish III Corps. SS-Infanterie Regiment 7 went to the 169th Infanterie Division, and the reconnaissance battalion moved south to screen for the Finnish 6th Infantry Division. These new assignments proved extremely beneficial to the men of SS-Division Nord, who learned from experienced, capable, and well-led German and Finnish soldiers. SS-Infanterie Regiment 9 benefited as well after *Generalleutnant* Dietl released the regiment from its security mission on the coast of the Arctic Ocean.

Within a matter of days, the XXXVI Korps attacked and by 1 September had captured Alakurtti. The corps consolidated its gains and settled into defensive positions—positions the corps would successfully occupy and defend until the Wehrmacht left Finland in September 1944.

In the south the Finnish III Corps attacked east toward Louhi and quickly gained ground. The Nord men soon learned from the Finns a new and highly effective technique for reducing small pockets of enemy resistance—smaller, multiple envelopments against the Russians called *mottis* that worked particularly well in the dense, wooded areas.

Despite the III Corps' successes, casualties ran high. By 25 August the Finns were too exhausted to continue. Even though the SS men were learning to fight with skill and courage beside their Finnish brothers-in-arms, the Russians still exacted a heavy toll on their ranks. Two of the three SS battalions could only muster 280 men between them at the end of August.

As the Finnish troops dug in, AOK Norwegen shifted Nord's remaining infantry troops (two battalions from SS-Infanterie Regiment 7) from XXXVI Korps to III Corps to help the Finns defend the area. The SS troops arrived in Kuusamo by 2 September, and SS-Division Nord existed as a combined force once again.

At the end of August, Nord saw the first influx of replacements since the war began. Nearly seven hundred well-trained Waffen-SS soldiers arrived at the SS replacement battalion in Kokosalmi to receive further training in forest warfare before moving forward to fill the many gaps in the division's ranks. Unlike the original police-trained members of Nord, these men received advanced training in infantry combat skills. In October *SS-Brigadeführer* Demelhuber left the division, and *SS-Standartenführer* Scheider, the commander of SS-Infanterie Regiment 6, assumed temporary command.[3]

AOK Norwegen ordered another offensive in November—the last one of the year—aimed once more at cutting the Murmansk rail line. The attack started on 1 November 1941 in bitterly cold temperatures at least two degrees below 0° Fahrenheit. Using the familiar *motti* encirclements to reduce enemy strongholds, the Finnish III Corps advanced toward Louhi led by a battle group from SS-Division Nord. Kampfgruppe Schreiber—commanded by *SS-Sturmbannführer* Franz Schreiber—encircled a large group of Russians north of the road to Louhi. The Russians defended doggedly. SS-Infanterie Regiment 7 alone killed at least 1,400 Soviet soldiers and took more than 500 prisoners. But the SS units lost at least one 100 dead from 1 to 13 November, and nearly 400 wounded. Similarly high casualty rates among the Finnish ranks drew shocked responses from the Finnish government.

Staggered by their losses and with winter at hand, the Finns halted the attack on 17 November. Pressure from the Finnish government about irreplaceable casualties (Finland only had a population of about 3.5 million in 1941) and the fact that the United States had warned the Finns about severing the Murmansk rail line and cutting off American lend-lease products to the Soviets caused both the Finns and the Germans to squander an opportunity for continued success. The November offensive thus became Germany's and Finland's last attempt to cut the Murmansk rail line—which would be a strategic blow for the German troops fighting on the Eastern Front farther south.

New replacements continued to fill the defending SS-Division Nord's ranks throughout the winter. The high casualty rates had caused nearly a complete turnover in personnel among the infantry units, thus reshaping the division dramatically with trained and professional infantry troops. One unique aspect of these replacements was that many of them were not German citizens but rather ethnic Germans, or *Volksdeutsche*, from Southeast Europe and former German provinces of the Austro-Hungarian Empire. These troops were German in culture and language and assimilated well into the ranks of the Nord Division, forming one of the first SS divisions to boast a truly multi-European flavor. But even by late January 1942, the division's ranks had not swelled to full strength. Nearly two thousand troop vacancies remained.

Even before AOK Norwegen launched the November attack against the Russians, Oberkommando der Wehrmacht (OKW; German Armed Forces High Command) issued new orders to the AOK to protect the nickel mines south of Petsamo and to prepare to seize the Fisher Peninsula and the Murmansk rail line sometime in 1942.

German preparations for a spring offensive stalled when the Russians attacked on 24 April 1942. The 23rd Guards Division, the 8th Ski Brigade, and the 80th Independent Brigade slammed into the northern section of SS-Division Nord's positions with terrific force. The SS men thwarted the Russian onslaught, but the 8th Ski Brigade managed to envelop the SS men from the north and nearly cut the German supply route. The Germans immediately counterattacked and blunted the Russian drive. Using numerous *mottis* to destroy the Soviet forces in bits and pieces, the SS men and their adjacent unit, Finnish Division J, spoiled the Russian effort. The Soviets lost nearly 15,000 troops in the month long offensive. Nord's losses included 2 officers and 157 men killed, and about 800 officers and men wounded.[4] By 23 May the entire operation dissolved and relative quiet returned to the German front line.

Continued supply problems for SS-Division Nord prompted OKW to reorganize the division into a reinforced mountain division. On 17 June 1942 SS-Division Nord became SS-Gebirgs Division Nord in an effort to solve the problems created by the division's nearly two-hundred kilometer supply line. The supply trains comprised two echelons for pushing supplies forward: a valley section (*talstaffel*) stockpiled the supplies in the rear, and a pack mule train—the mountain section (*bergstaffel*)—brought the supplies forward to the frontline positions. The SS men also received two battalions of twenty-four 75-mm pack howitzers in place of their slow-moving, heavy 105-mm artillery pieces, as well as one battalion (twelve guns) of truck-drawn light 105-mm howitzers and a heavy battalion with two batteries (eight guns in each) of 150-mm howitzers.

The shape of the infantry regiments changed dramatically as well. The 1st Battalion, SS-Infanterie Regiment 6, became the 1st Battalion, SS-Gebirgs Infanterie Regiment 6. Likewise, the 3rd Battalion, SS-Infanterie Regiment 7, became the 3rd Battalion, SS-Gebirgs Infanterie Regiment 6. SS-Infanterie Regiment 7's 1st Battalion converted to a separate motorized rifle battalion called SS-Schützen (Rifle)-Battalion Nord, motorized. Using the 1st and 3rd battalions, the division organized two complete mountain regiments with seasoned officers and noncommissioned officers from the other battalions. The absence of a third regiment was normal for a German mountain or infantry division at the time.⁵

Freshly trained replacements arrived ready to fight. But the new division commander, *SS-Brigadeführer* Mathias Kleinheisterkamp, who replaced Scheider on 1 April 1942, established a training site at Oulu to indoctrinate the new SS men into the combat peculiarities they would face in the heavily forested, arctic environment.⁶

In the summer of 1942, the Finnish III Corps returned to Finnish command. Responsibility for the Kiestinki-Louhi front now fell to a new formation, the XVIII Gebirgskorps (Mountain Corps) under the command of *General der Gebirgstruppen* Franz Böhme. This corps contained SS-Gebirgs Division Nord and the newly arrived 7th Gebirgs Division, creating a clear line between the German and Finnish forces. The Germans held the line from the Kiestinki-Louhi sector northward to the Arctic Ocean, while the Finns held everything to the south.

The rest of 1942 remained relatively quiet. The Nord Division continued to receive mountain-related equipment such as snowshoes, skis, and boat-like sleds (called *akjas*) to pull heavy equipment while sending out platoon-sized groups for a week at a time to infiltrate Russian lines and keep the Nord men's skills sharp.

❖

The division settled into a routine in 1943 that allowed the troops to sharpen further their defensive and patrolling skills. The Russians repeatedly attempted to outflank the Nord men's positions north of the division's flank. But the now-seasoned division consistently held the line, resulting in a reputation of reliability and battlefield worthiness that substantially raised the Nord Division's stock in the eyes of the senior German leaders.

The division's strength continued to increase throughout 1943. Nord began the year with 560 officers and 20,176 noncommissioned officers and soldiers, which left the division short by 165 officers and 950 troops.⁷ The quality of the average mountain-infantry replacement increased greatly in 1943 as well. The division's training battalion near Berchtesgaden and the Austrian border schooled new SS mountain-troop recruits vigorously in the art of mountain and cold-weather warfare.⁸

The Waffen-SS divisions throughout the Wehrmacht also completed a full reorganization program in 1943 that assigned a number to each SS division and regiment based on each unit's seniority. SS-Gebirgs Division Nord became the 6th SS-Gebirgs Division Nord, a designation that would remain with the division until the unit's final days in April 1945. Likewise, SS-Gebirgs Infanterie Regiment 6 and SS-Gebirgs Infanterie Regiment 7 changed to 11 and 12, respectively. In addition, the newly designated SS-Gebirgsjäger (Mountain Infantry) Regiment 11—commanded at this time by *SS-Obersturmbannführer* Paul Herms—received a name in keeping with a Waffen-SS tradition of awarding honorific titles to regiments and divisions based on the Teutonic and Third Reich heritage of the SS divisions.[9] In this case, SS-Gebirgsjäger Regiment 11 received the title "Reinhard Heydrich" after the former Sicherheitsdienst (State Security Service) chief of the same name and the architect of the so-called Final Solution against the Jews. British-trained Czech commandos had assassinated Heydrich the previous year in Prague, and the Waffen-SS hierarchy chose to recognize the regiment's earlier connection to that city by naming the 11th after this most feared and brutal man.

The 6th SS-Gebirgs Division Nord received another boost in combat strength in 1943 with the addition of a Norwegian volunteer police company and a Norwegian volunteer ski battalion—the SS-og Polit Company and SS-Ski Battalion Norge (Norwegian for "Norway"). In addition, young, well-trained Waffen-SS mountain-troop replacements continued to stream into the division from Germany throughout the fall and early winter of 1943. The new division commander as of 15 January 1944, *SS-Gruppenführer* Lothar Debes, would need these well-trained replacements and additional combat units in 1944 when the situation changed drastically on the northern front.

❖

The Soviet forces in the north had prepared throughout the winter of 1943 and 1944 to launch a powerful offensive against the German and Finnish forces defending the Ladoga-Karelia front. The Russian offensive began on 7 March 1944 at 0100 with an assault on the 6th SS-Gebirgs Division's extreme left flank near Shapkozero. A strongpoint on this flank manned by one platoon from SS-Gebirgs Reconnaissance Battalion 6 and the 2nd Company of SS-Ski Battalion Norge suffered the brunt of the enemy incursion. Dislodged but determined to retake their burned lodgments, the SS men counterattacked. By daybreak the shocked and disorganized Russian troops had fallen back. A counterattack a few hours later fizzled out, and the Russians fell back in disorder. The first part of the Soviet offensive of 1944 had apparently failed.

The Russian attack on the German left flank in March proved to be a precursor to the actual offensive, however. On 10 June 1944 the Soviets slammed into the Finnish forces defending the Karelian Isthmus to the south. The weight and scale of the Russian attack staggered the Finns. The Finnish people clamored for peace, and the Finnish Army could not weather the continued losses. Still smarting from Italy's surrender to the Allies in late 1943, Hitler and the OKW feared another alliance debacle in the north with the Finns.

As the fighting raged farther south in the Finnish sector, SS-Gebirgsjäger Regiment 12 received an honorific title just as its sister regiment, the 11th, had on 21 June. The title "Michael Gaissmair," a sixteenth-century South Tyrolean (Germanic) folk hero, sought to honor the presence of so many ethnic Germans assigned to the division.[10]

The rapid and inexplicable turnover in division commanders also continued. One month prior to the main Russian offensive on 10 June, *SS-Gruppenführer* Debes had relinquished command of the division to *SS-Obergruppenführer* Friedrich-Wilhelm Krüger, an aggressive and talented officer who would command the division briefly but skillfully during the summer months.[11]

A few days later German forces defending north of the Finns entered the fray at Sennozero. Nearly three Soviet divisions slammed into the extreme left flank of the Nord Division's positions. The Russians breached the German left flank and turned south behind the 6th SS-Gebirgs Division's frontline positions. Alarmed, *General der Infanterie* Friedrich Hochbaum released his XVIII Gebirgskorps reserve battalion, Ski Battalion 82. Krüger followed his commander's lead and released Nord's reserve, SS-Schützen Battalion 6 (motorized), as well. The two battalion commanders rushed their troops to the breakthrough area and, in a coordinated attack lasting several days, repelled the Russian forces. Both battalion commanders—*SS-Hauptsturmführer* Gottlieb Renz of SS-Schützen 6 and *Hauptmann* K. W. Lapp of Ski 82—received Germany's highest decoration for thwarting a possible Soviet encirclement—the Knight's Cross of the Iron Cross.[12]

Krüger ordered *SS-Hauptsturmführer* Walter Jensen's 3rd Battalion of the 12th Regiment to relieve the exhausted men of SS-Schützen Battalion 6 in place. At the same time, parts of SS-Gebirgsjäger Regiment 11 pulled out of their defensive positions along the road to Louhi and marched north to secure the front south of the lake at Sennozero.[13]

The Russians soon realized that a new German force blocked their repeated attempts to punch through the road position, so the Soviets opted to use a new tactic: propaganda. Loudspeakers belched forth messages from "converted" German prisoners that derided fascism and celebrated Bolshevism. The SS men ignored these oafish attempts to coax the German troops into surrendering.

On 23 August 1944 *SS-Obergruppenführer* Krüger departed the division for another assignment on the Eastern Front. He gave Knight's Cross–recipient *SS-Standartenführer* Gustav Lombard temporary command of the division until the new commander's arrival on 1 September.[14]

The brief pause in early August allowed *SS-Oberführer* Berthold Maack, the commander of SS-Gebirgsjäger Regiment 11 who had succeeded *SS-Obersturmbannführer* Herms in early 1944, to depart for Germany to attend a training course for division commanders. Maack's departure left no officer in the SS grade of lieutenant colonel or higher to lead the regiment. Therefore, *SS-Sturmbannführer* Ernst Rädeke, a senior member of the division staff, assumed command.[15]

On 1 September the last man to command the 6th SS-Gebirgs Division Nord arrived and took charge. He was *SS-Gruppenführer und Generalleutnant der Waffen-SS und Polizei* (Police) Karl-Heinrich Brenner; he had a long, distinguished history of military and police service. Born on 19 May 1895 Brenner volunteered for the army on 3 August 1914. After brief service in a handful of field artillery units, he joined Feldartillerie (Field Artillery) Regiment 10 "von Scharnhorst" and served with that unit through the First World War. In 1915 he joined the officer ranks as a lieutenant.

When that war ended in November 1918, Brenner remained in the Reichwehr, the 100,000-man, marginally equipped army dictated by the Treaty of Versailles. After leaving his artillery regiment on 15 January 1919, he was posted to a *freikorps* (free corps) unit, Baden Volunteer Battalion "Ost" (East), and Infanterie Regiment 7. A year earlier, he joined the police and served actively in that capacity while performing his other military duties.[16]

A strong supporter of Hitler, Brenner joined the Nazi party on 1 May 1933. His army assignments led him to attend the artillery school in Jüterbog in 1935 followed by a posting to Artillerie Regiment 4 in Ulm in September of that same year. By 1936 Brenner had earned the rank of *Oberstleutnant*. On 1 July 1938 Brenner transferred to the elite Waffen-SS with the equivalent grade of *SS-Obersturmbannführer*—a career move that Brenner must have thought would benefit his future military aspirations immensely.[17]

Brenner rose quickly through the ranks of the Waffen-SS. He experienced firsthand the Wehrmacht's new blitzkrieg tactics employed during the Polish and French campaigns in 1939 and 1940. When Germany invaded Russia on 22 June 1941, Brenner (an *SS-Standartenführer* since 20 April 1939) was in command of the Waffen-SS Polizei Division's artillery regiment. By 30 January 1942 he was an *SS-Brigadeführer*, and by October he was a member of the command group of an SS Panzer (Tank) Corps. His remarkable success and wartime career prospects in the Waffen-SS seemed almost limitless.[18]

In September 1944 Brenner's focus shifted to antipartisan warfare on the Eastern Front. He assumed command of Korpsgruppe (Corps Group) von Gottberg, which was charged with combating the nefarious *banden* (partisan) operations that consistently nagged the German armed forces' rear areas. As the commander of this antipartisan battle group in the Balkans, Brenner (an *SS-Gruppenführer* since 15 March 1944) learned to command forces fighting separately from one another and often against varying enemies and objectives. His up-front style of combat leadership earned him the esteemed Deutsche Kreuz in Gold (German Cross in Gold), which he added to his other numerous combat decorations such as the 1939 clasp to his 1914 Iron Cross, First Class, and the Infantry Assault Badge. Brenner's brand of leadership had cost him his left eye; he wore a black patch over the empty socket. His impressive combat résumé clearly lacked the mountaineering background required to command a mountain division, but the forty-eight-year-old Brenner's ability to act quickly and decisively under dynamic and chaotic circumstances would serve the men of the Nord Division well in the coming months.[19]

On 7 September 1944 Hitler's worst fears in the north were realized. OKW had learned that the Finns were meeting in secret with the Russians to discuss Finland's withdrawal from the war and a proclamation of neutrality. Nord Division messengers arrived at the regimental command posts bearing large, sealed brown envelopes outlining the details of Operation Birke (German for Birch), a phased withdrawal of all German forces from Finland back to Norway and finally to Germany (see Map 1.1).

The concept of Operation Birke seemed daunting. The entire 20th Gebirgs Armee Lapland would withdraw west and northwest over a mere two routes. The corps occupying the southern sector—the XVIII Gebirgskorps—would move first with the 6th SS-Gebirgs Division Nord and the 7th Gebirgs Division along a central route running northwest from Rovaniemi along the Swedish–Finnish border to a central route that intersected with the Norwegian coastal road the Germans officially named Reichsstrasse 50. The other two corps—the XXXVI and the XIX Gebirgs—would use this route as well once they had arrived in Norway.

Time became an essential factor in the withdrawal. The Germans learned that the negotiations included a concession by the Finns that the Finnish armed forces would disarm all Wehrmacht forces remaining in Finland after 15 September.

On 8 September SS-Gebirgsjäger Regiment 11 and Regiment 12 and the Nord Division's supporting troops began withdrawing from the frontline positions. The division was at more than full strength in both personnel and equipment (approximately 22,000 troops) due to an effort to expand the 6th SS-Gebirgs Division into a two-division corps. But the current departure from Finland prevented that plan from reaching fruition.[20]

Regiment 11 and Regiment 12 met on 10 September at a fallback position constructed for the XVIII Korps during the summer between two lakes west of the Sohjana River. Since the 11th Regiment was the rear-guard force for the entire corps during the move from Kiestinki to Kuusamo, the Reinhard Heydrich troops remained in place while the 12th Regiment continued west, crossing the Finnish frontier on 12 September.[21]

The pursuing Russian 26th Army harried SS-Gebirgsjäger Regiment 11 mercilessly. Near the small hamlet of Tuhkalla (about forty kilometers west of Kiestinki), the Russians bypassed to the west the overstretched SS column and blocked the road, cutting off the regiment from the rest of the Nord Division. Another Russian force separated the regiment from its rear-guard force, the 2nd Battalion, farther east of Tuhkalla.[22]

Map 1.1. Operation Birke (Birch): The German Withdrawal through Finland, September–October 1944. Credit/source: Based on a map in *Seven Days in January*, by Wolf T. Zoepf (Aberjona Press, 2001).

Determined to reunite his rear guard with the main body as quickly as possible, *SS-Sturmbannführer* Rädeke, the regimental commander, focused the regiment's attention on the eastern roadblock. *SS-Hauptsturmführer* Günther Degen led his 1st Battalion in a close-quarters assault against the Russians through thickly wooded terrain to rescue the encircled 2nd Battalion. Degen, a twenty-seven-year-old former druggist and longtime veteran of the SS (he enlisted with SS-Regiment "Germania" in July 1935), had joined the Nord Division in April 1943. This daring and energetic battalion commander led his 1st Battalion in helping the 2nd Battalion break through to the main body. The 11th Regiment was whole once more. The date was 20 September.[23]

Rädeke wasted no time in rearranging his forces for a breakthrough to the west—in the opposite direction. On the eastern side of the roadblock, SS-Gebirgsjäger Regiment 11's mountain battalions and supporting weapons organized to attack the Russian roadblock. Two Vierlingsflak 38 Wirbelwind (Whirlwind) four-barreled antiaircraft guns, each on an armored chassis, poured a steady stream of 2-cm rounds directly into the Russian defenses. *SS-Hauptsturmführer* Degen stood up in the middle of the road, raised his arm, and yelled for his three remaining infantry companies to follow him. Shocked by this brash display, the Russians vacated their positions and ran screaming into the nearby forest. The 11th Regiment had broken free of the Russian encirclement. The exhausted men of the 11th Regiment marched forth from the pocket and met the battalion from SS-Gebirgsjäger Regiment 12 that Brenner had sent to assist them. Realizing they were too late to help, the 12th Regiment's men lined up along the road and cheered their comrades.[24]

At Kuusamo, SS-Gebirgsjäger Regiment 12 met up with the division's service-support units and held fast. The Nord Division—minus the 11th Regiment—began preparing for the long foot march out of Finland.

Before departing Kuusamo, the commander of the 12th Regiment, *SS-Standartenführer* Schreiber, suspected that the Russian units pursuing the withdrawing German forces would occupy and raze the recently evacuated village. Still feeling a strong kinship with the Finnish people, Schreiber believed that the ultimate fate of the village at the hands of the Red Army was too terrible to contemplate. The seventeenth-century Lutheran church that stood in the town's center served as the centerpiece of the village community, and the two bells in the church (the larger one a gift from the Swedish king in 1698) meant a great deal to the local populace. In an act of compassion, Schreiber ordered his engineers to remove both bells and bury them near the village. The engineers documented the burial site with a precise sketch of the area so the villagers could locate and recover the hidden relics after the war.25

❖

SS-Standartenführer Franz Schreiber represented one of the Nord Division's finest and most respected leaders. He had assumed command of SS-Gebirgsjäger Regiment 12 nearly two years earlier on 1 December 1942 when the unit's title was still SS-Gebirgs Infanterie Regiment 7. Born in Dresden on 8 May 1904 as the seventh son of a businessman, Schreiber joined the small 100,000-man German Army (Heer) in 1920. As a member of Kavallerie Regiment 12, he aspired to become an officer but had failed to finish high school—a prerequisite for officer candidacy. Dejected, Schreiber served out his twelve-year stint in the army as a noncommissioned officer. He left the Reichwehr on 31 January 1933 as an *Oberfeldwebel*.

When Hitler came into power several months later, Schreiber saw an opportunity to become an officer in Führer Hitler's new army. On 19 March 1935 he rejoined the uniformed army, hoping to earn a commission as a reserve officer. But the army was not interested in reserve officers. They needed instructors. Disheartened, he served another two years as an instructor before his fifteen total years of service disqualified him from ever becoming an army officer. He finally left the army on 30 April 1937.

But Schreiber's army résumé held great weight in the fast-growing ranks of the SS. Hungry for experienced soldiers, the SS embraced Schreiber and offered him a chance to become an officer in the SS. A delighted Schreiber immediately joined SS-Regiment Germania as an *SS-Obersturmführer* on 1 June 1937. He commanded a company and quickly rose to the rank of *SS-Hauptsturmführer*; in 1941 Schreiber joined the Nord Division in Finland as a battalion commander.

Schreiber quickly earned an enviable reputation for exceptional combat leadership and bravery. His numerous decorations became a visible record of his battlefield successes and personal courage. By the time he became a regimental commander (and later an *SS-Standartenführer* on 9 November 1943), Schreiber had earned both the First and Second Classes of the Iron Cross, the Infantry Assault Badge, and the coveted German Cross in Gold. Remarkably, this frustrated, would-be army officer finally had found a home in the Waffen-SS and ultimately became one of the pillars of strength on which the Nord men depended for guidance and motivation.[26]

❖

SS-Gebirgsjäger Regiment 12 departed Kuusamo as the corps' rear guard on 26 September after the 11th Regiment passed through the village on the heels of the 7th Gebirgs Division.[27] The Soviets arrived the next day and occupied Kuusamo, burning the village to the ground as *SS-Standartenführer* Schreiber had anticipated.

The men of the 6th SS-Gebirgs Division Nord continued their trek westward to Rovaniemi. Since the 15 September deadline had long passed, the Soviets compelled the Finns to capture or expel all remaining Germans in Finland in accordance with the armistice signed a month earlier. Soviet liaison officers were attached to each Finnish unit to ensure compliance. This active role in expelling the Finns' former brothers-in-arms might convince the Russians that the Finnish–German partnership was truly shattered and thus avoid offering Josef Stalin a reason to occupy Finland. The Finnish troops grudgingly complied.

Following a grueling foot march, the SS men arrived in Rovaniemi on 14 October. The weary SS men soon crossed the Arctic Circle once more. The bulk of the Nord Division—minus the men comprising the rear-guard battalion—plodded northward toward Muonio and many kilometers beyond Kilpisjärvi. The frigid winter temperatures and the bitterly cold wind that whipped around the men and their horses from across the frozen tundra added to their physical burden. The mounted officers moved up and down the line to encourage and inspire their footslogging charges.[28]

❖

Farther north of SS-Gebirgsjäger Regiment 12 and that regiment's rear-guard battalion, SS-Gebirgsjäger Regiment 11 entered Muonio following a three-day forced march. The village of Muonio was nestled along the Muonio River, which marks the border between Sweden and Finland. At this critical nexus, the road from Rovaniemi meets the road from Tornio. This road (beginning in the south on the Gulf of Bothnia) runs the length of Finland up to the

Norwegian coast; at that time it was the only avenue out of Finland for the withdrawing German forces.

SS-Gruppenführer Brenner planned to have SS-Gebirgsjäger Regiment 12 defend the road from Kittilä and Rovaniemi while SS-Gebirgsjäger Regiment 11 defended the road south of Muonio leading up from Tornio. *SS-Sturmbannführer* Rädeke quickly marched his 11th Regiment troops through the village and then south into a defensive perimeter along both sides of the Tornio–Muonio road. Throughout the day mountain-troop units on foot and in vehicles poured forth from the south and through the 11th Regiment's defenses.

That night, on 26 October, a Finnish raid struck SS-Gebirgsjäger Regiment 11's supply trains just south of Muonio and behind the main defensive line. Another raid on the regimental headquarters resulted in Rädeke's death.[29]

During the night of 27 October, a Finnish battalion slipped behind the regiment and blocked the road to Muonio. The SS men again were cut off. The situation appeared grim, but preparations for a breakout began immediately. Heavily armed SS *gebirgsjäger* (mountain troopers) were soon rushing through the forest along the road to Muonio. A Wirbelwind antiaircraft gun lumbered along the road from the south, stopped, and barked a steady cadence of 2-cm rounds directly into the Finnish defenses. A motorcycle with sidecar came roaring up the road carrying *SS-Hauptsturmführer* Degen. The men could hear Degen shouting above the din, "Boys, we're in for it now! Come on now! Let's give them hell!"[30] Inspired by Degen's bravery, the SS men from all three battalions stood up and rushed the Finnish defenses. The Finns bolted. The 11th Regiment had cleared the road to Muonio.

The regiment finally reached the village and quickly occupied positions facing south in and among the cottages. On the village sign that read "Muonio" were the crudely written words "Das war . . . " ("That was . . . "). Below the words were nailed a series of Finnish decorations given to Degen and the regiment's other officers. The SS men had fully broken the bond they once shared with their former brothers-in-arms.[31]

The next day, 28 October, and two days after spotting their last Finnish patrol, the SS men of the rear-guard 3rd Battalion, SS-Gebirgsjäger Regiment 12, suffered the same fate the 11th Regiment had just experienced south of Muonio. On arriving at the road junction near Särkijärvi, the SS men discovered that the Finns had ambushed the supply trains.

The resolute SS men quickly salvaged the undamaged wagons and equipment and resumed the march. As the group approached the high ground six kilometers from Muonio, the ridgeline before them exploded with Finnish small-arms fire. *SS-Sturmmann* Werner Adam, a machine gunner in the 14th Company, felt a Finnish bullet slam into his chest, knocking him to the ground. Only days later did Adam realize that his dog tag, hanging by a string over his heart beneath many layers of clothing, had deflected the bullet and saved his life.[32] At 0000 on 29 October three rifle companies attacked the ridgeline and unhinged the Finns from their defenses. The road to Muonio was open.

As the sun rose on 29 October, the exhausted men of the 3rd Battalion, SS-Gebirgsjäger Regiment 12, assembled their gear, formed up on the road, and set out for Muonio. Learning of the successful breakout by his rearguard battalion, *SS-Standartenführer* Schreiber rushed south to greet his battle-weary regiment. Schreiber stood beside the road; as the men passed he saluted, greeting the troops with a smile and words of encouragement.

The entire 6th SS-Gebirgs Division Nord soon assembled north of Muonio along the frozen Muonio River, which bordered neutral Sweden to the west. Another 320 kilometers of road lay ahead before the SS men would reach the Finnish–Norwegian border. *General der Infanterie* Hochbaum published a corps order of the day (*korpstagesbefehl*) on 4 November 1944 wishing the Nord Division farewell and praising them for their battlefield achievements. In the message, Hochbaum wrote, "[Y]ou brave SS men have mastered all situations and won proud victories. The severe battle that lasted for weeks at Ssennosero and the battles at Kemi, Tuchkala-Suvanto, and Muonio are glorious chapters in the division's history. Where you SS-Gebirgsjäger stood, the Russians and the Finns received bloody heads. With sincere regret, the comrades of the Army give you your leave. We remember your fallen heroes, and we send our best wishes to the wounded."[33] With these plaudits echoing distantly in the SS men's ears, the division pressed northward along the frozen, narrow road to Norway without incident. The men marched between thirty to forty kilometers a day.[34] After more than a week, the Nord Division arrived at the Finnish village of Kaaresuvanto just short of the congested Reichsstrasse 50. The SS troopers moved through the village and paused along the road to spend one last bitingly cold night in Finland.

During that final night on Finnish soil, many of the SS men reflected on their time spent in Karelia. They were bitter about Finland's armistice with

Russia and the sudden loss of a close ally. A large number of SS officers and men had become friendly with the Finns on a personal level. Many recalled the mentoring the newly formed Nord troops received from the battle-hardened Finns—mentoring that helped shape the Nord Division into the combat-ready, highly trained, and well-led force that marched out of the country as an enemy. The stab in the back the SS men suffered in Finland only reinforced the patriotic fervor flowing strongly throughout the ranks.

The division crossed the Finnish–Norwegian border north of the Finnish town of Kilpisjärvi in the first week of November. The men of the 3rd Battalion, SS-Gebirgsjäger Regiment 12 finally received recognition on 9 November for their gallant rear-guard actions at Muonio. During a brief pause at Heiligskogen, Norway, many of the men received some much-deserved First- and Second-Class Iron Crosses for valor at the Muonio battle. In addition, thirty-two-year-old Sudeten-German Kurt Kreuzinger, former commander of the 6th Company, assumed command of the battalion.[35] Kreuzinger would later provide critical leadership during the Nord Division's first major action on the Western Front at Wingen-sur-Moder, France. During this period *SS-Gruppenführer* Brenner learned that, once the division assembled in Denmark, the SS men would be committed to combat on the Western Front.[36]

The 6th SS-Gebirgs Division continued the daunting trek north in subzero arctic conditions. Few SS men realized that the division had begun to pivot southward onto the heavily congested Reichsstrasse 50. Only motorized traffic could use the road during daylight hours, so the Nord men marched approximately thirty to forty difficult kilometers in the cold, dark, arctic night and then pitched hasty tent shelters on the roadside by day.

On their arrival at Gratangen, the SS men boarded Danish railroad ferries for the harbor north of Fauske and the port at Narvik. After a day-long journey by ferry, the SS men disembarked at Fauske and began the final, 185-kilometer leg of their foot march to Mo i Rana, the northern start point of the Norwegian railway system. The SS men arrived there on 10 December, marking the end of a 1,600-kilometer foot march that had begun two months earlier near Kiestinki and Louhi in Finland.[37] Following a brief respite that included delousing and the receipt of new supplies, the exhausted SS men boarded trains for a week long journey to the ports at Oslo and Moss, Norway. On 19 December they were headed to Denmark under German naval escort.

Few men in the division were aware that the Nord Division was moving quickly to the Western Front as OKW's top priority. The German Ardennes offensive (known to Americans as the Battle of the Bulge and to the Germans as Wacht am Rhein, or Watch on the Rhine) had begun on 16 December with some mixed results. The 6th SS Panzer Armee, the offensive's main effort, could not punch through the northern shoulder of the German bulge in the Allied lines, so OKW wanted to put as many units as possible into the fray to ensure success. Unfortunately for the German high command, the 6th SS-Gebirgs Division Nord would arrive too late to participate in Wacht am Rhein. Instead, the OKW would earmark the division for participation in another upcoming operation scheduled to begin in January. Elements of one regiment would barely arrive in time to participate in this operation.

❖

Once the freighters docked in Denmark on and after 20 December, *SS-Gruppenführer* Brenner gathered the regimental officers and informed them that OKW intended to employ the division in Wacht am Rhein.[38] The division's officers returned to their units to inform the troops about the forthcoming operation in the Ardennes. The worst part of this news was that no one could take the much-anticipated leave the SS men believed they deserved after their torturous and storied 1,600-kilometer trek from Finland. But the men's spirits lifted when the supply units produced some much-needed new uniforms, field gear, socks, underwear, and toiletries within forty-eight hours of each unit's arrival in Denmark.

The new equipment proved new not simply in terms of manufacturing, but also in terms of design. The Nord men had been fighting with equipment outfitted early in the war. The machine gunners still carried the dependable MG34 instead of the newer MG42, which fired nearly 1,200 rounds per minute compared to 800 to 900 for the MG34.

The troops also learned that each mountain rifle battalion would receive a newly constituted heavy company that consisted of one platoon of two 75-mm howitzers and one platoon of four 120-mm mortars. These companies would take several weeks to man, organize, and equip, and the resulting change in each company's unit designation created incredible confusion. Each regiment had fifteen companies numbered sequentially. Companies 1 through 5 comprised the 1st Battalion, companies 6 through 10 comprised the 2nd Battalion, and Companies 11 through 15 comprised the 3rd Battalion. The first three companies were the mountain rifle units, the fourth company was the heavy machine-gun company, and the fifth company was the headquarters company. The addition of these new heavy companies at the end of each battalion's numerical sequence caused each company's designation in the 2nd and 3rd battalions to increase by two. The 11th Company, for example, suddenly became the 13th Company. This sudden adjustment to the two mountain rifle regiments' organization fueled a great deal of communications and administrative problems and even confused the men who belonged to the companies. Most of the men simply continued to refer to their companies by the old numerical designation.

On 21 December *SS-Gruppenführer* Brenner and his staff arrived in Denmark. The next day Brenner received orders to form a *kampfgruppe* with the units already assembled on Danish soil and speed them south to the Saar-Palatinate. Most of the men already in Denmark hailed from SS-Gebirgsjäger Regiment 12, so Brenner gave the mission to *SS-Standartenführer* Schreiber.[39] Schreiber would assemble what troops he could and quickly head south by train. Brenner would remain in Denmark to oversee the assembly of the rest of the division.[40]

The Nord Division spent Christmas Eve in Denmark feasting on holiday victuals, but the order to depart for Germany dampened their Christmas spirit. The men would not spend Christmas Day peacefully in Denmark but would instead board trains headed for the Western Front.

The division received orders to send the units to Germany by battalion, but some of the battalions still lacked their heavy machine-gun companies, which were still moving to Denmark from Norway. In effect, the lead elements of Nord would be heading to Germany by train while the last units in the division were just arriving in Denmark by boat. The division was spread throughout Scandinavia, quite literally.

Loaded on trains by afternoon on Christmas Day, the available mountain rifle battalions started south for a four-day journey through a homeland they no longer recognized. By early evening the trains had crossed the German–Danish border. The last time many of the Nord men saw their beloved homeland was when Germany still rode the high tide of the war. At that time the empire was expanding, and the war clearly progressed in Germany's favor. But the fateful turn of events in 1943—the loss of the 6th Armee at Stalingrad and the 5th Panzer Armee in Tunisia—put Germany on the run. The Allied invasion of Normandy on 6 June 1944 brought the ground war closer to home while the German populace had long endured the air war—in the form of massive Allied bombing raids from England and Italy—for at least two years. The Nord men had simply never witnessed a beleaguered Germany or suffered from the Allies' air supremacy. The journey through their war-torn Fatherland in December 1944 would shake the SS men to the core.

❖

Nearly half a world away, at Fort Benning, Georgia, in the United States, newly promoted Maj. Gen. Willard G. Wyman spent Christmas Eve 1944 wondering whether his green 71st Infantry Division would be trained and ready enough to handle the rigors of combat. The division had only recently reorganized into a standard triangular infantry division after departing Camp Carson, Colorado, for Benning, seven months after a failed experiment as a mule-borne, mountain-type light division. After losing nearly all enlisted men as overseas replacements following months of rigorous, team-building training, the division was back to square one—a rough-and-tumble outfit with fresh replacements that needed to make every training minute count.

In command since November, Wyman knew the value of good, realistic combat training. A veteran of Omaha Beach on D-Day, then–Brigadier General Wyman watched as experienced, well-trained infantrymen overcame murderous German enfilading fire and rose to the incredible challenge of seizing the beachhead. Many, many young men died that day, and Wyman, haunted by those youthful bodies floating in the surf, was charged with training other young men for another battle. The responsibility weighed heavily on him.[41]

The "Red Circle" Division, so named for its red, circular patch with the blue number "71" inside, would soon deploy to the European Theater of Operations and meet a more weakened—but no less dangerous—German Army. What Wyman did not know on that Christmas Eve was how his division and a well-seasoned, well-blooded Waffen-SS mountain division named Nord—at that same moment moving south from Finland to the Western Front—would soon converge at a point in central Germany and engage in a sweeping, three-day battle during Easter weekend 1945 that would end in the destruction of one division and the rise of another. That Easter weekend was only three months away.

CHAPTER 2

Operation Nordwind and Beyond

The Western Front came as a shock to the men of the 6th SS-Gebirgs Division Nord. As their southward-bound trains passed Hamburg, the men witnessed firsthand the destructive might of the Allies' airpower. Germany's once beautiful northern metropolis was a bombed-out shell. For many SS men the destruction they witnessed on this train journey deepened their resolve and their will to fight. For others, their optimism about winning the war was waning rapidly.

On 28 December the first trains crossed the Rhine River south of Heidelberg. The lead battalions in the movement hailed from SS-Gebirgsjäger Regiment 12; SS-Gebirgsjäger Regiment 11—five days' travel behind Regiment 12—followed. The trains moved only at night to avoid the dreaded Allied aircraft.[1]

As night fell on 29 December, Regiment 12 and other Nord elements pressed onward to Pirmasens and Zweibrücken in the Palatinate. The first battalions to arrive would disembark and occupy two villages thirty kilometers from Pirmasens in the Hardt Mountains—also known on the French side as the Low Vosges. Following a hasty assembly of men and equipment, the 3rd Battalion, SS-Gebirgsjäger Regiment 12, marched toward the villages, which sat a few kilometers north of the German–French border and east of the historic, eighteenth-century citadel city of Bitche, France.

The 3rd Battalion's rifle companies arrived in deserted Ludwigswinkel and Eppenbrunn on 30 December as the vanguard of the regiment and the entire 6th SS-Gebirgs Division Nord. A potpourri of bedraggled German Army units shattered in the recent fighting occupied the local area. The obvious chaos shocked the SS men; their long journey had delivered them to a world where a seemingly obliterated German Army appeared to be fighting without hope.

Although the rest of the Nord Division was still traveling south by train, many 3rd Battalion men realized they might be thrown into the fray before the entire division arrived. The battalion commander, *SS-Hauptsturmführer* Kurt Kreuzinger, and his adjutant, *SS-Untersturmführer* Wolf Zoepf, visited the newly established SS-Gebirgsjäger Regiment 12 command post to meet with the commander, *SS-Standartenführer* Franz Schreiber, and learn of the battalion's future mission.[2] After congratulating Schreiber on his recent award of the Knight's Cross of the Iron Cross, Kreuzinger and Zoepf learned that orders to attack might come within twenty-four hours. SS-Gebirgsjäger Regiment 11 and the rest of the Nord Division would follow the 12th into the line as soon as possible. The New Year—1945—was just around the corner.

❖

The first units of the Nord Division trickling into the Western Front would not only enter a battle already joined, but also participate in a new offensive with aims nearly as ambitious as those of Wacht am Rhein. The Ardennes Offensive launched on 16 December sought to split asunder the British and American alliance by striking through the lightly defended Losheim Gap in the Ardennes with three strong armies, slicing between the U.S. and British forces and seizing the valuable Allied port of Antwerp. Hitler hoped that physically dividing the two forces on the ground might result in a separate armistice with each of the two former allies.[3] The Führer had just suffered from two such separate agreements that the Russians signed with his former allies, the Finns and the Rumanians. Ten days after the Ardennes offensive began, Wacht am Rhein's goals did not come to pass, but a new opportunity—a thinner American front line south of the Ardennes offensive's battle area—did not keep Hitler from trying to achieve a similar break in the Western alliance . . . but this time between the Americans and the Free French.

The new operation Hitler intended to launch on New Year's Day 1945 would be on a much smaller scale—one army attacking instead of three— and would focus on the American Seventh Army commanded by Lt. Gen. Alexander Patch. The Seventh and the French First Armies comprised Lt. Gen. Jacob Devers's 6th Army Group and the southern wing of Lt. Gen Omar Bradley's 12th Army Group. The Seventh Army had been advancing toward the Rhine River and Saarbrücken while the French First Army battled the Germans near Strasbourg and Colmar.

When General of the Army Dwight D. Eisenhower recognized that Wacht am Rhein was a major offensive, he shifted Lt. Gen. George S. Patton Jr.'s Third Army—then on the Seventh Army's left flank—northward to attack into the southern shoulder of the bulge created by the German assault. The Seventh Army then had to cover the hole left by the Third Army. On 21 December Devers ordered Patch to cease all offensive operations, assume a defensive posture, give ground when necessary, and extend the Seventh Army's frontage from 75 kilometers to a staggering 135 kilometers.

The limited U.S. withdrawals—including the one at the Bitche fortifications—did not escape *Generalfeldmarschall* Gerd von Rundstedt's experienced eye: von Rundstedt, the commander of Oberbefehlshaber (OB; Supreme Command) West and the overseer of Army Group B's attack into the Ardennes, quickly saw a weak spot in the U.S. lines near the Low Vosges. Wacht am Rhein had lost momentum, so on 21 December von Rundstedt ordered the commander of Army Group G, *Generaloberst* Johannes Blaskowitz, to attack. Hitler quickly agreed.[4]

Blaskowitz's concept had two corps attacking as the main effort with another corps launching a supporting attack. The main attack would punch through the American defenses, drive along the Rhine-Marne canal to the east, envelop the U.S. forces north of Strasbourg, and reconnect with the German 19th Armee, which the Americans had cut off from Army Group G in November in what became known as the Colmar Pocket on the Alsatian Plain.[5]

Hitler amended the plan and further directed that the 21st Panzer and 25th Panzergrenadier divisions remain in reserve. Blaskowitz could not employ these armored formations before seizing the Wingen-Ingwiller road well to the south. Hitler added one last item—a name for the operation. Germany's last offensive in the west would be known as Nordwind, or North Wind. Grudgingly, von Rundstedt and Blaskowitz accepted the meddling Führer's changes. On 25 December Blaskowitz informed the man responsible for carrying out Operation Nordwind, *General der Infanterie* Hans von Obstfelder, the 1st Armee commander, of the plan.

Like Wacht am Rhein, the preparations for Nordwind remained steeped in utmost secrecy. Hitler directed that only corps and division commanders—and their staffs—would know about the offensive in advance. The attack was set for 2300 on 31 December.[6]

Throughout the planning and preparation stages of Nordwind, the 6th SS-Gebirgs Division continued the long and difficult journey from Denmark and Norway. The only division elements that reached the front in time for Nordwind were the 1st and 3rd battalions of SS-Gebirgsjäger Regiment 12, SS-Panzergrenadier Battalion 506, SS-Gebirgs Artillerie Regiment 6, a *panzerjäger* (antitank) company, a signal company, a medical platoon, and a combat-engineer platoon.[7] *SS-Standartenführer* Schreiber commanded this advance element, which the 1st Armee designated as Kampfgruppe (Battle Group) Schreiber. The rest of the Nord Division would not arrive until a week after Nordwind commenced, but von Obstfelder could not wait and placed Kampfgruppe Schreiber under the operational control of the 361st Volksgrenadier Division.

Operation Nordwind began at 2300 on 1 January 1945. Schreiber received orders to form a smaller battle group with his two mountain infantry battalions, infiltrate the American lines, and seize the village of Wingen-sur-Moder to block the road leading through the Moder Valley against any counterattacking American forces.

Schreiber issued his movement orders at 0000 on 1 January and designated the battle group Kampfgruppe Wingen. The senior battalion commander, *SS-Hauptsturmführer* Alois Burgstaller of the 1st Battalion, was in command. Both battalions would occupy a designated assembly area, receive ammunition and rations, and then move to a link-up point before heading toward Wingen-sur-Moder.

Fresh snow had blanketed the area. The 3rd Battalion had only 62 percent of its full strength and five officers remaining. The heavy machine-gun company was still traveling from Scandinavia, and the heavy mortar platoon was undergoing conversion to the new howitzer platoon for inclusion in the new heavy company. The 1st Battalion suffered from similar problems and shortages.

The 3rd Battalion obtained fresh supplies and ammunition before departing Ludwigswinkel. The SS men also received a weapon they had not encountered before in the German arsenal—the *panzerfaust*, a hand-held, disposable antitank round the average soldier could fire at ranges of sixty to one hundred meters. The men received a crash course on the weapon before grabbing dozens of them for use in the coming battle.

By 1000 on 1 January, the 3rd Battalion's men had departed Ludwigswinkel on foot and trudged south toward the French and German border. A messenger led the 3rd Battalion commander, *SS-Hauptsturmführer* Kurt Kreuzinger and his adjutant, *SS-Untersturmführer* Wolf Zoepf, to the division command post where the 361st's operations officer, *Major* Ehlers, briefed them on the results of Nordwind's first twenty-four hours. The 361st had attacked at 2300 on 31 December and had taken Fischerhof and Thalhaeuseln. The regiment to the west failed to seize Bannstein and the key road junction leading south to Reipertswiller by sundown. Despite stubborn American resistance, though, Baerenthal fell, and the road to Reipertswiller lay open for possible employment of the 21st Panzer and 25th Panzergrenadier divisions.

On the 361st's left the 256th Volksgrenadier Division failed to seize the day's first objectives, potentially exposing the 361st's left flank. Ehlers explained the need to take Wingen-sur-Moder to stymie any U.S. counterattack attempts. Kreuzinger and Zoepf returned to the battalion after 2200 and told the men to rest for five hours. They would depart at 0300.

❖

The American Seventh Army troops that bore the brunt of the initial German assault in the Low Vosges were the ones least prepared to stave off a concentrated attack. The difficult terrain—marked by steep cuts, dense evergreen forests, and few roads—prompted the VI Corps commander, Maj. Gen. Edward H. Brooks, to screen this area with a task force built around Combat Command R, 14th Armored Division, and designated as Task Force Hudelson. The task force comprised two cavalry reconnaissance squadrons, the 117th and the 94th, and assorted combat and combat-support units. The attacking German *volksgrenadier* divisions slammed directly into the thinly held defenses of the 117th and 94th Cavalry Squadrons on the night of 1 January. By 0330 on 2 January, the 117th deemed their position untenable and fell back nearly nine kilometers. By 1700 the squadron's command post had jumped to Wingen-sur-Moder—Kampfgruppe Wingen's primary objective for 2 January.[8]

Lieutenant General Patch spent 2 January shifting forces around his threatened Seventh Army sector to block all passes through the Low Vosges leading south and thus frustrate any further German efforts to reach the Alsatian Plain. The 45th Infantry Division—the most combat-experienced of Patch's infantry—held the extreme left side of the VI Corps and covered a fifty-kilometer front that tied in with the 100th Infantry Division to the west. Maj. Gen. Robert T. Frederick—the 45th's commanding general—received all three infantry regiments of the 70th Infantry Division to reinforce his line.

The 70th's task force—designated Task Force Herren after its commander, Brig. Gen. Thomas Herren—went to the most threatened part of the sector, which included Wingen-sur-Moder. Frederick also shifted his 179th Infantry Regiment to this area. Remarkably, the regiment—like the 117th Cavalry Squadron—set up its command post in Kampfgruppe Wingen's primary objective—Wingen-sur-Moder.[9]

❖

The 3rd Battalion, SS-Gebirgsjäger Regiment 12, had moved out at 0430 and approached their first objective, the deserted town of Melch. *SS-Standartenführer* Schreiber arrived in Melch and explained to Kreuzinger that *SS-Hauptsturmführer* Alois Burgstaller's 1st Battalion would link up with the 3rd later in the afternoon. Schreiber further explained that SS-Panzergrenadier Battalion 506 would simultaneously attack Wimmenau four kilometers east of Wingen-sur-Moder with the help of one battalion from Grenadier Regiment 951. Like Wingen-sur-Moder, Wimmenau sat astride the Moder River and also commanded a portion of the east–west rail line.

Schreiber reiterated Kampfgruppe Wingen's mission: seize Wingen-sur-Moder and then prepare to take La Petite Pierre in the Saverne Pass to open a path for the German armor into the Rhine Valley. Unfortunately, Schreiber knew little about the American forces between Melch and Wingen-sur-Moder. Even before Kampfgruppe Wingen set out on 2 January, the day was rife with setbacks for the other attacking German forces, which meant the SS men would infiltrate the enemy's lines with little help from the stalled German Army troops.

SS-Hauptsturmführer Alois Burgstaller's 1st Battalion finally trudged into Melch after dark. Burgstaller, thirty-three years old and a highly decorated veteran battalion commander, had joined the Nord men in Norway in May 1940. After experiencing all the major battles in the north, he had taken command of the 1st Battalion eighteen months earlier.[10] Burgstaller explained to Schreiber the problems that plagued his battalion's journey from the assembly area—the loss of the battalion's radio car and repeated fighter-bomber attacks. Kreuzinger's battalion had already departed, so Burgstaller's men would have to hurry to catch up.[11] Both battalions eventually linked up at the mouth of the valley. After failing to come together days earlier, Kampfgruppe Wingen finally began moving toward Wingen-sur-Moder as a complete battle group.

The 3rd Battalion's lead element soon encountered some American soldiers in foxholes. After a brief but violent firefight, a lone American voice yelled out in broken German. The GI proposed a ceasefire to evacuate the wounded of both sides. Stunned, the SS men stopped firing. Such a truce with the Russians on the Eastern Front would have been inconceivable. Were the Americans trying to trick them? *SS-Hauptsturmführer* Bruno Schütze, commander of the 13th Company, agreed to the truce but with trepidation. The SS men then watched in amazement as medics from both sides—using small flashlights—worked feverishly to evacuate the wounded. Battle-hardened by combat with the Soviets, the SS men realized that they faced an altogether different enemy—an enemy with principles and a sense of humanity.

Before the sun rose on the third day of Nordwind, 3 January, *Generalmajor* Alfred Philippi realized that this day would herald either complete success or abject failure for his 361st Volksgrenadier Division. His troops were exhausted and nearly spent. Kampfgruppe Wingen would continue to drive for Wingen-sur-Moder, while one of his regiments and an additional battalion would attack Reipertswiller from the north and west. The plan must succeed if Philippi was to open a path south to the Alsatian Plain for the German armor. The most important part of the plan was the taking of Wingen, and he pinned his hopes on the SS men.[12]

In the hills north of Wingen-sur-Moder, the SS troops of the 3rd Battalion readied their weapons to continue the assault. The truce had ended, but in the soft glow of dawn the American soldiers had withdrawn. The battle group occupied a solid, defensible position on the Kaesberg.

Back at the 361st Volksgrenadier Division's command post, *Generalmajor* Philippi learned that his troops' attempt to seize Reipertswiller had failed. In the early afternoon Schreiber dispatched a messenger with instructions from Philippi to conduct a frontal assault on the American position and to split up to seize Heideneck—the 1st Battalion's objective—and Wingen—the 3rd Battalion's objective. Burgstaller countered with a plan to follow the ridgeline on the Weinbourg mountain undetected and split up just north of Wingen to seize each battalion's specified objective. At 1900 the messenger returned with good news: the senior leadership had approved the plan.

As the SS men prepared to move out, all offensive activity in the 361st Volksgrenadier Division's zone ceased (see Map 2.1). The Reipertswiller attack had failed. The only other Nord unit attempting to participate in the fighting, the dismounted SS-Panzergrenadier Battalion 506, had not yet reached the 361st's 2nd Battalion, Grenadier Regiment 951, to join in an assault on Wimmenau. In effect, Kampfgruppe Wingen would attack Wingen-sur-Moder with no additional German support.[13]

Unfortunately for Kampfgruppe Wingen, the American 45th Infantry Division knew that a sizable force occupied the Kaesberg and threatened Wingen-sur-Moder to the south, so Major General Frederick positioned three battalions to thwart any attempts to seize the town. The GIs did not know how the SS men would attack, so Kampfgruppe Wingen still had some measure of surprise on its side. The Nord men appeared to be Army Group G's last hope for achieving an armored breakthrough in the Low Vosges.

Kampfgruppe Wingen departed the Kaesberg shortly after 0000 on 4 January. At 0400 the column reached the main road leading south to the Moder Valley and into a foxhole line occupied by the surprised GIs of Company B, 276th Infantry, who gave ground quickly and headed south. Alarmed by the potential loss of surprise, Burgstaller set 0700 as the attack time on Wingen.[14] In the predawn light the outline of Wingen appeared to the SS men's south. The town's buildings straddled the Moder River, which runs east–west, while a complex system of railroad tracks and switch lines separated the forest to the north from the town itself. Two prominent church spires—one Catholic and the other Protestant—were connected by a north–south road that separated the village into eastern and western sections. The 1st Battalion would take the west while the 3rd Battalion took the east.

An American mortar round suddenly erupted in the dirt as the 3rd Battalion raced down the slope, across the railroad tracks, and into the northernmost edge of the town. The SS troopers quickly took up positions in the houses overlooking the fields. North of Wingen the rest of the 3rd Battalion occupied defensive positions facing north. The 1st Battalion's 1st and 2nd

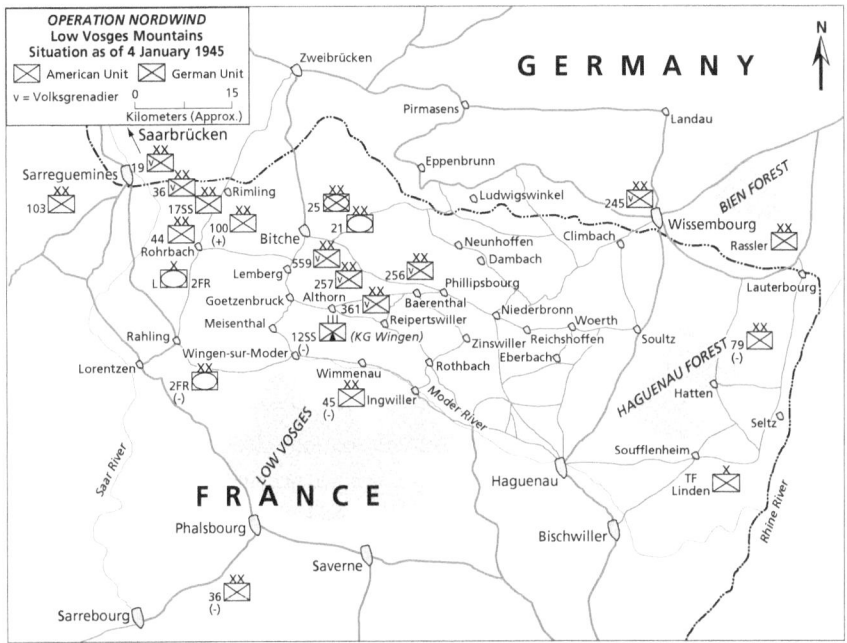

Map 2.1. Operation Nordwind: Low Vosges Mountains, 4 January 1945.

companies rushed into the town and across the train marshaling yards to seize a bridgehead over the Moder River and form the southern part of the *kampfgruppe*'s perimeter.[15]

The U.S. reaction to Kampfgruppe Wingen's rapid assault on the town was slow and poorly coordinated—in spite of the fact that the command posts of the 1st Battalion, 179th Infantry Regiment, and 117th Cavalry Squadron were both located in Wingen. The Americans seemed stunned.[16]

By 1200 the 1st and 3rd battalions had cleared all buildings in Wingen-sur-Moder. The 3rd Battalion established a command post in the Hôtel de la Gare and began collecting prisoners. *SS-Hauptsturmführer* Burgstaller quickly determined that his men had seized Wingen from approximately 350 GIs—all members of an American command post (no cavalrymen were around).[17] The American counterattack that Burgstaller feared began at 1330 along the railroad tracks from the west with infantrymen supported by tanks. *Panzerfaust* rounds destroyed two tanks; the American attack had failed.[18]

East of Wingen the 180th Infantry Regiment moved to close the gap in the American lines and blocked the eastern road to the Moder Valley and the Alsatian Plain. At 1200 the 2nd Battalion, 180th Infantry, struck the defenses of SS-Panzergrenadier Battalion 506. The GIs forced the SS men back with heavy rifle and machine-gun fire. The GIs still fell 1,500 meters short of closing the gap in the American lines, but they had effectively boxed in Kampfgruppe Wingen.

❖

As the sun rose on the morning of 5 January, the German offensive was at a standstill. *Generalmajor* Philippi, the commander of the 361st Volksgrenadier Division, wanted to regain the initiative, but his repeated attempts to crack Reipertswiller failed in the face of consistent—and determined—American counterattacks. Philippi and his staff devised an operation for a supporting attack against Reipertswiller while a much larger force enveloped the town from the east.[19] Such a plan required Philippi to reshuffle his forces on the ground, so he set the attack for 7 January—two days away. Kampfgruppe Wingen would have to hold for another forty-eight hours without the prospect of relief.

❖

The night of 4 to 5 January passed quietly in Wingen-sur-Moder. The SS men rested for the first time in many days while Col. A. C. Morgan, the commander of the 276th Infantry, devised another three-pronged attack on Wingen for the following morning.[20]

At 0800 U.S. artillery fire ripped into the roofs of the nearby houses. Sherman tanks positioned on the Kirchberg heights fired main-gun rounds directly into the buildings. Attacked from three sides by American infantrymen supported by tanks, artillery, and mortar fire, the SS men fought back furiously. The battle raged until the early afternoon, but Wingen remained firmly in the SS men's hands except for a few outermost buildings captured by some GIs.[21]

Lt. Col. Wallace R. Cheves, the commander of the 2nd Battalion, 274th Infantry, witnessed nothing but chaos when he came forward to see the battlefield. Cheves's battalion helped Company A, 276th Infantry, retain a hard-won foothold on some of Wingen's outermost buildings—a foothold that would provide a significant advantage the following day. Morgan's combined, concentric attack had achieved little. The attacks north of town had failed, and the combined tank–infantry assault on the underpasses collapsed in the face of well-prepared German defenses.

Frustrated and under extreme pressure from the top, Brigadier General Herren summoned Cheves to the 276th Infantry's command post in Zittersheim. Herren had lost confidence in Colonel Morgan and the 274th's regimental commander. Herren put Cheves in charge of seizing Wingen the next day and gave the startled officer most of the 276th Infantry Regiment for the operation. The attack would begin at 0800 the following morning.[22]

A bewildered Cheves acknowledged the order and gathered his commanders to formulate a plan. Cheves's battalion would exploit the existing foothold southwest of town and attack eastward while the 3rd Battalion, 276th Infantry, would continue the attack from west to east but north of the railroad tracks. Herren still thought that only fifty or so Germans held the town, but Cheves doubted this low estimate.[23]

Inside the town Kampfgruppe Wingen prepared for another day's fighting. The SS troops ushered all American POWs into one of the churches for their own safety while the dug-in German troops improved their positions. The SS men were suffering from a severe shortage of food, ammunition, and, above all, sleep. Their only hope rested in the possibility of German reinforcements reaching Wingen-sur-Moder in time.

East of Wingen the American effort to close the gap in the U.S. defenses raged for a second day. The 2nd Battalion, 180th Infantry, attacked at 0800 on 5 January, attempting a double envelopment of SS-Panzergrenadier Battalion 506 on the Rebberg and an attack on Kampfgruppe Stämmle—actually the 2nd Battalion, Grenadier Regiment 951, 361st Volksgrenadier Division. The Americans prevailed and overran the German defenses.[24] The 180th Infantry had finally achieved the previous day's objective—to reach the phase line that brought the regiment in line with the 179th on the left (or west) and the 313th on the right (or east). But a gap of nearly 1,500 meters still existed. The Americans had to narrow this gap in the U.S. defenses even further by continuing the attack the next morning at 0900. By that time, most of the German forces had withdrawn north, except for the SS *panzergrenadiers*.

On 6 January Operation Nordwind experienced a long operational pause. The senior German leaders at Army Group G and 1st Armee reassessed the situation and decided that the Zinswiller exit out of the Low Vosges—held by a battalion of the 361st Volksgrenadier Division—was too narrow and icy to facilitate passage of the armored reserve. Therefore, the staff at OKW—and within *Generaloberst* Blaskowitz's own Army Group G—realized that only the immediate commitment of the armored reserve offered them any chance at regaining the initiative. The 21st Panzer and 25th Panzergrenadier divisions moved north of Wissembourg to prepare for a breakout attempt on the Alsatian Plain. Other units within the 1st Armee spent 6 January shifting forces to support the commitment of the armored reserve.[25]

Just before dawn on 6 January, at 0600, Burgstaller met in Kreuzinger's 3rd Battalion command post to discuss new instructions from *SS-Standartenführer* Schreiber delivered by messenger. Schreiber wanted the *kampfgruppe* to withdraw from Wingen-sur-Moder as soon as possible and to occupy defensive positions in the Rothbach Valley. Burgstaller and Kreuzinger listened in stunned silence: they had to relinquish ground on which they had spilled so much blood. Schreiber did not want to sacrifice his two battalions needlessly, so he had chided *Generalmajor* Philippi to withdraw the SS battle group from Wingen-sur-Moder. Philippi grudgingly agreed.

The sun was almost up, so the SS men would have to hold the town for another day. The withdrawal would begin that night. Messengers set out with a stern warning from Burgstaller for both battalions' company commanders: "Don't let the Americans cut you off, or you and your men might have to remain behind!"

Lieutenant Colonel Cheves's artillery preparation began promptly at 0745. As soon as the barrage lifted, the GIs attacked and ousted some SS men from a few houses, but the rest of the Nord men refused to give ground.[26] Lieutenant Colonel Cheves resumed the attack at 1300. Following on the heels of another artillery barrage, two of Cheves's rifle companies moved forward at a low crouch, but rifle fire from the cemetery on their right and the high ground on their left caught the GIs in a cross fire.

Inside the Hôtel de la Gare, the SS staff members paused their withdrawal planning and listened. The sounds of battle were coming closer to the command post. Alarmed, *SS-Hauptsturmführer* Burgstaller rallied his staff—and every available man within sight—in the street outside the hotel and assaulted directly into the attacking GIs, who withdrew hurriedly. Lieutenant Colonel Cheves, still feeling that his forces were overextended, witnessed Burgstaller's counterattack and promptly ordered his troops to hold in place. The German counterattack had stalled the American effort for the moment.[27]

Burgstaller and his staff returned to their command post and renewed their planning efforts. Darkness was already upon them. After studying a map and the terrain along the planned egress route, Burgstaller realized that the terrain was too harsh for his wounded men to cross, so their best chance of survival rested in becoming American prisoners. He knew the Americans would treat his troops well.[28]

As Burgstaller and his officers planned Kampfgruppe Wingen's withdrawal, none of the SS men was aware that the American attacks that occurred north, west, and east of the town throughout the day had sealed the ten-kilometer gap in the U.S. lines, isolating the battle group. Two U.S. regiments and an additional infantry battalion attacked on a line from Meisenthal in the west to Wildenguth in the east early on the morning of 6 January—the 179th Infantry on the left, the 180th Infantry in the center, and the 1st Battalion, 314th Infantry, on the right. In the center the 2nd Battalion, 180th Infantry, slammed into the SS-(Gebirgs) Reconnaissance Battalion 6, which had recently arrived, finally entering the line after a long and exhausting journey from Denmark.

The SS reconnaissance men quickly dug in and strengthened the defenses of their beleaguered comrades in SS-Panzergrenadier Battalion 506, but the American infantrymen fought back violently and expelled the Nord men from their positions by late afternoon. Two battalions from the 180th Infantry also met stiff resistance from the 257th Volksgrenadier Division, but the GIs gained ground nonetheless. On the left the 179th Infantry plunged into the defenses of the 257th's Grenadier Regiment 457 and, by early afternoon, had gained the Kaesberg's eastern slope.

On the extreme right, near Wildenguth, the 1st Battalion, 314th Infantry, overcame scattered German resistance in and around the town. As the sun fell on 6 January, the Americans had resealed the hole torn into the U.S. defensive line at the onset of Operation Nordwind six days earlier. Kampfgruppe Wingen, the only German force located south of the American line, was completely cut off.

❖

Back in Wingen, *SS-Hauptsturmführer* Burgstaller approved the withdrawal plan. The 13th Company locked the 256 American prisoners in the Catholic church with no guard; the imprisoned GIs were unaware that the SS men had abandoned them.[29]

The withdrawal operation began as soon as both battalions passed word of the plan to their men. By 0000 most of the *gebirgsjäger* (mountain troopers) had left their positions and the town. The departure had gone smoothly. However, the Americans fully expected a withdrawal and, with elements of the 1st Battalion, 180th Infantry, blocked the eastern exits out of town. The GIs had no intention of letting their prey slip away easily.

❖

As the remains of Kampfgruppe Wingen trekked up the hill toward the assembly area, the nature of Operation Nordwind had already changed dramatically. Without reinforcements to bolster—or replace—the exhausted German troops in the line, the 1st Armee could no longer attack. Any chance for a breakthrough with German armor in the Low Vosges had all but vanished. Army Group G and 1st Armee depended on the success of the planned armored thrust near Wissembourg, which would begin at about the same time that the SS men vacated Wingen-sur-Moder. Unfortunately for the Germans, this attack would falter and Nordwind would end unceremoniously in failure.

❖

The new snow muffled the sounds of the withdrawing SS men's footsteps. The column soon crested the Weinbourg Heights, quietly traversed the ridgeline, then descended into the valley below. At 0530 the group paused to rest briefly at a small inn. During this respite Burgstaller learned to his dismay that his 1st Battalion had only six officers and 110 enlisted soldiers remaining; likewise, the 3rd Battalion could only muster three officers and 107 soldiers. Out of the original *kampfgruppe* strength of 725, Burgstaller was bringing out less than a third (205) of his force.[30] He also learned that—on the battle group's return—*SS-Standartenführer* Schreiber wanted the 3rd Battalion to occupy positions in the Rothbach Valley while the 1st Battalion remained in reserve. Burgstaller told Kreuzinger that the 3rd Battalion should lead.

At 0600 the column departed down into the Rothbach Valley, fully expecting to encounter the German lines within minutes. Instead, the 3rd Battalion ran into foxholes belonging to Company C, 180th Infantry—one of the companies that helped to close the gap in the American front line. A skirmish ensued, and the SS men scattered into the forest. The 1st Battalion, traveling behind the 3rd, ran directly into another American unit—Company C of the 179th Infantry.

Both SS mountain battalions, minus the twenty or so casualties sustained during the firefight and artillery barrage, eventually rallied after reaching the German lines—a mere shell of what the battle group had been a week earlier. Kampfgruppe Wingen had ceased to exist, and the survivors would eventually help reconstitute the remnants of SS-Gebirgsjäger Regiment 12. The Nord Division's baptism of fire on the Western Front was over; it had proved costly.[31]

Back in Wingen-sur-Moder Lieutenant Colonel Cheves's troops occupied the town at 0900 on 7 January and liberated a relieved and exhausted group of former prisoners from the Catholic church. In addition, the Americans captured the 420 wounded SS *gebirgsjägers* who manned the last line of defense in the town. The Americans had finally eliminated the only remaining salient in the U.S. front line and the farthest penetration in the Low Vosges made by a German unit during Operation Nordwind. With the loss of Wingen-sur-Moder, *Generaloberst* Blaskowitz, the commander of Army Group G, saw no way in which the 1st Armee could accomplish its tasks outlined in the Nordwind plan. The German effort shifted east—to the reserve panzer and *panzergrenadier* divisions. This effort would make modest gains but would ultimately end in failure as well.[32]

❖

As *SS-Standartenführer* Schreiber picked up the pieces of his freshly withdrawn 1st and 3rd battalions, the remaining units of the 6th SS-Gebirgs Division Nord finally arrived in the operational area. Waiting in the divisional assembly area was the newly assigned commander of SS-Gebirgsjäger Regiment 11, *SS-Standartenführer* Helmuth Raithel. Raithel was a seasoned mountain-troop officer of great skill who would lead the regiment through the most grueling fighting the Reinhard Heydrich men had yet to experience. He was a man with a remarkable background and great ambition.

Raithel was born on 9 April 1907 in Ingolstadt, Germany. An athletic boy who craved adventure, the sixteen-year-old Raithel stumbled into history on 9 November 1923. While walking his bike in downtown Munich on that fateful day, the young Raithel encountered a large crowd of armed, shouting men. What Raithel did not know was that he had blundered into Adolf Hitler and the Nazi Party's Beer Hall *putsch* (uprising).

Intrigued by the excitement, Raithel joined the crowd of Nazi followers (in this case Company Rossbach) who marched behind Hitler and the Party's cronies. Shots suddenly rang out. Hitler fell to the ground, and the crowd scattered. Bewildered, Raithel followed a small group of Nazis who rushed into an alley for cover. At some point a Party leader wrote down Raithel's name as a "Party faithful" who had participated in the failed action. Strangely enough, Raithel held no political beliefs and was not even a Nazi Party member, but this fact did not keep him from receiving the Nazi Party's most coveted decoration, the Blutorden (Blood Order).[33]

After finishing his secondary-school education, Raithel joined the 100,000-man army on 1 April 1926 as an officer candidate. He served with Infanterie Regiment 19 but later joined the newly formed Jäger Battalion Kempten, which became the foundation of the German Army's mountain troops. Raithel learned his craft from mountain-troop officers such as the future *Generalfeldmarschall* Schörner and the "Hero of Narvik," *Generaloberst* Dietl.[34]

When the war began in September 1939, Raithel was in command of the German Army's Mountain-Training School in Fulpmes (located in the Alps).

In 1940 he took command of the 2nd Battalion, Gebirgsjäger Regiment 143, of the 6th Gebirgs Division and fought in Greece and Crete.[35]

With two of his brothers in the army and commanding regiments, the always-competitive Raithel began pushing for increased command responsibility. In 1943 Raithel solicited the advice of his prior mentor, *Generalfeldmarschall* Schörner, who advised him that his best chances for regimental command rested in the rapidly expanding Waffen-SS. The Blood Order Raithel had earned during Hitler's *putsch* attempt in 1923 was highly regarded within the SS. Raithel took the advice and transferred from the German Army to the Waffen-SS on 30 November 1943.[36]

In the Waffen-SS Raithel's mountain-troop experience and skills earned him almost immediate command of the Freiwilligen (Volunteer) SS-Gebirgsjäger Regiment 28 in the 13th Freiwilligen (Volunteer) SS-Gebirgs Division Handschar. Raithel, now an *SS-Standartenführer*, immediately took his volunteers into combat against Tito's partisans in Yugoslavia. He fought bravely and led from the front, suffering a severe wound in mid-1944. After he was wounded, a forlorn Raithel was forced to relinquish his precious command.[37]

He returned to Germany to convalesce as part of the officer reserve pool. Within a few short weeks, Raithel clamored for a new command and received it: SS-Gebirgsjäger Regiment 11 Reinhard Heydrich. Raithel hastened to the 6th SS-Gebirgs Division's assembly area near Pirmasens to await his new charges.[38] The SS men of Regiment 11 did not realize that the commander they had yet to meet was an expert mountaineer and a selfless leader who would guide them adroitly along the dark, bitter path that awaited the division in its final months on the Western Front.

Raithel's new command, SS-Gebirgsjäger Regiment 11, was relatively fresh and fully manned in stark contrast to SS-Gebirgsjäger Regiment 12. Despite the losses suffered by the forces under *SS-Standartenführer* Schreiber's command in the first week of January (Kampfgruppe Wingen; SS-Reconnaissance Battalion 6; 1st Battalion, SS Gebirgs-Artillerie Regiment 6; SS-Panzergrenadier Battalion 506; and a variety of divisional support units), the 6th SS-Gebirgs Division was in much better shape and more combat effective than the depleted 361st Volksgrenadier Division had been. Even *SS-Hauptsturmführer* Kreuzinger's exhausted and depleted 3rd Battalion,

SS-Gebirgsjäger Regiment 12, after only a few hours of rest following the withdrawal from Wingen, still managed to conduct a hasty—and successful—counterattack on 8 January to push back a small U.S. penetration in the German lines.[39]

By 9 January the rest of the 6th SS-Gebirgs Division had assembled west of Pirmasens and was ready for deployment to the front lines. *SS-Gruppenführer* Brenner arrived that same day and located his division command post at Schweitzerländel (*La Petite Suisse* in French or Little Switzerland in English). Brenner was wearing his newly minted Knight's Cross of the Iron Cross that he had received on 27 December 1944 for his superb leadership in withdrawing the 6th SS-Gebirgs Division from Finland.[40]

The next day, 10 January, the 6th SS-Gebirgs Division relieved the 361st in place along the Rothbach Valley down to Reipertswiller. Brenner positioned his two mountain regiments forward to hold the main line while SS-Panzergrenadier Battalion 506 and SS-Reconnaissance Battalion 6 remained in reserve.[41]

Brenner no longer had SS-Ski Battalion "Norge," which was comprised solely of Norwegian, Danish, and Swedish volunteers. They had signed up with the Nord Division only to fight the Russians. The loss of this battalion, and the loss of a few other units, dropped the division's strength down to 15,000 from 22,000, which brought the 6th SS closer in size to a regular mountain division.

Brenner had great confidence in his troops. Morale was still relatively high, and his men were not "infected" like other units that had suffered one reverse after another on the Eastern and Western fronts in 1944. The Nord men had never really tasted defeat at the hands of the Russians and, later, the Finns. But Brenner was concerned about the one thing his SS men had yet to experience fully as a division: the Western Allies' total dominance in the air.[42]

Army Group G did not wait long before ordering the Nord men onto the offensive. Operation Nordwind had lost its impetus, and *Generaloberst* Blaskowitz wanted to regain the initiative. The modest gains made by the attacking panzer and *panzergrenadier* divisions near Wissembourg meant that the entire German offensive had ground to a halt.

On 11 January *SS-Standartenführer* Schreiber gathered his depleted battalions (the newly arrived 2nd Battalion was at full strength) and led them in an attack at 0700 against the American positions near the Rothbach Valley. The regiment assaulted through a position held by one company of SS-Panzergrenadier Battalion 506. A terrific American artillery attack ravaged the regiment's ranks. The attack—although initially gaining a few hundred meters of ground—ended abruptly. The long-suffering men of SS-Gebirgsjäger Regiment 12 staggered back to the German lines hauling dead and wounded comrades. Operation Nordwind had truly withered, stalled, and failed.[43]

Within a day of the 12th's ill-fated attempt to resume the offensive, the Americans launched a number of focused counterattacks against the German line. The depleted regiment bore the brunt of an assault by the American 100th Infantry Division. The GIs punched through the German line with relative ease. Schreiber immediately launched a powerful counterattack, forcing the 100th Division troops to withdraw.[44]

Soon after Regiment 12 repelled the American incursion, the 6th SS-Gebirgs Division was assigned on 13 January to Luftwaffe *General der Flieger* (Aviation) Petersen's XC Korps. *Generaloberst* Blaskowitz ordered another attempt to revive the ill-fated Nordwind operation using this corps to attack southeast toward Baerenthal. The 256th Volksgrenadier Division replaced the 6th SS in the line, thus freeing the SS men for the attack.[45]

On 15 January, without warning, a powerful thrust by the 45th Infantry Division unhinged the 256th Volksgrenadier Division after twenty-four hours, forcing the grenadiers back toward Melch. Alarmed by this unexpected turn of events, Brenner ordered SS-Gebirgsjäger Regiment 11 to initiate a counterattack on 17 January and regain the lost ground—two hills—near Reipertswiller.[46]

In spite of the presence of the American artillery and the harsh winter weather, Raithel launched his attack at 1630 on 15 January.[47] The SS men moved quickly down steep slopes through the hostile, dense forest and immediately encountered well-prepared American positions on the surrounding hilltops. Finally the seasoned SS *gebirgsjägers* could bring to bear the combat skills they had honed in Finland. Hidden from the GIs' prying eyes, *SS-Hauptsturmführer* Degen's 1st Battalion exploited the surrounding camouflage and attacked uphill, infiltrating behind the American positions in groups of two and three men. Once behind the U.S. positions, the SS men sniped at the GIs from the rear, creating panic and chaos. *SS-Sturmbannführer* Paul Schneider's 3rd Battalion worked its way up the slopes even farther behind the GIs' positions. American artillery continuously fell among the Nord men as they made their way deep into the American rear area.

As darkness fell on the first day of fighting, the SS men finally gained some high ground overlooking a ravine that fed into the saddle between the two American-occupied hilltops. When dawn came, the SS men witnessed the first attempt to reinforce the surrounded GIs on the hills north of Reipertswiller. A lone tank rumbled forward along the road leading through the ravine. A *panzerfaust* round tore through the air and slammed into the vehicle's flank. The Nord men cheered.[48]

Soon the Americans made another attempt to reach their encircled comrades. A massive artillery bombardment preceded the attack. As the GIs approached the bridge over the ravine, the SS men opened fire. German *nebelwerfer* rockets crashed among the attacking GIs, wounding many men and stalling their attack.[49] The Americans tried to crack the German line again in the afternoon with two more tanks, but failed.

The battle for the hilltops raged on for the next several days. *SS-Standartenführer* Raithel maintained steady frontal pressure on the 45th's GIs while his snipers did their damage in and among the American positions. Raithel had exploited the confusion masterfully. After nearly five days of fighting, he had led his troops in surrounding five American infantry companies (C, G, I, K, and L) of the 45th Division's 157th Infantry Regiment using Finnish *motti* tactics.[50]

On 20 January more than 450 American soldiers fell into captivity. By comparison SS-Gebirgsjäger Regiment 11 suffered 26 dead, 127 wounded, and 12 missing. The 12th Company alone dropped from 113 to a mere 8 men. Some of these casualties resulted from frostbite and starvation. But the SS men had made a deep impression on the Americans. Lt. Col. Felix L. Sparks, commander of the 3rd Battalion, 157th Infantry, later lamented the Nord men's prowess in battle: "They were the best men we ever ran into, extremely aggressive, and impossible to capture. There was no driving them out, for they fought till they were killed."[51]

Regiment 11's remarkable success near Reipertswiller apparently pleased the senior German leaders. The XC Korps commander ordered *SS-Gruppenführer* Brenner to attack at 0000 on 23 January to seize once again the main exits leading through Zinswiller and from the Rothbach Valley.

The attack proceeded well on the first day. SS-Gebirgsjäger Regiment 12 reached Zinswiller by 1200 in the face of little resistance. SS-Gebirgsjäger Regiment 11 raced through the local municipal forest during the day and, in a daring night attack, captured Rothbach, which the Americans had occupied in force.[52]

The SS men resumed the attack the next morning on 25 January in an effort to gain the Moder River. The fighting quickly intensified, but this time the GIs did not give ground. *SS-Hauptsturmführer* Kreuzinger's 3rd Battalion, SS-Gebirgsjäger Regiment 12, seized Schillersdorf and captured forty-eight Americans and a number of vehicles. However, American counterattacks forced Kreuzinger's men into a small corner of the town. The GIs then held fast.[53]

Long-range American artillery, guided by spotter planes, pounded both SS regiments. Casualties quickly accounted for nearly half the SS division's strength. Brenner, alarmed by his appalling losses, requested that the division withdraw. The corps commander acceded and pulled the Nord Division completely from the line.[54]

The division assembled just north of the German front lines to await replacements and to prepare to assume a defensive position in the line. As Brenner feared, the recent fighting had stripped the division of almost 50 percent of its infantry strength. The artillery regiment remained at nearly full strength in men and materiel except for a dearth of ammunition and fuel. The rest of the division's noninfantry units also retained much of their original strength. Additionally, the Nord men replaced the few assault guns they lost in battle with captured American tanks.[55]

New recruits trickled in, filling the ranks of both mountain-infantry regiments with inexperienced and extremely young soldiers. Many of the replacements were once again *Volksdeutsche* (ethnic Germans) like many of the SS recruits that filled the ranks back in Finland. But unlike these earlier recruits, the quality of these soldiers was poor at best. Many were no longer volunteers but simply draftees. By the end of January 1945, the 6th SS-Gebirgs Division was losing the shape and character it had developed after nearly three years of fighting in Finland. After spending less than a month on the Western Front, the division's combat efficiency had decreased noticeably. Many seasoned, highly experienced combat leaders had died or been wounded since entering combat in the West. The division was slowly becoming a mere shell of its former self.[56]

At the end of January, the Nord Division reoccupied the line as part of the XC Korps' newly established defenses and spent most of February resting and refitting. Operation Nordwind had long since ended. The SS men defended a stretch of difficult terrain east of the forest near Ingwiller that spread eastward to cover the gap between the Low Vosges and the Haguenau forest. Since this gap offered the Americans the best chance of resuming an armored assault north sometime in mid-March (as far as German intelligence predicted), the SS men would have to strengthen their defenses in this region over the next month.[57]

SS-Gruppenführer Brenner was surprised at the American inactivity immediately following Operation Nordwind—especially in light of the excellent weather conditions. Allied air activity had dropped off considerably. He took advantage of the situation by erecting strong obstacles throughout his sector and executing a vigorous training program for new replacements. Brenner also suffered another blow to his division's fighting strength in the first week of February: he received orders to detach SS-Panzergrenadier Battalion 506 for a mission in the Saarbrücken area. He never saw or heard from the battalion again.[58]

Before the end of the first week in February, the 256th Volksgrenadier Division left the front line and forced the 6th SS-Gebirgs Division to shift westward to cover the new opening. The 36th Volksgrenadier Division, on the division's left flank, also moved westward to help compensate for the move. During this period the Nord men captured a number of American reconnaissance patrols; vigorous debriefings of the stubborn GIs yielded little or no useful information, however.[59]

Some general reshuffling of German units in the line occurred once more during mid-February. The XIII SS Corps' 559th Volksgrenadier Division had become the right flank unit for the Nord Division following the withdrawal of the 256th a couple of weeks earlier. But the 559th had withdrawn and a mountain division, the 2nd SS-Gebirgs Division, took its place. Patrolling and routine artillery duels with the Americans continued, but the front line remained relatively stable during the middle of the month. During the last week of February, the 2nd SS-Gebirgs Division withdrew, and the Nord Division shifted again to the west and northwest to new defensive positions extending from Bitche in the west to Reipertswiller in the east.[60]

On 28 February the 6th SS-Gebirgs Division troopers turned their defensive sector over to the 16th Volksgrenadier Division. The Nord Division was assigned to the LXXXII Korps for employment in an offensive in the

Ruwer area. On 2 March the American 10th Armored Division had seized the German city of Trier. The corps immediately charged *SS-Gruppenführer* Brenner with retaking this beautiful, ancient German border city. The division's strength had increased greatly thanks to the influx of replacements, so Brenner believed that his two regiments were ready to attempt this difficult task.[61]

The division foot-marched to an assembly area near Hermeskeil and prepared for the coming operation. The preparations lasted for several days as the division rehearsed and dispensed supplies for the scheduled attack in early March. This offensive would mark the division's first operation for the month of March 1945—the last month the division would exist as a viable combat formation.[62]

❖

Not far to the west, the American 71st Infantry Division approached the German border with France by truck and by train to relieve another far-more-seasoned infantry division—the 100th—west of Bitche in German-speaking Alsace. The Red Circle men had endured a long, hard journey from Fort Benning, Georgia, to the European Theater of Operations. After off-loading troop ships at the French port of Le Havre in early February 1945, the GIs finally set foot on the European continent—and joined the war they had trained so hard to fight and win.[63]

Maj. Gen. Willard G. Wyman was still uncertain about the fighting prowess of his men, but their time would come to face the Wehrmacht's legendary war machine. After a month in a mud-infested assembly area called Camp Old Gold in Normandy's Seine-Inférieure department (now Seine-Maritime) and a personal inspection by General Eisenhower, the Red Circle men were deemed fit to fight and headed to the front. The time had come to test their mettle against a steadily dying German Army. Few of them, including Wyman, suspected that the division's greatest battle would be the one that would destroy one of the best German divisions left on the Western Front—the 6th SS-Gebirgs Division Nord.

CHAPTER 3

The Saar-Palatinate Falls

March 1945 began for the 6th SS-Gebirgs Division with the planned attack to recapture Trier as part of General der Infanterie Walter Hahm's LXXXII Korps. SS-Gruppenführer Brenner spent 28 February to 2 March moving the division's men and equipment north via truck and rail. By 2 March the bulk of the division was concentrated near Hermeskeil. A steady stream of replacements and ammunition gave Brenner confidence that his men could still fight effectively—offensively or defensively.

The original order called for an attack through the Ruwer area to regain Trier, which the Americans had captured at the end of February. The Nord Division would attack as far west as the Trier–Niederzerf road near Pellingen to cut the road from the south. Brenner reviewed the plan and noted the lack of artillery support. Hahm listened to Brenner's pleas but could offer little help. The attack was on.[1]

On 6 March Brenner moved his command post to Holzerath, roughly twelve kilometers southeast of Trier. The two *gebirgsjäger* regiments moved forward to attack positions in the heavy forest located halfway between Pellingen and Holzerath—Regiment 11 on the right and Regiment 12 on the left. Each regiment had one *pionier* company from the engineer battalion to assist the *gebirgsjägers* in crossing their only water obstacle, the Ruwer River. SS-Reconnaissance Battalion 6 remained in reserve.

The American 94th Infantry Division of the U.S. XX Corps (part of the Third Army) held a series of thinly manned defensive positions along a ridgeline west of the Ruwer River in the exact area where the 6th SS-Gebirgs Division planned to cut the Trier–Niederzerf road. The 94th's GIs had not detected the Nord men's combat preparations.

At 0200 on 7 March, both *gebirgsjäger* regiments crossed the Ruwer on hastily constructed footbridges. The temperature dipped below freezing, and a thin layer of snow covered the landscape. By sunrise the infiltrating SS men of both regiments, after overcoming a mixture of light resistance and fierce close-quarters fighting, occupied from north to south Ollmuth, Niedersehr, Obersehr, Lampaden, and Schömerich.[2]

The taking of Schömerich just south of Lampaden proved particularly difficult for Schreiber's SS-Gebirgsjäger Regiment 12. From his foxhole on Hill 468 south of Schömerich, Pfc. William A. Foley Jr. of Company G, 302nd Infantry, watched in awe at the disciplined and skillful approach of Schreiber's men. The SS men attacked with vigor and ruthlessness as a stunned Foley and his fellow GIs fought fiercely to repel the assault. Foley could not help but feel impressed that he and his fellow GIs faced such a worthy adversary.[3]

Soon after the *gebirgsjägers* occupied the villages on the ridgeline, the 6th SS-Gebirgs Division's antitank and artillery units crossed the Ruwer. The Nord men had achieved remarkable success up to this point despite the growing number of casualties. Impressed, *General* Hahm placed elements of the 256th Volksgrenadier Division under Brenner's control for reconnaissance purposes to the north and south. The 2nd Gebirgs Division provided scouting information directly to Brenner. Both of Brenner's flanks were now secure.

SS-Standartenführer Raithel pushed the three battalions of his SS-Gebirgsjäger Regiment 11 forward unopposed and, by late morning, had seized his primary objective: a stretch of the Trier–Niederzerf road one kilometer south of Pellingen. By contrast, SS-Gebirgsjäger Regiment 12's lead battalion had become lost in the early morning hours and once again encountered strong resistance from the 94th Infantry Division's GIs, who stalled the SS men's advance. Schreiber reorganized his men for a second assault, but the GIs counterattacked in the late afternoon with tank destroyers. The SS men fought fiercely to blunt the American counterattacks, but the GIs kept returning for more. The SS men's ammunition ran low. Darkness fell. The Americans encircled one of Schreiber's battalions, but the battalion was still in radio contact with the regiment's headquarters.[4]

SS-Gebirgsjäger Regiment 11's luck soon changed for the worse. Counterattacking units from the 94th Infantry Division hit Raithel's men near Pellingen with a force equal to the SS men's earlier attack. Raithel's men held their ground, but casualties began to mount alarmingly.

SS-Sturmmann Jochen Seeliger and his machine-gun squad from the 3rd Battalion had set up their MG42 in pitch darkness in an open field overlooking—as they learned at dawn—the village of Lampaden. When daylight came, the 94th's GIs began their attack near Pellingen and Lampaden. The American infantrymen, crouching behind a half dozen Sherman tanks, moved toward the Nord men's positions.

When the lead tank came within range, Seeliger's gunner, Heinrich, opened fire. The lead tank pivoted right. Seeliger and Heinrich watched in terror as the tank lowered its 75-mm main gun and fired directly at their position. The two SS men pressed their bodies into their shallow hole. The tank round exploded behind the dugout harmlessly. The tank fired again and missed.

"My God, are they playing cat and mouse with us?" thought Seeliger.

The tank fired a third time and scored a direct hit. The force of the blast lifted the dirt, the MG42, and the two SS men out of their hole. Dazed but unhurt, Seeliger and Heinrich staggered to their feet and raised their hands in surrender. Excited GIs shouted at the two German soldiers. Nearby, one of Seeliger's wounded machine-gun crewmen sought cover in his hole. The man's mangled leg bled profusely.

"Get up!" shouted Seeliger. "It's over."

The wounded man grabbed his rifle to prop himself upward. An alarmed GI yelled and threw a grenade, which exploded in a violent cascade of dust and dirt. Seeliger and Heinrich saw the body of their comrade ripped apart beyond recognition. An American infantryman grabbed Seeliger's helmet from behind and yanked it violently, snapping the chinstrap: informal protocol for surrender was to remove one's helmet immediately.

As Seeliger and Heinrich stood in the field among the American infantrymen and tanks, they saw before them the horrific sight of scores of their dead comrades. Depressed and stunned, both Nord men silently followed their American escort down the hill and into the village of Lampaden. Their war was over.[5]

❖

Concerned that the fighting along the Trier–Niederzerf road was bleeding his two mountain infantry regiments white, *SS-Gruppenführer* Brenner asked *General* Hahm for permission to withdraw his men. Grudgingly, Hahm acceded to Brenner's request. On the night of 7 to 8 March, Brenner withdrew the two regiments across the Ruwer River. *SS-Standartenführer* Schreiber succeeded in freeing his one encircled battalion and withdrawing the rest of his Regiment 12 with little difficulty. However, the GIs dogged Regiment 11's every step. The Nord men were fighting a pursuing enemy force while trying to attack through another enemy force to their front. Eventually, Raithel had to choose between carrying out his wounded and losing the entire regiment. He ordered the seriously wounded SS men to remain behind so the survivors could withdraw in the darkness. Mercifully, the bulk of the regiment escaped.[6]

Dejected and disheartened at their costly venture, the SS men reassembled near Hermeskeil and awaited their next mission. A dour Brenner tallied the "butcher's bill" for this failed action: 500 dead and wounded and 150 men missing. The *sturmgeschütz* (assault gun) company lost six precious assault guns, and the antitank battalion lost five guns. These losses resonated deeply with Brenner, who had lost nearly all the replacements he had received in February in this single two-day action. The 6th SS-Gebirgs Division had captured 356 GIs—nearly three full rifle companies—and six American officers. The SS men also had destroyed eight American tanks and captured two. One of these tanks was an M5 General Stuart light tank taken over by *SS-Rottenführer* Eberhard Hilger of the SS-Gebirgs Panzerjäger Battalion. Hilger, a veteran of the division since 1942, and his comrades operated the captured tanks because they had experience with armored vehicles. Brenner added the M5 General Stuart light tank to his shrinking arsenal since he would need every weapon at his disposal in the coming days and weeks.[7]

❖

As the 6th SS-Gebirgs Division licked its wounds from the battle south of Trier, the American senior leadership began plotting to eliminate the remaining German defenses south and west of the Rhine—the only obstacles standing between the U.S. Third and Seventh armies and the bridgeheads across the Rhine. Once across the Rhine the Americans could race into Germany's heartland and strangle the German war machine into capitulation. With the capture of the Ludendorff Bridge over the Rhine at Remagen farther north on 7 March, a renewed impetus to breech on all fronts this last great natural obstacle into central Germany obsessed the American senior leaders.[8]

The area west of the Rhine that the Third and Seventh armies had to conquer before jumping the river was the Saar-Palatinate (see Map 3.1). This nearly five-thousand-square-kilometer mountainous region sat south of the Moselle River and included the Saar industrial area, the Bavarian Palatinate,

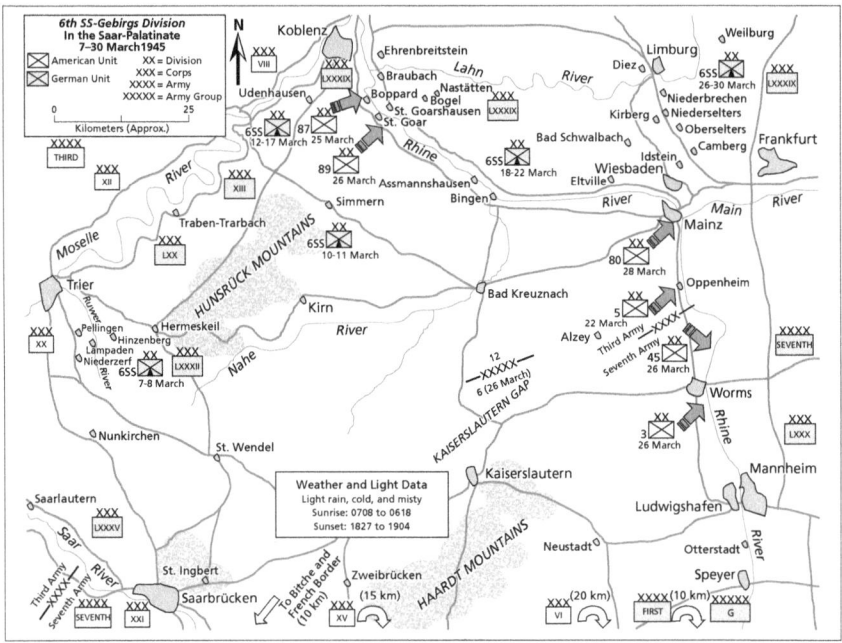

Map 3.1. 6th SS-Gebirgs Division in the Saar-Palatinate, 7–30 March 1945.

and a strip of French territory along the German border in the northeastern corner of Alsace. Lt. Gen. George S. Patton Jr.'s Third Army had already punctured the Siegfried Line by capturing Trier. If the Americans could further exploit this success on all areas of the Saar front, then the way would be open for the Third Army and Lt. Gen. Jacob Devers's 6th Army Group to capture crossing sites across the Rhine River between Mannheim and Mainz.[9]

The Saar was a vital logistical support base for Germany's armed forces and generated 10 percent of Germany's steel- and iron-producing capacity; it also included rich coalfields. Despite almost daily Allied bombing runs on the region, the Saar still pushed at least twelve trainloads of coal to manufacturing plants east of the Rhine River each day.

The area also was incredibly mountainous with deep, gorge-like valleys slicing through the terrain. The Hunsrück Mountains formed the Saar region's northern boundary while the Haardt Mountains of the Lower Vosges bordered the south near the Saar and Lauter rivers. The highway that led from Saarbrücken to Kaiserslautern—known to American planners as the Kaiserslautern Gap—represented the best place through which to funnel large numbers of troops and equipment.[10]

The man charged with defending the Saar-Palatinate from the Americans' grasp was the newly installed (as of late January) commander of Army Group G, *SS-Obergruppenführer* Paul Hausser, one of the Waffen-SS's most skilled and experienced leaders. Hausser's forces included the 1st Armee and—for a short time—the 19th Armee.

But the repeated American attacks throughout February—designed to straighten the front line—bled the 19th Armee of its divisions one by one. Finally, in early March, OB West shifted the 7th Armee to Hausser and withdrew the 19th—but this shift in forces did not remedy Hausser's overarching problem. He needed more troops to hold the German line, or his Army Group G faced imminent encirclement. *Generalfeldmarschall* von Rundstedt could not—or would not—compromise. He told Hausser to hold the Saar-Palatinate.[11]

For the U.S. Third and Seventh armies, seizing the Saar-Palatinate meant that these two forces could finish a task that began in December before Operation Wacht am Rhein and Operation Nordwind forced them to postpone the effort. Before these two German operations, Patton's Third Army had breached the Siegfried Line in two places. Only one of those breaches remained in Saarlautern. The Seventh Army had bounced the Lauter River at two points but had to withdraw from both bridgeheads when forced to expand to cover the line left open by the Third Army's commitment to the Ardennes farther north.

In the middle of February, General Eisenhower ordered Lt. Gen. Omar Bradley, commander of the 12th Army Group (which included Patton's Third Army) and Lieutenant General Devers's 6th Army Group (which included Patch's Seventh Army) to plan a joint offensive aimed at reducing the Saar-Palatinate and gaining bridgeheads across the Rhine River. Eisenhower told Bradley and Devers to shoot for 15 March as an attack date but that the offensive would not begin until British Field Marshal Bernard L. Montgomery's 21st Army Group had reached the Rhine farther north.

In the first week of March, Patch devised a plan with three corps attacking abreast directly through the Kaiserslautern Gap—Operation Undertone. Devers approved. Eisenhower also approved and further directed Devers to capture bridgeheads over the Rhine between Mainz and Mannheim. The Third Army would assist with diversionary attacks across the Moselle.

As the attack date neared, the Seventh boasted eleven infantry and three armored divisions for the operation while the Third Army had an even larger complement of twelve infantry divisions and four armored divisions. Since Patch's attacking corps had to stockpile fuel, ammunition, and other critical supplies, the Seventh Army could not attack earlier than 15 March. Patton, however, was ready to go on 12 March, and he saw no reason to wait. He knew the Germans were off balance, so Patton ordered his three corps—XX, XII, and VIII—to capture bridgeheads over the Rhine near Worms, Oppenheim, and Mainz. The fact that these three sites were in the Seventh Army's zone of attack did not seem to bother the imperturbable Patton.[12]

❖

Patton was correct about the German troops' problems. *SS-Obergruppenführer* Hausser's long defensive line forced him to defend a thinly manned front, so he shifted units from the 1st Armee to bolster the 7th Armee. But when the 7th Armee withdrew from the Eifel region before joining Army Group G, the army lost thousands of men and an entire corps headquarters. Hausser then pulled *General der Infanterie* Gustav Hoehne's LXXXIX Korps headquarters from the left flank of the 1st Armee and moved it to the 7th Armee. Hoehne's headquarters arrived on the Moselle River front on 9 March.

Hoehne's mission was to defend a forty-kilometer front from Koblenz to Cochem that included the snake-like convolutions of the Moselle River. His troops included an 1,800-man local defense force (Kampfgruppe Koblenz) and the greatly depleted 276th Infanterie Division. His last unit, the weakened 159th Infanterie Division (formerly of the 1st Armee), held the left flank. Hoehne pleaded for more forces, so Hausser released a unit intended for the 7th Armee's reserve—the 6th SS-Gebirgs Division.[13]

❖

On 9 March *SS-Gruppenführer* Brenner received the order to join *General* Hoehne's LXXXIX Korps while still struggling to reorganize and resupply his Nord men after their debacle along the Ruwer River south of Trier. Both mountain regiments and all divisional support units set out for Simmern that evening.

The next day, 10 March, 7th Armee messaged Brenner directing that the SS-Gebirgsjäger Regiment 12 turn off to the west for commitment near Traben-Trarbach on the Moselle River. Angered at splitting apart his command just before reaching a new sector, Brenner informed an equally irritated *SS-Standartenführer* Schreiber of the new orders. Both Brenner and Schreiber could not imagine that SS-Gebirgsjäger Regiment 12 would never again serve with the 6th SS-Gebirgs Division.

On 12 March Brenner met up with Hoehne at the LXXXIX Korps command post. Hoehne explained that the 6th SS-Gebirgs Division would reinforce the badly depleted 276th and 159th Infanterie divisions in the line by defending the corps' right flank south of Koblenz. Brenner immediately set up shop at Boppard on the western bank of the Rhine River and issued movement orders for the division.

The movement north progressed slowly owing to the fuel and truck shortage. Lack of fuel forced two artillery battalions to halt. The battalion commanders reported to the division artillery commander, *SS-Oberführer* Johann-Georg Goebel, that they would fight the Americans from where they were.

Before the sun set on 12 March, the lead elements of SS-Reconnaissance Battalion 6 arrived near Boppard. Brenner reported their arrival to Hoehne, who immediately ordered the battalion to plug the boundary shared by the 276th and 159th Infanterie divisions on the Moselle River.[14]

As SS-Reconnaissance Battalion 6 arrived in the 7th Armee area of operations, *SS-Obergruppenführer* Hausser released to the army the 559th Volksgrenadier Division. Hausser had to abandon some Siegfried Line positions—with Hitler's direct permission—before committing the 559th. The rest of the 7th Armee's defenses included XIII Korps (three *volksgrenadier* divisions and the understrength 2nd Panzer Division) on Hoehne's left. The rest of the Moselle River front leading south to Trier belonged to the LXXX Korps' three *volksgrenadier* divisions. South of the 7th Armee, the 1st Armee grew stronger thanks to the number of divisions absorbed from the 19th Armee following the collapse of the Colmar Pocket.[15]

Hitler had once again replaced the aging *Generalfeldmarschall* von Rundstedt. The new commander of OB West, *Luftwaffe Generalfeldmarschall* Albert Kesselring, visited the 1st and 7th Armee headquarters on 13 March for the first time. When Kesselring arrived, Hausser and the two army commanders argued that they could not hold the line against a concerted U.S.

attack. Kesselring acknowledged their concerns but could only repeat Hitler's order to hold the positions.

❖

Lieutenant General Patton planned his attack to exploit the weaknesses he sensed on the German side. XX Corps would attack first and draw off any German reserves in the area while XII Corps crossed the Moselle at one of the LXXXIX Korps' most thinly held points. The imminent convergence of the XX and XII Corps' drives would trap the 7th Armee's remaining two corps while the XII's southward penetration along the Rhine River might encircle all of Army Group G.

On the afternoon of 12 March, XX Corps' 3rd Cavalry Group launched a diversionary attack near the confluence of the Moselle and Ruwer rivers. At 0245 the night skies exploded as thirty-one divisional and corps artillery battalions erupted in unison. Fifteen minutes later the 94th Infantry Division (the Nord men's nemesis from the Trier attack), the 80th Infantry Division, and the 26th Infantry Division attacked. The advance was not easy, however. The deeply cut draws and ravines slowed the GIs' progress. The Germans resisted, but by nightfall on 13 March the 94th and 80th Infantry divisions held the first major ridgeline beyond the initial bridgehead. The 26th Infantry Division had even penetrated three kilometers beyond the Siegfried Line.[16]

On 14 March the American attack slowed. The Germans held their ground tenaciously. *SS-Standartenführer* Schreiber's SS-Gebirgsjäger Regiment 12, ordered to Trarbach along with SS-Panzergrenadier Battalion 506, counterattacked from the north to stall the American advance. Regiment 12 (serving under the command of the LXXXII Korps) had few troops available for a concerted effort, but the attack greatly slowed the 80th Infantry Division's advance.[17]

The damage inflicted by Schreiber's timely counterattack infuriated Patton. The Third Army's advance had slowed, and Patton feared that Lieutenant General Patch's Seventh Army, scheduled to attack the next day on 15 March, would beat him to the Rhine. But Patton's fears were ill founded: the German line showed no sign of imminent collapse.

The gains made by XX Corps on 15 March convinced Maj. Gen. Walton H. Walker, the corps commander, to launch his 10th Armored Division through the 94th and 80th Infantry divisions the next day and sprint the remaining forty kilometers to the Nahe River. On the lower part of the Moselle, Maj. Gen. Manton S. Eddy's XII Corps crossed the river on 14 March with three regiments. Anticipating success, he alerted his 4th Armored Division to move. On the far bank the GIs discovered that the 159th Infanterie Division defended villages converted into strongpoints. Farther downstream SS-Reconnaissance Battalion 6, sent in advance of the Nord Division's main body, arrived in time to assist in the defense.[18]

The first elements of SS-Reconnaissance Battalion 6 arrived at Niederfell on the east side of the Moselle River south of Koblenz on the evening of 12 March. The first unit to arrive was *SS-Hauptsturmführer* Karl-Hans Scheu's 4th Schwere (Heavy) Company, which consisted of an antitank platoon, an engineer platoon, and a 75-mm *infanteriegeschütz* (infantry gun) platoon.

The next morning, 13 March, Scheu led a small patrol across the Moselle to the town of Gondorf. To his surprise a four-person reception committee consisting of the town vicar, the *bürgermeister* (mayor), and two other local leaders greeted his patrol. The vicar wanted to know if Scheu and his men intended to "blow up" the town. Confused, Scheu simply answered, "No." The four-man group then led Scheu to two railway viaducts rigged with several large explosive charges (likely set by another German unit). Scheu's engineers expertly disconnected the charges.

The next day, 14 March, an American mechanized reconnaissance patrol entered Gondorf and clashed with the German outpost. The Americans withdrew after suffering several casualties. The following day, 15 March, a stronger American reconnaissance force arrived with more vehicles and troops. After a short but violent firefight, the outgunned SS men scattered. A horrified and angered Scheu watched from east of the Moselle as the local vicar, who had thanked him and his men so profusely for removing the explosive charges from the viaducts two days earlier, pointed out the 4th Company's positions in Niederfell across the river to an American officer. Feeling betrayed, Scheu withdrew his company eastward and away from the river by early afternoon.[19]

As darkness fell on 15 March, the XII Corps' 5th and 90th Infantry divisions had pushed three kilometers beyond the river. Using fog and smoke they created with machines as cover, engineers from both corps and division engineers built two treadway bridges across the Moselle. The armored exploitation was set to begin.[20]

General Hoehne quickly realized that the Americans had a solid bridgehead across the Moselle. His LXXXIX Korps' only hope was *SS-Gruppenführer* Brenner's 6th SS-Gebirgs Division, the main body of which was set to arrive the next day. But even Hoehne knew from Brenner's strength reports that the 6th SS had become too depleted to be fully effective.

The arrival late on 15 March of the Nord Division's main body motivated Hoehne to launch two counterattacks against the 90th Infantry Division's left flank before day's end. The first counterattack comprised two tanks supported by regular German infantry. The second counterattack involved the 6th SS-Gebirgs Division. The SS elements available for the attack were formed primarily around *SS-Standartenführer* Raithel's understrength SS-Gebirgsjäger Regiment 11—the division's remaining mountain infantry regiment.

The SS men's objective was the village of Pfaffenheck, nestled deeply in a forested area midway between the Moselle and Rhine rivers. The SS troopers—supported by a lone panzer—soon slammed into a battalion from the 90th Infantry Division. The Nord men fought furiously to keep the GIs from seizing the road through the village and to the east. A severe shortage of heavy weapons and ammunition kept Raithel from ordering a counterattack. Meanwhile, the 90th's other regiments expanded the bridgehead by another nine kilometers, allowing Combat Command A of the 4th Armored Division to pass through and gain two full kilometers before darkness set in. On the XII Corps' right wing, Combat Command B ruptured the German line and, in five hours, had plunged twenty-six kilometers beyond the Moselle River, rallying in Simmern for the night. Pleased with this progress, Patton pulled the 11th Armored Division from Maj. Gen. Troy H. Middleton's VIII Corps and sent it in the wake of the 4th Armored Division.[21]

Combat Command B's penetration of the German lines had sliced Hoehne's LXXXIX Korps in two. The 7th Armee commander, *General der Infanterie* Hans Felber, pleaded for help from *SS-Obergruppenführer* Hausser at Army Group G. Hausser released the first two battalions of the reassigned 559th Volksgrenadier Division and ordered the 1st Armee to release another *volksgrenadier* division.

But Felber, without consulting Hausser, ordered Hoehne to conduct a fighting withdrawal with those elements of the LXXXIX Korps still east of the American penetration. Hoehne also had the option of withdrawing across the Rhine. The XIII and LXXX Korps were still defending the Moselle River, and the American breakthrough threatened to encircle both commands.

Back in the XX Corps' zone, the 10th Armored Division passed through the 94th and 80th Infantry divisions at daybreak on 16 March. The German LXXXII Korps had reorganized during the night to strengthen the lines. *SS-Standartenführer* Schreiber's SS-Gebirgsjäger Regiment 12 was still under the corps' command. The Americans were going to aim a powerful armored thrust at the corps and eventually get through. In fact, Patton, during a meeting with the visiting supreme Allied commander, asked for the Seventh Army's reserve armored division, the 12th. Eisenhower agreed. To Patton's delight, XX Corps—like XII Corps—would have six divisions.

The XII Corps continued pushing forward with the 4th Armored Division's Combat Command B. After assembling for the night in Simmern, the tankers seized Soonwald, covered another twenty-three kilometers of ground, and bounced the Nahe River near the corps' objective, Bad Kreuznach. On the northern edge of the Soonwald, the American tankers felt the teeth of the defending SS-Reconnaissance Battalion 6. Still operating in small groups, the fatigued and ill-supplied SS men fought tenaciously but eventually gave ground. Combat Command A, 4th Armored Division, finally reached the Nahe by nightfall only to discover that the Germans had destroyed all bridges.[22]

German hopes of holding onto the Saar-Palatinate crumbled on 16 March. In the XIII Korps sector, the American 89th Infantry Division crossed the Moselle River with two regiments while the 11th Armored Division waited expectantly to follow. Farther north VIII Corps sent the 87th Infantry Division across the Moselle to seize Koblenz.

Hoehne's LXXXIX Korps had few troops in the area to stop the attack, so the 87th Infantry Division's 347th Infantry Regiment crossed the Moselle without firing a shot. But they soon encountered SS-Gebirgsjäger Regiment 11 on a narrow strip of land between the Moselle and Rhine at Waldesch. Raithel's troops resembled a menagerie of mixed equipment and men. As more Nord troops arrived, Brenner sent them forward to Raithel. Fortunately, Raithel's ad hoc battle group was still combat effective. Brenner had two forces at his disposal: his own regiment defending between Pfaffenheck and Udenhausen and another *kampfgruppe* of divisional units assembled around the remaining senior-ranking officer in the division, the Nord Division's artillery commander, *SS-Oberführer* Johann-Georg Goebel.

Johann-Georg Goebel was born the son of a schoolteacher on 30 June 1893 in Osterwieck in the Harz Mountains. He joined a foot artillery regiment on 12 October 1910 and later fought with that regiment on the Western Front in World War I. Following the war Goebel left the army, attended the police school in Eiche near Potsdam, and later became a police lieutenant. He became politically active with the National Socialists in the late 1920s, but his superiors in the police unit disciplined him for this behavior.

After Hitler assumed power in 1933, Goebel's career progressed without incident. When the Germans invaded Poland on 1 September 1939, Goebel, a member of the SS since July of that year, assumed command of a police battalion in East Prussia. On 28 May 1940 he resumed the life of an artilleryman and was assigned to the artillery regiment of the SS-Polizei Division until the defensive fighting around Leningrad (Saint Petersburg) began.

A gifted artillery officer, Goebel rose quickly in rank and, on 20 April 1943, assumed command of SS-Gebirgs Artillerie Regiment 6 in the Nord Division as an *SS-Standartenführer*. His adept and highly effective handling of this regiment against the Russians in the north earned him another promotion to *SS-Oberführer* on 21 June 1944, and later earned him the German Cross in Gold. As the commander of a *kampfgruppe*, Goebel would command ground maneuver forces in direct contact with a highly motivated enemy.[23]

❖

Goebel's *kampfgruppe* held the line between Udenhausen and Buchholz, but Raithel's regiment completely stalled the 347th Infantry Regiment's advance north of Pfaffenheck at Waldesch. SS-Reconnaissance Battalion 6 still operated in small groups on either side of the division's flanks but had no contact with any other units.

Throughout the day the GIs advanced toward Boppard on the Rhine River, but Raithel's men held tenaciously. The bitter fighting robbed Raithel of his best battalion commander, *SS-Hauptsturmführer* Günther Degen of the 1st Battalion, who was killed near Pfaffenheck on the morning of 16 March. The loss of this great leader and Knight's Cross recipient cast a terrible shadow over the regiment.[24]

The chaos and confusion that characterized Raithel's spirited defensive efforts made command and control for his officers at all levels extremely difficult. The previous day, 15 March, *SS-Hauptsturmführer* Walter Tank's 3rd

Battalion, SS-Gebirgsjäger Regiment 11, advanced as far as the small village of Herschwiesen, twenty kilometers south of Waldesch. Tank's attack stalled in the face of unrelenting American artillery fire. Since his radios functioned only intermittently, Tank had to rely on messengers to request further instructions. He dispatched his messenger, *SS-Sturmmann* Egon Krüger, with a note explaining the battalion's circumstances to Raithel.

Krüger's odyssey for the next two days—15 and 16 March—highlighted the chaotic nature of the violent clash between the attacking Americans and Raithel's defending SS troops. Krüger, a one-year veteran of the division and a former member of the 12th Company, was a dependable messenger. A reasonably skilled navigator, he would have to find Raithel's headquarters somewhere between Buchholz and Boppard.

Krüger trudged eastward across numerous open fields and arrived in Buchholz unharmed. American artillery, directed by slow-flying spotter planes, dogged his every step. He found Raithel's regimental headquarters in a nearby forest and ceremoniously delivered his message to a staff officer, who promptly returned with a reply. A weary and anxious Krüger set off once more toward Herschwiesen.

American spotter planes and artillery again dogged Krüger's every move. Sherman tanks began firing main-gun rounds from an unknown location directly into a nearby Luftwaffe flak (*flieger abwehrkanone*, or antiaircraft) position. The Germans dove for cover and waited until the shooting ended. Exhausted and stressed from his day's exploits, Krüger decided to spend the night of 15 March in the cellar of a bomb-damaged house with his new Luftwaffe friends.

Krüger awoke the next morning, 16 March, to bright sunshine and the sound of artillery shells falling throughout the area. Alarmed, he rushed from the house and toward two wooden bunkers south of the road from Buchholz. In the first bunker he encountered *SS-Oberführer* Goebel, who arranged a ride for him back to the 3rd Battalion's headquarters. Krüger delivered the message to Tank, who then told his exhausted messenger to get something to eat and prepare to return with a response.

Krüger set off once more on another dangerous journey back to regimental headquarters. After running a gauntlet of American artillery fire, he arrived after several hours of cross-country travel. A staff officer informed Krüger he would not be returning to his battalion. Instead, Krüger would become part of a small rear-guard force consisting of three other men and an officer. One thing quickly became clear to Krüger: the division was not going to remain west of the Rhine for long.[25]

As Egon Krüger's odyssey ended and the battle between his SS comrades and the 347th Infantry developed north of Pfaffenheck at Waldesch on 16 March, another regiment of the 87th Infantry Division crossed the Moselle River and attacked into southern Koblenz. At the end of the day, two American battalions were in the city. *General* Felber ordered *General* Hoehne to withdraw the LXXXIX Korps across the Rhine but to leave Kampfgruppe Koblenz behind to fight to the last man. Hoehne complied. By nightfall on 16 March, a heavy fog allowed Hoehne to withdraw his remaining 1,700 soldiers across the Rhine. Meanwhile, the 1,800-man Kampfgruppe Koblenz defended valiantly against the American offensive. By 19 March only 50 members of this *kampfgruppe* would escape across the Rhine.[26]

Farther south the Seventh Army attacked at dawn on 15 March. Patch's army, although consisting of several inexperienced divisions, boasted a solid backbone of seasoned combat veterans such as the 3rd, 36th, and 45th Infantry divisions organized into three corps—VI, XV, and XXI.

Two badly depleted German corps and the elements of another corps faced the Seventh Army. The XXI Corps would strike part of the LXXXV Korps while the XV Corps—the American main effort—faced the XIII SS Korps, the strongest of the two.[27]

Throughout the Seventh Army zone of attack, German resistance all but melted. The XV Corps advanced nearly ten kilometers while, on the right flank, the 100th Infantry Division gained the high ground overlooking the fortress town of Bitche by day's end. The 5th Infantry Regiment, 71st Infantry Division, was attached for this assault to the 100th Division, which had taken Bitche in December before withdrawing from their bloody prize. On the army's right flank, near the Wissembourg Gap, the VI Corps met little opposition. The corps' four divisions crossed the Moder River with little trouble.[28]

On 16 March, the second day of the Seventh Army's offensive, the Germans were merely delaying as best they could. The XV Corps made swift gains; as the sun set on 16 March, the 3rd and 45th Infantry divisions had punctured the German lines and crossed into Germany. The race was on to push the Germans back into their precious homeland—even though *Generalfeldmarschall* Kesselring staunchly continued to back Hitler's demand that no German units give ground.[29]

Although part of the XV Corps (the main effort), most of Maj. Gen. Willard G. Wyman's 71st Infantry Division had yet to get into the fight except for the 5th Infantry Regiment, which was attached to the 100th Division for the assault on Bitche. The Red Circle men joined the XV Corps, Seventh Army, on 10 March following an initial arrival-in-theater assignment to the new Fifteenth Army. Wyman's first mission was to relieve, occupy, and defend the positions of the veteran 100th Infantry (Century) Division in and around the fortress town of Bitche. On 11 March the division's artillery settled into fields near Montbronn, France; at 1150 that same day, the division fired its first shot against Germany's armed forces.[30]

By 12 March Wyman had moved his division command post forward to Ratzwiller, France. From 13 to 14 March, the regiments—organized as combat teams each with an engineer, medical, tank, and tank-destroyer company—relieved the Century men in the line.[31]

❖

The birth of the 71st Infantry Division arose from the U.S. Army's need not just for more ground troops, but also for units designed to meet the daunting threats posed on difficult terrain by two enemies in two separate theaters of war. The jagged mountains near El Guettar in North Africa and the hilly jungles of islands in the Pacific signaled the need for infantry units designed to fight where tanks and half-tracks could not venture. Consequently, the summer of 1943 heralded the advent of the first of three planned, compact striking forces capable of fighting in the most difficult terrain imaginable—the 71st Light Division.[32]

The 71st Light Division was activated on 15 July 1943 and formally entered active service on 21 August 1943 at a ceremony at Camp Carson, Colorado. Nearly eight thousand spectators witnessed the division's nine thousand soldiers leading 1,800 pack mules—bells jangling noisily—in review before the newly appointed division commander, Brig. Gen. Robert L. Spragins, a battle-hardened, thirty-year Army veteran. The Army's chief expert in mountain warfare, Brig. Gen. Onslow S. Rolfe, served as Spragin's Assistant Division Commander. A 1917 West Point graduate and World War I veteran, Rolfe had commanded the 87th Mountain Infantry Regiment and the Mountain Training Center at Camp Hale, Colorado.[33]

The 71st Light Division represented the amalgamation of two veteran regular-Army infantry regiments, the 5th and 14th, and the creation of a third, the 66th. The light concept reduced these regiments from the normal 3,087 troops found in the standard infantry regiment to 2,075 soldiers. The newest regiment, the 66th Infantry, began as the 1st Tank Regiment (Light Tanks) in 1929 but became an infantry regiment in 1943 by combining one battalion each from the 5th and 14th regiments, a cadre from Hawaii's 34th Infantry, and troops from the 89th Infantry Division. Most of the artillery, engineer, and support units were organized in much the same way. The men within the division did not come from any one region within the United States but instead represented a rich variety of backgrounds from across the country.[34]

The 71st's light infantry experiment began immediately for the Red Circle men, so named for the division's newly designed patch of the blue numbers "71" resting diagonally on a white field surrounded by a red circle. By December of 1943 training with the division's pack mules on Pike's Peak and Cheyenne Mountain demonstrated that the light concept could work. The division soon packed off to Hunter-Liggett Military Reservation in the mountains of California for a more intense twenty-one-day, three-phased training regimen against another experimental light division, the 89th. Torrential rains, ubiquitous mud, and supply problems that had GIs instead of the stubborn mules packing food and ammunition into the hills convinced the Army and the War Department to deem the light experiment a failure. The 71st returned to Camp Carson, put the mules out to pasture, and awaited orders.[35]

Labor shortages soon forced the Army to strip the division of all 3,200 of its privates and privates first class as overseas replacements. In May 1944 the Army ordered the Red Circle Division to Fort Benning, Georgia, and converted it into a standard, triangular division. The conversion increased the division's overall authorized strength from nearly 9,000 men to more than 14,000 and made the loss of the 3,200 enlisted men even more difficult to weather. The Army Specialized Training Program (ASTP) had selected soldiers of higher aptitude for advanced civil schooling and subsequent commissioning in technical branches such as the Engineer Corps but canceled the program in 1944 due to manpower shortages. Many of those ASTP men filled many of the gaps, but many troop positions remained vacant. In August Brigadier General Spragins departed the 71st to command a division in Europe, and the 71st welcomed a new commanding general, Maj. Gen. Eugene M. Landrum, a veteran of the Aleutians. Landrum had commanded the division for barely three months before a new commanding general stepped forward in November, a combat veteran with an enviable combat record—Brig. Gen. Willard G. Wyman.³⁶

Born in Augusta, Maine, on 21 March 1898, Wyman graduated West Point in November 1918—the month World War I ended—as a second lieutenant in the Coast Artillery Corps; he later transferred to cavalry. For the next seven years, he served in cavalry units in California and Texas. From July 1928 to August 1932, Wyman studied the Chinese language in Peking (now Beijing), China, while serving as a topographer for the Central Asiatic expedition in Mongolia. He first saw combat with the Chinese 19th Route Army in the defense of Shanghai against the Japanese in 1932.

Wyman returned to the United States and a more traditional Army career pattern for the next eight years. He was assigned to the China-Burma-India theater as Gen. Joseph Stilwell's G-3 (operations) representative to the Chinese 5th Army. A few months after the Allied forces landed in North Africa in November 1942, Wyman arrived there as a colonel and chief of Plans Subsection, G-3, Allied Forces Headquarters. Despite his service in two theaters, assignment to frontline troop units still eluded him. Operation Husky, the invasion of Sicily, loomed on the horizon, and Wyman's wish was granted in July 1943 when he received orders—and a brigadier general's star—to serve as the assistant division commander of the storied 1st Infantry Division, known as "the Big Red One."

Wyman's new duties allowed him to see combat at all levels in Sicily and as the Allies chased the Germans onto the Italian peninsula. But his most troubling combat experience—an event that would later compel him to train the 71st Division rigorously and realistically at Fort Benning—was the debacle he witnessed at Omaha Beach on D-Day, 6 June 1944. As the Big Red One landed in the first wave on the Normandy coast, the defending Germans cut down the flower of the division's troops mercilessly. Only true leadership from the front and vigorous training back in England allowed the Big Red One to carry the day on this most daunting and horrific of tasks.

Wyman fought with the Big Red One until the fall of 1944 before learning that the senior U.S. leadership had deemed him worthy of commanding his own division. He arrived at Fort Benning and took command of the 71st Division in November with great pride. His second star would soon follow, but Wyman was more interested in how well he could prepare the former mountaineers for the true realities of combat. Wyman's stock with the division immediately soared when he retracted an earlier order by Brigadier General Spragins that forbade the Red Circle men from blousing their trousers inside the tops of their new two-buckled, high-top combat boots—despite the protests of Benning's paratrooper community as the only soldiers allowed the right to do so. The Red Circle men never forgot this act of respect.[37]

The newly promoted Major General Wyman—with Omaha Beach still fresh in his mind—began vigorous, realistic, combined-arms training exercises with his Red Circle men. He insisted on combat conditions and tactical awareness at all times. Live-fire exercises with mortar rounds impacting one hundred meters from the troops reinforced the reality of the training.

But after only a short training period at Fort Benning, the order came to deploy the Red Circle Division to Europe. The GIs loaded weapons, vehicles, and other equipment on trains while Brigadier General Rolfe led an advance party to France. After a short stay at Camp Kilmer, New Jersey, the GIs boarded troop ships on 28 January 1945 and, after an overnight port stop in England, trundled down gangplanks on 6 February at the war-ravaged port of Le Havre and onto French soil. The GIs loaded trucks in the cold night air for a fifty-six-kilometer journey to Normandy's Seine Inférieure and a muddy tent city named Camp Old Gold—one of several "cigarette" camps used to stage arriving American units.[38]

Initially assigned to the newly activated Fifteenth Army, the Red Circle men spent an uncomfortable month in Camp Old Gold training and preparing for combat. A brief inspection from the supreme Allied commander, General Eisenhower, heralded the GIs' commitment to the front lines. On 6 March the Red Circle Division boarded "forty-and-eight" railroad cars (cars that held forty men or eight horses) and headed east toward the French–German border.

As of 10 March the 71st operated under the Seventh Army's XV Corps, the army's main effort for the spring offensive aimed at penetrating the Siegfried Line, taking that part of the Maginot Line not already in Allied hands, and pushing toward the Saar-Palatinate region of Germany.[39] Several special units soon appeared for attachment to the division, such as the 635th Tank Destroyer Battalion, the 530th Army Antiaircraft Battalion, and the 749th Tank Battalion.

The 71st's first mission was to secretly relieve the 100th Division, which defended positions just inside the French border with Germany (see Map 3.2). After a two-month static interlude of patrolling and artillery duels, the Century men were pulling out of the line to receive much-needed replacements and prepare for the Seventh Army's spring offensive to retake Bitche, crack the Siegfried Line, and seize the Saar-Palatinate. The 71st Division stepped in to fill the gap and guard the XV Corps' right, or eastern, flank. A lone GI spoke for everyone when he said, "This is it!"[40]

The relief-in-place operation occurred smoothly. The 5th and 66th infantry regiments—commanded by Col. Sidney C. Wooten and Col. Augustus J. Regnier, respectively—moved into positions near Lemberg and Enchenberg while Col. Donald Beeler's 14th Infantry Regiment occupied Meisenthal and Soucht on the division's right flank. Col. Carl E. Lundquist would replace Beeler on 19 March after Beeler was evacuated through medical channels following an unspecified—but serious—illness.[41]

By 15 March the 71st Infantry Division was firmly in place with the 42nd Infantry Division on their right and the 100th Infantry Division on their left. While guarding the XV Corps' right flank during the opening hours of the attack, the Red Circle men captured their first two German soldiers. A thorough interrogation of these prisoners at the division command post revealed that the XV Corps attack had already prompted a regiment of the weakened 16th Volksgrenadier Division to withdraw through the Siegfried Line toward Pirmasens.

The news of hastily withdrawing Germans emboldened the Red Circle men into thinking that Germany's finest could not stop the American war machine. The GIs wanted to get into the action—to fight a foe more worthy than the German units already bled white by months of fierce combat. Their commander, the veteran Major General Wyman, knew his men would get their chance soon enough.[42]

❖

Farther north in the German 7th Armee's sector, the beleaguered LXXXIX Korps enjoyed a brief respite from the attacking 4th Armored Division, which paused to regroup after establishing a bridgehead over the Nahe on 16 March. The delay helped *General* Hoehne withdraw his corps to the eastern side of the Rhine River.

The rest of the 7th Armee—and the right flank of the 1st Armee—did not enjoy a similar break from the fighting, however. The 12th Armored Division kept up the pressure and reinforced XX Corps on 17 March while the 10th Armored Division captured a bridge over the tiny Prims River. On the XII Corps' right flank, the 89th Infantry Division expanded the bridgehead over the Moselle as the 11th Armored Division made a final drive to the Nahe.[43]

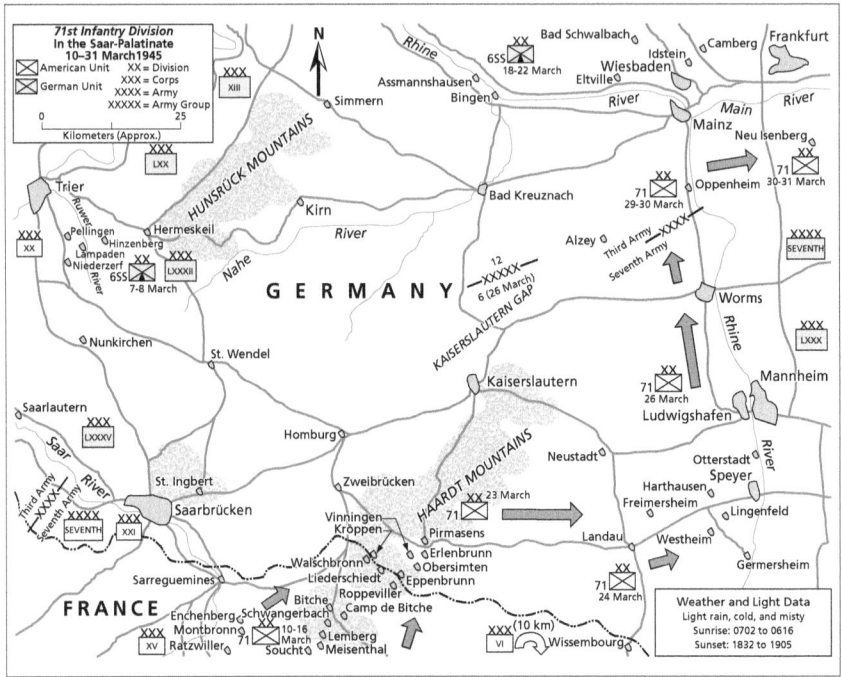

Map 3.2. 71st Infantry Division in the Saar-Palatinate, 10–31 March 1945.

At dawn on 17 March, XIII Korps attacked the 4th Armored Division, but the counterattack's rapid failure signaled to *General* Felber that the defense of the Saar-Palatinate was no longer possible. Even *SS-Obergruppenführer* Hausser, the commander of Army Group G, begged *Generalfeldmarschall* Kesselring to withdraw behind the Rhine. Felber and Hausser both knew the Americans would encircle the XIII Korps and the LXXX Korps in a matter of days—or even hours.

Late in the day on 17 March, Kesselring issued an ambiguous order to defend the Saar-Palatinate but to avoid encirclement. Hausser understood this order as implied permission to withdraw his forces at least behind the Nahe River.[44]

Hausser immediately ordered a general withdrawal. Hoehne's LXXXIX Korps headquarters, in Boppard on the west side of the Rhine River, received instructions from the 7th Armee to disengage and withdraw east of the Rhine. The 6th SS-Gebirgs Division would hold their present positions and block the American forces from Boppard while the rest of the corps crossed the river.

SS-Gruppenführer Brenner—even before receiving word from the corps headquarters—had already planned to send his rolling stock, horses, medical company, and support units across the Rhine via ferry on the night of 16 to 17 March. The American commanders clearly sensed that the Germans were trying to escape. However, Brenner's service and support troops still traversed the Rhine unscathed.

The Americans even targeted their propaganda efforts directly at the 6th SS-Gebirgs Division. Perhaps in recognition of the SS men's battlefield prowess, the Americans wanted to keep the Nord men from escaping across the Rhine to fight another day. The Americans launched artillery-delivered propaganda leaflets addressed directly to the 6th SS. One of those leaflets read as follows (see Figure 3.1):

6. SS

Many of your comrades with the 6.SS already walked the way into captivity. Thereby, the opportunity opened for them, as well as for all other German soldiers in Allied captivity, to return to a peaceful home after the war. Now they know, like nearly one million other German soldiers, what it means to enjoy fair treatment in captivity.

Many of your comrades with the 6.SS are all the more impressed with their happy experience in Allied captivity as they felt disdained in their own ranks. All those among you who were put into the SS uniform through bitter coercion, who by chance or by Himmler's orders found yourselves in the SS instead of a unit of the Wehrmacht, all those finally who realize the senselessness of further self-sacrifices in a lost sector of the front, to all those we call

Look for the OFFICIAL PASS

which we'll give you as well as to all other German soldiers. Read it carefully, point by point, and it applies to you point by point—and note that under all the promises made in it the name of the supreme Allied commander, Gen. Eisenhower (pronounced Eisenhauer) is signed. Use it if the opportunity is there.[45]

This particular propaganda effort may have resulted in a handful of defections, but most Nord men viewed the leaflets with disdain.[46]

Fog enshrouded the Rhine River crossing site at Boppard on the morning of 17 March, but Brenner had yet to receive word from *General* Hoehne that his main force could withdraw. The Americans resumed their tank and infantry assaults against SS-Gebirgsjäger Regiment 11 near Pfaffenheck and Udenhausen, but the American attacks seemed weaker than usual. Finally, Brenner received permission to send his two combat forces—SS-Gebirgsjäger Regiment 11 and Goebel's battle group—across the river by ferry. The two units—under the protection of heavy fog—crossed the Rhine at Boppard and Brey.[47]

SS-Sturmmann Egon Krüger, the messenger turned rear-guard soldier from the 3rd Battalion, SS-Gebirgsjäger Regiment 11, spent the night on the east bank of the Rhine only to return to the west side before dawn. When he awoke inside the house occupied by his small rear-guard force, he encountered two German civilians sitting outside cooking over an open fire. One civilian casually offered Krüger some civilian clothes so the SS man could desert from his unit. Krüger answered angrily, "Whether the war is lost or not, I will never voluntarily surrender and become a traitor—whether my country is right or wrong!" He then boarded a ferry, crossed the Rhine, and occupied a rear-guard outpost in the ruins of an ancient *schloss* (castle). The first group of withdrawing SS men soon emerged from the darkness. To his surprise, Krüger saw *SS-Hauptsturmführer* Tank, his battalion commander, leading the 3rd Battalion's remnants—a mere thirty or forty men. He waved his comrades toward the riverbank and the ferry that would take them across. His mission complete, Krüger returned to the east bank just in time for another long march to the east.[48]

By the morning of 18 March, Brenner's new command post was in Braubach east of the Rhine. The division's main body was already across, and rear-guard forces west of the river detected no pursuing American troops. Aside from some U.S. artillery fire on the crossing sites, the Nord Division had crossed the Rhine with little incident.[49]

As reports arrived at the command post, Brenner noted that his remaining units had crossed intact but with significant personnel losses. The division staff and signal battalion remained together and functioning. SS-Gebirgsjäger Regiment 11's three battalions could barely assemble fifty combat-effective men except for the 3rd Battalion, which managed to muster one hundred men into two companies of fifty, armed only with submachine guns or MG42s. Eighteen-year-old Egon Krüger, formerly the battalion messenger, joined one of these ad hoc companies. Krüger believed that this company, under

6.SS Viele von Euren Kameraden in der 6. SS sind jetzt bereits den Weg in die Gefangenschaft gegangen. Ihnen wie allen anderen deutschen Soldaten in alliierter Gefangenschaft hat sich damit die Möglichkeit der Rückkehr in eine befriedete Heimat nach dem Krieg eröffnet. Sie, wie fast eine Million anderer deutscher Soldaten, erfahren jetzt, was es bedeutet, in Kriegsgefangenschaft das Recht fairer Behandlung zu geniessen.

Viele von Euren Kameraden in der 6. SS sind umso tiefer von ihrer glücklichen Erfahrung in alliierter Kriegsgefangenschaft beeindruckt, als sie sich in ihren eigenen Reihen oft missachtet fühlten. Allen denen unter Euch, die der bittere Zwang in die SS-Uniform gesteckt hat, die Ihr Euch durch einen Zufall oder auf Grund von Himmlers Befehlen in der SS findet anstatt in einer Einheit der Wehrmacht, all den SS-Männern ferner, die die Sinnlosigkeit weiteren Opfertodes in einem verlorenen Frontabschnitt einsehen, rufen wir zu:

HALTET AUSSCHAU NACH DEM

AMTLICHEN PASSIERSCHEIN

den wir Euch wie allen anderen deutschen Soldaten zukommen lassen. Lest ihn aufmerksam durch, Punkt für Punkt — und er gilt Punkt für Punkt für Euch — und beachtet, dass unter den dort gemachten Versprechen der Name des alliierten Oberkommandierenden, Generals Eisenhower (sprich: Eisenhauer) steht. Nutzt ihn, wenn die Gelegenheit sich Euch bietet.

Figure 3.1. U.S. propaganda leaflet directed at the 6th SS-Gebirgs Division.

the command of an incompetent SS officer alleged to be a former political leader (or Gauleiter), was a wretched and sorry gang. The company consisted of younger recruits and older men transferred from the Kriegsmarine or rear-echelon supply units. Krüger believed that only he, along with a misplaced sergeant from the lost SS-Gebirgsjäger Regiment 12 and the 12th Company's former tailor, were the most experienced soldiers in the lot.[50]

Brenner's personnel woes were further compounded when he had to detach one mountain-troop company to the commander of the Koblenz garrison. However, the reconnaissance battalion still held strong with 150 men while the artillery regiment's fully manned staff—serving *SS-Oberführer* Goebel—controlled two light mountain artillery battalions totaling sixteen guns. The antitank battalion managed to retain twelve guns, and the *pionier* battalion survived with two companies of 60 SS combat engineers each. The division's field-replacement battalion from the Pfalz even managed to send 500 minimally trained replacements. In spite of the SS men's recent setbacks, morale remained reasonably high.[51]

As Brenner reorganized his exhausted troops, *General* Hoehne received orders to establish a new front line along the Rhine once all of the LXXXIX Korps' units were east of the river. He directed the 6th SS-Gebirgs Division to occupy the left wing of this new line from Nastätten southward in an arc to Eltville, just west of Wiesbaden. The 276th Infanterie Division would hold the right wing from Nastätten north to Ehrenbreitstein (in the suburbs of Koblenz). A composite group of forces commanded by army *Generalleutnant* Ludwig von Berg (the commander of Wehrkreis [Military District] XII in Koblenz) held a thin security line east of the river in Brenner's new sector that consisted mostly of flak units, two police companies, and Volkssturm (German People's Army) forces. Hoehne, knowing that von Berg's troops had little combat value, placed these forces under Brenner's control.[52]

When the sun rose on 19 March, the Americans had yet to initiate a crossing of the Rhine. After reviewing the situation, Brenner kept the current security line in place but with officers detached from the division staff to serve as local commanders for the poorly trained Volkssturm and flak units. He opted to use his two *kampfgruppen* (battle groups) led by *SS-Standartenführer* Raithel and *SS-Oberführer* Goebel as mobile (truck-mounted) reserves positioned back from the river but within striking distance. Goebel would have at his disposal one *gebirgsjäger* battalion from SS-Gebirgsjäger Regiment 11, a mountain artillery battalion, a *pionier* company, and four antitank guns positioned five kilometers northeast of St. Goarshausen, a possible crossing point for the Americans. Kampfgruppe Raithel, positioned farther south near Eltville, boasted two *gebirgsjäger* battalions, a mountain artillery battalion, a *pionier* company, and eight antitank guns. Brenner's most skilled and experienced ground-troop commander, Helmuth Raithel, had the larger of the two groups to thwart any crossing efforts north of Mainz, the most probable American crossing point.

By nightfall on 19 March, the 6th SS-Gebirgs Division's two battle groups were set in their assembly areas. The next night, 20 March, American reconnaissance patrols attempted to cross the river on rafts south of St. Goarshausen. The SS officers who presided over the Volkssturm soldiers set their charges to work. The older men opened fire and forced the GIs to paddle back from whence they came. The Americans were boldly searching for ways to jump the Rhine quickly. Clearly, the worst was yet to come.⁵³

By 18 March SS-Gebirgsjäger Regiment 12 was awash in a sea of advancing American units. *SS-Standartenführer* Schreiber had lost contact with his higher headquarters, the LXXXII Korps, and knew nothing about the larger situation. Schreiber's radio operators intercepted a Wehrmacht communiqué that mentioned a new line of resistance east of the Rhine. In the absence of further information, Schreiber decided to move his regiment across the river at Worms, but his men lacked vehicles that would allow them to outpace the rapidly advancing Americans.

To enable his men to escape through the American lines undetected, Schreiber reorganized his dwindling regiment into several small groups. He issued each group leader handwritten orders to proceed eastward to Worms, cross the Rhine, and then rally with the rest of the regiment. When darkness fell, the groups headed toward the Rhine River through a landscape rife with enemy troops. Unfortunately, few of Schreiber's men reached the water. The Americans intercepted most of the escaping German troops as they crossed open fields near the river's west bank. Only a handful of officers and men evaded capture. Within a matter of days, SS-Gebirgsjäger Regiment 12 had dissolved from the field of battle.⁵⁴

As the senior German commanders struggled to control their steadily deteriorating situation, General Eisenhower saw new opportunities on the horizon. The supreme Allied commander, impressed by Patton's rapid gains, wanted to shift boundaries and have Patton attack across the northern zone of Patch's Seventh Army but perpendicular to the Seventh's attack axis. The objective was to cut off and destroy the remaining German forces in the Saar-Palatinate. After this maneuver, Patton would withdraw from the Seventh Army's zone of attack.[55]

To the corps commanders in the Third Army, the new plan meant that the race was on. Patton turned up the heat and chided his commanders to take to the roads and trap the Germans before they—the Americans—lost their opportunity. As the sun rose on 19 March, XX Corps, beefed up by the addition of the 12th Armored Division, started their trek. During that one day they covered about thirty-seven kilometers, an extraordinary amount of ground; by nightfall the men could see the Nahe River. Likewise, by dark the 10th Armored Division was only nine kilometers from Kaiserslautern.

To the north in the XII Corps area, the 4th Armored Division failed to regain momentum on 18 and 19 March; German resistance had stiffened as the tankers approached the Rhine. But on the corps' right flank, the 11th Armored Division met little resistance and, on 18 March, dashed thirty-two kilometers to the Nahe River. The following day, the tankers raced another twenty-one kilometers and reached Kaiserslautern. The combined advances of XX and XII Corps clearly meant encirclement for the German XIII and LXXX Korps.[56]

By 20 March the German 7th Armee and the right wing of the 1st Armee—*General* Hahm's LXXXII Korps—were on the verge of total collapse. German formations were in full flight. Burning panzers and other vehicles were strewn across the countryside. White sheets—a sign not just of surrender but of submission—hung from the buildings and homes in each German town.

The end was at hand for the German forces defending the Saar-Palatinate. By day's end XX Corps owned the high ground overlooking the city of Mainz on the Rhine River and, by nightfall, would enter the Rhine plain. Finally, the withdrawal order came. *General* Felber was one of the last to leave as he and his 7th Armee staff crossed to the east side of the Rhine. The 1st Armee units still fighting from within the Siegfried Line fortifications near Saarbrücken and Zweibrücken withdrew to avoid American entrapment and then moved to block the main avenue of approach leading into the Kaiserslautern Gap.[57]

On 19 March the XXI Corps breached the main fortification line near St. Ingbert. That night the XIII SS Korps withdrew in front of the XV Corps. By 20 March the enemy was gone. VI Corps further compounded the threat to the withdrawing 1st Armee forces by striking the Siegfried Line in the Wissembourg Gap with four American divisions concentrated along a thirty-two-kilometer front. It was only a matter of time before the German defenses had collapsed.[58]

Up north in the XX Corps zone, the 12th Armored Division headed toward Ludwigshafen on the Rhine River while the 10th Armored Division turned southeastward. When the sun set on 20 March, the 10th Armored Division was a few hundred yards from the main road leading through the Pfaelzer Forest—a primary German escape route. As the 10th's tanks penetrated the forest late on 20 March, the XC Korps fell back. When the 42nd Infantry Division on the VI Corps' left flank attacked the Siegfried Line on 21 March, the enemy troops were gone.

When darkness fell on 22 March, the remaining German forces in the Saar-Palatinate had only a few hours left before the region west of the Rhine collapsed. The 12th Armored Division was within nine kilometers of Speyer—the last gap open to the retreating Germans.

Three days earlier, 19 March, the Germans had blown up all bridges over the Rhine River north of Ludwigshafen. The next day, 23 March, German engineers destroyed the bridge at Speyer. The last bridge over the Rhine was east of Landau at Germersheim. Escaping German troops frantically pushed vehicles, assault guns, tanks, and other equipment across this bridge.[59]

On 23 March VI Corps broke through the final German defenses. A spirited defense at Speyer by some remaining German units kept the 12th and 14th Armored divisions from linking up that day. By 24 March the two armored divisions swept aside all German resistance and raced for the bridge at Germersheim.

The time had come for the 71st Infantry Division to get into the fighting. After spending the last several days leapfrogging behind the advancing armored and infantry divisions, Major General Wyman's men received the mission to grab the bridge at Germersheim.

The Red Circle men's combat experiences had been modest up to this point. The 71st had conducted a series of moving relief-in-place operations with the advancing 100th Infantry Division. On 21 March, though, the division shifted to the XXI Corps, and the pace of operations increased. The Red Circle men soon encountered the outer belts of the Siegfried Line.[60]

Following some brisk and spirited fighting near Eppenbrunn, the Red Circle men breached the German defenses. Colonel Regnier's 66th Infantry Regiment neutralized all enemy bunkers in the regiment's zone and then pushed forward to take Pirmasens, a major German supply center.[61]

With their feet planted firmly on German soil, the Red Circle men advanced quickly by foot and by truck. Colonel Wooten led his 5th Infantry Regiment against and through Landau, while Colonel Lundquist's 14th Infantry Regiment kept pace and covered the division's open right flank. By 23 March the 5th Infantry cleared Landau, and patrols from each of three regiments struck eastward toward the Rhine River. The 71st Infantry Division occupied positions that put them within striking distance of the bridge at Germersheim. Wyman promptly issued Field Order Number Eight—the field order that gave the Red Circle men the chance to seize a bridge over the famed Rhine River.[62]

The primary mission of seizing the bridge rested with the 5th Infantry Regiment's 2nd and 3rd battalions (the 1st Battalion, 5th Infantry, would follow in reserve). The entire 66th Infantry Regiment would attack and seize the bridge, supported by tanks from the attached 749th Tank Battalion in close coordination with the 12th Armored Division, which had already stopped and was planning to attack the town as well. (The 12th had been reassigned from the Third Army to the Seventh Army on 23 March.)[63]

The attack began at 1000 on 24 March. A planned aerial bombardment tortured the town of Germersheim while sparing the still-intact bridge. The Germans had three working ferries at the site frantically shuttling troops and equipment across the Rhine. The 12th Armored Division moved forward and quickly seized Westheim to the north of Germersheim. The 5th and 66th infantry regiments attacked shortly thereafter at 1015.[64]

The 3rd Battalion, 5th Infantry, rushed north of the 12th Armored Division's GIs to take Lingenfeld on the left flank. The Red Circle men slammed into a wall of intense German artillery and small-arms fire that stopped them in their tracks. Earlier reports suggested that the Germans had evacuated Lingenfeld, but the reports were clearly false. White sheets fluttered deceptively from the windows of several buildings.[65]

Company L, 3rd Battalion, soon rallied, and the GIs sprinted for Lingenfeld, firing as they ran. The heavy volume of German artillery and machine-gun fire continued unabated. On reaching the outskirts of Lingenfeld, the GIs cleared the first few houses with hand grenades. The Red Circle men tossed more grenades through windows, killing many of the occupants inside. The GIs knew some of the dead included civilians, but they had no sympathy for them. The townspeople had draped white sheets throughout their town as a sign that Lingenfeld had surrendered. The GIs would not be duped again.[66]

Advancing on the 3rd Battalion's right flank, Lt. Col. Charles M. Gettys's 2nd Battalion, 5th Infantry, also ran into fierce small-arms fire along the Lingenfeld-Westheim rail line. Gettys's mission was to attack across the open farmland between Lingenfeld and Westheim and then on to Germersheim to seize the bridge. To further compound the battalion's woes, the GIs began receiving harassing fire from the southern outskirts of Lingenfeld. Several Red Circle men cursed the 3rd Battalion for failing to seize that town on time.[67]

Farther north, the 3rd Battalion, 5th Infantry, eventually secured most of Lingenfeld on 24 March. The battle for Lingenfeld had become the single bloodiest day in the combat history of the 5th Infantry Regiment and—for that matter—the 71st Infantry Division. The 5th Infantry suffered a staggering twenty-three killed and sixty-nine wounded.[68]

As the 5th Infantry Regiment fought to take Lingenfeld and advance on Germersheim, the 66th Infantry and 12th Armored Division pressed their main attack into Germersheim proper, but the going there proved difficult as well. At 1020—mere minutes after the attack began—the Germans blew the bridge sky high. Wyman radioed his troops to hold fast. The Red Circle men and the tankers of the 12th Armored Division waited until 1630 to resume the attack, but darkness quickly set in. The attack petered out. The race to grab the bridge had failed.[69]

Dismayed at failing to seize an intact bridge, the Red Circle men and the American forces west of the Rhine spent the rest of 24 March and all of 25 March mopping up stragglers. The men of the 71st Infantry Division were no longer green by the standard definition. The price had been high for the experience gained that day. After mopping up, the 5th and 66th infantry regiments moved northeast toward Speyer to join the 14th Infantry Regiment, which had moved to that area during the Germersheim operation.[70]

The attack to seize the bridge at Germersheim signaled the culmination of the Saar-Palatinate campaign, which ended with tremendous losses to the German 1st Armee and 7th Armee. The Seventh Army staff estimated that the Germans lost 75 to 80 percent of their infantry strength during the fighting.[71] The German prisoner count was high as well: the Seventh Army captured 22,000 Germans while the Third Army nabbed more than 68,000. Casualties on the American side were not as great as on the German side but were significant nonetheless. The Third Army suffered 5,220 casualties, of which 681 were killed in action. The Seventh Army incurred 12,000 casualties with 1,000 dead. The campaign was a brilliant display of offensive maneuver on the American side; but the Germans, for their part, had skillfully handled their forces in effective delaying actions that frustrated many of the American efforts.[72]

CHAPTER 4

Convergence

The stunning American success in the Saar-Palatinate did not prompt Lieutenant General Patton to rest on his laurels. He wanted to beat British Field Marshal Montgomery's 21st Army Group in the north across the Rhine. Fortunately, Lieutenant General Bradley's new instructions allowed Patton to jump the Rhine (ostensibly near Mainz) and then drive northeast up the Frankfurt–Kassel corridor to converge with the First Army along the Lahn River—a convergence that would ultimately bring the 71st Infantry Division into direct contact with the Nord Division. Patton was clearly pleased.[1]

German resistance near Mainz suggested that a crossing there might prove difficult, so Patton instructed his XII Corps commander, Maj. Gen. Manton S. Eddy, to conduct a feint, a limited-objective attack, near Mainz but to traverse the Rhine seventeen kilometers farther south at Oppenheim. Patton knew that Montgomery planned to cross the Rhine the night of 23 March, so Eddy charged his 5th Infantry Division, commanded by Maj. Gen. S. LeRoy Irwin, to cross that night—on 21 March!

After the first two regiments of the 5th Infantry Division were across, Eddy planned to push the 4th Armored Division over the river, bypass Frankfurt-am-Main, and jump the Main River at Hanau. The XII Corps would then advance northward and link up with the First Army along the Lahn River. This convergence of armies would hopefully trap thousands of German troops in the Ruhr industrial region.[2]

❖

A mere two days had passed since *General der Infanterie* Felber's 7th Armee had crossed to the east side of the Rhine River. He still held an eighty-kilometer sector of the Rhine—from Wiesbaden to Mannheim—with only a handful of bedraggled German units. Felber's only hope of blunting an American crossing near Oppenheim was his sole reserve force, the understrength 159th Volksgrenadier Division. Felber had lost the LXXXIX Korps to Army Group B in the north, and his staff had lost communications with the 1st Armee in the south.³

A few minutes before 2200 on 22 March, the 3rd Battalion, 11th Infantry, 5th Infantry Division, stormed across the Rhine at Nierstein against little German opposition. To the south, the 1st Battalion's assault at Oppenheim met only brief resistance. By 0000 the entire 11th Infantry Regiment was across the Rhine, and a second regiment was loading the boats.

By early afternoon on 23 March, the entire 5th Infantry Division and a regiment of the 90th Infantry Division were east of the Rhine. Within twenty-four hours the bridgehead was more than eight kilometers deep, and Major General Eddy sent orders to the 4th Armored Division to cross the Rhine early the next day.

General Felber struggled to mount a counterattack against the American bridgehead. At 0000 on 23 March, he launched a regimental-sized unit drawn from students of the Wiesbaden officer candidate school into the northern edge of the bridgehead. Amid the chaos and confusion, the GIs ran off the German attackers. Lieutenant General Bradley then joyously proclaimed to the press that Patton was across the Rhine.⁴

Meanwhile, Patton was already planning two more assault crossings of the Rhine River with Maj. Gen. Troy H. Middleton's VIII Corps. Middleton planned to send the 87th Infantry Division across the Rhine at Boppard near the confluence with the Lahn River at daybreak on 25 March. Twenty-four hours later the 89th Infantry Division (recently transferred from XII Corps) would cross at St. Goar thirteen kilometers to the south. Patton ordered both crossings to occur at the Rhine gorge, a deep, canyon-like valley bordered on the west by the Hunsrück Mountains and on the east by the Taunus Mountains. The shear four-hundred-foot cliff facings made the gorge an unlikely place for a crossing.⁵

Defending the Rhine gorge was the overstretched LXXXIX Korps commanded by *General der Infanterie* Gustav Hoehne. Hoehne and his corps had spent more than a week east of the Rhine preparing for future operations. Yet on the eve of the VIII Corps' first assault crossing of the Rhine gorge, *Generalfeldmarschall* Kesselring of OB West transferred the 6th SS-Gebirgs Division from Hoehne's corps and sent the Nord men southeast toward Wiesbaden—possibly to assist against the Oppenheim crossing. The move angered Hoehne, who had lost his most combat-effective division, rendering his corps nearly unfit to defend against a concerted American crossing effort.

SS-Gruppenführer Brenner had actually received word of Kesselring's decision on 22 March. The decision surprised Brenner, who had just disposed his SS and Volkssturm troops along the Rhine from Nastätten southward to Eltville to blunt any American crossing efforts. Brenner's staff managed to find enough trucks to transport all units within the Nord Division except for one *gebirgsjäger* battalion. That battalion—from SS-Gebirgsjäger Regiment 11—would have to remain behind temporarily. The 6th SS-Gebirgs Division's last march element closed on the new assembly area northwest of Frankfurt and north of Wiesbaden on 24 March—a scant few hours before Middleton's VIII Corps would attempt to jump the river at the Rhine gorge.[6]

Just before 0000 on 24 March, the 87th Infantry Division's assault boats launched into the Rhine at both crossing sites. After some stiff resistance from the LXXXIX Korps' troops, both assault regiments crossed and, by late afternoon, held the high ground across from Boppard and the heights at Oberlahnstein near the confluence of the Rhine and Lahn rivers.[7] On the VIII Corps' southern right flank, the 89th Infantry Division's crossing at 0200 on 26 March near St. Goar and Oberwesel drew heavy German fire, but the lead infantry companies traversed the river and moved on St. Goarshausen. By mid-afternoon, two light task forces were across the river. At Major General Middleton's corps command post, reports pointed toward a general collapse of the German defenses east of the Rhine. Middleton told his 6th Cavalry Group to split into light task forces and head east at daybreak.

The real explosion in the Oppenheim bridgehead occurred on 24 March when the 4th Armored Division's Combat Command A struck out for Darmstadt and, by sunset, had pushed twenty-four kilometers beyond the

Oppenheim bridgehead. *General* Felber promptly ordered his 7th Armee to abandon Darmstadt.

On 25 March the pace of the American exploitation quickened. The 6th Armored Division crossed at Oppenheim and rushed northeast in search of crossing sites over the Main River between Frankfurt and Hanau. Combat Commands A and B of the 4th Armored Division also struck out for crossing sites over the Main River at Hanau and twenty-four kilometers south at Aschaffenburg; fortunately, each command found an intact railway bridge over the tributary.

The next morning, on 26 March, the 6th Armored Division sped through the forest south of Frankfurt and discovered a bridge over the Main as well. Vehicles could not cross, but the 5th Infantry Division's foot soldiers sprinted across the damaged bridge and swarmed the southern suburbs of heavily bomb-damaged Frankfurt.[8]

With his troops pouring eastward at a rapid pace, Lieutenant General Patton saw an opportunity to launch an armored combat command to liberate American prisoners at a camp fifty-six kilometers inside German lines. The raid—known as the Hammelburg Raid—fell to an armored infantry task force from the 4th Armored Division called Task Force Baum (named for the commander, Capt. Abraham Baum). Despite protests from his most senior commanders, Patton launched the raiding party shortly after 0000 on 25 March. Many of Patton's subordinates saw the effort as a thinly veiled attempt to save his son-in-law, Lt. Col. John K. Waters, who had been captured in North Africa a couple of years earlier and was believed to be in the camp. After a daunting two-day blitz into enemy territory, the task force liberated an overwhelming 1,200 American officers from the camp. Unfortunately, Baum lacked the vehicles to transport them all. Waters was indeed inside the camp, but an errant bullet fired during the rescue attempt wounded him in the hip, and he had to remain behind.

Quick countermoves allowed the Germans to surround the task force and capture Baum and his men after the forty-eight-hour operation. Remarkably, as the task force had advanced toward Hammelburg, Baum's men had passed Lohr and driven within three kilometers of *General* Felber's 7th Armee command post.[9]

South of Patton's Third Army, Lieutenant General Patch's Seventh Army had completed mopping up the German troops remaining in the Saar-Palatinate triangle. The time had come for the Seventh Army to join the Third Army in bouncing the Rhine River. Patch wanted to cross near Speyer, but General Eisenhower recommended Worms, which was close to the Third Army boundary.

Patch charged Maj. Gen. Wade H. Haislip's XV Corps to serve as the main effort; the VI and XXI Corps would plan secondary crossings near Speyer. The 45th Infantry Division would cross just north of Worms while the 3rd Infantry Division would cross to the south. Haislip set the attack time as 0230 on 26 March.[10]

The German XIII Korps holding the tenuous Oppenheim sector had already suffered greatly at the hands of the Third Army troops breaking out from the bridgehead. Seventh Army would actually attack before the German forces could reorganize after the breakout at Oppenheim, which physically severed the boundary between the 1st Armee and the 7th Armee. This situation would result in XIII Korps being assigned to the 1st Armee by the end of the day. The 1st had actually fared better than the 7th when withdrawing east of the Rhine. The army still had three corps headquarters and twelve divisions, two of which were on their way to reinforce the 7th Armee.[11]

The American assault crossings commenced at 0230 on 26 March and happened as planned. By day's end the 45th Infantry Division's GIs had contacted Third Army units on their left and crossed the *reichsautobahn* (improved highway) connecting Darmstadt and Mannheim—a full thirteen kilometers beyond the Rhine River.

The 3rd Infantry Division advance lagged due to German resistance, but the 3rd eventually caught up with the 45th by midday on 27 March. Lieutenant General Patch, pleased with the rapid successes, ordered the transfer of the 12th Armored Division to the XV Corps for immediate exploitation. The Seventh Army had suffered few casualties and nabbed nearly 2,500 German prisoners.[12]

Major General Wyman's 71st Infantry Division also played a part in the overall river-crossing operation. Attached to the VI Corps from the XXI Corps since 25 March, the Red Circle men had encroached on Speyer, Otterstadt, and Harthausen following the Germersheim attack. As part of Patch's plan, the VI and XXI Corps would conduct secondary crossings near the medieval town of Speyer to support Major General Haislip's XV Corps as it crossed the river farther north near Worms. The 71st would conduct a feint across the river at Speyer and capture a mock bridgehead intended to draw German troops away from the main effort near Worms. Wyman selected Colonel Lundquist's 14th Infantry Regiment; in turn, Lundquist tapped his 2nd Battalion, commanded by Lt. Col. Philip D. Brant, to lead the feint.

Brant, a 1937 graduate of West Point, had moved his 2nd Battalion, 14th Infantry, to medieval Speyer on 24 March while the 5th and 66th infantry regiments fought at Lingenfeld and Germersheim farther south. Brant's troops relieved Combat Command B, 12th Armored Division, in the town.[13]

The feint mission called for one platoon to cross the Rhine in engineer assault boats, spend twenty minutes on the far side, and then return—a ruse designed to draw German reserves away from Worms. At 0100, 2nd Platoon, Company E, dashed across the Rhine in four engineer assault boats under the cover of smoke and artillery. The Germans responded with small-arms and mortar fire. An hour later the entire platoon had returned to the near side with only light casualties. Brant greeted the boats personally and gave each returning GI a swig from a bottle of Seagram's whiskey.[14]

By 26 March Lt. Gen. Omar Bradley's 12th Army Group boasted four well-established bridgeheads and crossing sites over the Rhine River. The First Army owned Remagen, the Third Army had Oppenheim and the Rhine gorge, and the Seventh Army had Worms. Lieutenant General Patton wanted his XX Corps to grab a fifth bridgehead at Mainz; this bridgehead promised a superb network of roads and railways that would allow Patton to move more of his forces quickly to the east and eventually link up with the First Army. Major General Walker, the XX Corps commander, ordered his 80th Infantry Division to cross at Mainz before daylight on 28 March and clear the arc formed by the confluence of the Rhine and Main rivers.[15]

Few German forces actually defended the Rhine-Main arc. *General der Infanterie* Kniess and his LXXXV Korps staff arrived on 25 March and inherited two poorly manned and equipped infantry divisions. Two other divisions were on their way but became embroiled with the American units breaking out of the VIII Corps bridgehead. These divisions were the 11th Panzer Division and *SS-Gruppenführer* Brenner's 6th SS-Gebirgs Division Nord, which had been ordered out of the LXXXIX Korps on the eve of the VIII Corps' assault across the Rhine gorge.

Defending Frankfurt, Hanau, and Mainz along the Rhine and Main rivers would prove impossible. Kniess and the 7th Armee commander, *General* Felber, conspired to leave a thin line of troops to defend while withdrawing the bulk of their forces farther east to form a new line starting north at Frankfurt. Unfortunately for Felber someone had to be blamed for the failed defense of the Rhine at Oppenheim, so *General der Infanterie* Hans von Obstfelder replaced him late on 26 March. Kniess followed Felber into the doghouse three days later.[16]

Before sunrise on 28 March, two regiments of the 80th Infantry Division assaulted across the Rhine and Main rivers and, in spite of German resistance, were across both rivers by day's end. The Third Army's third Rhine crossing had come at a remarkably cheap price.[17]

❖

Back to the north, *General* Hoehne's LXXXIX Korps began to collapse on 27 March. Before the VIII Corps crossed at the Rhine gorge, OB West had transferred the corps to Army Group B's 15th Armee, but Hoehne never established contact with that headquarters. Likewise, on the eve of the Rhine gorge assault, *Generalfeldmarschall* Kesselring at OB West pulled the 6th SS-Gebirgs Division from Hoehne to help blunt Patton's crossing at Oppenheim. But when Kesselring heard that American armor was streaking toward the Lahn, he countermanded that order and returned the SS division to Hoehne's control.

On 24 March *SS-Gruppenführer* Brenner received the new order to move the division from its day-old assembly area north of Wiesbaden to Limburg and Diez on the Lahn River. Transportation problems and a severe gasoline shortage meant that the weary, battle-worn SS men had to march to their new area of operations. Hoehne intended to use the nearly six thousand–strong SS division to hold the line around Limburg and the Lahn River, but traveling on foot meant the SS men would not reach Limburg in time.[18]

Brenner emplaced his division command post six kilometers south of Limburg on the afternoon of 26 March, but his SS men would not arrive until sometime that night. The Nord men, traveling in two separate columns as Kampfgruppe Goebel and Kampfgruppe Raithel, arrived late on 26 March—

well after American tanks had penetrated Limburg and Diez. Throughout the night as the division arrived piecemeal, Brenner ordered them to build a defensive line facing north astride the *reichsautobahn*. Reports stated that the Americans were already across the Lahn River, but Brenner believed his troops still had a chance to stall the American drive southward toward Idstein.

The combined strength of the division at this point was dwindling rapidly. Brenner still had three *gebirgsjäger* battalions, but each was severely understrength. (The *gebirgsjäger* battalion left in the LXXXIX Korps area when the Nord men moved to Wiesbaden had rejoined the division.) Brenner still had his two light mountain artillery battalions (low on ammunition), two very weak *pionier* companies, a handful of antitank guns, and the scattered remnants of SS-Reconnaissance Battalion 6. These units quickly built a defensive line facing northward along the Limburg–Kirberg road.[19]

But on the morning of 27 March, Combat Command R of the 9th Armored Division sliced through Brenner's hastily constructed defenses and, by nightfall, took Idstein twenty-five kilometers to the southeast. During their rapid, two hundred–tank drive on Idstein, the American tankers received several bloody noses from the SS men but eventually bypassed and encircled them west of the main Limburg–Idstein *reichsautobahn*.

Exhausted from a fifty-kilometer night march, *SS-Sturmmann* Egon Krüger and his ad hoc company from the 3rd Battalion, SS-Gebirgsjäger Regiment 11, witnessed the steady stream of American armor as the SS men made their way to Limburg. From a concealed position near the road, Krüger counted exactly two hundred Sherman tanks driving southward. Aware that the American thrust had encircled them, Krüger and his company marched through the night toward the *reichsautobahn* leading southeast from Limburg toward Frankfurt am Main—their only hope of breaking free of the American trap.[20]

With the U.S. VIII Corps pushing hard against his own corps and the 9th Armored Division well into his rear area, *General* Hoehne appealed to OB West to withdraw. As usual, *Generalfeldmarschall* Kesselring denied the request. But Kesselring's permission no longer mattered. Hoehne had lost contact with the 6th SS-Gebirgs Division, which was still holding the Limburg–Kirberg–Idstein *reichsautobahn* position behind the American front line. Hoehne's remaining division was faring poorly in the face of the American pressure. Without OB West's permission, he ordered his troops to withdraw. The LXXXIX Korps had finally collapsed, severing the final—albeit tenuous—link that existed between Army Groups B and G. The entire German front had ruptured.[21]

Although Brenner had lost contact with Hoehne, the division's communications center was still intercepting radio traffic suggesting that a continuous German front west of Frankfurt no longer existed. Brenner began moving his division eastward in search of a more cohesive German defensive line that must surely exist somewhere. On 28 March Brenner jumped his command post to Schwickershausen east of the Limburg–Idstein *reichsautobahn* in preparation for this eastward move. Both battle groups were still encircled west of the highway, so Brenner sent messages to Raithel and Goebel to break out, cross the *reichsautobahn*, and occupy new positions facing west along the highway at Niederbrechen, Oberbrechen, Niederselters, and Oberselters. The American tankers of Combat Command R, 9th Armored Division, had since turned about and returned north.[22]

By late afternoon on 28 March, the two SS battle groups were in place east of the *reichsautobahn*. The weary SS troops had just finished digging in when the Americans—having abandoned their drive to the south—pushed eastward along the autobahn. Frenetic and fierce fighting occurred, but the exhausted and underequipped SS men held their ground.

One of the SS units embroiled in this fierce fighting was *SS-Sturmmann* Krüger's company from the 3rd Battalion, SS-Gebirgsjäger Regiment 11. After crossing the *reichsautobahn* the previous night, his company occupied a small hill in Oberselters overlooking the *reichsautobahn* and Niederselters. Krüger was part of a smaller reconnaissance group of seven men within the company led by a more capable combat leader: *SS-Standartenoberjunker* Kainhaus, an officer candidate.[23]

When the GIs of the 9th Armored Division attacked across the *reichsautobahn*, they attempted to push past the 6th SS-Gebirgs Division's defensive line east of the highway. Krüger's patrol had left the hilltop position to probe the area near the *reichsautobahn* when the attack began. The patrol stumbled on the attacking Sherman tanks. The SS men scattered into the forest. Krüger leveled his MG42 at the tank and fired. He then turned on his heels and sped into the darkened wood line.

For Egon Krüger the horror and hopelessness of the situation began to sink in. The fact that the 6th SS-Gebirgs Division was constantly on the run began to take a toll on the exhausted SS man. As he ran through the woods, images of his long-dead comrades and the face of his brother, who died at Stalingrad, flashed before his eyes. A dazed and frightened Krüger finally reached his company's hilltop position in Oberselters. Feeling safe for the moment, Krüger gave his MG42 to a comrade and lapsed into a stress-induced sleep.

Krüger awoke before 0800 the next morning, 29 March, to the sound of explosions and rifle fire. The Americans had renewed their attack and sought to expel Krüger's company from the hilltop overlooking Niederselters and the autobahn. American infantrymen, followed closely by Sherman tanks, entered the forest. The younger recruits shouted "Americans!" and ran off into the woods. Krüger held his ground. Kainhaus appeared suddenly at Krüger's side with a *panzerfaust*. Another SS soldier, a long time Nord veteran, appeared with an MG42 machine gun and opened fire. The GIs scattered. The American attack stalled.

The Americans renewed their drive within a few minutes, but the SS men held their ground. The GIs tried to bypass and encircle the SS troops throughout the day. Both sides fought bitterly. Low-flying fighter-bombers strafed the hill. Exploding cascades of dirt showered the SS men. Krüger just wanted to hang on long enough for the sun to go down.

Night finally arrived. Kainhaus developed a plan to abandon the hill. He picked Krüger to be the last man out—a one-man rear guard. The SS men rallied at a small shed in the center of the hill. The group of more than one hundred Nord men then marched off into the darkness, down the hill, and east toward a nearby village. The village was clear, so the SS men moved through onto a hill and, to their delight, found empty foxholes dug by an unknown German unit. Exhausted, the SS men collapsed into the holes and slept soundly.

But their sleep did not last long. By daybreak, the American tankers and infantrymen resumed their drive east. The Sherman tanks fired directly into the wood line on the SS men's new hilltop position. Krüger took aim and fired his rifle, but suddenly the shooting stopped. The Sherman tanks, gears grinding, backed down the hill and stopped firing. Puzzled, the SS men slowly emerged from their holes and watched in disbelief as the American infantrymen withdrew.

The SS men did not mull over the situation for long. They quickly consolidated their position and took stock of their dead and wounded. A veteran 12th Company machine gunner, a former tailor, was dead. Kainhaus had suffered a severe bullet wound to the leg. One man moaned, bleeding from a neck wound. A bullet had grazed Krüger's right shoulder.

Krüger walked among the foxholes to offer assistance and discovered at the edge of the wood line an American soldier who had been shot in the neck. The man had lost too much blood and was dying. Krüger reached into his tunic, produced a bandage, and wrapped it gently around the dying man's wound. Krüger stayed with the GI until he died.

The SS men then took their dead and brought them to the village graveyard below the hill. After arranging the bodies neatly, the SS men, led by one of the 6th SS-Gebirgs Division's few captured tanks, struck out to the east once more on foot. A handful of American prisoners walked with them.[24]

Several stragglers who had become separated from the division during the numerous shifts to the east found their way back to the 6th SS-Gebirgs Division. *SS-Rottenführer* Walter Becker, a radio operator in the 3rd Company, SS-Gebirgs Nachrichten Battalion 6, crossed the *reichsautobahn* at Camberg and rejoined the division after a harrowing journey through enemy-held territory. Becker and his fellow platoon members became separated from the division after they crossed the Rhine at Boppard. Once on the far side of the river, American tanks opened fire and destroyed one of the radio vehicles, killing one man. By 28 March the small band of SS *funkers* (radio operators) had crossed the autobahn between Camberg and Erbach and rejoined the division. The division needed every able-bodied man it could muster, and these returning stragglers helped to stabilize the division's rapidly dwindling strength.[25]

On that same afternoon of 28 March, the deputy commander of the German Army's officer-candidate school at Weilburg (located west of Wetzlar and fifteen kilometers from the 6th SS-Gebirgs Division's current positions) arrived at *SS-Gruppenführer* Brenner's command post. An amazed Brenner listened as the deputy school commander—speaking on behalf of the school's commandant—offered up the entire school's cadre and students to the division's control. Brenner gratefully accepted this new battle group of fifty officers and six hundred students. If led effectively, this new force—Kampfgruppe Weilburg—could help relieve the ever-increasing American pressure from the west.[26]

Since SS-Reconnaissance Battalion 6 had recently reported that the Americans were scouting the areas near Camberg, Walsdorf, and Esch in an effort to bypass the Nord Division's southern defenses, Brenner disposed the new battle group of officer candidates in these three towns. By nightfall Kampfgruppe Weilburg was in place in the forested areas east of the towns—just in time to repel a strong American attempt to move through that area. The officer candidates were already earning their keep.[27]

The next day, 29 March, the Americans pushed hard all along the 6th SS-Gebirgs Division's front. Although Kampfgruppe Goebel and Kampfgruppe Raithel held their villages throughout the day, both battle groups ultimately had to relinquish Niederbrechen, Oberbrechen, Niederselters, and Oberselters by nightfall. Like *SS-Sturmmann* Krüger's group that had abandoned the hill overlooking Oberselters and Niederselters, the SS men simply withdrew to a new defensive line a few kilometers east and dug in once more.

The fighting had cost the SS men some precious equipment. *SS-Rottenführer* Eberhard Hilger's captured 37-mm M5 General Stuart light tank suffered a hit from an American M9 bazooka, destroying the vehicle and wounding several of the crewmen.[28]

Remarkably, Kampfgruppe Weilburg's officer candidates fought steadfastly and gallantly against the assaulting GIs at Camberg, Walsdorf, and Esch. The German Army students did not submit to their American adversaries but instead held fast throughout the day and night.[29]

By 30 March Brenner recognized that he could not hold the line any longer. For all he knew the Americans had already bypassed the entire division. Brenner knew of no other German units on his flanks. Radio traffic had all but ceased, and Brenner's radio operators could not raise the LXXXIX Korps command post or any other German headquarters. Brenner realized that holding his present position was futile. He sent his staff to Neuweilnau in preparation for a rapid move to the east and, hopefully, a new German defensive line.

In the late afternoon Brenner ordered all Nord troops to disengage and move eastward. Few vehicles were available to transport the troops and gear. The division could only withdraw at a snail's pace. Most of the SS men were using a potpourri of captured enemy equipment, handcarts, and private cars to haul their equipment. The artillery troops depended on horses and mules to pull the light field guns and ammunition wagons. German Army troops—such as Kampfgruppe Weilburg—were mixed in among the division's SS troops. Many of the remaining battalion commanders were dead or captured: *SS-Hauptsturmführer* Degen of the 1st Battalion fell at Pfaffenheck and *SS-Hauptsturmführer* Tank of the 3rd Battalion had been taken prisoner during the recent fighting. The once powerful 6th SS-Gebirgs Division was simply another weakened German unit on the run.

The month of March ended for the 71st Infantry Division with a change of pace for the Red Circle men. This time, another division would relieve the 71st in place so the Red Circle men could move north and cross the Rhine at Oppenheim. On 26 March, the day of the 14th Infantry Regiment's feint at Speyer, the 5th and 66th infantry regiments moved north to an area below Ludwigshafen to relieve elements of the 100th Infantry Division. The 14th joined the other two regiments following the feint at Speyer—but the 103rd Infantry Division would move forward and assume the 71st's positions beginning on 28 March.

Freed from their defensive responsibilities, the Red Circle men loaded up on trucks and spent 28 and 29 March driving northward to the Third Army's crossing site at Oppenheim. As the division moved out, the 749th Tank Battalion bid farewell to the division. In their stead the legendary all-Black 761st Tank Battalion joined the division; it would remain with the Red Circle men until the war ended in May. One company of tanks would go to each regiment: Company A went to the 5th, Company B to the 14th, and Company C to the 66th.[30]

By nightfall on 29 March, the relief operation with the 103rd Infantry Division was complete. Major General Wyman received orders that he and his Red Circle men belonged to the XX Corps of Patton's mighty Third Army. The Red Circle men had felt privileged to serve with the Seventh Army in the Saar-Palatinate campaign, but nothing swelled the GIs with pride more than proclaiming to their friends and family that they were part of Patton's Third Army.[31]

The motorized movement of men and materiel continued north throughout the night of 29 March. Finally, on 30 March, the first elements of the 71st Infantry Division crossed the Rhine at Oppenheim under an enormous smoke screen. Pfc. Bill Hefner of Company K, 66th Infantry, even caught a glimpse of the famed Third Army commander visiting the bridgehead to observe the Red Circle Division's crossing.

As soon as the Red Circle men were across the Rhine, they became members of Maj. Gen. Manton S. Eddy's fast-moving XII Corps. Wyman's first orders placed the division in assembly areas near Neu Isenburg and Heusenstamm south and southeast of Frankfurt with orders to be prepared to protect the corps' right flank behind the advancing 26th Infantry Division. During their first twenty days of combat, the Red Circle men had traveled an incredible 288 kilometers by foot and by truck.[32]

For most of the month of March, the 71st Infantry Division had moved east with—and nearly parallel to—the 6th SS-Gebirgs Division Nord. The Nord men operated in the northern part of the Saar-Palatinate while the Red Circle men fought farther south. But, with the 71st's assignment to the Third Army father north, the two divisions shared the same area of operations. Their respective and converging journeys to the east would ultimately result in a battle that both sides would never forget.

❖

As the month of March 1945 came to a close, the American 12th and 6th Army Groups were well across the Rhine River south of Frankfurt and heading unchecked into the heart of Germany. *Generaloberst* Johannes Blaskowitz's Army Group H in the Ruhr industrial region faced imminent encirclement as part of General Eisenhower's grand design. Since Berlin no longer held any military value to Eisenhower, the supreme Commander on 28 March issued a plan for the Ninth and First U.S. Armies to converge east of the Ruhr and encircle the remaining forces within that pocket. The Ninth Army then would revert to Lieutenant General Bradley's control for the 12th Army Group's drive eastward to seize the Leipzig-Dresden area and link up with the Russians.

The American forces were on a full-fledged pursuit of their German foes, bypassing larger, slower-moving German formations in favor of rushing ahead and gaining a foothold in Germany's heartland. Many of the commanders who drove these fast-moving units forward—among them the always impatient Patton—expected follow-up divisions and units of Maj. Gen. Leonard T. Gerow's newly activated Fifteenth Army to clean up these bypassed pockets of resistance. What these commanders did not expect was that some of this resistance might be rather difficult to eliminate—as in the case of the 6th SS-Gebirgs Division Nord.[33]

CHAPTER 5

Nord Falls Behind, 31 March 1945

By 31 March 1945 the Third Army had ruptured the entire German front. Charged with driving on Kassel, a town on the Fulda River, in order to protect the right flank of Lt. Gen. Courtney H. Hodges's First Army, Lt. Gen. George S. Patton Jr. unleashed his armor in an eastward race that quickly outpaced the Seventh Army in the south and easily closed up with the First Army's easternmost units in the north, which had already pivoted northwards to encircle the Ruhr industrial region. As Patton's tidal wave of tanks and infantry surged forward, many German units—some still eager to fight and others that had ceased resisting—were left behind and bypassed.

Maj. Gen. Manton S. Eddy's XII Corps made the most impressive progress. The corps had crossed the Rhine and—led by the 4th Armored Division—bounced the Main River near Hanau on 26 March. When the sun set on 28 March, the 4th Armored Division had already plunged forty-eight kilometers toward Giessen. The 6th Armored Division, also part of Eddy's corps, jumped the Main River with the 90th Infantry Division west of Hanau and gained an impressive twenty-four kilometers. The two armored divisions—the vanguard not just of Eddy's corps but also of the entire Third Army—resulted in shifting boundaries that threatened to pinch out Maj. Gen. Troy H. Middleton's VIII Corps and Maj. Gen. Walton H. Walker's XX Corps.[1]

Lt. Gen. Omar N. Bradley, the 12th Army Group commander, soon adjusted the First and Third Army boundaries to compensate for the First Army's northward turn toward Paderborn, thus finally pushing the XX and VIII Corps to the rear of the front lines. Alarmed that his XII Corps was advancing alone with open flanks, Patton split the XII Corps zone and assigned the left flank to the XX Corps. Patton chopped the advancing 6th

Armored Division and the 5th Infantry Division (embroiled in the fighting to seize Frankfurt am Main farther west) to Walker's corps. The VIII Corps problem would resolve itself later. Patton was eager for the other two corps to advance alongside each other rapidly and unchecked toward Kassel.²

❖

Patton's success rested largely on the gap he was exploiting between Army Group B in the north and Army Group G in the south. When *General der Infanterie* Gustav Hoehne's LXXXIX Korps headquarters disintegrated, the tenuous link between both German Army groups dissolved. Hoehne had already lost contact with the 6th SS-Gebirgs Division, and his only remaining infantry division, the 276th, was signaling imminent collapse. Hoehne and his staff ultimately surrendered to a Third Army Quartermaster unit in the first days of April.³

Likewise, LXXXV Korps, last charged with holding the Rhine–Main arc, had disintegrated. The only viable German defense facing the Third Army and the Seventh Army advancing farther south was *General der Infanterie* Hans von Obstfelder's 7th Armee, the northern part of which had *General der Infanterie* Walther Hahm's LXXXII Korps holding the Main River bridgeheads. But Patton's forces had already bested Hahm's three remnant divisions by crossing the Rhine and advancing north and northeast. Obstfelder watched helplessly as both XX Corps and XII Corps raced past his 7th Armee and deeper into Germany. Organized German resistance in front of the Third Army all but evaporated on Saturday, 31 March, the day before Easter Sunday.⁴

❖

On 29 March Major General Eddy committed the 11th Armored Division to the right flank of his advancing 4th Armored Division so XII Corps could proceed with two armored divisions abreast. The 11th's task was to drive northeast for the open terrain near Fulda. On the left and behind the 4th Armored followed the 90th Infantry Division, while on the right and behind the 11th Armored followed the 26th Infantry Division. The 71st Infantry Division, the corps' third infantry division reassigned from XX Corps as of 31 March, was still crossing the Rhine and closing on assembly areas south of Frankfurt in preparation for commitment to the XII Corps' advance. Screening the corps' right flank was the 2nd Cavalry Group, charged with maintaining contact with the Seventh Army, which had fallen behind the Third Army's swift advance.[5]

By sunset on 31 March, the 4th Armored Division, the fastest-moving unit in the entire Third Army, stuck out like a lone finger jutting northeastward thirty-two kilometers beyond Hersfeld and a few kilometers short of the Werra River. The 11th Armored Division on the right had already gained the high ground overlooking the town of Fulda. Eddy's corps headquarters occupied Lauterbach (captured by the 4th Armored on 28 March) well behind his advancing divisions but also dangerously ahead of most of his supply elements and flank units. The corps' main supply route (MSR) leading to Lauterbach was still not fully secure since the corps had bypassed so many German units in the dash for Kassel and Fulda. Concerned about his overstretched logistics lines of communications, Eddy also understood Patton's intent—"Forward, ever forward!"[6]

On 31 March the 6th SS-Gebirgs Division was on the move (see Map 5.1). Off balance and withdrawing eastward, the Nord men had relinquished their last major defensive line at Oberbrechen, Niederselters, and Oberselters more than twenty-four hours earlier in the face of relentless American attacks. The division was still organized roughly into two *kampfgruppen*. Many recently liberated German Army troops were intermeshed and fighting with the SS men as well, to include the students of Kampfgruppe Weilburg. Most of the division's vehicles were captured American jeeps or trucks—and even a couple of Sherman tanks. Although these captured vehicles numbered three hundred or more, the Nord men still traveled on foot, dragging most of their equipment and the few remaining artillery pieces. Men hauled small-arms ammunition and other supplies in handcarts and—in some cases—baby carriages. When advancing U.S. forces closed on the Nord men from the west, the SS troops would stop, dig in, and fight until the GIs withdrew. The severe fuel shortage forced the SS men to abandon many vehicles and larger stores of ammunition and equipment, including much of the division's engineer gear.

SS-Gruppenführer Brenner and his staff abandoned Neuweilnau and moved to the eastern part of the town of Usingen. At Usingen, *SS-Unterscharführer* Georg Stöwe's intelligence communications group jumped from frequency

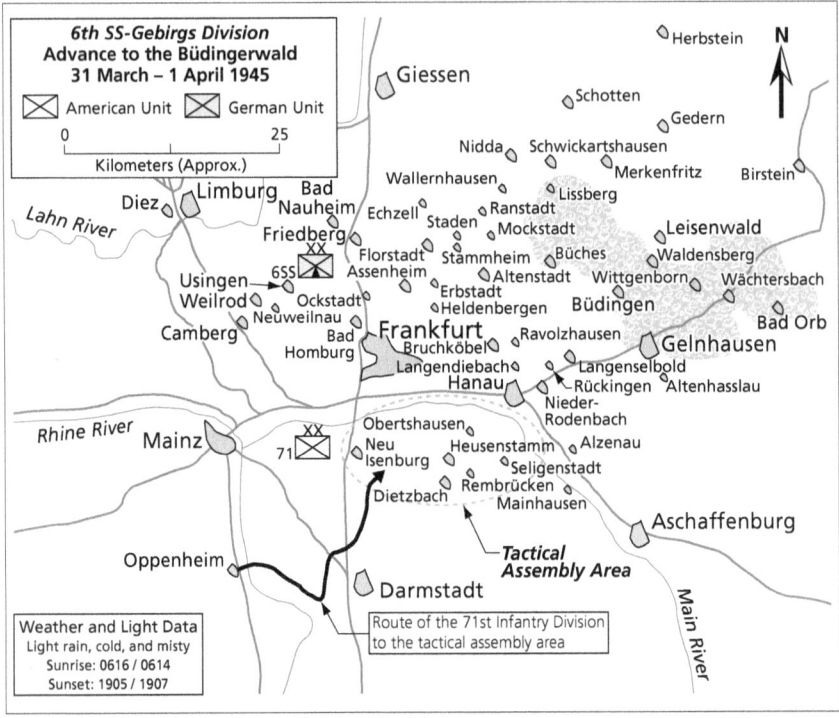

Map 5.1. 6th SS-Gebirgs Division's advance to the Büdingen forest, 31 March–1 April 1945.

to frequency in search of information about the current German situation, but the *funkers* could learn nothing of value. The division had absolutely no communications with German forces on either flank.

The small bits of information Brenner received from his two *kampfgruppe* commanders, *SS-Standartenführer* Raithel and *SS-Oberführer* Goebel; from his reconnaissance troops in the ubiquitous SS-Reconnaissance Battalion 6; and from recently captured American prisoners confirmed his earlier suspicion: the Americans had advanced well to the east of the division's current position. Stöwe reported some intercepted American transmissions, which mentioned the names of towns and villages far to the east of Usingen. In effect the division had become an island trapped on all sides by a sea of advancing American forces. Brenner decided to move east in search of a German defensive line. The last information he received about such a line was that one existed near Gelnhausen on the southern fringe of the Büdingen forest—nearly fifty kilometers east of Usingen.[7]

Brenner ordered the two *kampfgruppen* to prepare for a nighttime withdrawal to Gelnhausen. The Americans continued to push at Altweilnau and Neuweilnau, but the GIs made no significant attempts to overrun the Nord men. The chaotic state of the SS troops—replete with their caravan of dilapidated vehicles, horse-drawn wagons, and handcarts—probably convinced the GIs that the SS men were nothing more than a bunch of stragglers trying to keep out of harm's way. But the SS men were still very much under the command and control of *SS-Gruppenführer* Brenner, who adeptly ordered Kampfgruppe Weilburg into position in time to blunt a late-afternoon attack on Usingen from the southeast by the American 76th Infantry Division.[8]

These concerted American attacks demonstrated to Brenner that the division had to move east quickly, away from these constant skirmishes, if the 6th SS-Gebirgs Division was going to contribute to the further defense of the German Reich. The potential futility of these efforts never seemed to concern Brenner: he still had a potent combat force at his disposal, and he intended to use that force as long as the division existed. To increase the division's march speed, Brenner ordered all American prisoners—both officers and enlisted men—to remain with the German military hospital in Usingen. All excess baggage had to be dropped. The time for rapid movement was now.[9]

As the Nord men prepared to move east from their location northwest of Frankfurt am Main, Maj. Gen. Willard G. Wyman was just settling his 71st Infantry Division into an assembly area south of that same city. After a long truck movement that began with the division crossing the Rhine River at Oppenheim, the first complete infantry regiment to arrive, the 5th, settled into the assembly area at 0815 on 31 March near Neu Isenburg, which sat along the north–south *reichsautobahn* connecting Frankfurt to Darmstadt. Exhausted and physically drained from their long, nighttime journey in open-backed trucks (at least eighty road kilometers), the GIs moved into their positions, established security, and prepared to bed down there that night. The unlucky ones ran security patrols outside the regimental perimeter.[10]

As the other two infantry regiments—the division artillery, the engineers, tank destroyers, and supporting units—arrived in the area, Wyman's staff monitored the movement from a new division command post at

Heusenstamm. Wyman zipped around in his jeep from one march unit to the next to check their progress, assess troop morale, and meet with his regimental commanders.[11]

Wyman was clearly anxious about getting his division committed to the bigger fight at the tip of the XII Corps spear farther east. As a new member of Patton's Third Army, the 71st Division's chances of getting into real, up-front fighting increased greatly. Combat operations experienced by the division to this point, except for smaller but fierce battles such as the battle at Lingenfeld, had been of the mop-up variety. Wyman had yet to maneuver his entire division against a larger enemy force in a pitched battle.

Wyman had seen the worst of combat. As assistant division commander of the 1st Infantry Division, he had walked bravely up and down Omaha Beach on D-Day, 6 June 1944, dodging German bullets while motivating and inspiring his Big Red One soldiers to press on. War correspondent Don Whitehead was on Omaha Beach that day with Wyman and later wrote, "There were many heroes on Omaha Beach that bloody day, but none of greater stature than [Brig. Gen. Willard G.] Wyman and [Col. George A.] Taylor. They formed the core of the steadying influence that slowly began to weld the 1st Division's broken spearhead into a fighting force under the muzzles of enemy guns."[12] Wyman's courage that day earned him the undying respect of both officers and enlisted men alike. That day he also learned about the true abilities of trained and ready soldiers. On 31 March 1945 Wyman knew that his trained and disciplined Red Circle men could rise to any challenge—but they needed the opportunity to do so.

Before the 71st Infantry Division even closed fully on their assembly area south of Frankfurt, Eddy's XII Corps' staff already sending mission requirements to Wyman. The corps' G-3 (operations officer) contacted the division G-3, Lt. Col. Norman H. Lankenau, with instructions to guard on short notice the open right flank of XII Corps with at least one regiment. The corps had dramatically outpaced the Seventh Army to the south, leaving the right flank wide open. A mission of this nature might allow Wyman and his Red Circle men to take on some better-organized and better-led German forces.[13]

The fact that the 71st Infantry Division might soon become the glue that connected the seam between both armies prompted Wyman to seek out and contact the nearest Seventh Army unit on the ground. The XV Corps, on the Seventh Army's left flank and charged with seizing Fulda, was still back somewhere along the Rhine River. Wyman had to establish contact with that corps, or any other units in the area, to link both armies and deny the Germans an assailable gap.[14]

In the meantime the remainder of the division continued to stream into the assembly area. Lt. Col. Paul L. Bates's newly attached, all-Black, veteran 761st Tank Battalion already occupied positions within the assembly area; as the infantry regiments closed on the perimeter, the individual tank companies split off and linked up with the regiments they would support. Bates was White and a former All-American football star from Western Maryland College who had spent ten years as a high school teacher and coach before joining the Army. His compassion, decency, and modest humanity neutralized the issue of race in his battalion. His soldiers loved and respected him for his fairness and his undying belief in them, which made the battalion a highly combat-effective force.[15] Tank-destroyer companies from Lt. Col. Wint Smith's 635th Tank Destroyer Battalion (towed) remained attached to the regiments they supported. The attachment of these and other combined-arms assets resulted in the regiments being permanently labeled as combat teams (such as Combat Team 66).

The armored and tank-destroyer strength of the division was very strong on 31 March. All thirty-six 3-inch towed antitank guns and the battalion's one 90-mm M36 self-propelled gun were fully operational. Twelve of the 761st's fifty-three M4 Sherman medium tanks were down for maintenance, but all seventeen light tanks and six assault guns remained operational. The infantry strength and that of the supporting units remained high as well. Although weary from a hectic two weeks of fast-paced maneuvers, the division was ready for major combat action.[16]

The first complete infantry regiment to close on the assembly area was Col. Sidney C. Wooten's 5th Infantry Regiment. Maj. Irving Heymont, the regimental S-3 (operations officer), led an advanced party to Neu Isenburg and opened the forward command post at 0400 on 31 March. Company A, 761st Tank Battalion, arrived in the 5th's assembly area at 0630, and the rest of the regiment detrucked there at 0815. Exhausted from nearly forty-eight hours of constant movement, the men of the 5th Regiment needed rest if they were to be of value in the near future. No one was more aware of this fact than Wooten.[17]

Wooten, born in Kentucky on 16 May 1907 and a 1930 graduate of West Point, was a tough-as-nails, no-nonsense commander who had earned the respect of his men long before the regiment arrived in Europe. He had driven his men relentlessly and had demanded much from them during their training at Fort Benning. No one had a neutral opinion of the man. Some troops disliked him while others adored him. Major Heymont found Wooten to be personally brave but sometimes arrogant. At just over six feet tall with close-cropped hair, Wooten cut a larger-than-life image in the minds of his men. He smoked cigarettes eccentrically, using a long, black cigarette holder, and he always carried a wooden swagger stick with a silver band around the end.[18]

First Lieutenant Lewington Ponder, the regimental liaison officer to division headquarters, considered Wooten to be the most influential, natural-born leader he had ever met. On signing in at the regiment's Fort Benning headquarters, Ponder was discussing his new assignment with the regimental S-1 (personnel officer) when Wooten stormed into the office and demanded that the young officer follow him to the Headquarters Company mess hall to "get some blood." Shaken, the young lieutenant followed apprehensively and then asked his commander what the man meant by "blood." Wooten snapped, "To get a cup of coffee, the blood of life!" Ponder enjoyed a brief conversation with his commader over that cup of coffee and only later realized that Wooten had expertly interviewed him and learned everything he wanted to know about the new lieutenant.[19]

At 1150 Major General Wyman arrived at Wooten's command post and explained that one of the regiments might have to move on short notice to protect the corps' right flank. The mission, said Wyman, would fall to the more rested 66th Infantry Regiment. He was concerned about the exhausted state of Wooten's men, and the 66th had had at least two more nights' rest than Wooten's troops. Wooten could expect to follow the 66th Regiment to Rückingen east of Hanau for eventual deployment along the corps' right flank.[20]

Col. Carl E. Lundquist's 14th Infantry Regiment was the second regiment to close on the division assembly area. Currently the division reserve, the 14th set up shop in the small village of Obertshausen northeast of Heusenstamm. The final truck-mounted elements of the regiment pulled into the assembly area at 1745 just as the sun began to hang low on the horizon.[21]

Lundquist, who had replaced the medically relieved Colonel Beeler two weeks earlier, instructed his battalions to establish roadblocks and outposts in the vicinity of the new assembly area. Foot patrols searched wooded areas for German stragglers while motorized patrols ran every two hours at irregular intervals to cover gaps between the units. Company B, 761st Tank Battalion, remained in regimental reserve in Obertshausen. Lundquist recognized that his tired and dirty Red Circle men needed a morale boost, so he rotated the troops through a shower point and planned religious services for the following day, Easter Sunday.[22]

Lundquist also received a special mission from Major General Wyman for one battalion to occupy Hanau and secure the two bridges over the Main River near the village of Klein-Auheim. Lundquist selected Maj. Samuel E. Hubbard's 1st Battalion for this task. Hubbard's men had already relieved elements of the 26th Infantry Division at the two bridges, of which the northern bridge was a repaired civilian structure designed for one-way traffic while the southern structure was an Army treadway bridge capable only of sustaining foot traffic. A second requirement compelled Lundquist to detach one rifle company and a machine-gun platoon from the 3rd Battalion to guard German prisoners at the corps' POW cage located in a quarry twelve kilometers north of Bad Nauheim near Eberstadt. Lt. Col. Paul G. Guthrie, the battalion commander, sent one machine-gun platoon from 1/Lt. W. P. Sims's Company M and 1/Lt. Caleb H. Paul's Company I.[23]

As the division reserve, Lundquist probably believed his men would not see any direct combat for several days, so routine personnel and supply activities continued. The commander of the 2nd Battalion, Lt. Col. Philip D. Brant, finally found time to relieve his S-3, Capt. Lloyd A. Lafargue. Lafargue had proved himself ineffective as the battalion operations officer, but the earlier pace of operations did not afford Brant the opportunity to replace him. The regiment's short break from combat would not last long, however. Both Lundquist and Brant would soon find themselves at the forefront of the Red Circle Division's coming duel with the 6th SS-Gebirgs Division Nord.[24]

The advance elements of the 66th Infantry Regiment arrived at the southernmost portion of the division assembly area on the night of 30 March. Col. Augustus J. Regnier located his command post in Dietzenbach at 2115 just three kilometers south of Heusenstamm. The final elements of the regiment arrived by truck at 1945 the next day, 31 March. Regnier, a stern disciplinarian, ordered security patrols dispatched immediately. As the most rested of the three regiments, Regnier had already received word that the 66th would spearhead the next action.[25]

The G-3, Lieutenant Colonel Lankenau, warned Regnier that the regiment should be ready on one hour's notice to extend the southern flank of XII Corps along the line Langenselbold–Hailer–Gelnhausen. Lankenau likened the mission to "a leapfrog deal" where the individual battalions would have to move past each other to keep pace with the corps' units.[26]

Regnier was confident in his troops and enjoyed the support of some very capable battalion commanders. The men of the 2nd Battalion revered their commander, Lt. Col. Gaston B. Eikel, who was somewhat older than most of the other battalion commanders and had served as a college professor in New Orleans prior to the war. Eikel knew most of his men by sight, which never ceased to amaze them. The 3rd Battalion commander, Lt. Col. Bryce F. Denno, already boasted an impressive combat résumé that included action in North Africa and Sicily with the 1st Infantry Division. A recipient of the Distinguished Service Cross for valor in Sicily, Denno led from the front and often acted on his own initiative.[27] Regnier was well served by such an impressive cadre of leaders, and these very same men would tip the scales in the coming battle with the 6th SS-Gebirgs Division Nord.

Capt. Bernard C. Johnson's 71st Calvary Reconnaissance Troop (mechanized), the real eyes and ears of the division, crossed the Rhine River on Good Friday, 30 March, and became one of the first units to arrive near Heusenstamm. As the division's units streamed into the assembly area on 31 March, Major General Wyman, ever mindful of his flank-protection mission, sent the troop southeast along the Third Army boundary to contact the nearest Seventh Army units. Lt. Edward W. Samuell Jr.'s 1st Platoon contacted the XV Corps' 106th Cavalry Group near Seligenstadt and the 44th Infantry Division in Babenhausen farther south. Samuell's platoon and the rest of the reconnaissance troop then rallied in Mainhausen later in the day to await further instructions.[28]

The division reconnaissance troop was Wyman's most effective source of battlefield information. The troop received its reconnaissance and counter-reconnaissance missions directly from the division G-2, Lt. Col. Kenneth W. Foster, a meticulous intelligence officer who enjoyed the unwavering support of Wyman and, subsequently, a great deal of independence. Foster gave the troop its missions carefully because Johnson's cavalrymen were not a combat capability to be squandered needlessly.

The 71st Cavalry Reconnaissance Troop (mechanized) comprised four elements: a headquarters and headquarters platoon and three reconnaissance platoons. Each platoon consisted of three sections each comprising a quarter-ton scout truck (often called a bantam), a six-wheeled M8 Greyhound armored car, and a second bantam with an M2 60-mm mortar crew. The troop's heaviest armament was on the M8 armored car, which boasted an M2 .50-caliber machine gun and a turret-mounted 37-mm gun that the troops jokingly called a "paint remover" because of its minimal effect on German armor. The cavalrymen had also become enamored of the white phosphorus rounds used in the M9 bazooka: the smoke generated by these rounds offered the frequently outgunned cavalrymen the precious obscuration needed to break contact with the enemy.[29]

The M8 armored car also doubled as the command car for each section and carried both an FM and an AM radio. The FM version, the SCR-508, had limited range and was nearly useless, given the large distances within which the sections and platoons operated relative to the division command post's location. The AM version, however, was the SCR-506 and had a range of more than 240 kilometers. The cavalrymen relied exclusively on this AM radio to send back critical spot reports on the enemy. This reliable communications asset would prove crucial in the coming engagement with the Nord Division.[30]

By late afternoon on 31 March, XII Corps finally issued the order that Major General Wyman had been eagerly awaiting: protect the advancing XII Corps' open right flank. Wyman and Lieutenant Colonel Lankenau immediately devised a concept for the operation. Lieutenant Colonel Bates's 761st Tank Battalion—which consisted of the battalion headquarters, Service Company, and Company D—and the newly attached 71st Cavalry Reconnaissance Troop would depart the assembly area at 0630 on Easter Sunday (1 April), cross the Main River over the repaired civilian bridge, and occupy positions south of the Hanau-Lieblos road to cover the occupation of Gelnhausen by the 66th Infantry Regiment. The 761st and the reconnaissance troop would then assemble near Langenselbold and await further instructions.

As planned, Regnier's 66th Infantry Regiment would be the principal force to cover the corps' right flank. The regiment's truck-mounted battalions would follow the 761st Tank Battalion and division reconnaissance troop across the bridge over the Main at 0700 and then occupy positions facing south along the Hailer-Gelnhausen line; the GIs expected to encounter only light resistance. The regiment's direct-support artillery battalion, the 609th, would follow and cover the Red Circle men as they moved to their new positions.[31]

Brig. Gen. Frank Henning's division artillery—minus the 609th Artillery Battalion—was next in line behind the 66th and would move at 1000 into firing positions northeast of Hanau to support the 66th Infantry. Once in place the 609th would return to Henning's control. The 5th Infantry Regiment came next as the unit designated to leap ahead of the 66th as the XII Corps forged eastward. Since the division G-4 (logistics officer) did not have the truck assets to motorize the entire regiment, the 5th would be split into a truck-mounted element and a foot element. The foot element would cross the treadway bridge over the Main River at 0700, and the motorized element would follow the division artillery across the civilian bridge at 1300. Both forces would assemble northeast of Hanau. The reserve regiment, the 14th, would remain in place guarding the Main River bridges, the corps' POW cage, and the city of Hanau until further notice.[32]

At 1800 Lieutenant Colonel Lankenau issued Field Order Number 12 outlining the next day's plan. Regimental liaison officers, such as First Lieutenant Ponder of the 5th Infantry, carried the new orders back to their respective headquarters. A great deal of coordination had to occur throughout the night, to include an information exchange with the 2nd Cavalry Group, which was somewhere near Gelnhausen screening the corps' right flank. Few leaders at any level could expect to sleep on this night.[33]

❖

Col. Charles H. Reed's 2nd Cavalry Group had begun screening forward of the 71st Infantry Division on the XII Corps' right flank near Gelnhausen on 30 March. Deactivated in May 1942 as a horse cavalry regiment and then reactivated in December 1942 as a mechanized cavalry regiment, the 2nd Cavalry Group finally received its group designation in December 1943. The group boasted an impressive combat lineage dating back to the Seminole Indian Wars in 1836 up through—and including—World War I. Organized with two cavalry squadrons, the 2nd and the 42nd, the group came ashore on Utah Beach in Normandy in mid-July 1944 and fought through northern France, the Rhineland, the Ardennes, and into central Europe. A seasoned combat unit, the 2nd Cavalry's men had proven themselves both efficient and highly dependable.[34]

The group was organized with a headquarters structured for the tactical control and coordination of two squadrons. Each squadron had a headquarters troop, three reconnaissance troops (A, B, and C), an assault gun troop (E), a light tank troop (F), and a headquarters and service troop. The reconnaissance troops principally contained M8 armored cars and M3A1 half-tracks. The squadrons were organized for reconnaissance and infiltration missions; direct combat with the enemy came as a last resort since they lacked the firepower to overcome heavy resistance.[35]

The 2nd Cavalry Group crossed the Rhine River on 26 March. For the cavalrymen, combat in March 1945 resembled their mad dash across France in the heady days of the Normandy campaign the previous summer. Like the French campaign the group would make long jumps across broad expanses of terrain, meet minor resistance, engage in sporadic—but sharp—firefights with German troops, then make another long jump that repeated the cycle all over again.

After crossing the Rhine movement became so rapid for Colonel Reed and his cavalrymen that the group headquarters received new orders daily. On 27 March the group helped the 26th Infantry Division secure the bridgehead over the Main River at Hanau. The next day, orders arrived placing the group directly under XII Corps control to screen the corps' right flank. On 29 March Lt. Col. William A. Hill's 42nd Cavalry Squadron crossed the Main River on ferries, followed by Lt. Col. Walter J. Easton's 2nd Cavalry Squadron. The 42nd's Troop A took up positions near Wasserlos just south of Alzenau, while the 2nd Squadron contacted elements of the Seventh Army's 106th Cavalry Group at Oberrodenbach.[36]

Since the XII Corps had pushed so far ahead of the Seventh Army, the corps' southern right flank stood wide open to assault by a flanking enemy force. Colonel Reed recognized this danger immediately and sent Hill's 42nd Squadron leapfrogging more than twenty-five kilometers eastward toward Spielberg on the easternmost fringes of the Büdingen forest—the principal march objective of the withdrawing 6th SS-Gebirgs Division Nord, which was thirty-five to forty kilometers away from the cavalrymen moving on a straight line toward them from the west.[37]

On 31 March Lieutenant Colonel Easton's 2nd Squadron advanced along the corps' flank near Gelnhausen to the right rear of its sister squadron, the 42nd. For the first time after crossing the Main River, the 2nd Squadron's cavalrymen encountered stiff German resistance in the towns of Eidengesäss and Altenhasslau a few kilometers south of Gelnhausen. After sharp small-arms and mortar exchanges with the German defenders, the cavalrymen seized both towns. All resistance in Altenhasslau ended the following day, 1 April, with the taking of more than 250 German prisoners.[38]

When Major General Wyman received his instructions to guard the corps' left flank near Gelnhausen, the 2nd Cavalry Group had already been operating in the area for a full day. Wyman recognized the need to coordinate his efforts with Colonel Reed to avoid a clash between friendly forces. Wyman requested a liaison officer from Reed to coordinate troop dispositions and locations. At 2020 that evening Captain Calloway, traveling from Reed's command post near Altenhasslau, arrived at the 71st Infantry Division headquarters and reported that in the vicinity of Gelnhausen the 2nd Squadron's Troop A occupied Niedermittlau, and Troop B was at Hailer moving east. He then explained that elements of the 42nd Squadron were still moving through Lieblos and Hain-Gründau to assemble with the rest of the squadron at Spielberg. From Spielberg the squadron would skirt the eastern periphery of the Büdingen forest southward through the Gelnhausen-Wittgenborn gap toward Bad Soden to link up either with elements of the 71st Division's infantry or with the 2nd Squadron moving north of—and through—Gelnhausen. Neither Wyman nor Reed could know that this maneuver would place the unwitting cavalrymen of the 2nd Squadron directly in the path of *SS-Gruppenführer* Brenner's eastward-moving columns.[39]

Wyman was pleased with the level of coordination between the cavalry troops and his staff. And now, on the eve of Easter Sunday, his regiments and battalions were busy planning. The stage was set for the Red Circle men to take an active part in the frontline operations of the advancing Third Army. Wyman believed in his men, and he would see his faith in them bear fruit before the sun set on 1 April.

For the 71st Infantry Division and the 2nd Cavalry Group, current operations had focused on protecting the XII Corps' right flank near Gelnhausen—a focus that would shift when the 6th SS-Gebirgs Division entered the Büdingen forest farther north. Nestled in a small valley and along an east–west tributary of the Main River called the Kinzig, Gelnhausen occupied the southern edge of the Büdingen forest. The ancient town of Büdingen (the forest's namesake) to the northwest and Wächtersbach to the east framed the limits of this hilly and densely forested twelve-square-kilometer region. The town of Breitenborn sat in the very center of the great Büdingen forest. Gelnhausen was the Nord Division's march objective because *SS-Gruppenführer* Brenner believed that a cohesive German defensive line still existed there. He was wrong.

War came to Gelnhausen and the surrounding region during one of the holiest times of the year for Christians: *Ostern* (Easter). Preparations for celebrating the death and resurrection of Jesus Christ continued despite the rumblings of war approaching from the west. (Approximately two-thirds of Germany's citizens were Protestant in 1945 and most of the rest were Catholic.) For the Protestant population of Gelnhausen and its surrounding villages, war seemed like a perverse violation of such a holy celebration. But the XII Corps' advance did not pause for any religious celebration or holiday. The time for greater celebration would come when the war ended.[40]

The vanguard of the XII Corps, the 11th Armored Division, arrived in Gelnhausen on a gray, overcast Good Friday, 30 March. The American tanks pushed past unmanned Volkssturm roadblocks effortlessly. By 1200 on 31 March the bulk of 11th Armored Division and the follow-on 26th Infantry Division had moved through Gelnhausen headed northeast. Support units and the M8 armored cars of the 2nd Cavalry Group were the only U.S. forces the citizens of Gelnhausen and the surrounding villages witnessed throughout the day. Except for some minor battle damage to homes and sporadic looting, the citizens in the communities surrounding Gelnhausen believed they had come through their thirty-six hours of war relatively unscathed. Only a handful of civilians died as a result of the brief skirmishes in the area. Many breathed sighs of relief and prayed in gratitude. Unfortunately, they had no way of knowing that the war in their area—especially to their north in the Büdingen forest—was far from over. The worst was yet to come.

❖

As the sun set on 31 March, *SS-Gruppenführer* Brenner assembled the remaining elements of the 6th SS-Gebirgs Division Nord outside Usingen (northwest of Frankfurt) for an eastward move to Gelnhausen. Elements of the American 76th Infantry Division and the 16th Cavalry Group were swarming around Usingen, but Brenner's troop concentration went undetected—or so he thought.

Maj. Gen. S. LeRoy Irwin's 5th Infantry Division had attacked the city of Frankfurt am Main some twenty-five kilometers south of Usingen on 28 March as part of the XII Corps' speedy advance. By 30 March the division had cleared much of the mammoth city and paused to rest and regroup. The 5th Division was one of the few American divisions that had been going strong since the fall of 1944 without a break. Seizing Frankfurt gave the Red Diamond Division (the division patch was a plain, red diamond) an opportunity to consolidate, rest, and reorganize while ferreting out German stragglers, seizing German ammunition stores, maintaining general law and order, and guarding vital installations and bridges. The division's three regiments—the 2nd, 10th, and 11th—soon pushed outward and cleared Frankfurt's surrounding suburbs. On that same day, 30 March, the 5th Division was detached from Major General Eddy's XII Corps and assigned to Major General Walker's XX Corps as the corps reserve (and subsequently Third Army and Supreme Headquarters Allied Expeditionary Force reserve).[41]

At 1130 on 31 March, Colonel Snyder, the XX Corps G-3, called the 5th Division command post in downtown Frankfurt and spoke to the G-3, Lt. Col. Randolph C. Dickens. Dickens and his staff were busy preparing to move the division to a new assembly somewhere northeast in preparation for future operations. Snyder informed Dickens of a reported enemy troop concentration in the VIII Corps zone near Usingen. Dickens agreed to send the 5th Cavalry Reconnaissance Troop (mechanized) to investigate.[42]

Dickens sent word to Capt. Donald E. Robinson, the reconnaissance troop commander, to check on the enemy force purportedly gathering near Usingen, which sat on the extreme northern edge of Frankfurt and roughly along the boundary between the VIII Corps and the XX Corps. Robinson, a dynamic and aggressive officer, was about to earn some national recognition in *Life* magazine. On 29 March, as the bulk of the Red Diamond Division fought to clear Frankfurt, Robinson, acting on a tip from a captured German medic, dashed ahead seventeen kilometers into enemy territory with two of his reconnaissance platoons and liberated a hospital in which fifty-eight captured Allied airmen were being held. A *Life* photographer went along for the ride and documented the daring venture. Stateside newspaper accounts in the coming days would further recount the troop's audacious rescue mission.[43]

When Robinson received the mission to investigate Usingen, he had already dispatched his 2nd Platoon to reconnoiter and mark a route for the 10th Infantry Regiment along the *reichsautobahn* heading northeast toward new assembly areas near Alsfeld some seventy-five kilometers distant. Therefore, Robinson sent only one platoon, the 3rd, to explore Usingen. By late afternoon the platoon had encountered Company B, 385th Infantry Regiment, of the 76th Infantry Division. The 76th's infantrymen told the reconnaissance platoon that at least "400 SS troops" were in the town and that the company would "mop them up."[44]

After taking stock of the situation, the 3rd Platoon leader radioed back to Robinson that perhaps two hundred Germans were concentrating in and around Usingen and that these Germans might escape if someone did not contain them. Robinson passed the report to division headquarters at 1800. He and the division's staff officers quickly became concerned about the proximity of this enemy force to the *reichsautobahn*, which the 10th Infantry Regiment was using for a rapid move toward Alsfeld. If the Germans moved eastward, they might cut the road. Robinson radioed the 10th Infantry's command post that his troop would keep an eye on the German force throughout the night but that he might need an infantry battalion to deal with the situation the next morning.[45]

What Robinson did not know was that the estimates of the German force assembling near Usingen were wildly off the mark. Instead of a couple of hundred German troops assembling in the nearby forest, a force of more than two thousand was gathering. *SS-Gruppenführer* Brenner's efforts at assembling his troops covertly had failed, but the element of surprise still remained in his favor. The Americans had underestimated the size of his command. The American armored vanguard had bypassed not simply a group of poorly organized stragglers, but instead a strong, cohesive force that—although battered and exhausted—could still deal the Americans a heavy blow.

Back in the 5th Infantry Regiment's assembly area near Neu Isenburg, 2/Lt. Joseph Edinger of Company H, 2nd Battalion, penned his last diary entry for the month of March before settling down for some much-needed sleep:

> This month marks the first days of real combat in my life. Now, I am scared and I'm not afraid to admit it. It's no fun watching your fellow man fall around you, never to rise again. Worse yet, is to hear them cry and not be able to do anything about it.
>
> God was good to me; I might easily have been killed by that sniper's bullet, but he spared me. I pray I can do what he has in store for me in the days to come. May I keep on being courageous, soldierly and an example to my platoon and may I never, above all things, let them down.
>
> Tomorrow is Easter, and we may march right into another fight. May God grant us strength and wisdom in our decisions. May his will be done, and we pray his will, will be conformed to in our way of life.[46]

CHAPTER 6

The First Day: Assenheim and Altenstadt, 1 April 1945

As the officers and men of the 71st Infantry Division planned their flank-protection mission during the night of 31 March to 1 April, SS-Gruppenführer *Brenner finished assembling his 6th SS-Gebirgs Division in the forest around Usingen. The division comprised two battle groups of about one thousand men each, commanded by* SS-Oberführer *Goebel and* SS-Standartenführer *Raithel. These two* kampfgruppen *were mixed not just with original SS troops of the Nord Division, but also with smaller German Army units and some individual Luftwaffe troops that had attached themselves to the division to continue fighting. By contrast, many other fragmented German Army units and troops avoided the division. For them, the war was over.*

Raithel's *kampfgruppe* still represented the division's main fighting force. The core of the *kampfgruppe* was SS-Gebirgsjäger Regiment 11, but many of the experienced senior leaders were gone. *SS-Hauptsturmführer* Alfred Steurich, formerly Raithel's adjutant, commanded the 1st Battalion as the most experienced and senior officer the regiment could muster. The SS officers and noncommissioned officers used Army troops as replacements to fill out their ranks.[1]

The second *kampfgruppe*, led by *SS-Oberführer* Goebel, the division artillery commander, consisted of mountain troops from Raithel's regiment and the remnants of the division's artillery—a total of six light, horse-drawn, ammunition-starved artillery guns. Like Raithel's battle group, Goebel's command reflected a blend of German Army stragglers and SS troops. Both battle groups even had a few officer candidates from Kampfgruppe Weilburg, which had lost all semblance of a separate force and merged with the two groups.[2]

By 0000 on 31 March the bulk of the Nord Division was assembled in the forest near Usingen. Brenner conferred with his two *kampfgruppe* commanders. Radio transmissions suggested that the division was well behind the advancing American forces, but some German units were still resisting at Gelnhausen. The Nord Division would move there as quickly as possible to bolster those German units—speed and stealth were essential to slipping through the American rear area undetected. Brenner therefore split the division into two movement columns: a motorized column and a horse-drawn column. Since Goebel's *kampfgruppe* had the most horses (used principally to pull the remaining artillery pieces), that *kampfgruppe* would serve as the horse-drawn column. The motorized column, which included Brenner and his staff, would form around Raithel's *kampfgruppe*. Each *kampfgruppe* would still be slowed by the numerous foot troops that would accompany them. The division did not have enough horse-drawn carts or motorized vehicles to mount everyone, so each column could advance only at the pace of the marching foot soldiers.[3]

Brenner directed his two commanders to move eastward immediately that night. The darkness would protect the columns from American fighter aircraft and artillery spotter planes. And since the Americans tended to limit their operations at night, the SS men had a good chance of slipping past the unsuspecting support units following the American vanguard. The overcast sky and the slight drizzle would obscure the moon and make for an extremely dark night. The Nord men could move in relative security until sunrise at 0614.[4]

Raithel sent a patrol of four or five SS men to scout the underpass at the north–south Bad Nauheim–Frankfurt *reichsautobahn* eight kilometers east of Usingen. *SS-Sturmmann* Egon Krüger, the former messenger from the 3rd Battalion, SS-Gebirgsjäger Regiment 11, was one of the members of this scouting party. When the SS men arrived at the underpass on the other side of the *reichsautobahn* from Ockstadt, they noticed heavy American traffic on the highway in both directions. Jeeps and supply trucks rumbled on the highway over their heads. The men moved carefully from tree to tree expecting to receive American gunfire at any moment, but the underpass was clear.[5]

The SS men then made their way back to Usingen through the pitch-black night to report their findings to Raithel. One of the men suddenly shouted, "Panzer! Panzer!" The SS men scattered and dropped to the ground, listening to the sound of a vehicle approaching from the west. Krüger, his head pressed firmly to the damp ground, listened as the vehicle slowly passed. He quickly rose and aimed his *panzerfaust* at the rear of the vehicle, twenty-five meters past his position. The vehicle suddenly stopped. It was not a tank but an American jeep with two occupants. The Nord men leapt to their feet and encircled the jeep. The SS sergeant in charge of the patrol ordered Krüger to speak to the two prisoners. In his best school-learned English, Krüger ordered the men out of the jeep. The Americans moved slowly, towering over the SS men in the darkness. Both men were officers, one a captain and one a major. The major declared, "Germany is defeated." Puzzled by this arrogant response, Krüger did not translate it to his sergeant. One of the SS men jumped into the driver's seat, turned the vehicle around, and led the rest of the patrol and its two American prisoners, on foot with Krüger and his comrades, back to Usingen.

By the time the patrol returned with the prisoners and information about the underpass, the columns were already lined up and ready to move. Raithel was happy to know the route was clear. His motorized column and the division's headquarters, followed by Goebel's horse-drawn column, immediately departed, led by an advance guard of SS *gebirgsjägers*.

The division made steady but slow progress during the night. The combined columns advanced eastward through Pfaffenwiesbach to the highway underpass scouted earlier by Raithel's patrol. The columns crossed under the heavily trafficked Bad Nauheim–Frankfurt *reichsautobahn* unmolested. Some SS troops even traversed the highway at other locations north and south of the Ockstadt underpass without incident.[6]

As the columns passed through several small villages in the dark of night, *SS-Rottenführer* Walter Becker, riding in a radio car as part of the 3rd Company, SS-Gebirgs Nachrichten Battalion 6, was pleased to see Easter cakes and other treats being tossed to the troops from supportive civilians. Most villages were clear of American troops, but Becker was surprised that, as the motorized column wended its way slowly along the many narrow streets common to these small towns, small units of occupying American troops equipped with jeeps would suddenly appear. On nearly every occasion these GIs were taken prisoner, and the SS men readily confiscated their jeeps and added the vehicles to the long, winding motorized column. Some SS troops could not drive the jeeps, so they impressed into service several reluctant American drivers.

On one occasion the motorized column entered a village with several GIs standing guard outside some buildings. Trucks and jeeps were parked everywhere. The GIs seemed to ignore the enemy column as it passed. Becker was surprised to see a truck loaded with German prisoners cheering the passing column. Becker heard one German soldier shout, "Go on! The *Amis* [the German nickname for Americans] are still asleep!"[7]

Before the sun rose at 0614, the lead elements arrived in a small forest east of Assenheim (see Map 6.1). Raithel's scouts—among them *SS-Sturmmann* Egon Krüger—crept along the main east–west road leading east out of Assenheim in search of American troops. The nighttime drizzle had created a low-hanging morning mist that obscured the rising sun. Just before sunrise one of the SS men spied the dark outlines of several large tents beside the road in a strip of woods on the eastern fringes of Assenheim. The SS men advanced at a crouch. As the sun peeked through the morning mist, the Nord men saw other tents with several vehicles parked beside them farther down the road.

Shots suddenly rang out. Krüger could not determine who fired first or what had happened. A sergeant ordered him to drop his *panzerfaust* and head to the freshly tilled rye field next to the tents. The shooting continued. SS troops ran in and out of the tents, firing as they ran. Krüger saw some American soldiers standing a scant ten meters from him, but they did not spot him as he sprinted through the woods toward the field.

As he approached the edge of the pasture, Krüger came across a dead American soldier, a Black man. Krüger had never before seen a Black man and was stunned. Shouts echoed throughout the tents as the shooting slowly abated. Near the woods beside the road, Krüger saw what appeared to be a kitchen tent. Rising cautiously, he crept toward the tent and entered. Inside he discovered three containers of what looked like rice (probably grits) that had been cooked with milk and sugar. Tables were arranged in preparation for breakfast, with bread, cans of corned beef, and tomato juice laid out. Krüger quickly stuffed his mouth with as many delicacies as possible while reading the labels on the cans.

After eating his fill—and barely tasting the food he had so rapidly consumed—Krüger emerged from the tent and noticed a series of other tents through some pine trees across the field. Unsure if his comrades had already cleared these tents, he sprinted across the field to check on them. Surprisingly, none of his comrades followed. As he approached the entrance to the first tent, he encountered a Black GI—the first living Black man he had ever seen. The GI's sudden presence shocked Krüger. If more GIs were in the tents, he would have to handle them alone since his comrades were busy mopping up the rest of the American encampment. The GI, armed with an M3 submachine gun and a large knife, was taller and thinner than Krüger. Asking the man for chocolate was the only thing that came to Krüger's mind. Krüger shrieked, "Chocolate! Chocolate!"

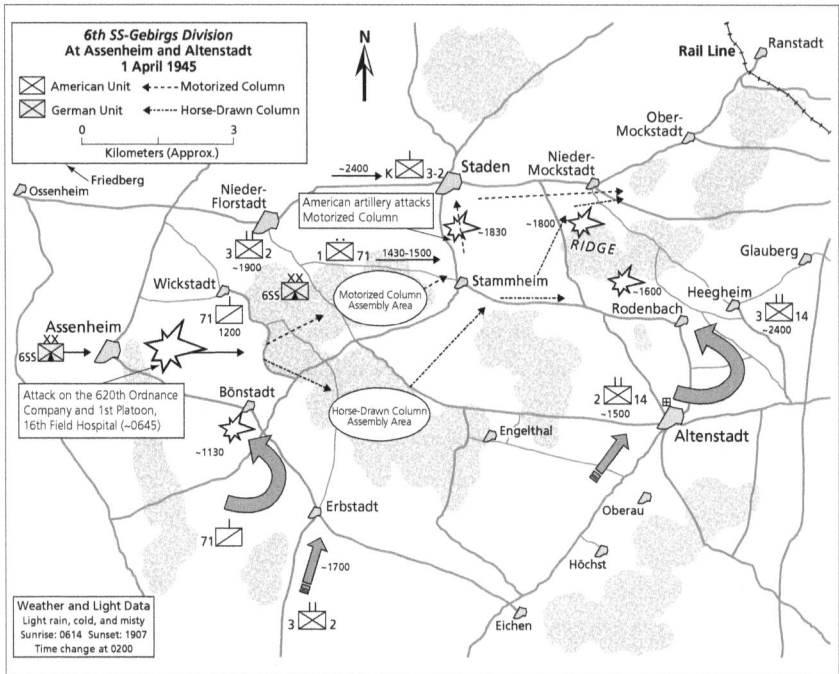

Map 6.1. 6th SS-Gebirgs Division at Assenheim and Altenstadt, 1 April 1945.

Puzzled, the GI simply stared at Krüger. Two more German soldiers appeared suddenly behind Krüger. The three men disarmed the GI and, after briefly checking the other tents, marched their prisoner back to the main road. Krüger saw several other American GIs, most of whom were Black, sitting on the road under German guard.

Krüger and his comrades quickly learned that they had stumbled onto the 620th Ordnance Company, an all-Black unit that supplied the advancing Third Army troops with ammunition. The Nord men had had little exposure to the American Army's support troops up to this point. Many of the supporting units in the segregated American Army consisted of all-Black units led by White officers. The U.S. Army had only recently (as of March 1945) begun allowing Black soldiers to serve in the front lines as infantrymen, and the Nord men had yet to encounter any Black infantry or even support troops.[8] Lieutenant Nemeth, one of the 620th's White officers, also had been taken prisoner.

The Nord men had struck gold by capturing the 620th, which had stores of ammunition in tents and trucks all around the area. Many Nord men used captured American weapons, so the ammunition was a boon to them. Remarkably, a German civilian from nearby Assenheim arrived on the scene and pointed out to the SS troops the location of the American ammunition stores.[9]

Krüger walked across the road toward two other tents marked with large red crosses where some of his SS comrades were conferring. Several American trucks and ambulances were parked at varying angles around the tents. In addition to the 620th Ordnance Company, the SS men also had captured the 1st Platoon of the 16th Field Hospital, which was displacing from Dieburg to Lauterbach. The platoon had stopped temporarily near the ordnance troops to set up a few tents and check on some patients whom the hospital was carrying forward.

Twelve trucks from 1/Lt. Foster C. Burns's 136th Quartermaster Truck Company was helping with the hospital's move. The SS men fought a fierce but short gun battle with the drivers, who did not surrender easily and killed at least ten German soldiers.

The hospital platoon was attached to the 4th Armored Division, driving eastward as the XII Corps vanguard. In the initial assault, only a couple of Americans in the hospital were wounded. The commanding officer of the 106th Evacuation Hospital was taken prisoner. His chief of surgery, Major Fonde, was killed.[10]

When *SS-Sturmmann* Krüger arrived at the scene, the skirmish for the field hospital was already over. SS troops were busy segregating the captured American officers from the enlisted men. They separated First Lieutenant Burns, the truck company commander, from his spirited and headstrong drivers. The SS men thoroughly searched each GI for weapons and the occasional watch or other booty. But the thing that caused Krüger to stop and stare was the sight of eight women from the Army Nurse Corps standing beside the road and fidgeting nervously. Although the SS men were searching the GIs, no one touched the women. Krüger had never before seen female American prisoners; these were the first women from XII Corps ever captured by the Germans.[11]

Krüger watched as an SS officer approached the women and, in a calm voice, addressed the nurse at the front of the group, 1/Lt. Helen R. Cosma, in perfect English.[12]

"You need not worry as no harm will come to you," he said. "You are not prisoners of war but merely under the protection of the Third Reich until the tactical situation changes."[13]

The man's words calmed the young nurses. But the SS officer's tone and choice of words clearly suggested that he suspected the situation would soon change for his division—for the worse.

The Nord men also captured another senior officer: the commander of the 10th Armored Infantry Battalion, Lt. Col. Harold Cohen. Cohen was a patient in the hospital recovering from a debilitating case of hemorrhoids. Cohen was one of Patton's favorite officers in the 4th Armored Division and a close friend of Lt. Col. Creighton Abrams, commander of the division's 37th Tank Battalion. Cohen had been set to lead Patton's ill-fated raid a couple of weeks earlier through German lines on the POW compound at Hammelburg, which held Patton's son-in-law, Lt. Col. John K. Waters. But Cohen's hemorrhoids kept him from leading the foray. Patton showed up and balked at the man's alleged ailment. The officer dropped his pants and bent over. Patton personally inspected Cohen's hemorrhoids and, after viewing what seemed like six or seven large eggs clustered around the man's rectum, declared, "That is some sorry ass. Terrible." Cohen immediately went to the field hospital for treatment and, after a couple of weeks, was nearly ready to return to duty when the Nord men attacked. A shamefaced Cohen found himself plucked from a hemorrhoid bath and forced into captivity with bare, dripping buttocks.[14]

After capturing an ordnance company and a field hospital, the SS men realized just how far behind the American lines they were. The SS troops immediately began checking the American vehicles and loading them with German equipment and captured American food and ammunition. The Nord men could not figure out how to drive the ordnance company's wreckers so they abandoned them. The rest of the division's main body was still closing on the wooded area in search of cover from the growing daylight.

Krüger was walking among the hospital tents in search of more American supplies when he stumbled across a wounded Black GI covered in a blanket. "Water, water," gasped the man. Krüger was deeply sorry for the suffering man but had no water to give him. He ran back to the group of prisoners and sought out a German medic treating the wounded. The medic immediately brought water to the man. Both he and Krüger then carefully carried the grateful GI over to the group of prisoners.

At that point the senior noncommissioned officer from Krüger's company, the 12th Company, appeared and took charge of the situation. The sergeant ordered Krüger to call for doctors and nurses from among the prisoners who could treat the wounded. Immediately, four GIs wearing red-cross armbands emerged from the group; they were followed by some doctors, nurses, and litter bearers. The sergeant told the GIs that the care of the wounded was in their hands. The doctors, nurses, and litter bearers quickly began transferring the wounded into the tents, where they treated them. When one American soldier approached Krüger and asked him what would happen to the prisoners, Krüger asked his sergeant for the answer. The sergeant simply said to ask the division headquarters, which was still moving and out of contact. Krüger could only shrug at the man's question.

Krüger then joined some Nord soldiers manning a checkpoint at one of the wooded road entrances east of Assenheim. SS troopers continued to search the surrounding forest for GIs who had scattered following the initial assault. Soon, four or five American jeeps—traveling at about two-hundred-meter intervals from each other—came roaring up the road through the woods and the checkpoint. The two GIs in the lead jeep instantly realized that something was not right and stopped. The SS men jumped up from their concealed positions beside the road and leveled their rifles at the surprised Americans. The GIs scrambled from the jeep and sprinted up the slope toward the woods. The SS troops fired but missed.

The next jeep stopped about forty meters away. The GIs dismounted and crouched near their vehicle. Krüger rose and approached them as they raised their hands in surrender. He disarmed the GIs and sent them down the road into captivity. The SS men then hid once more as the next vehicle approached. Once again, the GIs stopped the jeep and dismounted. The SS troops watched carefully as the three GIs leveled their M1 carbines at the partially concealed SS sergeant in charge of the checkpoint. The third GI, crouched behind the first two, raised his rifle with a white cloth attached to the end. The SS sergeant stood up in full view of the GIs to accept their surrender. The first GI, perhaps not realizing that the man behind him had shown the white flag, fired his carbine. The round hit the SS sergeant in the head.

Krüger immediately aimed his captured American M3 submachine gun at the GIs and fired. The bolt slammed forward with a loud, metallic click, but the weapon did not fire. Krüger, irritated at himself for not checking the weapon earlier, tossed it away and leveled his K98k rifle at the GIs. The other SS troops had not yet fired. The three GIs stood up with hands held high. The SS men sprang from the woods and surrounded the three Americans. They separated the one who killed the sergeant, a GI wearing spectacles, and sent the others down the road. Krüger could hear the SS men discussing a summary execution.

Krüger was dumbfounded. Were his comrades really going to execute the American? A German Army *Leutnant* attached to the Nord Division suddenly appeared from the forest brandishing a pistol. The *Leutnant* prevented the execution and sent the bespectacled GI to the rear with the other two Americans.

The SS men captured without incident a few more jeeps coming through their checkpoint. Krüger squinted in disbelief at one group of American soldiers captured in a jeep. He noticed long hair bundled up under their helmets—more women! More than likely, these women were also nurses traveling with the 16th Field Hospital. The vehicles passing through the checkpoint were probably the remainder of the hospital personnel arriving from the previous location, Dieburg. Krüger and his comrades even allowed a bus full of more women in American uniforms (probably more nurses) to pass unmolested. The SS men simply did not want to bother with a busload of females.[15]

❖

While *SS-Gruppenführer* Brenner moved his columns from Usingen, across the *reichsautobahn*, and into Assenheim on the night of 31 March and 1 April, the report of the SS division's presence the previous evening resonated throughout the headquarters of Major General Irwin's 5th Infantry Division. The initial strength estimate of the German force was two hundred to four hundred, as reported by Capt. Donald E. Robinson, the commander of the 5th Cavalry Reconnaissance Troop. But that number began to grow throughout the night. By 0300 on 1 April, the 11th Infantry Regiment reported nearly seven hundred German troops near Rosbach just south of the Ockstadt underpass. Two jeeps from the regiment's Intelligence and Reconnaissance Platoon stumbled onto the Nord Division's motorized column during a nighttime message-center run. A brief firefight ensued. One jeep escaped, but the Germans grabbed the other one, shooting the driver and capturing the other two occupants. The GIs who escaped reported the column to be at least seven hundred strong, composed of captured American jeeps and other vehicles towing at least sixteen big guns. (The Nord Division had only six remaining artillery pieces pulled by horses.)[16] "Seven hundred German troops" was still an inaccurate estimate but one that generated consternation at the division—and the XX Corps—headquarters.

XX Corps had scheduled the 5th Infantry Division to move to new assembly areas on the morning of 1 April using the *reichsautobahn* between

Bad Nauheim and Frankfurt. These assembly areas would position the division for future commitment as part of the Third Army's rapid advance. The Nord Division's presence in the area now placed that plan in jeopardy.

A spirited discussion between the staffs of both XX Corps and the 5th Infantry Division took place throughout the night. Corps reported that Third Army had placed the Red Diamond Division's move on hold until further notice. Something had to be done about the German columns spotted in the area before the route could be considered secure.

Major General Irwin arrived at the command post at 0427 and received an update from his G-3, Lieutenant Colonel Dickens. Tall and russet-haired, Stafford LeRoy Irwin—"Red" to his peers—was one of Eisenhower's former classmates and a skilled artilleryman. He switched to artillery from cavalry in 1917 because, to Irwin, calibrating gunnery seemed more challenging than determining the proper mixture of hay and oats for horses. He was born and raised in Virginia, and loved poetry and painting with watercolors. As the 9th Infantry Division's artillery commander in North Africa in February 1943, he deftly massed the division's artillery fires to blunt an attack by the 10th Panzer Division against the British position at Thala north of Kasserine. This achievement alone cemented Irwin's reputation in the Allied ranks as a skilled battlefield commander who could think and react quickly to challenging and dynamic situations.[17]

After Irwin discussed the situation with Dickens, he postponed the division's scheduled move that day, Easter Sunday, until further orders. He directed that Col. A. Worrell Roffe's 2nd Infantry Regiment, still located in Frankfurt, be prepared to move on two hours' notice to react to the German column—or columns—reported to be moving eastward south of Bad Nauheim and across the division's planned route. Irwin further charged Captain Robinson's reconnaissance troop and the 803rd Tank Destroyer Battalion's reconnaissance company (attached at the time to the 2nd Infantry Regiment) with executing a screening mission ordered by XX Corps along a line running north and south along the Bad Nauheim–Frankfurt *reichsautobahn*. The basic concept called for these two reconnaissance units to locate the German column and then call for the 2nd Infantry Regiment to capture or destroy the enemy troops. In addition, one platoon was to be detached from the 803rd's reconnaissance company and sent on another scouting mission in a forest west of Frankfurt. Irwin wanted both reconnaissance companies moving by 0800.[18]

❖

As the Red Diamond troops prepared for the coming day, the Nord Division's motorized column was already closing on the small town of Assenheim well inside the XII Corps' rear area. The XII Corps' night-shift staff, operating from the Forward Echelon (or Main) command post at Offenbach (on the northern outskirts of Frankfurt), first received reports of the seven hundred enemy troops from XX Corps through Third Army at 0400. The XII Corps' staff dutifully informed the 71st Infantry Division staff at 0415 since the Red Circle Division would have troops moving in the general area not long after daybreak.[19]

Major General Eddy was still controlling the corps' rapid advances from the main command post in Offenbach because the communications troops had yet to string wire and activate telephone lines at the Advance (or Tactical) command post in Lauterbach. Without those lines in place, Eddy could not communicate with Third Army headquarters. A small group of representatives from each staff section operated the Advance command post as a communications bridge between the Forward Echelon command post in Offenbach and the two advancing armored divisions. The signal troopers finally completed their wiring task at the Advance command post on the night of 31 March. Before the sun rose on 1 April, Major General Eddy; his chief of staff, Brig. Gen. Ralph J. Canine; and the corps' artillery commander, Brig. Gen. John M. Lentz, departed for Lauterbach in Stinson L-5 Sentinel spotter planes.[20] The rest of the Forward Echelon staff in Offenbach vacated the buildings they occupied and formed a lengthy column of vehicles for the long journey to Lauterbach. The corps' provost marshal and several military police vehicles had scouted two easterly routes during the night and deemed them both safe for travel. The Forward Echelon command post normally infiltrated to subsequent forward locations in small vehicle groups and along a variety of different routes for security reasons. But speed was essential on this day, so the entire command post would move in one convoy. Some staff members chose not to wait until the main column departed but instead struck out on their own. Capt. George Gorry and Pfc. Joseph Kaczor had departed in Brigadier General Canine's car before the long vehicle column even formed.

At sunrise the convoy departed for Lauterbach. The three general officers were already on their way by air when the first report about the seven hundred enemy troops came into the Forward Echelon command post in Offenbach. The report did not raise much concern until *SS-Standartenführer* Raithel's advance guard struck the ammunition company and field hospital east of Assenheim at dawn. A wild-eyed and panicked medical soldier from the captive 1st Platoon, 16th Field Hospital, burst into the command post at Offenbach after escaping capture by the Nord Division. The shaken soldier had sped off in a vehicle before the SS men could stop him.

Lt. Col. George Dyer, a special assistant to the corps' chief of staff, tried to calm the man. Dyer soon learned from the medic that nearly two thousand German troops had captured the field hospital's halted convoy near Assenheim—along precisely the same route the Forward Echelon command post's convoy was using at that very moment. Although Dyer doubted the man's seemingly inflated estimate of the enemy's strength (the GI was actually closer to the truth than anyone suspected), he immediately dispatched the provost marshal and some military police troops to catch up to the column, stop it, and lead it to Lauterbach along a newly scouted and cleared route. Unfortunately, many of the vehicles were beyond communications range. While driving Brigadier General Canine's car forward to Lauterbach, Captain Gorry and Private First Class Kaczor slammed into the rear of the Nord Division's march columns. After an SS trooper flipped the vehicle on its side with a *panzerfaust* round, the Germans took the two bewildered, but fortunately uninjured, XII Corps' staff members prisoner.

Soon a medical service corps major who also escaped the Nord Division's morning attack arrived at the command post and verified the other escaped medic's earlier report. The major further confirmed the Nord men's eastward direction of march. Dyer immediately sent word of the field hospital's capture to the XII Corps Advance command post in Lauterbach. Eddy and the other two generals had just arrived. Until that moment the XII Corps—and Major General Eddy—had no idea that a German force of any size posed a direct threat to the corps' rear area and MSR.

The reports immediately concerned Eddy. The corps' command post was already on edge because of an incident in Offenbach. A railroad car full of ammunition had caught fire a day earlier in the Frankfurt rail yard across the Main River and had exploded violently.[21] The corps' staff—and Eddy—thought the command post was under attack. Naturally, when the staff learned of the fire they breathed easier. No one in the corps headquarters underestimated the dying Wehrmacht's ability to inflict further casualties on American high-value targets—even at this late date. But numerous other incidents of messengers disappearing and vehicles being ambushed in the corps' rear area began to haunt the corps commander. Perhaps this group of Germans in the rear area was responsible for these incidents. If so, then Eddy's back was not secure—and something had to happen fast.

Major General Wyman and his Red Circle Division planned throughout the night for the move to Gelnhausen to guard the XII Corps' right flank with the 2nd Cavalry Group. The troops stood ready to move the next morning until the first report of seven hundred enemy troops moving into the corps' rear area reached division headquarters. The report—sent by XII Corps headquarters at 0415—did not seem to concern the corps' staff officers. Col. Oscar R. Johnston, the chief of staff, monitored the reports while Wyman caught some much-needed sleep.[22]

But the seriousness and intensity of the reports changed as daylight approached. The corps' staff, growing steadily more concerned, ordered the 71st Infantry Division to send the division reconnaissance troop to the enemy's reported location (at that time somewhere between Friedburg and Nieder-Florstadt). At around 0500 corps reported that the enemy was moving with horse-drawn wagons in a column approximately a half-kilometer long.[23]

Johnston sent for Capt. Bernard C. Johnson, the commander of the 71st Cavalry Reconnaissance Troop. Johnson's troop was scheduled to move out that morning with elements of the 761st Tank Battalion to cover the movements of the 66th Infantry Regiment, the Division Artillery, and the 5th Infantry Regiment as those forces relocated to Gelnhausen. Johnston cancelled that plan and later informed the 761st's commander, Lieutenant Colonel Bates, that he would have to execute his mission without Johnson's troop.[24]

Johnson arrived at the division command post at 0516. Colonel Johnston outlined the numerous reports of enemy troops moving with horse-drawn vehicles and told Johnson to head to Assenheim, the largest town in the area and three kilometers southwest of the enemy's last-reported location at Nieder-Florstadt.[25] The cavalrymen, Johnson later learned, would be operating just east of Captain Robinson's 5th Cavalry Reconnaissance Troop of the 5th Infantry Division.

Johnson dispatched his first vehicles northward at 0530. As the reconnaissance troop departed, Colonel Johnston instructed the division staff to keep the regiments abreast of the reconnaissance troop's new mission.[26] Johnston told the 14th Infantry Regiment, the division reserve, to prepare in particular to act on any information the troop sent back.

Meanwhile, the 5th and 66th infantry regiments, along with Brigadier General Henning's artillery, began rising from their brief slumber as daylight approached. The move to Gelnhausen would take place as scheduled. As the Red Circle men prepared to depart, they were still unaware of the attack on the ammunition company and field hospital more than twenty kilometers to the north. Further reports from the few GIs who escaped the carnage filtered into the XII Corps headquarters at Lauterbach between 0700 and 0800. Major General Eddy ignored his advancing armored divisions for the moment and pored over the reports.

The corps' staff sent a flurry of messages to the 71st's command post requesting updates from Johnson's troop. Johnson had been moving north with no enemy contact for nearly ninety minutes but had been unable to raise the division command post since 0655 on his normally reliable SCR-506 AM radio set. For the moment the troop was out of contact, and the 71st's reports to XII Corps outlining that fact only increased the anxiety level at corps headquarters. The Nord men's mere presence in the area was already raising alarms.[27]

By 0800 Major General Wyman was awake and in the division command post. He discussed the situation with Colonel Johnston and Lieutenant Colonel Lankenau, the G-3, then decided to contact Major General Eddy personally. The conversation between the two commanders was brief. Eddy expressed his deep concern over the enemy force and the damage it might be doing to the corps' support elements. The agitation in Eddy's voice struck Wyman. Eddy was a seasoned combat leader not usually prone to overreacting to enemy reports. He enjoyed Patton's full confidence, but others on the Third Army staff, particularly the chief of staff, Maj. Gen. Hobart R. Gay, thought Eddy to be "very nervous." Eddy clearly displayed that nervous quality.[28]

When the conversation concluded at 0824, Wyman turned to Lankenau and demanded to know why the headquarters could not talk to Johnson's troop. Lankenau could offer no explanation. At 0852 Johnson finally regained radio contact with the division command post and sent his first report after nearly two hours of silence. The troop was still moving north and had yet to contact any German forces.[29]

As Wyman listened to the troop's report, the rest of the division was on the move. Colonel Regnier's 66th Infantry Regiment—mounted on trucks dutifully supplied by the division G-4, Lt. Col. Clifton D. Blackford—crossed the regiment's initial point at 0720 (twenty minutes later than planned) without incident and proceeded for the bridge across the Main River near Hanau. The 761st Tank Battalion (minus), without the reconnaissance troop, had arrived at the battalion objective north of the Hanau–Lieblos road at 0805 and was in position, ready to overwatch the 66th Infantry Regiment's move down that same avenue. The 5th Infantry Regiment's foot element, scheduled to use the treadway bridge over the Main River, departed the planned initial point at 0700, on time.[30]

Wyman was pleased that his troops were moving as scheduled, but the reported enemy column in the corps' rear area cast a shadow over the operation. He was eager to get his troops into the frontline fighting and did not want to allow a rear-area scuffle with enemy stragglers to detract from that opportunity. The time for his men to test their mettle against a more worthy opponent had come. What Wyman did not realize was that the 6th SS-Gebirgs Division would be the worthy opponent he sought—and the most challenging battle his Red Circle men would face in the entire war.

❖

SS-Gruppenführer Brenner was pleased with the booty his advance guard had snatched from the ammunition company and the field hospital at Assenheim. The vehicles would prove particularly useful in transporting his troops to Gelnhausen. The American ambulances were especially valuable since each could carry ten or more fully equipped SS troops in the back.

The brief combat action at Assenheim convinced Brenner to pause so his advance guard could consolidate and reorganize while the division's two overextended—and strung-out—columns closed up with one another before continuing east. Daylight placed the columns at risk of detection by American artillery spotter planes and attack by American aircraft, but Brenner believed that his motley crew of SS, Heer, and Luftwaffe troops had made good progress throughout the night.

Brenner decided that the division would spend the morning assembling in the forest east of Assenheim before proceeding. He sent word to his two commanders to gather the columns in the woods, redistribute ammunition and supplies (especially the stores captured at Assenheim), and then continue eastward in the early afternoon. The temporary pause would allow Brenner's staff to account for the number of troops, vehicles, artillery pieces, and other equipment the division still had at its disposal. The staff set up shop in the forest two kilometers east of Wickstadt.[31]

Several local Volkssturm leaders, all older men, sought out Brenner's headquarters and, after greeting the division commander, offered their services to him. Brenner politely refused and instructed the men to return home to their families, but he readily accepted their gifts of weapons and ammunition. Brenner explained to them that he intended to keep his vehicles and troops away from the local villages to avoid putting the civilian populations at risk.

Once the men departed, Brenner sat down with his *funkers* and monitored the radios for information about the current situation.³²

❖

Captain Johnson's 71st Cavalry Reconnaissance Troop continued northward toward Assenheim in search of the enemy column. Johnson was unaware that the force he was moving to locate did not number in the hundreds but in the thousands.

The cavalrymen sped unopposed along the improved secondary roads in their M8 Greyhound armored cars. They occasionally paused at small villages along the way and learned from civilians that bands of German soldiers were moving throughout the area and looting the nearby towns for food. Johnson radioed these reports to the division and kept his troop moving. At 1115 the troop approached the southern outskirts of Assenheim near the small hamlet of Bönstadt two kilometers southeast, on the forest's western edge.³³

The cavalrymen deployed west and east and moved slowly toward the forest's edge nearest Assenheim. As the armored cars inched forward, Johnson learned from division headquarters that elements of the 5th Infantry Division were nearby. XII Corps had informed Lieutenant Colonel Lankenau of this fact at 1030, so Lankenau passed word through corps to the 5th Infantry Division that Johnson's troop was in the area as well. The 5th, also, was preparing to send truck-mounted infantrymen from the 2nd Infantry Regiment to the area, but Lankenau did not yet know of that mission. This hodgepodge commitment of forces from two divisions to the same general area was already proving to be a coordination challenge for both division staffs.³⁴

As both staffs sorted through the coordination problems, Johnson's M8 Greyhound armored cars crept along the western edge of the Assenheim forest. Visibility for the cavalrymen was only fair given the gray, overcast sky and the occasional drizzle. Mist and some fog still clung tightly to the undulating folds of open ground, covering the cavalrymen's movement.

By 1130 the entire troop had traversed the wood line near Bönstadt. As Lt. Delno Burns's 3rd Platoon approached the southern fringe of the town, a young woman shouting in Polish (probably a refugee) ran screaming up to the lead jeep. A Polish-speaking GI understood the woman to say that SS troops were in the town, and that they had slit her husband's throat and killed her infant son. Burns immediately placed T/4 Mason "Mickey" Dorsey's M8, nicknamed "The Four Rebels," in the lead. The nickname reflected the fact that the four-man crew all hailed from Southern states: Tennessee (driver Pvt. Jim Mathis), Florida (gunner Pvt. Marvin Eiland), South Carolina (vehicle commander T/4 Mason Dorsey), and Texas (Sgt. Carl R. Williams).

Dorsey's M8 crept slowly into Bönstadt, the crew watching carefully for Germans peering from windows and doorways. The town consisted of one narrow main street lined with quaint shops and houses. To the right, at the end of a small side street, sat a church on a parapet six feet high with two sets of stairs fifteen feet apart leading from the street to the church doors. The main street ended sharply with a left turn.

Dorsey had Mathis stop the M8 next to the first building at the town's entrance. The 3rd Platoon's other M8s and bantams followed thirty meters behind. Dorsey was scanning the main street and the fields behind the shops and houses when he spotted nearly sixty German soldiers in a field of small, randomly planted trees. The Germans were walking leisurely through the pasture carrying their weapons at the ready but seemingly unaware that American troops were nearby.[35]

Dorsey jumped from the turret and repositioned himself behind the M2 .50-caliber machine gun. He yelled down to his gunner, Private Eiland, "When I say go, you start firing the 37-mm and .30-caliber machine gun from the left, and I'll fire the .50 from the right."

But Lieutenant Burns, watching from the rear, yelled, "Don't shoot!"

Dorsey glanced over his shoulder at Burns and barked back, "What the hell? Do we have to have a hunting license to kill these sons-of-bitches? What the hell are we over here for, anyway?"

By now, Burns's jeep had closed on the rear of Dorsey's M8. Burns dismounted, approached the armored car, and said, "Our orders are not to fire unless fired upon."

Burns instructed Dorsey to proceed farther up the main street. Dorsey and his crew grudgingly complied. As the Greyhound edged deeper into Bönstadt, a German soldier, rifle slung casually over his shoulder, stepped from a doorway, spotted the M8, and ducked back inside. Dorsey reported the incident via radio to Burns, who simply replied, "Move on."

The M8 covered the length of the main street and, on turning left at the end, encountered a stone wall surrounding a cemetery. The road turned right, so Dorsey told Mathis to follow the road and hug the wall. A Nord man suddenly stood up from behind the wall shouldering a *panzerfaust* aimed directly at the M8. Dorsey shouted, "Shoot, Eiland, shoot!"[36]

A flash of smoke appeared over the Nord man's shoulder and, to Dorsey's horror, the projectile sailed through the air toward the armored car. Everything seemed to happen in slow motion. Dorsey dropped inside the turret just as the *panzerfaust* round exploded. A wall of flame swept past Dorsey and his driver, Private Mathis. The concussion slammed Dorsey's head against the inside edge of the turret hatch, rendering him momentarily unconscious. Mathis blacked out as well.

When Dorsey came to, the car's interior was filled with pungent, hazy smoke. Eiland was squatting behind the driver's seat and kicking Mathis on the shoulder. Eiland kept yelling, "Back up!" Mathis had apparently regained consciousness because he threw the M8 into gear and, relying on directions from Eiland, backed up. But Mathis could not see (M8 drivers had no vision ports to their rear), so he turned too sharply and slammed the vehicle into the church wall. Mathis turned the vehicle around and sped back down the street toward Lieutenant Burns's location. By this time Dorsey had realized that the *panzerfaust* round had not struck his armored car but instead had burst in the air above his and Mathis's hatches. Both men were unscathed except for two splitting headaches.[37]

The *panzerfaust* attack on Dorsey's M8 sparked a sharp exchange with the Germans occupying Bönstadt. Several houses crackled with flickers of German small-arms fire. The cavalrymen just entering the town ducked inside their M8s as German rifle and machine-gun rounds pinged against the thin armor. The rushing sound of several more *panzerfaust* rounds launched from within the village filled the air, but the projectiles missed their marks and impacted harmlessly into the cobblestone roads or nearby farm fields.

Captain Johnson shouted into the radio for all platoons to return fire. The M8 crews swung their 37-mm guns toward the village and opened fire. The rounds burst on the walls and roofs of the village homes. Several M8s sought better firing positions as German soldiers rushed from one house to another. Johnson radioed back to division headquarters that at least 125 German troops occupied the village.[38] He had no way of knowing he was up against seasoned SS troops.

Enemy rifle fire suddenly rang out behind the Red Circle men from the western edge of the forest. The GIs swung their turrets around and sent a flurry of 37-mm rounds into the darkened tree line. S/Sgt. L. B. "Whitey" Rhatican, the 1st Platoon sergeant, grabbed an M9 bazooka, loaded a white phosphorous round, and fired into the forest. Since Rhatican had fired from atop his M8 armored car, the round arced downward in a large loop and burst above the ground. Searing white phosphorous cascaded downward and scorched the earth, creating a blanket of smoke that obscured the Germans from the cavalrymen. Rhatican fired another round into the haze. The white phosphorus again burst at nearly treetop level. Germans screamed in agony. The small-arms fire ceased abruptly, and several Germans appeared from the woods with hands held high.[39]

The American volume of fire proved too much for the SS men in Bönstadt. The Germans quickly withdrew to the east. A few Nord men stumbled from the village with their hands up. The GIs gathered the prisoners—about thirty in all—and sent them to the rear. Had the cavalrymen checked what uniforms the Germans were wearing, they would have seen that the prisoners sported distinctive collar tabs with the two silver lightning runes of the Waffen-SS.[40]

Recognizing that he had contacted the reported enemy column, Johnson ordered his troop to rush north toward Wickstadt on the northern edge of the forest. Wickstadt sat on higher ground and would give the cavalrymen a better view of the valley below and the forest to the east. The troop sped across two kilometers of open ground and entered Wickstadt from the south unopposed. At some point during the maneuver, the Red Circle men encountered a badly shaken Black soldier from the 620th Ordnance Company—a survivor of the clash with the Nord men earlier that morning. The GI anxiously related to Johnson and his men the incident between the SS troops and the ammunition company. Johnson reported the GI's account to division headquarters and sent the man to the rear.[41]

From his troop's mounted observation posts scattered along the high ground below Wickstadt, Johnson could see scores and scores of German troops assembling in the forest. Vehicles maneuvered within and without the wooded area, and the sounds of activity echoed across the open fields between Assenheim and the forest.

After receiving multiple reports from his three platoons, Johnson concluded that the enemy had concentrated in the forest's center and was preparing to move out for the Assenheim forest's easternmost exits. Johnson radioed Lieutenant Colonel Lankenau that the enemy had trucks lined up at close intervals in the center of the woods and had set fire to some apparently inoperable vehicles that were burning on the road leading into the forest. The Germans appeared ready to pull out. Johnson told Lankenau that local civilians had reported seeing SS troops in the area an hour or so earlier—the troop commander's first realization that he was dealing with first-rate soldiers and not simply stragglers.[42]

Johnson informed Lankenau that he planned to deploy his platoons on the other side—the eastern side—of the Assenheim forest to block the roads leading eastward to Stammheim and Altenstadt. Blocking these roads would stall the German advance and buy time for friendly forces to arrive.[43]

Lankenau concurred with Johnson's plan. Major General Wyman had already decided to commit a larger force to meet the German threat. Earlier that morning Wyman tasked Colonel Lundquist, the commander of the 14th Infantry Regiment and currently the division reserve, to send a battalion to the same area where the reconnaissance troop had located the enemy force. Lundquist selected Lt. Col. Philip D. Brant's 2nd Battalion and alerted that battalion at 0930 to prepare to move out. The division staff had received news from corps of a new contact point at Heldenbergen (eight kilometers south of Assenheim) so that Brant could link up with the 5th Infantry Division troops in the area and coordinate activities to avoid friendly-fire incidents—or worse.[44]

By 1200 on Easter Sunday, the 71st Infantry Division was on the move. The Division Artillery had departed for Gelnhausen on time at 1000 behind the 66th Infantry Regiment. The foot elements of the 5th Infantry Regiment continued to march while the regiment's truck-mounted forces eagerly awaited clearance to cross the bridge over the Main River. But a battalion from the 14th Infantry Regiment was ready to move northward to attack an enemy force of unknown size. The Red Circle men also had one critical piece of information about this German force—it hailed from the Waffen-SS.[45]

❖

Back at the 5th Infantry Division command post, the focus of the day's events remained on locating and eliminating the threat posed by the Nord Division. At 0850 Captain Robinson reported that his reconnaissance troop, and the attached reconnaissance company from the 803rd Tank Destroyer Battalion, were moving slowly northward and screening as ordered. Robinson and his men had yet to encounter any enemy troops, but he found his movement slowed by constant, intermittent American artillery rounds falling in and around his zone. He speculated that other American units farther west were firing in the hope of hitting the Nord Division's column. An artillery observation plane buzzing high overhead confirmed Robinson's suspicions.[46]

Although Captain Robinson's troops had yet to encounter *SS-Gruppenführer* Brenner's columns, the contact that Captain Johnson's 71st Cavalry Reconnaissance Troop would have with the Nord men in the woods east of Assenheim a couple of hours later would clearly command the attention of the XII Corps' staff. Recognizing that the 5th Infantry Division was west of Johnson's troop, the corps' chief of staff, Brig. Gen. Ralph J. Canine, decided to call the 5th's commanding general, Major General Irwin, to coordinate the actions of both the 71st and 5th divisions. The 5th belonged to Major General Walker's XX Corps, so Canine was bypassing another corps headquarters and speaking directly to one of that corps' subordinate organizations.[47]

When Irwin picked up the phone, Canine summed up the situation quickly.

"About this business of the Germans east of Assenheim. Just heard about it at 0500. Sent a reconnaissance troop out and a cub [artillery observation plane] up."

"We sent two reconnaissance companies up," replied Irwin.

"[The] cub got shot at and came down," continued Canine. "Figure it is a couple of battalions regrouped in the woods east of Assenheim and the woods to the southeast. [The] 71st Reconnaissance Troop is up there. The 71st Division is sending a battalion up there and some tanks. [Third] Army said you were sending something up, and I told them to get liaison with you."

"[XX] Corps told us not to move, and we are still holding in town," answered Irwin. "I am anxious to go up."

Irwin ended the call. Moments later, at 1130, he contacted Major General Walker, the XX Corps commander. Irwin described his conversation with Canine and the corps' concern with the situation near Assenheim. Irwin further reminded Walker of the Third Army's orders for the division to stand fast until further notice. Walker dismissed Third Army's instructions. He said, "Give them [XII Corps] all the help you can."

Irwin hung up and told his G-3, Lieutenant Colonel Dickens, to send a reinforced battalion from the 2nd Infantry Regiment to Assenheim to help the 71st Infantry Division flush out the two suspected enemy battalions hiding in the nearby woods. Although the strength estimate of the Nord Division was starting to grow (from seven hundred troops to two battalions), Irwin still had no idea that the SS formation numbered in the thousands. Two reinforced battalions, both from two different divisions operating as members of two different corps, might not be sufficient to cope with the German force at hand.

Dickens contacted the XX Corps G-3, Colonel Snyder, to coordinate the efforts of both the 2nd Infantry Regiment's battalion and the 71st Infantry

Division's battalion as these two units converged on the enemy at Assenheim. Dickens explained that XII Corps had already identified Heldenbergen as the contact point between the two forces, but Dickens did not know from which regiment the other battalion hailed. Snyder's staff officers reported that the regiment was the 14th Infantry.

As soon as planning for the 2nd Infantry Regiment's battalion mission went into effect, Major General Irwin contacted Brigadier General Canine at XII Corps and updated him on the situation. Irwin explained that he too was sending a reinforced battalion, organized with tanks, up to Assenheim to locate the enemy force. He intended to send the battalion around from the northwest to capitalize on the high ground above Assenheim. The battalion would be operating out of its zone but would pull out when the mission was complete. Canine thanked Irwin and notified the 71st Infantry Division of the plan.

Lieutenant Colonel Dickens contacted Col. A. Worrell Roffe, the 2nd Infantry Regiment's commander, and spelled out the nature and scope of the mission to Roffe in direct terms: "[T]he CG [commanding general] has directed that [you] reinforce a battalion, send them there to clean it up, [and] destroy all Bosche [Germans] within. You can reinforce your battalion with whatever you think it will need in armor and such."[48] Dickens explained that the 14th Infantry Regiment would be moving to the same area and that the contact point was Heldenbergen. He identified the reported German locations in and around Assenheim, the enemy's reported strength, and where the 14th Regiment's battalion planned to attack.

Roffe acknowledged and selected the 3rd Battalion to serve as the nucleus of the combined-arms task force that would move north against the German force. The battalion commander, Lt. Col. Robert E. Connor, was a seasoned combat leader who had assumed command of the battalion in Normandy the previous summer. Roffe gave Connor the regiment's tank company from the 737th Tank Battalion, the regiment's Cannon Company, and a platoon of tank destroyers from the 803rd Tank Destroyer Battalion. In addition, Roffe notified Lt. Col. William R. Calhoun's 50th Field Artillery Battalion, the 2nd Infantry's direct-support 105-mm artillery battalion, to abandon its current mission of transporting infantry troops and to support the 3rd Battalion's move north. Roffe further explained that the enemy was gathering in the woods south and east of Assenheim, so the 3rd Battalion should head to Erbstadt, just south of those woods, to locate the German force. Roffe also mentioned the contact point with the 14th Infantry Regiment's battalion, which would move against the enemy somewhere near the woods west of Altenstadt. Connor understood his mission fully.[49]

Roffe, an experienced commander himself, was not taking any chances—especially when a message arrived from division headquarters identifying the enemy troops as members of the Waffen-SS. The report, communicated via radio, seemed dismissive of the SS men's capabilities and expressed a cavalier attitude about the coming operation. The division staff officer said, "We have . . . identification on these people. They are out of an SS Ack Ack [antiaircraft] outfit. They probably don't have anything but rifles, so they won't be hard to knock over. There is no point in any mercy tactics."[50]

Roffe undoubtedly winced at the last remark, but the fact that these SS troops were armed only with rifles and hailed from an antiaircraft unit changed nothing. Roffe knew they would fight doggedly. They were Germany's best, and SS troops always proved that point in each and every engagement. The coming battle would not be easy.

❖

By 1200 on 1 April, the bulk of the 6th SS-Gebirgs Division Nord had gathered in the nearly five-kilometer-wide stretch of forest east of Assenheim. Heer and Luftwaffe stragglers coming down from the nearby hills continued to attach themselves to the division for security and—more importantly— to help keep up the fight. Intermittent American artillery rounds fell in and around the forest, undoubtedly directed by observers in the ever-present XII Corps artillery spotter plane that buzzed high overhead. The constant explosions and the occasional direct hit frayed the nerves of the exhausted SS troops. The brief but sharp engagement with the 71st Cavalry Reconnaissance Troop less than an hour earlier also kept the SS men on their toes. *SS-Gruppenführer* Brenner was fully aware that the Americans knew his troops were gathering in the forest and that time was a precious commodity. The division would have to move quickly; the Americans would not keep their distance for long.

As the rest of the troops and vehicles assembled in the forest, *SS-Unterscharführer* Stöwe's communications section continued to intercept American transmissions that mentioned German towns and villages far to the east of the Nord Division's location. Brenner reviewed several reports assembled by his staff that summarized what local villagers and prisoners had stated about the Americans' progress. He could only conclude that the Americans had pushed much farther east than previously suspected. However, transmissions supposedly emanating from a German unit near Gelnhausen still gave Brenner hope that a German line was continuing to hold in that town. He was unaware that the 2nd Cavalry Group had already overcome the few German forces in Gelnhausen and that the 71st Division was moving into the town in force.

Brenner met with his two commanders, *SS-Oberführer* Goebel and *SS-Standartenführer* Raithel, and told them that the mission to Gelnhausen still stood. The division would remain organized in two columns—a motorized column and a horse-drawn column—and strike out along parallel routes for the Büdingen forest north of Gelnhausen. Goebel's horse-drawn column would depart on a northerly route at 1200, followed by Raithel's motorized column (moving along a more southerly route) at 1300.

Brenner's staff managed to tabulate the division's strength in personnel, equipment, and horses. When Brenner read the report, he saw only a shell of his former division. The staff estimated that the division had two thousand men, six hundred horses or other pack animals, three hundred vehicles of all types (both German and American), six German light mountain guns, three antitank guns, one *sturmgeschütze* (assault gun), two captured American Sherman M4 tanks, and two hundred American prisoners (twenty of whom were officers).

Goebel's horse-drawn column, along with a complement of foot-marching troops, prepared to depart the Assenheim forest at 1200. Brenner had been clear in his instructions to the artillery commander: avoid the main roads and larger villages, get to the Büdingen forest, and establish contact with the German troops believed to be in Gelnhausen.[51] The motorized column would soon follow. The captured American field hospital—complete with doctors and female nurses—also would move with the Nord men and provide medical care for troops of both sides.

The horse-drawn column, after struggling to organize in the woods, finally exited the forest well after 1200 and moved in the direction of Stammheim. Lt. Col. Harold Cohen, the 10th Armored Infantry battalion commander who had been captured with the field hospital earlier that morning, was amazed at the exceptional discipline displayed by the SS men—and even by the stragglers who had become part of the force. Cohen marveled at the Nord men's spirit and the fact that, in spite of the current situation, they remained well equipped. Most SS troopers still wore the distinctive SS camouflage smock, camouflaged cloth covers on their helmets, and full complements of personal field gear.

Each man sported an automatic weapon either in the form of a German Sturmgewehr (StG) 44 or MP40—or some form of captured American weapon. Nearly every man carried a *panzerfaust*.

But the Nord men's march discipline amazed the veteran battalion commander the most. The troops stayed in step, together, and responsive to the commands of their sergeants. No one complained. The SS men were proud and, at every opportunity, reminded Cohen that they lived up to the requirements of the Geneva Convention. They interrogated Cohen and the other prisoners at length, but they did not mistreat them. Cohen was surprised that the SS men seemed to know so much about the American units and their battle records. Some Nord men even told Cohen a story that a group of Americans had taken some SS troops, forced them to dig their own graves, and then shot them. Cohen did not respond to the tale.[52]

The SS troops placed Cohen and other prisoners too injured to walk on either a motorized vehicle or horse-drawn cart. The prisoners who could walk formed a column guarded by SS troops or helped to push some of the carts.

As Goebel's procession of troops slowly emerged from the forest, Raithel gathered his motorized column—which included the division headquarters—and prepared to move out. Raithel's column departed late as well—long after 1300 had passed. The lead element began creeping slowly toward the eastern exit of the Assenheim forest headed for Altenstadt.[53] The entire Nord Division was back on the move—but later than planned, in broad daylight, and vulnerable to the ubiquitous American artillery spotter planes overhead and the prying eyes of American reconnaissance troops manning outposts on the forest's fringes. But Brenner believed that speed would be their security, so he accepted the risk.

SS-Sturmmann Egon Krüger, still guarding his checkpoint at the entrance to the woods with other members of his battalion, heard the vehicles from the motorized column roar to life. Alarmed, Krüger and his comrades abandoned their post and ran into the forest just in time to leap onto one of the captured American trucks at the tail end of the column. Krüger was relieved; he had almost been left behind. The intermittent American artillery and the threat posed by the 71st Cavalry Reconnaissance Troop had distracted the men at the checkpoint; they kept their eyes glued to the west, waiting for the next artillery barrage or for another attack by the cavalrymen. If Krüger and his friends had not heard the sound of engines revving in the forest, they would have missed the division's last battle![54]

As the lead vehicles of the 6th SS-Gebirgs Division's motorized column emerged from the eastern fringe of the Assenheim forest, Col. Augustus J. Regnier's 66th Infantry Regiment was already taking up positions along a line extending from Hailer to Gelnhausen. At 1220 Regnier opened his new command post in Lieblos, a small village two kilometers north of Hailer and west of Gelnhausen. Keeping his 1st Battalion in reserve, Regnier moved his 2nd and 3rd battalions forward to positions north of Gelnhausen on the high ground overlooking the town—high ground that marked the southern limits of the Büdingen forest.[55]

As the 66th settled into position along the XII Corps' right flank, the division artillery occupied firing positions northeast of Hanau to support the 66th. The artillery battalion that initially moved with the 66th across the Main River, the 609th, had broken off from the regiment and returned to Brigadier General Henning's control. Elements of Lieutenant Colonel Bates's 761st Tank Battalion, in place since that morning along the Hailer-Gelnhausen road, oversaw the movement into Gelnhausen.

Farther north and west, above the Assenheim forest, Captain Johnson's 71st Cavalry Reconnaissance Troop watched as captured American vehicles, German-made motorcycles, and a hodgepodge of other rolling stock crept slowly out of the Assenheim forest. Johnson sent his 1st Platoon, led by Lt. Ed Samuell, around to the east to block the German columns heading out of the forest. However, not all Germans troops opted to forge ahead with the Nord Division. Some Heer stragglers emerged from the forest and, with white flags held high, walked across the fields toward Wickstadt and surrendered. Johnson reported the trend of surrendering German troops to division headquarters, but a handful of surrendering stragglers did not mean the Nord Division was ready to concede.[56]

Back in the south the 71st Division's move to Gelnhausen progressed smoothly until a traffic jam at the repaired civilian bridge stopped everything in the early afternoon. Support elements of the 11th Armored Division, anxious to cross the Main River to keep up with their advancing division, did not wait until the 71st Division's march columns had cleared the bridge before attempting to cross. The 11th's supply troops were scheduled to use the bridge only after the Red Circle Division was across the river. Supply truck convoys became snarled with the 5th Infantry Regiment's motor convoy on both sides of the bridge. Lieutenant Colonel Brant's 2nd Battalion, 14th Infantry, heading north toward Altenstadt and the Nord Division, managed to slip across the main bridge with its tanks and other vehicles before the traffic jam materialized. The 5th Regiment's foot-marching element, using the treadway bridge farther downstream, crossed without incident and by 1425 was already on the far side of the river. Major Heymont, the regimental S-3, predicted that, once the traffic jam at the main civilian bridge subsided, the rest of the 5th Regiment could close on the Rückingen area sometime around 1630 that afternoon.[57]

As the 5th Regiment's motor convoy struggled to squeeze through the congested bridge site, Colonel Wooten's foot-marching troops entered Nieder-Rodenbach at 1330 on their way to Rückingen and found the town unoccupied by German troops. Wooten believed that Nieder-Rodenbach (a short distance from Rückingen to the south and east) offered excellent short-term billets for his men, so he requested that division headquarters allow him to occupy the town. He received approval within minutes.[58]

By 1455 Brigadier General Rolfe, the assistant division commander, reported to the G-3, Lieutenant Colonel Lankenau, that the traffic jam was cleared and that all rolling stock was moving across the river nicely. A few moments earlier Major General Wyman had directed Lankenau to work out a plan to move the rest of the 14th Infantry, and the division (minus its service elements), across the river as soon as possible. The frustrating situation at the bridge signaled to Wyman that he needed to move all combat forces across the Main River in case something happened to any of the outfits already on the far side. He wanted to be able to reinforce his forward troops quickly and not have them separated by a river with only two crossing points. Wyman's thinking was prescient at this juncture. His task force from the 14th Infantry, led by Lieutenant Colonel Brant, was only minutes away from slamming headlong into the 6th SS-Gebirgs Division's horse-drawn column near Altenstadt.[59]

❖

Lieutenant Colonel Brant's task force of tanks and truck-mounted infantry, assembled around his 2nd Battalion of the 14th Infantry Regiment, had cleared the main civilian bridge across the Main River just in time to avoid the traffic jam. The task force's timing was fortuitous: if Brant's troops had become ensnarled in the congestion at the bridge, the battalion would have missed the 6th SS-Gebirgs Division's eastward-moving columns as they emerged from the Assenheim forest.

Lt. Col. Philip D. Brant, the 1937 West Point graduate whose 2nd Battalion had previously occupied Speyer on the Rhine River, was eager to accomplish the mission his regimental commander, Colonel Lundquist, had given him: round up the roughly 750 German troops massing in the woods east of Bönstadt. Brant received the mission at 0930 on 1 April at his command post in the tiny hamlet of Hausen—barely one kilometer north of the 14th Regiment's command post in Obertshausen. At that time the German strength estimate was low but growing. Brant would lead his men into the coming battle still thinking he was taking on a group of German stragglers comparable in strength to his own task force.[60]

On receiving the mission Brant immediately canceled Easter church services. The regimental chaplain, Capt. (Father) John J. Fahy, was preparing to say Easter Mass for the battalion's Catholic soldiers in a small German church when word arrived for everyone to report to their companies immediately. Many of the men were disappointed at missing Easter Sunday Mass, especially Cpl. Robert V. Reno, an assistant squad leader in the 1st Platoon of Company E. A devout Catholic, Reno had written his mother the day before, 31 March, to express his hope that this Easter would be the last one he would spend away from his family, including his pregnant wife and infant son. He wrote, "Tomorrow I'll be thinking of you all and missing you all, but this Easter I have a feeling that it will be our last Easter apart God willing. We should all be together again for next Easter." What Reno did not know was that his platoon would soon lead the charge against the 6th SS-Gebirgs Division Nord.[61]

Brant quickly convened a meeting of his company commanders. Although not eager to thrust his men into the cauldron of battle, Brant insisted on competence, initiative, and aggressiveness in his subordinate leaders. These characteristics, in Brant's mind, would save lives on the battlefield.

Capt. Harry T. Goldman commanded Company E and enjoyed Brant's full confidence. Brant often gave Goldman's company the more difficult missions to perform. When Colonel Lundquist asked the 2nd Battalion for a platoon to help the 1st Battalion guard the bridges over the Main River at Hanau, Brant gave the mission to Company E. As a result of the guard mission, however, the company could muster only two rifle platoons and a weapons platoon for the coming mission.[62]

Capt. Thomas W. Alvey had just assumed command of Company F that morning after learning from Colonel Lundquist on 31 March that he would replace Capt. William R. Swope in that position. Alvey previously commanded the regimental headquarters company before earning the opportunity to lead a rifle company. Alvey met with Brant at the company command post earlier that morning and barely had a chance to meet his four platoon leaders before the battalion received the order to move out.[63]

Capt. Andrew J. Bass commanded the third of Brant's three rifle companies, Company G. Bass had proved to be a very effective and reliable leader in the past. And Capt. Hank Brewer, the commander of the heavy weapons company, Company H, was always where Brant needed him—with machine guns and mortars in place, ready to support the rifle companies.

Brant's company commanders gathered to learn of their latest mission. Brant explained that Lundquist had given the battalion the regiment's tank company—Company B, 761st Tank Battalion, led by Captain Long—a platoon of tank destroyers (3rd Platoon, Company C, 635th Tank Destroyer Battalion, led by 1/Lt. Walter E. Standfield), and a psychological warfare public address system mounted on an M8 armored car. With the addition of these assets, the battalion was a full-fledged, combined-arms task force.

The mission called for the task force to move—with the infantry mounted in trucks—to an area twenty-five to thirty road kilometers north and engage—and capture if possible—a group of 750 or so German soldiers in the woods between Bönstadt and Altenstadt. Brant directed that Company E, minus one rifle platoon, lead the task force mounted on Captain Long's tanks—ten men to a tank. Companies F and G would follow in trucks, and the tank destroyers and heavy weapons company, Company H, would bring up the rear. Speed was essential: the Germans might move out before the task force could engage them.[64]

The company commanders raced back to their companies to issue instructions and movement orders. Colonel Lundquist soon arrived with the five jeeps of 1/Lt. Nat R. Freeman's regimental Intelligence and Reconnaissance (I&R) Platoon. Lundquist, who had yet to command his regiment in a significant action against the enemy, believed strongly in reconnaissance and in seeing the prospective battlefield. He directed Lieutenant Colonel Brant to accompany him and the I&R Platoon on a scouting mission of the suspected German locations. Once the two commanders pinpointed the Germans' location, both men could employ the arriving task force directly against the enemy. Lundquist was fully aware of the urgency that Major General Wyman and Major General Eddy placed on this mission; rapid action was critical.[65]

The task force, led by Company B's tanks, lined up in Hausen and at 1215 departed northward. The task force's objective was the forest between Bönstadt and Altenstadt east of Assenheim and the Nord troops assembled therein. The column's planned route took the task force across the Main River bridge south of Hanau, north to the contact point at Heldenbergen, and then northeast toward the Assenheim forest. Brant told both Captain Long and Captain Goldman that he and Lundquist would contact the column via radio and direct the task force toward the enemy once the I&R Platoon located them.

Lundquist and Brant then sped off in advance of the column along the same planned route. The five jeeps moved quickly, crossing the bridge over the Main River with ease. Although the roads were generally improved and, in many cases, paved, the going was slower than Brant and Lundquist had expected. Many of these secondary roads were narrow, two-lane tracks that meandered through a combination of low, confining wooded areas and across vast expanses of open farm fields topped by high ridgelines. The low-hanging clouds and occasional drizzle limited observation. Lundquist wanted to locate any support elements from the 4th Armored Division still moving through the area so he could coordinate the task force's movement, but found no one on the open, desolate roads.[66]

Farther north in the Assenheim forest, *SS-Gruppenführer* Brenner was frustrated that his columns were not moving faster. He intended for speed to give his men security during daylight, but speed was the thing his columns clearly lacked. Although *SS-Oberführer* Goebel's column of horse-drawn carts and vehicles had departed after 1200, only the leading elements had cleared the forest by 1500. Despite the Nord troops' remarkable march discipline, the onerous task of guiding exhausted horses and foot-marching men, all overburdened with supplies and ammunition, across open fields slowed the movement to a maddening crawl. The column had advanced barely one kilometer in three hours.

The progress of *SS-Standartenführer* Raithel's motorized column—complete with the division staff and headquarters—was not much better. The captured American ambulances and other vehicles moved quickly when using hard-surface roads but slowed to a crawl when negotiating forest roads and trails. By 1500 the lead elements of both columns were still creeping along west of Stammheim—resembling their long, bitter trek from Finland nearly eight months earlier.

Back near Wickstadt the 71st Cavalry Reconnaissance Troop prepared to move east of the Assenheim forest and block the roads toward Altenstadt. Johnson opted to move his troop in sections for security and stealth. He wanted the bulk of his cavalrymen to keep their eyes on the SS troops in the woods while selected sections skirted the northern edge of the forest and swung around to the eastern side of the woods. After consulting his map Johnson believed a blocking position in Stammheim would be the best location for the first section. From Stammheim the section could report on all activity east of the forest while forcing the German troops to disperse if necessary.

Johnson called Lt. Edward W. Samuell Jr., the 1st Platoon leader, and told the lieutenant to send one section to the troop command post. Johnson planned to start with the 1st Platoon's sections followed by the rest of the troop in sequence. Samuell selected S/Sgt. L. B. "Whitey" Rhatican's section for the mission. Rhatican was Samuell's platoon sergeant and his most experienced cavalryman.

Rhatican sped off to Captain Johnson's command post with his section's two bantams and one M8 Greyhound armored car. As soon as the section arrived, Johnson briefed Rhatican. The platoon sergeant acknowledged his orders and departed for Stammheim at 1430.

As the cavalry section skirted the northern fringe of the forest east of Wickstadt, Rhatican and his men spotted a group of heavily armed SS troops—about twenty-five in all—moving toward the town and the troop's locations. The SS troops clearly intended to attack Wickstadt. Rhatican radioed Lieutenant Samuell immediately. Alarmed, Samuell sent his other two sections to meet the advancing Germans on the open ground outside the village. As soon as the SS men appeared, Samuell ordered his sections to fire. The Red Circle men sprayed the Germans with machine-gun fire. The outgunned Germans threw down their weapons, tossed aside their helmets, and reached for the sky. The Red Circle men rounded up twenty-two prisoners to send back for interrogation.[67]

Staff Sergeant Rhatican and his section continued on their five-kilometer journey to the other side of the Assenheim forest. Stammheim was supposedly clear of German troops, but Rhatican knew the number of Germans roaming the area would mean that some were probably inside the village as well. Soon, the section rounded the northeastern corner of the forest two kilometers below Staden. Stammheim appeared in the southern distance nestled in a small valley.[68]

The lead bantam, driven by Pvt. Brunislaus "Bruno" Kieslewski, stopped abruptly. Kieslewski, the troop's "Polish giant," had encountered several Polish displaced persons on the road heading north out of Stammheim and he stopped to question them. The clearly agitated rag-tag group explained that the SS troops had dug into the cellars in Stammheim and were ambushing all American vehicles (probably XII Corps supply troops) that entered the town. The SS men had attempted to bribe the Poles into fighting for the Germans.

An American truck suddenly sped past Rhatican's section heading south along the road from Staden into Stammheim. Rhatican led his troops to a small knoll and watched as the truck entered Stammheim. As soon as the truck had passed the first few buildings inside the village, several SS men leapt onto the road and fired. The truck screeched to a halt. The SS troops pulled the driver and his passenger from the truck, searched them, and led them off. A German soldier then jumped into the driver's seat and drove his new prize away. The other SS men quickly cleared the battle debris from the road and returned to their positions to await another vehicle.

Rhatican raced back to his M8 Greyhound armored car and radioed what he had seen to Lieutenant Samuell. Samuell considered his options. He wanted to keep the Germans under observation, but he did not want to put Rhatican's section at risk. He instructed Rhatican to move to a defensive position two kilometers farther north at Staden but to keep a small observation post on the knoll overlooking Stammheim. Samuell then sent a report to Captain Johnson.

Staff Sergeant Rhatican left one bantam and a few men on the knoll and departed for Staden in his M8 Greyhound, followed by the other bantam. The two vehicles had barely reached Staden when the distant sound of mortar rounds reached the GIs' ears. Rhatican radioed the observation post and learned that the Germans, after detecting the GIs on the knoll, were mortaring them. Rhatican informed Samuell, who immediately ordered the section back to Wickstadt. Samuell's men were outgunned and outnumbered, so he wanted them back with the rest of the troop. Rhatican ordered the bantam out of Stammheim just as the German mortar rounds found their mark. The GIs hunkered down inside the bantam as it raced north and away from Stammheim under a gauntlet of German indirect fire. The men—and the bantam—emerged unscathed.[69]

As soon as Rhatican's section returned to Wickstadt, Captain Johnson changed the plan and told Rhatican to go back and stay put until a larger force arrived to deal with the Germans. Johnson's men were clearly outnumbered, so the best the Red Circle cavalrymen could do was hunker down and report the German activity. For the moment Johnson would have to settle with being the eyes and ears of the 71st Division until more troops arrived.

At 1500 the jeeps of the 14th Infantry's I&R Platoon entered Altenstadt. The long, three-hour journey northward proved uneventful for First Lieutenant Freeman and the two senior officers in his charge, Colonel Lundquist and Lieutenant Colonel Brant. Lundquist had directed Freeman's jeeps toward Altenstadt to determine if the enemy had moved east out of the forest. At Heldenbergen, the platoon took the road heading northeast and soon arrived. Altenstadt seemed strangely quiet, perhaps owing to the solemnity of Easter Sunday.[70]

The jeeps crept slowly through the town, the I&R men watching the windows for German snipers. A few faces glanced from behind curtains but then quickly disappeared. The jeeps passed the town's small church and continued along the road leading north out of town. At the northern edge of town, Lundquist and Brant found the village's cemetery, surrounded by a low, waist-high brick-and-plaster wall. Both officers scanned the horizon and the small patch of woods to the northeast for any sign of German troops.

As they searched for the enemy, a sudden burst of rifle and machine-gun fire crackled from a small patch of woods. Lundquist and Brant dove for cover. The jeep drivers threw their vehicles into reverse and sought cover behind the cemetery wall and some nearby houses. The German fire, although well aimed, was ineffective since the forest was nearly a kilometer and a half away. The Nord men who fired, part of the foot-marching element of *SS-Oberführer* Goebel's horse-drawn column, caught only a glimpse of the I&R Platoon's jeeps before shooting.[71]

Freeman's jeeps moved to better positions and returned fire with M2 .50-caliber and M1 919 .30-caliber machine guns. Only the .50-caliber rounds had the range, and several Nord men in the distant column fell wounded or dead. The Germans returned fire sporadically, but the American fire did not cause the column to waver. The highly disciplined Nord men forged ahead undeterred.[72]

Lundquist, a large man with an impressive physique, immediately stood up and scanned the horizon with his binoculars. He could see in the distance, among the patch of woods east of the Assenheim forest (but not connected to that forest), at least five hundred German troops skirting the edge of the wood line moving east. Their discipline impressed him. He turned to Brant and proclaimed, "We need to get to Stammheim." Lundquist believed that the main German force was centered around the town just visible beyond the patch of woods, so Brant's task force would probably have to attack there.[73]

Lundquist instructed Freeman to leave one jeep with a light machine gun at the cemetery and to have the other jeeps cover all entrances into Altenstadt.[74] He also told Freeman to radio the task force with instructions to head for Altenstadt. Lundquist intended to locate a route to Stammheim and possibly the main body of the German force. He instructed his jeep driver to move slowly along the road past the cemetery in the direction of Stammheim.

Lieutenant Colonel Brant, after consulting his map, believed he had discovered a better route to Stammheim via Rodenbach, which sat two kilometers northeast of Altenstadt along a road that paralleled the north–south Stammheim–Altenstadt road (see Map 6.2). This route was a kilometer farther east and provided better cover. Brant directed his jeep driver to follow the road to Rodenbach but to keep Lundquist's jeep in sight. Brant and his driver sped along the road. On seeing Rodenbach, they looked west and realized that Lundquist was out of view. The Rodenbach road offered more protection from the enemy, but Brant did not venture into the town because he did not want to leave his regimental commander alone on the road to Stammheim—and in the midst of the enemy.

Brant's driver spun the jeep around, and both men soon caught sight of the cemetery. Lundquist's jeep was stopped in the open, just north of the graveyard. When Brant arrived he found Lundquist tending to a Black soldier who, only moments before, had been shot in the stomach. The man, most likely a member of the 620th Ordnance Company, happened on Lundquist minutes earlier. The GI likely escaped from the Nord Division's column and had been wounded in the process.[75]

Without warning, the main body of *SS-Oberführer* Goebel's horse-drawn column became fully visible on the east–west ridgeline from Stammheim to Rodenbach. The sudden appearance of such a large and impressive enemy force stunned the two officers. The two jeeps sat on open ground north of Altenstadt's cemetery, clearly observable to the German troops. Lundquist jumped into his jeep, swung the pedestal-mounted .30-caliber machine gun toward the column—less than a kilometer away—and opened fire.[76]

Brant shouted for him to stop. In the distance, the slow, muffled squeal of tank tracks reached Brant's ears.

"I can hear my tanks in the distance!" shouted Brant.[77]

Brant jumped into his jeep and ordered his driver to race toward the sound of the tanks. The GI threw the jeep into gear and sped off through the center of Altenstadt. The time was nearly 1600.[78] As Brant's jeep emerged from the south side of Altenstadt, the column's lead tank appeared at the bend in the road. Brant signaled for the tank commander to follow him and sped back into town.

The tanks and truck-mounted infantry meandered through Altenstadt's narrow, cobblestone streets. Frightened residents peeked from behind curtains. Realizing that the war had finally come to Altenstadt, many citizens hung white bedsheets from their windows to show their submission to the Americans. The GIs ignored this now-common practice.

As Brant guided the first tank up to the cemetery, Colonel Lundquist stepped into the street and began directing the vehicles into firing positions. Brant leapt from his jeep and, after a hurried exchange, convinced Lundquist that the better tactic would be to swing the entire task force to the right through Rodenbach along the route Brant had scouted earlier. That option would put the task force in front of the German column creeping along the ridgeline. Lundquist agreed.

Brant jumped into his jeep and ordered the lead tank to follow him. He led the column down a side street and onto the road heading north toward Rodenbach. The soldiers of 2/Lt. Frank J. Hagney's 1st Platoon, Company E, clung to the tanks' exteriors and scanned the horizon for enemy troops. The GIs did not understand what was happening until the large German column moving in the distance toward Rodenbach came into full view.

About five hundred meters south of Rodenbach, Brant stopped the column and mounted the lead tank with Second Lieutenant Hagney. He told Hagney that the task force had to move through Rodenbach and gain the high ground as quickly as possible to block the German column on the ridgeline so the rest of the task force could deploy and attack.

As the column entered the southern outskirts of Rodenbach, the first few tanks opened fire with their .30-caliber coaxial machine guns, spraying the village homes. Brant, alarmed by the unexpected shooting, banged on the hatch of the lead tank. One of the 761st Tank Battalion's crewmen popped his head out. Brant demanded to know why the tankers had opened fire. The crewman simply replied that they were conducting a reconnaissance by fire to

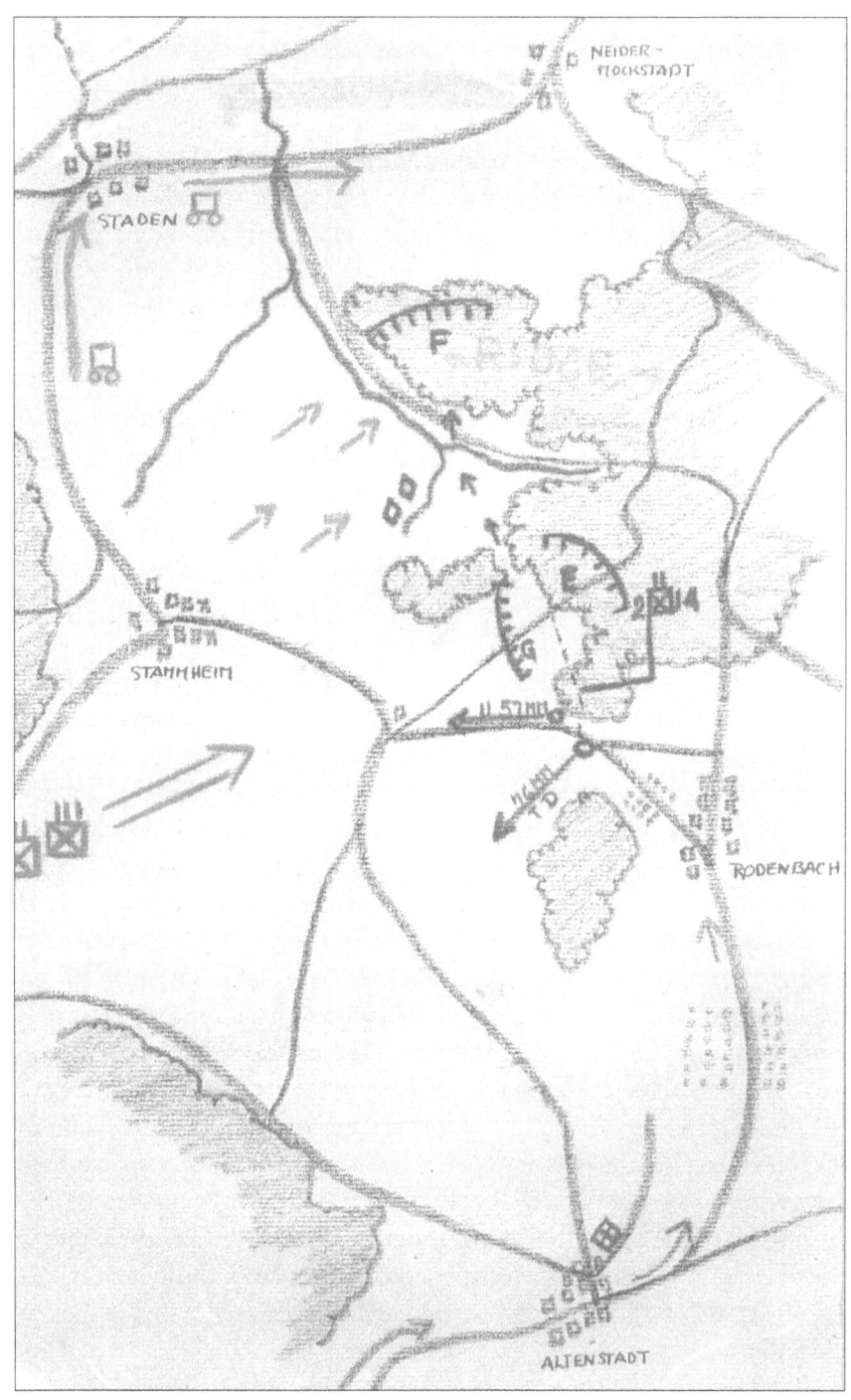

Map 6.2. 2nd Battalion, 14th Infantry's attack north of Rodenbach, 1 April 1945 by Lt. Col. Philip D. Brant. From Brant's scrapbook of his war exeriences.

draw out enemy troops hiding in the town. Brant did not tell them to stop, deferring instead to the seasoned tankers' judgment. But Brant was anxious that the machine-gun fire had showed the enemy Brant's hand.[79]

The tanks raced quickly through Rodenbach, firing their machine guns as they moved. As the column emerged northeast of town, Brant ordered Company E's infantrymen to dismount the tanks, deploy, and move up to the ridgeline north of Rodenbach. He intended to follow with the tanks in support. Captain Goldman had yet to arrive with the rest of Company E, so Brant momentarily took charge of the company's lead platoon and part of the weapons platoon.[80]

Second Lieutenant Hagney assembled his GIs into a broad skirmish line along the open ground west of the wooded area above Rodenbach. Sgt. John F. Cecula, a squad leader riding on the third tank with his assistant squad leader, Cpl. Robert V. Reno, ordered his troops off the tanks and to the right. The Sherman tanks spread out in a linear formation and slowly followed the GIs uphill toward the ridgeline. Brant stood behind the turret on the lead tank and guided the troops.[81]

Second Lieutenant Ray K. Mortensen, the Company E weapons platoon leader, placed his 60-mm mortar sections into action on the slope just behind the tanks and infantry. Mortensen's troops could clearly see the SS troops moving slowly along the ridgeline—seemingly oblivious to the Americans' presence. Horses unhurriedly pulled carts and artillery pieces among the foot-slogging Nord men. Mortensen ordered his gunners to fire with all powder increments on the rounds for maximum range. Within minutes several mortar rounds arced through the sky toward the German column. The rounds exploded harmlessly in the open just short of the column. The SS men ignored the explosions and kept marching. Mortensen told his mortar crews to stop firing; they were only wasting ammunition. He then directed his machine-gun sections into position along the ridge to support the 1st Platoon's advance.[82]

Thinking his Red Circle troops had still beaten the German column to the forest's edge, Lieutenant Colonel Brant urged his tanks and infantrymen forward to the crest of the ridgeline. Brant, from his vantage point on the lead tank, scanned the woods to the right and, to his amazement, saw German troops in the wood line less than one hundred meters away. The foot-marching advance guard of *SS-Oberführer* Goebel's column had beaten Brant's men to the forest.

Brant ordered the tanks to swing their turrets eastward—away from the main German column—and fire on the SS troops in the woods. The lead tank fired several 75-mm main-gun rounds at the German *gebirgsjägers*, scattering them into the dark forest beyond. Brant hopped down from the lead tank and moved toward Second Lieutenant Hagney's platoon. The tank directly behind Brant's Sherman suddenly sprayed the forest's edge and the ground around Brant with machine-gun rounds. Brant dove for cover. The third Sherman moved forward into position and fired several main-gun rounds at another stretch of woods to the north. The crew probably had seen more German troops in that area.

When Brant got to his feet, he was standing on the crest of the ridgeline looking down into the valley east of Stammheim. What he saw stunned him. Multiple columns of eastward-marching German soldiers covered the valley floor. The column still advancing on the ridge toward Brant was consistent in size and strength with earlier reports—around 750 troops. But the large enemy concentration in the valley below easily doubled that estimate—and Brant was only looking at the Nord Division's horse-drawn element. The motorized column was still west of Stammheim and not yet visible. Brant had to employ his tanks against this greater threat immediately if his outnumbered troops were to prevail.[83]

Meanwhile, Second Lieutenant Hagney's 1st Platoon pressed on toward the wooded area east of the ridgeline. Hagney moved one squad left into the open and kept Sergeant Cecula's squad thirty meters to the right near the wood line. The tanks continued to fire into the woods north and east—in some cases over the heads of the advancing Red Circle men. German small-arms fire suddenly crackled from the forest. The GIs rushed forward, firing as they moved. A German bullet struck Hagney in the chest and exited his back. The shock of the impact staggered Hagney, but he continued to shout for his men to advance.[84]

Cecula's squad raced for the tree line as German rounds tore at the dirt near their feet. One soldier dropped, writhing in agony. Corporal Reno, Cecula's assistant squad leader, immediately rushed to the man's side and, fully exposed to enemy fire, rendered aid. A Nord man in the forest took careful aim at Reno's head and fired. The round struck Reno's helmet and punctured it. Reno fell beside the man he had tried to help. Sergeant Cecula ran to Reno's side. Gasping for air, Reno asked Cecula to give his love to his wife, son, and mother before drifting into momentary unconsciousness. Cecula called for a medic and then rejoined the battle. A medic arrived and bandaged Reno's head wound. One of the platoon's noncommissioned officers, Sgt. Edward Reinsmith, paused briefly beside the well-liked Reno and asked the wounded man how he was faring. Reno, barely conscious, told Reinsmith he would be fine.[85]

Hagney and his men were soon inside the wood line, shooting wildly at the German troops scattered inside and along the forest's edge. Wounded twice more Hagney led his platoon as the Red Circle men chased the German troops deeper into the woods. The Germans fled, leaving behind several casualties. But Hagney could no longer press on. He bit down on some sulfadiazine tablets—designed to prevent infection in wounds—and turned over command of the platoon to one of his noncommissioned officers. Hagney then staggered out of the woods and back over the top of the ridgeline in search of a medic. He stumbled past an alarmed Second Lieutenant Mortensen, who could clearly see the bullet hole in the front and back of Hagney's field jacket. The sulfadiazine tablets that Hagney chewed were causing him to froth at the mouth. Mortensen quickly called for a medic as the gallant first platoon leader fell and lapsed into unconsciousness. Hagney would later receive the Distinguished Service Cross for his heroic actions on this day, one of only a handful of such medals awarded to members of the 71st Infantry Division.[86]

As Hagney's platoon chased the Germans into the woods, Captain Goldman, the Company E commander, finally arrived on the ridgeline with his other platoon. He found Lieutenant Colonel Brant, who told him to attack east with Company E into the forest to cover the rest of the battalion as it arrived on the ridgeline. Goldman gathered his men and moved out.[87]

Aid men were carrying off Goldman's wounded troops and sending them back to the battalion aid station, which had set up shop below the ridgeline. When Corporal Reno arrived, he was still alive—in spite of his severe head wound. But the young father of two, a devout Catholic who had hoped to spend his next Easter at home with his family, died peacefully at the aid station several days later.[88]

As Captain Goldman led his men into the forest, Lieutenant Colonel Brant scanned the valley below for a route his tanks could follow to get into better firing positions against the German column. The tanks sat dispersed on the ridgeline and fired sporadically at the Germans on the valley floor, but the range was too great. The horse-drawn column, the one first seen by Brant and Colonel Lundquist moving along the ridgeline toward Rodenbach, responded to the American presence by veering northward and down into the valley with the rest of the Nord troops. Although *SS-Oberführer* Goebel's column represented only one of two larger forces in the Nord Division, the column could move only in smaller elements—or subcolumns—as the terrain demanded. These subcolumns, moving across the valley floor, were clearly heading for another ridge northeast of Stammheim, and Brant wanted to stop them before they reached that high ground. The time was 1700.

Lundquist joined Brant on the ridgeline just as Captain Alvey's Company F arrived. Brant explained that the enemy was reacting to the battalion's attack by abandoning the ridgeline for the valley below and moving northeast to another ridge leading into a forest southeast of Staden. Brant intended to send Alvey's company to that ridge to stop the Germans from gaining the high ground and a potentially faster route through the woods to the east. Lundquist agreed.

Captain Alvey approached, and Brant outlined Company F's mission. He directed Alvey to mount his men on Captain Long's tanks and proceed to the ridge southeast of Staden to prevent the Germans from entering the woods and disappearing to the east. The route to the ridge two kilometers away would take Company F through the small patch of woods west of Company E's present location, over the crest of the ridgeline, and down into the valley through a steep draw that fed into a small tributary of streams on the other side. Company F would then move out of that draw, gain the high ground, and block *SS-Oberführer* Goebel's columns as they climbed the ridgeline to enter the forest.[89]

Alvey sped down the hill toward his infantry platoons, which were dismounting the trucks that ferried them to the area. The rest of the 2nd Battalion task force was still crawling at a maddeningly slow pace toward the ridge and Alvey's location; traffic congestion within Altenstadt had made for extremely sluggish progress.

Alvey gathered his platoon leaders and issued hasty instructions. He had no time that day to learn the names of his platoon leaders—Lt. Arthur Metcalfe, Lt. Lowell Arrington, Lt. Felix Gossum, and a Lieutenant Barstow—so he simply referred to them as 1st Platoon Leader, 2nd Platoon Leader, and so on. Alvey wanted a small patrol to precede the company equipped with hand-held SCR-536 radios to report any enemy contact. The 1st and 2nd platoons would follow in extended formation on line with machine guns on the flanks under control of the Weapons Platoon Leader. The 3rd Platoon would follow in reserve. Although Lieutenant Colonel Brant specified that he wanted Company F to move mounted on the tanks, Alvey opted to place just a handful of his men on the Shermans to communicate with the crews.[90]

Alvey's patrol soon departed, followed by the rest of Company F. The tanks followed the dismounted infantrymen closely, traveling on the flanks of the GIs and only collapsing into single file when the terrain became restrictive. The GIs crested the ridgeline and then negotiated a narrow gap in the forest leading down a steep slope to the valley below. The engines squealed as the Sherman tanks traversed the increasingly more difficult terrain. The German column moved a scant five hundred meters away and parallel to Company F, but neither the Germans nor the Americans could see each other due to the deep folds in the open, rolling fields below.

As the tanks entered the valley below and the soft, marshy soil adjacent to the streams, two Shermans became mired. The tanks rocked back and forth, racing their engines and emitting a thick, black smoke from their exhausts. But no amount of movement could dislodge the bogged vehicles. The crews abandoned them and joined the infantrymen on the ground for protection.[91]

The remaining tanks avoided the mud and moved across the valley floor in the open. The infantrymen followed at a crouch. Pfc. Irving A. Boone, a 60-mm mortar gunner with the Weapons Platoon, was particularly impressed by a tank officer who stood on the valley floor and, using hand and arm signals, skillfully guided his tanks past the numerous tree stumps and other natural obstacles.[92] Captain Alvey could no longer see his advance-guard patrol toward the front. The forest along the ridgeline southeast of Staden was in sight—but so was the SS column moving parallel to the company on the left.

Rifle fire suddenly echoed throughout the valley. The GIs dropped to the ground and leveled their rifles and machine guns at the tree line to the north. No one was in sight.

Alvey called the patrol on the SCR-536s. The GIs reported contact with some Germans in the forest to their front. Apparently, *SS-Oberführer* Goebel's dismounted advance guard had already reached the woods, so Alvey had to move quickly. He ordered the patrol to break contact and return to the main body. As soon as the patrol returned to the company, sitting in the open on the valley floor, Alvey ordered the two leading platoons, the 1st and the 2nd, to resume the advance.[93]

As the platoons entered the outer fringes of the wood line, small-arms fire crackled. A rapid and violent exchange of rifle and machine-gun fire ensued. GIs shouted and rushed for the woods, firing as they ran. The tanks sprayed the forest with coaxial machine-gun fire, but the fact that they were firing uphill limited their effectiveness. Several puffs of smoke appeared from the wood line. A flurry of *panzerfaust* rounds screeched from the forest above, hitting two of Company B's Sherman tanks in quick succession. The crews bailed out as the vehicles burst into flames on the valley floor. Remarkably, the driver of the second tank braved a hail of small-arms fire to return to his damaged Sherman. He climbed aboard the burning tank, threw it into gear, and backed it out of the field and into the cover of the nearby forest. His gallant actions spared the vehicle for future repair and use on the battlefield.[94]

Alvey rushed forward with his radio operator to learn what was happening, but the shooting soon stopped. He could hear his men shouting for the Germans to drop their weapons and put their hands in the air. Nearly out of breath, Alvey crested the ridgeline and saw his men hustling scores of German soldiers into small groups. The GIs searched the prisoners and threw their weapons into small piles on the forest floor.

Captain Alvey was amazed at the fifty or sixty prisoners Company F had captured. All of them were either young boys aged fourteen to fifteen or old men aged fifty to seventy-five. The older men wore either complete German uniforms or civilian garb with Deutsche Volkssturm armbands. The young boys all wore ill-fitting German uniforms and clearly represented the dregs of the German manpower pool. A couple of the more talkative prisoners explained to some German-speaking GIs that Waffen-SS sergeants from the 6th SS-Gebirgs Division had been leading them (some claimed involuntarily), but when the shooting started and the boys and old men began to surrender, the SS men fled into the forest. Several Red Circle men then marched the German prisoners down into the valley and toward Altenstadt.

Alvey ordered his platoons to move through the forest to the other side of the ridgeline and take up positions overlooking the valley east of Staden. As the GIs emerged on the far, or northern, side of the ridge, they spotted the slow-moving German column in the valley below. The American attacks concerned *SS-Oberführer* Goebel, so he directed his officers to bypass the ridge to the north and head toward the small village of Nieder-Mockstadt two kilometers east of Staden.

Alvey watched in awe as the German columns changed direction and moved steadily away. Several large, canvas-topped Dodge trucks were intermingled with the horse-drawn carts and wagons. Scores of dismounted German troops either rode in the trucks or carts or marched on foot alongside them. The Germans clearly outnumbered Company F. But Alvey knew his mission was to take the high ground and hold, so he ordered his platoons to dig in facing the long German columns.[95]

As the GIs dug foxholes along the tree line, four or five of Company B's tanks managed to climb the ridge and advance through the sparse forest until reaching Company F's position on the far side. The American infantry did not alarm *SS-Oberführer* Goebel as long as the GIs continued to dig foxholes in the distance. But the tanks, clearly visible to Goebel from his command car, alarmed him. He ordered his light howitzers, pulled by horses, to deploy into firing positions. The SS artillerymen expertly unlimbered the guns from the horses, swung all howitzers around and toward the southern tree line, and, aiming over open sights, fired on the Sherman tanks.[96]

High-explosive artillery rounds burst in and among the exposed GIs digging their foxholes. The men dove for cover and pulled their helmets down low over their heads. Several rounds burst among the tanks but with no effect. Private First Class Boone set up his 60-mm mortar but quickly realized that his German targets were well out of range. A Sherman tank burst suddenly from the tree line to Boone's right and started across the open field with its main gun and machine guns blazing. Instantly, two German artillery rounds bracketed the tank on either side. Cascades of dirt and grass clods filled the air. The next round would certainly hit the tank. The crew bailed out and sprinted for the wood line just as the next round struck the exposed vehicle. Black smoke engulfed the burning tank.

A second Sherman tank maneuvered to Boone's left and tried to remain below the crest of the ridge. The tank popped above the crest and fired its main gun. But, to Boone's horror, the Germans returned fire nearly simultaneously, striking the tank's main gun barrel with an artillery round. The crew bailed out, hauling an injured tanker with them. Amazingly, the driver crawled back to the tank, climbed inside, and backed the vehicle out of the line of fire and into the forest.[97]

The rest of the 761st's tankers did not return fire but instead slowly withdrew their tanks inside the forest. The SS artillerymen, already running low on ammunition, seemed satisfied that the American tanks no longer posed a threat. The Nord men reconnected their howitzers to the horses and joined the tail end of the retreating German column.[98]

Captain Alvey tried to report his situation and new defensive position to Lieutenant Colonel Brant via SCR-300 radio, but the range was too great. Alvey was unaware that Brant had been actively trying to reach Company F by radio as well but was also unsuccessful.[99]

After Company F departed for the ridgeline southeast of Staden, a machine-gun platoon from Capt. Hank Brewer's Company H arrived. The tail end of the enemy column was still visible moving through the valley below, so Lieutenant Colonel Brant led the machine gunners to the top of the open ridge and positioned them to fire on the long line of German troops.

Rifle fire crackled suddenly from the small patch of woods barely one hundred meters from Brant and the machine gunners. Brant dropped to the ground as his machine gunners swung their barrels toward the forest, but the firing had ceased as suddenly as it had begun. A German straggler had obviously remained hidden in the woods but, after firing his weapon, was gone. Brant wondered why the German had fired at him and then realized he was the only one carrying a khaki-colored canvas map case. He quickly emptied the map case, stuffed the maps and pencils into his field jacket, and threw away the canvas bag.[100]

❖

While Lieutenant Colonel Brant deployed his slowly arriving task force, an unusual event occurred with the 2nd Battalion's support units, which were still crawling through Altenstadt and into Rodenbach. A couple of SS men under a white flag appeared in Altenstadt at 1600 (the approximate time the task force initially made contact with the SS column) escorting Capt. W. B. Swiggert, one of the officers who had been captured with the 16th Field Hospital platoon earlier that morning. The SS men—probably part of *SS-Standartenführer* Raithel's motorized column, the bulk of which was still inside the Assenheim forest—demanded plasma from the support personnel for wounded Americans and Germans and then safe passage back to their division. Swiggert explained that the SS troops had captured the field hospital earlier that day and were using the hospital's vehicles and ambulances as transportation. The Germans were holding the hospital staff as hostages—presumably in exchange for the plasma. The deal never materialized, and the SS men went away empty handed. Brant would learn of the incident later that night.[101]

❖

Nearly an hour after Lieutenant Colonel Brant's men first clashed with the Nord men north of Rodenbach, Lt. Col. Robert E. Connor's 3rd Battalion, 2nd Infantry Regiment, from the 5th Infantry Division, arrived in Erbstadt south of the Assenheim forest. Connor's task force, consisting of a tank company, the regimental cannon company, a platoon of tank destroyers, and an artillery battalion, had departed Frankfurt at 1400. With infantrymen clinging to tanks and others mounted in trucks, the task force sped along the improved road network leading north to Assenheim. After more than three hours on the road, Erbstadt suddenly appeared in the distance. The time was 1700.[102]

Connor, unaware of the enemy's disposition in and around the small town, proceeded cautiously. He directed Company I, mounted on the 737th Tank Battalion's Sherman tanks, to advance directly on Erbstadt while Companies K and L circled around either flank on foot. The 50th Field Artillery Battalion occupied firing positions to the southwest, and one of the battalion's spotter planes was buzzing overhead.

As the task force encroached on the town's southern outskirts, a small group of Nord men, probably manning an outpost, fled across the open fields toward the forest. The GIs fired a few sporadic shots at the fleeing Germans but hit no one.[103]

The task force entered Erbstadt and found no other German troops present. Connor ordered his companies to keep moving north along the western fringe of the forest in the direction of Bönstadt and, farther north, Wickstadt, the current location of the 71st Cavalry Reconnaissance Troop. Connor hoped to spot enemy troops hiding in the forest before dark.

Connor did not realize, however, that he was out of contact with Colonel Roffe at the 2nd Infantry Regiment's headquarters. Major General Irwin pressed Roffe for reports about the 3rd Battalion's progress, but Roffe could report only what he was learning from the 50th Field Artillery Battalion and its high-flying spotter plane. Irwin, ever mindful of the mission's urgency to the XII Corps commander, Major General Eddy, was eager to develop the situation north of Erbstadt. He and Roffe had already discussed committing the rest of the regiment to the area later that night. In fact, within minutes of the 3rd Battalion's departure for Erbstadt, Irwin ordered Col. Robert P. Bell's 10th Infantry Regiment to send a reinforced battalion to clear the forest east of the *reichsautobahn* between Bad Homburg, Friedberg, and Bad Nauheim. The forest bordered the route Irwin intended to use to move his 5th Infantry Division north as previously planned. If any German stragglers were still hiding in those woods, Irwin wanted them out.[104]

Back near Erbstadt, Lieutenant Colonel Connor moved his task force north along the western edge of the forest. He did not realize how much his communications problems were concerning both his regimental and division commanders. He was not receiving their radio messages and, obviously, they were receiving only a few of the many reports sent by his staff.[105]

As the lead elements of Company I, still mounted on tanks, approached the forest's edge, the GIs hopped off, formed a skirmish line, and entered the woods. The rest of the task force followed in trucks; some GIs rode on the tops of the tank destroyers. The 2nd Platoon's lead scout, Private Roberts (nicknamed "Young" by his friends), spotted a walled farm complex at the edge of the woods. Roberts moved quickly through a clearing and edged his way along the stone wall until he came to a large barn. Before he could look inside, the doors burst open. Six or seven American nurses (including 1/Lt. Helen R. Cosma) pounced on him and began kissing the young GI as they shouted for joy. These women were part of the 1st Platoon, 16th Field Hospital, that had been captured that morning. The overjoyed young women showered their American liberator with hugs and kisses. The rest of Roberts's comrades soon arrived on the scene, shouldered their rifles, and began catcalling and poking fun at the embarrassed private. Roberts accepted the nurses' momentary affections with quiet dignity—and even loitered close by for a few minutes hoping for a repeat performance. Clearly, the SS troops had decided not to take the nurses along and instead sequestered them in the farmhouse—unguarded—until American troops came along and found them. Those troops had arrived, and the unharmed nurses were free once more and back on duty.[106]

Once the joyous moment subsided, several GIs ushered the nurses to the rear of the task force while the rest continued to clear the wood line. Lieutenant Colonel Connor intended to press ahead until reaching Wickstadt, Nieder-Florstadt, and then Staden in the hope of pushing the SS troops toward Lieutenant Colonel Brant's task force near Altenstadt and Rodenbach. But Connor had not yet contacted Brant's battalion. No one was at the contact point at Heldenbergen when Connor's troops passed through the town on their way to Erbstadt. A boundary between the two forces was not yet clear to either the 5th or 71st divisions, but that boundary, and its implied no-fire lines and other restrictions, would soon become an issue that XII Corps and the two divisions would have to resolve quickly. Connor even had Captain Johnson's 71st Cavalry Reconnaissance Troop in his zone near Wickstadt but was unaware of the troop's presence. Improved coordination between the divisions was imperative.[107]

As Lieutenant Colonel Connor's 3rd Battalion, 2nd Infantry Regiment, cleared the western edge of the Assenheim forest, Lieutenant Colonel Brant continued to organize his slowly arriving 2nd Battalion, 14th Infantry, on the ridgeline just seven kilometers farther east. The trucks offloaded the infantry troops north of Rodenbach, and the GIs trudged uphill to the ridge. Tank destroyers and other vehicles still struggled to squeeze through the narrow, cobblestone streets of Rodenbach.

Brant decided to check on Captain Goldman's progress in the forest to the east. He found Goldman and Company E dug in facing east—in the direction the Germans had fled less than an hour earlier. The company had suffered nine casualties in the skirmish, among them the gallant Second Lieutenant Hagney. Brant noticed a loaded German antitank gun emplaced at the edge of the woods directly behind Company E's position. He looked over the top of the barrel and a chill ran down his spine. The gun was aimed precisely at the spot where he had stopped and dismounted the lead tank during the initial brush with the Germans. The antitank gun sat a mere 150 meters from where the lead Sherman had halted. If his men and the 761st's tankers had not reacted so quickly to the German fire, the gunner might have fired the antitank gun, destroyed the lead tank, and possibly killed Brant.

Satisfied that Goldman had things well in hand, Brant emerged from the woods to find his S-3, 1/Lt. E. E. Smith, racing toward him. (Smith had replaced the recently relieved Captain Lafargue.) Huffing from his uphill sprint, Smith explained that an L-5 spotter plane (probably from XII Corps' artillery) had just landed south of Rodenbach with news that two full German regiments were approaching in columns from the southwest.

The news stunned Brant. Two more regiments clearly shifted the balance in favor of the Germans. Capt. Andrew J. Bass's Company G had just detrucked and was moving onto the ridge, followed by 1/Lt. Walter E. Standfield's 76-mm tank-destroyer platoon and the battalion's 57-mm antitank platoon. Brant ordered Bass and the antitank troops to dig in along the open ridge and block the two reported enemy regiments. The GIs hurriedly scraped out shallow holes facing southwest.

As Brant scanned the horizon in front of Company G, he soon realized that the German columns the aerial observers had spotted were the same ones that had crested the ridgeline earlier and descended into the valley below. The report had reached Brant much later than the L-5 crew intended. Brant told his men to stop digging.

Brant then turned his binoculars north toward Staden. Sunset at 1907 was less than an hour away. The day had been long, but Brant's task force—after sporadically engaging the Nord Division's horse-drawn columns for nearly three hours—had dispersed many of *SS-Oberführer* Goebel's men into the nearby forests and forced the column to change direction to the northeast. The size of the German force precluded further action, however. Brant's task force was not strong enough to deal with the German troops Goebel had at his disposal—even though those troops were moving slowly and in the open. Brant lacked artillery support at that moment, support that might have shifted the balance in his favor.

Just as Brant prepared to lower his binoculars, something on the horizon caught his eye. He focused on the north–south road between Stammheim and Staden, and what he saw surprised him. The vanguard of *SS-Standartenführer* Raithel's motorized column had finally emerged, after a long delay, from the eastern fringe of the Assenheim forest west of Stammheim. The vehicles quickly gained the improved road leading to Staden and soon filled it bumper to bumper with trucks and assorted vehicles, with scores of captured American jeeps, and, above all, with ambulances.

SS-Gruppenführer Brenner had monitored the horse-drawn column's painfully slow progress and repeated brushes with Brant's task force. Brenner soon realized that he could not keep both groups moving along parallel trajectories heading east, so he directed Raithel to move the motorized column northward to a forest exit closer to Stammheim that would avoid the Americans. The motorized column then could follow Goebel's column around to the north and split off on a parallel path somewhere farther east. But changing the column's direction inside the Assenheim forest had taken Raithel and his men several hours. Brant's attack had cost the Nord Division nearly a half day of progress, so Brenner wanted to get things moving—quickly!

Brant recognized that he had to do something to the German motorized column—but what? His troops were disposed in various battle positions in and around the woods north of Rodenbach. Dismounted infantry could not catch a fast-moving motorized force. Brant's only option rested in Captain Long's command tank that remained with Brant as a communications link to the other tanks with Company F. Brant directed Long to fire on the motorized column and disperse it. The German vehicles seemed well out of range—nearly two kilometers away. But Long complied and fired the Sherman's 76-mm main gun at the distant convoy. The rounds fell short. The Germans did not even flinch.[108]

The massive German motorized column on the road between Stammheim and Staden did not go unnoticed by the 50th Field Artillery Battalion's spotter plane flying in support of Lieutenant Colonel Connor's 5th Infantry Division task force farther west. The aircraft's crew watched Captain Long's Sherman tank ineffectively firing at the column. The liaison officer in the plane contacted the 50th's fire direction center: within minutes, 105-mm rounds from the 50th and the regiment's Cannon Company began dropping around the slow-moving motorized column. The rounds tore into the enormous traffic jam on the road, hitting several trucks and other vehicles. But the determined SS troops simply used undamaged vehicles to push damaged ones from the road.

The spotter plane reported the column's size and location back to the 5th Division's headquarters. Word soon reached Major General Irwin of the artillery strike on the enemy column. Without delay, Irwin directed his division artillery commander to coordinate all indirect-fire efforts with the XII Corps' Artillery and the 71st Division's Artillery. Irwin also ordered a second spotter plane up to verify the enemy column's size and disposition.[109]

In the German column itself, an impatient and concerned *SS-Gruppenführer* Brenner, sitting in a staff car among other vehicles containing his division staff, ordered *SS-Standartenführer* Raithel to get the column moving. The time was 1815, and Brenner did not want his troops decimated by American artillery less than an hour before sunset simply because of a traffic jam. Raithel ordered the lead element, approaching Staden, to move out as quickly as possible. Soon, the column gained speed in fits and spurts and began moving toward Nieder-Mockstadt. But the 50th Field Artillery and the 2nd Infantry's Cannon Company had done considerable damage. The 185 105-mm rounds expended by the battalion had inflicted a number of casualties among the Nord Division's ranks, including the destruction of several precious vehicles needed to move troops and stores to the east.[110]

Colonel Lundquist arrived on the ridge above Rodenbach at 1830 and asked Lieutenant Colonel Brant for a situation report. Brant explained the battalion's current disposition and then pointed out the motorized column. Lundquist, squinting through his binoculars, shared Brant's amazement. Although American artillery rounds from an unknown source were clearly inflicting damage on the column, the German force was too large to be attacked just yet.

Lundquist also recognized that the sun was about to set, and he did not want the 2nd Battalion attacking in the dark against an enemy whose size seemed to increase hourly.[111]

Lundquist explained that he had ordered Lt. Col. Paul G. Guthrie's 3rd Battalion to move up to strengthen the 2nd Battalion's right flank and extend the task force's line one kilometer eastward to Heegheim. Major General Wyman wanted the regiment to push against the German troops vigorously and clear up the situation. Lundquist told Brant to bring the 2nd Battalion's companies back to Rodenbach for the night. He intended to attack early the next morning with two infantry battalions supported by artillery to clear the forest north and east of Rodenbach. The 14th Infantry Regiment's main command post was moving farther north to Langendiebach (north of Hanau and about ten kilometers south of Altenstadt) while establishing a smaller tactical command post in Altenstadt with a handful of regimental staff personnel led by the S-1. Lundquist intended to use this tactical command post to control the next day's operation. Brant immediately set out to withdraw his companies to Rodenbach for the next day's attack.[112]

As Brant walked away, a voice speaking in German through a public-address system mounted on an M8 Greyhound armored car echoed in his ears. Lundquist had attached this Psychological Warfare section to Brant's battalion for the mission that day. The German-speaking GI directed the loudspeaker at the darkening forest north of Rodenbach and repeatedly chided the Germans to surrender because they were surrounded. Brant chuckled. If only his men knew that the Germans were probably the ones who had the Red Circle men surrounded.[113]

As the 2nd Battalion, 14th Infantry, withdrew to Rodenbach, Colonel Lundquist brought Major General Wyman up to date on the situation. He had kept Wyman apprised of the situation soon after Lieutenant Colonel Brant's troops made contact with the SS troops. At the time Wyman did not see a need to readjust his staff's—and the division's—focus from protecting the flank of the advancing XII Corps. Wyman recognized Major General Eddy's concern about the security of the corps' rear area but directed his staff to continue planning the leapfrog maneuvers the 66th and 5th infantry regiments would make to keep pace with the fast-moving corps' spearheads. The division command post had jumped well forward to Langenselbold at 1615 in anticipation of the continued advance.[114] In spite of the current fighting near Altenstadt, the primary mission for the division, from Wyman's perspective, was protecting the corps' right flank.

At 1530, just as Brant's 2nd Battalion was about to make contact with the Germans near Rodenbach, the G-3 staff issued instructions to the liaison officers of the 66th and 5th infantry regiments for the next day's movement. The 66th Infantry would depart at daylight to occupy a new line farther to the northeast while the 5th Infantry would move from the south along the corps' MSR and defend the same Hailer-Gelnhausen line abandoned by the 66th. But after Lundquist began sending reports about the size and capabilities of the German force near Altenstadt, Wyman grew concerned. The estimated size of the German columns that Lundquist was reporting were much greater than previously described.[115]

Fearing that his new command post in Langenselbold might be vulnerable to attack from other bypassed enemy troops, Wyman ordered Lieutenant Colonel Bates, commander of the 761st Tank Battalion, to send the battalion's light tank company to Langenselbold and defend the headquarters. The tanks arrived an hour later.[116]

Lieutenant Colonel Lankenau kept XII Corps headquarters apprised of the situation near Altenstadt and Rodenbach. When the corps' G-3 requested an update, Lankenau outlined the growing size and nature of the German force. The corps' G-3 simply replied, "Kill every one of them."[117]

By 1830 the picture that Lundquist painted for Wyman suggested that the entire division might have to commit to the battle farther north and abandon, for the moment, the corps' flank-protection mission. Lundquist suspended operations for the night and outlined his plan for the next day via radio. Wyman approved Lundquist's plan to send the 3rd Battalion, 14th Infantry, and the 608th Field Artillery Battalion northward for a morning attack to clear, once and for all, the woods northeast of Rodenbach and Altenstadt.

Wyman further realized that Captain Johnson's reconnaissance troop at Wickstadt could better support the 14th Infantry's attack the next day from blocking and observation positions north of the forested areas that Lundquist's troops planned to clear. Wyman attached the troop to the 14th Infantry and then, at 1950, ordered Johnson's cavalrymen into Stockheim and Selters along a three-kilometer line nearly six kilometers east of Staden. The cavalrymen could support the operation from vantage points in these towns by reporting to Lundquist the movement of German troops flushed from the woods.

Blocking positions in these two towns also would compel Germans seeking to escape in that direction to turn back and into the advancing 14th Infantry GIs. This new mission would remove the troop from the 5th Infantry Division's zone of attack for the following day.[118]

Major General Wyman then sent word to the 66th and 5th infantry regiments that none of their units would move the next day—or at all—until the regiments received direct orders from division headquarters. At 2015 Wyman informed XII Corps of his plans and the fact that the entire 71st Division, minus some service and support elements, would be north of the Main River by daybreak.[119]

The 71st and 5th Infantry divisions had shared with each other information about the day's operations throughout the afternoon. The XII Corps' staff attempted to coordinate the efforts of both attacking forces on either side of the Assenheim forest in the hope that the two task forces would meet near Staden and encircle the German columns, but Wyman balked since a clear boundary between the two divisions had yet to be established. He did not want attacking forces from different divisions (and corps) to converge without the proper controls—such as boundary and artillery no-fire lines.[120]

Wyman then turned his attention to working out a boundary between the 71st and the 5th Infantry Division. The 5th proposed a boundary originating at the contact point in Heldenbergen and along a northeast line to Eichen, through Altenstadt, and up to Glauberg. Wyman agreed. Convinced that on-the-ground contact between both forces was essential, he sent his assistant division commander, Brigadier General Rolfe, to Heldenbergen a few hours earlier in the day to ensure that a physical link-up occurred. Rolfe was present when representatives from the 2nd and 14th infantry regiments met in the town at 1730.[121]

After contemplating Colonel Lundquist's planned attack for 2 April, Wyman decided to delay the movement of the 66th and 5th infantry regiments until the situation with the SS troops was cleared up. Lieutenant Colonel Foster, the G-2, had already informed Wyman that the enemy troops hailed predominantly from the Waffen-SS, a fact that weighed heavily on the division commander. Waffen-SS soldiers were no slouches and would fight fiercely and skillfully. He knew he not only had to support Lundquist's attack the next day with a full complement of division resources, but also that he had to eliminate this German threat to the corps' advance—a threat just as great as an open right flank.

Wyman intended to use the minimum amount of force necessary to trap and destroy the SS troops. He decided to send a battalion task force from Colonel Regnier's 66th Infantry Regiment through the Büdingen forest and then sweep back north and west in a maneuver designed to bag the escaping SS troops as the 14th Infantry's two battalions pushed them north and east the next day. The 5th Infantry Regiment would remain in reserve. Earlier that day, Wyman visited the 5th Infantry Regiment's forward command post near Rückingen (the regiment had closed on the area at 1750 that afternoon) and told Colonel Wooten to prepare to move one battalion by truck on a moment's notice. Wooten selected Lt. Col. Charles M. Gettys's 2nd Battalion.

Wyman coordinated his plan with the 5th Infantry Division through the XII Corps' staff. The Red Diamond Division intended to follow a similar plan and push north along the boundary between both divisions to the northeast and then east, pinning the Germans against the north–south railroad line at Ranstadt. Wyman also sent an artillery liaison officer to the 5th Division's 50th Field Artillery Battalion to help coordinate fire missions between both attacking forces the next day.[122]

At 2250 the division staff informed Regnier of Wyman's instructions. The 2nd Battalion, 66th Infantry, mounted on trucks and tanks (from Company C, 761st Tank Battalion), would move from Gelnhausen northeast and through the Büdingen forest to Breitenborn, Wittgenborn, north to Waldensberg, and up to Wolferborn. Once north of the Büdingen forest, the battalion would patrol an east–west line from Gelnhaar to Ortenberg to contain and capture as many enemy troops as possible. The battalion would depart at 0715.[123]

Colonel Regnier, initially puzzled by the orders, soon understood and informed the 2nd Battalion's commander, Lt. Col. Gaston B. Eikel of the plan. Regnier designated the battalion as Task Force X. Eikel also would have one platoon from the regiment's Cannon Company and a platoon of tanks from Company C, 761st Tank Battalion, at his disposal. The regimental and battalion staff then began coordinating for trucks. The G-4, Lieutenant Colonel Blackford, agreed to have twenty trucks at the 66th Infantry's command post in Lieblos at 0615.[124]

Wyman hoped the planned attack set for the following morning, 2 April, would finally eliminate the threat to the corps' rear area, but lots of troops and units would be moving into position throughout the night. Things could go wrong, so Wyman had to carefully watch the battle unfold. He knew that he might have to commit even more forces to the fray before the sun set the next day. Lieutenant Colonel Lankenau had reminded Wyman earlier that evening that daylight savings time would occur at 0200. With everyone switching their watches ahead one hour, something was bound to go awry.[125]

❖

The staff of the 14th Infantry Regiment prepared furiously for the next day's attack. Colonel Lundquist, concerned about the enemy's intentions, ordered his S-2 to send an interrogation team to Rodenbach to interview the numerous German prisoners taken by the 2nd Battalion that day. Lundquist wanted to know if these prisoners could provide information about the enemy's plans.[126]

Information gleaned from hasty interrogations by the 2nd Battalion S-2 and other reports from a variety of division- and corps-level sources identified the enemy not as just a hodgepodge group of Waffen-SS troops but definitively as the 6th SS-Gebirgs Division. Estimated strength reports of the enemy jumped from seven hundred to three thousand, but no one was certain of the Nord Division's actual size. Division G-2 Periodic Report Number 19, issued at 1600, did not mention SS troops in the area whatsoever.[127] But with information pouring in from a variety of sources (to include the information from Lundquist's troops), Lieutenant Colonel Foster, the G-2, began piecing together a better picture of what the 14th Regiment, and the rest of the division, faced north and east of Rodenbach and Heegheim. The identification of an intact Waffen-SS division in the corps' rear area was sobering not just for Lundquist, but also for everyone up the chain to XII Corps and the Third Army.

As the S-2 and his team of interrogators made their way to Rodenbach, Lt. Col. Paul G. Guthrie's 3rd Battalion, scrambled by Lundquist several hours earlier to join the 2nd Battalion up north, finally departed Weiskirchen (just southeast of Obertshausen) on trucks at 2008. Guthrie's battalion was shy one infantry company and a machine-gun platoon for the coming mission. First Lieutenant Caleb H. Paul's Company I and a machine-gun platoon from 1/Lt. W. P. Sims's Company M remained on guard duty at the corps' POW cage near Eberstadt. Guthrie could only muster two infantry companies—Capt. Tommy L. Long's Company K and Capt. Milo D. Krichbaum's Company L—for the coming operation. First Lieutenant Sims's Company M had only one machine-gun platoon and an 81-mm mortar platoon available.[128]

After a long, slow journey through the pitch-black countryside, the 3rd Battalion's trucks reached Langendiebach at 2130 and, after a brief pause, continued north to Altenstadt, arriving at 2300.[129] The road-weary Red Circle men detrucked and formed single-file columns on each side of the road to Rodenbach. Although Colonel Lundquist and his staff had yet to formulate—and issue—a detailed operations order for the next day, the regimental commander had given Guthrie specific instructions on how he wanted the battalion disposed in preparation for the next day's attack. The 3rd Battalion would extend the 2nd Battalion's line eastward from Heegheim out toward Glauberg nearly two kilometers distant. The general scheme of maneuver would call for both battalions to enter the forest to the north on line—the 2nd Battalion on the left and the 3rd Battalion on the right. But since Lundquist was unsure of the enemy's location farther east, he did not want his troops, vulnerable while traveling in the backs of trucks, to ride any farther than Altenstadt.

The GIs lined the road to Rodenbach and, on Guthrie's command, moved out. The low-hanging clouds overhead masked all moonlight. After traveling two kilometers, the GIs reached Rodenbach and turned eastward for Heegheim and Glauberg. In Heegheim, Guthrie paused and set up his battalion command post. He then directed his companies onward to assembly areas between Heegheim and Glauberg. They arrived sometime after 0000 on 2 April. The troops, although exhausted, remained alert for enemy movement. Word had already spread that the GIs were facing an SS division—so no one took victory for granted.[130]

The regiment's main command post finally arrived in Langendiebach at 2300—ninety minutes after the 3rd Battalion had passed through the town. Once settled, the staff, led by the regimental S-3, Captain Borden, quickly began planning for the next day's attack. With guidance from Colonel Lundquist, Borden expected to issue Operations Instruction Number Nine for the next day's mission well before sunrise. Borden and key members of the staff would then join Lundquist at the tactical command post in Altenstadt and issue the operations instruction to the battalion commanders there. Maj. Clay O. Collier's 608th Field Artillery Battalion began arriving in the Altenstadt area during the night to support the 14th Regiment's morning attack.[131]

Lundquist further requested that his 1st Battalion be released from the mission of guarding Hanau and the bridges across the Main River. He wanted a reserve force at his immediate disposal. Major General Wyman agreed and at 2245 Maj. Samuel E. Hubbard's 1st Battalion departed Hanau for Langendiebach.[132] The battalion would remain in an assembly area near the main regimental command post until needed. No one—not even Lundquist—

was certain how the clash with the 6th SS-Gebirgs Division would unfold the next day.

❖

With the issues of boundary lines and contact points resolved, Lieutenant Colonel Connor's 3rd Battalion, 2nd Infantry Regiment, 5th Infantry Division pressed northward toward Wickstadt along the western fringes of the Assenheim forest. Enemy resistance proved light. The few German troops encountered by the Red Diamond troops fled into the forest after firing a few token shots. Six German soldiers surrendered.[133]

By 1820 the 803rd Tank Destroyer Battalion's reconnaissance company, relieved from its screening mission along the Bad Nauheim–Frankfurt *reichsautobahn*, had arrived under orders from the division and attached itself to the 3rd Battalion. Elements of this company manned the contact point at Heldenbergen. Major General Irwin ordered Colonel Roffe to keep the contact point manned at all times to ensure close coordination with the 14th Regiment along the new boundary and no-fire line. A great deal of coordination was already in the works in the artillery channels to ensure that the various artillery units in the area—from both divisions and XII Corps—did not fire on friendly troops.[134]

When the sun finally set at 1907, Connor's 3rd Battalion occupied the northwestern portion of the Assenheim forest east of Wickstadt. The Nord Division had already exited the forest to the east, but a few stragglers still roamed the dark forest. Connor ordered his troops to stop and hunker down until he had received further instructions from Roffe.

Likewise, Roffe solicited further orders from Irwin. The 2nd Regiment staff was already busy preparing instructions for the 1st and 2nd battalions to move to the Assenheim area the following morning, but Roffe was unsure just how far Irwin wanted the 3rd Battalion to go that night. Irwin and his G-3, Lieutenant Colonel Dickens, had been busy working out the boundary and the next day's plan with the XII Corps and 71st Division staffs. By 2100 Irwin was ready to issue Roffe instructions for the remainder of the night's operations.

Dickens, with Irwin at his side, contacted Roffe at 2105 and instructed him to send the 3rd Battalion's Company K, mounted on tanks, to the northeast and east along the new division boundary to seize the woods some five kilometers east of Staden. The route would take the company north to Nieder-Florstadt, east through Staden to Nieder-Mockstadt, and then northeast to Ober-Mockstadt. The woods in question were in the vicinity of both Nieder- and Ober-Mockstadt. The company's limit of advance was the railroad line at Ranstadt. The rest of the battalion, minus tank support, would follow and then drop down to Stammheim and, on foot, clear the woods there. The fact that the Nord Division's motorized column emerged from the forest at that point undoubtedly drove the decision to clear that immediate area. Roffe immediately communicated the orders to Lieutenant Colonel Connor.[135]

Within minutes of receiving his new instructions, Connor had his troops on the road. Company K, mounted on tanks, sped to Staden in the pitch-black night. The tankers were squinting to see the road before them under the soft glow of blackout headlight markers when suddenly the lead tank lurched to a halt. On the roadside outside Staden sat forty or fifty wounded GIs. The Red Diamond troops dismounted the tanks and, after a brief discussion with the wounded GIs, learned that they were from the 4th Armored Division, the division spearheading the XII Corps' drive many kilometers northeast. The company commander radioed Connor for ambulances to transport the wounded.[136]

Despite a flurry of questions from Company K's GIs, the wounded American soldiers could not explain how they arrived at their location. More than likely, the SS troops had captured the wounded Americans that morning with the field hospital. Once the Nord Division came under fire along the Stammheim–Staden road, the SS men probably decided that the wounded GIs were slowing them down and decided to deposit their human cargo where the advancing Americans would likely find them. Company K was now forced to guard these wounded troops until ambulances arrived to evacuate them. The SS men through this act, either wittingly or unwittingly, had stalled the 3rd Battalion's nighttime pursuit of their escaping columns.

Companies I and L, however, reached the Stammheim–Staden road by 2145 and were busy running patrols up and down the length of the thoroughfare. Connor realized he could not expect Company K to fulfill its original mission that night owing to the wounded GIs, so he instructed Company K to go as far as possible once the ambulances arrived and relieved the company of its injured charges. Nothing more was bound to happen for the rest of the night.

Lieutenant Colonel Dickens informed Major General Irwin about the incident with the wounded GIs. The injured troops were a priority. Like Lieutenant Colonel Connor, Irwin could not expect much more from the 3rd Battalion that night. Unexpectedly, at 2220 Irwin received a call from an agitated Major General Eddy. Eddy had received word that the German columns (actually elements of *SS-Oberführer* Goebel's horse-drawn column) were moving along the corps' MSR south of Ortenberg, some fifteen kilometers northeast of Altenstadt. Eddy asked for help in blocking the German column's advance along the MSR.

Irwin quickly decided that Captain Robinson's 5th Cavalry Reconnaissance Troop was best suited for this mission; it was still screening the Bad Nauheim–Frankfurt *reichsautobahn* to the west with elements of the 10th Infantry Regiment. He told Lieutenant Colonel Dickens that he wanted the troop detached from the 10th immediately and, with a platoon of light tanks from the 737th Tank Battalion (the light tank company was already with the 10th Regiment), race for Nidda twenty kilometers north of Ortenberg. From Nidda an improved road to the east provided a rapid route to a point along the MSR just short of Gedern, where the troop could block the advancing German column. If the Germans had already passed that point, continued Irwin, Robinson was authorized to chase them. He ended by saying, "Here is a chance for Robbie [Robinson] to strut his stuff."

Captain Robinson soon received his orders and, after a quick analysis of his mission, called the G-3 and refused the light tanks since they would slow his progress. He further recommended that, after arriving in Nidda, he would take his troop all the way to the corps headquarters at Lauterbach some thirty kilometers distant and then come back down the MSR from the opposite direction. He intended to block the German column, if it was indeed moving along the MSR, no matter how far the column had progressed. Irwin agreed to Robinson's change in plans but insisted on the light tanks. In fact, Irwin added a second platoon of light tanks from Company D, 737th Tank Battalion, and a platoon of tank destroyers to the mix. Robinson acknowledged the orders and immediately put his reinforced troop on the road to Nidda. The time had come to contain the SS troops and limit their ability to affect the corps' support operations. The coordinated efforts of both the 5th and 71st divisions, scheduled to begin early the next day, was intended to achieve this very goal as quickly as possible.[137]

❖

As the 5th and 71st divisions focused their attention on the 6th SS-Gebirgs Division in the XII Corps' rear area, Col. Charles H. Reed's 2nd Cavalry Group continued to screen the corps' right flank. The situation with the SS men near Altenstadt had momentarily distracted Major General Wyman from the division's task to guard the corps' flank, so Reed's cavalrymen continued to go it alone until the Red Circle men could resume the mission. Despite the problems in the rear area, the corps was still steamrolling ahead unchecked, so someone had to focus on keeping the flank safe. Captain Calloway, the group's liaison officer at the 71st's command post, kept Reed apprised of the developing situation around Altenstadt.[138]

Lt. Col. Walter J. Easton's 2nd Squadron continued attacking the German Army troops defending Altenhasslau south of Gelnhausen—an attack begun the previous day. The engagement lasted most of the day before the Germans finally surrendered. Easton then received word from Reed that a POW compound housing thousands of Allied troops (more than half of which were American) was located in Bad Orb ten kilometers northeast of Altenhasslau. Easton quickly redirected his troops to the town and the POW compound. By day's end Troop A pushed five kilometers to Höchst and Wirtheim while Troop B occupied the tiny village of Kassel south of Wirtheim. The 2nd Squadron could advance no farther on 1 April, so Easton began moving his rear-echelon troops and trains forward in preparation for the squadron's onward movement the next day.[139]

Lt. Col. William A. Hill's 42nd Cavalry Squadron had rallied at Spielberg the day before on the eastern fringe of the Büdingen forest and then moved southeast to Bad Soden and Salmünster to close the gap between the 42nd and 2nd Squadrons. The original plan had the 42nd closing with troops from the 71st Division, but the delay caused by the Nord Division meant the two squadrons would have to leapfrog forward along the corps' flank by themselves.

As the 42nd swept through the forested area north of Wächtersbach, a small but sharp skirmish erupted between the cavalrymen and some German Army stragglers. The GIs quickly bested the disorganized Germans before pressing forward. By 1300 the 2nd Squadron's occupation of Höchst and Wirtheim (and the 2nd's clearing of the small hamlet of Haitz just west of Gelnhausen) allowed the 42nd to push into Salmünster and the Bad Orb forest. By nightfall the 2nd Squadron's Troop A was in place on the outskirts of Schlüchtern while Troop C, with one platoon from Troop F, occupied positions deep inside the Bad Orb forest near Mernes. Lieutenant Colonel Hill then moved his squadron command post forward to Ulmbach in preparation for the next day's movement.[140]

Meanwhile Lieutenant Colonel Easton moved his 2nd Squadron headquarters forward to the town of Wittgenborn on the eastern edge of the Büdingen forest. Three kilometers to the northwest sat the tiny village of Waldensberg on the northern fringe of the forest. During the night the 2nd Squadron's rear-echelon support troops and trains occupied Waldensberg. With truck and jeep engines roaring, the GIs entered the village noisily, much to the dismay of the town's occupants. But the cavalrymen soon settled down into a standard guard routine.

After demanding admittance to several homes, the GIs unrolled sleeping bags and lapsed into a deep sleep. The newsletters and *Stars and Stripes* newspapers that had circulated among the GIs stated that the Germans were on the run much farther east. This news had had a calming effect on the cavalry troops, who felt safer now that they were, according to the newspapers, well behind friendly lines. As a result, they only posted four guards in the town for the night and kept someone awake in the rear-echelon's sole M8 armored car, which the support troops used exclusively for radio communications. The cavalrymen, slumbering snugly in their sleeping bags, had no way of knowing that four guards would not be enough to protect them that night. The quiet town of Waldensberg would soon become the flashpoint of a major clash between the cavalrymen and the Nord Division.[141]

The assaults on the Nord Division's columns near Stammheim and Staden had exacted a heavy toll on the SS troops and the other German soldiers attached to the division. The artillery and direct-fire attacks destroyed several of the captured and organic trucks, jeeps, and motorcycles in *SS-Standartenführer* Raithel's motorized column, while many of the horses pulling the division's artillery and ammunition stores in *SS-Oberführer* Goebel's column had fallen victim to fatal bullet wounds and shell fragments. *SS-Hauptsturmführer* Steurich's 1st Battalion, SS-Gebirgsjäger Regiment 11, one of the few remaining organized formations within Raithel's column, could only claim two officers and sixty men on its rolls, despite reinforcement by the 2nd Company of SS-Gebirgs Pioneer Battalion 6 and the 3rd Battalion's 14th Company.[142] The problems resulting from these losses had the effect of reducing the division's ranks even further—not just through those wounded or killed, but also through the desertion of German Army or Luftwaffe stragglers who had attached themselves to the division but who now thought better of their decision and, taking advantage of the American attacks, fled into the surrounding forests. Most of these deserters wisely surrendered to the first GIs they encountered.

Despite the damage inflicted on the Nord Division, the German columns forged eastward and away from the American infantry, armor, and artillery. The overcast night shrouded the moon and gave the SS men the concealment they needed to travel unmolested by the omnipresent American artillery spotter planes and other watchful eyes. The fact that the Americans had ended their attacks and subsequent pursuit of the German columns was a boon for the Nord Division. The few SS officers and noncommissioned officers still controlling the columns used this respite to reorganize their march units and keep them moving.

Both columns converged east of Staden in the vicinity of Nieder-Mockstadt immediately following the clash with the Americans. *SS-Gruppenführer* Brenner radioed his two *kampfgruppe* commanders to separate and travel along different paths as planned to the Büdingen forest and the German defenses believed to be somewhere north of, or near, Gelnhausen.

Goebel was the first to disentangle his troops from the mass of foot-marching soldiers, vehicles, and horse-drawn carts. He quickly ordered his lead units to continue northeast toward Ortenberg, which would put the column on a parallel course astride the XII Corps' MSR. The presence of Goebel's column in this area would soon alarm Major General Eddy and result in the 5th Cavalry Reconnaissance Troop's mission that night to clear the MSR of all German forces. But Goebel had learned that, nighttime or not, the Americans would not wait long before again pursuing his battle group. The slow-moving nature of his horse-drawn vehicles and foot-marching soldiers put his column at risk of encirclement or capture, so Goebel positioned his few remaining light artillery howitzers at the end of the procession to provide covering fire against pursuing American forces.

Goebel's column first crept toward Stockheim before turning northeast to Ortenberg (see Map 6.3). The hungry and exhausted SS men executed the movement in the pitch-black darkness with great skill and discipline. Although haggard, dirty, hungry, and heavily laden with as much equipment as each man could carry (to include at least one *panzerfaust* per man), the spirit of the SS troops remained unbroken.

As the slow-moving column approached Stockheim, Goebel ordered his six horse-drawn howitzers onto a hill, identified on American maps as Hill 267, just east of Glauberg. Goebel wanted to pause and rest his troops in the nearby forest before pressing on, and the howitzers would provide cover for the resting troops. These six howitzers, the final remnants of SS-Gebirgs Artillerie Regiment 6's 4th, 5th, and 6th Batteries under the command of a senior noncommissioned officer, *SS-Sturmscharführer* Plösch, represented the last of the division's artillery. Goebel had only a few hours to spare until daylight. The column would have to begin moving again long before the sun rose.[143]

Once *SS-Oberführer* Goebel's column departed, *SS-Standartenführer* Raithel directed his motorized column, complete with the division commander and his staff, along the same general route as the horse-drawn column. At Stockheim both columns separated, and Raithel's advance guard, mounted in captured American jeeps and accompanied by scouts on German motorcycles, sped eastward to Bleichenbach before veering south toward the tiny hamlet of Wolf—just two kilometers north of Büdingen. Brenner wanted to gain the Büdingen forest quickly so the column could reorganize and close up. The gaps between vehicles and march units increased owing to the darkness and the narrow, poorly defined farm tracks leading through the fields.

The German advance guard cleared Wolf quickly and changed direction northeast toward the small village of Dudenrod, nestled snugly in the very heart of the Büdingen forest. The rest of the motorized procession followed noisily, engines racing as transmissions strained to carry the heavy vehicles and their cargoes up and down the steep, winding hills that marked the entrance to the forest. Exhausted and nearly asleep at their wheels, the drivers squinted to see the darkened roads. But few mishaps occurred and the vehicle column slowly entered the heart of the Büdingen forest.

The advance guard's jeeps and motorcycles then left the main road at Dudenrod and struck eastward along the narrow logging trails that paralleled deep ravines in the dense, heavily canopied pine forest. Raithel told his scouts to stop at the tiny village of Michelau at the eastern exit of the forest. The column—strung out for several kilometers—would have to pause so the rest of the vehicles could close the gaps that had formed. Some vehicles were still as far back as Glauberg. But *SS-Gruppenführer* Brenner could spare only a few hours before resuming the march. Like *SS-Oberführer* Goebel, Brenner was concerned that the Americans might not wait until dawn to resume their pursuit of the column. Therefore, Brenner intended to use the concealment of the thick forest and the dark of night to assemble the column properly before continuing to move. The column could then swing south toward Gelnhausen and join whatever German forces were still fighting there. Brenner still did not know that the Americans occupied that key town.

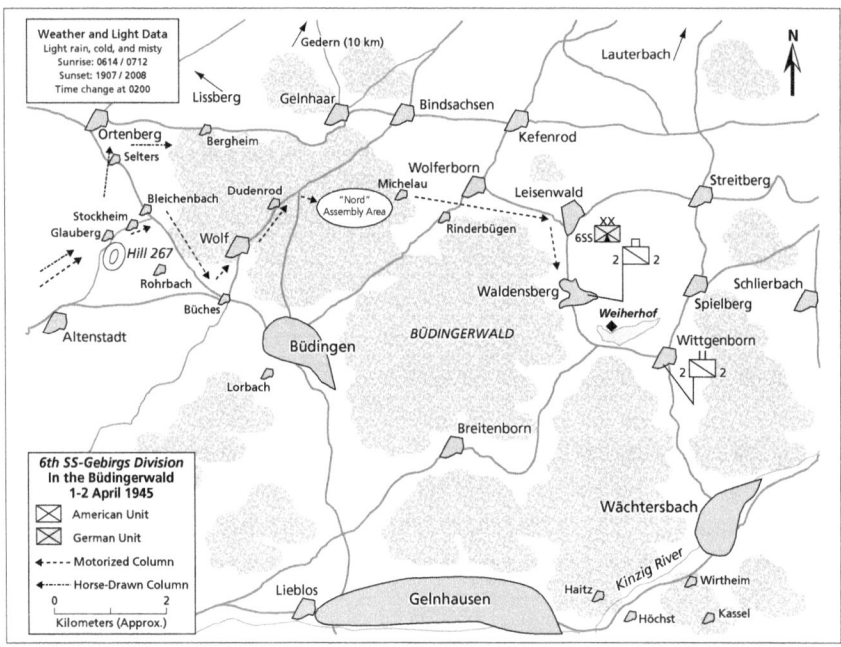

Map 6.3. 6th SS-Gebirgs Division in the Büdingen forest, 1–2 April 1945.

Not long after 0000 the motorized column finally assembled in a three-kilometer area in the Büdingen forest between Dudenrod and Michelau. The last of the straggling vehicles had closed on the rear of the column. After a brief pause for food, water, and a nap, the Nord men resumed the march. Raithel directed his advance guard to exit the forest at Michelau and head for Wolferborn. From there the road to Leisenwald, Waldensberg, and points south lay wide open. Speed and darkness would continue to be the column's only security, so Raithel ordered his troops and their vehicles to remain closely together. The time had come to race to the final objective: Gelnhausen.[144]

❖

Sometime around 0000 on 1 April Lt. Gen. George S. Patton Jr., the Third Army commander, arrived at his command post to consider the guidance he had recently received from Lt. Gen. Omar N. Bradley, the 12th Army Group commander. Bradley warned that Patton's lead elements, predominantly Major General Eddy's XII Corps, were pushing too far ahead and risked German counterattacks from the flanks. If Third Army could not gain Weimar that night, then the army would have to stop and wait for the First and Ninth Armies to come abreast. Patton asked Bradley for another day to advance since the going was so smooth for his fleet-footed armored troops. Bradley conceded and allowed Patton to keep moving until 1700 on 2 April. After that time, however, the Third Army would have to allow the other two armies on the northern flank to come abreast.

Patton then received updates from his staff about the general Third Army situation. Among the numerous reports made available to Patton, one caught his eye. The report outlined an atrocity committed in the Third Army area of operations. Earlier that day troops from the 6th SS-Gebirgs Division, bypassed by advancing American forces, had escaped from the hills north of Frankfurt and cut across the XII Corps' rear area. The report, assembled from several initial accounts, alleged that the Germans had overrun a field hospital and ammunition dump, murdered everyone, raped the nurses, and destroyed the dump. Patton winced and demanded further information.[145]

The staff scrambled and requested further clarification from XII Corps and the other units involved. Patton wanted to know for certain if the reports were accurate. Soon, during the late hours of the night, the staff was able to report to Patton that the Germans had indeed captured a field hospital and ammunition company that day but, after killing one officer and a couple of enlisted men in the initial clash, simply stole vehicles and supplies. The Germans did not kill everyone and did not rape the nurses. In fact, the Germans were in such a hurry to depart that they did not even destroy the ammunition stores they left behind.[146]

Patton was satisfied that the earlier report was nothing more than a wild rumor. He wrote in his diary that night, "This is simply another illustration of my opinion that the report of no incident which happens after dark should be treated too seriously. They are always overstated."[147]

Patton mused that such rumors might enhance the fighting spirit and ferocity of the GIs going up against the Nord men and result in more dead Germans and fewer prisoners. What Patton did not realize was that the rumors that drove the initial atrocity report were not widespread among the GIs of the 71st and 5th Infantry divisions. The thing that drove the GIs to fight was their healthy respect for the fighting prowess and dedication (often perceived—perhaps justifiably—as fanaticism) of their Waffen-SS opponents. The GIs had learned, mostly through propagandized hearsay about the "fanatical SS," that battling a Waffen-SS soldier meant a tough fight. The men of the 71st Division in particular suffered no illusions about the difficulty they would face in defeating the Nord Division.[148]

CHAPTER 7

The Second Day: Waldensberg, 2 April 1945

SS-Standartenführer *Raithel watched patiently as his advance guard exited the Büdingen forest at Michelau on their way toward Wolferborn. The captured American jeeps and German motorcycles crept slowly up to the forest's edge and then roared off into the darkness through the heart of Michelau. Then, one by one, the captured American ambulances, Dodge trucks, and tanks—all heavily laden with stores and troops—emerged from the forest on the road to Wolferborn. Losses had been significant earlier that day, as reflected by the smaller number of men and vehicles lining up in the forest.*[1]

Raithel checked his watch. The time was nearly 0400. Daylight savings time had prompted everyone, including the Americans, to push their clocks ahead by one hour. The sun would rise at 0712, which meant the motorized column had two, maybe even three hours of total darkness remaining in which to conceal the battle group's movement to Gelnhausen. Raithel was optimistic that his troops could make the journey before the sun rose. The SS troops had abandoned all slow-moving or damaged vehicles in the Büdingen forest, also leaving behind scores of American prisoners. Speed was essential if what remained of the *kampfgruppe* was to arrive in Gelnhausen to bolster the German defenses that *SS-Gruppenführer* Brenner believed still existed there.

Brenner's decision to leave behind most of the American prisoners eased the burden on some of his men but created a problem for others. GIs drove the jeeps for their captors since few SS men knew how to drive the vehicles. Most Nord men would have to catch rides on other vehicles or walk. A couple of junior leaders even suggested that some of the men head off on their own through the forest to Gelnhausen or elsewhere. Most Nord men ignored such advice and remained with the division. Oddly, some of the Americans remaining behind requested certificates from the Nord men identifying them as former prisoners of the Germans. A number of SS sergeants dutifully complied and issued the GIs the required papers.

The lack of American drivers meant that several captured vehicles had to remain behind. *SS-Rottenführer* Walter Becker and his comrades from the 3rd Company, SS-Gebirgs Nachrichten Battalion 6, found themselves abandoning several captured jeeps after first disabling them by removing the distributor caps. Becker's American jeep driver was among those prisoners staying behind in the forest, but Becker knew how to drive a jeep. He climbed into the driver's seat and prepared to follow the departing motorized column. But Becker's comrade, a fellow *funker* named Gerd Weber, had yet to find a jeep or German *kübelwagen* he could not drive. Weber had a passion for driving and enjoyed demonstrating his skills whenever possible. Becker readily surrendered the driver's seat to his delighted friend.

Becker then called for passengers to climb aboard until the jeep was full. Becker's other friend and fellow *funker*, Walter Bärenklau, hopped in, followed by an unnamed *funker* from another company and two *SS-Unterscharführers* from one of the *gebirgsjäger* companies. Becker, sitting in the passenger seat beside Weber, warned the driver not to fall behind in the column. If the *Amis* were to identify the lead part of the column as German, he explained, the rear vehicles would bear the brunt of their attack. Weber nodded, started the vehicle, and pulled in behind the main column on the narrow logging trail headed east out of the forest. Becker would not realize until later that morning how fortunate he and his comrades were to have such a skilled driver at the helm of their jeep.[2]

At the head of the column, the advance guard was busy clearing the hamlet of Wolferborn. Low-hanging morning fog drifted slowly across the open countryside on either side of the group's motorcycles and jeeps as they sped through the darkness and into Leisenwald. Like Wolferborn, Leisenwald showed no signs of life. White sheets hanging from numerous windows perturbed the SS men, but the town appeared completely asleep. The roar of vehicle engines undoubtedly roused many of the town's occupants, but no one dared emerge from their homes this Easter night.[3]

After a quick inspection of the town's desolate side streets, the advance guard re-formed in the center of Leisenwald and sped off toward Waldensberg a kilometer south. The SS men hoped the way through this town would be clear as well. If so, nothing would impede their progress to Gelnhausen, their ultimate objective. As the lead motorcycle crested the small, undulating hillside overlooking Waldensberg, the clock struck 0430.[4]

Technician 5th grade Walter S. Wojciechowski shivered in the damp, early morning chill that surrounded the small town of Waldensberg. As one of four guards posted in the town to secure the slumbering troops of the 2nd Squadron, 2nd Cavalry Group's rear echelon, Wojciechowski expected nothing to happen. The newspapers and recent scuttlebutt suggested that the war had moved east and that Waldensberg was well to the rear of any potential fighting.[5]

The townspeople of Waldensberg had been relieved when the first Americans of the XII Corps' advance guard finally arrived in the town two days earlier, on Good Friday. After a brief but harmless artillery barrage, American troops and tanks appeared from the west. *Bürgermeister* (mayor) Wilhelm Schmidt urged Landrat (District Administrator) Heinrich Kress to hoist a large white bedsheet from the belfry of the church steeple. Soon, the Americans entered the town. The loud tank, truck, and jeep engines momentarily frightened the people of Waldensberg, but the GIs moved on quickly without encountering a single German soldier. The last German troops seen by the townsfolk had left a day earlier headed east, dragging their equipment on carts or in baby carriages. A follow-on American contingent of jeeps laden with GIs quickly followed the advance guard and occupied most of Waldensberg's houses. Stoically, the displaced townspeople took up residence in the village church and town hall, thankful the war had passed them by without incident. The GIs even allowed the women to return to their homes, do their housework, and prepare for Easter. The GIs soon departed; after only a daylong hiatus from American occupation, though, more GIs arrived in the dark of night in the guise of the 2nd Squadron, 2nd Cavalry's rear echelon. The townspeople, torn between their feelings for their own German soldiers and the American troops, clearly saw the GIs as agents of peace while they saw the German troops as harbingers of combat and destruction.[6]

The town of Waldensberg was quiet once again except for the occasional loud snore emanating from the American-occupied houses. Besides guarding the rear-echelon troops, Wojciechowski and his fellow sentries guarded several nearby houses filled with nearly five hundred captured German soldiers. The rear echelon had served as a mobile prisoner collection point during the 2nd Squadron's fast-moving advance. The rear echelon troops sent captured Germans to the rear as soon as possible, but the growing number of prisoners bagged in the past few days forced the cavalrymen to transport them until delivered to the corps' POW cage farther west. But Wojciechowski was unconcerned about prisoners. Tired, disheveled, and dispirited, the prisoners—predominantly soldiers from the Heer and a few Luftwaffe flak troops—showed no will to fight. Most were just happy to have survived the war up to that point.[7]

The roar of slow-moving jeep and motorcycle engines suddenly broke the near-silence. Wojciechowski and the other three guards—posted nearby and around the rear echelon's command post—glanced toward the northern entrance of the town. Who could be driving through town at this hour?

The guards squinted into the waning darkness. The overcast sky kept the early morning twilight from illuminating the vehicles, but the GIs certainly recognized the sound of American jeeps. A total of eight jeeps and motorcycles paraded slowly past Wojciechowski and his fellow guards. The vehicles' occupants obviously did not see the guards and the various American vehicles parked along the town's side streets.

Wojciechowski leaned forward to catch a better glimpse of the vehicles' occupants. Instantly, he identified the familiar outlines of a German helmet. All the occupants wore German helmets! Before Wojciechowski could speak, the advance guard of *SS-Standartenführer* Raithel's motorized column disappeared down the road toward Wittgenborn. Wojciechowksi ordered another guard to run to the command post and inform the rear echelon's commanding officer (and squadron motor officer), Capt. John W. Mayfield, of what he had seen.

The bewildered guard burst into the command post and unceremoniously roused Mayfield from his bedroll. He shouted that a German vehicle column had just moved through town toward the 2nd Squadron's command post in Wittgenborn. Startled, Mayfield jumped up and told radio operator T/4 Marion E. Harsla to alert squadron headquarters. Mayfield then sent several runners to rouse the rest of the rear echelon and put them on full alert. Sgt. Godfrey V. Dwyer, T/5 Rodney Bridges, and T/5 Sidney Berg—the crew of the rear echelon's sole, fully functioning M8 armored car—quickly mounted their vehicle and began breaking out ammunition.

At the 2nd Squadron's headquarters in nearby Wittgenborn, the executive officer, Maj. Eben R. Wyles, listened to Harsla's radio transmission with concern. He hastily assembled the few M8 armored cars and light tanks that traveled with the headquarters and deployed them along the road leading from Waldensberg to the north. Within minutes the German advance-guard column appeared. The vehicles' dark shapes, barely visible to the waiting cavalrymen, provided sufficient targets to the M8 and the light tank gunners.

Wyles ordered his men to open fire. Machine-gun and main-gun fire from the armored cars and light tanks erupted around the lead jeep. The Nord men scrambled from the jeeps and sought cover among the dense underbrush lining the road. Several jeeps burst into flames. The motorcyclists quickly abandoned the road and attempted to speed off through the forest. The GIs tracked them with rifle fire, forcing the motorcycles to ground and wounding or killing the drivers.[8]

SS-Rottenführer Walter Becker's jeep, driven by his friend Gerd Weber, was at the end of the advance guard's column when the shooting started. Becker, his friend Walter Bärenklau, and the three other occupants bailed out of the jeep and sought cover beside the road. Weber remained behind the wheel and, in a remarkable display of driving skill, swung the jeep around on the narrow road without decelerating, speeding off in the direction from which they had just come. Becker and the others jumped up from their hiding places and chased after Weber, barely able to climb back onto the speeding jeep.

Out of breath and hearts racing, the SS men pleaded with Weber to stop so they could assess their situation. But Weber ignored their entreaties and drove like a man in a trance. After following a maze of darkened dirt roads and other trails, Weber eventually reached the Kinzig River west of Wächtersbach. He crossed the river and drove into the town unmolested. The group ultimately rejoined another German unit near Schweinfurt, thanks to Weber's skilled driving. He had saved himself and his handful of comrades from death or imprisonment by the Americans. Becker never regretted allowing his good friend to drive.[9]

Back near Wittgenborn, several Nord men from the advance guard tried to counterattack the cavalrymen. Major Wyles gathered a group of dismounted GIs and led them through the woods to flank the German column. The GIs fired into the column's flank, stalling the German counterattack and catching the SS men in a deadly cross fire. The surviving Nord men returned fire sporadically but refused to give ground or surrender. Soon, the firing waned as both sides became deadlocked in a lethal standoff. Wyles ordered his men to stand fast. He intended to fix the enemy in place until more help arrived.

Back in Waldensberg, Captain Mayfield and his men remained on alert. At 0500, half an hour after the German advance guard had passed through the town, one of the guards rushed into the command post and reported an even larger German column of approximately thirty-eight vehicles led by a tank entering Waldensberg from the north. Technician 5th grade Berg, one of the M8 armored car's crewmen, sent a flash message to the 2nd Squadron headquarters. Mayfield's rear-echelon troops were no match for a German force of this size, so he sent runners to tell the troops to hold their fire and allow the German column to pass. The early morning darkness still concealed the cavalrymen's vehicles parked along the side streets. A few of Waldensberg's civilian residents braved a peek through curtained windows but otherwise remained quiet and out of sight. The German column, an odd mixture of ambulances, trucks, jeeps, and assorted German vehicles, moved quietly through the town. The column would soon encounter Major Wyles's roadblock near Wittgenborn.

After a short break in the German column, another smaller column of ten to twelve German vehicles led by a captured American jeep appeared. The time was 0530 and the glow of morning twilight had begun to permeate the overcast skies. As the lead jeep moved slowly through the main avenue, an SS officer glanced down a side street and noticed T/5 Dwight Gardner, a water-truck driver, standing next to an M8 armored car brought to the rear echelon for repairs. The jeep screeched to a halt as the officer cried, "*Amerikaner!*" Gardner instantly leapt onto the armored car, swung the turret-mounted M2 .50-caliber machine gun toward the column, and opened fire. Every vehicle in the column slammed on its brakes. The SS men piled out of the vehicles and returned fire.

Captain Mayfield, realizing that he and his men had to stand and fight, ordered Sergeant Dwyer to take his M8 armored car around to the western edge of town and engage the enemy column from the flank. The vehicle quickly sped off down a side street and emerged on the open ground west of Waldensberg. Dwyer and his crew could see scores of German vehicles stacked up on the road at the northern entrance to the town. They opened fire with the 37-mm gun and the .30-caliber coaxial machine gun. The rounds ripped into the stalled vehicle column, forcing several German troops to dismount and go to ground. Dwyer saw a group of SS men on foot moving toward the armored car from the right. He informed Berg, who swung his machine gun toward the Germans and opened fire. The Nord men immediately sought cover among the nearby houses.

While the crew was preoccupied with the advancing German foot troops, several Nord men set up a towed antitank gun (probably a 3.7-cm gun) on the road north of Waldensberg. Within seconds, several antitank shells exploded around the exposed M8 armored car. One round glanced off the vehicle's left front. Dwyer ordered Technician 5th grade Bridges to back up and move through the town to engage the column from the other flank east of the village. The armored car quickly sped off.

Farther inside Waldensberg the S-4 supply section was busy holding off the SS mountain troops swarming throughout the town. T/Sgt. Charles A. Franz promptly woke his men; before some of the men could get fully dressed, though, the sound of machine-gun fire reached their ears. Technician 5th grade John E. Donohue was so surprised by the sound that he grabbed his bedroll and prepared to walk outside to place it in his vehicle. Technician 5th grade Joseph V. Ferrizzi, busy shooting at the German troops from a nearby window, shouted, "Get the hell out of the doorway! The streets are full of Krauts!" Donohue instantly came to his senses and ducked back inside.

Within minutes the S-4 troops found themselves surrounded. No one could venture forth from the house without coming under German rifle or submachine-gun fire. When the Germans began tossing grenades toward the house, Technical Sergeant Franz ordered everyone into the cellar. The S-4 men had no choice but to hunker down and wait for their fellow cavalrymen to rescue them.

One of the four guards on duty that morning was T/5 Frank Veldhuis. After giving an update to Captain Mayfield, he ran down to where the men of the transportation platoon were sleeping and promptly alerted them to the situation. S/Sgt. Mike Bellanca roused his men, but the shooting had already started by the time the GIs were dressed and ready. The fast-moving German mountain troopers were everywhere; they had already isolated the transportation platoon from the rear-echelon command post. Pfc. Roland R. Guay started out the back door and ran into two SS men. He called for Bellanca, who charged forward and opened fire, felling one of the men. The other returned fire, but Pfc. Ben Sowers rushed out the door and shot him dead.

Within seconds the transportation platoon was standing in the street behind the house wondering what to do next. The early morning sky was rapidly brightening. One of the men suddenly spied Pfc. William E. Roots standing beside the corner of a nearby building. Roots was holding his M1 carbine by the barrel and cocking it over his shoulder like a baseball bat. The

GIs quickly understood. When a German poked his head around the corner, Roots swung his carbine and busted the man squarely in the face. The Nord man fell into a heap on the ground.

Bellanca decided that the transportation platoon should make a break for the command post. The GIs started trotting down the street, but the small-arms fire crisscrossing the roads proved too intense for the men to continue. As the GIs turned to go, a stray round struck Pfc. Glenn T. Page. Bellanca started toward the wounded man, but German rifle fire kept him from advancing. Two other cavalrymen in a nearby house, Cpl. Paul H. Brooks and Pfc. Harold H. Friedly, yelled from a window that they could reach Page from their position. They told Bellanca to keep on moving out of the area. Both Brooks and Friedly would later be seriously wounded in the fighting.

Bellanca and his thirteen men began fighting house to house in search of better cover and fellow cavalrymen, but the fighting had become too intense. Ammunition quickly was running low. Bellanca and his men made a break for the nearby forest on the western edge of the town. After sprinting across several hundred yards of open field, the GIs gained the woods and sought cover. Oddly enough, the group encountered a German Army major, a captain, and two lieutenants who wanted to surrender to them. The officers had likely attached themselves to the Nord Division at some point but wanted no part of the fighting. Bellanca was at a loss since he did not know where he was or where he should go. The German major said that American troops were in Büdingen, so the officer led the group on a long journey through the forest to Büdingen where Bellanca and his men met up with an American engineer unit that took charge of the German prisoners and eventually returned the cavalrymen to the 2nd Cavalry Squadron.

While Staff Sergeant Bellanca and his men made their break for the forest, Sergeant Dwyer's M8 had reached the eastern side of Waldensberg. Just as the armored car emerged into the open to fire on the backed-up German column, a cavalryman shouted from a nearby house that some Germans were approaching the car from behind. Dwyer grabbed his Thompson submachine gun and opened fire, scattering the Germans. Technician 5th grade Bridges swung open the hatch above his driver's compartment, leveled his M1, and shot two SS men who were approaching with grenades in hand.

Bridges gunned the engine and sped out onto the open ground to a position from which Dwyer and Berg could engage the enemy column. As Bridges edged the vehicle onto a muddy slope, Dwyer spotted ten German soldiers advancing on the armored car from five hundred meters away. Berg swung the turret around and opened fire with the vehicle's .30-caliber machine gun. The Germans fell dead or wounded. As the fighting continued, Bridges broadcast on the radio a running account of the battle to the 2nd Squadron headquarters until German small-arms fire severed the car's antenna.

At Captain Mayfield's command post in town, approximately fifteen GIs remained to defend the house. German mortar shells fell into the town relentlessly, setting several houses alight. The burning buildings cast an eerie glow as the SS men surrounded the command post and peppered the building with rifle and machine-gun fire. The odds were clearly against the small group of stalwart defenders. Mayfield and his driver, T/4 Perry J. Long, stepped outside briefly to assess the situation, but a German marksman shot them both dead. Capt. Winston C. Hill immediately assumed command.

Hill recognized the situation as hopeless, so he ordered the remaining men in the command post to rush outside, board the two jeeps and one M8 armored car parked beside the building (the M8 was there for repairs but could still function), and speed off into the forest. Within seconds the GIs were racing west toward the Büdingen forest. The Germans followed the three vehicles with a hail of rifle and machine-gun fire. The jeeps and armored car bounced wildly over the open fields; the excessive speed and uneven terrain made the drive a death-defying venture for the few cavalrymen hanging on for their lives.

About two hundred meters from the town, the three vehicles encountered a small stream and became mired. The recent rains had swelled the stream and turned its banks into a sea of mud. With the Germans still pursuing them, the GIs abandoned their vehicles and disappeared into the forest. The fighting inside Waldensberg soon waned. Captain Hill's group had represented the final resistance inside the town. Waldensberg now belonged to the Nord Division.

Uninjured but out of the breath, Hill and his men rallied several hundred meters inside the forest. S/Sgt. Harold T. Cooley volunteered to lead a patrol to find a nearby American unit. The radio operator, T/4 Marion E. Harsla, offered to crawl back to the M8 armored car and radio their situation to squadron headquarters. Hill agreed. Harsla soon returned and told Hill that the squadron was aware that Waldensberg was in enemy hands. Hill then gathered his men and, using a map and compass, went in search of a friendly unit. The men eventually found their way back to the 2nd Squadron.[10]

Back inside Waldensberg some of the town's male residents ventured forth from their hiding places. The other townspeople cringed in their cellars or inside the church, terrified to emerge for fear of injury or death. *Bürgermeister* Wilhelm Schmidt stepped outside the Rinkenberger Hall and saw SS troops running throughout the town, most of them shouldering *panzerfäuste*.

Alarmed that Waldensberg had become a battleground, Schmidt approached a passing Nord man and asked, "Whatever are you doing? You're endangering the whole place!"

The SS man looked at Schmidt and replied, "You stay quietly in your hall. For the most part, we have mopped up the place from top to bottom."

The sound of vehicle engines coming from the south caused the Nord men to freeze. A sergeant quickly waved the SS troops off the main road and into the side streets and alleyways. Schmidt hurried back inside the hall and told the citizens to take cover.

A dozen American cargo trucks led by a jeep soon appeared from the south (probably driving up from the road leading back to Breitenborn). Waldensberg seemed quiet once again. The unsuspecting GIs pulled up in front of a large barn, turned off their vehicle engines, and dismounted. A couple of GIs went to the barn door, unlocked it, and began waving into the street the German prisoners held there by the cavalry troops. The prisoners had no idea what was happening and could not make sense of the shooting they had heard minutes earlier. Likewise, the SS men did not know the barn housed several hundred of their fellow troops from the Heer and Luftwaffe.

As the American truck drivers and co-drivers stood around smoking and laughing, a handful of GIs herded the bewildered German prisoners into the backs of the trucks for movement to the rear. As the German troops climbed aboard, the unseen Nord men crept forward from the side streets and emplaced two MG42 machine guns on either side of the road beside the barn.

Bürgermeister Schmidt peered from a window in the Rinkenberger Hall to see what was happening. He watched as the prisoners loaded the American trucks. The Germans seemed genuinely happy to get on the trucks and, more than likely, to move back to a place of safety. They probably thought that for them the war was over.

After forty-five minutes the trucks were fully loaded. Just as an American sergeant stepped into the street and gave the signal for the drivers to mount up, the sudden ripping sound of two MG42 machine guns firing simultaneously broke the stillness. Three GIs fell dead beside the trucks, blood pouring profusely from their torsos.

The SS men rushed into the street seemingly from out of nowhere, shouting and firing short bursts from MP40s and other weapons. The GIs quickly raised their arms in surrender. Several Nord men herded the GIs into the street and searched them. The SS men then led the stunned Americans along the main road to the northern part of town.

The Nord men motioned the newly liberated German prisoners off the trucks. Clearly dejected, the Heer and Luftwaffe troops climbed down from the truck beds and gathered in the street. The Nord men searched the trucks for American weapons and ammunition and then gave what they found to the former prisoners. Several SS men then jumped in the truck cabs, turned over the engines, and sped off to the north. The German Army soldiers took the weapons hesitantly. They had thought their war was over. Now they had been drafted to fight once more under the direction of the Waffen-SS. The former prisoners slowly shouldered their rucksacks and followed the Nord men to the center of town, presumably to help with the mopping-up operation. The war had found them once more.[11]

Major General Wyman and his 71st Division staff in Langenselbold were unaware of the predawn clash at Waldensberg. They had spent the night fine-tuning their preparations for the coming attacks scheduled for the next morning. Lieutenant Colonel Lankenau had informed both XII Corps and the 5th Infantry Division of the plan to send one battalion from the 66th Infantry Regiment (designated by Colonel Regnier as Task Force X) northward through the heart of the Büdingen forest while two battalions of the 14th Infantry Regiment pushed through the woods from the northeast and east. The staff also learned that the 5th Infantry Division's 5th Cavalry Reconnaissance Troop, led by Captain Robinson, was already well to the north above Ranstadt and on the way to Schotten after passing though Nidda along the Ortenberg road.[12]

Colonel Lundquist reported during the night that Lt. Col. Paul G. Guthrie's 3rd Battalion, 14th Infantry, had settled into positions between Heegheim and Glauberg at 0200. Both Guthrie's battalion and Lieutenant Colonel Brant's 2nd Battalion had foot patrols out for security as well as for listening posts. The situation remained quiet, however.[13]

Lundquist further informed the G-2, Lieutenant Colonel Foster, of the results of his own interrogations of captured German soldiers. Lundquist's report squared with the information Foster had been receiving from various sources throughout the night. Lundquist's report indicated that a large number of enemy troops had concentrated at Staden and that the enemy columns were fleeing along American supply routes and ambushing supply vehicles—a situation that had caused Major General Eddy, the XII Corps commander, much angst. In fact, a message from corps headquarters at 0725 instructed all corps units that service trains moving in rear areas would travel only under armed escort.[14]

Lundquist's report helped Foster provide Major General Wyman with a clearer picture of the enemy situation. Wyman intended to commit three battalions against the SS troops, but the reported size of the enemy force—growing with each new report—suggested that he might be forced to commit the entire division to the attack. Not prone to impulsive decisions, Wyman opted to wait and see how the morning attacks would further develop a murky and confusing situation.

❖

Lt. Col. Gaston B. Eikel's 2nd Battalion, 66th Infantry—now designated as Task Force X—was scheduled to attack at 0715 that morning along a route leading northeast from Breitenborn to Wittgenborn, then north to Waldensberg, and finally northwest to Wolferborn. The maneuver was intended to push the escaping SS troops back into the forest toward the two advancing battalions of the 14th Infantry farther west. Eikel, like his regimental and division commanders, was unaware of what had transpired at Waldensberg a few hours earlier. The assigned route would lead Eikel and his men directly into the German-held town.

Late arrival of the trucks delayed the task force's move by fifteen minutes. The trucks finally appeared a few minutes after 0700, but the platoon from the regimental Cannon Company failed to show. The platoon of medium Sherman tanks from Company C, 761st Tank Battalion, arrived on time, though, and was ready to move out with the task force. The Red Circle men mounted the trucks and loaded all necessary equipment, but by 0715, the scheduled departure time, the platoon from Cannon Company still had not arrived. The sun had risen just three minutes earlier, and the gray, overcast sky glowed brighter. A misty morning rain dampened the GIs' uniforms.[15]

After a flurry of radio traffic and a vain attempt to locate the missing platoon from Cannon Company, Colonel Regnier slapped his thigh with his ever-present riding crop and ordered the task force to depart. At 0740 Maj. William J. Merrill, the regimental S-3, reported to division that Task Force X had crossed their line of departure fifteen minutes late, at 0730.[16]

Eikel's truck-mounted task force departed Gelnhausen and gained the narrow, meandering road to Breitenborn. Tall, heavy pine and spruce trees canopied the road, nearly eclipsing the emerging daylight. The trucks and tanks sped swiftly through Breitenborn unopposed and past their first phase line; as the lead vehicles approached the Weiherhof between Wittgenborn and Waldensberg (roughly Phase Line Two), though, the column slowed. A messenger from the lead company reported that the enemy was manning a roadblock three kilometers ahead. Eikel relayed this message back to Colonel Regnier and Major Merrill, who immediately informed the division command post.[17]

Major General Wyman received the news of the enemy's presence near Task Force X's second phase line with great consternation. He had expected the task force to encounter enemy troops farther north near Wolferborn. Colonel Lundquist's nighttime report that the SS troops had clustered around Staden made Wyman believe that a force spread out so far had to be much larger than he or his staff previously believed. The mission would require the attention of his entire division.

At 0840 Wyman called Major General Eddy at the XII Corps advance command post in Lauterbach and made his case for the full commitment of the 71st Infantry Division against the 6th SS-Gebirgs Division. The 66th Regiment's task force was already receiving small-arms fire, and a considerably larger force than previously determined was trying to break out. Wyman needed all three regiments to swing through the woods and sweep up the enemy. Wyman also asked for a greater commitment of troops from the 5th Infantry Division to support the operation.[18]

Wyman's argument found a sympathetic ear in Eddy, who was already deeply concerned about the threat to his corps' rear area. Committing whatever resources necessary to allay that threat made perfect sense to him. Eddy gave Wyman permission to commit the entire Red Circle Division to the fray.

As soon as the call ended, Wyman radioed Colonel Wooten and told him to move the 5th Infantry Regiment north to Ravolzhausen for imminent commitment to the Büdingen forest. Wooten would stand ready to attack in a northeasterly direction with two battalions abreast along the road leading into the town of Büdingen. When Wooten asked for Wyman's intent, the division commander simply replied, "I want to clean these woods up."[19]

❖

The clash with the American cavalry troops in Waldensberg did not surprise *SS-Gruppenführer* Brenner, who had come to expect that the Nord Division would continue to bump into scattered U.S. units throughout the American rear area. Brenner knew, however, that each clash cost him dearly in personnel and vehicles. The enemy always managed to destroy several of the division's precious transport vehicles and kill or wound several soldiers. Stragglers from the Heer and Luftwaffe who had recently attached themselves to the division often ran off into the woods to avoid direct combat with the Americans. These troops obviously believed that dying in the last days of a war that Germany had already lost was not worth the sacrifice. Few of Brenner's Waffen-SS troops felt this way, however, and continued to fight bravely during each skirmish.

As the fighting abated in Waldensberg, *SS-Standartenführer* Raithel immediately committed more troops to clear the town. The experienced SS troops quickly occupied the village and sought out any remaining GIs from the 2nd Squadron's rear-echelon trains. Despite a thorough search, several American cavalrymen managed to remain undetected in houses and cellars.

The brief but violent clash at Waldensberg had forced Raithel to halt the motorized column on the road north of Waldensberg; the long, serpentine column already stretched back along the road leading from Leisenwald and northwest to Wolferborn. Daylight made the stalled column vulnerable to American spotter planes and the merciless artillery attacks these planes brought with them.

Raithel quickly ordered *SS-Hauptsturmführer* Steurich, the 1st Battalion commander, to bring as many of the battle group's vehicles and troops into Waldensberg as possible to limit their exposure on the open roads. Likewise, Brenner ordered the division staff and the rest of Raithel's Gebirgs troops bringing up the column's rear to abandon the open roads and enter Leisenwald. The SS troops quickly closed on both towns.

Raithel had lost contact with his advance guard and assumed they had met an unfortunate fate south of Waldensberg. Actually, the advance guard remained stalled at Major Wyles's roadblock just outside Wittgenborn. Many of the advance guard's troops had already slipped away undetected into the forest and had begun to work their way back toward Waldensberg. They knew that Wyles and his men would not allow the SS men to advance any farther.

In Leisenwald the Nord Division staff quickly set up shop in the hay-filled stalls of a cattle barn adjacent to one of the many homes in the town's center. Many of Leisenwald's homesteads were constructed in a similar manner so the proprietors could easily step from a side door and pass directly into their barns to milk the cows or gather eggs.

Until now the citizens of Leisenwald had experienced little of the war. A four-hundred man foreign labor force of Polish, Russian, French, Belgian, and Dutch slave laborers, transported into central Germany in the face of the advancing American forces, was billeted in the town temporarily on 18 March but left quickly thereafter. By 29 March the last German infantry troops deployed in the area moved east through the town and away from the advancing American forces. On the afternoon of Good Friday, 30 March, the first American tanks rolled noisily through Leisenwald. Before 0000 on 31 March scores of GIs roused the town's inhabitants out of every second house so American support troops could occupy them. The GIs then departed on the morning of 1 April, Easter Sunday, and left the town in relatively good order, much to the townspeople's relief. Looting and damage had been minimal.

But the numerous explosions and cacophonous sounds of fighting in nearby Waldensberg—and the town's occupation by a large contingent of SS troops—greatly alarmed the citizens of Leisenwald. Without prompting by the Nord men, the townspeople quickly gathered their most precious possessions and took to the cellars. As the citizens hustled to their hiding places, Johannes Kaltenschnee overheard some Nord men complaining about the numerous white sheets adorning the town. The SS troops were clearly unhappy about the lack of fighting spirit displayed by the denizens of Leisenwald in these days of total war.

Kaltenschnee and his family moved into a large, vaulted cellar beneath a farmhouse with about 120 men, women, and children from the northern part of town. After settling his family into their dank but secure subterranean hiding place, Kaltenschnee departed for his home to remove the white flag he had hoisted when the Americans first arrived. He was afraid the Nord men might torch his house in a fit of pique.

Kaltenschnee arrived safely at his home and removed the sheets. He decided to inform some of the SS troops that the Americans had already passed through the town within the last thirty-six hours. He grabbed a pitcher of milk from his wife's pantry, stepped onto the cobblestone street, and began filling the mess kits of passing SS troops. The Nord men thanked Kaltenschnee profusely for his kindness.

Kaltenschnee soon encountered a Waffen-SS officer, who approached him for some milk. As Kaltenschnee poured milk into the officer's cup, he explained how the Americans had only recently moved off to the east and deeper into Germany. Concerned about the safety of Leisenwald, Kaltenschnee stated that any further fighting would only damage the town and prove futile. To Kaltenschnee's dismay, the officer only replied, "Nothing is futile."[20]

Inside the new division command post, *SS-Unterscharführer* Stöwe and his *funkers* set up their radios inside a cattle stall and began listening for any clues to the location of the German defensive front. Instead, the traffic they intercepted originated from American radios—and the Americans were talking about plans to bring in reinforcements to destroy the 6th SS-Gebirgs Division in the Büdingen forest![21]

Stöwe informed *SS-Gruppenführer* Brenner of the American plans and the fact that the *Amis* had identified the Nord Division by name. Brenner knew that his troops could go no farther than Leisenwald and Waldensberg in daylight, so he decided to consolidate the remaining forces from the motorized column in both towns—at least until nighttime when the SS troops could move again. Brenner was already out of contact with *SS-Oberführer* Goebel's horse-drawn column, which was moving east but father north somewhere along the Ortenberg road. Goebel and his troops would have to find the German defensive front somewhere to the east on their own.

Brenner sent a message to Raithel in Waldensberg to hole up there for the day. The Americans might try to wrest Waldensberg from the SS troops, so Brenner instructed Raithel to defend the town in strength and to establish outposts for early warning. Raithel had already sent out a truck-mounted, platoon-sized force of Nord men to erect a roadblock along the intersection of the Waldensberg–Wittgenborn road near the Weiherhof and the road to Breitenborn. The SS troops had this barricade in place by 0845 when the lead company of Task Force X slammed into it.

The lead company of Task Force X, Captain MacArthur's Company E, approached the Nord Division's roadblock near the Weiherhof slowly and cautiously. Lieutenant Colonel Eikel sent the Sherman tanks forward to follow closely behind Company E's troops, which had dismounted from the trucks and were advancing through the woods along both sides of the road. The tall, dense pines canopied the road and prevented the morning light from illuminating the area. Day seemed more like night to the Red Circle men.

MacArthur's lead platoon had already pinpointed the roadblock's position, so the GIs knew what to expect and where to expect it. As Company E approached the well-camouflaged barricade, a single shot from a German sniper shattered the morning stillness. The GIs instantly went to ground and returned fire with M1 rifles and Browning automatic rifles (BARs). The familiar ripping sound of German MG42s echoed throughout the dark forest, sending shards of bark and wood through the air.

MacArthur called the Sherman tanks forward. The armored behemoths crept slowly up the road, the drivers wary of any Germans hiding nearby with *panzerfäuste* at the ready. As the tanks came on line with the prone GIs, their turrets erupted with coaxial machine-gun fire that drowned out the sound of the German machine guns. SS men fell wounded or dead around the few logs and dead trees they had dragged onto the road for cover. The tanks fired main-gun rounds at the defending SS troops, sending shards of metal and bark whipping dangerously through the woods. Tracer rounds from American and German machine guns crisscrossed throughout the forest, forcing soldiers on both sides to seek cover. But the advancing Sherman tanks, impervious to the German small-arms fire, continued to creep forward.

MacArthur assembled part of his company and led them in a flanking maneuver against the German barricade. Within minutes, the men were behind the Germans and firing mercilessly into the enemy's ranks. Obviously caught in a trap, the Nord men attempted to withdraw, but as soon as they left their covered positions, they fell victim to the GIs' rifle and machine-gun fire.[22]

Within minutes the German troops were either dead or wounded. Two SS men stood up with arms raised and helmets removed. Company E's soldiers swarmed the roadblock position, checking the dead and assisting the wounded. Company E suffered no casualties in the fray. Captain MacArthur immediately questioned the two prisoners. After several minutes of conversing in broken German and English, MacArthur learned that the Germans had occupied Waldensberg with one Mark VI Tiger tank and twenty-five to thirty truckloads of SS mountain troops. MacArthur quickly radioed this information to Lieutenant Colonel Eikel, who in turn reported it to Colonel Regnier at the regimental command post in Lieblos.²³

The report disturbed Eikel, who realized that in order to accomplish his mission he had to fight through a heavily defended Waldensberg. What Eikel did not know was that the Nord Division did not have any Tiger tanks; the estimate on the number of German troops in the town was reasonably accurate, however. In any case Task Force X had a fight on its hands in Waldensberg. The time was 0900.

The information gathered by the 14th Infantry Regiment's S-2 from the prisoners captured by Lieutenant Colonel Brant's 2nd Battalion the previous day allowed Colonel Lundquist and his regimental S-3, Captain Borden, to formulate a plan for clearing out the forest north of Rodenbach and Heegheim. The prisoners' admissions caused Lundquist to revise his estimate of the Nord Division's strength from several hundred to nearly three thousand. The prospect of tackling an enemy force that outnumbered his two attacking battalions by a margin of two to one seemed daunting, but there was reason for optimism: the prisoners had disclosed that the SS troops lacked mortars and were using two artillery battalions as infantry—crucial information for Lundquist. The few artillery pieces the SS troops dragged along with them were dangerously low on ammunition as well. The prisoners further revealed that the Nord men were destroying all vehicles that ran out of fuel. Lundquist's S-2, Capt. Spencer P. Edwards, estimated that the SS troops would continue to move northeast to escape their pursuers but might counterattack in battalion strength only when forced to do so, taking as many Americans with them as possible in the process.²⁴

Lundquist and Borden, with suggestions from Edwards and the rest of the regimental staff, completed Operations Instruction Number Nine during the night. At 0500 the battalion commanders arrived at the regiment's forward command post in Altenstadt. Present for the briefing were Lieutenant Colonel Brant, 2nd Battalion; Lieutenant Colonel Guthrie, 3rd Battalion; and Major Collier, 608th Field Artillery Battalion. Collier's artillery troops were still moving into position south of Altenstadt, but he promised Lundquist the howitzers would be in position in time for the attack.²⁵

Lundquist explained the scheme of maneuver for the attack. Two infantry battalions—the 2nd and the 3rd—would attack on line north into the woods above Rodenbach and Heegheim to clear the forest of SS troops and drive the enemy into the 66th Infantry's 2nd Battalion, which was attacking farther east in a northwesterly direction. The operation would ultimately trap the escaping SS troops and force them to surrender or fight to the last man. The 608th Field Artillery Battalion would support the attack from firing positions south of Rodenbach and Heegheim. Lundquist gave each infantry battalion three M4 Sherman tanks for the attack. He would control the movement using a series of phase lines to ensure that one battalion did not outpace the other and needlessly expose a flank. Lundquist set the attack time for 0900. The battalion commanders departed to issue their own respective orders.[26]

The time had come for Lundquist to worry about minute details associated with the operation. Confusion during the night about transportation restrictions nearly prevented the 2nd Battalion from replenishing its ammunition supply, but the trucks finally arrived with the necessary ordnance. Lundquist was concerned about the 608th getting into firing positions in time for the attack, however. By 0719 the first batteries had arrived at Oberau a kilometer south of Altenstadt. Rifle fire from a group of unknown German stragglers in a nearby forest had delayed the artillerymen's northward progress.[27]

The 608th brought with them a welcome capability that allowed Colonel Lundquist to see another dimension of the battlefield in real time: an artillery spotter plane. Even though the howitzer batteries had not yet pulled into their planned positions, Major Collier sent the spotter plane into the air at sunrise (0712) to survey the forest the two infantry battalions planned to clear.[28]

The plane's crew detected few German troops in the woods north of Rodenbach and Heegheim. Instead, they spotted German columns stretched out farther east moving slowly into the northern part of the Büdingen forest above Glauberg and Stockheim. The columns hailed from *SS-Oberführer* Goebel's battle group, which was still closing on the forest after a night of painfully slow progress. The six howitzers, which Goebel had ordered onto the hill overlooking Glauberg, had yet to occupy their positions and provide cover for the SS troops slowly assembling for a brief rest in the forest east of Selters and south of Ortenberg.

The report stunned Lundquist. The SS troops had obviously slipped past his men during the night and occupied an area several kilometers east of his battalions' planned objectives. Lundquist and Borden huddled and revised the plan. Instead of two battalions attacking due north into the forest, the 2nd

Battalion would attack northeast while the 3rd Battalion would proceed due east toward Glauberg. The battalions would remain on line, and Lundquist still planned to control their movement using phase lines. By the time Lundquist and Borden revised the plan, Major Collier's firing batteries were in position with four hundred rounds of ammunition.[29]

Lundquist radioed Collier and explained the changes to the plan. Collier stated that his batteries could not fire effectively on the enemy's positions from their current locations, so the artillerymen had to move farther north and then face east to support the attack. Lundquist postponed the attack to 1000. At 0759 he notified the infantry battalions of the change in plans. Messengers would deliver a new operations overlay within thirty minutes. By 0803 the 608th was already on the road and speeding north to firing positions between Heegheim and Glauberg.[30]

At 0830 Brig. Gen. Frank A. Henning, the division artillery commander, arrived at the 14th Regiment's forward command post and met with Lundquist. Lundquist explained what the artillery spotter plane had learned about the enemy's current location and the effect this updated information had on the original attack plan. Henning agreed with Lundquist's decision to postpone the attack and promised to inform Major General Wyman personally of the reasons for the delay. Henning departed at 0830.[31]

Ten minutes after Henning's departure, the liaison officer for Company C, 635th Tank Destroyer Battalion, arrived and reported that he had encountered someone from the 5th Infantry Division. Up to this point communications at the ground level between the 71st and 5th divisions had been poor despite an initial link-up and exchange of information in Heldenbergen. Both units abandoned the contact point soon thereafter, and no one from either division remained in the town to exchange plans or coordinate future operations. Lundquist had no idea what the 5th Division planned to do on his left flank that day.

The liaison officer described to Lundquist the 5th Division's planned operations for the coming day. The 3rd Battalion, 2nd Infantry, intended to attack from Staden to the rail line at Ranstadt and two infantry companies would cross through Stammheim. The 3rd Battalion's command post was located in Erbstadt. Lundquist promptly reported this information to the division command post.[32]

An hour before the attack, Brigadier General Henning called and offered Lundquist two more tanks and two assault guns for the coming attack. Lundquist accepted the additional firepower and immediately assigned the vehicles to Lieutenant Colonel Brant's 2nd Battalion. Henning also told Lundquist that Captain Johnson's 71st Cavalry Reconnaissance Troop headquarters had already departed for the 14th Infantry's command post and would operate from there for the regiment's coming attack. Major General Wyman had attached the troop to the 14th the day before to provide flank security and establish blocking positions in and around Stockheim and Selters to support the regiment's attack. The reconnaissance platoons were already on their way to those locations. By locating his troop headquarters with Lundquist's command post, Johnson could provide immediate spot reports of enemy activity that might threaten the operation.[33]

After some last-minute preparations, Lundquist departed at 0945 for the 3rd Battalion. He believed the 3rd Battalion's attack across the open ground toward Glauberg would prove decisive in the coming operation, so he planned to lead the attack from that vantage point. All was ready. The artillery was in place, and the battalions sat like coiled springs at their lines of departure. The time had come to strike.

❖

Colonel Lundquist's report concerning the 5th Division's planned actions prompted Major General Wyman to call Major General Irwin and work out better communications between both divisions. Wyman asked Irwin how things were moving for the 5th Division. Irwin replied that his task force had made little contact so far. He then asked Wyman if both divisions could improve on exchanging information—even though they had linked up at least once at Heldenbergen. Irwin said that his artillery spotter planes had located German troops near Glauberg but were afraid to send fire missions since no one from the 71st was available to give them clearance. The 5th Division artillerymen did not want to fire unless they knew for certain that they were shooting at enemy troops.[34]

Puzzled, Wyman proclaimed that he thought both sides had exchanged liaison officers, but Irwin said he could not reach his liaison folks at Heldenbergen. Wyman told him that if they could get liaison officers back at the contact point, both divisions could coordinate their efforts better. Irwin agreed. Wyman promised to send his assistant division commander, Brigadier General Rolfe, back to Heldenbergen to ensure that liaison occurred. Irwin promised to send someone there as well. Both commanding generals ended their call after exchanging situation reports. Close coordination between the two divisions was essential to ensuring that the Nord Division did not slip through any gaps in their common boundary.[35]

❖

The attack on the 2nd Squadron, 2nd Cavalry's rear echelon at Waldensberg reverberated rapidly throughout the 2nd Cavalry Group. An alarmed Col. Charles H. Reed, the group commander, immediately dispatched the group's security platoon to the 2nd Squadron's headquarters at Wittgenborn. As soon as the platoon arrived, Major Wyles gathered his troops from their roadblock position outside Wittgenborn and, with two light tanks in the lead (presumably M24 Chaffee light tanks sporting 75-mm main guns), advanced toward Waldensberg to relieve the besieged forward-echelon troops. The surviving SS troops that Wyles and his men blocked from advancing farther south had already melted back into the forest. Although slightly wounded earlier that morning, Wyles remained at the head of the relief column.[36]

The 42nd Squadron, operating between Bad Orb and Bad Soden, immediately sent forces to assist their beleaguered brethren at Waldensberg. The 42nd's rear echelon dispatched a relief column comprising a few light tanks and several trucks mounted with all available troops the support units could muster. Lieutenant Kraatz of the 42nd organized a light tank platoon and several cavalrymen from the squadron's headquarters company and sped off toward Waldensberg.

Both columns arrived on the eastern edge of the town at around 0900—just as Lieutenant Colonel Eikel's Task Force X dealt a final blow to the German roadblock on the Wittgenborn–Waldensberg road. The rear echelon's column entered eastern Waldensberg unmolested after traversing nearly three kilometers of open, rolling terrain. Although the Nord men had seized the town, they had not yet finished clearing it of all remaining cavalrymen. A few GIs, notably from the 2nd Squadron's S-4 section, remained hunkered down in the cellar of a house in the heart of Waldensberg.

As the cavalrymen of both columns converged on the town from the east, they could still hear sporadic firing within the settlement. But the SS troops soon spotted the new threat emerging on their eastern flank and opened fire as the first light tanks entered the side streets. The GIs dismounted the accompanying trucks and scattered, returning fire as they moved from house to house.

Sergeant Peterson from the 42nd's rear echelon attacked like a man possessed, racing from house to house, firing from the hip. His actions accounted for fifteen dead SS men. He even captured eighteen Germans in one house after surprising them by bursting through a side door. But German counterattacks compelled Peterson and his fellow cavalry troopers to relinquish their prisoners and abandon the house for the safety of woods nearby.

The GIs from the S-4 section hiding in a nearby cellar listened as the sounds of battle increased substantially. The cavalrymen had no idea what was happening outside, but the sound of tanks boosted their morale. Their fellow cavalrymen had finally come to rescue them. The sound of a tank pulling up beside their house gave the men pause. They listened with bated breath, hoping to hear the sounds of fellow GIs telling them the worst was over . . . but no such words came.[37]

The light tank that had pulled up outside the house hailed from Lieutenant Kraatz's relief column. The tanks had managed to work their way into the town's center, drawing intense rifle and machine-gun fire from the German defenders. Technician 5th grade William A. Stehley stood on the tank's rear deck, reaching over the turret and firing the .30-caliber machine gun mounted on top. Stehley continued to fire despite the numerous grenade and mortar explosions impacting near the tanks. Out of the corner of his eye, Stehley saw a *panzerfaust* warhead streak through the air and slam into the tank's side. The resulting blast knocked Stehley from the tank, painfully wounding him in the neck and killing two crewmen.

Although severely injured, Stehley grabbed a rifle and continued to fight. But after killing or wounding several other German soldiers, Stehley and the remaining tanks withdrew to the eastern edge of town. Lieutenant Kraatz was wounded, and the GIs recognized that they simply lacked the firepower to take back Waldensberg. Unfortunately, none of the cavalrymen realized that an entire U.S. infantry task force was maneuvering to attack the town from the south.[38]

Task Force X quickly gained the road leading from Waldensberg to Wittgenborn and turned north. Lieutenant Colonel Eikel chose to proceed cautiously since the two SS men captured at the roadblock had reported that the defenders of Waldensberg had Tiger tanks at their disposal—an erroneous assertion but one that Eikel could neither prove nor disprove. Companies E and F advanced along both sides of the road, moving slowly through the forest as the Sherman tanks, led by a jeep carrying several GIs, edged forward cautiously on the road between. The ground sloped gently upward as the tanks and GIs closed on Waldensberg.

A single shot suddenly rang out, forcing the dismounted GIs to ground. Then a German MG42 opened fire. The jeep rolled to a stop as the occupants slumped over dead in their seats. The tank turrets quickly swiveled left and right, seeking targets in the darkened woods. Cautiously, the surrounding GIs rose to their feet and continued forward. A quick burst of German machine-gun fire forced the GIs to ground again, dogging their advance. This pattern resumed for the next several hundred meters, reducing the GIs' progress to a crawl.[39]

Farther back in the column, Eikel sat in his jeep with his driver and radio operator, Pfc. John H. Wagner Jr. A clearly agitated messenger from one of the lead companies ran up to Eikel's jeep and blurted, "Our convoy has been ambushed by some SS troops on the hill this side of the town. The Krauts are flopping around the forest on the hill beside the road!" Eikel, in his usually calm manner, simply replied, "Well, we'll just 'flop' them right out of there."

Eikel instructed his jeep driver to move to the front of the column. Wagner noted his commander's calm manner while remembering that certain things Eikel had said in the past suggested he was eager for a taste of some close combat.[40]

Eikel's jeep soon arrived at the ambush site, but the two lead companies had already pushed ahead. Eikel and Wagner could see SS troops in the distance surrendering to his men as the Sherman tanks crept up the hard-surface road. The bullet-riddled jeep and its dead occupants still sat near the middle of the thoroughfare. Eikel and Wagner dismounted and approached the jeep. Both men winced at the sight of the blood-spattered bodies with their exposed intestines.[41]

Wagner soon heard a call from the two lead company commanders on the SCR-300 radio. Captain MacArthur and Capt. John L. Sullivan, the commanders of Companies E and F, respectively, reported to a now-frustrated Eikel the increasing sniper activity that was impeding the battalion's advance. Eikel also learned that small groups of Germans delayed the two lead companies by firing and then withdrawing, forcing the GIs to give chase. Eikel told both captains to move forward as quickly as possible.

Eikel and his staff soon learned what had transpired at Waldensberg from an eyewitness. A radio operator from the 2nd Squadron's rear echelon, T/4 Chester Harmon, had escaped the town soon after his radio failed. After dodging German bullets while running across the open fields west of Waldensberg, Harmon bumped into some GIs from Task Force X. These GIs now brought Harmon to Eikel's jeep.

An out-of-breath Harmon quickly related the events that had transpired in Waldensberg earlier that morning. He explained that the Germans occupied the town in strength and that several cavalrymen remained hidden in some cellars. Harmon offered to lead the task force into Waldensberg. Eikel now had a better picture of the German forces in the town and their capabilities. Tiger tanks were no longer a concern. He agreed to Harmon's offer and sent the radio operator, now armed with an M1 rifle, forward to the lead infantry companies as a guide.[42]

By 1030 Companies E and F climbed a slight rise and spied the southern edge of Waldensberg from the forest's edge. Lieutenant Colonel Eikel came forward and surveyed the scene with his company commanders. Capt. Fred J. Kratz, Company G, and Captain Charleton, Company H, were there as well. The officers scanned the town with binoculars in search of the SS men's defenses. The town, situated in the open on a slight rise and nearly a kilometer from the forest in all directions, appeared easily defensible. A steady concentration of German machine-gun fire spewed forth from a small patch of woods on a slight rise west of town. The tracer rounds probed the woods for American troops. Eikel did not like what he saw. The attacking GIs would clearly lack the advantage—especially since the task force did not have artillery support at that moment.

Eikel quickly developed a scheme of maneuver for the attack. The numerous snipers and delaying forces employed by the Germans up to this point meant that Task Force X lacked the element of surprise. Eikel believed that a rapid, aggressive assault on the town would bring success. He directed Captain MacArthur to attack frontally with Company E while Company F maneuvered to the left flank and attacked the small patch of woods to the west. The tanks and Company H's 81-mm mortars would support the two companies with main-gun and indirect fire from the forest's edge. The commanders quickly agreed on several other details and departed to issue orders.[43]

At 1100 Company E's GIs rushed from the forest and onto the open ground south of Waldensberg with 2/Lt. John Tripp's Third Platoon in the lead. A mortar section from Lt. Roy J. Long's mortar platoon (part of

Company H) supported the attacking troops with a barrage of 81-mm mortar rounds. The rounds impacted on the edge of town, erupting on rooftops and sending orange tiles scattering through the air. Company C's Sherman tanks barked as main-gun rounds streaked across the open fields beside Company E's GIs and slammed into numerous buildings, setting alight several houses. The burning homes disgorged columns of black smoke, helping to conceal the vulnerable Red Circle men as they rushed across the open, rolling terrain.[44]

The Germans opened fire as the GIs approached the outskirts of town. Second Lieutenant Tripp directed his men to the right side of the main road. The GIs thundered down the street and entered the houses, firing as they moved. Tripp and his men passed a damaged M8 armored car and saw an unknown American captain lying on the ground beside it. The man was obviously dying, but the GIs were too preoccupied to call for a medic. A Nord man popped up from behind some nearby bushes only be cut down by a BAR-toting GI.

The Sherman tanks advanced with the GIs, firing into the houses and other buildings as the Red Circle men sprinted down the cobblestone streets and ducked into doorways. Tripp looked up at one tank to see a pair of hands rising up from the turret and pressing down the butterfly trigger of the vehicle's .50-caliber machine gun.[45]

The GIs kicked open doors and entered houses with rifles blazing. The Red Circle men tossed hand grenades through windows and doorways. The muffled explosions sent shards of glass and wood spraying into the streets. Nord men appeared from the houses with hands held high. Tripp's men waved them back down the road to the southern part of town.

The GIs discovered a Nord man changing into civilian clothes in the attic of a house. The Red Circle men dragged the man downstairs and out into the street. Angered by the SS man's subterfuge, Tripp forced the prisoner back to the rear down the main street while bullets flew in all directions. Civilians who had hunkered down inside their homes appeared and pointed out the hiding places of other German soldiers. The GIs quickly rooted them out.[46]

Chaos engulfed the town once more that day as fierce house-to-house fighting ensued. The tanks sprayed the building walls with coaxial machine-gun fire, sending plaster and brick shards spiraling into the air. The Germans fired frantically from windows and doorways but soon gave ground, abandoning the houses and running down side streets to find alternative fighting positions.[47]

The civilians hiding inside the town quickly realized that remaining in Waldensberg was pointless. The group, hiding inside the local pub, rushed outside and headed west for the low ground and culverts that surrounded the town. *Bürgermeister* Schmidt led the way. The group of townspeople—several elderly folks, women, children, and two babies—ran a gauntlet of rifle and machine-gun fire to get to the low ground. The civilians slid down into the trench-like culverts on the town's periphery only to find them occupied by Heer and Luftwaffe soldiers—the former prisoners released by the Nord men that morning and drafted to fight once more. These soldiers had no desire to participate in the battle. A withdrawing SS man ran by the group but paid those soldiers scant heed. Schmidt called to the man and begged him not to destroy the village. The Nord man looked over his shoulder and shouted derisively, "Your mud huts! We lost women and children, and you hoist the white flag!"[48]

Lieutenant Long advanced with his mortar jeeps behind Company E. Other Company H jeeps loaded with the heavy machine-gun platoons followed. Long dismounted his mortars at the edge of town and launched mortar rounds into the streets and among the buildings held by the German defenders, wounding or killing several of them.[49]

As Long worked, sniper fire suddenly erupted from one of the first buildings on the left near the southern edge of town. Long and his mortar troops scrambled for cover as the heavy machine gunners scanned the upper windows and rooftops for the invisible sharpshooter. The sniper fired again, wounding a nearby GI, but this time a machine gunner had spotted the SS man in an attic. The German would raise a tile shingle, fire, and then drop the shingle back into place. The machine gunner swung his .30-caliber weapon toward the roof and opened fire. The rounds shattered the tile shingles, scattering them into the air and onto the street below. The machine gunner paused and waited for a response from the sniper. Nothing happened. The sniper was finished.[50]

Several Germans concealed in the forest southeast of town began firing on Company E from across the open fields. The German MG42 rounds peppered the buildings on the town's outer edge, forcing the GIs to take cover and return fire. Although inaccurate, the German fire hampered the GIs' advance into the northern part of town. Fearing a German counterattack from these woods, Captain MacArthur sent his 2nd Platoon to eliminate the threat. The 1st and 2nd Squads sped down a side street for the open fields as the 3rd Squad provided covering fire from the town's edge. A sniper dogged the GIs' movement, but could not score a hit.

As they reached the edge of town and swung southeast toward the open fields, an MG42 opened fire from the woods. The GIs dove into the plow furrows for cover. A steady stream of German machine-gun fire swung back and forth over their heads. Several GIs screamed for medics. Staff Sergeant Ogden, the 2nd Squad Leader, knew his men were in trouble. Each time a Red Circle man raised up to fire, he gave away his position and drew another burst from the MG42. Finally, Sergeant Howard sprang to his feet and raced back into town. Minutes later he returned with Company C's three tanks. The tankers saturated the forest with machine-gun and tank fire. The surviving Nord men either fled or surrendered. As the tanks lumbered forward into the woods and overran the German defenses, the 2nd Platoon's GIs got to their feet and moved back into town. Ogden felt fortunate that he and all of his men had survived the ordeal.[51]

Lieutenant Colonel Eikel arrived in his jeep at the southern entrance to Waldensberg and dismounted. Private First Class Wagner hopped down from the jeep and slung the heavy SCR-300 radio onto his back. Eikel set off on foot with Wagner in tow, the radio's antenna swaying conspicuously from the radio operator's back. The sounds of combat echoed loudly inside the town as Eikel walked calmly forward, watching as his infantrymen rushed from house to house. Bodies of dead American and German soldiers littered the streets.

Both men passed the roadside culvert where *Bürgermeister* Schmidt and his group of twenty-five to thirty civilians huddled for safety. Eikel and Wagner could not help but feel pity at the sight of these elderly folks, women, children, and two babies shuddering in fear at the deafening sounds of combat.

Eikel quickened his pace and soon was behind the leading infantry troops as they tossed grenades into houses and kicked open doors. Eikel loudly encouraged the GIs to press on, exposing himself to the dangers shared by his troops. His calm, professorial demeanor belied an aggressive, courageous spirit that inspired his men.

But Eikel and Wagner proved tempting targets for a German machine gunner farther inside the town. The SS man opened fire, sending a stream of bullets whizzing above Eikel's head and splattering against the buildings behind him and Wagner. Both men took cover behind the burned-out hulk of an American tank. Wagner ran awkwardly under the uneven weight of his backpack radio. The long, swinging antenna made him easy to spot.[52]

Explosions sounded nearby and the houses next to the burned-out tank burst into flames. In the confusion Wagner became separated from Eikel. He pressed himself flat against the street to avoid the hundreds of machine-gun rounds that crisscrossed the main road. During a lull in the firing Wagner rose up, sprinted across the road, and tucked himself between two houses, only to discover that Eikel had taken cover in the same spot.[53]

Eikel remained with Wagner between the two houses until the fighting moved off to the north. An elderly man and woman soon appeared from one of the two houses and tried to communicate with Eikel. Despite the language barrier, the man and woman managed to explain that the SS troops had taken to shooting some of their own soldiers for refusing to fight the Americans. Eikel thanked them and told the two civilians to seek cover from the fighting.[54]

On the left flank Captain Sullivan's Company F attacked from the forest and moved on the small, forested patch on a small rise west of town. As they attacked, several SS men suddenly opened fire from a fence line along a row of houses at the town's western edge. Company F's GIs took cover and returned fire. Sgt. Melvin Denslow, the company communications sergeant, fell in the opening hail of bullets. Severely wounded and trapped in the open, Denslow moaned loudly for help.

Sullivan spied two Sherman tanks sitting on the southern edge of the main road ready to move into the center of town. He ran across the open field and hailed one of the tank commanders from the 761st Tank Battalion. Sullivan directed the crew to fire some main-gun rounds into the line of houses along the fence line.

"Heavy stuff?" asked the tank commander.

"Yes," replied Sullivan.

Within minutes, the two tanks pounded the exteriors of several buildings with main tank rounds. Rubble rained down on the Nord men firing from the fence line. The SS troops quickly withdrew toward the center of town.

Sullivan then asked the tank commander to put his tank between the wounded Denslow and the fence line in case any more Germans were hiding there. The tank commander rolled the Sherman tank onto the open field, shielding the injured GI from further harm.

Sullivan and the company medics rushed up to Denslow and began administering aid. The medics lacked a litter, so Sullivan and one of the medics ripped a door off a nearby tool shed. The medics gently laid Denslow on the door and lifted him off the ground. Sullivan held his hand as the faithful, hard-working sergeant, his face deathly white, said softly, "I'm sorry, Captain." Denslow later died of his wounds.[55]

Sullivan rejoined his company, and the GIs pressed on toward their primary objective, the forested patch of woods in the middle of the open field west of

Waldensberg. As the GIs approached, the Germans concealed in the wooded patch opened fire, but a steady rain of 81-mm mortar rounds forced the Nord men to seek cover.

Sullivan's men soon gained the forest and assaulted the SS troops' dug-in positions. The Red Circle men tossed grenades and rooted out the German defenders one by one. The fighting proved fierce and intense. Lieutenant Tarbell fell, severely wounded, as did several other Company F GIs. The battle quickly ended and Company F held the hill.[56]

Back in town Captain Kratz's Company G followed in reserve behind Company E. As the GIs approached some smoldering ruins at the town's edge, the evidence of a pitched battle became obvious. Company G's troops witnessed Company E's GIs advancing from house to house up the main street. Pfc. Thomas Tomich, a Company G radio operator, knew the fighting was fierce when he saw a bullet-riddled M8 armored car by the side of the road. As Tomich inspected the ruined scout car, he saw a medic running forward up the street to help some injured GIs. As he ran, the medic tripped on some communications wire strewn across the road just as an SS man opened fire with an MP40 from a nearby window. The submachine gun's burst barely missed the lucky medic.

Kratz's men began mopping up the outer edges of the town and relieving Company E's troops from guarding several SS prisoners taken in the fighting. First Lieutenant John Pfeiffer, the 3rd Platoon Leader, led his men in searching the captured SS troops. Pfeiffer enjoyed studying the legal aspects of combat and often expounded to his men on the Articles of War. Therefore, he set about searching the SS prisoners by the book. The few sullen prisoners remained defiant and uncooperative. An aggravated Pfeiffer quickly dispelled with any courtesy. He drew his trench knife and cut open the tunic pockets of several astonished SS men. Their personal papers and belongings soon littered the rubble-strewn street. The other prisoners quickly emptied their pockets with little prompting.[57]

On the outskirts of Waldensberg, *Bürgermeister* Schmidt and his group of twenty-five to thirty civilians huddling in the culvert west of town saw an opportunity to make a break for the forest. The civilians struggled to their feet but instantly came under rifle fire. An elderly woman, Elizabeth Nagel, fell dead; her husband had been shot through the arm. Despite the rifle fire, Schmidt managed to get the group of several elderly folks, women, and children to the forest's edge in the direction of Rinderbügen. Three Dutch men joined the group. They had previously been forced laborers who were making their way home to The Netherlands. The men had unfortunately chosen Waldensberg as a rest stop in their travels.

The group pressed on until reaching the tunnel of an old mine, seeking refuge inside. But soon, the two babies, hungry and tired, began crying loudly. The three Dutch men volunteered to return to Waldensberg for milk. They soon departed, but Schmidt and the townspeople never saw them again. Schmidt then led the group to a hay-filled hunting lodge deeper in the Büdingen forest. The solid roof overhead and the dry hay kept the people warm. Here they could wait until the war passed them by—once more.[58]

On the northern edge of Waldensberg, *SS-Standartenführer* Raithel recognized the futility of trying to hold Waldensberg from such an aggressive American assault. He began sending selected vehicles back to Leisenwald so the Americans would not destroy or capture them. Among those vehicles were two large American fuel trucks captured from the 2nd Squadron's rear echelon. Raithel also sent the newly liberated German prisoners—released from American custody by the Nord men during the fighting—back toward Leisenwald on foot under escort by several of his Waffen-SS soldiers. Although the former prisoners numbered nearly five hundred, Raithel could see that these unarmed and dispirited Heer soldiers would not prove useful to the division. They seemed deeply perturbed at having been thrust back into combat, preferring instead the safety of an American POW cage well behind the front lines.[59]

Raithel intended to hold Waldensberg as long as possible—buying time for *SS-Gruppenführer* Brenner to find another way out of the area, but his SS troops were running low on ammunition. Without artillery or air support, the Germans could not dominate their adversaries. The incessant American mortar barrages and tank attacks had resulted in several dead and wounded SS men. In addition, fighting in an urban setting expended an enormous amount of resources that the SS troops lacked. Raithel might have to abandon the town in order to save his men to fight another day. But perhaps this battle would be—and should be—the last engagement fought between the SS men and their American antagonists.

In their basement hiding place, the cavalrymen from the 2nd Squadron's S-4 section listened to the battle raging outside and prayed. The first tank they heard outside met a terrible fate from a German *panzerfaust*, but then the sound of more tanks approaching met their delighted ears. At the same moment they heard the tanks, the building suddenly rocked with explosion after explosion. Dust and plaster rained from the ceiling and blanketed the frightened GIs. Within seconds, the sounds of battle ceased. The men heard a voice outside say, "Give me a grenade. There's somebody in the cellar."

The American voice was like the sound of an angel from heaven to the cavalrymen. One of the GIs hiding in the cellar, T/5 Henry A. Harrison, thrust open the door and shouted, "Hold it, fellows! We're GIs!" The Red Circle men entered and, following an emotional moment shared by all, the cavalry troops offered their services to the Red Circle men. The GIs promptly armed their new comrades and together they continued to clear the town of German soldiers.[60]

As the men of Companies E, F, and G—and the accompanying cavalry troops—advanced through Waldensberg, the scope and nature of the calamity that had occurred there became apparent. Scores of dead GIs and Germans littered the streets. Many houses were reduced to rubble. Several buildings continued to burn, obscuring the streets with thick, black smoke. As the GIs cleared each house, they discovered dead American soldiers still inside their sleeping bags. In one case, they found several dead GIs with their hands bound behind their backs. Did their captors murder them? Or were they simply caught in the cross fire of the ensuing battle? These horrific scenes sickened the Red Circle men and strengthened their resolve to fight through the town.[61]

By 1200 Company E had reached the northern outskirts of Waldensberg. During their advance, the Red Circle men encountered the remains of the two relief columns sent by the 42nd Squadron. The third column, led by Major Wyles of the 2nd Squadron, already arrived from Wittgenborn and linked up with the main body of Task Force X south of Waldensberg. The 42nd's cavalrymen had managed to hold out until the Red Circle men arrived, and both forces joined the battle to wrest the town from the 6th SS-Gebirgs Division. The cavalrymen's light tanks were a welcome addition to the battle, and Company E progressed more rapidly thanks to this added firepower. But the Nord men gave ground slowly, preferring to fight to the end instead of surrendering. The Red Circle men had managed to take only nineteen prisoners to this point.[62] Captain MacArthur radioed Lieutenant Colonel Eikel at 1200 and reported that the town was almost in American hands. Eikel, the balding, congenial former college professor from New Orleans, appeared greatly pleased with his men's gallant efforts that morning.

❖

As the battle for Waldensberg intensified, Major General Wyman met with Lieutenant Colonel Lankenau in the division command post to discuss the continuing employment of the division against the 6th SS-Gebirgs Division Nord. Wyman had just received a report that the 2nd Cavalry Group, along with a few elements of the 66th Infantry Regiment (presumably the regimental I&R Platoon), had just liberated 6,533 Allied prisoners from a German POW camp in Bad Orb. At least 3,328 of the liberated prisoners were Americans. Several tank-destroyer men of Company A, 635th Tank Destroyer Battalion (directly supporting the 66th Infantry Regiment), were present at the camp's liberation.[63]

Wyman told his G-3 that the camp's liberation east of the division's zone suggested that everything was moving eastward. He wanted to bring the 5th Infantry Regiment forward quickly so he could commit all his forces in unison. The 5th Infantry Regiment's liaison officer, 1/Lt. Lewington S. Ponder, reported that by 1025 the 1st Battalion was moving by foot and the 2nd Battalion by motor to Ravolzhausen to clear the wooded areas to the northwest as previously instructed. The 3rd Battalion, the regimental reserve, was foot marching to a forward assembly area at Langendiebach. The regimental command post, Headquarters Company, Cannon Company, and Antitank Company remained back at Rückingen.[64]

Wyman told Lankenau to contact Colonel Wooten and instruct him that when the 2nd Battalion reached Ravolzhausen the trucks were to go back for the 3rd Battalion. Major Heymont, the regimental S-3, set the plan into motion.[65]

In the meantime, both the 1st and 2nd battalions had arrived at Ravolzhausen. After a brief respite both battalions deployed into the woods abreast and began clearing the thick, evergreen forest to the northwest. By 1045 both battalions had encroached on the 14th Infantry's area of operations, prompting a call from the 14th's regimental executive officer, Lt. Col. Bryan S. Halter, to the G-3. Halter reported that the 5th Infantry's two battalions had suddenly appeared in the 14th's rear area, but Lankenau told him the two battalions would be there for only a short time and would move quickly into their own zone.[66]

But by 1100 the two battalions had slowed their movement to a crawl. Colonel Johnston, the chief of staff, directed Lankenau to tell Wooten that the two battalions should not move through the woods in deployed formation. Instead, the two battalions should remain close together behind the I&R Platoon. When the I&R Platoon contacted enemy troops, both battalions could deploy into wider formations. Since both battalions traveled on foot, speed was essential if the 5th Infantry Regiment planned to come on line with the 14th and 66th regiments on their left and right boundaries, respectively. Major General Wyman further directed that the Division Artillery send up another spotter plane (in addition to the one circling above the 14th Regiment's zone of operations) to provide Wooten's battalions with early warning of enemy troops to their front.[67]

At 1129 XII Corps forwarded an intelligence report to Wyman that captured his immediate attention. An unnamed ordnance officer had identified two dismounted German regiments moving ahead of Kefenrod while another unnamed soldier had bumped into a hornet's nest of German troops in the town of Büches. The report convinced the corps' staff that the enemy moving in strength between Büdingen and Kefenrod further threatened the corps' MSR and other rear-area troops.[68]

Reports of the Nord men's dispositions did not reflect their precise locations, however. *SS-Standartenführer* Raithel's motorized column had already passed through Büches during the night. If any German troops remained in the town, then they represented stragglers who had dropped off from the column. *SS-Oberführer* Goebel's horse-drawn column remained concentrated near Bleichenbach just south of Ortenberg and clearly did not figure in to the corps report. The report about Kefenrod was more accurate since the concentration of Raithel's troops, along with the division headquarters, occupied Leisenwald only three kilometers farther south. In both instances the report was dated and did not accurately reflect the Nord Division's true disposition at 1200 on 2 April. In fact, the tail end of Raithel's column remained in the forest near Michelau and Wolferborn due to the delay caused by the fighting in Waldensberg earlier that morning.

Unaware of the report's inaccuracies, Lankenau passed the information to Colonel Wooten since the enemy's reported locations would affect the 5th Infantry Regiment's current sweeping operation. Lankenau initially directed the 1st and 2nd battalions to a newly developed phase line (Phase Line One) stretching from Büdingen down to Vonhausen. At the time both battalions were moving abreast through the woods in a northwesterly direction behind the 14th Regiment's area of operations. But the report that the enemy's column stretched from Büches through Büdingen and up through Kefenrod meant that the 5th Infantry should shift northeast. After receiving the G-3's instructions, Wooten ordered his two battalions to the new phase line. He ended his message to both battalion commanders with these words: "All possible speed essential."[69]

Lankenau briefly discussed the XII Corps report with Major General Wyman, who decided that the 5th Regiment should seize Büches and Büdingen directly instead of continuing with the sweeping operation. Lankenau contacted the 5th Infantry Regiment and issued new orders. Major Robertson's motorized 3rd Battalion would move immediately to seize Büches while the other two battalions would shift northeast and head for Büdingen. Lankenau's instructions for taking Büdingen were unambiguous: "Clear it out." He further directed the 5th Infantry to contact the 14th Infantry at Rohrbach to ensure the regiment's left flank remained secure. Lankenau spoke directly with Colonel Wooten at 1230 and confirmed the change in plans. Wooten had already countermanded the previous orders. He placed his 1st Battalion in reserve and instructed the 3rd and 2nd battalions to seize Büches and Büdingen, respectively. The time had come to begin pushing against the 6th SS-Gebirgs Division—not just from the flanks, but also from the center.[70]

❖

The 14th Infantry Regiment's two infantry battalions finished making preparations to attack the forest north of Rodenbach and the hill above Glauberg (Hill 267) at 1000 (see Map 7.1). An artillery spotter plane's report confirming the Nord men's new locations prompted Colonel Lundquist to change his attack plan and time to allow the 3rd Battalion to face east toward Glauberg and afford the 608th Field Artillery Battalion time to move into better firing positions.[71] Just before H-Hour at 1000, the men of both infantry battalions had adjusted their attack positions, and the last firing batteries from the 608th finished moving into positions above Rodenbach and Heegheim.

The commander of Battery B, Capt. Stanley Jagoda, had just finished designating firing positions for his gun section chiefs at 0900 when the big, crew-cut-sporting battery commander departed for the 608th's headquarters for a last-minute update. The battery executive officer, 1/Lt. Douglas Kinnard, supervised the positioning of the guns in an open field north of Heegheim.

THE SECOND DAY: WALDENSBERG, 2 APRIL 1945   207

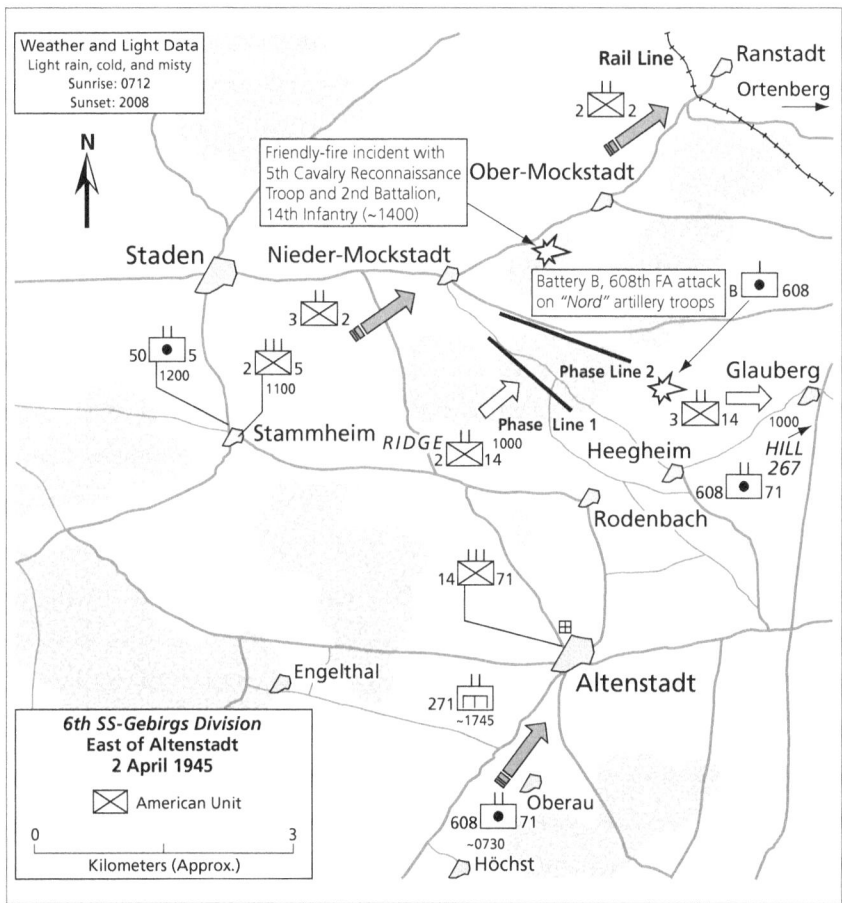

Map 7.1. 6th SS-Gebirgs Division east of Altenstadt, 2 April 1945.

Kinnard, a Paterson, New Jersey, native, had graduated from West Point less than a year earlier as a member of the D-Day class of 6 June 1944.[72] Kinnard assembled the section chiefs and stressed the importance of providing good security. The fluid nature of the current situation suggested that the enemy might attack from any direction, so Kinnard urged his men to remain vigilant. As soon as Kinnard finished speaking, one of the gun section chiefs, Sgt. George Orseske, pointed to the left beyond the howitzers and exclaimed, "What the hell is that?"

Kinnard and the section chiefs lifted their binoculars and scanned the horizon. What they saw startled them. A slow-moving column of German horse-drawn artillery pieces crested the hill to their left front. The column was no more than 150 meters distant. Unknown to the Red Circle artillerymen, they were witnessing the final remnants of the 6th SS-Gebirgs Division's artillery guns, an amalgam of three depleted batteries led by *SS-Sturmscharführer* Plösch, moving toward positions on Hill 267 east and southeast of Glauberg. *SS-Oberführer* Goebel had ordered Plösch to position his six remaining guns on the hill to provide cover for the rest of his horse-drawn battle group, which was assembling in the woods east of Selters and south of Ortenberg before moving east.

Kinnard immediately decided to fire on the SS artillerymen to prevent them from escaping. He ordered Sgt. Joe Gliessner onto a small knoll nearby to act as observer while the other section chiefs rushed to their guns and alerted the crews. Kinnard wanted to fire his howitzers in unison to maximize the element of surprise he held over the Nord men, who had yet to spot Battery B.[73]

Kinnard turned to his radio operator and said, "Tell battalion what we are doing, but I can't talk to them now." The radio operator promptly radioed Major Collier's command post.[74]

The gun section chiefs reported that the howitzers were ready. Kinnard barked, "Fire!"

The Red Circle men launched four volleys at the exposed SS troops before the Nord men realized what was happening. The rounds impacted in and around the moving column, scattering the SS men. Cascades of dirt and mud sprayed upward in all directions. One of the German artillerymen, *SS-Rottenführer* Karl Müller, instinctively ran for cover with his fellow Nord men. Plösch shouted above the din for his men to head for the hill. Despite the confusion the six 105-mm light field howitzers remained hitched to the wildly galloping horses. Some of the men chased after their frightened horses, but other Nord men ran back to the forest north of Rodenbach for cover from the murderous volleys.[75]

The SS troops soon moved out of sight, dropping below the contours of the open fields and hastening toward Hill 267. Wounded or dying German soldiers and horses lay scattered on the muddy road in front of Battery B, but all six artillery pieces managed to survive the direct-fire American artillery. After many painstaking minutes, the distressed and bedraggled SS artillery troops, with howitzers intact, gained the heights of Hill 267 out of Battery B's view and range. The surviving Nord men paused and regained their composure before positioning their guns on the hill as ordered. They knew another American attack would be forthcoming.

Kinnard praised his men for their rapid action and, after establishing wire communications with the 608th's command post, described in detail to the S-3 what had happened. Kinnard explained that the situation was one of "kill or be killed."[76]

❖

When Colonel Lundquist heard from Major Collier about Battery B's clash with the SS artillerymen, he knew he had to attack on time at 1000 if the 14th Infantry expected to destroy the Nord men and not simply chase them through the neighboring countryside. Lundquist arrived at Lieutenant Colonel Guthrie's command post as the rest of the 3rd Battalion lined up to attack Hill 267 from a position northwest of Glauberg. Lundquist intended to remain with Guthrie's battalion since he believed the SS troops had concentrated somewhere near Glauberg and Stockheim.

On the 3rd Battalion's left flank, Lieutenant Colonel Brant readied his 2nd Battalion to attack into the forest north of Rodenbach. Brant planned to attack with Captain Goldman's Company E on the left and Captain Bass's Company G on the right. Both companies would advance northeast, clear the wooded area up to Stockheim, and close with the 3rd Battalion on the right. Captain Alvey's Company F would follow in reserve. Brant planned to control the movement using phase lines. The first phase line sat along the Nieder-Mockstadt and Heegheim road while the second phase line ran along the Nieder-Mockstadt and Stockheim road. Both companies' immediate objectives lay just beyond Phase Line Two and due east of Nieder-Mockstadt. Company F's first objective sat along the very center of Phase Line Two.[77]

A few minutes before the attack began, Brant was surprised to see Lt. Col. Robert E. Connor, the commander of the 5th Infantry Division's 3rd Battalion, 2nd Infantry, pull up in a jeep. Connor had been eager to coordinate with the unit on his right—in this case Brant's battalion. The two battalion commanders exchanged information about each other's planned operations for the day. Connor then sped away in his jeep to report to Colonel Roffe, the 2nd Regiment's commander.[78]

At 1000 Brant's 2nd Battalion moved into the woods north of Rodenbach. The cool, damp conditions made movement easier for the GIs. The wet leaves under their feet deadened the sounds as they stepped on branches so the Red Circle men could move in relative silence through the forest.

As Company G approached the first small hill before Phase Line One, the GIs detected movement in the underbrush. The Red Circle men halted and went to ground. A few GIs shouted toward several figures they observed cowering in the brush along the hill's crest. Seven German soldiers slowly emerged from the hilltop with hands held high. Captain Bass's men had taken the day's first bag of prisoners—stragglers who had likely broken off from SS-*Oberführer* Goebel's horse-drawn column.[79]

Up to this point things had been going smoothly for Brant and his men. The only problem arose when one of the 3rd Battalion's rifle companies, Company K, followed the wrong azimuth and moved across the 2nd Battalion's front along Phase Line One. Brant and Capt. Tommy L. Long, the Company K commander, quickly sorted out the mess in time for Long to turn his men around and cover the one kilometer east to Glauberg, where the 3rd Battalion prepared to assault Hill 267.[80]

Long's navigation error concerned Lieutenant Colonel Guthrie greatly since he was afraid Company K would not be able to attack on time with the rest of the battalion. Unlike the 2nd Battalion attack, the 3rd Battalion's advance would follow a twenty-minute artillery and mortar preparation on Hill 267 designed to soften up the German artillery positions. First Lieutenant Kinnard and his Battery B artillerymen had seen the SS artillerymen escape up the hill less than thirty minutes earlier, so Colonel Lundquist and Guthrie knew that taking the hill would not come without a fight. Fortunately, those twenty minutes allowed Long and his company to arrive in time to attack with the battalion. Unlike the 2nd Battalion, Guthrie's battalion only had two-thirds of its normal strength since 1/Lt. Caleb H. Paul's Company I and a machine-gun platoon from Company M remained back at Eberstadt guarding the corps' POW cage.[81]

Guthrie chose to attack Hill 267 from a small open area north of Glauberg along the Glauberg–Stockheim road. This location—approximately eight hundred meters of open, upward-sloping farmland—allowed Guthrie to employ his three M4 Sherman tanks more effectively with standoff range from the enemy's weapons systems. Unfortunately for the dismounted troops, they would have to traverse this open part of the hill before gaining the thickly wooded hilltop and, finally, some natural cover and concealment. This attack position also put the town of Glauberg on the battalion's right and Stockheim, in the distance, on the battalion's left.

Guthrie planned to attack with Captain Long's Company K on the left, 1/Lt. W. P. Sims's Company M in the middle, and Capt. Milo D. Krichbaum's

Company L on the right. Company K would attack through a large patch of young pine trees to the north while Company L, supported directly by the three tanks from Company B, 761st Tank Battalion, would attack straight up the hill. In addition, the 2nd Platoon, Company C, 635th Tank Destroyer Battalion, occupied firing positions more than a kilometer south of Hill 267 and west of Düdelsheim to support the attack.[82]

The companies moved into position under sparse concealment along the Glauberg–Stockheim road. Company E's GIs, on their way from the 2nd Battalion's zone, would soon gather near a large pile of neatly stacked firewood among a stand of trees west of the pine saplings on the battalion's left flank. First Lieutenant Sims located his Company M command post with his 3rd Platoon of 81-mm mortars, which the platoon leader, Lt. Willard E. Prekker, had placed in a small gravel pit west of the road. To the right of the mortars sat two 105-mm howitzers from the 608th Field Artillery Battalion. The three tanks moved forward and parked squarely in the middle of the open field east of the road. Company L's GIs lay in the open all around the Sherman tanks with rifles and BARs at the ready. Lt. Harry W. Thode's 2nd Platoon of .30-caliber machine guns from Company M were mixed with Company L. Pfc. Edward G. Rimple, an ammunition bearer in the mortar platoon's 1st Squad, watched from the gravel pit as Company's L's GIs huddled in the open field next to the tanks. Rimple believed the men were a bunch of sitting ducks.[83]

❖

On Hill 267, *SS-Sturmscharführer* Plösch scrambled to put his howitzers into position, but Battery B's direct-fire artillery attack less than an hour earlier had spooked the horses so severely that many of them had run off into the forest after the SS men unhitched them from the howitzers. Plösch knew an attack on his position was imminent, so he spread his troops out to provide all-around security in case the Americans attacked from several directions at once.

Despite the carnage his small artillery column had suffered north of Heegheim, Plösch's men still managed to transport several American prisoners. The SS men led the GIs to a quarry in the center of Hill 267 and spread a large sheet on the ground with a Red Cross in the center. Nearby sat a small wooden shack on which some SS men hastily painted a large Red Cross. They hoped that this mark would keep the artillery spotter planes from sending artillery fire onto the hill and killing American prisoners and German soldiers alike.[84]

At the forward edge of the hill, Plösch put his men into improvised firing positions everywhere. The SS men located several small root cellars on the hill—undoubtedly belonging to residents of nearby Glauberg—and converted the small dugouts into fighting positions. The gun section chiefs swung the howitzers into position and stacked as much ammunition nearby as possible. Plösch had perhaps fifty men at his disposal, but some troops had already abandoned the position and fled northeast. *SS-Rottenführer* Müller remained and took refuge behind a small pile of firewood. He hoped this cover would prove adequate in the coming fight.[85]

A few minutes after 1000, Hill 267 erupted as scores of American artillery and mortar rounds ripped apart the earth and forest. Trees fractured and split as the artillery rounds exploded above them, showering the ground with deadly white-hot shell fragments.[86]

The 3rd Battalion's men covered their ears and hunkered down as the artillery and mortars did their deadly work. A kilometer south and west of Düdelsheim, the antitank crews from the 2nd Platoon, Company C, 635th Tank Destroyer Battalion, detected movement on the hill. Sergeant Goodspeed observed four Nord men rapidly digging in on the back slope of the hill as American artillery shells impacted around them. Goodspeed's crew quickly fired two three-inch, high-explosive rounds, which exploded among the SS troops and threw their injured or dead bodies to the ground. Through his binoculars, Sergeant Linquist watched as several German medics braved the artillery barrage and carried away all four wounded men on litters. Goodspeed's next target was a horse-drawn wagon some Nord men were driving down the backside of Hill 267 to escape the barrage. Goodspeed estimated their distance at two kilometers from the gun position. The gun crew fired three high-explosive shells at the wagon as the SS troops gesticulated frantically at the four horses pulling the vehicle. The rounds hit their mark, splintering the wagon and killing the SS troops and all four horses.[87]

Back at the 3rd Battalion's attack position west of the hill, the preparatory barrage continued to pound away at Hill 267. Small clods of dirt suddenly spewed upward next to Company L's GIs. The Red Circle men, exposed among the three tanks in the open field, quickly searched for the source of the gunfire. One GI looked toward the town of Glauberg several hundred meters away. He saw a tiny flash appear from the small church spire rising up from the center of town and realized a German sniper was firing at them from the steeple. The GIs alerted the tank crew closest to the town. The turret swiveled to the right. The crew fired a main-gun round, missing the steeple. A second round struck the spire squarely, collapsing the structure in a cloud of dust. The GIs later learned that the sniper was a young German teenager who did not survive the steeple's collapse.[88]

At 1020 the artillery and mortar barrage ceased. An eerie silence swept the area as smoke and dust blanketed the summit of Hill 267. The Red Circle men rose to their feet and advanced up the hill. The tank engines roared to life. The Shermans slowly followed the dismounted infantrymen as the turrets moved back and forth in search of enemy targets in the tree line above.[89]

Companies K and L advanced without incident. First Lieutenant Sims left his mortar platoon in the small gravel pit, crossed the Glauberg–Stockheim road, and followed behind Lieutenant Thode's machine-gun platoon, which was supporting Company L. As the GIs covered the eight hundred meters to the hill's summit, only silence met their ears. Everything on Hill 267 seemed dead.

From behind his pile of firewood on Hill 267, a dazed *SS-Rottenführer* Müller struggled to his feet. Dust hung in the air everywhere. Huge, gaping holes of churned, black earth dotted the landscape. Large pine trees and other evergreens lay toppled and shredded everywhere. Müller's ears were ringing. He could neither hear nor see any of his comrades.

Müller looked down at his rifle and saw a large shell fragment jammed into the wooden stock. The metal shard had just missed killing him. Uncertain of what to do or where to go, Müller staggered into the woods and headed northeast, away from the American guns that had just shattered his world. Perhaps he would meet up with other comrades farther east—maybe even the main body of the horse-drawn column. In any case, Müller felt fortunate to be alive.[90]

Lieutenant Colonel Guthrie's 3rd Battalion quickly gained the heights of Hill 267. The GIs promptly fanned out in search of surviving SS troops. In the distance on the left, several explosions echoed throughout the forest—possibly some German artillery ammunition still burning from the American barrage. Soon the dust settled and the Red Circle men saw first hand the results of their artillery's handiwork.[91]

Pfc. William L. Asay, a member of Lieutenant Thode's 2nd Platoon, Company M, scoured the hilltop in search of German survivors. Asay met his company commander, the much-admired First Lieutenant Sims, on the hill. Sims was easy to spot because of his thin, Clark Gable–like mustache. What both men observed of the carnage struck them to their core. Six dead German soldiers lay scattered on the ground in grotesque positions. Shell fragments had torn their bodies asunder, exposing entrails and scattering limbs. One dead Nord man lay with his head split in two; one-half was missing, exposing the empty skull cavity. Sims and Asay grimaced.[92]

The smell of smoke from the small fires that burned everywhere mixed with the strong stench of pine resin from the shattered trees. The combined odors turned the men's stomachs. But the most disturbing aspect of the carnage to Sims and Asay was not the smell or the sight of dead Germans. Instead, the horrific vision of several large, eviscerated horses lying next to their overturned wagons and demolished artillery pieces proved extremely disturbing. The entrails of one horse originated from the poor creature's torn belly and extended nearly five meters down the side of the hill. Several men retched and vomited. Among those men was Private First Class Asay, who would not be able to eat anything for several days.[93]

As the men of Companies K and L searched the hill, they discovered the shack with the hasty Red Cross painted on it next to the small quarry. However, they did not find any American prisoners or other Nord men. The German survivors must have escaped with their prisoners during the barrage. The six SS men who remained behind with the horses and the howitzers, however, had not survived. Company K's GIs captured four SS men taking cover inside a root cellar but discovered no other survivors.[94]

Sims ordered Lieutenant Prekker's mortar platoon to leave the gravel pit and come onto the hilltop with the rest of the battalion. Once the mortars were in place, Prekker's men began searching the German debris for anything useful and discovered in one of the German wagons a cartload of neatly packaged and crated German Reichmarks. Sims told his men the money was no longer any good, but many GIs stopped by the wagon and took several bills as souvenirs.[95]

As the 3rd Battalion consolidated and reorganized on Hill 267, Lieutenant Colonel Guthrie issued orders at 1200 for the companies to continue moving east. Lt. Ed Samuell's 1st Platoon, 71st Cavalry Reconnaissance Troop, had established a blocking position at 1100 in Stockheim that would protect the 3rd Battalion's left flank until Lieutenant Colonel Brant's 2nd Battalion on the left could come on line with Guthrie's troops. Colonel Lundquist wanted to keep up the pursuit, so he ordered his reserve battalion, Maj. Samuel E. Hubbard's 1st Battalion, forward from Langendiebach to Altenstadt. Pleased with the results of the regiment's attack so far, Lundquist wanted to keep up the momentum so the Nord Division would not escape the Red Circle Division's grasp.[96]

When Lieutenant Colonel Eikel reported to Colonel Regnier that his Task Force X (2nd Battalion, 66th Infantry) had nearly taken Waldensberg by 1200, he did not realize that his men would spend another two hours clearing each building in the town. *SS-Standartenführer* Raithel had already moved back to Leisenwald all surviving vehicles and equipment, so the only SS troops remaining to hold the northern limits of the town were mountain troops armed with MG42s, rifles, submachine guns, and *panzerfäuste*.

By 1200 Captain MacArthur's Company E had taken nineteen German prisoners and suffered only a few wounded men. But the SS men clung tenaciously to each house, forcing the GIs to fight for each dwelling in a deadly cat-and-mouse game that involved a running exchange of grenades and small-arms fire. In an effort to hasten his battalion's progress, Eikel sent Captain Sullivan's Company F into the town to assist Company E. Earlier, Sullivan's men had successfully cleared the small patch of woods west of the town. Captain Kratz's Company G and Captain Charleton's Company H followed closely behind the two leading rifle companies, mopping up and escorting captured SS troops to the south of town.[97]

Eikel was confident that his troops had the situation well in hand, so he moved his command post into an abandoned house near the town's center. Many houses continued to burn fiercely, obscuring the side streets with thick, black smoke. Battle debris littered the main street. The bodies of cavalrymen and SS mountain troopers lay along the cobblestone walkways in distorted, grotesque positions. Eikel's support troops had begun the distasteful task of removing these bodies, but German snipers bypassed by Companies E and F remained hidden and made Waldensberg a dangerous place to move around.⁹⁸

From his command post in Lieblos, Colonel Regnier was pleased to learn of the 2nd Battalion's progress in Waldensberg. Casualties were extremely light. The reports suggested that in taking Waldensberg, Task Force X was also forcing many SS troops into the towns and forests to the west, north, and east. Regnier saw an opportunity to cut off and bag these escaping SS troops with his 3rd Battalion. Even before receiving Eikel's most recent report, though, Regnier had already decided to commit the 3rd Battalion, which was located in a blocking position facing Gelnhausen in the Büdingen forest southwest of Wittgenborn. At 1125 Regnier had asked Major General Wyman to motorize at least two companies from the 3rd Battalion for immediate commitment to Waldensberg. Wyman agreed and further instructed Regnier to keep the 66th's 1st Battalion intact and to maintain communications with all three battalions in case something else developed. Regnier notified Lt. Col. Bryce F. Denno, the 3rd Battalion commander, to move north quickly to assist Task Force X. The trucks would come from the 2nd Battalion—trucks that Regnier had ordered Eikel to return after arriving at Waldensberg. Denno had monitored the situation from afar and was aware of what was happening several kilometers north of his position. He warned his company commanders and staff that the battalion should prepare to move out.⁹⁹

In the meantime Eikel's men fought house to house to clear the final remnants of the Nord men from Waldensberg. By 1300 the GIs were down to a handful of remaining homes. Many SS troops evaded their attackers and fled west across the fields to assemble in the forest a kilometer away. Once there *SS-Hauptsturmführer* Steurich, the commander of the 1st Battalion, SS-Gebirgsjäger Regiment 11, gathered his battle-weary troops and reorganized them. *SS-Standartenführer* Raithel had already departed Waldensberg for Leisenwald to report to *SS-Gruppenführer* Brenner the loss of the town.

As the fighting raged on the Red Circle men's prisoner count jumped from nineteen at 1200 to more than fifty by 1330. The GIs searched each house carefully. As a patrol passed a farmhouse on the northern edge of town, the Red Circle men heard a voice shout from inside in English, "Don't throw your damned grenades in here. I'm an American colonel, and this place is full of dying and wounded men and two women." The voice clearly belonged to an American, but the GIs still approached the farmhouse door cautiously. A sergeant pushed open the door with the muzzle of his M1 rifle. On seeing the colonel the GI relaxed, pushed his helmet back up on his head, and said with a grin, "I believe y'all really is an American colonel. I'm a Georgia boy myself."¹⁰⁰

When the GIs entered the farmhouse, they were surprised to discover that the voice belonged to the commander of the 10th Armored Infantry Battalion, Lt. Col. Harold Cohen, whom the SS men had captured with the field hospital near Assenheim the previous day. With Cohen was Lieutenant Nemeth of the 620th Ordnance Company who had been captured near Assenheim at the same time. On the ground lay several dead and dying Waffen-SS soldiers under the care of two clearly exhausted German nuns. The German guards and medics had already fled. After an emotional reunion with their rescuers, Cohen and Nemeth quickly explained that the SS troops did not mean to give up easily. The GIs understood and promptly sent the newly liberated officers to the battalion command post. Lieutenant Colonel Eikel greeted the two officers warmly and sent them—along with nearly fifty German prisoners—back to the regimental command post.[101]

Before long Lieutenant Colonel Cohen and Lieutenant Nemeth were sitting inside the division command post in Langenselbold talking to Lieutenant Colonel Foster, the G-2. The information given by both officers proved invaluable. Foster could confirm that many of his current reports were in fact accurate, but the other information that Cohen and Nemeth provided the G-2 was equally enlightening.[102]

Cohen estimated that the 6th SS-Gebirgs Division had at least four thousand troops with more than 150 horse-drawn carts, wagons, and other vehicles. Cohen remembered seeing only five or six horse-drawn artillery pieces and one self-propelled tank destroyer or howitzer. Every other SS trooper carried a *panzerfaust*. The division moved in three serials, as far he could determine; one serial moved by foot, the second by horse, and the third by motor. The SS troops mainly used captured American vehicles with colored panels on them—ostensibly to show that the vehicle was in German hands. When a vehicle broke down or was destroyed, they stripped it of all useful equipment and removed the colored panel. Cohen explained that he traveled with the motorized column, which moved very slowly and carefully. As the column moved, stragglers from the hills nearby joined the column, and the Nord men quickly assimilated these wayward Heer and Luftwaffe troops into their ranks.

Cohen explained to Foster that as the SS troops moved through each German town, the civilians came out and cheered them. Cohen's overall impression of the Nord Division was that they were a good, well-disciplined outfit. They fed him and the other prisoners once in a twenty-four-hour period and interrogated him at great length. The SS men always insisted that they were living up to the requirements of the Geneva Convention. In fact, the SS men discovered Cohen's cache of souvenir Iron Crosses but did not punish or abuse him for his wartime "hobby."

Foster thanked Cohen and Nemeth for the information and began preparing G-2 Periodic Report Number 20. The information Foster and his staff members had gleaned from Cohen, Nemeth, and other SS prisoners captured at Rodenbach and Waldensberg helped to form a more detailed picture of the enemy troops.

Foster learned from several Waffen-SS prisoners about the division's exploits in Finland and their long march through Norway and into Denmark. He also learned the name of the division commander, *SS-Gruppenführer* Brenner, and some personal details about the man, such as his missing eye. Aside from the information on the few howitzers and vehicles used by the SS troops and the fact that they traveled in various columns (actually two columns, but mistaken by Cohen and others as three or more), Foster managed to gather other information. He identified specific units within the division as well as units from which many of the Heer stragglers attached to the division belonged, such as Grenadier Ersatz Battalion 116 and Grenadier Ersatz Battalion 459, both of which were infantry replacement training battalions.

Foster and his G-2 staff compiled this information into a new intelligence estimate (G-2 Periodic Report Number 20) for dissemination at 1600 that afternoon. The information would prove sobering to Major General Wyman and his regimental commanders since they could clearly see what type of force they faced and its capabilities. Although the Nord Division no longer boasted anywhere near four thousand troops (the combined horse-drawn and motorized columns, separated from each other, perhaps had two thousand men), the 6th SS-Gebirgs Division, in part or as a whole, still proved a force capable of putting up a good fight.[103]

❖

Task Force X finally had cleared the last few houses in Waldensberg by 1400. The town was secure. Companies E and F quickly dug hasty defensive positions north of Waldensberg in preparation for a counterattack while Company G remained in reserve in the town's center. Lieutenant Colonel Eikel jumped his command post farther north and behind his defending companies.

In addition to his two companies' forward defenses, Eikel ordered Captain Charleton, the Company H commander, to use his two heavy machine-gun platoons to block the main north–south road running through Waldensberg. Company H's mortar platoon would continue to support the rifle companies. Lt. Roy J. Long positioned his 81-mm mortar sections behind each of the two defending companies to buttress their defenses. Most of the SS troops had withdrawn toward Leisenwald. Since the Red Circle men had observed many of the SS troops taking refuge in the woods farther west, though, Long ensured that a mortar section and observation post faced that direction in case the SS troops launched an attack from the woods.[104]

Second Lieutenant Tripp's Third Platoon, Company E, dug in northwest of town and watched for the expected German counterattack. As the GIs dug their holes outside some houses, they witnessed perhaps the most gruesome, unnerving sight they had seen during the entire war. Several hogs freed from their pens during the fighting were rooting around the bodies of fallen GIs and German soldiers. The pigs had partially eaten some of the bodies before the Red Circle men came across them and ran the animals off.[105]

In the center of town Pfc. Thomas Tomich and other signal troops from Company G strung wire from the command post to the houses occupied by the company's platoons. They worked among streets filled with bodies and bullet-riddled American vehicles. Many houses still burned brightly. Some of the wire strung too closely to these buildings melted and required constant repair.

Private Marx, one of Company G's wiremen, was repairing some burned wire along the main street when the sound of a roaring jeep engine met his ears. Marx turned to see an SS man behind the wheel of a jeep that was racing toward him. Pfc. James Cook of Company H had seen the Nord man rush from a building and jump into the jeep, which another Company H soldier had left parked on the street with the engine running. The SS man had obviously remained hidden in town and decided to make his break. The Nord man adeptly lifted with one hand an MP40 submachine gun and fired it at Marx. The rounds missed. Marx spun and raced down a side street and directly into Private First Class Tomich, who started running toward the intersection when he heard the shots. Marx, his face pale as a ghost, and Tomich watched the SS man race the jeep frantically through the intersection. The man gunned the engine, seemingly unaware that it was in low gear.[106]

The machine gunners from Company H manning the roadblocks along the main street ignored the jeep at first. But when the SS man fired on Marx, they realized the driver was not American. The gunfire brought several men into the street. Lieutenant Long rushed from his mortar platoon's command post in time to see the jeep zip past his building. The battalion motor officer, 1/Lt. Richard J. Berthelot, rushed from a doorway and yelled, "Don't shoot up that jeep! We need it!"[107]

At the same moment Private First Class Cannon poked his head from a second-story window to see about the commotion. The SS man in the jeep saw Cannon and fired a burst at the GI, hitting the man. Cannon screamed and fell backward into the house. Pfc. Gilbert Gongeware, a Company H machine gunner manning a nearby roadblock, had seen enough. He rushed into the street carrying his M1917A1 heavy, water-cooled, .30-caliber machine gun still on its tripod. A belt of ammunition dragged along the ground behind him. Gongeware fired from the hip, riddling the rear end of the careening jeep with red tracer rounds. The bullets punctured the jeep's gas tank, and the vehicle burst into flames. The burning jeep slammed into a building and came to rest, with the SS man burned to death in the driver's seat.[108]

The GIs' attention quickly shifted as field-phones began ringing and the shouts of GIs met their ears. The SS troops were counterattacking from the west. Lieutenant Long ran back to his mortar section northwest of town and saw several groups of SS troops advancing on foot across the open ground. These Nord men were the same ones organized by *SS-Hauptsturmführer* Steurich as they escaped from Waldensberg and gathered along the eastern edge of the Büdingen forest less than a kilometer west of town.

The SS troops were well outside rifle and machine-gun range when Lieutenant Long spotted them, but he decided not to wait. Long ordered his mortar crews to open fire. The rounds burst among the advancing SS mountain troopers, forcing them to ground. Brisk winds from the southwest caused some rounds to miss their mark, but most shells fell directly on the attacking German soldiers—perhaps fifty or sixty in all. Soon, the staccato of American .30-caliber machine-gun fire filled the air as Company E's troops opened fire. The combined mortar and machine-gun fire caused the attack to falter. The SS troops grabbed their wounded and dragged them back to the woods. The dead lay abandoned in the open field. The counterattack had failed.[109]

Lieutenant Colonel Eikel promptly sent word to Colonel Regnier about the counterattack. The attack had begun at 1430 and was over by 1455. The report pleased Regnier, who believed that his men had a good hold on the town. The stage was now set for the second part of Regnier's plan: Lieutenant Colonel Denno's 3rd Battalion would swing around from the east and take care of the rest of the SS troops still hiding in the woods and in Leisenwald.

The walls were closing in on the last remnants of this once-powerful SS mountain division.[110]

❖

The 5th Infantry Division's operations on 2 April resulted in far less enemy action than the Red Circle men experienced on 1 April. Captain Robinson's 5th Cavalry Reconnaissance Troop, reinforced with two light tank platoons from Company D, 737th Tank Battalion, and a platoon of tank destroyers, departed at daybreak to interdict any German forces moving along the XII Corps MSR. Robinson planned to take his troop along a path north of the MSR through Nidda and east to Lauterbach, the location of Major General Eddy's XII Corps advance command post. Robinson and his troop would then drop down to the corps' MSR and follow it backwards toward Ortenberg to locate any enemy troops moving along the route.

By 0815 Robinson's reinforced troop had cleared Echzell and pressed on toward Nidda. At 1100 the troop entered Nidda, where Robinson separated the three platoons, each organized with tanks and tank destroyers, to follow three independent routes to the south, southeast, and east. The platoon that headed south eventually contacted elements of Colonel Roffe's 2nd Infantry Regiment at Ober-Mockstadt. While there, the platoon bumped into some elements of the 76th Infantry Division, which would be detached from XII Corps to XX Corps the next day. The troop's movement throughout the morning proved uneventful except for a few fire missions called against German stragglers spotted throughout the area.[111]

After his mid-morning conversation with Major General Wyman, Major General Irwin realized that Colonel Roffe's lone battalion, the 3rd, would be spread too thinly for the day's operation. Wyman had given Irwin a clearer picture of a much larger enemy force spread out over a greater area. Irwin informed Roffe to truck another battalion to the area to help clear the enemy in zone. When Roffe received the message, he called back and requested twenty trucks for his 2nd Battalion located in Seckbach. Roffe added that if the division planned to use his regiment for pursuit purposes, he would need more tanks and tank destroyers.[112]

Irwin acknowledged Roffe's request, and Lieutenant Colonel Dickens and his G-3 staff began working to shift the necessary forces within the division. Irwin realized that Roffe needed help coordinating the reconnaissance, infantry, and artillery troops in the area, so he sent the assistant division commander, Brig. Gen. Alan D. Warnock, forward to liaise with the 71st Division and synchronize the efforts of the Red Diamond forces involved in the operation.

Some confusion already existed with regard to coordinating artillery fires between the 5th and 71st divisions despite the previous day's exchange of artillery liaison officers. The 50th Field Artillery Battalion's spotter planes had located *SS-Oberführer* Goebel's horse-drawn column concentrated around Hill 267 (where the 3rd Battalion, 14th Infantry, destroyed Goebel's remaining artillery pieces) and the forest south of Ortenberg. The liaison officers quickly resolved the fire mission that the spotter planes called on Hill 267 since the 14th Infantry Regiment had already fired a preparatory barrage on the hill before their attack. But the fire mission on Goebel's assembled Nord men southeast of Ortenberg confused the 5th Division Artillery's staff and its commander, Brig. Gen. Harnold C. Vanderveer. The fire request appeared to fall outside the previously established boundary between the two divisions, so Vanderveer's staff hesitated to sanction the mission. The designated targets also exceeded the 50th's present range, and the battalion could not displace forward fast enough to provide timely fires. Vanderveer immediately ordered the 50th Field Artillery Battalion forward to positions near Stammheim and then attached the 21st Field Artillery Battalion (155-mm howitzers) to reinforce the 50th for the longer-range fire missions.[113]

As the Red Diamond artillerymen sorted out these and other cross-boundary artillery fire missions, Lt. Col. Robert E. Connor's 3rd Battalion, 2nd Infantry, departed Staden and Stammheim at 0800 to finish clearing the woods of SS troops to the south, east, and northeast. After a quiet, uneventful night in the Staden and Stammheim area, Companies I, K, and L were well rested and ready to go. Having relinquished to the regimental medical troops the wounded 4th Armored Division prisoners discovered near Staden during the night, Company K's tank-mounted troops pressed onward from Staden toward Nieder-Mockstadt unmolested. By 1045 the company occupied Ober-Mockstadt with a handful of newly acquired German prisoners in tow.[114]

But Companies L and I, after clearing the woods west of Stammheim, could not press eastward into the forest north of Rodenbach due to the 2nd Battalion, 14th Infantry's current operation, which began at 1000. Connor's conversation with Lieutenant Colonel Brant at the latter's command post just before the attack that morning convinced him that both battalions would almost certainly cross paths at some point. As a result, Connor could not follow through with Colonel Roffe's orders to clear the woods east of Stammheim for fear that his troops would converge with Brant's men.[115]

As Connor prepared to contact his regimental commander, Colonel Roffe was already on the radio with Major General Irwin discussing his S-2 section's interviews with the 4th Armored Division casualties abandoned by the Nord Division near Staden (the same ones discovered during the night by the 3rd Battalion's Company K). Roffe related to Irwin what the division commander had already learned about the enemy, the 6th SS-Gebirgs Division. The division had about 1,500 troops, one tank, three field guns with little ammunition, and horse-drawn vehicles carrying captured rations, supplies, and other booty. Although these details varied slightly with other reports, Irwin was confident that the information was reasonably accurate.

Roffe added, "They're spread all over the woods in no particular group and they have no particular destination except to get back to their own lines. They have no resistance qualities."

Irwin responded confidently: "I think they can be cleaned up without any trouble."

Roffe replied, "Yes, sir. I'd like all the TDs [tank destroyers] and [tanks] we can get."

"I'll see about that," said Irwin.[116]

Roffe finished by informing Irwin that he was moving forward not only the regiment's 2nd Battalion, but also the 1st Battalion, since the enemy force covered such a large area. Irwin agreed to move the entire 2nd Infantry Regiment forward if their combined efforts would quickly eliminate the threat to the XII Corps' rear area.

As soon as Roffe ended his conversation with Irwin, Lieutenant Colonel Connor contacted him about the problem with the 2nd Battalion, 14th Infantry, blocking their planned zone of attack through the forest between Nieder-Mockstadt and Rodenbach. Roffe understood the problem and quickly called Irwin. After listening to Roffe outline the dilemma, Irwin said that Connor did not need to enter the woods there. He instructed Roffe to find Brigadier General Warnock and have the assistant division commander contact the 71st Division. Warnock should tell the 71st to stay below a general line from Düdelsheim to Büdingen and leave the north and west part to the 5th Infantry Division. Roffe agreed, not realizing the 14th Infantry's forces were attacking well above that line, and headed east into the forest just north of Büdingen. Once again, minor coordination problems continued to nag both divisions despite concerted efforts on both sides to synchronize their actions.

Roffe told Connor to assemble his battalion in Ober-Mockstadt until the rest of the regiment arrived later in the day. He then ordered Maj. Beryl J. Pace's 2nd Battalion to mount the trucks when they arrived in Seckbach and proceed to an assembly area around Ranstadt. He further directed Lt. Col. William H. Blakefield, commander of the 1st Battalion, to move to the same area that day. Roffe then jumped his command post forward from Frankfurt to Stammheim, setting up shop in the town by 1100. An hour later Lt. Col. William R. Calhoun's 50th Field Artillery Battalion arrived in Stammheim and settled into firing positions northeast of town.[117]

At 1155 Lieutenant Colonel Dickens, the G-3, called Roffe and told him that Company A, 737th Tank Battalion, was detached from the 11th Infantry Regiment and belonged to the 2nd Infantry. Roffe thanked Dickens and asked him to send the tanks to his 1st Battalion's location. Roffe wanted the 1st Battalion to use the tanks to transport Blakefield's infantrymen to the Staden area. He was in the process of bringing forward his entire regiment so that, once assembled, he could resume clearing the forests of SS troops in accordance with the newly established boundary set forth by Major General Irwin.[118]

At 1330 Roffe received a call from the division command post telling him that the regiment would receive an additional four tank companies from the 13th Armored Division. Roffe marveled at the resources his division commander provided for him, but his excitement was short-lived. The tank companies would arrive in Staden between 0000 and 0800 on 3 April—not in time to help accelerate the pace of the day's operations.[119]

❖

The bulk of *SS-Oberführer* Goebel's horse-drawn column finally assembled in the northwestern edge of the Büdingen forest at 1300—nearly two hours after the 3rd Battalion, 14th Infantry's attack on Hill 267. Goebel's slow-moving troops had followed a northerly route from Nieder-Mockstadt to Stockheim and up toward Ortenberg during the night before settling into a temporary assembly area just south of Bergheim—and directly below the XII Corps' MSR. Goebel had hoped to have his remaining artillery guns in position on Hill 267 before daylight to cover the horse-drawn column's movement into the woods, but he was unaware of the earlier attack that decimated his artillerymen.

Despite moving all night and throughout the morning, Goebel's dismounted troops, shepherding scores of horses pulling an odd mixture of wagons, carts, and other assorted vehicles, had only begun entering the planned assembly area at 1000. The previous day's attack on the column had created enough confusion to send many troops scattering throughout the countryside only to re-form in smaller groups during the night and early morning. Many of these groups and other individual stragglers eventually found their way back to Goebel's column in the assembly area.

But as the SS men assembled in the woods and collapsed in exhaustion, Goebel anguished over how long he could wait before moving out. He knew his worn-out troops needed rest, but he also knew the American troops were hot on his heels. Since daylight American artillery spotter planes had buzzed endlessly overhead, seeking clues to the Nord men's location. Only the protective canopy of evergreen pines concealed the SS men from view.

Goebel also recognized that his underequipped and poorly armed troops could not survive another clash with the Americans. Two of his artillery battalions had functioned as infantry since the long march began two days earlier in Usingen. Although skilled as artillerymen, these troops lacked the basic weaponry necessary to serve as effective infantry troops. Only the significantly depleted *gebirgsjäger* battalion from SS-Gebirgsjäger Regiment 11 that traveled with them had enough machine guns, submachine guns, and *panzerfäuste* to match a similarly sized American force—and then only for a short period.

As Goebel pondered his battle group's predicament, he finally received word (presumably from survivors who managed to return to the battle group) of the debacle on Hill 267 that had occurred a few hours earlier. The destruction of his six remaining howitzers came as a shock. Those howitzers represented the only remaining firepower at his disposal. Alarmed, Goebel realized the time had come to roust his slumbering SS troops and move out. The Americans might arrive at any moment and catch his men napping, literally. He gathered his few remaining officers and issued movement orders. The column would head east and follow the road leading from Ortenberg to Gelnhaar, Bindsachsen, and Kefenrod. What Goebel did not know was that this route was the XII Corps MSR—the very route patrolled by Captain Robinson's 5th Cavalry Reconnaissance Troop.

Lt. Col. Bryce F. Denno, the commander of the 3rd Battalion, 66th Infantry, had monitored the situation in Waldensberg all morning via radio, so Colonel Regnier's instructions at 1200 to move out in support of Task Force X did not come as a surprise. Denno had already anticipated such orders and decided to move on his own initiative. Just minutes before receiving Regnier's instructions from the regimental S-3, Denno had dispatched his own S-3, Capt. George Kaminsky, to the 66th's command post in Lieblos to explain that the 3rd Battalion planned to move out to support the 2nd Battalion in Waldensberg and attack the enemy from the rear. Denno's battalion also would receive enough trucks from the 2nd Battalion to motorize at least two companies for the movement. But Denno had no intention of waiting for these trucks to arrive.[120]

Denno's battalion had occupied a blocking position the day before on high ground overlooking Gelnhausen along the southern fringes of the Büdingen forest four kilometers southwest of Wittgenborn—part of the regiment's original mission of protecting the XII Corps' right flank. But news of the fighting near Altenstadt and Waldensberg told Denno the action was to his north and not south. Throughout the morning Denno's motorized Ranger platoon (a nonregulation formation organized with handpicked volunteers from the rifle companies) had busily patrolled the southern forest along the outskirts of Gelnhausen and Wächtersbach. The Rangers failed to discover any traces of German troops in the area and radioed hourly negative situation reports back to Denno's command post. Denno soon realized that his men were of little value to the regiment or to the division in their current position.

Radio traffic suggested that the enemy was moving eastward, so Denno consulted his map. He did not know how quickly the 6th SS-Gebirgs Division was moving, but he saw three possible routes to intercept them. The first led directly northwest to Leisenwald while bypassing Waldensberg. The second led through Spielberg to Streitberg, and the third led to the east from Spielberg to Eisenhammer. Denno chose the second option—the route through Spielberg to Streitberg to Leisenwald.

Denno knew he enjoyed the confidence of his regimental commander and did not hesitate to put his plan into action without first clearing it with Colonel Regnier. As a decorated veteran of the 1st Infantry Division in North Africa and Sicily, Denno was one of the most combat-experienced officers in the division. After graduating from West Point in 1940, he joined the 16th Infantry Regiment of the 1st Infantry Division. He landed in Oran in North Africa in November 1942 as the cannon company commander; by the end of the Tunisian campaign, he was the executive officer of the 2nd Battalion, 16th Infantry.

In July 1943 the Big Red One landed on the shores of Sicily. On the second day of the invasion, the tanks of Panzer Division Hermann Göring overran the 2nd Battalion. Denno, as second in command, took charge and led the way to seize the regiment's objective, earning for the battalion a Presidential Unit Citation. Recommended for the Medal of Honor, Denno instead received the Distinguished Service Cross and a battlefield promotion to major. Shortly thereafter Denno was wounded and spent seven months recuperating in various hospitals. While assigned stateside to the Infantry Branch, Training Division, G-3, Army Ground Forces, Denno visited Fort Benning and met with Major General Wyman, the 1st Infantry Division's former assistant division commander and a hero of Omaha Beach. Denno asked to command a battalion in Wyman's new division, and the commanding general readily agreed. A seasoned combat leader like Denno would prove essential to the division's future success in combat.

But Denno, now in combat with his own battalion, remained concerned about how his less-seasoned troops might fare in action. To date his men had done little more than mop up after other major actions and had yet to engage the enemy directly in combat. The fact that a long journey north awaited his battalion at this late time of day meant that his men might go into action after dark, something Denno wanted to avoid since he was unsure how his troops might perform under those conditions.

Denno quickly gathered his staff and outlined his plan. He explained that the 6th SS-Gebirgs Division had withdrawn from Waldensberg thanks to the 2nd Battalion's attack. Denno speculated that the SS troops were probably assembling in Leisenwald in preparation for an eastward move out of the area. He recommended that the 3rd Battalion leave immediately, swing south and east of Wittgenborn up to Spielberg, and assemble in an attack position west of Streitberg. This maneuver would block the SS troops' eastward movement and squeeze them between the 2nd and 3rd battalions.

Since the Ranger platoon was still kilometers away patrolling to the south, the battalion would have to depart without the benefit of jeep-mounted screening patrols forward. Denno planned to personally scout the planned route by jeep. He charged his executive officer, Maj. Obediah Spencer, with moving the battalion by shuttle with all available transportation assets. The battalion could not wait for the trucks to arrive from the 2nd Battalion. Lt. Horace B. Ellison, the commander of Company M (the heavy weapons company), would lead the overall shuttle effort. The vehicles would drop off the first group of riflemen in the attack position and return along the route for another group. In the meantime, the battalion would march on foot until picked up by the trucks somewhere along the route. Denno was confident in this shuttle technique since his battalion employed it habitually.

Denno still had two towed 105-mm howitzers from the regiment's Cannon Company and two 105-mm assault guns attached to his battalion for the blocking mission. The assault guns—105-mm howitzers mounted in the turret of an M4 medium Sherman tank—belonged to the regiment's tank company, Company C, 761st Tank Battalion. These assault guns provided close-fire support for the infantry and would prove useful to Denno and his 3rd Battalion later that day.[121]

Denno soon sped off in his jeep as Major Spencer and Lieutenant Ellison organized the battalion's movement north. Denno and his driver raced quickly through narrow logging trails and secondary roads northward to Spielberg. The numerous, unmapped trails and roads made navigation confusing. The pair often found themselves turning around and following other roads to remain on a northerly heading. Denno was surprised, however, that he did not encounter any enemy troops.[122]

Back at the 3rd Battalion command post, Major Spencer watched the first load of infantry-laden trucks depart northward for Streitberg at 1245. The trucks sped along steadily, easily negotiating the narrow logging trails and roads except for the occasional navigational error. The Ranger platoon normally moved ahead of the battalion and marked the route, but not today: the truck drivers had to follow their maps carefully.[123]

The trucks followed the route east of Wittgenborn and sped northwest to Spielberg. The lead truck driver suddenly slammed on his brakes. The vehicles had encountered a bridge out over a large stream one kilometer west of Schlierbach. The commanders of Companies I and L, moving with the first group, radioed the problem to Denno. They would have to find another route. The time was already 1333. Denno was concerned that delays such as the collapsed bridge would force his Red Circle men to fight in the dark—something he did not want them to do on their first big attack.[124]

Back at the 66th Regiment's command post in Lieblos, Colonel Regnier considered not just sandwiching the SS troops between his 2nd and 3rd battalions but instead pocketing the Nord men between both of his battalions and Colonel Wooten's 5th Infantry Regiment, which was moving up on the left. Regnier directed his S-3, Major Merrill, to contact Lieutenant Colonel Lankenau, the G-3, and find out where the 5th Infantry Regiment was currently located. If both regiments could coordinate their efforts closely, they would be able to fulfill Major General Wyman's intent of bagging the SS division in its entirety.[125]

Merrill called and learned that Wooten's 5th Regiment was still on the road to both Büches and Büdingen. The 5th Regiment's two battalions were at least an hour away by foot from both locations. The 5th Regiment might not advance far enough before sunset to make a difference in the day's operations. Regnier's 2nd and 3rd battalions would have to handle the bulk of the SS troops for the moment.[126]

❖

Lieutenant Colonel Brant's 2nd Battalion, 14th Infantry, continued moving through the forest northeast of Rodenbach without incident. The only excitement had come from Company G's capture of seven German soldiers shortly after the battalion's 1000 departure time. Companies E and G continued their advance slowly through the heavily canopied pine forest. Company F followed closely in reserve. Deep ravines, cut into the terrain by age-old streams, slowed the Red Circle men's movement.

By 1400 both companies had reached Phase Line Two. The town of Nieder-Mockstadt, invisible to the GIs through the thick forest, was less than a kilometer away. Artillery rounds suddenly impacted in the trees overhead and on the ground directly behind Captain Goldman's Company G. The GIs scattered and sought cover. Within seconds the artillery fire lifted. No one had been hurt. Goldman reported the barrage to Brant. The rounds most likely originated from the 5th Division's 50th Artillery Battalion located back near Stammheim. With several spotter planes still buzzing low overhead, the pilots and their accompanying observers probably mistook Goldman's company for SS troops. Once again, coordination problems bedeviled units of both divisions.

Brant radioed both Captain Goldman and Captain Bass and instructed the two lead companies to continue moving and to seize the wooded hill due east of Ober-Mockstadt. The GIs gathered their gear and moved out. Both companies had barely advanced three hundred meters when rifle fire erupted from the woods directly in front of Company E. Strangely, the fire was not directed against Goldman's men but at Bass's Company G, which was visible through a small clearing just east of Company E.

Goldman quickly ordered the men of Company E forward to attack the source of the small-arms fire, which had pinned down Company G less than five hundred meters away. As Company E closed on the suspected enemy location, they were surprised to find several bantams and an M8 armored car parked along a logging trail to their front. The strong smell of cordite hanging in the air revealed these reconnaissance troops as the source of the shooting. Goldman approached the platoon leader, who explained that he was part of Captain Robinson's 5th Cavalry Reconnaissance Troop. The platoon had just split off from the troop at Nidda and contacted Red Diamond soldiers from Colonel Roffe's 2nd Infantry Regiment near Ober-Mockstadt.

Lieutenant Colonel Brant arrived in his jeep and quizzed the reconnaissance platoon leader on his mission. The young officer explained that his troop was in the process of patrolling the XII Corps MSR and had split up to cover a larger area. Brant told the officer that his 2nd Battalion planned to seize the high ground due east of Ober-Mockstadt. The cavalry officer explained that another battalion from the 5th Infantry Division (Lieutenant Colonel Connors's 3rd Battalion, 2nd Infantry) was headed for that same objective. That battalion also planned to drop an artillery barrage on that hill sometime soon. After exchanging other pertinent information with Brant, the cavalry platoon departed.

Brant quickly huddled with his company commanders and discussed what he had learned from the cavalry officer. Coordination problems with the 5th Infantry Division were becoming too troublesome for the battalion to continue. The men could not press on without possibly running into another friendly unit or coming under friendly artillery attack. Brant's men had already emerged unscathed from two friendly-fire incidents that day; he did not want to create the potential for a third. Brant told his commanders to hold fast while he contacted Colonel Lundquist for further information.

Brant radioed Lundquist (who was still with the 3rd Battalion east of Glauberg) and reported what had transpired. Lundquist recognized the dilemma faced by Brant, so he ordered the battalion commander to abandon his drive northeast and instead move to Bleichenbach just north of Glauberg. This move would place Brant's battalion on line and left of the still-advancing 3rd Battalion. Brant informed his commanders of their new orders and told them to be ready to move in two hours—at 1700. They would need the two hours to reorganize into tank-infantry company teams for the move to Bleichenbach.[127]

Lieutenant Colonel Guthrie's 3rd Battalion had reorganized on Hill 267 following the attack on the Nord Division's few remaining artillery pieces. A couple of sniper attacks from Glauberg nagged the GIs on the hill, but no other resistance materialized. Lundquist told Guthrie to head northeast toward Wolf and Dudenrod as quickly as possible. Guthrie's reorganized and resupplied troops promptly departed the hill at 1245 and surged forward into the forest north and east of Glauberg. The Red Circle men moved slowly and cautiously. While reorganizing on the hilltop, they had spotted German survivors of the attack on Hill 267 heading toward the forest beyond Bleichenbach, so the GIs knew the Germans occupied those woods. The SS men might have set up ambushes or other traps for the advancing GIs.[128]

As the 3rd Battalion GIs carefully advanced, the lead infantrymen scouting ahead reported seeing SS troops with horses moving into the woods east of Selters—undoubtedly other Nord men closing on *SS-Oberführer* Goebel's assembly area. The GIs could see American vehicle traffic in the distance moving along the Ortenberg–Gedern road. A sharp-eyed Red Circle man with binoculars managed to make out vehicle bumper numbers identifying the 4th Armored Division—the vanguard of the XII Corps' drive to the northeast.[129]

As the 3rd Battalion's lead companies emerged from the woods into a clearing, a screeching sound caused the Red Circle men to look skyward. In the distance—and coming in low—was a fast-flying German aircraft headed straight for the GIs. First Lieutenant Sims, the Company M commander, ordered his mortar men and machine gunners to abandon their vehicles and seek cover in the plowed field. Companies K and L hit the dirt. The plane zoomed low over the field but did not strafe the men. The GIs had never seen a plane move so quickly. The aircraft came around for a second pass, and the men quickly realized that they were witnessing the new German Me262 jet in action—one of Hitler's last-ditch "secret weapons" that entered the war too late to turn the tide in the Third Reich's favor.

The jet failed to strafe the GIs on the second pass, and the men breathed a sigh of relief. Mortar and artillery rounds suddenly impacted around the prone GIs. The barrage ended within seconds, and no one was injured. Once again, no one was certain of the artillery fire's origin. Did the low-flying German jet request it? If so, who fired it? The Nord men might have mustered some mortar rounds for a barrage, but the SS troops lacked artillery pieces. And the jet was almost certainly not in contact with *SS-Oberführer* Goebel in his assembly area northeast of Bleichenbach. Perhaps the 5th Infantry Division had fired another salvo on friendly troops that occurred coincidentally with the Me262's flyover. After a few moments, the confused but thankful GIs resumed their trek to the towns of Wolf and Dudenrod.[130]

The push against the center of the Büdingen forest by the 5th Infantry Regiment continued without incident during the mid-afternoon. Lieutenant Colonel Gettys's 2nd Battalion, still on foot, departed for Büdingen at 1400. Lieutenant Colonel Broyles's dismounted 1st Battalion followed in reserve. The trucks Gettys's men had used to move forward that morning had returned to Langendiebach to motorize Major Robertson's 3rd Battalion for seizing Büches on the northwest outskirts of Büdingen. An intelligence report received from XII Corps before 1200 indicated Büches was swarming with German troops—an inaccurate report but one that prompted Major General Wyman to want the town in his division's hands quickly.[131]

The trucks arrived at Langendiebach and quickly loaded Major Robertson's troops for their twelve- to thirteen-kilometer journey northeast to Büches. Soon the battalion was on its way, rumbling across the secondary roads leading to the western fringes of the Büdingen forest. The damp, dreary weather chilled the GIs as they huddled in the open-backed trucks. These same GIs, ever vigilant, also scanned the countryside for possible threats. The GIs had received word that the enemy hailed from the Waffen-SS—a fact that heightened the Red Circle men's senses out of respect for the fighting abilities of their intended foe.

Colonel Wooten already moved his forward regimental command post northward toward Büdingen in anticipation of occupying the town. He shifted his advance command post to Ravolzhausen at 1100 that morning and jumped his S-2 and S-3 sections there beginning at 1340. At 1444 Wooten received a radio message from Lieutenant Colonel Gettys reporting that the 2nd Battalion's advance elements had cleared Hüttengesäss roughly eight kilometers southwest of Büdingen. Thirty minutes after receiving that report, Wooten's rear command post closed on the regiment's forward headquarters at Ravolzhausen.[132]

The 5th Regiment's progress continued smoothly throughout the afternoon. At 1510 the motorized 3rd Battalion edged into the outskirts of Calbach—three kilometers from Büches. Major Robertson advanced by truck to within several hundred meters of the town and, after crossing a small bridge over a narrow stream, dismounted and deployed his companies. At 1520 lead patrols from the battalion entered Büches uncontested while the 2nd Battalion, coming in on foot from the 3rd's right rear, cleared Altwiedermus seven kilometers farther south.[133]

Robertson and his men encountered no enemy troops in Büches, immediately contradicting the earlier XII Corps' report. Robertson promptly established outposts around the hamlet and sent foot patrols southeast to investigate Büdingen. Wooten phoned Lieutenant Colonel Lankenau that Büches was in friendly hands, and that the enemy was nowhere in sight. Lankenau told Wooten that after clearing Büches the 3rd Battalion should leave some troops behind to contact the 14th Infantry to the north and then seize Büdingen. (The 3rd Battalion, 14th Infantry, was headed for Wolf less than a kilometer away.) When the 2nd Battalion arrived on foot, the men would assemble south of Büdingen and prepare to move east. Both battalions were to hold in place until Lankenau transmitted further orders. Wooten agreed and informed his two battalion commanders of the plan via radio.[134]

A mere twelve minutes had passed before Lankenau was back on the phone with Wooten. Lankenau explained that the previous instructions for the 3rd Battalion remained unchanged but that the 2nd Battalion should instead head for a confluence of roads a kilometer south of Büdingen and west of a small *schloss* near a lake. After seizing this small, secondary road network on the western fringe of the Büdingen forest, the battalion should hold fast until further orders. Lankenau further directed that Wooten motorize his 1st Battalion with the same trucks used by the 3rd Battalion. The 1st Battalion would become the division reserve. The time was 1605.[135]

CHAPTER 8

The Second Day: Leisenwald, 2 April 1945

By mid-afternoon in Leisenwald, SS-Gruppenführer *Brenner had taken stock of his remaining divisional elements. After* SS-Hauptsturmführer *Steurich's failed counterattack against the 2nd Battalion, 66th Infantry, at Waldensberg at 1430, Brenner knew the Nord Division could no longer proceed south.* SS-Standartenführer *Raithel had returned to Leisenwald with the grim news of the failed attack and had with him but a handful of survivors—including Steurich.*

Raithel and the division staff—still operating from their command post in a cattle barn adjoining a farmer's house—quickly determined what troops they still had at their disposal and how to deploy them. Brenner's intelligence radio section—led by *SS-Unterscharführer* Stöwe—could not contact *SS-Oberführer* Goebel's *kampfgruppe* thought to be moving eastward somewhere farther north, so Brenner assumed that Goebel had either reached the German lines or fallen prey to the Americans.

Raithel and the division staff soon conjured up a troop estimate based on reports from the remaining divisional units—or their remnants—located within Leisenwald. Raithel reported that his SS-Gebirgsjäger Regiment 11 could produce no more than six hundred mountain infantry troops armed with rifles, grenades, and *panzerfäuste*, loosely organized into small groups. The newly liberated prisoners from Waldensberg—numbering more than five hundred—and the other Heer and Luftwaffe stragglers that had attached themselves to the division, lacked either weapons, fighting spirit, or both. Raithel soberly assessed their value to the command as insignificant. A hasty estimate of the remaining equipment included a captured American tank, an antitank gun, and a few MG42 machine guns.[1]

The reports disheartened Brenner. His command of several thousand had been reduced to several hundred in the span of a day. Reports that American armored vehicles were visible on the ridgelines south and east of Leisenwald meant that a determined enemy attack would soon be forthcoming. He could not advance east, west, or south—and north was probably out of the question as well. In effect, the last surviving remnants of the Nord Division were surrounded, but Brenner had no intention of giving up (see Map 8.1).

Brenner issued instructions to shore up the town's defenses in every way possible, especially to reinforce the houses ringing the town's perimeter. Many of Leisenwald's residents—frightened by the prospect of a coming battle—remained hidden in cellars or fled into the nearby countryside. The town remained ghostly quiet except for the clacking of German hob-nailed boots tramping over cold, damp cobblestones and the hushed whispers of leaders issuing instructions. Brenner and Raithel conferred and decided on establishing an outermost defense north of town in a strip of woods five hundred meters above Leisenwald. The SS men could not venture far outside the town's limits since Leisenwald sat squarely in the middle of open countryside bounded on all sides by rolling farmland recently plowed into neat furrows, a stark reminder that spring had arrived.

Soon the SS troops had dispersed their vehicles throughout the town for protection from American artillery and air attack. The Nord men fortified many houses on the town's outskirts with expertly concealed MG42s in windows or in the small, neatly manicured yards. Tank-killer teams armed with *panzerfäuste* ventured into the surrounding fields and dug in, hoping to ambush any encroaching American armored vehicles. Within a few hours, the town of Leisenwald had become a *festung* (fortress) that would hold as long as the Nord men had weapons to fire and blood running through their veins. Surrender to the Americans never crossed Brenner's mind or the minds of his men. They would fight to the end.[2]

Lieutenant Colonel Denno, commander of the 3rd Battalion, 66th Infantry, and his jeep driver sped through the narrow logging trails south of Spielberg. Denno's driver quickly found a more improved road heading north to Streitberg and punched the accelerator, racing for the town and Denno's planned attack position. The first two companies of the battalion, I and L, followed in the battalion's few assigned trucks using a shuttle system. The rest of the battalion marched on foot until the trucks returned to pick them up along the route and take them to the attack position.[3]

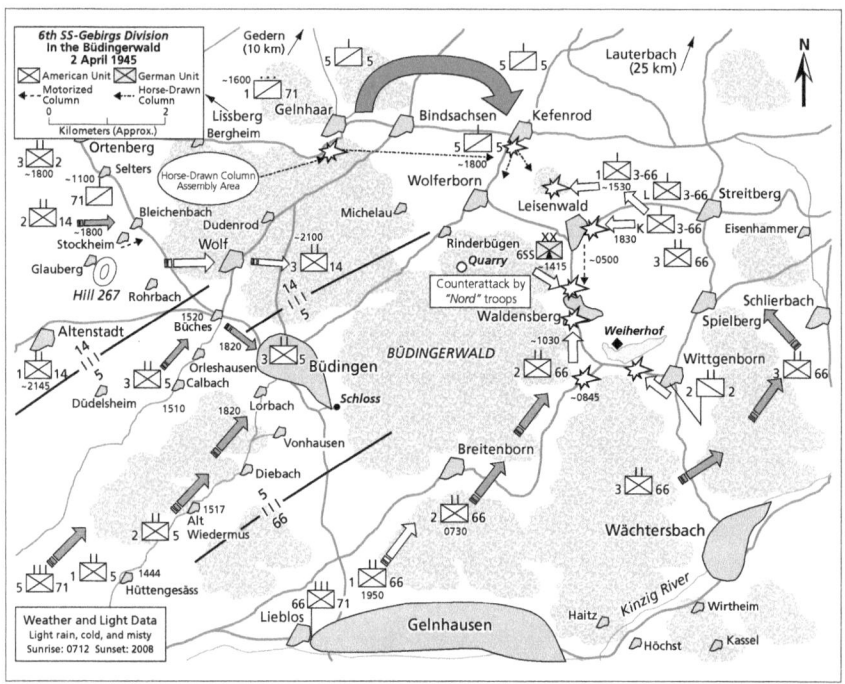

Map 8.1. 6th SS-Gebirgs Division in the Büdingen forest, 2 April 1945.

Denno soon reached Streitberg. The town seemed strangely quiet except for the soft fluttering sound made by numerous white sheets suspended below second-floor windows. A few civilians roamed the streets, but Denno saw no sign of German soldiers. The jeep quickly gained the road to Leisenwald and sped west toward the town. Denno still had not managed to contact Lieutenant Colonel Eikel's 2nd Battalion in Waldensberg. He knew Eikel's troops occupied the town, but he did not know if Eikel planned to continue attacking north toward Leisenwald.[4]

Denno's driver slowed the vehicle as they approached a small rise overlooking Leisenwald. To Denno's surprise, four M24 Chaffee light tanks from the 2nd Cavalry Group sat evenly spaced along the small ridgeline scanning the town's eastern outskirts. Denno dismounted and walked between the tanks, asking for the officer in charge. A lieutenant appeared and explained that his squadron (presumably the 2nd Squadron) had sent his tanks to help the rear echelon in Waldensberg. Waldensberg was now back in American hands, but the enemy had withdrawn to Leisenwald and occupied that town in strength.

Denno scanned Leisenwald with his binoculars but detected no movement. The disciplined SS troops, aware the light tanks were there, limited their movement through the streets. Denno shifted his binoculars to the wooded plot north of town and saw numerous German soldiers digging fighting positions. He still was unsure if the SS troops planned to stay and fight or attempt an eastward breakout. He had to attack quickly if he intended to thwart the SS troops' plans—whatever they may be.

Denno asked the cavalry officer if he could rely on fire support from the four light tanks. He explained that two rifle companies would arrive soon, and he wanted them to attack immediately. Denno's self-propelled 105-mm howitzers and assault guns would not arrive in time to support such a hasty attack.

The officer agreed to support Denno's attack, but the lieutenant refused to bring his tanks into Leisenwald due to the threat of hidden SS troops armed with *panzerfäuste*. As they argued, artillery rounds suddenly impacted in and around the light tanks. Denno and the lieutenant dove for the dirt as the tank crews buttoned up. Denno immediately recognized the artillery as American. He sprinted for his jeep and managed to contact someone via radio from regimental or division headquarters to stop the fire mission. The barrage quickly ended with no casualties. Denno suspected that an artillery spotter plane had seen the tanks in the open and, unable to distinguish friend from foe, called for fire from a nearby artillery unit—probably from a XII Corps artillery battalion somewhere farther east.

No sooner had Denno and the lieutenant brushed the mud from their field jackets than the first trucks bearing 1/Lt. Frederick L. Tyler's Company I and Capt. Everett W. Gray's Company L arrived. The Red Circle men quickly dismounted, and the trucks sped away to retrieve the foot-marching Company K. Company M's mortar jeeps also arrived behind the trucks pulling trailers laden with ammunition and 81-mm mortars.

Denno briefed the two company commanders on his plan. He wanted Companies I and L to seize the wooded area north of town from the dug-in German troops he observed there earlier. Both companies would attack abreast—Company L on the left and Company I on the right. After seizing the woods from the German defenders, he instructed Gray to set up Company L's light machine guns in the wood line to fire into Leisenwald. These machine guns would support Company K's eventual assault into the town when that company arrived with the platoon from Cannon Company. In the meantime the 2nd Cavalry's four M24 Chaffee light tanks would cover the companies' movements.

The two commanders assembled their men in the open field behind the tanks. The companies would have to cross five hundred meters of open field before gaining the woods, but the deep folds in the rolling terrain would conceal them from German observation until they reached the forest.

The GIs shouldered their weapons and struck out across the freshly plowed farm fields. The time was 1500 and the sun was already dropping behind the overcast sky. A slight drizzle blanketed the Red Circle men as they moved toward their objective. They scanned the town and surrounding fields for German ambushes or patrols.

As the two companies maneuvered over the fields, Lieutenant Ellison's Company M mortar troops, led by 2/Lt. John F. Steinmetz, unloaded their jeeps and trailers. Each gun crew quickly thrust the base plates firmly into the rain-dampened soil and installed the bipods, mortar tubes, and sights. A two-man observation party moved forward to the rise above Leisenwald and dug in. From this vantage point, the observers could see both the town and the woods to the north.[5]

Pfc. Henry B. Mathews, a wireman in Company M, went forward with the observation party and unfurled a spool of wire as he walked. As soon as he had rigged the GIs' EE-8B field phone with wire, Mathews began the long, dangerous journey back across open ground to the mortar positions. As he hurried along at a crouch, his eye caught something in the field nearby. Four SS troops armed with *panzerfäuste* occupied a shallow hole on the approaches to Leisenwald. If the tanks moved forward any farther, this tank-killer team would easily destroy or disable them.

Recognizing the immediate danger posed by the Germans, Mathews stood up and sprinted across the field to warn the tank crews. The Nord men realized the GI had spotted them and opened fire. Bullets whizzed past Mathews's head as he ran. Within seconds he reached the nearest tank and pounded on the side armor, yelling for the crew. The hatch popped open, and a cavalryman's head jutted out. Mathews pointed toward the tank-killer team's location.

The tank crewman dropped back down inside the tank, swiveled the turret toward the Nord men's location, and opened fire. The main-gun rounds chewed up the dirt in front of the Germans' shallow dugout. The impact of each tank round flung the bewildered SS men backward. When the smoke cleared, Mathews saw four bodies strewn across the open field in grotesque positions. The tank-killer team was no more. Private First Class Mathews later received the Silver Star for his valorous effort to warn the tanks.[6]

As soon as the tank fire subsided, companies I and L entered the woods north of Leisenwald and ran into a hornet's nest of German rifle and machine-gun fire. The SS troops had dug in along the outermost fringes of the forest and engaged the GIs as soon as the lead element entered the woods. The Red Circle men rushed from tree to tree, ducking for cover while trying to return fire. But the Nord men had prepared their positions well. The hail of small-arms fire forced the GIs to ground, but many Red Circle men crawled forward and lobbed grenades into the shallow German trench works.

Screams soon echoed throughout the forest as GIs and SS troops fell. The Nord men began firing 5-cm mortar rounds into the trees. The airbursts rained hot metal splinters onto the exposed GIs below. Lt. James E. Bangs of Company L fell to the ground in extreme pain. Hot fragments from a mortar shell had punctured one of his knees, severely damaging the joint. Private Saucier, a Company L radio operator, also fell wounded, the weight of the SCR-300 radio strapped to his back slamming into his head as he plunged face first onto the forest floor. Bangs's and Saucier's injuries would later earn them a visit from Lieutenant General Patton in a field hospital near the Rhine River. Another member of Company L, Sergeant Wallan, received a severe wound that crippled him for life.

Several Nord men also screamed out in pain as the Red Circle men shot the Germans in their holes or scored direct hits with hand grenades. Despite the fierce German resistance, the two companies' attacks did not stall completely—but their momentum had slowed greatly. As always, though, the Waffen-SS soldiers had no intention of surrendering.[7]

Captain Gray and First Lieutenant Tyler radioed their situation back to Lieutenant Colonel Denno, who watched the battle unfold from the ridgeline overlooking town. Through his binoculars, Denno observed his men firing and maneuvering in the woods through a hail of gunfire. The light tanks could not fire in support since both sides were too closely enmeshed in the woods. All Denno could do was hope for reinforcements to arrive in the form of Capt. Freddie W. Grambling's Company K. The time was 1600.

Capt. Donald E. Robinson's 5th Cavalry Reconnaissance Troop of the 5th Infantry Division reassembled north of Ortenberg later in the afternoon. Earlier that morning each platoon had split off on reaching Nidda and scouted separate routes to the south, southeast, and east. The individual scouting missions yielded no information on the 6th SS-Gebirgs Division or the enemy's alleged interdiction of the XII Corps MSR. Robinson's troop now re-formed to move eastward along the MSR in search of the evasive SS troops. Robinson still had with him the light tanks of Company D, 737th Tank Battalion, and a platoon of tank destroyers from Company C, 803rd Tank Destroyer Battalion.

The troop's M8 armored cars soon sped off along a path parallel to the MSR and generally east from Ortenberg to Gelnhaar. Robinson's original plan was to travel along a northerly route parallel to the MSR and, on reaching Lauterbach, head back along the MSR from the opposite direction. But numerous reports of enemy troops east of Ortenberg caused him to alter his itinerary and follow a more easterly route south of the MSR, which ran northeast up to Lauterbach. Except for a few service and supply vehicles moving along the Ortenberg-Gelnhaar road, the cavalrymen observed nothing out of sorts. The troop then moved in tandem across the main thoroughfare west of Gelnhaar to follow the road to Kefenrod before turning northeast once more.

The Red Diamond cavalrymen, led by 1/Lt. Norman Sterling's 1st Platoon, gained the high ground just south of Gelnhaar and paused. Sterling and his troops were scanning the horizon to the south and the distant wood line when they suddenly spotted a caravan of horse-drawn carts accompanied by scores of dismounted German troops emerging from the wood line nearly a kilometer away. Squinting through their field glasses, the GIs could see that each German soldier carried a submachine gun or rifle and, in most cases, a *panzerfaust*. The stunned Red Diamond men had spotted the lead element of *SS-Oberführer* Goebel's horse-drawn column as it uncoiled from its assembly area inside the forest southwest of Gelnhaar.[8]

The SS troops did not see Robinson's armored vehicles on the heights above them. The Nord men simply trudged through the open fields in an easterly direction. Sterling radioed Robinson, whose M8 armored car soon appeared among Sterling's vehicles. The troop commander squinted through his binoculars and absorbed the image of several hundred SS troops and numerous horses on the open ground before him. A few motorized vehicles—mostly captured American jeeps and Dodge trucks—were intermeshed with the massive column, but the troops traveled mostly on foot or rode in horse-driven carts and wagons. A few individual soldiers pushed baby carriages overflowing with ammunition and other stores.[9]

Robinson called his 3rd Platoon forward to come on line with Sterling's 1st Platoon. The M8 armored cars lined up along the commanding ridgeline and aimed their 37-mm main guns into the valley below. Interspersed among the armored cars were Company D's M5 light tanks sporting 37-mm main guns and Company C's M10 tank destroyers with 76.2-mm M7 guns. As soon as most of the troop was in firing position, Robinson gave the word to open fire.[10]

The tanks, tank destroyers, and armored cars barked and crackled, shattering the afternoon stillness. The main-gun rounds and machine-gun fire raked the left flank of the German column mercilessly. From his jeep farther back in the column, *SS-Oberführer* Goebel watched helplessly as scores of his men and horses fell to the murderous fire. The SS troops raised their weapons, took aim, and returned fire, but the Americans were hopelessly out of range. Several terrified men broke ranks and sprinted for the woods, but the remainder held fast and manhandled the frantic horses to keep them from bolting.

The 37-mm and 76.2-mm rounds chewed up the ground around the SS troops. Many Nord men fell wounded, but the American fire proved less accurate due to the kilometer-wide distance between the shooters and their intended targets. Goebel raced his captured American jeep through a hail of fire to the head of the column and ordered his Nord men to follow. He quickly led the foot-marching column farther south and away from the cavalrymen's vehicles.

The column's main body soon faded into the distance and out of range. Robinson ordered his men to cease fire as the SS troops moved southeast and then veered east below Bindsachsen in the direction of Kefenrod. Robinson ordered his troop to turn about and move north. He planned to head off Goebel's column by swinging north of Gelnhaar, bypassing Bindsachsen, and dropping down to Kefenrod. At Kefenrod, mused Robinson, he could spring another ambush on the Nord men's column—a closer ambush that would prevent them from escaping the trap. But Robinson would have to hurry. The time was nearly 1700; only a couple of more hours of daylight remained. Visibility was already poor due to the steady drizzle and mist-enshrouded fields. If the sun set before the troop could attack the SS column again, then the Nord men would have a chance of escaping into the darkness.[11]

As Captain Robinson's troop attacked *SS-Oberführer* Goebel's horse-drawn column, Colonel Roffe, the 2nd Infantry Regiment commander, was just finishing a face-to-face discussion with a visiting Major General Irwin, the 5th Infantry Division commander, at the 2nd's command post in Stammheim. Earlier that day Irwin had agreed to Roffe's request to bring forward the entire 2nd Infantry Regiment for the ongoing operation against the 6th SS-Gebirgs Division. But Lieutenant Colonel Connor's 3rd Battalion, 2nd Infantry, had stalled its eastward advance when the Red Diamond men ran into Lieutenant Colonel Brant's 2nd Battalion, 14th Infantry, in the forest north of Rodenbach. Irwin told Roffe to keep his troops above the line running generally from Düdelsheim to Büdingen, and Roffe agreed. But Roffe quickly learned that the 14th Infantry Regiment was operating well above that line. He could not proceed with his operation until further coordination with the 71st Division occurred. Irwin had already dispatched his assistant division commander, Brigadier General Warnock, to the 71st for this purpose, but coordination did not improve.

At 1420 a frustrated Roffe radioed the division command post and stated that the regiment's assigned mission, at present, was impossible to execute—even though the regiment's GIs were attempting to move forward in accordance with the newly established boundary between the 5th and 71st divisions. Roffe soon received a message from the division headquarters that Major General Irwin was on his way to Stammheim.[12]

Irwin arrived at Roffe's command post just before 1500. Roffe immediately briefed his commander on what appeared to be the facts regarding where the 2nd Regiment and the 71st Division were operating. After consulting a map with Roffe, Irwin began to understand what was happening. The 71st Division was indeed farther north than Irwin previously believed. Coordination problems between both divisions continued to be a major concern despite the exchange of numerous liaison officers. XII Corps' misunderstanding of the situation further exacerbated the confusion. Roffe told Irwin that the regiment would compensate as necessary and continue to clear the woods to the north and away from the 71st Division's zone. Irwin agreed and departed the command post at 1530.[13]

Irwin wanted to confirm the 14th Infantry Regiment's dispositions and the location of other 71st Division units, so he drove straight from Stammheim to the 14th's command post in Altenstadt. Irwin met with Colonel Lundquist and discussed the situation. Lundquist's map confirmed what Irwin had learned from Colonel Roffe: the 71st Division was operating well above Büdingen, so the 2nd Infantry Regiment would indeed have to limit their advance to an easterly zone above a line generally running from Nieder-Mockstadt to Ober-

Mockstadt to Ortenberg. Irwin thanked Lundquist for the information and departed for his command post in Frankfurt.

At 1700, only twenty minutes after Irwin arrived, Major General Eddy called to discuss the current situation. Eddy's phone connection was weak, but the XII Corps commander stated that he believed the 6th SS-Gebirgs Division had generally confined themselves to the forests south of Stockheim but were as far south as Wächtersbach. Irwin agreed after explaining that he had just returned from a visit to the 2nd and 14th Infantry command posts. At just that moment Eddy's line went dead.

At 1715 Col. Albert C. Lieber Jr., the XII Corps deputy chief of staff, called and relayed Eddy's message. Lieber explained Eddy's belief that the enemy was well below the Staden-Ortenberg road and that Major General Wyman and Colonel Reed (2nd Cavalry Group) were well engaged with them. According to Lieber, Eddy believed the 71st was driving the 6th SS-Gebirgs Division northeast and that the 5th Infantry Division should move its committed forces (presumably the 2nd Infantry and the 5th Cavalry Reconnaissance Troop) up to the towns of Schotten and Herchenhain some twenty kilometers in that direction.

Irwin could only explain that such a move would be impossible due to a lack of trucks and because the situation on the ground was far different from what Eddy believed it to be. Irwin replied to Lieber, "The picture you give me is not in accord with the facts I have found out there." All of his troops were committed to various missions, and he had only two uncommitted battalions left with no transportation. Irwin also outlined to Lieber the 5th Division's current operations in the Büdingen forest :

> I have [two] units attempting to [advance] in that general direction but between them and those points are considerable [enemy] as far as we know. I don't think [Major General] Eddy has the picture of what we are doing very well. Actually we are attacking [northeast] on [a general] axis ... which is heading for those places. We are fighting in that direction and not just marching. You can see we are headed for the [two] points you indicate but we cannot just march there as we have to push our way [through enemy] in the woods between us and those points. I think what we are doing is still in accord with [Major General Eddy's] idea.

Lieber sensed the frustration in Irwin's voice and agreed to pass the information to Major General Eddy for a reply. He also agreed to send a liaison plane to Irwin's command post in Frankfurt to pick up a current overlay identifying the correct positions of the units involved in the operation.[14]

Irwin could only hope that his discussion with Lieber would shed some light at the XII Corps level on the complex coordination problems faced by him and the 71st Division. The fact that both divisions belonged to different corps did not appear to be the problem. The problem stemmed from a fluid, rapidly changing operational situation and the independent decisions made by each division commander about how many forces to commit to the battle and when those forces should be committed. The orders given to the troops in the field were fragmentary orders—mostly oral and only followed up later with written operations instructions and graphics. The fact that the XII Corps' main focus was on a rapid eastward advance did not help matters. Fighting the enemy both in front and behind clearly showed the complexities and difficulties inherent in such an operation. But, as Irwin hoped, a clearer picture at all levels now existed, and the Red Circle and Red Diamond men could concentrate on the business of eliminating the 6th SS-Gebirgs Division as an effective fighting force.

❖

Colonel Wooten jumped the 5th Regiment's advance command post to Büches at 1645. With Büches protected by patrols and other outposts from the 3rd Battalion, Wooten directed Major Robertson to follow the first patrols into Büdingen with the remainder of the battalion. Wooten wanted Büdingen in the regiment's hands before the sun set in just over two hours.[15]

By 1700 Major Robertson's 3rd Battalion had entered the heart of Büdingen unopposed. White sheets hung from the windows of most houses as a sign that the town would not resist American occupation. The XII Corps' leading elements had already passed through the town, and the civilian populace had become accustomed in the last forty-eight hours to American vehicle traffic running through the ancient cobblestone streets at all hours of the day and night.

The Red Circle men, although not the first GIs to enter Büdingen, observed the town's medieval beauty with awe. Büdingen lay reasonably untouched by the horrors of war except for the recent cast-offs of battle littering the streets such as empty ammunition crates, shell casings, and other battlefield debris. Founded in the twelfth century, Büdingen became a city in 1321 and boasts a wonderful Jerusalem Gate built in 1503 that marks the entrance to the heart of the town. Attached to the gate are magnificent and elegantly preserved defensive walls made of red sandstone. Modern Büdingen has grown up and prospered along the outskirts of this walled medieval city and surrounded it with tile-roofed homes and businesses sitting astride the narrow cobblestone streets typical of many German towns.[16]

Robertson's rifle companies quickly fanned out through the town and checked the environs for hidden or stray German troops. The Red Circle men found none. Robertson directed his company commanders to settle in and post guards. He then radioed his report to Colonel Wooten, who seemed satisfied that Büdingen was clear of the enemy.

In Büdingen Robertson's 3rd Battalion surgeon, 1/Lt. (Dr.) James M. Paul, found the walled city to be starkly beautiful. He quickly directed the trucks and jeeps that carried his medical equipment to the town square. Paul found a nearby shoe store to his liking and designated it as the battalion aid station. Soon the battalion medics were busy off-loading medical supplies and other equipment into the store. Much to Paul's surprise, the store also held a large cache of food—undoubtedly gathered by the store's missing owners in preparation for an uncertain future.[17]

Back in Büches Wooten sent patrols into nearby Rohrbach to the northwest to establish contact with the 14th Infantry on the regiment's left. The patrols soon returned and reported that no one from the 14th was in or around the town; the 3rd Battalion, 14th Infantry, was actually farther north and moving east to Wolf.

At 1710 Wooten reported to division headquarters that he was unable to locate the 14th Infantry and that his new forward command post was in Büches. He explained that he had contact with the 66th Infantry Regiment in the form of a liaison officer located with the 5th's advance command post in Büches.[18]

Wooten then contacted his own main command post in Rückingen and ordered Major Heymont, the regimental S-3, and the rest of the staff to displace north to Büdingen. He further directed that Company A, 271st Engineer Battalion, and Company B, 635th Tank Destroyer Battalion, move forward to Orleshausen south of Büches. He wanted all his combat power forward for an anticipated push eastward into the Büdingen forest.[19]

In the meantime the trucks that had transported Major Robertson's 3rd Battalion to Büches had returned and retrieved Lieutenant Colonel Broyles's foot-marching 1st Battalion. At 1820 the truck-mounted battalion arrived in

Büches, dismounted, and took up positions in and around the town. At the same time Lieutenant Colonel Gettys's foot-marching 2nd Battalion arrived in the nearby hamlet of Lorbach.[20]

Now that the 2nd Battalion had closed on the southern outskirts of Büdingen, Major Heymont called the division G-3 staff and asked for further clarification of the 2nd Battalion's orders. One of Lieutenant Colonel Lankenau's G-3 officers, Major Hurt, informed Heymont that the 2nd Battalion's instructions remained unchanged: move farther east by another three kilometers and cover the road network near a *schloss* southeast of Büdingen. Hurt further informed Heymont that the 14th Regiment was indeed farther north near Bleichenbach and that a new boundary between the two regiments extending along the road from Büdingen northeast to Rinderbügen would go into effect immediately. Hurt also told Heymont that Lankenau wanted the 2nd Battalion to stop at Diebach, but that word had not reached the 5th Regiment in time. The 2nd Battalion would simply proceed with its current mission to cover the road network east of Lorbach. The 1st Battalion should remain in place in Büches. In effect the 5th Regiment had moved as far forward as possible for the day since darkness was coming on. Heymont ended the call and helped prepare the regimental staff for the last movement of the day—the new main command post in Büdingen.[21]

In Waldensberg the Red Circle men of the 2nd Battalion, 66th Infantry, improved their positions throughout the town following the Nord men's failed mid-afternoon counterattack. Ammunition and supplies arrived from the battalion's supply trains, and the GIs grabbed handfuls of M1 Garand rifle clips and belts of .30-caliber machine-gun ammunition. The GIs also carried off cases of ten-in-one rations (ten meals in one box) for their fellow Red Circle men in the lines and outposts. The men were not looking forward to a wet, chilly night with soaked uniforms and foxholes that had become muddy pits.

As the GIs watched Leisenwald for possible signs of another enemy attack, Lieutenant Colonel Eikel's staff took stock of the "butcher's bill." Despite the day's fierce house-to-house fighting and close combat, only eleven Red Circle men had perished—all enlisted men. Twenty GIs were wounded, including two officers. Eikel's men had captured 105 German soldiers. Many were SS men, but the balance hailed from various other German armed services such as the Heer and Luftwaffe.[22]

As Eikel's men rounded up these prisoners, the Red Circle men learned how frightened some of the Germans were of the Black soldiers manning the 761st Tank Battalion's Shermans. Many of the Black officers had already learned from German civilians that this fear was due to the savage reputation earned by French-Senegalese soldiers in World War I. The tank officers warned their Black crewmen to stay buttoned up until all prisoners had passed to avoid panicking the Germans. But one of the Company C tankers mistakenly opened his hatch when some German prisoners were still nearby. Several Germans shouted, "*Schwarze Soldaten!*" ("Black soldiers!") and ran for the woods. A warning volley from the GIs stopped them in their tracks.[23]

Eikel still did not have communications with Lieutenant Colonel Denno's 3rd Battalion to the east and remained unaware of what was happening in and around Leisenwald. His men heard shooting to the east and northeast, but no one—not even the staff members at the 66th Regiment's command post—could verify what was happening.[24]

Eikel had ordered an all-around defense of the town, and his men had been steadily at work digging foxholes or fortifying houses as the sun set. Eikel's men promptly gathered all civilians who had not fled. Among the civilians was thirty-three-year-old Johanna Jende who, with her family, had already escaped her burning home earlier in the day. After the civilians had briefly taken refuge in the basement of a *gasthaus* (an inn), several angry Red Circle men loudly evicted the civilians from their dark sanctuary and ushered them into the street. The GIs then herded the civilians, many shivering in the cold rain, into a field south of town. Jende noticed several young men in the group dressed in civilian clothes whom she did not recognize as citizens of Waldensberg. She was further disappointed that the GIs kept the residents in the open and away from the shelter of the nearby forest—perhaps because the GIs were fearful that everyone might break and run for the woods. The GIs then systematically searched each resident, always starting with the legs. Once a Red Circle man detected military boots under the civilian clothes, he pushed the man to the side and said, "*Du* (you) *SS*." A saddened Jende could only watch as the GIs searched everyone against the backdrop of Waldensberg's burning, shattered remains. In the field nearby, she looked in abject pity at the figure of a woman, an evacuee from Offenbach, staring blankly into space as she sat beside the dead body of her ten-year-old son.[25]

As the GIs searched the town for Nord men who had escaped detection, Pfc. Thomas Tomich and his team of wiremen from Company G continued to string wire from each platoon position back to the company command post inside the town.[26] The GIs soon spotted an undamaged .30-caliber machine gun on top of an M24 Chaffee light tank from the 2nd Cavalry Group. As Tomich and his men approached the tank, they could see two small holes the size of baseballs underneath the chassis and just under the top track. Germans armed with *panzerfäuste* had clearly made short work of the tank. An inspection of the tank's interior revealed a grim sight to Tomich and his men. The crew was dead, killed by the ricocheting, white-hot metal shards that bored through the side armor and then flailed around in the tank's interior, mauling the crew. Outside the tank lay the lifeless crew of a 57-mm anti-tank gun—undoubtedly operating under the supposed protection of the light tank. Tomich and his wiremen quickly retrieved the machine gun from the Chaffee's turret, transferred it to their jeep for some additional armament, and departed the depressing scene as quickly as possible.[27]

As Tomich and his men attached the machine gun to their jeep, a distressed German woman approached two Company G privates, Laverne G. Fisher and a fellow named Parsley, as both men worked on their foxholes near a house on the edge of town. One of the men asked, "What is it?"

The woman replied in broken English, "Will you bury my daughter?"

Touched by the woman's request, the men stopped working and asked her what had happened. In a conversation marked by broken English and German, the woman explained that before the GIs had arrived her daughter had been very sick. She had asked an SS officer who had occupied the town that morning for assistance. The officer, an *SS-Hauptsturmführer*, said that he could do nothing for the girl. In a fit of pique, the woman declared to the SS officer, "The Americans are here, and they have medicine. I will go to *them*!" The officer then drew his pistol and shot the little girl.

"That settles it, does it not?" asked the German officer.[28]

The two GIs winced at the woman's story. Although they could not verify her account, the fact that her daughter was dead clearly agitated the distraught, sobbing woman. The GIs grabbed their entrenching tools and set off to help the mother bury her child.[29]

Lt. Roy J. Long's 81-mm mortar platoon continued to dig gun pits along the northern edge of town behind Companies E and F. After putting his mortars into position, S/Sgt. Jack Inciarrano walked back into town to Long's command post to learn about the "big picture." Since the sun was already setting, Inciarrano knew he would return to his squad well after dark. After meeting with Lieutenant Long and gathering as much information as possible, Inciarrano phoned his section to let them know he was returning to the gun position. He suspected his men would have itchy trigger fingers that night after the day's excitement, and he did not want to take any chances in the dark.

Inciarrano set out for his section's position, keeping in mind that the body of a dead SS soldier was lying somewhere near his position. He would have to watch his step. As he emerged onto the town's outskirts and followed the road, he sensed that he was near the dead German's body. He squinted through the ever-increasing darkness and spotted the Nord man's lifeless form. He carefully stepped over the body; but, before his other foot touched the ground, a communication wire slapped him in the face. At the same time, he heard a GI loudly yelling, "Halt!"

The frightened staff sergeant, with sheer terror consuming his senses, dove headlong into the mud. The thick, soupy sludge covered his entire face and body. After pausing a few moments to gain his composure, Inciarrano realized he had run into a piece of wire strung at head level (improperly, no doubt) and that the challenge had come from one of his own men. Inciarrano slowly got to his feet and sheepishly approached his gun position. As he wiped mud away from his face to the jeers and laughter of his men, Inciarrano realized that this night in Waldensberg would be a long and edgy one.[30]

❖

Lieutenant Colonel Brant's 2nd Battalion, 14th Infantry, departed the forest north of Rodenbach for the town of Bleichenbach promptly at 1700. To avoid colliding further with 5th Infantry Division troops on the battalion's left flank, Brant instructed his companies to face due east and head for Stockheim two kilometers southwest of Bleichenbach. Lieutenant Colonel Guthrie's 3rd Battalion would continue to move south and right of Brant's troops in the direction of Wolf.[31]

Captain Alvey's Company F led the way while Captain Goldman's Company E and Captain Bass's Company G followed. The Red Circle men moved quickly through the woods and onto the open ground east of the Rodenbach forest. Three kilometers distant the GIs could see their first objective—the small town of Stockheim. Brant had organized the rifle companies into tank-infantry company teams, so the GIs walked briskly in the welcome company of Sherman tanks from Captain Long's Company B, 761st Tank Battalion. Each company had two tanks, one towed 76-mm anti-gun from the tank destroyer platoon, one 57-mm antitank gun, and a section each of heavy machine guns and 81-mm mortars from Captain Brewer's Company H.

The GIs quickly gained the outskirts of Stockheim and moved into the heart of town. As the Red Circle men marched into town with rifles at the ready, they passed what appeared to be a German labor camp filled with Polish refugees. No German guards were in sight. The Poles cheered the GIs loudly from behind the compound's barbed-wire fences. The Red Circle men smiled and waved back. The Poles apparently realized that remaining inside the compound until rear-echelon American troops arrived was their safest bet, given the rapid flow of forces through the area in recent days.

The battalion soon passed through Stockheim and ventured toward Bleichenbach two kilometers distant. Brant sent Company F along a parallel route to the north while Companies E and G followed the main road directly into town. When Company E approached to within several hundred meters of the town, a German civilian met them on the road. In broken English the man informed Captain Goldman that the SS troops had just left town and now occupied the wooded hills north of Bleichenbach. Lieutenant Colonel Brant pulled up in his jeep and consulted Goldman and the German civilian. The man's report concerned Brant. He did not want his men to blunder into a German trap, so he told Goldman to form a small reconnaissance party and scout the town.

Within minutes a small group of GIs from Goldman's lead platoon departed for Bleichenbach. The GIs entered the town cautiously, ducking from doorway to doorway. Frightened civilians peeked from behind curtained windows. But for these few civilians, the town seemed deserted.

As the men reached the center of town, they followed a stream on their left named, coincidentally, the Bleichenbach. Near the town square, a small stone footbridge spanned the creek and led to various houses on the other side. Inside the town square sat an ornate, stone-crafted water fountain surrounded by a low wall. The GIs circled through the town and met back in the town square. The town appeared to be clear of SS troops.

The patrol returned and reported to Brant and Goldman that the town was clear. Brant then instructed Goldman to gather his men and enter the town as planned. As Company E departed, Captain Alvey's Company F arrived after dropping down from a parallel northern route.

The battalion entered Bleichenbach without incident, and the rifle companies quickly fanned out to conduct a more thorough search of the town. Brant and his battalion staff rolled noisily into the town square with several jeeps and trucks. He selected a house on a nearby street corner as his command post. A small medical building or clinic sat directly across the narrow street. The staff began unloading field tables, boxes, radios, and other items into the house to set up shop. Brant stayed by his jeep parked beside the fountain to monitor the radio.

A sudden shot rang out from across the creek. A nearby Red Circle man dropped to the ground, severely wounded. Brant sprang from his jeep and crouched down behind the low stone wall surrounding the fountain. More shots rang out. Several bullets ricocheted wildly off the cobblestone street. The staff officers and men quickly sought cover.

From Brant's position, he could see the German sniper's location. The Nord man—probably left behind by *SS-Oberführer* Goebel to harass the American troops pursuing his battle group—fired from a window on the top floor of the third house from the small footbridge. Brant radioed Captain Long to send a tank to the fountain.

A lone Sherman tank from the 761st Tank Battalion soon rumbled into the square from a side street. The crewmen popped their heads up from the turret and spotted Brant near the fountain. He motioned the tankers toward a house across the creek. The crewmen dropped back inside and slammed the hatches shut. The tank then moved to the right of the fountain and swung the turret toward the house. A large tree beside the fountain obscured most of the house from the tank's view, but the tankers intended to shoot right through it and into the house beyond. Several battalion staff members crept carefully into the street with necks craned to watch the show.

To ensure the round did not pass directly through the house and miss the sniper, the tankers loaded a super-quick fuse round. The gunner took aim and fired. The round belched forth from the gun tube and exploded in the tree, creating a near muzzle burst that sent shards of hot metal spraying outside the tank and into the streets. A GI standing outside the command post building fell wounded, bleeding from a severe leg wound; a shell fragment from the tank round's premature burst had severed an artery in the man's leg. First Lieutenant E. E. Smith, the battalion S-3, rushed forward, ripped open the Carlisle-model bandage pack from his first-aid pouch, and stopped the bleeding with a gauze dressing and some sulfanilamide powder.[32]

The tank crew, angered by the near muzzle burst, loaded a high-explosive round into the gun tube. The gunner took aim and fired. The round tore through the tree and into the house, sending large chunks of mortar and rubble tumbling into the street below. Large branches snapped from the tree as the tankers fired three more rounds into the house, blowing out the sidewall and exposing the house's interior to the world. The sniper had been silenced.

Brant stood up from behind the fountain wall and ordered his men to rush the building. Armed with M1 rifles, the Red Circle men charged across the bridge and through the shallow creek. They invaded the severely damaged building and searched it thoroughly. The GIs found nothing—no body, no sniper rifle, nothing.

Lieutenant Colonel Brant soon had the town *bürgermeister* standing out in the square. He warned the dapper, well-dressed old man that if any more snipers fired at his troops, he would reduce the town to ashes. The frightened old man quickly proclaimed in German that he would personally hang any SS troops that he caught!

Satisfied that the *bürgermeister* understood the severity of the situation, Brant ventured into his new command post to consult the operations map and confer with his staff. Inside, Brant's men were still clearing each room. A beautiful young German woman with red hair suddenly stormed into the building, presumably to protest the GIs' occupation. The woman's beauty disarmed Brant for a moment. A nearby GI proclaimed loudly that he thought she had a pistol. Alarmed, Brant stepped forward and bodily searched the woman from top to bottom. He discovered nothing on her person. The young woman, exasperated and embarrassed at the manhandling she had just endured, turned on her heels and stormed angrily out of the building.

The rifle companies soon reported that Bleichenbach was clear of German troops. The company commanders then huddled with Brant in the command post to receive further instructions. Only one hour of daylight remained, but Brant did not want to spend the night in town with a possible concentration of German troops in the woods nearby. The German civilian who met the battalion on the road into town was adamant that the SS troops were somewhere in the forest beyond Bleichenbach.

Brant directed Captain Bass to take Company G to Bergheim two kilometers distant while Captain Alvey took Company F directly into the forest to occupy the high ground three kilometers east of town. If the Germans were in the forest between Bleichenbach and Bergheim, Brant wanted to know about it. He then told Captain Goldman that Company E would remain in Bleichenbach to secure the town and serve as battalion reserve.

Companies F and G were soon on their way to their respective objectives. The GIs covered the ground quickly while daylight remained. Within an hour, Bass and his men had occupied Bergheim without incident. However, Company F had just entered the exact location of the assembly area recently vacated by *SS-Oberführer* Goebel's battle group. The battle group had departed a few hours earlier only to clash with the 5th Cavalry Reconnaissance Troop south of Gelnhaar. Abandoned German stores, equipment, and assorted broken vehicles littered the forest. The GIs picked carefully through the debris to see if they could find anything useful such as documents and the like.

Surprisingly, the Red Circle men encountered several American prisoners abandoned in the woods by Goebel's men. The liberated GIs—mostly from the 9th Infantry Division—explained that the Germans had no way of taking them along, so the Nord men had just left the GIs in the forest. The former prisoners explained that the SS troops had treated them well but worked them hard. The Nord men had little food but lots of liquor, both of which they shared with the prisoners. One weary and disheveled GI stated that the Germans had taken a 9th Division signal operation instruction from them. The tired and hungry men also mentioned that at one point captured American nurses were with them.[33]

The Red Circle men distributed rations to the former prisoners and sent them back to Bleichenbach. The regimental command post had transmitted messages to each battalion stating that all American soldiers who escaped from the enemy were to be sent to the rear immediately for debriefing. But Brant requested that the regimental S-2 come forward to question the newly released prisoners on site. These former prisoners were his best source of information about the elusive Nord Division.[34]

Back in Bleichenbach Brant radioed Colonel Lundquist and reported the day's events. He explained that the former prisoners had stated that two thousand SS troops might be moving toward the 3rd Battalion's area. Lundquist told Brant that since the sun was going down (sunset that day was at 1908), the 2nd Battalion should remain in its current positions for the night. Orders concerning the next day's operation would follow. Brant acknowledged the instructions, hoping that the next day would bring a decided conclusion to his battalion's pursuit of the 6th SS-Gebirgs Division.[35]

❖

Captain Johnson's 71st Cavalry Reconnaissance Troop enjoyed a far less eventful day than their 5th Infantry Division counterpart, the 5th Cavalry Reconnaissance Troop. Johnson's troop spent the day supporting the 14th Infantry Regiment's offensive in the woods north of Rodenbach and on Hill 267 near Glauberg. After placing platoon-blocking positions in Selters and Stockheim, the troop encountered no enemy activity on the 14th's left flank.

At 1225 Johnson—located with the 14th Regiment's command post in Altenstadt—received a message from the G-3 staff that the troop might soon revert to division control. The purpose would be to maintain contact with the 5th Infantry Division troops on the division's left and the 14th Infantry Regiment on the right—presumably to help mitigate the nagging coordination problems suffered by both divisions. In the meantime the troop would continue to support the 14th Regiment.[36]

At 1453 Lieutenant Colonel Lankenau, the G-3, called Johnson once more and told him the troop was once again under division control. Major General Eddy had just contacted Major General Wyman and instructed him to send the troop to patrol a portion of the XII Corps' MSR between Stockheim and Gedern, a fifteen-kilometer stretch of improved roadway heading northeast toward Lauterbach. Eddy continued to be genuinely concerned about the threat posed to his supply lines. The 5th Infantry Division's 5th Cavalry Reconnaissance Troop, commanded by Captain Robinson, had engaged in a similar mission along the same MSR but farther north. Robinson's mission, unknown at the moment to Captain Johnson, was to follow the MSR along a parallel path to the north and, on reaching Lauterbach, head back along the route from the opposite direction. If Robinson had not chosen a different course that afternoon south of the MSR along a more easterly path toward Gelnhaar, the two cavalry reconnaissance troops would have been on a collision course. Lankenau further informed Johnson that the troop should not simply patrol the roadway, but also clear the woods on either side. Johnson was to render a report the first time the troop completely navigated the route.[37]

Johnson contacted his two forward platoons, the 1st and 2nd, and told them to recall all patrols and prepare to move. The 1st Platoon's command post had remained in Stockheim since 1100 that morning; the 2nd Platoon had advanced to a wooded hilltop position a kilometer southeast of Ortenberg. Johnson kept the 3rd Platoon in reserve.[38]

Johnson radioed Lieutenant Samuell and told him to depart with the 1st Platoon immediately and clear the designated stretch of road. The other platoons would soon follow. Samuell gathered his M8 armored cars and bantams and headed toward Ortenberg. On reaching the town, the platoon veered northeast and began the laborious task of moving along the road from its wooded flanks, scouting for enemy activity and ambush sites. The M8s and bantams wended their way slowly through the underbrush and tightly packed pine forest. Occasionally the cavalrymen dismounted and investigated wood thickets and ravines where the M8s could not venture. The setting sun and the overcast sky darkened the forested areas further, and the drizzling rain that had nagged the Red Circle men all day continued to fall. What Samuell and his men did not know was that their route reconnaissance mission was leading them directly across the front of two advancing battalions from the 5th Infantry Division.[39]

❖

The three battalions of the 5th Infantry Division's 2nd Regiment continued to advance northeast but away from the 14th Infantry Regiment's troops on their right flank. Coordination problems forced the regiment to veer northward to avoid friendly-fire incidents with the Red Circle troops. After a long day fraught with such troubles, the three battalions could not advance much farther during the remaining daylight before stopping and hunkering down for the night.

Lieutenant Colonel Connor's 3rd Battalion pressed onward from Ober-Mockstadt, through Ranstadt, and then eastward to Ortenberg and beyond toward Lissberg. The Red Diamond GIs, field jackets and equipment soaked through from the day's steady drizzle, encountered no one. On reaching Ortenberg, Connor moved his command post into the town and sent his three companies, I, K, and L, another kilometer to the north, northeast, and east. The companies' movements proved uneventful and, on reaching their designated locations, they paused for the night. Their positions formed a battalion-sized semicircle facing Lissberg.[40]

Major Pace's 2nd Battalion offloaded at Ranstadt late in the afternoon after a long, uncomfortable ride in open-backed trucks from Seckbach. The wet, sore GIs dismounted, assembled just short of the railroad tracks outside town, and moved out toward Nidda, clearing the roadways and forests as they went. Like the 3rd Battalion the GIs encountered no enemy troops. After a slow trek northeast along a five-kilometer stretch of open road bordered by thick clusters of pine trees, the GIs reached Nidda—their final destination for the day. The descending darkness prevented the men from venturing any farther.[41]

Lieutenant Colonel Blakefield's 1st Battalion finally arrived after an equally difficult journey clinging to the backs of Sherman tanks from Company A, 737th Tank Battalion. The tanks rumbled through Ranstadt and passed directly through Major Pace's 2nd Battalion on the way to Nidda. The tanks soon arrived at the outskirts of Nidda and thundered noisily through the town before turning east toward Glashütten eight kilometers distant.

Blakefield's orders from Colonel Roffe were to turn south at Glashütten, take Merkenfritz, proceed southeast to link up with Captain Robinson's 5th Cavalry Reconnaissance Troop near Kefenrod, and cut off any remaining enemy troops in the area. Aware that Robinson's troop had engaged—and now pursued—one of the Nord Division's columns in that area, Blakefield planned to provide the added firepower needed to destroy the enemy column.[42]

The GIs dismounted the tanks in Glashütten and began moving in a series of squad-sized formations toward Merkenfritz. One squad scouted the road ahead. Coincidentally, heading in the direction of Merkenfritz from the southwest along the corps MSR was Lieutenant Samuell's 1st Platoon, 71st Cavalry Reconnaissance Troop. As the platoon's M8 armored cars and bantams approached the town along both sides of the MSR, Samuell ordered his vehicles to halt when he spotted the 5th Infantry Division troops approaching Merkenfritz from the north. Samuell guided his vehicles onto the high ground south of town and watched as the 1st Battalion's scouting patrol approached the town's outskirts. He and his men recognized them as friendly troops and scanned the town for enemy activity. Samuell was aware the 5th Division's troops were in the area, but he had no way of hailing them via radio or any other means except for direct, on-the-ground contact, which could prove dangerous in limited visibility. Samuell opted instead to wait until the Red Diamond troops cleared the town before contacting them.[43]

The ripping sound of a German MG42 suddenly cut through the air. Lieutenant Colonel Blakefield's scouting party dove for the ditches alongside the road. Samuell watched the GIs raising their heads slowly above the road's shoulders to locate the German machine gun. The GIs then crawled back from whence they came—this time off the road.

Samuell ordered his men to stand fast. If the GIs needed help, the M8s could rush forward. But the potential for a friendly-fire incident existed, so Samuell wanted to be very careful before proceeding. From his turret position in his command car, the bespectacled platoon leader pressed his binoculars against his face and watched the situation develop. The rest of the 1st Battalion, 2nd Infantry, and their supporting tanks were barely visible on the road north of town.

Soon, two GIs appeared on the road, each carrying a wooden chair. Puzzled, Samuell and his men watched as the two men carried the chairs to within three hundred meters of the town's entrance. They positioned the chairs on opposite sides of the road facing each other and then sat down. They placed their M1 rifles across their laps and then waited a moment. One GI gave the other a signal, and both men rushed across the road simultaneously. The

MG42 hidden deep inside Merkenfritz barked again as the GIs crossed the center of the road. The rounds missed their mark. The men then occupied the other's chair on the opposite side.

Samuell scratched his head as the GIs kept up this game of musical chairs for at least twenty minutes. Each time they crossed on a predesignated signal, the MG42 opened fire but missed. The machine gun was positioned too far inside the village; the few houses on the village's outskirts kept the MG42 from traversing left and right and hitting the men in their chairs.

Samuell and his cavalrymen watched transfixed as this strange tableau unfolded before them. Small-arms fire suddenly rang out inside the village. The sound of exploding grenades sent dark wisps of smoke emanating above the rooftops. In a matter of minutes, the town fell silent. GIs were visible moving through the streets and entering houses. Shouts filled the air as GIs proclaimed the town clear. Samuell and his men quickly realized that these seasoned, highly experienced infantrymen from the 5th Division had used the musical-chairs ruse to occupy the German troops' attention while a separate force—probably a platoon or larger—maneuvered around Merkenfritz from the east and attacked from the rear.[44]

Samuell and his platoon drove down off the hill and contacted the Red Diamond GIs in town. He told the Red Diamond men that he thought their unusual tactic was amazing—especially since they suffered no casualties. The few Germans who defended the town were dead or wounded, but the GIs were unable to discern if they hailed from the much-hunted 6th SS-Gebirgs Division. Scores of enemy stragglers from several disbanded German formations still roamed the countryside, and this group likely did not belong to the Nord Division.

Samuell and his platoon soon bid the Red Diamond men farewell and departed for Gedern to complete their route reconnaissance and clearing mission. Lieutenant Colonel Blakefield opted to hold fast in Merkenfritz for the night. The sun would set within an hour, and he did not want his troops searching for an enemy column in the dark of night. The SS troops would have to wait until morning.

After narrowly escaping the 5th Cavalry Reconnaissance Troop's ambush south of Gelnhaar, *SS-Oberführer* Goebel led his long, meandering column of dismounted SS troops and their accompanying caravan of horses, horse-drawn carts, trucks, jeeps, and baby carriages along an easterly route through open farm fields toward Kefenrod. Goebel hoped to regain contact with the Nord Division's main body somewhere to the east or southeast. He had lost radio contact with *SS-Gruppenführer* Brenner and the rest of the division long before departing the battle group's temporary assembly area southeast of Ortenberg earlier that afternoon. The *kampfgruppe* commander desperately wanted to keep his force intact in order to rejoin the division or to find the German main line of resistance that he, like Brenner, believed existed somewhere farther east. But Goebel's immediate concern was to evade the American forces pursuing his column—particularly the 5th Cavalry Reconnaissance Troop that had attacked his battle group less than an hour earlier.

❖

Captain Robinson realized that his 5th Cavalry Reconnaissance Troop's attack on the column of 6th SS-Gebirgs Division troops south of Gelnhaar had forced the German battle group to swing southeast to avoid total destruction. The SS troops suffered few casualties in the initial clash and managed to carry away their wounded and most of their equipment and vehicles. The Red Diamond troops quickly inspected the kill zone and discovered only a handful of bodies and a smattering of German equipment and arms left behind.

Robinson now planned to swing his troop north of Bindsachsen and drop down to Kefenrod in an effort to interdict or block the German column. He believed that the firepower his troop could bring to bear—a combination of armored cars, light tanks, and tank destroyers—would be enough to destroy the German column or, at the very least, to scatter the SS troops until American infantrymen from either the 5th or 71st divisions could mop them up.

The troop made good time traveling the four-kilometer distance through the muddy fields north of Bindsachsen. The armored cars, light tanks, and tank destroyers easily negotiated the rolling terrain even as the day's constant drizzle turned to a steady rainfall. A small curtain of low-lying fog hugged the small valleys among the rolling hills. Only an hour of daylight remained; the overcast sky darkened more with each passing minute.

As the troop approached the western outskirts of Kefenrod, Robinson directed the vehicles south onto the fields below the town. He wanted to gain the high, open ground to the southwest to observe the valley floor below and locate the German column.

First Lieutenant Sterling's 1st Platoon led the way up the high ridgeline outside Kefenrod. As his vehicles crested the hill, an astonished Sterling yelled through his radio headset for his men to stop. Less than fifty meters to the platoon's front moved the lead elements of *SS-Oberführer* Goebel's horse-drawn battle group. The long column was moving in the open across the field below from west to east. The SS men spotted the cavalrymen behind them and yelled, "*Achtung!*"[45]

Sterling shouted through his radio headset for his men to fire. The M8 armored cars launched scores of 37-mm main-gun rounds at point-blank range against the startled German troops. The Nord men scattered and went to ground, returning fire with rifles and MG42 machine guns. The 3rd Platoon came on line with Sterling's men and joined the cacophony of barking main guns and crackling machine guns.

Robinson sped forward in his armored car to observe the clash. He witnessed hundreds of German soldiers lying prone in the field below, many of whom were returning fire. Several SS men braved the maddening torrent of 37-mm and machine-gun fire to kneel upright and launch *panzerfaust* rounds at the armored cars. The rounds all missed their marks.

The 37-mm cannon fire tore up large hunks of dirt and mud that saturated the prone SS troops. Many SS men bolted for the safety of small folds in the terrain farther away or sprinted toward Wolferborn barely visible a kilometer away. Several Nord men struggled to calm the spooked horses that tried to wrench free from the wagons they pulled. Their panicked reactions overturned several carts, spilling their stores onto the damp fields underfoot. SS men screamed in pain as machine-gun bullets and shell fragments rent their exposed flesh. A distraught *SS-Oberführer* Goebel could only watch helplessly and shout from his jeep for his men to run for cover.

Within minutes Robinson had the light tanks and tank destroyers on line with the armored cars and was firing into the column's ranks. The tanks took careful aim and fired at the now chaotic, panicked column of SS troops and horses. The 37-mm and 76.2-mm rounds slammed into their targets at point-blank range, obliterating the motorized and horse-drawn vehicles and their occupants. Several vehicles burst into flames.

The tanks fired on the horse-drawn carts as well, blasting the wagons to pieces and freeing the terrified horses that pulled them. The horses immediately ran away, dragging their yokes and damaged carts. Scores of SS troops joined the horses in a mad dash for safety.

Goebel's heart sank as he watched his *kampfgruppe* of nearly one thousand men disintegrate. He abandoned his jeep—now an easy target for the tanks and tank destroyers—and set off on foot to the south with members of his staff. The rest of the *kampfgruppe* had already scattered; men were sprinting across the open fields.

Robinson quickly ordered his armored cars and tanks to assault through the column and pursue the escaping SS troops. The vehicles sped down the ridgeline through the field and drove between the dead and wounded Nord men. Equipment and ammunition lay scattered across the fields. Wounded SS troops moaned as a handful of German medics rushed from one man to another to administer aid.

As his vehicles moved through the mass of German wreckage, Robinson ordered his men to stop and round up the surviving SS troops. He did not want to pursue individual soldiers into the woods since his cavalry troop's real firepower advantage rested in the open with unrestricted fields of fire. Mopping up the woods for individual Nord men was a job best left to the infantry.[46]

The Red Diamond troops soon dismounted their vehicles and rounded up the few SS troops who now stood up slowly, removing their helmets and raising their hands high. The GIs signaled the SS men to approach and then promptly searched them. They found fighting knives and grenades well hidden on the prisoners. The GIs also retrieved from the breast pockets of the SS troopers' tunics the SS *Soldbuch* each man carried that quickly identified the prisoners as members of the 6th SS-Gebirgs Division Nord.

Robinson's armored car soon pulled up and stopped in the midst of his men, who were busy searching the wreckage for survivors and anything useful that might provide further clues about the Nord Division and its intentions. The platoon leaders approached Robinson with reports on the number of Germans killed and captured—49 prisoners and 150 dead. The rest, a significant number, had escaped in small groups or as individuals into the surrounding countryside. Among the SS men who escaped was *SS-Oberführer* Goebel, the *kampfgruppe* commander.[47]

Robinson radioed his report to the G-3 and then sent mounted patrols to the outlying countryside in search of stragglers. The time was 1830, and only thirty-eight minutes of daylight remained. Robinson wanted to grab as many SS troops as possible before the day finally ended.[48]

❖

Companies I and L of Lieutenant Colonel Denno's 3rd Battalion, 66th Infantry, finally cleared the woods north of Leisenwald nearly two hours after their assault began at 1530 that afternoon. After hours of dogged, close-quarters combat, the Red Circle men expelled the dug-in Nord men from their positions overlooking the town, taking several prisoners and killing scores of others in numerous small-arms exchanges. Numerous SS troops escaped west into the woods toward Wolferborn more than a kilometer away.[49]

The sun had nearly set by the time Captain Gray's Company L troops occupied firing positions from the wood line overlooking Leisenwald. Lieutenant Tyler's Company I used the German foxholes (or dug new ones) and provided all-around protection for the two companies. Gray directed his light .30-caliber machine guns to the forest's edge and ordered the crews to fire on any enemy troops in and around Leisenwald. Within minutes, the gunners spotted German troops moving on the town's outskirts less than six hundred meters away. The GIs opened fire. The cadence of their sporadic machine-gun bursts broke the temporary evening stillness. The rounds impacted against houses and along the streets, sending SS troops running for cover.[50]

As the machine gunners fired into Leisenwald, Gray and Tyler both radioed situation reports to Lieutenant Colonel Denno, who waited impatiently on the hill overlooking Leisenwald for the rest of the 3rd Battalion—consisting of Company K, the towed 105-mm howitzers, and the 105-mm assault guns—to arrive. Denno had expected them to appear soon after the two companies assaulted the woods north of town at 1530, but the time was now 1800 and the rest of the battalion had yet to arrive. Denno told the two company commanders to dig in and wait. As soon as Company K arrived, explained Denno, he would assault Leisenwald.

Inside the heart of Leisenwald, *SS-Gruppenführer* Brenner sat on a small wooden stool in his division command post—still situated inside a cow barn—and listened to the American machine guns firing in the distance. *SS-Standartenführer* Raithel, still energetic and coordinating the remaining SS troops' defensive efforts, had already reported to Brenner the assault by the two American companies in the woods north of town. *SS-Unterscharführer* Stöwe, the radio section chief, had reported no contact with *SS-Oberführer* Goebel's horse-drawn *kampfgruppe* or any other German unit in the area.

The situation was beginning to look hopeless. Raithel reported that the division still had approximately six hundred able-bodied Waffen-SS soldiers and various troops from other services to defend Leisenwald. They had about five hundred former prisoners liberated from American captivity in Waldensberg. However, most of these men—predominantly from the Heer—were unarmed and lacked the will to fight.

The report depressed Brenner. His division of several thousand had been reduced to a mere six hundred in less than forty-eight hours. Waldensberg to the south was in American hands, GIs were firing on him from the north, an unknown number of U.S. units were undoubtedly advancing from the west, and several light tanks on a hill overlooked the town from the east. The situation was clear to Brenner: the remaining troops of the 6th SS-Gebirgs Division Nord were surrounded.[51]

Despite the clearly hopeless situation faced by his Nord men, Brenner did not plan to surrender. He ordered Raithel and the handful of remaining officers to dig in and prepare to defend the town from an assault on all sides. The division would fight to the very end.

Raithel and his mountain-troop officers quickly spread Brenner's orders to the men in position inside houses and outbuildings along the outskirts of the town. The Nord men stockpiled ammunition, drove their one captured American tank into position, and braced for the worst. Brenner's orders to his division staff officers were equally pointed and stark: prepare to destroy the division's records and fight to defend the command post. The final battle was coming.

❖

As Lieutenant Colonel Denno scanned Leisenwald with his binoculars, the sound of truck engines and squealing tank tracks met his ears. He turned to see several trucks laden with Company K's GIs approaching from the direction of Streitberg. The trucks and 105-mm guns had finally arrived. When Denno saw the two slow-moving 105-mm towed howitzers and the two self-propelled 105-mm assault guns slogging through the muddy fields, he understood the group's delay. The rain-soaked trails through the woods had become muddier throughout the day and slowed their progress considerably.

Captain Grambling, the Company K commander, and Lieutenant Ellison, the Company M commander, jumped down from the first two trucks and approached Denno. The Red Circle men dismounted the trucks, stretched, and began checking their equipment and offloading boxes of ammunition and grenades. The 2nd Cavalry Group's four light tanks continued to scan Leisenwald for enemy activity.

Grambling told Denno that he had only Company K's 1st and 2nd platoons with him. The trucks would have to go back for the 3rd Platoon, which was still on foot several kilometers away. They had not had enough trucks to bring everyone forward at once. Denno, disappointed that he did not have all of Grambling's troops present, immediately told the two company commanders that he intended to attack Leisenwald before the sun set within the hour. He directed the four 105-mm howitzers to take up firing positions beside the M24 Chaffee light tanks. Ellison's 81-mm mortars and the howitzers would fire a pre-attack barrage onto Leisenwald. Once the sun was down, the mortars would have to use illumination rounds to allow the Red Circle men to see as they cleared buildings and houses within Leisenwald.

Denno then turned to Grambling and instructed him to attack the town from the east as soon as the barrage ended. The tanks and assault guns would cover the GIs' movement over the several hundred meters of open ground until they reached the village itself. The tanks would then follow in close support. What Denno did not tell the two men was that he privately doubted their ability, and the ability of his entire 3rd Battalion, to fight effectively at night since they had yet to conduct an attack in limited visibility. Denno would be pleased to learn later that his fears had been unfounded.[52]

As Grambling prepared his men for the assault, Denno instructed Ellison to send two men to observe the road to the north leading into Leisenwald from Streitberg. Denno was concerned that a German force might try to relieve the SS troops in Leisenwald along this road; if so, he wanted some early warning. Denno then assembled Grambling and his two platoons and gave them a pep talk. He warned the GIs to keep their helmets on their heads; any Red Circle man failing to conform could expect to report to him. Denno was concerned for his troops and, as a seasoned combat leader, knew the dangers inherent in house-to-house fighting.[53]

Lieutenant Ellison found Second Lieutenant Steinmetz, the 81-mm mortar platoon leader, and instructed him to set up the observation post directed by Denno along the Leisenwald–Streitberg road. Steinmetz approached Private First Class Knapp and Pfc. Alec C. Burton, one of the platoon's ammo bearers, and assigned them the observation post mission. Both men had nearly completed their own foxholes near the mortar positions when

Steinmetz told them to stop. The two dismayed privates shouldered their gear, grabbed their weapons, and trudged off to the north. The evening drizzle had become a steady rain, causing the two GIs' feet to stick in the mud.⁵⁴

Knapp and Burton soon crested the small rise over which stretched the main road leading east to Streitberg. The two GIs had no option but to dig foxholes on the open hillside on either side of the road. They could not see a single tree or bush anywhere in sight. Burton and Knapp immediately began digging in the steady rain but, after removing ten inches of dirt, they hit solid rock. Frustrated, the two men decided to convert their ten-inch holes into body-length slit trenches into which they could lie prone and observe the road. But, as Knapp and Burton settled down inside the holes, their rear ends protruded above the top edges. Their only recourse was to cover themselves with their resin-fibered raincoats. However, the various folds in the raincoats created small reservoirs of water that spilled down each man's neck with the slightest movement. For Private First Class Burton, whose M1 carbine lay saturated in the mud, this night would be the most miserable one in all his days in combat.⁵⁵

Back on the hill overlooking Leisenwald, Captain Grambling assembled his two platoons directly behind the light tanks and assault guns. The time was 1830 and Grambling had less than forty minutes of daylight remaining—even though the overcast sky and steady rain had darkened the landscape considerably. Denno stood next to his jeep beside the tanks and howitzers. Grambling looked over to his battalion commander and nodded. Denno ordered the tanks and assault guns to fire.⁵⁶

The countryside exploded in a cacophony of steady, ear-splitting reports as the light tanks, howitzers, and assault guns belched flame and steel at the tiny village of Leisenwald. To their rear Second Lieutenant Steinmetz's 81-mm mortar platoon went into action. The assistant gunners dropped round after round into the tubes, sending the ordnance skyward with loud, hollow popping sounds. Mortar gunner Pfc. Leo A. Sims marveled at the incredible number of rounds his platoon was firing into Leisenwald.⁵⁷

Within seconds Leisenwald was ablaze. The 105-mm rounds slammed directly into the houses on the eastern edge of town. Mortar shells burst on rooftops and in the streets. Orange tile fragments from the roofs spun into the air as houses disintegrated in the explosions. The spackled stone exteriors of other houses crumbled. SS troops ran into the streets to avoid the falling rubble in their doorway and window positions. Several wooden houses caught fire. Numerous barns burned brightly as the hay inside burst into flames. Cows and horses, freed from their stalls, galloped madly from the town and into the surrounding countryside. Gaping holes appeared in the sides of buildings as the assault guns and light tanks systematically belched main gun rounds at each house, barn, or building on the town's eastern edge. The tower atop the town's school, complete with a beautiful clock and bell erected in 1924 by the citizens of Leisenwald, crumbled to the street. In the woods north of town, machine gunners from Companies I and L saturated the streets and houses with steady streams of tracer-laden .30-caliber fire.[58]

As the massive barrage pounded Leisenwald mercilessly, Grambling and his men rushed down the hill toward the town firing M1 Garand rifles, BARs, and belt-fed .30-caliber machine guns from the hip. Denno was amazed at the ferocity and gallantry of the GIs' assault. As the infantrymen approached the outskirts of town, the tanks and assault guns shifted their fires to the northern and southern edges of Leisenwald. The mortars began seeking deeper targets within the village.[59]

Terrified by the massive barrage destroying their town, the citizens of southeastern Leisenwald no longer felt safe in their cellars. They quickly abandoned their hiding places and rallied in a rain-filled hollow along the road heading east out of town. Elderly men and women, together with crying children and terrified young mothers, huddled in the open as the rain fell steadily on them. Many of them raised their heads above the hollow long enough to witness their beloved Leisenwald in flames.[60]

From his hilltop position east of town, Denno watched as the assault unfolded with precision. He knew the German troops in Leisenwald outnumbered the seventy or so men in Company K's two platoons, but he counted on the tremendous fire support provided by the tanks, assault guns, and mortars to shift the balance in the GIs' favor. He further planned to commit Companies I and L to the assault as soon as the timing seemed right.

As the GIs approached the town's edge in the heavy rain, the German defenders remained silent. Only a few dead and wounded, writhing in agony, lay sprawled on the streets. As the GIs came within fifty meters of the nearest house, though, the burning, partially demolished outer buildings crackled loudly with MG42, rifle, and MP40 fire. The small-arms rounds raked the exposed GIs' ranks, wounding several Red Circle men and sending them to the ground writhing in agony.[61]

Undaunted the GIs pressed their attack and swiftly gained the first series of buildings in town. The GIs quickly spread out, bayonets fixed. They expertly shot SS soldiers firing from doorways and windows. The Red Circle men kicked down doors and entered with rifles and machine guns blazing wildly. Burning buildings nearby illuminated the streets and created dancing shadows that toyed with everyone's imaginations. The streets became an instant no-man's land as German and American tracer rounds crisscrossed from one side to the other.

Several Red Circle men rushed from doorway to doorway, dodging heavy German rifle fire. A determined antitank crew, firing the SS men's lone antitank gun, launched several rounds down the streets at the seemingly ubiquitous American attackers. The antitank rounds exploded against building corners and walls, sending chunks of cement and stone and shards of wood into the air. Several GIs fell wounded, but the rest kept coming. The SS troops gave ground grudgingly, many falling back to the town's inner defenses.

❖

In his command post barn near the center of Leisenwald, *SS-Gruppenführer* Brenner received numerous sketchy reports about the unfolding attack. The constant, steady barrage of mortar rounds and 105-mm rounds impacting the town deafened Brenner and his staff. Some reports suggested that the town's outer defenses had crumbled when in fact the Nord men were still holding. The ferocity of the American attack surprised Brenner, who had become accustomed to the Americans' more methodical, deliberately executed assaults.

Brenner's confidence in his ability to defend Leisenwald quickly began to wane. He watched his staff scrambling to make sense of various messengers' reports. A quick look outside the barn's entrance revealed to Brenner that the town was in flames. Nord men rushed about frantically in an effort to push men and ammunition to the village's eastern defenses. Brenner knew the end had come. The time to disband the 6th SS-Gebirgs Division Nord had arrived.

❖

As Company K's two platoons fought bitterly for the heart of Leisenwald, Lieutenant Colonel Denno heard the sound of truck engines roaring across the field to his rear. The 3rd Platoon of Company K had finally arrived. The time was 1915.

Denno briefed the platoon leader on the situation and immediately sent the GIs into the fray. The men gathered their weapons and equipment and headed for the eastern edge of town. Denno directed the light tanks to follow the platoon. The 3rd Platoon's presence brought Captain Grambling's company up to full strength—121 men. This opportune addition of fresh troops would reinvigorate Company K's assault and increase its chances for a rapid denouement to the situation.

Denno could not help but feel proud of Grambling and his troops. An outnumbered Company K had rushed gallantly into a close-quarters battle with a seasoned enemy force and held its own. The battle was still in full swing; from Denno's vantage point, though, the Red Circle men were clearly gaining ground and advancing steadily. If they could get to the heart of town without delay, they could eliminate the SS troops' command post and crush all resistance—once and for all.[62]

❖

At the 66th Infantry Regiment's command post in Lieblos, Colonel Regnier struggled to make sense of the various reports coming in concerning the fighting in and around Waldensberg and Leisenwald. Regnier was confident that Lieutenant Colonel Eikel had Waldensberg well in hand. But the sporadic reports from Lieutenant Colonel Denno's 3rd Battalion in Leisenwald—reports hampered by the technical and range limitations of the battalion's radios—did not allow Regnier to grasp fully the high-intensity nature of combat in that town. He believed Denno was only trying to tie in with Eikel's 2nd Battalion at Waldensberg. As a result of this confusion, Major Merrill, the regimental S-3, mistakenly reported to Lieutenant Colonel Lankenau at division headquarters that both battalions were attacking west from Waldensberg, which was clearly not the case.[63]

Eikel's 2nd Battalion had continued to defend Waldensberg after taking the town in heavy fighting earlier that afternoon. Eikel remained unaware that Denno's 3rd Battalion was assaulting Leisenwald to the north although many of the 2nd Battalion's men reported hearing firing and explosions to the northeast. Communications problems kept the two battalions from sharing information and coordinating their efforts, thereby preventing the regimental and division headquarters from grasping the true situation.[64]

Earlier in the afternoon Lieutenant Colonel Lankenau had contacted the 66th's command post and told Colonel Regnier that he had a free hand in running the situation developing in and around Waldensberg and Leisenwald. Lankenau suggested that the regimental reserve, Lt. Col. Everett C. Thomas's 1st Battalion, begin moving toward Breitenborn to assist in the fighting. The 1st Battalion had occupied the forested high ground north and northeast of Lieblos since the previous day. Regnier still had at his disposal the trucks used by the 2nd Battalion to move Thomas's GIs, but Regnier asked permission for the 1st Battalion to avoid using the trucks and instead travel dismounted through the woods and clear the forest of German troops as they moved. Lankenau agreed. After a flurry of instructions from Major Merrill, Thomas began moving the battalion toward Breitenborn by late afternoon.[65]

Lankenau further informed Regnier that Major General Eddy, anxious to clear the Büdingen forest of the 6th SS-Gebirgs Division, had sent a battalion from the 26th Infantry Division (which was following in the wake of the advancing 11th Armored Division) to the Waldensberg area. This battalion, explained Lankenau, would be attached to the 66th and employed at Regnier's discretion.[66]

But Major General Eddy's anxiety about the presence of the Nord Division in the XII Corps' rear prompted the corps commander to grow more concerned about the security of his advance command post in Lauterbach. The 4th and 11th Armored divisions were advancing quickly, followed by their supporting infantry divisions, the 80th and 26th, respectively. As these infantry divisions moved farther away from the corps command post, Eddy believed that his command group had become considerably more vulnerable to any action the 6th SS-Gebirgs Division might take—especially since the 71st Division appeared to be pushing the Nord men east and northeast. The corps command post needed added protection, so Eddy called Major General Wyman for help.[67]

At 1840, as Colonel Regnier struggled to piece together the tactical situation of his 2nd and 3rd battalions, Lieutenant Colonel Lankenau called with an urgent message: move the 1st Battalion northeast and secure the corps command post. Lankenau explained that the battalion should travel by truck back toward the division command post in Langenselbold to meet halfway with a liaison officer who would provide directions to Herbstein (five kilometers southwest of Lauterbach). The battalion would halt at Herbstein and await further orders. In the meantime, explained Lankenau, the battalion commander (Lieutenant Colonel Thomas) would head directly for Lauterbach and report to Major General Eddy for instructions.

Regnier told Lankenau that the regiment's trucks were gassed and ready to go, so the 1st Battalion would be on the road within twenty minutes. Regnier ordered Thomas to assemble his battalion near Lieblos, load up on the trucks, and depart immediately. The battalion's attached tank destroyers would remain behind and, with the regimental antitank company, pull in tightly around the regimental command post and defend Lieblos. Thomas quickly issued instructions to his staff and company commanders. By 1950 the battalion had plotted the route and was on the way preceded by Thomas, who raced ahead by jeep to Lauterbach and the corps advance command post.[68]

Although Regnier had quickly obeyed Major General Wyman's instructions, he expressed concern to Lankenau about the gap left open to the south by the 1st Battalion's departure. The battalion had been the only unit on the corps' right flank that covered the gap between the XII Corps and the lagging Seventh Army to the south. Lankenau told Regnier that units from Major General Robert L. Spragins's 44th Infantry Division, part of the Seventh Army's XV Corps, would arrive to fill the gap. In the meantime the 2nd Cavalry Group would watch the gap. Regnier's concerns proved short-lived, because the first elements of the 44th arrived in Hailer within an hour of the 1st Battalion's departure. Regnier's back was now covered, so he could concentrate his full efforts and attention on clearing the SS troops from the area around Waldensberg and Leisenwald.[69]

❖

SS-Sturmmann Egon Krüger emerged from the basement of the house in Leisenwald where he had managed to catch a few hours sleep before Company K's attack began at 1830. After the motorized column had nearly left him behind in the Assenheim forest the previous day, Krüger opted to stay close to SS-Gebirgsjäger Regiment 11's headquarters—or what remained of it.[70]

As Krüger stepped onto the cobblestone street in the evening dusk with his rifle firmly in hand, a scene of pure chaos met his eyes. SS men ran from one building to the next carrying ammunition and shouting that the Americans were on the next street. The deafening clatter of machine-gun and rifle fire echoed through the town. The rain fell steadily. American mortar rounds burst on the rooftops of nearby houses, sending shards of orange-tiled shingles clattering to the ground. Several mortar rounds struck two American fuel trucks that had been captured in Waldensberg a day earlier. The trucks burst into flame, brilliantly illuminating many nearby buildings and streets with dancing, red-hot flames.[71]

As though in a trance, Krüger walked through the streets and watched the horror of the fighting unfold. No one seemed to notice him or stop to give him orders, so he kept on walking toward the eastern edge of town where the combat seemed most fierce. He walked past German trucks and an occasional *kübelwagen* (German jeep) parked outside a building. Captured American jeeps and trucks lined the streets and alleyways all throughout Leisenwald; many of these vehicles now burned intensely.

Krüger walked past a courtyard and saw a large group of frightened, wild-eyed American prisoners huddled there under German guard. They sat curled up in the rain, flinching at the numerous shell bursts that peppered nearby rooftops. The Nord men had captured many of these Americans in and around Leisenwald and Waldensberg in the previous twenty-four hours.[72]

As Krüger approached the eastern edge of town, he noticed the American light tanks and assault guns edging toward the village from the open, freshly tilled ridgeline. The vehicles' main guns fired on the move. GIs rushed from building to building, firing rifles and carbines from the hip as they ran. Krüger quickly realized that the Americans had Leisenwald surrounded. He crouched low and ran up to the four-man crew manning the lone antitank gun firing down the side streets. The *panzerjäger* crew struggled to aim the weapon by sighting it from the top of the barrel. American rifle bullets had cracked the aiming sight's glass aperture. Krüger asked if he could help, but one SS soldier simply replied that they only had five rounds left and would have to abandon the gun shortly.

The sudden drone of an airplane engine caused Krüger and the *panzerjäger* crew to glance upward. In the overcast sky above circled a low-flying spotter plane from the 71st Division Artillery. Krüger could clearly see the plane's two occupants peering downward into the town. The Nord men raised their rifles and fired, peppering the aircraft's fuselage. The plane sputtered, coughed, and sputtered again before descending rapidly toward the forest's edge well east of town. In the rapidly waning daylight, the SS men watched the plane's two occupants, having survived the crash landing, run for cover into the nearby forest.

Krüger turned and hurried back toward the center of town. All around him he recognized members of *SS-Sturmbannführer* Walter Nestler's SS-Gebirgs Panzerjäger Battalion 6. The antitank men were armed with rifles and *panzerfäuste* and were fighting as infantrymen. But where was Nestler? Where were the rest of the division's leaders?

Krüger soon came to the entrance of an undamaged cow barn on the right side of the main road to Wolferborn. He entered and saw *SS-Gruppenführer* Brenner standing in the midst of numerous staff officers gathered around a map laid flat on a crude, wooden table. The men mumbled to each other and pointed to various areas on the map. Brenner stood nearby with the handset of a field phone pressed firmly to his ear, trying to hear reports of the fighting that consumed the village. Several oil-burning lamps barely illuminated the barn's dark interior.[73]

SS-Unterscharführer Georg Stöwe and his six-man communications section sat on stools huddled around several radio sets. The men listened at American Morse-code transmissions crackling through the static. Stöwe's interpreter, Army *Oberfeldwebel* Dr. Martin Gladenfeld, strained to hear what the American voices were saying. The transmissions were short and clipped: "Reached point A; we're under small-arms fire." "Wait," came the response. "We'll send tanks." Within minutes, another voice would bark, "Tanks arrived." A few moments later, the same voice would say, "Enemy silenced. We're moving on." Gladenfeld wrote the short missives furiously on a small pad of paper. The other four listening operators (all *SS-Rottenführers*)—Kurt Bauer, Karl-Heinz Wommer, Herbert Schröder, and Josef Bielita—switched frequencies continuously in search of German transmissions.[74]

One of the *funkers* shouted to Stöwe. The man quickly handed his communications chief a handwritten message. Stöwe read it and then immediately walked over to Brenner, who read the message intently. Brenner then looked down at the ground and shook his head. The message originated from the German high command and ordered all surviving German formations (including the 6th SS-Gebirgs Division) to disband into groups of "Werewolves" seven to twenty men strong. These groups would carry on a guerilla campaign against the Americans using hit-and-run and sabotage tactics. Brenner tossed the paper aside. He refused to allow his men to fight as partisans. His Nord men were soldiers and would fight as soldiers—not as criminal marauders.[75]

At that moment the door burst open. A Nord medic shouldering a bleeding officer pushed past Krüger and sat the injured man on a bench. Brenner approached and saw that the injured man was *SS-Standartenführer* Raithel. Blood-soaked paper bandages covered one part of Raithel's head. His camouflage smock was smeared with blood and bits of flesh. The Nord medic explained that Raithel had lost an eye in the fighting. Raithel seemed barely conscious and sat slumped with his back against the wall.[76]

The loss of Raithel meant only one thing to Brenner: the time had come to evacuate Leisenwald. The continued defense of the town seemed pointless. A motorized breakthrough was out of the question. The SS men lacked heavy weapons and vehicles. Brenner's only recourse was to disband the remaining divisional units, organize them into small groups, and escape Leisenwald on foot—but not as Werewolves. The objective of each group would be to find the German front lines, which Brenner mistakenly still believed to be south in Gelnhausen.

Brenner assembled his staff and informed them of his decision. The officers could only agree with their commander's assessment of the situation. Brenner told his staff to send messengers to the fighting units with instructions to begin assembling into groups. The wounded and the American prisoners would remain behind. Brenner still wanted to move as one large entity if possible and split up into the smaller groups only if pressed by the Americans. Even at this stage of the fighting, Brenner still envisioned keeping as much of his command intact as possible.[77]

Brenner ordered the staff members and orderlies to burn all classified materials and render inoperable any remaining vehicles that still functioned. Staff officers promptly threw documents into small barrels and pails then set them alight. Orderlies departed the barn and spread the word. *SS-Unterscharführer* Stöwe and his *funkers* grabbed all radios, pulled out the tubes, and buried them in a manure pit outside the barn along with engine parts from the working vehicles. Each *funker* then donned his camouflage smock, field gear, and helmet and awaited instructions to depart.[78]

An orderly approached *SS-Sturmmann* Krüger, who remained standing near the barn's entrance. The orderly barked at Krüger to leave the village immediately either alone or as part of a group and to find the new front line. Confused and bewildered, Krüger stepped outside, looked around at the town's burning buildings, and then headed for the southern outskirts of town. He soon disappeared into the surrounding farm fields, concealed by the night's inky blackness.[79]

❖

As word spread for the Nord men to assemble in the center of Leisenwald, Captain Grambling's Company K pressed their attack for the heart of the town. Darkness enveloped the village and the surrounding countryside. The

Red Circle men dashed from house to house and doorway to doorway in the eerie light of burning buildings. Lieutenant Colonel Denno, now at his command post in a small house on the eastern edge of town, continued to receive reports from Grambling about the ferocity of the fighting. Denno urged Grambling to press his attack. The Nord men were giving ground, and the GIs clearly had the advantage.[80]

With night upon them, Company M's 81-mm mortar platoon began firing illumination rounds over the center of Leisenwald. The rounds popped high above the town as the small, white parachutes opened and slowly floated to earth; the attached flares burned brightly, leaving a smoky trail in their wake but providing the GIs with enough light to advance quickly and deliberately. As the first flares burst above the GIs' heads, the sporadic drizzle turned to a steady downpour, soaking the men as they rushed from building to building. The rain began to extinguish many of the house fires burning throughout town.[81]

Pfc. Lewis W. Ashforth and his fellow Company K GIs rushed down side streets, firing as they ran. Ashforth watched as a fellow infantryman named Kendall W. Emde, on hearing the crackle of rifle fire from the upper floor of a nearby house, swung his BAR around and, firing from the hip, knocked a Nord man from a balcony.

Two Company K mortar men, William N. Kasson and Jerry Orona, followed behind the advancing riflemen and stopped to set up their light 60-mm mortar in a tank trap the Nord men had dug on the edge of town. As they set up the base plate and mortar tube, rifle bullets began kicking up dirt around the edge of the shallow hole. Kasson and Orona quickly realized that some of their own men had mistaken the two mortar men for Germans and opened fire. Kasson was low inside the hole and avoided injury, but Orona was exposed. As Orona jumped for cover, a bullet struck him in the helmet, penetrated the shell and liner, and plowed a crease in the wool jeep cap he wore underneath. The bullet did not even part Orona's hair—a remarkable instance of pure luck.[82]

Kasson and Orona quickly waved off their friendly attackers, who recognized their mistake and stopped firing. The two Red Circle men then finished setting up their mortar in the shallow pit and began sending rounds into the town. Soon, Kasson and Orona noticed a dead German motorcyclist at the far end of the pit. The mangled remains of the man's motorcycle lay nearby. Kasson crawled over to the body and rolled the corpse over. The man's arm, frozen in death, was cocked up near his face. The SS man appeared to be thumbing his nose at the two GIs, even in death.[83]

The machine-gun and rifle fire crisscrossing the streets grew more intense as the GIs approached the center of Leisenwald. One infantry squad, moving rapidly in single file at a crouch and closely hugging the buildings' outer walls, turned a corner and stumbled onto a stationary MG42 position. The German machine gunner opened fire, shooting away the lightweight gas masks the men carried on their hips. The surprised but unharmed Red Circle men kept moving forward undeterred.

Sgt. Rex Chamberlain's rifle squad jogged quickly down a side street, scanning the upper windows of each building for the seemingly ubiquitous German snipers who dogged the GIs' every move. As the GIs stood below the second floor window of one house looking for signs of SS troops in the building across the street, a shower of clothing and gear landed on the Red Circle men. The GIs recognized an American field jacket and a pair of brown boots. They aimed their rifles upward just as a scantily clad man jumped from the window and landed on the riflemen in one big heap. The GIs fell to the ground with arms and legs flailing. After a great deal of cursing, the GIs disentangled themselves from the half-naked man, who stood up and exclaimed, "Boy, am I damned glad to see Americans again!"[84]

Captain Grambling's men encountered several well-defended houses that seemed impenetrable to the average infantryman—even with well-aimed M9 bazooka rounds. The SS troops had fortified the doorways and windows backed up by several MG42 machine-gun positions. As the GIs approached these small fortresses, rifle and machine-gun fire crackled and sent the Red Circle men scurrying for cover. The GIs heard whooshing sounds as the SS men fired *panzerfaust* rounds from the upper floors. The warheads burst on the rain-soaked cobblestones and stone buildings, sending shards of white-hot metal fragments and rock flying through the air.

Grambling immediately called forward the cavalrymen's light tanks, which were moving slowly throughout town stalking SS troops. The M24 Chaffee light tanks pulled up in front of the houses and opened fire at point-blank range, punching large holes in each building. The Nord men withdrew from their small fortresses with their wounded in tow. The GIs then stormed the buildings and cleared them room by room.[85]

Despite close-quarters combat in the town (some of which had been hand to hand), the GIs suffered remarkably few casualties. Initial reports to Grambling suggested fewer than ten soldiers killed and an equal amount wounded. The number of Germans killed was clearly much higher yet not possible to tabulate. Grambling passed these figures back to Denno's command post with a request for more ammunition. The GIs were running low on rifle bullets and grenades. One tank crew had already told Grambling that they only had two main-gun rounds remaining.[86]

Civilian casualties in Leisenwald proved much more difficult to ascertain. A seven-year-old boy died along with some of Company K's men when a shell impacted on the first floor of the Möser pub. The local carpenter, Karl Wagner, was killed, as were nearly all members of the Schmidt family. Many more civilians undoubtedly lay dead throughout town.

In the central part of Leisenwald, Johannes Kaltenschnee, his wife and children, and nearly 120 other residents were still huddled in the cellar of a large barn when the door to the cellar suddenly flew open. Children and women screamed in terror. A GI crept down the steps, rifle at the ready, and spotted the fearful crowd of civilians. Smiling, he said, "Don't cry. You're saved!"

Other GIs quickly joined the first. Together they searched the basement for SS troops. Satisfied that the cellar contained only civilians, the GIs departed and then returned after a short time. The Red Circle men yelled, "All come out!" Slowly, the civilians emerged from their subterranean hiding place and stepped onto the street. The GIs assisted the elderly and the children. Kaltenschnee and several other men motioned to the GIs that they wanted to return to their homes to extinguish fires and try and save as much property as possible. The GIs blocked them from doing so and instead herded them into a column facing east.

Kaltenschnee and his fellow townspeople could only look back and watch their beloved town engulfed in a sea of flames as the Red Circle men marched the civilians along the road toward Streitberg. Lieutenant Colonel Denno planned to house the displaced citizens there until his troops had finished mopping up Leisenwald. As the despondent Kaltenschnee marched eastward past burning vehicles and buildings, he and his fellow Leisenwald residents firmly believed that not one single building in town would escape total destruction.[87]

In the forest north of Leisenwald, Companies I and L continued to provide supporting fire to Company K. Denno had opted not to commit the two rifle companies to the fray due to the obvious confusion that reigned within the town. His fear was that the companies would converge on each other from various directions and, due to the darkness and chaos of street fighting, engage each other mistakenly.

Both companies remained hunkered down in their foxholes along the forest's edge. The steady downpour drenched the miserable GIs, whose holes quickly filled with ankle-deep water. The temperature had dropped as well, chilling everyone.

A wet, tired, and miserable Pfc. Coy Wicker from Company L cursed the Germans under his breath for his current predicament. He watched from afar the flash of explosions and exchange of tracer rounds in Leisenwald, fuming and wishing for revenge on the SS troops.

Suddenly, three dark forms appeared in the field to Company L's front. A voice from a nearby foxhole called out, "Halt!" The three figures stopped. In a low voice, Wicker heard one of the figures mutter, "*Was ist los*? (What is happening?)"[88]

That phrase was all Wicker needed to hear. The incensed infantryman grabbed two M1 carbines—one in each hand—and stood up from his foxhole. He yelled, "*Das ist los*! (This is happening!)" and emptied each carbine's magazine into the three shadowy forms. Two figures dropped to the ground while the third spun and ran away into the darkness. Wicker approached the two German bodies to check for signs of life as his fellow GIs marveled at the man's cowboy-like actions. Both Germans were dead. They had obviously attempted to flee Leisenwald but had clearly chosen the wrong way out.

❖

On the western edge of the Büdingen forest, Colonel Lundquist's 14th Infantry Regiment settled in for the evening along a line running generally from Bergheim in the north to just east of Wolf. Despite only sporadic contact with the Nord men throughout the day, the 14th Regiment accounted for 149 SS prisoners, 80 wounded, and 20 killed.[89]

Lundquist ordered his three battalions into position along the Bergheim–Wolf line with instructions to tie in with each other in preparation for resuming the advance in the morning. Major Hubbard's 1st Battalion was already moving forward and would arrive in Altenstadt—the location of the 14th's command post—by 2145. Major General Wyman had already instructed Lundquist that he could commit the 1st Battalion only on division order and that the regiment could advance no farther in the morning than the eastern edge of the Büdingen forest.[90]

Lieutenant Colonel Brant's 2nd Battalion command post remained in Bleichenbach. Two of his companies, F and G, had dug in east of Bleichenbach and south of Bergheim, respectively. The battalion would stand fast in these positions for the night.⁹¹

Southeast of the 2nd Battalion, Lieutenant Colonel Guthrie's 3rd Battalion had advanced through Wolf; by 2100 they occupied a line well inside the Büdingen forest four kilometers due east of Dudenrod. Guthrie, concerned about his right flank, directed First Lieutenant Sims, the Company M commander, to position some heavy machine guns along the battalion's right rear flank south of Wolf. Sims placed Lt. Harry W. Thode's 2nd Platoon of heavy, water-cooled, .30-caliber machine guns in a defensive arc facing south from the forest below the tiny hamlet. The rain fell steadily as the GIs unpacked entrenching tools and began digging in the rain-soaked soil.⁹²

Just beyond the forest to the platoon's front lay an open area Thode believed he must explore. As his machine gunners labored with their entrenching tools, Thode struck out on his own to scout the woods. He had only traveled a short distance when he saw a dark figure—clearly sporting the standard German, flared-rim helmet—duck behind a pile of neatly stacked logs.

Thode dropped to the ground, crawled to the base of a large tree, and leveled his M1 carbine at the pile of logs. The officer squeezed off two rounds into the rain-soaked woodpile. Breathing heavily, Thode waited a few moments for the German soldier to return fire. Nothing happened.

Thode raised his head up slightly and, in his best German, called out, "*Alles kaputt! Aufgeben!*" (Everything is over! Give up!). An astonished Thode then watched as not one but four dark figures slowly emerged from behind the woodpile with hands held high. Thode stood and motioned the men toward him. In the darkness, he could not discern if they wore uniforms with Waffen-SS, Heer, or some other service's insignia. With one hand on his M1 carbine, Thode searched the men for weapons and then directed them back toward his platoon's position.

Thode marched the prisoners through his platoon's foxhole line and directly to the nearest rifle company position—Company L. He handed the Germans over to Captain Krichbaum, the company commander, who listened in earnest as Thode explained the circumstances of their capture. First Lieutenant Sims arrived and listened as well.

After Thode recounted his tale, Sims met with his company officers privately and discussed issuing new guidance to the men about taking prisoners in the dark. The officers speculated on the merits of calling for the Germans to surrender each time the GIs entered a wooded area. Simply calling out into the forest for hidden Germans to surrender would give away the GIs' position and might get someone shot. Sims and his officers quickly communicated this new guidance to Company M's men. Ignoring these fundamental lessons would only cost lives needlessly and prolong the operation.[93]

❖

At the 71st Infantry Division command post in Langenselbold, Major General Wyman voiced his frustration to Lieutenant Colonel Lankenau about the infrequent situation reports from his units. At that moment he was unaware of the 3rd Battalion, 66th Infantry's ongoing battle to seize Leisenwald. Colonel Regnier and his staff, like the other divisional units, were having difficulty transmitting messages to the division command post via radio. Transmissions came through sporadically, giving Wyman an incomplete picture of the division's moment-to-moment activities. The fact that the entire division was operating in a twenty-two-square-kilometer area did not facilitate communications. Jeep-mounted liaison officers and messengers had long distances to travel in the dark under blackout conditions.[94]

As the G-3 staff struggled to gather up-to-date reports from the units, Wyman and Lankenau used the best information available to devise a plan for the following day that would net the remnants of the Nord Division. It was already 2100 and the infantry regiments needed instructions from the G-3 in order to plan the next day's operation.

Wyman and Lankenau knew that Colonel Lundquist's 14th Infantry Regiment held positions in the northern part of the Büdingen forest. To the 14th's south Colonel Wooten's 5th Infantry Regiment occupied the towns of Büches and Büdingen along the southwestern edge of the forest. The 5th's command post had opened in Büdingen at 2100, and Wooten's troops had already made contact with the 14th Regiment on their left. Farther east Colonel Regnier's 66th Infantry Regiment occupied Waldensberg and, as far as Wyman and Lankenau knew, the area around Leisenwald. In addition, most of the division's support troops and other units had already advanced to locations just behind the 5th and 14th regiments. Major Eddy's 271st Engineer Battalion, for example, had arrived in Altenstadt at 1745 that afternoon, 2 April.[95]

The disposition of the infantry regiments quickly led Wyman and Lankenau to conclude that the 71st Infantry Division now had whatever troops remained of the 6th SS-Gebirgs Division completely surrounded. If the 5th and 14th infantry regiments advanced northeast through the Büdingen forest, they would drive the SS troops into the waiting arms of the 66th Infantry Regiment—a classic hammer-and-anvil maneuver. After a brief discussion with Lankenau, Wyman agreed on the concept and informed the infantry regiments of the plan. The attack time would be 0700—twelve minutes before sunrise.

In addition, both 1st battalions of the 5th and 14th regiments would remain in reserve. The regimental commanders could only commit those battalions on division order. The 1st Battalion, 5th Infantry, would also receive trucks from the G-4 to motorize that force for rapid commitment to any part of the battlefield. Lankenau notified the regiments that an operations overlay would be forthcoming.[96]

Wyman also was concerned that two of his regiments would be converging on another regiment, so he directed the 5th and 14th regiments to halt at the northeastern edge of the Büdingen forest and advance no farther. The 66th Regiment would pick up the battle from there.[97]

Wyman then tried to learn more about the status of his reconnaissance troop and the battalion moving to guard XII Corps headquarters. As far as Wyman knew, Captain Johnson's 71st Cavalry Reconnaissance Troop still remained on patrol along the road to Gedern. Johnson had reported earlier that the troop had completed their first round-trip reconnaissance of the fifteen-kilometer route at 1900. Johnson had not sent another report since that time. Wyman also learned from Colonel Lundquist that the forward elements of the 1st Battalion, 66th Infantry, tasked to guard the XII Corps advance headquarters in Lauterbach, had passed through the 14th Regiment's command post at Altenstadt at 2215 and continued northeast. Wyman passed that information to corps headquarters.[98]

Wyman and the division staff would spend the rest of the night poring over reports delivered via messenger or liaison officer along with sporadic radio messages from the regiments. These reports would slowly confirm Wyman's estimate of the situation and validate his plan for the next day's operation.

Intelligence reports also continued to arrive from XII Corps headquarters throughout the night. One report (received before 0000 on 3 April) stated that prisoners from the 6th SS-Gebirgs Division had revealed that isolated enemy groups planned to use American trucks to move their personnel through the lines. The German drivers would dress as GIs, and the German troops in the back of each truck would pose as prisoners. Wyman remained nonplussed by such reports. He believed that his plan for the next day would bag the rest of the Nord Division—no matter what tactics they used or ruses they employed.

As far as Wyman was concerned, all enemy troops would be killed or captured by 1200 on 3 April.⁹⁹

In the center of Leisenwald, *SS-Gruppenführer* Brenner stood outside the barn that housed his command post and watched as scores of his men organized into groups in the darkness. The time was 2145. The Nord men checked their gear and emptied rucksacks of all but the essentials. The SS men would have to move swiftly and stealthily if they planned to escape the attacking Americans.

The sound of sporadic rifle and machine-gun fire echoed along the side streets on all sides of the barn. Illumination rounds fired by American mortars still burst high above the town. The Nord men froze until the brightly burning orbs descended to earth.

Brenner knew the situation he and his men now faced was extremely dangerous—more dangerous than even close-quarters combat with the enemy. His men, organized in groups of various size and composition, had to slip out of Leisenwald undetected while some groups remained in contact with the Americans. The GIs had pressed their attack vigorously and—despite more than two hours of sustained, bloody combat—never lost momentum. The Americans would reach the center of town and the division command post in a matter of minutes.

Brenner walked among the shadowy figures and called out the names of officers and sergeants alike. Each man responded that his particular group was ready. Brenner asked if the wounded, about 150 in all, were safely sheltered in houses along with the division's remaining medics. An officer replied in the affirmative. Another officer chimed in that the thirty or so American prisoners remained in a nearby courtyard out of harm's way. These prisoners would remain behind as well.¹⁰⁰

The division staff officers and orderlies finished tossing the remaining files and other documents into burning barrels and feed pails inside the barn. Thick smoke filled the structure. The staff officers soon emerged and took up positions next to Brenner. A staff orderly supported *SS-Standartenführer* Raithel, who still managed to stand despite the severe head wound and loss of an eye.¹⁰¹

The rain continued to fall steadily, and a light mist hung low along the side streets and buildings of Leisenwald. The surrounding mud-soaked countryside disappeared in a foot-high layer of fog as the nighttime temperature dropped.

The sounds of voices shouting commands in English soon met Brenner's ears. The GIs were almost on them. Several Nord men came running toward the various groups of crouching SS troops. Brenner estimated that eight hundred or so men were gathered in the street outside his command post. Their discipline awed him. The situation was grave and filled each Nord man with a level of anxiety that had undoubtedly reached a near crescendo. On the surface, though, the SS troops appeared calm and patient, awaiting word to move out.

The sound of the GIs' voices told Brenner that the time had come to leave. He issued a brief command to a nearby officer, who in turn muttered instructions to several other SS soldiers. The Nord men quickly formed into a single-file column and, led by Brenner and the division command group, moved out down a side street for the southwestern part of town. The main group of SS men, standing patiently in the center of town, slowly uncoiled into a long, serpentine column that made its way to Leisenwald's outskirts and into the surrounding countryside. The men flinched as explosions and rifle fire neared their position, but waited patiently for their turn to move out. The Nord men knew that many of their fellow SS troopers who were still in contact with the Americans would never join the group. Their rear-guard actions would unquestionably end in their deaths or capture.

After several minutes—minutes that seemed like hours—the last members of the group moved out. The head of the column reached the southwestern outskirts of Leisenwald undetected. At the edge of town, Brenner stopped and looked back over his shoulder at the remnants of his division. The Nord men were following as planned. Brenner turned, looked ahead into the pitch-black countryside before him, and disappeared into the darkness. The time was 2200.[102]

❖

At precisely 2200 Company K's lead platoon reached the center of Leisenwald. The GIs approached the barn that formerly housed the Nord Division's command post. A GI pushed open the main door, coughing as he entered the smoke-filled room. Several GIs followed and quickly extinguished the numerous fires.

Captain Grambling arrived, entered the barn, and surveyed the scene. Piles of documents littered the hay-strewn floor. Grambling and some of his men flipped through the partially burned documents. The files, largely intact and undamaged, appeared to be personnel records. Several files had small photographs of SS officers and enlisted men attached by a single staple.

One GI approached Grambling and stated that he and his buddies had found a pile of German banknotes, Reichmarks, in a nearby stall—probably the division's payroll. Grambling instructed several men from his company headquarters to gather the German money and files for delivery to the battalion S-2.

Grambling stepped outside and saw his men swarming throughout the heart of Leisenwald. The shooting had stopped. GIs marched scores of SS troopers, arms held high, down the main street to a holding area near the center of town. Other GIs stacked captured German weapons in a pile on the sidewalk. A few Red Circle men jumped into nearby jeeps and trucks, captured by the Nord Division, and turned over the engines. Many of the vehicles functioned, and the sound of idling engines soon mixed with the shouts of Red Circle men rousting SS soldiers from their hiding places and into the streets.

Grambling immediately requested situation reports from his platoon leaders. Within minutes messengers brought him handwritten notes from the three officers. The reports told him that Company K had seized Leisenwald in its entirety. The Red Circle men had captured nearly 250 SS men, many of whom were wounded, and liberated approximately thirty Americans from captivity.[103]

Among the thirty liberated GIs were men captured in Waldensberg as part of the 2nd Squadron, 2nd Cavalry Group's rear echelon. As the exhausted but happy GIs walked onto the streets in freedom, they noticed the scorched hulk of a captured American M3 half-track on the street at the far end of town. The blood-drenched body of an SS sergeant hung over the machine gun he had been firing when killed. Another dead Nord man sat in the driver's seat, hands firmly grasping the wheel, his eyes wide open. The back of his head had been shot away. An American bazooka round had punctured the light armored plating on the side of the vehicle.

The sight of the two dead SS men evoked no sympathy from the liberated cavalrymen. They explained to the Company K GIs that the SS troops had moved them from Waldensberg to Leisenwald on foot. The same captured half-track and driver that now sat in ruins at the end of town had followed behind the group of captured GIs. The driver terrorized the prisoners by accelerating toward them and then slamming on the brakes at the last minute. One of the Company K GIs listening to the story simply replied, "He got his kicks, but you fellows got in the last licks."

Grambling continued to receive reports from his platoon leaders and soon learned that the "butcher's bill" for Company K's attack on Leisenwald amounted to nine enlisted soldiers dead and ten wounded. One officer was wounded as well. Grambling also learned that his men had recovered ten working American trucks and a number of jeeps. When Lieutenant Colonel Denno later learned of these working vehicles, he kept them for the battalion's use—spoils of war, as Denno later remarked.[104]

Grambling radioed the battalion command post—located in a house on the eastern edge of town—and reported that Leisenwald was now in American hands. Denno was delighted. He ordered Grambling to consolidate and reorganize inside the town and continue to mop up as necessary. Denno wanted his men to get some rest as soon as possible. The company could finish clearing all buildings at daybreak. He further instructed Grambling to send a large patrol west to Wolferborn to ensure that any enemy troops expelled from Leisenwald were not gathering there for a counterattack. (The patrol would later occupy Wolferborn a few minutes before 0000.) Grambling acknowledged his commander's instructions and set to work. The men of Company K still had a long night ahead of them.[105]

CHAPTER 9

The Third Day: Dissolution, 3 April 1945

The cold rain drenched SS-Gruppenführer *Brenner and his column of eight hundred troops as they marched quietly across the open ground southwest of Leisenwald and entered the Büdingen forest a kilometer west of Waldensberg. The night was especially dark due to the ominous rain clouds that hung so low they seemed to touch the very ground on which the Nord men walked. The drop in temperature heralded a light dusting of snow that would fall before sunrise.*

Few Nord men carried much equipment. They had shed most of their gear in Leisenwald—gear that would slow them down or prove too noisy to carry. *SS-Unterscharführer* Georg Stöwe, the radio section chief, moved with Brenner's group. He carried a lightly packed rucksack and his K98k rifle. He wore his helmet and carried, in one of his trouser pockets, a lone clip of five rounds for his rifle. The other eight hundred or so Nord men in the group were equipped in the same manner—although several SS men carried MP40s, MG42s, and *panzerfäuste*. Many men, particularly the Heer and Luftwaffe troops traveling with the group, lacked weapons.[1]

As Brenner led his long, serpentine column into the Büdingen forest, he could not help but marvel at the men's stealth and their luck at avoiding detection. The time was now a little past 0000 on 3 April, and the SS troops had been walking for more than two hours without rest. GIs were outposting Leisenwald and Waldensberg and running occasional foot patrols on the outskirts of each town, but the large column had managed to slip into the forest undetected.

The SS men forged ahead in a southwesterly direction until they crested an area of high ground in the pitch-black forest. Brenner paused, consulted his map with some staff officers, and then proceeded due south. That direction would take them into Gelnhausen and, hopefully, the German lines. But

Brenner's plan of reaching a German defensive line was nothing more than wishful thinking. In fact, the Americans occupied Gelnhausen and its environs in force. If Brenner and his men even reached the town before sunrise, they would be trapped and forced to either fight or surrender. But Brenner, despite his misgivings, continued to express confidence to his men; he encouraged them to take heart and press on.[2]

The rain-soaked deadfall littering the forest floor muffled the SS men's footsteps. The column paused periodically for rest breaks. The men were exhausted, and many of them fell into a deep sleep on settling back against a tree or large rock. Officers and sergeants had to rouse the men from these deep slumbers and help the weary troops to their feet. Many men remained behind, undetected in the darkness. They would awake later to find that the column had long since departed. Men even fell asleep on their feet: an exhausted *SS-Unterscharführer* Stöwe dropped off while walking and fell to the ground. His comrades helped him to his feet and shook him awake.[3]

By 0300 the column had reached a point three kilometers southwest of Waldensberg. The SS men were deep in territory that now belonged to the 71st Infantry Division. Brenner halted the column once more and allowed the men to catch some sleep. After an hour or so, they could move out and reach Gelnhausen before the sun rose at 0710. Brenner needed the cover of darkness to march his men safely into the town. He had no time to waste.[4]

Soon after Lieutenant Colonel Lankenau and his G-3 staff officers issued the next day's operations instruction, planning at the lower echelons began in earnest. The regiments finally received the plan sometime after 0000 on 3 April. Exhausted and bleary-eyed regimental staff officers pored over maps and worked out details. Staff assistants forwarded fresh intelligence data from division headquarters directly to the individual battalions.

An example of one of the many intelligence messages passed down to the regiments throughout the night was a response to the XII Corps report that the Germans planned to escape the 71st's net by masquerading as GIs who would drive captured American trucks full of German troops posing as prisoners. Colonel Lundquist immediately forwarded the report to his three 14th Infantry Regiment battalions. But the information seemed inaccurate. Lieutenant Colonel Brant received the message at 0015 in his 2nd Battalion headquarters and quickly examined it. The text read, "Troops of enemy 6th SS vicinity M9090 will be using US trucks. Troops dressed like PWs [prisoners of war]. Drivers dressed in GI clothes. Check closely on trucks hauling PWs to determine if they are really who they claim to be."[5]

The message confused Brant, who thought the SS troops were farther east than the report suggested. The grid reference of 9090 placed the German troops a kilometer south of Glauberg, which meant the enemy was behind the 14th Infantry Regiment. Brant was correct. The SS troops were indeed farther east, but the message caused the 14th Regiment needless consternation. Exhausted GIs would expend needless effort throughout the cold, damp night scouring the terrain south of Glauberg for Germans who simply were no longer there. The information was obviously inaccurate and would have made more sense if rendered the previous day.

Brant turned his attention back to the attack set for 0700. Like all commanders and staffs in the other battalions that night, Brant and his officers worked into the early morning hours to put the finishing touches on their attack plans. Details such as scheme of maneuver, axis of advance, ration- and ammunition-issue times, artillery fire plans, and other coordinating instructions began to take shape.

Brant briefed the completed plan to his assembled company commanders a couple of hours past 0000. His instructions and operational concept were clear and direct: The battalion would attack with two companies abreast, E and F, followed by Company G in reserve. Both lead companies would advance on the high ground near Gelnhaar. Company E on the left would sweep the woods north of Bergheim while Company F moved to the south. Both companies would depart at 0600—an hour earlier than the planned division attack time. Company G would follow and at 0700 would swing left of Company E and clean out the tiny hamlet of Usenborn two kilometers west of Gelnhaar. Brant directed his commanders to "sweep the woods as fast as possible" and halt along the eastern edge of the Büdingen forest. The attached platoon of tanks from Company B, 761st Tank Battalion, would follow in general support. Lieutenant Colonel Guthrie's 3rd Battalion would attack along a similar axis on the battalion's right, or south. And, on the 14th Regiment's right, the 2nd and 3rd battalions of the 5th Infantry Regiment would proceed eastward into the forest.[6]

With the plan completed and briefed to the companies, Brant, like his fellow battalion commanders throughout the division, settled down for some much-needed shut-eye. The operational tempo of the previous forty-eight hours had exhausted all Red Circle men in the division, and everyone needed as much rest as possible before 0700. If 3 April was going to be anything like the past two days, the GIs would need the rest.

A good night's rest evaded the 71st Division staff, though. Although the G-3 section had issued the plan for the next day's operation, the main command post in Langenselbold remained a beehive of activity throughout the night.

Message traffic passed constantly between and among the division and three regimental headquarters throughout the night. At 0204 Colonel Regnier's 66th Infantry forwarded a report to the division that detailed all battalion locations and the fact that the 2nd and 3rd battalions occupied the towns of Waldensberg and Leisenwald, respectively. Up to this point, Major General Wyman and Lieutenant Colonel Lankenau had only assumed that both units had taken the two towns. This planning assumption now became a fact and validated the scheme of maneuver outlined in the operations instruction issued earlier that night. Regnier's report also tallied the "butcher's bill" for Company L during the previous day's fighting in the forest north of Leisenwald: one officer dead and two officers and eleven GIs wounded.[7]

The 5th Regiment reported no change from their positions in and around Büdingen. The 5th had made contact with the 14th Regiment during the night at Büches with a liaison officer from the 14th's 3rd Battalion. On the 5th's left flank, the 14th Regiment's two battalions were set to attack along a line running generally north from Lissberg and south to the forest above Büches.[8]

Much of the back-and-forth radio exchanges throughout the night involved the 66th Infantry Regiment. The regimental staff continued to query division headquarters throughout the early morning hours concerning attachment of a battalion from the 26th Infantry Division (engaged in heavy fighting farther east in Schlüchtern and Fulda) and a cavalry squadron. The 66th had yet to make contact with these units, both of which XII Corps had attached to the 71st Division to assist in the operation scheduled to begin at 0700 on 3 April. In turn, the 71st Division staff contacted the XII Corps' staff concerning the attachments. At 0450 XII Corps finally responded. The message stated that the 1st Battalion, 328th Infantry (from the 26th Infantry Division) and the 2nd Cavalry Squadron (2nd Cavalry Group) were under the operational control of the 71st. The corps had messaged the two units with instructions to report immediately to Colonel Regnier at his command post in Lieblos. Likewise, Lieutenant Colonel Thomas's 1st Battalion, 66th Infantry, had finally closed on the XII Corps command post in Lauterbach at 0655—five minutes before the day's established attack time.[9]

In addition to the concerns about new attachments, the 71st and 5th Infantry divisions both exchanged disposition and planning information during the night to ensure better coordination for the next day's operations. A 71st Division messenger delivered the Red Circle Division's attack plan in person to the Red Diamond Division's command post in Frankfurt. On examining the 71st's plan for 3 April, the 5th Division staff quickly realized that their plans for the next day would have to change.[10]

Not long after the 5th Infantry Division's night-shift staff forwarded the 71st Division's plan to the 2nd Regiment's staff in Stammheim, the regimental staff radioed at 0325 with a message: the regiment's two plans for the next day—Plans A and B—were not feasible given the Red Circle Division's planned actions on 3 April. The objectives indicated in those plans would bring the 2nd Regiment directly into the paths of the 71st Division's two attacking regiments, the 5th and the 14th.

When Colonel Roffe entered the command post before sunrise for his morning update, he learned that his regiment's plans for the next day, sent up to Major General Irwin the night before for approval, were no longer realistic. The center of gravity for the day's coming operation to destroy the 6th SS-Gebirgs Division rested with the 71st Division to the south.

Yet Roffe believed that stragglers from the Nord Division might still be scampering throughout the woods in his regiment's zone, so he instructed his three battalion commanders to move northeast and east to clear the forests in the area and prevent the SS troops from escaping northward. The battalion farthest north, Major Pace's 2nd Battalion, would proceed from Nidda and move northeast. Lieutenant Colonel Blakefield's 1st Battalion, which had occupied Merkenfritz the previous day, would advance east and southeast toward Burgbracht nine kilometers distant. On the regiment's right flank, Lieutenant Colonel Connor's 3rd Battalion would press forward six kilometers toward Wenings, a small village five kilometers north of Kefenrod.[11]

Roffe's plan, although slow and plodding for his Red Diamond infantrymen, would at least create a northern east–west line against which the Red Circle men could drive the SS troops from the south. For the moment, this slow-moving operation was the best way Roffe could see to help the 71st Division troops round up the Nord Division. Roffe did not realize, however, that the woods his troops would clear still hid many members of *SS-Oberführer* Goebel's now-scattered horse-drawn column. Goebel himself was taking refuge in a small forest directly in the path of the advancing Red Diamond men.[12]

❖

Throughout the night the Büdingen forest and its environs remained a no-man's land rife with loose bands of German soldiers from a variety of destroyed or disbanded Wehrmacht units. Many of the Germans just wanted to surrender and end the war, while others, such as the Nord men, were determined to fight on. American patrols engaged in nighttime activities found themselves bumping into these German bands or individual stragglers. Jeep-mounted liaison officers whose primary mission was to travel throughout the night from one command post to another were particularly at risk.

First Lieutenant Lewington S. Ponder, the 5th Regiment's liaison officer to division headquarters, had a nerve-wracking experience around 0000 on 30 April while trying to find his way to Büdingen from the division command post in Langenselbold. When Ponder was assigned as the regiment's liaison officer, he felt fortunate to get Cpl. Samuel E. "Red" Kennerly as his jeep driver. Kennerly was in his late twenties and hailed from North Carolina. Kennerly had made his living running bootleg whiskey across the border into South Carolina—runs usually made at night without lights and on back roads. He honed his driving skills during such nighttime runs, and the police only caught him the night his car broke down. The judge gave Kennerly a choice: enlist in the Army or go to jail. Red enlisted.

Ponder and Kennerly had departed Langenselbold sometime before 0000 on 30 April to deliver the next division operations instruction and map overlay to the 5th Regiment's command post in Büdingen. Ponder had not yet been to the Büdingen command post and did not know the way. He and Kennerly made certain they both knew the challenge and password since riding around at night without that information might mean a quick death from friendly fire. Kennerly knew to stop immediately if a sentry ordered "Halt!"

As the two men drove under blackout conditions along a secondary road heading toward Büdingen, Ponder sat in the passenger seat with a Thompson submachine gun across his lap. As they drove quickly down the road in the dark, the shape of a figure suddenly appeared beside the road. Kennerly, thinking they had encountered an American security post, slammed on the brakes.

The man approached and began speaking German. Ponder, shocked by the man's identity, scrambled to raise his submachine gun, but the barrel caught under the dashboard. Ponder clambered out of the jeep but almost fell on his face in the process. When Ponder finally managed to level his weapon at the German, he went cold all over when he realized he had not pulled back the bolt.

In the meantime the German soldier just stood and watched patiently. When the young officer had finished fumbling around, the German began speaking as if both men could understand him, and approached the jeep and tried to climb into the back seat. He clearly wanted to surrender, but Ponder was carrying sensitive material and could not allow it. Ponder yanked the man from the jeep, pointed down the road to the next town, and said, "*Amerikaner Soldaten.*"

The man tried to climb back into the jeep once again, but Ponder raised his weapon as if to give the man a butt stroke. The German soldier jumped back. Ponder then hopped back into the jeep, and Kennerly sped off, leaving the German standing in the road.

Ponder quickly realized that if the German soldier had wanted to fight, he might easily have killed him and Kennerly. Feeling foolish that the German had caught him flat-footed, Ponder rested his Thompson submachine gun with the muzzle now pointed up and to the right. He also kept the bolt back on "load" and his finger on the safety release. As far as Ponder was concerned, he and Kennerly had survived a close call.[13]

❖

The sun rose at 0710 on Tuesday, 3 April, illuminating a deeply overcast sky. Wet, cold, and tired Red Circle men from all three regiments had stirred an hour earlier from a fitful night's slumber exposed to the elements. GIs who managed to avoid guard duty or a foot patrol received the most rest. But even when trying to sleep under a tree, in a foxhole, or hunched over in the front seat of a jeep, the damp night air still invaded every bit of exposed skin and chilled the men to the bone. The rain had stopped sometime during the night, but many GIs had climbed into sleeping bags or foxholes with soaking wet field jackets and boots.

As the temperature dropped during the night, the rain turned to snow in some parts of the region. In Waldensberg, Pfc. Bob Abbott of the 2nd Battalion, 66th Infantry's Company H, and the other members of his machine gun squad arose from the comfort of a warm barn a couple of hours before sunrise. Distant small-arms fire had interrupted their much-needed slumber. When the GIs looked outside, they were surprised to see an inch of snow on the ground.

The small-arms fire Abbott and his men had heard resulted from the only real bit of excitement the 2nd Battalion experienced during the night in Waldensberg. A jeep had come roaring up the road through the center of town and right through Company F's positions, which were in a line of houses on either side of the main road. Captain Sullivan, the Company F commander, poked his head outside his command-post building just in time to see three Nord men speeding away in a stolen jeep. The SS troopers had obviously hidden in town and awaited the right moment to grab a vehicle and escape. The only problem was that the SS man driving the vehicle did not know how to shift, so he kept grinding the gears loudly as he tried to shift out of low.

Sullivan shouted to alert his men just as a wayward cow, wandering like many other escaped farm animals throughout the smoldering ruins of Waldensberg, casually walked onto the main road and directly into the path of the speeding jeep. The Nord man seated behind the driver leveled his rifle and felled the cow with one shot. The jeep then veered around the cow's prone carcass and sped for the road out of town. But one of Sullivan's machine-gun crews outposting the edge of town heard the shot and swung their .30-caliber weapon around. As soon as the jeep came into view, the gunner fired a single burst and killed all three German soldiers. Thus ended the only real excitement of the night except for Company F's 1st and 2nd platoons, both of which had to move several times when the fires still burning throughout town spread to their buildings.

In Company E's position along the northwest corner of Waldensberg, an unfortunate incident occurred during the night. Company E's GIs had been on edge waiting for another German counterattack to materialize. Tired and nervous, the Red Circle men spent a long, cold night scanning the fields for signs of enemy infiltrators. A fresh replacement to the company, a young private new to combat, wandered toward some outbuildings on the edge of town, possibly in search of a latrine. A GI saw the man's shadowy form, took aim, and fired. The young private fell dead.[14]

In Leisenwald a kilometer to the north, Lt. Col. Bryce F. Denno emerged from his 3rd Battalion, 66th Infantry, command post located in a house on the eastern edge of town. The men of Company K had spent the night mopping up the remaining Nord men hunkered down inside the village. The morning glow of the rising sun allowed Denno to see the destruction that resulted from Company K's head-on clash with the SS troops.

As he walked down the narrow, debris-strewn streets of Leisenwald, he passed scores of German dead scattered about the entranceways to houses and small buildings. The steady drizzle throughout the night had doused the flames of many burning buildings. Denno noticed the body of an SS sergeant sprawled across the hood of a captured, bazooka-damaged American half-track; the man had apparently been killed while manning the vehicle's .50-caliber machine gun. He also took note of the sturdily built stone houses with their outer walls lined with neatly stacked firewood. Strong, earthy smells filled the air. Ever since they had crossed the Rhine, noted Denno, they had encountered more and more of these small villages, which the men called "cow towns."[15]

Denno stopped and entered one building to find it filled with German wounded. SS medics—*sanitäter* to the Nord men—worked feverishly to treat and comfort the wounded. The medics paid Denno little heed and went about their work. Denno turned and left the exhausted medics to their grim labors.[16]

Back in Waldensberg Lieutenant Colonel Eikel wanted to contact the 3rd Battalion to the north. He had not heard from them all night and was uncertain if Denno and his battalion had taken Leisenwald. The communication line to the 3rd Battalion had been cut during the night. Pfc. Thomas Tomich and two other communications men had set out in a jeep to find and repair the break, but with no luck. Communications within the 66th Regiment throughout the night had been sporadic at best, and Eikel was concerned that the Germans might counterattack once more from the direction of Leisenwald.

Eikel instructed Captain MacArthur to send a platoon from Company E, mounted on tanks, north to Leisenwald. If the 3rd Battalion was not there, he explained, the platoon could expect a fight to take the town. If so, the rest of the battalion would follow and support the attack.

MacArthur selected his Third Platoon for the mission. He called for the platoon leader, 2/Lt. John Tripp, and briefed him on the plan. Tripp was shocked. He thought such a daylight operation with only one platoon was foolish and needlessly risky. The plan called for Tripp to enter the town, fight if necessary to gain control of it or simply link up with the 3rd Battalion, and then return to Waldensberg.

Tripp dutifully accepted the orders and set about loading his men onto a platoon of tanks from Company C, 761st Tank Battalion. What made Tripp even more apprehensive about the mission was that his platoon would be heading in the direction from where the previous day's counterattack had originated. Tripp could not help but think that his battalion commander, Lieutenant Colonel Eikel, was crazy.

Tripp soon ordered the tanks to move out on the road to Leisenwald. On the way out of town, the platoon passed a large wooded plot thick with underbrush and tall pine trees, a type of pine-forest oasis standing alone in the open farm fields. The trees showed clear signs of mortar and small-arms damage. Dead Germans lay scattered on the open ground nearby.

Tripp was scared. He could see that his men felt like sheep being led to the slaughter, and that the sight of the dead Germans heightened their fear. Tripp remained calm despite his own trepidation. His men needed to see him confident and in charge.

The outskirts of Leisenwald quickly came into view. Black smoke was rising from the town. Tripp ordered the tanks to stop and the men to dismount. He split his infantrymen into two groups to advance alongside the tanks, which would remain on the road between them. Just before he ordered the troops to move out, an American jeep popped into view on the road ahead leading south out of Leisenwald. A man was standing up in the passenger's side of the vehicle. Behind the jeep followed several other American trucks and vehicles.

Tripp ordered his men to hold their fire. As the jeep approached, Tripp recognized Major Spencer, the 3rd Battalion's executive officer, standing in the jeep. Tripp ran up to the jeep and listened with great relief as Spencer explained that the 3rd Battalion had seized Leisenwald during the night. Tripp was elated. When he told his men the news, they felt as though they had received a reprieve from a death sentence. Tripp could not help but think that the 3rd Battalion's taking of Leisenwald had saved his life and the lives of his men.[17]

Farther west in the area of Bleichenbach, Lieutenant Colonel Brant's 2nd Battalion, 14th Infantry Regiment, had formed up in company attack positions prior to 0600, the scheduled departure time. But, based on instructions Brant had received from Colonel Lundquist during the night, he revised the attack time to 0700.

At 0700 Brant radioed orders to Captain Goldman of Company E and Captain Alvey of Company F to move out. Brant left Bleichenbach and followed Company E in his jeep. Goldman led his GIs into the mist-enshrouded Büdingen forest and headed northeast for his first objective, the tiny hamlet of Usenborn five kilometers distant. Company E had spent the night in Bleichenbach as the battalion reserve and had the farthest to travel. Captain Bass's Company G, now the designated reserve for the morning's operation, was already forward in the town of Bergheim, so Goldman would have to lead his men though Company G's positions on the way to Usenborn. On Company E's right flank, Alvey was leading Company F toward Bindsachsen from an attack position on the high ground three kilometers east of Bleichenbach.[18]

Company E's movement to Usenborn proved uneventful. The Red Circle men slogged through the wet deadfall that carpeted the forest floor. As Lieutenant Colonel Brant followed the GIs to Usenborn, he attempted to reach Bass or someone in Company G via radio but with no luck. Company G was scheduled to depart Bergheim soon after Company E had passed through the town, so Brant expected them to be moving along a northeast axis to a point just above Gelnhaar.

Frustrated, Brant broke away from Company E at Usenborn and headed back to Bergheim in search of Company G. When he arrived at the town, the company was gone. He told his driver to follow the company's planned northeast axis and catch up to them. After nearly an hour of on- and off-road driving through the darkened forest, Brant saw the tail end of Company G's formation. The GIs had advanced quickly through the forest and were nearly at their day's objective north of Gelnhaar. Brant had expected them to reach that point by 1200, but now he feared they had far outpaced the other companies to the south.

Brant left his jeep and walked quickly through the company formation until he met up with Captain Bass. He instructed Bass to hold fast until the other companies came on line farther south. Company G was already approaching the battalion's limit of advance—the eastern edge of the Büdingen forest. Brant was pleased with Bass's rapid progress—especially since the company had netted some German prisoners along the way. When Brant examined the German prisoners, he identified them as young officer cadets but not members of the 6th SS-Gebirgs Division Nord. Brant then conducted a brief jeep reconnaissance forward of Company G's location in the direction of Gelnhaar—alone and without an escort except for his driver and radio operator.[19]

A little more than seven kilometers south of the 14th Infantry Regiment, Colonel Wooten's 5th Infantry Regiment crossed the line of departure at 0700. With his two attacking battalions, the 2nd and the 3rd, located in and around Büdingen, Wooten was in an excellent position to push eastward into the forest and round up the SS troops that remained between his regiment and Colonel Regnier's 66th Regiment farther east.

Major Robertson's 3rd Battalion, in Büdingen along with the regimental command post, set out into the damp, chilly forest and advanced northeast along the road leading to Rinderbügen six kilometers distant (see Map 9.1). The GIs walked briskly along either side of the improved road, squinting to see through the dimly lit forest and morning haze. Despite the wet and near-frigid conditions, the GIs made good time, covering a full kilometer in just over fifteen minutes. They encountered a few enemy troops, whom they quickly took prisoner. Since resistance was light Robertson told his lead company to press on to Rinderbügen as quickly as possible. On the other side of the road, the jeep-mounted regimental I&R Platoon paralleled the battalion and swept through the forest. Like Robertson's men, they encountered only a few enemy troops.[20]

On the 3rd Battalion's right flank, Lieutenant Colonel Gettys's 2nd Battalion entered the Büdingen forest from a crossroads area southeast of the medieval town. The battalion's march objective was Waldensberg, eight kilometers distant and slightly northeast. Companies E and F led the way while Companies G and H followed in jeeps and other vehicles. Company G's men, the battalion reserve, rode atop a platoon of tanks from Company A, 761st Tank Battalion. The tanks and other vehicles were confined to the numerous logging and switchback trails that ran throughout the forest. Gettys and his staff followed Company E in two jeeps. Three 60-mm mortar squads (led by S/Sgt. Morton Cree) from Captain Neal's Company G followed Gettys in several Company H jeeps. Like Robertson's men, Gettys's infantrymen stepped

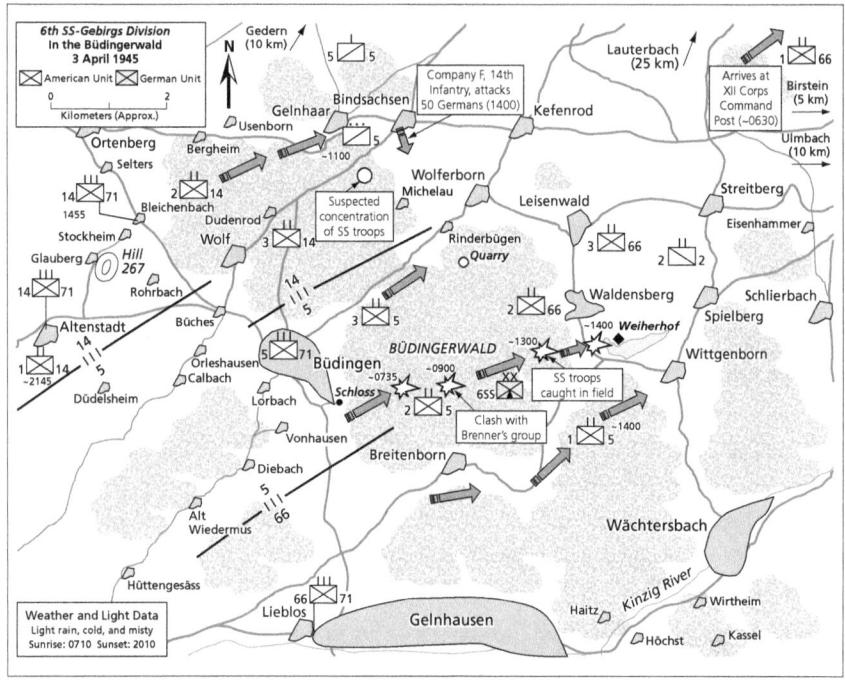

Map 9.1. 6th SS-Gebirgs Division in the Büdingen forest, 3 April 1945.

out smartly and searched the misty woods for wandering SS troops. The men covered two kilometers in thirty minutes without meeting any resistance.[21]

As they walked quietly through the humid forest, a sudden shot rang out. Company E's GIs dove for cover. Word traveled in a flash through the battalion formation, and everyone sought cover behind trees and fallen logs. GIs dismounted jeeps and tanks and took up all-around firing positions. Tank turrets swiveled back and forth in search of targets.

From his position behind Company E, Gettys listened to the sounds of a sharp firefight at the head of his battalion formation. Within minutes, the shooting stopped. Everyone stood slowly as a couple of GIs herded a small group of Nord men toward Gettys's jeep. The SS men looked dirty and exhausted. Their camouflage smocks were soaking wet, they were exhausted, and they could barely hold their hands high as they trudged into captivity. Gettys quickly ordered his company commanders to resume the advance.

Back to the north Major Robertson's 3rd Battalion progressed quickly through the forest unopposed. By 0825 his men had reached the outskirts of the battalion's objective—the small town of Rinderbügen. Robertson had already reached his limit of advance since Rinderbügen was on the eastern edge of the Büdingen forest. According to Major General Wyman's plan, no element from either the 14th or 5th infantry regiments was to advance beyond the forest's eastern edge.[22]

Although Robertson and his men could proceed no farther, they had yet to occupy Rinderbügen, a mere two kilometers west of Leisenwald. Robertson dispatched a patrol to scout the town and its environs. Perhaps members of the 66th Infantry might be there. He then radioed his position back to the regimental command post.[23]

At the regimental command post in Büdingen, Colonel Wooten had already radioed the division headquarters with news of the 2nd and 3rd battalions' smooth progress. Concerned the regiment may be missing the bulk of the SS troops hidden in the forest, Major General Wyman decided to cast a wider net. He instructed Wooten to send the truck-mounted troops of Lieutenant Colonel Broyles's 1st Battalion in a broad sweeping maneuver from their present location in Büches south to Hain-Gründau. From Hain-Gründau the GIs were to dismount and clear the woods along the road to Breitenborn and then move due east into the woods. Wyman's instructions were to round up every German male of fighting age—whether in uniform or in civilian clothes.[24]

Back in the Büdingen forest, the 3rd Battalion moved out a bit more cautiously due to the recent firefight. Lieutenant Colonel Gettys paused with his S-2 and briefly interrogated the small group of SS men. The Nord men were all that remained of a mountain-troop platoon, and Gettys prodded them for information on the whereabouts of the rest of the SS division. The Germans grudgingly admitted that at least two hundred to three hundred other SS troops were somewhere in the woods but could offer no specific locations. Gettys dismissed the prisoners. A handful of GIs, bayonets fixed, escorted them to the rear.[25]

Gettys radioed his company commanders to watch out for a large concentration of enemy troops somewhere in the forest. As he sped off in his jeep to catch up with Company E, he never imagined that he and his men would be the ones to bag the command group of the 6th SS-Gebirgs Division— huddled in the forest not two kilometers away!

Just before the sun rose at 0710, *SS-Gruppenführer* Brenner decided that his slumbering group of Nord men and other troops (many from the Heer and Luftwaffe) would simply rest in the forest by day and wait for sunset before moving on. His exhausted men desperately needed sleep. Only a few men still had rifles and machine guns, and none of them had much ammunition. A handful of SS troops outposted the woods as security. *SS-Standartenführer* Raithel, a blood-caked bandage wrapped around his head, remained barely conscious and in obvious pain.

By Brenner's rough count his group of nearly eight hundred men had dwindled greatly in size since departing Leisenwald the night before. Perhaps only four hundred men remained with the group. Several men, principally individuals from the Heer or Luftwaffe who had attached themselves to the division, had decided to become masters of their own fate and slipped away in the night. Many of those individuals had had a bellyful of war and lacked the will or desire to continue fighting for an obviously lost cause.[26]

The motley group of sleeping SS troops was spread out beneath the trees as night faded to day; it was 0900. Brenner wanted to move quickly to Gelnhausen and join with any German forces still there, but daylight was as much an enemy as the ubiquitous American infantrymen swarming the Büdingen forest. If Brenner moved his group by day, the SS men would be easy prey for American aircraft—especially the slow-moving artillery spotter planes that frequently buzzed overhead. Brenner's only hope of getting his remaining group to Gelnhausen intact was under cover of darkness.[27]

❖

The GIs of Company E, 2nd Battalion, 5th Infantry Regiment, moved east cautiously through the Büdingen forest. The Red Circle men knew a larger number of SS troops were out there somewhere, so they carried their M1s and BARs at the ready. Following the dismounted infantrymen closely along crude logging trails were several jeeps and a platoon of Sherman tanks carrying men from Company G. One jeep carried the battalion commander, Lieutenant Colonel Gettys; several more jeeps, loaded with three mortar squads from Company G, followed.[28]

The lead Company E infantrymen soon approached a small clearing with tall grass, surrounded by trees. The grass was nearly waist-high and sparkled with frost. Just as they entered the clearing, the sound of a German MG42 ripped through the air. The lead GIs returned fire quickly. The ripping sound of other German machine guns fired by the Nord men's security outposts soon filled the air, followed by the ratatat of numerous rifles. Shouts in both German and English filled the air as officers and men from both sides barked out orders. What the Red Circle men did not realize was that they had encountered the last remaining organized element of the very unit they were seeking—the 6th SS-Gebirgs Division.[29]

Behind Company E the entire 2nd Battalion column of tanks and jeeps lurched to a halt. The GIs, including Gettys and his staff, paused and listened. No one moved. Everyone sat transfixed with engines idling and listened to the distant sounds of combat echoing through the forest. As the small-arms fire rapidly grew in intensity, everyone quickly dismounted and sought cover behind trees and felled logs. Gettys stood long enough to wave two Sherman tanks forward to help Company E.

In the jeeps behind Gettys's command vehicle, Company G's 60-mm mortar men listened to the sounds of battle from prone positions beside their vehicles. Sgt. Johnny Rohan, one of the mortar squad leaders, realized that Company E needed help, so he ordered all mortar men armed with rifles and carbines to follow him. The mortar gunners and assistant gunners—armed only with pistols—would remain with the mortars on the jeeps. Pfc. Dean P. Joy, one of the rifle-bearing squad members, was nearly paralyzed with fear when Rohan barked his instructions. Others hesitated as well but quickly moved out when Rohan screamed, "C'mon, you guys, goddammit, let's go!"[30]

Back toward the front of the column, Company E and the Nord men continued their small-arms duel in the tall grass. *SS-Gruppenführer* Brenner moved calmly among his men at a crouch, encouraging them to return fire. His long, glistening leather overcoat moving through the forest became a welcome sight to the Nord men, who returned fire furiously. Unlike his men, who mostly wore helmets or mountain caps, Brenner wore a side cap with the sparkling insignia of the Waffen-SS *totenkopf* and eagle. The men recognized him because of the plastic cap he wore over his missing left eye.

Brenner soon moved to where his intelligence signals section, led by *SS-Unterscharführer* Georg Stöwe, was positioned. Stöwe fired his rifle into the tall grass—the first time he had actually fired his weapon at an enemy soldier in the entire war. The firing quickly intensified as Stöwe's *funkers* took aim and squeezed triggers. A loud gasp beside Stöwe caused him to stop shooting and turn. Beside him lay the lifeless form of one of his *funkers*, *SS-Rottenführer* Herbert Schröder. An American bullet had struck the young man dead.

As the firefight continued the sound of Sherman tanks moving up on the left caught the ears of several SS men. A Nord man, clearly irritated by the situation, exclaimed that nothing was going right. Brenner, always calm, heard the man and replied, "All is well. We'll come out of it."[31]

The Sherman tanks came into view above the tops of the tall grass. The crews fired their coaxial machine guns into the prone ranks of the SS men. Scores of Nord men jumped upright and retired to positions farther into the forest. Company E's GIs, emboldened by the tank support, began maneuvering on the SS troops in quick rushes. SS men screamed as the tanks raked the grassy area with long bursts of machine-gun fire.[32]

Stöwe watched in amazement as an SS man, armed with a *panzerfaust*, stood and hid behind a nearby tree. The man prepared the antitank weapon for firing and, as the lead Sherman moved within range, stepped from behind the tree and shouldered it. A loud rushing sound soon filled the clearing as the warhead streaked through the air and struck the tank with a loud thunderclap. The round glanced off the tank's thick frontal armor. The second Sherman tank stopped. The turret swiveled toward the source of the *panzerfaust* round. Before the SS man could take cover, the tank loosed a main-gun round at him. Stöwe gasped as the man's body disintegrated.

Just at that moment, a German soldier arose from the grass with his hands held high and started walking toward the Americans. Stöwe thought the man's behavior to be stupid but not cowardly. Bullets were still flying through the air, and the surrendering man risked almost certain death. Other SS men, Heer soldiers, and Luftwaffe troops soon stood with arms raised high. The firing quickly died down.

Brenner used the pause to rally his remaining troops—possibly a hundred or so—and move away from the larger group of surrendering troops. Despite the disaster that had just befallen all that remained of the Nord Division, Brenner was determined to avoid capture with as many men as possible. Stöwe and his signals section gathered around the group led by the division supply officer and followed Brenner to the east. For the moment, Brenner and perhaps one hundred of his men had evaded capture—but they could not hold out for long.[33]

As Sergeant Rohan and his Company G mortar men arrived at the trail leading to the clearing, the Germans had already begun surrendering. They walked past a GI lying on a stretcher as a medic tended to his wounds. Private First Class Joy heard German voices in the distance faintly shouting "*Kamerad! Kamerad!*" as the bareheaded SS men emerged from the woods and tall grass with hands raised high. As Rohan and his men approached the clearing, they encountered several Company E GIs, bayonets fixed, leading a group of SS men with hands on heads in the opposite direction.[34]

For Private First Class Joy, these SS troops were the first he had ever seen. He thought his imagination might be playing tricks on him, but the SS men seemed bigger, tougher, and meaner than any German prisoners he had yet encountered during the war. As the guards prodded the prisoners past the mortar men, Joy could not help but think that the rumor of SS men fighting to the last or committing suicide before surrendering was just that—a rumor.[35]

As Rohan, Joy, and the mortar men entered the clearing, they saw GIs combing the surrounding forest and rounding up numerous German prisoners. The tall figure of Captain Neal, the Company G commander, met their eyes. Neal stood in the clearing's knee-high grass speaking to Lieutenant Colonel Gettys. Several battalion staff officers stood nearby and observed the mopping-up operation. German soldiers squatted in small groups around the clearing. In one of those groups sat the wounded *SS-Standartenführer* Raithel, the commander of SS-Gebirgsjäger Regiment 11, who had been incapable of following Brenner's small group to the east to avoid capture.[36]

Sitting on a stump near one side of the clearing was an *SS-Sturmbannführer* (probably a member of Brenner's divisional staff) with a severely injured arm. Blood ran down the man's tunic sleeve as the officer clutched the wounded arm with his good hand. A GI, cigarette clenched in his teeth, stood guard near the officer, holding his M1 with fixed bayonet.

As Joy and his group approached the wounded officer, the arrogant look on the SS man's face became readily apparent. Someone behind Joy said, "Lookit the fancy braid on that sumbitch's shoulder straps! What is he, a general?"

The guard took a long drag on his cigarette, threw the butt to the ground, and said, "Naw, he's just a major, but he speaks good English." The guard said that if the SS man griped about calling a medic to look at his arm one more time, he would stick him with the bayonet. "He kin just sit here an' bleed t' death as far as I'm concerned," proclaimed the GI.[37]

The *SS-Sturmbannführer*, overhearing the conversation and grimacing in pain, looked pleadingly at Joy and his group and said, "I demand to speak with an officer! It is my right according to the rules!" The guard raised his rifle menacingly at the officer and pointed the bayonet at the man's stomach. "Shut yer goddamn mouth, you!" he snarled.

Rohan, Joy, and the other mortar men kept moving east behind the advancing 2nd Battalion, which had moved off in pursuit of *SS-Gruppenführer*

Brenner and the remaining members of the Nord Division. GIs fired occasional shots at straggling SS troops, taking them prisoner and sending them back to the rear under guard.

As the 2nd Battalion's GIs entered another clearing farther east, Lieutenant Colonel Gettys, confident that he was hot on the trail of the remaining SS troops, radioed Colonel Wooten from his jeep's SCR-300. An excited Gettys blurted into the handset, "Got 'em in the bag, Sid!" Gettys described his battalion's maneuver concept to Wooten: all rifle companies—E, F, and G—were on line in pursuit of the SS troops supported by tanks moving southeast. The maneuver, explained Gettys, would certainly trap them.

Several Red Circle men overheard Gettys's conversation, and the prospect of bagging a large Waffen-SS formation electrified them. A current of excitement carried throughout the battalion like an epidemic. To add to the exhilaration, several prisoners revealed that *SS-Gruppenführer* Brenner was with the group of remaining Nord men. Gettys was even able to get a physical description of Brenner, which he immediately reported to Wooten. The time was 0922, and the 2nd Battalion was moving in for the final kill.[38]

After Lieutenant Colonel Brant had stopped his rapidly advancing Company G, 14th Infantry, west of Gelnhaar, he conducted a quick reconnaissance of the town with his jeep and driver. Farther south, on the right flank of Brant's 2nd Battalion, Lieutenant Colonel Guthrie's 3rd Battalion had crossed the line of departure at 0930—much later than the 2nd Battalion since Guthrie's troops were positioned farther east than Brant's GIs. Like the 2nd Battalion, the 3rd Battalion encountered no enemy troops and moved quickly toward the eastern edge of the forest.[39]

As Brant and his jeep driver crested the high ground west of Gelnhaar along the main road into the town, he encountered several M8 armored cars. Brant dismounted and spoke with the crew members. He learned that these cavalrymen hailed from Captain Robinson's 5th Cavalry Reconnaissance Troop of the 5th Infantry Division. The cavalrymen were still scouring the Gelnhaar-Kefenrod area in search of the scattered remnants of *SS-Oberführer* Goebel's horse-drawn column.[40]

The cavalrymen described to Brant their attack on the horse-drawn column the previous day. He said that they thought they had cornered a large concentration of SS troops in the forest a kilometer south of Gelnhaar. Brant checked his map and was alarmed to see that this alleged enemy concentration was in the path of his rapidly moving Company F. Brant thanked the Red Diamond cavalrymen for the information, hopped into his jeep, and sped off toward Bergheim and Company F.

After cutting back along some narrow trails leading east, Brant encountered Captain Alvey and his company as they crested a ridge within the forest—a few hundred meters from the suspected enemy concentration. Brant informed Alvey that SS troops may be in the woods just ahead. He walked along with Alvey and Company F as they forged cautiously ahead, anticipating enemy contact at any moment. As the GIs emerged from the eastern edge of the forest and onto the open farmland beyond, though, they realized the enemy either had departed or had never been there. However, the GIs discovered an American jeep and a trailer-mounted engineer compressor that had apparently been captured and then abandoned. An intact German trailer also was nearby. The GI hopped behind the jeep's wheel, pushed the ignition button, and the engine turned over. Brant directed Alvey to confiscate the equipment and take it along.

When Brant returned to his jeep, a call from Captain Goldman crackled over the radio. Company E had contacted about ten to fifteen enemy troops in the woods just east of Usenborn. Goldman's men quickly overcame the small enemy force in a sharp but brief firefight.

As soon as Goldman finished his report, the radio crackled again. This time the message originated from the 2nd Battalion's command post in Bleichenbach. The radio operator explained that the message had come directly from Colonel Lundquist moments earlier, at 1215 (the message was based on information reported to Lundquist from Colonel Wooten). Brant listened intently to the message: "Tamer Six [call sign for Colonel Lundquist] directs following be transmitted to you at once. A German Major General, in civilian clothes and rain coat and SS hat, with false left eye and plastic cover on left side of face, looks like refugee, accompanied by two full colonels, also probably in civilian clothes, is wandering around in our area, last observed last night, vicinity Gelnhaar 0097. Tamer Six extremely anxious to capture this individual. Notify all troops."[41]

Brant listened to the message with great interest. This information clearly suggested that the 6th SS-Gebirgs Division had come undone as an organization and that the division commander was on the run. Better yet, everyone now had the general's description. Brant had no way of knowing that

SS-Gruppenführer Brenner had not been near Gelnhaar the previous night and was no longer traveling with two full colonels (one of the two, *SS-Standartenführer* Raithel, was in the hands of Wooten's men at that time). Yet the prospect of having the enemy division's command group on the run— and possibly in the 14th Regiment's area—excited Brant. He quickly transmitted the information to his companies and then began looking to advance beyond the eastern edge of the Büdingen forest—possibly into Bindsachsen and beyond in the hope of earning the distinction of nabbing the SS general!

❖

Thin rays of the noontime sun peeked through the dense canopy of the Büdingen forest as Lieutenant Colonel Gettys's 2nd Battalion, 5th Infantry, pursued the remaining Nord men eastward. *SS-Gruppenführer* Brenner had escaped with this group, which had remained together despite the pressure of the American pursuit. Gettys traveled on foot along an eastward logging trail with Captain Neal's Company G. Company F was somewhere on the right, and Company E maneuvered through the forest on the left.

The logging trail soon became a sunken lane with high banks lined by dense brush rising on both sides. Staff Sergeant Cree's Company G mortar section still followed closely behind Gettys. Gettys's jeep and the other mortar vehicles followed from a distance.

Company G navigated the sunken lane until reaching an open area. The company had nearly reached the eastern limits of the Büdingen forest at a point just southwest of Waldensberg where Lieutenant Colonel Eikel's 2nd Battalion, 66th Infantry, waited.

Gettys and Captain Neal turned suddenly and signaled for the Red Circle men to halt. Gettys grabbed the handset from his radio operator and spoke quickly into the mouthpiece. He issued some rapid orders to the lead infantrymen, and the men quickly turned about and ran back along the sunken road. Staff Sergeant Cree led the way, followed by two machine-gun squads and several riflemen. Gettys and Neal followed.

Private First Class Joy and the rest of the Company G mortar section simply watched from beside the road. As Cree ran past his mortar section, he breathlessly told them that a report identified a large force of SS troops trying to escape south behind Company G. The machine-gun crews were to run back along the sunken road, link up with the tanks, and form a firing line along the crest of the high bank facing north.

Just then, a red-faced Gettys, followed by a huffing Captain Neal, arrived at the location where the mortar men stood. He gestured toward the line of underbrush on the left—facing north—and said, "Quick! Some of you men get up there on that bank and hit the dirt!" He told the GIs to keep their eyes peeled on the open area and that Company F would be coming up on the right soon. Then Gettys asked, "Who's in charge here?"

Neal quickly replied that Sergeant Rohan was in charge and pointed out the other mortar squad leader, Sergeant Bailey. Gettys told Rohan to leave five or six men on the bank overlooking the open area while Rohan, Bailey, and the rest followed Gettys and Neal, retrieved a mortar and rounds from one of the jeeps farther down the road, and set it up in case they needed it.

Rohan told Joy, Corporal Zarimba (the weapons platoon runner), and four ammunition bearers—all armed with M1 carbines—to man the bank overlooking the open field. The men scrambled up the small rise as Gettys, Neal, and the rest of the mortar section disappeared down the road.

The six GIs reached the bank's crest and assumed prone positions. They crawled forward through the tall grass and bushes until they could see the open area to the north. Zarimba and Joy scanned the horizon with their binoculars. Joy's glasses fogged as he pressed the optics to his face. He and Zarimba were the only ones armed with M1 Garand rifles. Joy brushed aside some deadfall to clear a small area next to his right arm. He spread his handkerchief and lay two eight-round ammunition clips on it.

Just then, Zarimba whispered hoarsely that he saw something coming out of the trees. Joy jammed his binoculars to his face and looked to where Zarimba pointed. Three or four hundred meters distant was a long column of men walking through the open area from left to right. "Maybe that's Fox Company, do ya think?" asked one of the ammunition bearers. Another GI stated that Company F was on the right, so the column could not be them.

The discussion continued for several minutes while the column moved closer. Joy could see through his binoculars the distinct outline of German helmets and, in particular, the MG42 carried by a man in the column's center. They had discovered the remaining group of Nord men.

"They're Krauts! They're Krauts!" exclaimed Joy. One of the ammunition bearer's carbines crackled first. Joy took aim and squeezed off two rounds at the German machine-gun bearer. The man stumbled and fell. A nervous and frightened Joy quickly realized that he had just fired his rifle in anger for the first time in the entire war.

As the GIs fired, they quickly realized that the German column, now scattering in all directions, was too far away for the carbines to be effective. Only Joy's and Zarimba's M1s could range the enemy. The ammunition bearers stopped firing and instead spotted for Zarimba and Joy. Joy had loaded his clips with a tracer round after every other bullet. He shouted to the man to his right, Private Vincent, "Watch my tracers; tell me if I'm over or under!"

The two men fired as rapidly as possible as the SS men, unaware of the source of the firing, scrambled, stumbling for cover. Nearly a dozen Nord men fell wounded or dead. The distinctive pop-pop-popping sound of a BAR suddenly echoed from the right. Several SS troops stopped and raised their hands above their heads as a long skirmish line of Company F GIs appeared from the woods. An out-of-breath Sergeant Rohan suddenly rushed up the bank behind the mortar men, crouched down beside them, and said, "Cease fire—they're surrendering." The noisy rumbling of tank engines soon filled the air as the Shermans clattered toward the open area along the sunken road.

Rohan told Joy to follow him into the field to help Company F disarm the SS troops. The other five men would remain on the bank and cover them. A reluctant Joy, nervous and feeling sick to his stomach, rose and followed Rohan, who gestured to the lead Sherman to follow him into the field. The crewman in the turret nodded, and the tank turned onto the field.

As the two men walked onto the field, Joy averted his eyes from the numerous dead Germans littering the ground. Instead, he looked ahead at the Company F GIs who now occupied the field in force and herded the surrendering Nord men. The GIs would not find *SS-Gruppenführer* Brenner among this remaining group of SS troops. Brenner once again had eluded capture—for the moment.

Rohan walked across the field and began conversing with a Company F sergeant. The lead Sherman followed slowly behind Joy. From the corner of his eye, Joy suddenly saw a large SS man lying on his back flinch. The man's helmet had come off, and one arm was stretched out beside him. The man moved his other arm to his face—but something was in the Nord man's hand. Joy froze as he thought, "The bastard has a hand grenade!"

Before Joy could react, he heard the tank lurch to a stop behind him. A short sergeant, wearing a tanker's helmet and armed with a Thompson submachine gun, jumped down from the turret. The tanker fired a quick three-round burst into the SS man. The man's body jerked violently, and his hand dropped the unknown article.

The sergeant and Joy approached and saw what appeared to be a dull mess-kit knife near the man's hand. A deep, bloodless cut ran across the man's neck: he had been trying to slit his own throat. Shaken, Joy turned away and walked toward Rohan. Before he had walked a few feet, Joy heard the tank sergeant growl, "Still breathin', ya bastard? Okay, now die!"

Joy turned as the tanker fired his Thompson into the SS man once again. Shocked by the violence he had just witnessed, Joy looked blankly at the sergeant. The man shot a scowling glance back at Joy as if to say, "You want to make something of it?" Sickened, Joy turned and walked away.[42]

Company F continued to gather and search the remaining SS troops, who readily cooperated with their captors. The final dissolution of the 6th SS-Gebirgs Division Nord was now nearly complete, but Major General Wyman and his Red Circle men could not be certain. They suspected that many of the stragglers had changed clothes and blended into the civilian population. The challenge would now be to ferret out the stragglers.

❖

Major General Wyman watched the situation develop from his command post in Langenselbold throughout the morning before setting out to visit his attacking units in the early afternoon. He recognized that the operation was rapidly pushing his forces eastward, so by mid-morning he instructed Lieutenant Colonel Lankenau to move the division command post forward to Büdingen. Since the 5th Infantry Regiment command post already occupied Büdingen, Wyman sent word to Colonel Wooten to move the 5th's command post forward into Wittgenborn, the same town occupied by the headquarters of Lt. Col. Walter J. Easton's 2nd Squadron, 2nd Cavalry Group. The division advance party arrived in Büdingen at 1130 and quickly selected buildings in the town's center to house the displacing headquarters.[43]

Colonel Reed's 2nd Cavalry Group also continued to maintain liaison with the 71st Division. Sometime during the night Major General Eddy had given Wyman operational control of Easton's 2nd Squadron so the Red Circle men and cavalrymen could better coordinate their actions. With liaison officers sending him constant reports from the 71st's command post, Reed was able to deploy the 2nd Squadron in a way that would best support the Red Circle Division's operation and net any German stragglers escaping eastward from the advancing infantrymen. Reed realized that as the Germans were pushed up against the 2nd and 3rd battalions of the 66th Infantry Regiment in Waldensberg and Leisenwald, respectively, they might find ways around and between the two towns and flee eastward. Reed instructed Easton to deploy the 2nd Squadron in a screen between Waldensberg and Spielberg to prevent such an occurrence. Reed then positioned his remaining 42nd Squadron in the twenty-kilometer gap between Wächtersbach and Flieden in the east to screen for German stragglers headed in that direction.[44]

Reports of enemy concentrations and activity continued to flood Lieutenant Colonel Foster's division G-2 shop even as the staff pulled up stakes from Langenselbold. Major Merrill, the 66th Infantry Regiment's S-3, reported that the enemy might be concentrating due east of Breitenborn while an artillery spotter plane radioed in at 1235 that the enemy was on the road north of the gravel pit (probably the quarry south of Rinderbügen). The pilot gave no direction of march and no number of enemy troops in the report. Other reports from newly captured German soldiers provided Foster and his intelligence troops with information that was no longer timely, such as SS troops moving in trucks—accompanied by two tanks—moving north through Wolferborn with American prisoners in tow. The estimated time of this enemy movement—according to the prisoners—had been 2100 the night before. Collectively, these reports suggested to Foster that the 6th SS-Gebirgs Division had completely dissolved and was on the run—a supposition made all the more accurate by the 2nd Battalion, 5th Infantry's attack on the last organized group of Nord men in the woods southwest of Waldensberg.[45]

❖

Lieutenant Colonel Gettys quickly got his 2nd Battalion, 5th Infantry, moving again after Company F finished searching and guiding rearward the numerous SS men captured in the clearing southwest of Waldensberg. Company F's troops counted more than one hundred prisoners in the field—the strength of a full German company. Patrols struck out to investigate further the fields and wooded areas north and east. These patrols made contact with members of Lieutenant Colonel Eikel's 2nd Battalion, 66th Infantry, south of Waldensberg shortly before 1200. By early afternoon the 5th Regiment as a whole had bagged more than five hundred prisoners. But continued rumors of the SS troops slipping out of uniform and into civilian clothes—along with the report of the one-eyed German major general on the run—prompted Colonel Wooten to push his battalions forward without stopping.[46]

Concerned that many of the SS troops might evade the Red Circle Division's trap by heading south, Wooten committed his motorized 1st Battalion to the regiment's right flank. He instructed the battalion commander and fellow West Point graduate, Lieutenant Colonel Broyles, to depart Büches quickly, swing south to Breitenborn, and head toward Wittgenborn. The 3rd Battalion had advanced toward Rinderbügen in the north without incident, and Wooten wanted to ensure that he cast as wide a net as possible on both of the regiment's flanks to ensure that few SS men escaped to fight another day.[47]

While Broyles's truck-mounted 1st Battalion sped to the area, Lieutenant Colonel Gettys's lead company, Company G, soon encountered the main road connecting Waldensberg and Wittgenborn. On the other side of the road, Captain Neal and his GIs spied a small hamlet consisting of some stone barns, small houses, and several outbuildings. This small hamlet, identified on the map as the Weiherhof, was nestled snugly against a kilometer-wide pond that was surrounded by thick underbrush. As Neal and his men crossed the road and approached the Weiherhof, shots rang out. The Red Circle men dove for cover and returned fire. A handful of SS men had garrisoned the tiny hamlet, and they did not intend to relinquish it easily.[48]

In the 3rd Battalion zone on the 2nd Battalion, 5th Infantry's left flank, Lieutenant Colonel Guthrie's GIs had advanced quickly during the day without encountering many Germans. Yet one tragic incident resonated deeply throughout the ranks of Captain Long's Company K and the rest of the battalion. After clearing the town of Wolf, the battalion, led by Company K, set out toward Dudenrod. Just before reaching the town, the GIs paused for a quick rest break. The Red Circle men flopped down alongside a road lined with young conifer trees barely eighteen inches tall. T/Sgt. Edward R. Utrup walked into one of the small conifer-tree clusters to urinate when he surprised an SS officer and two enlisted men hiding there. The officer drew his P08 Luger and shot Utrup dead.

The GIs swiftly rushed the area and took the three Nord men prisoner. Private Guzzo, a BAR man and close friend of Utrup, wept profusely on learning of the sergeant's death. Perhaps unwisely, Captain Long detailed Guzzo to escort the three SS men back to the prisoner collection point. Guzzo marched the Germans away at the point of his BAR and, presumably, did just as he was told without harming his charges.

Utrup's death particularly shocked the men of First Lieutenant Sims's Company M. The GIs became more sensitive about potential hiding places for German soldiers in the woods. Rampant rumors about cornered SS men sworn to kill the highest-ranking American possible or die trying still echoed in the GIs' minds. An order had gone out several days earlier for all sergeants and officers to remove any visible rank insignia from their uniforms. Most men had complied. But Utrup, in response to the cold, rainy conditions, had just pulled on his field jacket before entering the woods to urinate. He had failed to remove his stripes from that particular jacket since it was packed away when the rank-removal order surfaced. Company M's GIs quickly surmised that the rumor was true and that the SS officer shot Utrup because of his stripes. Those men who failed to comply with the order earlier quickly stripped their sleeves of all chevrons.[49]

❖

First Lieutenant Lewington S. Ponder, the 5th Regiment's division liaison officer, and his driver, Cpl. "Red" Kennerly, departed the 71st Division's main command post in Langenselbold earlier that morning as the staff organized themselves for their move to Büdingen. Ponder's only information on the whereabouts of his regiment was that they were moving generally along an eastward axis extending from Wolferborn in the north to Waldensberg farther south. Ponder had the latest map overlay and division operations instruction to deliver to Colonel Wooten.

Armed with only general information on the regiment's whereabouts, Ponder and Kennerly drove into the woods from a point south of the forest's namesake town of Büdingen. Kennerly drove his jeep along several narrow logging trails before reaching a more improved secondary road northeast of Breitenborn.

As the two men approached the three-way intersection just short of the Weiherhof, Ponder and Kennerly saw shell holes that were still smoking. As the jeep entered the intersection, both men observed thick, black smoke rising from the small hamlet to their front. They had clearly stumbled on a battle in progress.

The staccato sounds of rifle fire echoed throughout the Weiherhof as Kennerly eased the jeep behind a stone wall on the hamlet's outskirts. Ponder and Kennerly dismounted and, at a crouch, worked their way through some rubble and entered the tiny village. As they rounded a corner, Ponder and Kennerly spotted a hand extending from behind the edge of another building. The sallow, gray texture of the hand told Ponder the person was dead. Ponder rounded the corner to identify the hand's owner only to face the gruesome sight of a dead German soldier with most of his head missing and several bayonet wounds in his back.

Just beyond the dead German lay the body of an American soldier with a bullet hole between his eyes and a shattered leg. The GI did not appear to be from the 71st Division, though. In a nearby field, Ponder saw the body of another German soldier. The man lay on his back and appeared to gaze peacefully at the sky. Ponder knew the man was dead, though, since the body had flattened and lost all sense of normal proportion.

Ponder and Kennerly cautiously advanced into the village toward the sound of the fighting. They came across the charred remains of an M8 armored car with the scorched body of a crewmember hanging halfway from a hatch. The man's body looked like a chunk of burnt cork. The dead Americans were clearly from the 2nd Cavalry Group and had most likely died violently a day earlier in the initial fighting that erupted when the 6th SS-Gebirgs Division entered the area.

As Ponder and Kennerly moved farther into the hamlet, they encountered some of Company G's men being treated by medics. A few more steps into the village brought Ponder and Kennerly into the heart of the fighting. The small-arms fire became louder. Peering from the cover of a severely damaged house, Ponder saw a Nord man dash from a burning building into the street. Several shots rang out, and the man collapsed in a heap in the doorway of a barn. At that moment, several American mortar rounds burst in the street in front of Ponder and Kennerly. The street filled with smoke as several machine guns opened fire in a loud, sustained staccato. When the gray smoke cleared, Ponder saw white flags popping out from windows in the buildings ahead. Company G's GIs suddenly appeared from covered positions and rousted the SS troops from their hiding places. The street soon filled with numerous Germans standing with hands held high.

Ponder and Kennerly stood to survey the situation. Ponder could see the enormous frame of Captain Neal, the Company G commander, moving about the handful of surrendering prisoners. Ponder approached Neal and learned that the rest of the regiment had moved off to either the north or the south. Colonel Wooten and the command group had most likely headed for Wittgenborn, which is where Wooten had ordered Lieutenant Colonel Broyles to bring up the reserve 1st Battalion.

As Company G's men settled down in the rubble-strewn streets of the Weiherhof to eat their rations, clean weapons, or hunt for souvenirs, Ponder and Kennerly returned to their jeep and took off in search of Wooten. As they drove down the road toward Wittgenborn, Ponder and Kennerly encountered numerous destroyed vehicles left from Major Wyles's ambush a day earlier. Wyles, the 2nd Squadron, 2nd Cavalry Group's executive officer, had waylaid the Nord Division's advance guard on the road in the early morning hours of 2 April. The damaged and destroyed vehicles, along with other debris such as field gear, ammunition crates, and crippled weapons, littered the route. Many of the vehicles were German while others were American—captured and used by the SS troops so effectively during their dramatic eastward drive. Several German bodies also lay among the wreckage.

As Kennerly steered the jeep through the debris, Ponder noticed an American "Ike" jacket on the seat of a *kübelwagen*, the German equivalent of a jeep. The jacket, copied from the short-waisted British battle-dress jacket, had not yet received wide distribution to troops in the European Theater of Operations, and getting one was as much a status symbol as a fashion statement. General Eisenhower had popularized the jacket by being the first to wear one, thus giving the garb its nickname. Ponder looked closer at the jacket and saw the insignia of a medical corps major on it (undoubtedly taken from an officer the Nord men had captured with the field hospital two days earlier). Ponder was tempted to reach for the jacket, but the prospect of a booby trap warned him away from grabbing it.

As Ponder and Kennerly drove farther down the road to Wittgenborn, they began to see Red Circle men from the 1st Battalion, 5th Infantry, moving through the forest. Ponder stopped and asked where he could find the battalion or regimental commander. A GI pointed out where Lieutenant Colonel Broyles and Colonel Wooten stood conferring in the woods. As Ponder approached Wooten and Broyles, Major Irving Heymont, the regimental S-3, pulled him aside. Heymont could not believe that Ponder and Kennerly had just come down the road. Reports had indicated that roving German bands had moved in behind the 1st Battalion and cut the road. Ponder explained that he and Kennerly had navigated the wreckage-strewn road and encountered no one. Heymont dispatched a patrol back down the road. The patrol returned quickly and reported contact with a German group directly on the route. The GIs drove off the Germans after a brief but sharp firefight.

Ponder believed that he and Kennerly were indeed lucky and had narrowly missed the roaming band of Germans encountered by the patrol. He perhaps had been equally lucky by not grabbing the "Ike" jacket from the *kübelwagen*, since it might have been booby-trapped. Later that night, in the 5th Regiment's new command post in Wittgenborn, Ponder saw Captain Boggs, the regimental S-1, wearing a new "Ike" jacket. On closer scrutiny, Ponder realized the jacket was the same one he had spotted in the *kübelwagen*. Boggs, clearly not concerned with booby traps, had evidently snatched it from the German jeep when the rest of the command post displaced from Büdingen to Wittgenborn. Still, Ponder was better safe than sorry.[50]

❖

In his 3rd Battalion, 5th Infantry, aid station located in a main-street shoe store in Büdingen, 1/Lt. (Dr.) James M. Paul and his medics found themselves treating more wounded Germans than Americans. Most of the German wounded hailed from Heer or Luftwaffe units. Paul and his aid men had yet to treat a member of the Waffen-SS—even though the regiment was taking numerous SS prisoners farther east.

The medics greatly admired Paul for his medical skill and humanity. When a truckload of wounded arrived, Paul would immediately set to work on them—even though he may have already been working for hours with little or no sleep. He treated all wounded troops—American and German—with the same care and attentiveness.

Pfc. David L. Ichelson served as one of Paul's litter bearers at the aid station. Since most of the wounded arrived by truck, the litter bearers had little to do except assist Paul and the other medics. Ichelson soon became bored. He had been itching to get back to Company K as an aid man and get an opportunity to kill Germans, which was well outside his job description as a medic: his mission was to save lives and not to take them.[51]

After treating some wounded GIs, Paul told Ichelson and the other aid men to start packing since they would have to drive quickly to catch up to the eastward-advancing 3rd Battalion, which had already had several engagements with the Nord men that day. As soon as the men began repacking the medical supplies into equipment chests, a GI entered the shoe store and casually mentioned that a lot of SS prisoners were now starting to show up. Ichelson, eager to get a look at some SS "supermen," dropped what he was doing and went to the collecting point east of town.

When Ichelson arrived, he found several GIs (presumably from Company I, 5th Infantry) herding the SS men into groups. The SS men kept their hands held high as the GIs shoved them roughly into their respective groups. When one Nord man asked in broken English if he could drink from his canteen, a GI violently slapped the aluminum container to the ground and shouted, "No!"

Ichelson returned to the aid station and rejoined the other medics as they loaded the trucks outside the shoe store. First Lieutenant Paul and his medics hopped aboard and prepared to speed off in pursuit of the 3rd Battalion when a truckload of thirty wounded SS men pulled up directly in front of the shoe store. The GI behind the wheel leaned out the window and explained to Paul that he had been driving the wounded SS men around since 0300 that morning in search of medical help. Two of the men had died during the journey, and the driver had had no choice but to leave their bodies beside the road.[52]

Paul removed his helmet, muttered that he was supposed to keep up with the infantry, and then instructed the aid men to set up shop in the shoe store once more. Ichelson and the other medics quickly unloaded the instrument chests, the sterilizer, and the collapsible operating table. Within minutes, the aid station was back in business.[53]

Paul began by treating the moderately wounded. Most of the Nord men were suffering from wounds apparently received two or more days earlier. Some men were missing arms and legs. One man had had the flesh blown off the backs of his legs. Paul took one wounded prisoner at a time and treated each one quickly and efficiently. He carefully cleaned and debrided each wound, administered plasma, and applied clean dressings. Paul also offered some of the Nord men morphine, which they usually refused. The SS men appeared at ease while sitting on the floor or in chairs inside the shoe store. They seemed convinced that they were receiving good care.[54]

The SS men had never before seen plasma. One of the English-speaking prisoners asked Private First Class Ichelson about the plasma as Ichelson administered the solution to another SS man. Ichelson, a Jew with no love for the German people, answered that it was "Jewish blood"—administered so that the prisoner would feel "like one of us." The Nord man quietly accepted this response. The man then asked why the plasma was so yellow, and Ichelson explained that the red cells had been removed.

Paul and the medics treated each wounded prisoner as quickly and as thoroughly as possible. None of the wounds was minor, however. In particular, one Nord man suffered from a badly infected hand wound that was black with gangrene and emitted a strong fetid odor. Ichelson winced at the injury and was certain the man would eventually lose the hand.

Finally, Paul reached the last of the thirty patients. The medics gingerly lifted the overcoat-wearing SS man onto the operating table. The man had suffered a horrific torso wound that exposed his intestines. The large, protruding intestinal mass emitted a powerful fecal odor that nearly made Paul and the medics gag. Paul treated the man last because, in his estimation, the man would probably not survive.

Paul worked quickly and feverishly to clean and debride the man's stomach wound and administer plasma. After dressing the SS man's gaping stomach injury, Paul stepped back from the operating table, his surgeon's apron smeared with gore.

The wounded man suddenly reached into the pocket of his overcoat and produced a stick grenade. The man held the grenade in front of Paul's face. Paul blanched and froze. The entire aid station fell silent. Paul's gut reaction was that this SS fanatic was about to commit suicide and take everyone with him.

The wounded Nord men on the floor seemed unperturbed by the act—probably because the screw cap on the bottom end of the grenade was still intact. The SS man would have had to unscrew this cap and pull a small lanyard inside to arm the grenade. Instead, the man simply handed the grenade to the surgeon. Visibly relieved, Paul took the grenade and then barked to his aid men, "Time to move out!"[55]

Back in the north on the division's extreme left flank, Lieutenant Colonel Brant ordered his 2nd Battalion, 14th Infantry, forward into Bindsachsen. The message he had received from Colonel Lundquist about the SS general possibly hiding near Gelnhaar sparked him into action at the prospect of netting such a highly valued prize. Brant directed Captain Alvey's Company F into Bindsachsen to search the town thoroughly while Captain Goldman's Company E moved northeast through the gap between Gelnhaar and Bindsachsen.

Alvey's men met no resistance on entering Bindsachsen and quickly searched the town. Brant soon arrived by jeep leading Captain Brewer's Company H. He quickly ordered Brewer and Alvey to outpost the town with roadblocks guarded by tanks and riflemen.[56]

Colonel Lundquist, eager to act on the message received by Colonel Wooten about the SS general, raced to Bindsachsen by jeep to link up with the 2nd Battalion. On his way there Lundquist stopped by the 3rd Battalion's command post in Dudenrod. Lieutenant Colonel Guthrie reported that all was quiet except for a couple of small German patrols encountered by his men. The 3rd Battalion was at the limit of advance and could proceed no farther without additional orders.[57]

Lundquist believed that if the report about the SS general roaming the area was true, then the remaining enemy forces were probably farther north in the 2nd Battalion's zone. Just to be safe, he planned to reinforce Brant's men with some armor and additional infantrymen. Lundquist directed Guthrie to dispatch a platoon of three tanks and a rifle platoon from Captain Tommy L. Long's Company K to Bindsachsen. Lundquist would travel ahead and meet the platoon and tanks in the town. Lundquist also radioed back to his command post in Altenstadt and told Captain Borden, the S-3, to scratch up three more tanks and send them to Bindsachsen. Borden quickly contacted Captain Long (not to be confused with Company K's Tommy L. Long), the commander of Company B, 761st Tank Battalion, who promptly dispatched the three requested tanks to Bindsachsen. Borden and the rest of the regimental staff troops packed up the command post and moved northeast to Bleichenbach, finally settling there at 1455.[58]

When Lundquist arrived in Bindsachsen, he toured the 3rd Battalion's roadblocks with Lieutenant Colonel Brant. He wanted to keep Brant's armor and the freshly arriving tanks from the 3rd Battalion in reserve in case Brant's men detected a large concentration of SS troops in the outlying areas. Lundquist instructed Brant to replace his tanks at the roadblocks with machine guns and mortars from Captain Brewer's Company H while Companies E and G screened the woods and terrain north and east of the town. The platoon from Company K had arrived along with the tanks, so Brant positioned them and his own tanks in the center of town to reinforce the rifle companies on short notice. Brant then sent Captain Alvey's Company F southeast to investigate a large wooded hill sitting in the open—about a kilometer east of where the 5th Division cavalrymen had been searching for a concentration of SS troops earlier in the day.[59]

Alvey and his men struck out across the open ground south of town and advanced on the hill unmolested. After crossing nearly eight hundred meters of open terrain, the GIs were climbing the slope leading to the densely wooded crest of the hill when, suddenly, shots rang out. The Red Circle men scattered.

GIs rushed up the hill in pairs with their rifles leveled at the woods above them. Alvey directed his platoons to the flanks and, within minutes, the GIs were swarming through the trees and dense underbrush on the hill.

A sharp exchange of gunfire ensued as several Nord men, taking refuge within the woods, now concentrated their rifle and machine-gun fire on the invading GIs. The Red Circle men assaulted the SS men's positions with vigor, firing from the hip as they ran. Within minutes, the battle was over. SS men stood with arms raised. GIs ordered them forward. A handful of SS troops slipped away undetected and avoided capture.

Alvey was surprised to notice that as his men herded the prisoners into small groups and searched them, the count exceeded fifty Nord men. Perhaps his men had bagged the concentration of SS troops sought by the 5th Division's cavalrymen. In any case, this engagement proved to be the 14th Regiment's final encounter with SS troops in the Büdingen forest. Lundquist and Brant would later learn—much to their chagrin—that the notorious SS general was not among the prisoners.[60]

By 1500 reports from his regimental commanders suggested to Major General Wyman that the day's sweeping operation had reached its high-water mark. Personal visits to the regimental command posts throughout the day indicated that all organized resistance had ended. The prisoner count increased dramatically throughout the day, and Wyman could only conclude that his troops had shattered once and for all the 6th SS-Gebirgs Division Nord. In the 5th Regiment's zone, the Red Circle men had bagged 544 enlisted men, nine officers, and a German nurse. The regiment had killed forty-six SS men and wounded fifteen at a cost of seven GIs killed and four wounded. The 14th Regiment had netted 149 prisoners while killing twenty and wounding eighty, and the 66th Regiment had claimed 307 prisoners. By day's end, the prisoner count would exceed 2,700 SS troops and numerous stragglers from Heer support units and various infantry soldiers separated from their now defunct or disorganized units. Wyman planned to outline the details of the day's events in person to Major General Eddy later that evening when the XII Corps commander flew into Büdingen. Eddy had arranged earlier in the day to meet the 71st Division commander at his command post for dinner to discuss the situation.[61]

Yet a few hours before that dinner meeting was to occur, Major General Eddy had already sensed from the reports Lieutenant Colonel Lankenau sent to his corps' staff that the Nord Division had dissolved and no longer posed a threat. But reports from prisoners sent up through the G-2 staffs of both the 71st Division and the XII Corps hinted that even though the SS troops no longer operated as an organized combat unit, they planned to carry on the fight by shedding their uniforms, blending into the population, and using hit-and-run guerrilla tactics to harass the American rear areas. One report from some prisoners captured by the 5th Infantry Regiment suggested that one hundred or more SS troops were concentrating northwest of Wittgenborn and planned to raid Waldensberg after dark to seize U.S. vehicles and weapons, and possibly some horses. Colonel Wooten promptly forwarded this report to Colonel Regnier's 66th Infantry command post (Lieutenant Colonel Eikel's 2nd Battalion was still in Waldensberg) as well as to the division G-2. The report eventually reached Major General Eddy in Lauterbach.[62]

Eddy decided to keep up the pressure on any guerrilla-type SS units forming in the corps' rear area. He issued instructions to Wyman to push the three infantry regiments eastward out of the Büdingen forest to occupy new assembly areas behind the advancing corps units. In addition, Eddy directed Wyman to conduct motorized patrols on key portions of the corps' MSR and other eastward-oriented traffic arteries that, if impeded or interdicted by renegade SS troops, might hinder the corps' continued advance. Eddy also planned to return to the division the numerous trucks that transported the 1st Battalion, 66th Infantry, to Lauterbach.

Eddy also wanted all villages and towns through which the Red Circle men would pass on their way to the new assembly areas to receive a thorough vetting for SS troops who may have blended into the population. In particular Eddy wanted those villages in close proximity to the new assembly areas to undergo systematic house-to-house and room-to-room searches for all males between the ages of eighteen and forty-five. Men in this age group were to be taken into custody and placed in a POW enclosure until the man could prove his right to be in the area. In addition, the owners of homes where GIs discovered German soldiers or snipers would be taken to the town *bürgermeister*, the situation explained, and the homes destroyed by thermite grenades or some other incendiary device.[63]

As Eddy issued these instructions to Wyman, the division and corps G-2 staffs began preparing and disseminating propagandized information to the troops on blue-inked leaflets that provided a brief history of the SS and warnings not to fraternize with them or with members of the local population. These leaflets painted the SS troops as undying fanatics and, using clumsy and inflammatory rhetoric, outlined the dangers of fraternizing. One leaflet, received by Lieutenant Colonel Brant's 2nd Battalion, 14th Infantry, ended with a stern warning in all capital letters: "You would not fraternize with an SS man any more than you would handle a rattlesnake. But every German, wrinkled grandmother, pipe-smoking old brewer, soft-limbed young girl, barelegged schoolboy, are SS men at heart. Listen to your talk. They have voices you can still hear—20 million of them from Russia to France. They keep saying: D-O-N-'T F-R-A-T-E-R-N-I-Z-E!"[64]

Wyman acknowledged Eddy's instructions and set to work developing a new plan that would push the division eastward into forward assembly areas. These assembly areas would not only position the Red Circle men directly behind the fast-moving armored and infantry divisions, but also would allow them to clean out, once and for all, any lingering threats to the corps' rear area. Wyman also acknowledged from Eddy the release of the 2nd Squadron, 2nd Cavalry Group, back to Colonel Reed's control and the return of the 1st Battalion, 328th Infantry, back to the 26th Infantry Division—a battalion that never arrived in time to participate in the operation.[65]

Wyman and Lieutenant Colonel Lankenau quickly devised a plan that would push the regiments eastward through territory where SS troops who escaped the Red Circle Division's grasp might be hiding. The 14th Infantry would head due east by fifteen kilometers to an assembly area in Ulmbach while the 66th Infantry's two remaining battalions, the 2nd and 3rd, abandoned the hard-won towns of Waldensberg and Leisenwald and headed for Birstein just seven kilometers away. The 5th Infantry Regiment would push southward toward Wächtersbach with one battalion, the 1st, while the 2nd Battalion would advance through Spielberg and the 3rd Battalion would move northeast from Rinderbügen. Each regiment would travel with their attached tank and tank destroyer companies. The 71st Cavalry Reconnaissance Troop would continue to patrol the corps' MSR but extend the patrolling effort all the way to the XII Corps command post in Lauterbach. And, on reaching Ulmbach, the 14th Infantry would provide a rifle company to protect the division command post.[66]

Lankenau and his G-3 staff hurriedly prepared the new map overlay and order—Operations Instruction Number 7—to issue to the regiments. With darkness falling quickly the eastward advance to the new assembly areas would not occur until the next morning.[67]

Wyman sat back in his command post inside Büdingen and pondered the success of his division's actions against the 6th SS-Gebirgs Division. He had just employed his entire division in a massive operation to destroy an enemy division that, for all purposes, may have bested his men at a different time and under different circumstances. But, despite nagging coordination and communication problems, his regiments worked well together in a complicated envelopment of a large, enemy-infested forest region that ultimately resulted in the destruction of the SS division. His Red Circle men had a right to be proud of their accomplishment—the first real employment of the division as a whole in a coordinated action. In Wyman's mind, his men had proved their mettle.

But where was the notorious one-eyed division commander of the Nord Division? How had this man slipped through the ever-tightening net cast by the three regiments? Wyman had one SS regimental commander in custody—the injured *SS-Standartenführer* Raithel—but he knew that another senior officer, a colonel, was out there, along with the division commander. Would the Red Circle men nab them both during the night? One of these men would evade capture until much later. But, with the war in its waning days, capture for both men was inevitable.

As darkness fell on the Büdingen forest, Major General Irwin, the 5th Infantry Division commander, called Major General Eddy, the XII Corps commander, from the 5th Division's command post in Frankfurt to discuss the very thing that was nagging Major General Wyman—the location of the elusive 6th SS-Gebirgs Division's commanding general and the rest of the SS troops that may have melted away into the forest and surrounding towns. When Irwin phoned Eddy at 1940, he began by explaining that Colonel Roffe's 2nd Infantry Regiment had reached the day's objectives and bagged a total of 174 prisoners that day. Eddy then explained the next day's plans.[68]

> "We are giving Wyman a goose egg which some of your troops are in [and] directing him to make a house-to-house check up and bring in all men between 18 to 45 years of age and asking you to do the same thing in the towns you are located in. Does that sound OK?"
>
> "Yes, we are working on that now," replied Irwin.
>
> "Keep a close lookout for a man 40 years old with a plastic [cover] over

his eye," continued Eddy. "[T]hat's the General. Every house that harbors a soldier, where you can give proof that it is a soldier, burn the house down. Just drop a couple of thermite grenades in them."

"Okay," answered Irwin.

"I'm also sending back an officer of mine who was a prisoner who saw a soldier coming out of those towns vicinity Stockheim and had been harbored for a few days and wherever he saw soldiers come out I'm going to burn those houses down."

Irwin responded, "We got close to 1,000 PWs [prisoners of war] from everybody."

"I think we broke it up," remarked Eddy. "I'm interested in those SS PWs."

"Yes," replied Irwin.

"I'm an easygoing guy," continued Eddy, "but I think we'll have to give the population here a lesson. I'll assume all responsibility. I'll tell you a good way to tell these fellows: Most of them have their pay cards in their shoes or underneath their underwear. Now is the time to be very harsh. Thanks for all you've done. I appreciate it, Red."

"Oh the boys had a fine time," quipped Irwin.

"We're going fine up ahead," said Eddy. "[T]he armor has taken Gotha."

"Good," answered Irwin as he hung up the phone.⁶⁹

As far as Red Irwin was concerned, his Red Diamond men had done all they could to help the 71st Division and XII Corps rid the Büdingen forest and its environs of the threat posed by the 6th SS-Gebirgs Division Nord. But, little did Irwin know that at that moment, somewhere in his 2nd Regiment's area, his men were actually rounding up the final remnants of the Nord Division.

A damp chill hung in the night air as *SS-Oberführer* Goebel and the handful of Nord men in his group trudged through the small forested areas north of the Büdingen forest and along desolate back roads and logging trails. Goebel thought he was heading northeast somewhere near Gedern and away from the American forces pursuing him. If only he and his men could find a German unit somewhere to the east, he might once again offer his services to the Third Reich before the final cataclysm befell his nation.

As Goebel and his men trudged through the forest, an American voice suddenly called out in the darkness: "Halt!" The men froze. Shadowy figures of GIs quickly appeared all around the men. Goebel, the commander of SS-Gebirgs Artillerie Regiment 6, was a prisoner. He raised his arms high as the GIs searched each SS man and stripped him of his gear and weapons.[70]

In the bright beam of an American flashlight, Goebel noticed the shoulder patch sewn to the field jacket of one of his captors. The patch was a simple design, a red diamond with a thin, olive drab border. Goebel wondered what this patch meant and which unit had captured him. He would soon learn that these men hailed from Major General Irwin's 5th Infantry Division—the Red Diamond Division.[71]

As the Red Diamond men led him and the other SS troops away, Goebel wondered if *SS-Gruppenführer* Brenner and the rest of the Nord Division had escaped to fight another day. Goebel would be surprised to learn later that his capture had marked the end of the American operation aimed at destroying the 6th SS-Gebirgs Division Nord. The battle was over. The Nord Division's dissolution was complete.

CHAPTER 10

Completing the Record

As morning broke on 4 April, three days after Easter Sunday, Major General Wyman's Red Circle men still had not found the fabled one-eyed commander of the 6th SS-Gebirgs Division Nord. With his three regiments moving eastward to new assembly areas and searching each town, village, and hamlet for wayward SS troops and German men of fighting age, Wyman had hoped to ensnare the man who had given his division and the XII Corps commander so much grief—SS-Gruppenführer Karl Brenner. But Brenner had somehow eluded his American pursuers and was not captured until the war ended five weeks later.

A message from the 5th Infantry Division during the night about the capture of a senior SS officer—as well as coordination problems resulting from the 71st Division's move to the east—prompted Wyman to call Major General Irwin and close the loop concerning the operation against the Nord Division. Wyman hoped that Irwin's men had captured Brenner.

Wyman phoned Irwin at 0855 and began by explaining the coordination problem his troops in the north were having with members of the Red Diamond Division. The 5th Division troops were already in an area that 71st Division troops were to occupy.

"I am in kind of an embarrassment this morning," began Wyman. "You know that task force on your left in my area. That is in a goose egg that I am supposed to be going into this morning. I didn't know it was right there."

"We can pull them out," replied Irwin.

"I would appreciate it," responded Wyman. "Actually, my people are all underway."

"They will help clean it out," said Irwin.

"I wonder if your task force could go north of the 08 grid somewhere," Wyman added.

"I will move them up. Do you think the place is cleaned up now?" asked Irwin.

"Yes," answered Wyman.

"I want to move my people out," said Irwin.

"I believe you can as far as I am concerned," replied Wyman. "I hear you got the big one last night."

"We got the artillery commander," answered Irwin.

Wyman was disappointed to hear that Irwin had not captured Brenner. Both men thanked each other for their respective division's cooperation in the fighting against the Nord Division and ended the conversation. Irwin phoned Major General Eddy, the corps commander, and reported his discussion with Wyman. When Irwin mentioned the capture of the artillery commander, *SS-Oberführer* Goebel, Eddy answered, "Good work. That looks like it is pretty well busted up."[1]

Eddy told Lieutenant General Patton, the Third Army commander, that the operation against the 6th SS-Gebirgs Division was over. He said that he could focus solely on his XII Corps' rapid advance and the capture of a possible secret German government headquarters in the Thüringer Wald (Thuringian Forest) around Gotha and Ohrdruf (unfortunately, no such headquarters existed). However, fears of a vulnerable MSR still haunted Eddy, prompting him to request permission from Third Army for an armored task force from the 13th Armored Division to patrol the route.[2]

The 5th Infantry Division, pinched out of the line by an adjustment in the First and Third Army boundaries and relieved that day of assignment to the XX Corps, was available for other missions. In fact, on this same day, 4 April, General Eisenhower returned the Ninth Army to Lieutenant General Bradley from British control, thus giving Bradley command of four field armies, twelve corps, and forty-eight divisions—more than 1.3 million troops and the largest American field command in U.S. history. Bradley's mission with these four armies—as the new Allied main effort—was to reduce the Ruhr pocket while cutting a wide swath eastward across central Germany toward Leipzig and Dresden, split Germany in half, and link up with the Russians. The resulting adjustment in boundaries placed most of Major General Walker's XX Corps of the Third Army in the new First Army zone. Patton received orders from

Bradley's 12th Army Group headquarters to slow his advance so the First and Ninth Armies, deeply engaged in cleaning up the Ruhr pocket, could process the thousands of German prisoners captured in that encirclement. Patton loaned Major General Irwin's 5th Infantry Division and the 13th Armored Division to the First Army to assist in the mopping-up operations.³

Back in the 71st Infantry Division, Major General Wyman and his Red Circle men pressed on toward their new assembly areas and with their village-clearing missions. As the division that ultimately destroyed the 6th SS-Gebirgs Division, the 71st Division's Red Circle men seemed to have a renewed sense of pride and confidence. Greater challenges in the next five weeks awaited them. A reinvigorated self-assurance in their ability to take on the toughest troops the Wehrmacht could throw at them led the 71st's GIs to achieve an enviable combat record that took them farther east in Hitler's Reich than any other American division. Wyman had good reason to be proud of his men. They had performed superbly.

The public's only knowledge of the battle surfaced that very day, 4 April, in a small article in London's *The Times* newspaper. Even though the 71st Infantry Division played the greatest role in destroying the Nord Division, the Red Circle men received no mention. Instead, the news item singled out the 5th Infantry Division, possibly because a war correspondent traveling with the Red Diamond Division submitted the story. Although generally accurate for wartime reporting, the news column lent credence to the rumor of a massacre perpetrated by SS troops but dismissed by Patton himself days earlier. The five-paragraph article, featured under the Imperial and Foreign column of the newspaper, began with a small headline that read, "A German Army of Stragglers."

> Americans' Pursuit: From Our Special Correspondent: Frankfurt, April 3—The 5th Infantry Division, with tanks and tank destroyers, is engaged in a big man-hunt north of Frankfurt, where between 4,000 and 5,000 German troops are struggling hard to break out of encirclement.
>
> The quarry is a motley army which includes remnants of the 6th *S.S.* (Heydrich) Mountain Division and other units who hid in the woods when the allied [sic] tank columns drove through, and a group of armed civilians. The civilians, apparently, do not wear Volkssturm armlets, and are therefore liable to be shot at sight.
>
> Cut off northwest of Frankfurt, these Germans crossed the Autobahn that leads north to Cassel [sic], and thrust eastward 25 to 30 miles to a

point near Bad Soden. They are moving at walking pace, and are towing 16 captured jeeps, some 88mm guns, and one or two trucks. Though they are believed to have little ammunition, they have been mining roads and ambushing vehicles.

Negroes Shot: The presence of this enemy force was discovered when two jeeps ran into a German column. An American negro [*sic*] ordnance company was overrun and four or five bodies were found later at the spot each with a bullet through the head. An eyewitness states that two *S.S.* guards told a negro [*sic*] to run and then shot him as he ran.

On a main supply route the Germans waylaid a field hospital on the move, killing a medical major. An *S.S.* divisional surgeon said that American and German patients would be brought to the hospital, and later came along himself with shell fragments in the shoulder. Finally the enemy troops made off with unwounded prisoners and the ambulances, but left the 16 nurses and the patients behind. Now the United States forces are hard on the Germans' heels.[4]

The correspondent's report did little service to the Nord Division by propagating an unfounded rumor about the murder of Black soldiers near Assenheim. The article, like most reports during the war about SS troops, painted the 6th SS-Gebirgs Division as a group of brutal fanatics, an image further exacerbated by the division's unfortunate association with the late and very vicious Reinhard Heydrich—the man behind the Holocaust and the gestapo. Although the division's actual name was Nord, SS-Gebirgsjäger Regiment 11's official title was "Reinhard Heydrich," a name woven on the black-and-white cuff titles sewn to each SS man's left sleeve.

Although probably unaware of the news report, Wyman likely would have been frustrated at the omission of his division from the article. But Wyman was already looking ahead to other missions of greater importance. And these missions would certainly come in a fast-moving, five-week period that would end in Steyr, Austria.

After searching the towns east of the Büdingen forest, the Red Circle men occupied their new assembly areas, rested for a day or so, and then struck out on 6 April for Fulda. The division took Meiningen on 8 April; with that town came the discovery of the central records depository for all POWs in Germany. After seizing Meiningen, the division veered southeast. Within a week the 71st Division was through Coburg and Bayreuth and racing for Regensburg on the Danube River. After a perilous crossing of the Danube on

26 April, the Red Circle men raced ahead to Landau, bounced the Isar River, and paralleled the southeast-running Danube across the Inn River and over the Austrian border on the night of 2 May. The Red Circle men seized Steyr on 5 May and then moved to a link-up point farther east with the 5th Guards Airborne Division of the Russian Red Army on 7 May. On that same day, 7 May 1945, the day before VE (Victory in Europe) Day, elements of Captain Johnson's 71st Cavalry Reconnaissance Troop persuaded the commander of German Army Group South, *Generaloberst* Dr. Lothar Rendulic, to surrender. With Rendulic's capture came the brokering of the final German surrender of troops in the southeast. Approximately 60,000 German prisoners crossed the Enns River near Steyr and into the 71st Division's zone. With this massive surrender of German troops, the war ended for the Red Circle Division.[5]

Unfortunately for Major General Wyman and his GIs, the 71st Infantry Division was not spared the horrors of Hitler's Final Solution. Hidden in the dense forest near Lambach, Austria, the Red Circle men discovered—and then liberated—the people being held in a concentration camp, Gunskirchen Lager. Inside the camp were unspeakable examples of cruelty, genocide, and torture—the same things that Allied troops were now finding throughout Germany at places like Dachau and Buchenwald. The scores of malnourished bodies littering the woods outside Lambach starkly reminded each GI why he was there to defeat Nazi Germany.[6]

Praise for the Red Circle men's accomplishments from the highest levels of command proved effusive and widespread. Major General Eddy never forgot the role the Red Circle men played in protecting the XII Corps' rear area at a crucial time when the corps was in fast pursuit of the withdrawing German Army. Unfortunately for Eddy, the nervous and high-strung corps commander was unable to see the war through with the rest of his men. In Patton's words, Eddy had "cracked up" and needed to go home. On 20 April 1945 Patton replaced Eddy with Major General Irwin of the 5th Infantry Division. Coincidentally, both Eddy and Irwin had served together as brigadier generals in the 9th Infantry Division a few years earlier.[7]

Before Eddy relinquished command, he sent a letter to Willard Wyman that specifically highlighted what Eddy clearly believed to be the 71st's greatest battlefield success—the destruction of the 6th SS-Gebirgs Division Nord. The letter read, "Before I leave I want you and your command to know how thoroughly satisfying your brief service was under this command. Few divisions have acquired the spirit of veterans as quickly and as thoroughly as the 71st. At a period in which our lines of communication were dangerously threatened by the SS Mountain Division Troops, you joined the Corps and proceeded to eliminate this threat with skill and dispatch. Your subsequent advance into Germany is surely the auspicious beginning of a fine combat record."[8]

For Wyman and his men, no praise could have been greater—especially coming from one of Patton's most respected and storied corps commanders. The Red Circle Division had clearly made its mark.

Wyman expressed his pride for his men in a letter he crafted and then issued as General Order Number 20 a day after hostilities in Europe ended, 9 May 1945. Wyman wrote:

The war with Germany is ended.

Before we turn to a new mission, I wish to extend my heartfelt congratulations to the members of this Division for the splendid accomplishment of the many tasks that have been given it.

From the day you left your concentration area in Le Havre, in a period of 92 days, you have marched, fighting a large part of the way, a distance of 1060 miles. You have captured over 80,000 prisoners of war, the bulk of them being captured the hard way. From the day you were committed with the Seventh Army south of Bitche, with the XV Corps and XXI Corps, there has been no break in the intensity of effort. Historic names are emblazoned on your memories by the heroic deeds of members of the Division. You were cast through the Siegfried Line to capture Pirmasens, which you did without faltering. Your advance continued to the Rhine where the record of your valor was written in the blood of brave comrades at Speyer and Germersheim.

A sudden change in directive transferred the Division from the Seventh to the fast moving Third Army where you were thrown across the Rhine to cover the rear of XII Corps. East of Hanau you were confronted with hard fighting elements of the 6th SS-Mountain Division Nord, which you destroyed with every battalion of the division working smoothly together as a team. On through Fulda and Meiningen, constantly opposed by small fighting groups of the enemy which you did not permit to delay you, seizing Coburg and Bayreuth in your path.

A transfer to the XX Corps gave us new missions when we swept southeast to Velden, Sulzbach, and Amberg. You crossed the Regen River at Regonstauf, the Danube at Regensburg, the Isar at Landau, the Inn on dams east of Braunau which were secured only after vicious fighting and major labors of our Engineers. We stopped only on our objective, the River

Enns, at Steyr, but with patrols thrusting deeply into enemy territory at Waidhofen and Amstetten, the eastern-most point reached by American Ground Forces of any U.S. Army in the European Theater.

You have refused to let fatigue, the physical obstacles of mountains and rivers stop you. The enemy has only delayed you momentarily. You have written a glorious page in the military history of our beloved country. You are veterans, proven in battle. May you continue to live up [to] the high standards you have set for yourselves, whether it be in further battles in Asia, or in an occupational role in Europe.

I salute you.[9]

Wyman remained in command of his beloved 71st Infantry Division on occupation duty in Germany until August 1945, when he received orders to report to Headquarters, Army Ground Forces, in Washington, DC. After an emotional farewell to his troops and staff, Wyman left for the states while the Red Circle Division remained in Germany under the command of Brigadier General Rolfe, the assistant division commander. In October Rolfe passed command to Maj. Gen. Arthur A. White; just after Christmas 1945 elements of the division began redeploying to the states. The regular Army regiments, the 5th and the 14th, remained behind to augment the occupation forces along with the reconnaissance troop and the division's ordnance company. By late winter the rest of the division had closed on Camp Kilmer, New Jersey—the same location from whence the division deployed overseas a little more than a year earlier. On 12 March 1946 the Red Circle Division was inactivated.[10]

Major General Wyman remained with Headquarters, Army Ground Forces, and followed the command to its new home at Fort Monroe, Virginia, in October 1946. Wyman's star continued to rise quickly, and he returned to combat once again as commanding general of IX Corps in Korea in December 1951. In March 1956 Wyman became a four-star general and assumed command of the U.S. Continental Army Command, which consisted of more than 450,000 officers, soldiers, and civilians, one half of the standing Army. Wyman retired in 1958 and settled in Damariscotta, Maine. He died at Walter Reed Army Hospital in Washington, DC, on 29 March 1969. His beloved Red Circle men never forgot their commanding general and kept his memory alive at the reunions that still occur every year.[11]

Many of the division's officers and men also enjoyed distinguished Army and civilian careers following their combat exploits while wearing the Red Circle patch. The 5th Infantry Regiment's commander, Colonel

Sidney C. Wooten, left the regiment in 1946 wearing a Distinguished Service Cross only to command another regiment in combat, the 17th, during the Korean War. He quickly became a general officer following the Korean War and commanded both Fort Dix, New Jersey, and Fort Devens, Massachusetts. As the last surviving regimental commander from the Red Circle Division, Maj. Gen. Sidney Clay Wooten, West Point Class of 1930, died of pneumonia in Chevy Chase, Maryland, on 26 December 2003 at the age of ninety-six.[12]

Wooten's S-3, Maj. Irving Heymont, remained in the regiment and took command of the 2nd Battalion, 5th Infantry Regiment, from Lt. Col. Charles M. Gettys. Following the battle with the 6th SS-Gebirgs Division, Heymont typed a V-Mail letter to his wife, Joan, on 5 April 1945 using a captured German typewriter. As a Jew, Heymont expressed delight at chasing down the remnants of the Nord Division. He wrote,

> Our last operation was a very pleasant task. We pocketed the remnants of an SS division in a large woods and it was a case of hare and hounds to root them out. The SS people are the bastards we hate. They are fanatics who fight to the end and then calmly give up. Even after capture they are still an arrogant bunch. We finally rooted them out. It was a pleasure to kill them off and capture the remnants. All through this area we constantly run into stragglers.[13]

Heymont's sentiments undoubtedly reflected the same attitude of many of the Red Circle men toward all Waffen-SS soldiers throughout the war. Heymont remained in the Army and later commanded an infantry battalion in Korea, earning a second award of the Combat Infantryman's Badge. He retired as a full colonel and took a job in the private sector in northern Virginia before finally retiring once and for all. He remained close with his former regimental commander, Major General Wooten, up until Wooten's final days. Irving Heymont died on 17 March 2009 in a military retirement community on Fort Belvoir, Virginia.[14]

Two of the 5th Regiment's battalion commanders, Lieutenant Colonel Broyles of the 1st Battalion and Lieutenant Colonel Gettys of the 2nd Battalion, both stayed in the Army as well and retired after full careers. Broyles, a 1936 West Point graduate, went on to serve in the Korean War from 1950 to 1951, followed by an assignment to the Pentagon in 1952. He retired in Raleigh, North Carolina, as a colonel in 1964. Broyles's fellow battalion commander, Charles M. Gettys, followed a similar career path and reached the rank of major general before leaving the service. In 1968 he deployed to Vietnam and assumed command of the 23rd Infantry (Americal) Division. He retired from the Army in 1973 and died in Washington, DC, in 1982.[15]

The regimental liaison officer to division headquarters, 1/Lt. Lewington Ponder, also remained in the Army and retired as a full colonel in 1976. A 1943 graduate of Syracuse University, Ponder took command of Company L in the 3rd Battalion for a few months after the war before becoming the regimental S-3 after Major Heymont left to command the 2nd Battalion. When he returned from Europe in 1946, Ponder decided to make the Army a career and eventually commanded a brigade. He lives today in retirement in North Carolina.[16]

One of the regiment's enlisted soldiers went on to a distinguished career in the field of medicine. Pfc. David L. Ichelson, the Company K medic who received his first taste of combat outside Lingenfeld, was inspired by a man he greatly admired, 1/Lt. (Dr.) James M. Paul, the 3rd Battalion surgeon and graduate of Harvard University and Johns Hopkins Medical School. Ichelson eventually graduated medical school and enjoyed a successful decades-long medical practice in California before retiring in 1997. In his spare time Dr. Ichelson wrote a detailed and insightful monologue of his wartime experiences entitled, "I Was There." Like his regimental S-3, Irving Heymont, Ichelson was of Jewish descent and hated the SS troops he encountered. He remained in close contact after the war with his mentor, Dr. Paul. Dr. Ichelson died in 2008.[17]

Pfc. Dean P. Joy, the bespectacled mortar man from Company G, 2nd Battalion, left the Army but continued to serve the armed forces as an engineer. Joy returned to school on the GI Bill, earned a degree in Aeronautical Engineering from the University of Colorado, and began a forty-two-year career in the aerospace defense industry. Upon retirement he wrote and published in 2004 a memoir of his combat time with the 71st Infantry Division entitled *Sixty Days in Combat: An Infantryman's Memoir of World War II in Europe*. Dean P. Joy was a resident of Los Gatos, California, until his death in 2009.[18]

Like many in the 5th Infantry Regiment, several of the 14th Regiment's officers remained on active duty and had long Army careers. Col. Carl E. Lundquist, the regimental commander and 1927 graduate of West Point who replaced Col. Donald Beeler before the division's commitment to combat in March, remained in command of the regiment until he received orders returning him to stateside duty. In early 1948 Lundquist—then assigned to Headquarters, Army Field Forces, at Fort Monroe, Virginia—received a letter through the 71st Division's postwar association from the mother of a 14th Regiment soldier killed north of Rodenbach on 1 April 1945 requesting information about the soldier's death. The soldier was Cpl. Robert V. Reno of Company E's 1st Platoon—the very platoon that led the 2nd Battalion's tank-mounted assault on a wooded area infested with Nord men. Reno was wounded and died later at a medical aid station.[19]

Lundquist's two-page response written on 28 May 1948 to Reno's mother, Mrs. Warren Middleton of Ridgeville, Indiana, was both sincere and heartfelt. He explained the circumstances of Reno's death and the impact of the young man's sacrifice: "I have always been proud of the way those men performed that day. By their swift and fearless action that day against superior numbers they saved General Patton's Army from a severe setback at the beginning of his victorious thrust across Germany. Had the German division succeeded in cutting off the XII Corps, the war might have lasted weeks longer than it did. Both General Patton and General Eddy acknowledged this and were strong in their praise."[20]

Lundquist, who had already commanded a regiment—the 141st Infantry, 36th Infantry Division—prior to assuming command of the 14th Infantry, went on to command the 4th Regimental Combat Team at Ladd Air Force Base from 1952 to 1954. He retired as a colonel in 1957 with an impressive array of decorations that included the Distinguished Service Cross, two Silver Stars, and the Combat Infantryman's Badge. He died on 3 March 1980 in Panorama City, Maryland.[21]

Second Lieutenant Frank J. Hagney, Corporal Reno's platoon leader, received a remarkable honor for his gallantry on 1 April north of Rodenbach. Hagney, severely wounded in the same assault that mortally injured Reno, received the Distinguished Service Cross in July 1945—the third such medal received by a member of the Red Circle Division. A front-page news item in the 14th Regiment's newsletter, "Right of the Line," on 28 July 1945, quoted the citation for Hagney's award: "Inspiring his men by his heroic, indomitable leadership he pressed forward against the enemy and, although wounded seriously twice more, continued his gallant, aggressive actions. Lieutenant Hagney's tenacious courage and unflinching devotion to duty exemplify the highest traditions of the military service."[22]

Hagney's battalion commander, Lt. Col. Philip D. Brant, also was decorated for valor for his actions that same day. Brant, the 1937 West Point graduate from Washington, DC, received the Silver Star for leading the division's first assault against the 6th SS-Gebirgs Division Nord. The award citation described how Brant

> was present in the front lines of his battalion during the action in which his command was attacking elements of an enemy division, with the mission of cutting off and destroying an enemy force estimated at 750 men. Upon encountering the enemy, he found their strength to be from 1500 to 3000 men. Despite the smallness of his force, he pressed the attack unhesitatingly. He continuously exposed himself to enemy small arms and artillery fire in order to exercise maximum control of his battalion. This action resulted in the disorganization and dispersal of the enemy units.[23]

Brant remained a career officer in the Army after the war like his father, who graduated West Point in 1904 and retired as a major general in 1944. The younger Brant retired in 1965 and died on 29 March 1985 in San Antonio, Texas, at the age of seventy-two. His son, Philip Jr., also graduated West Point but did not make the Army a career like his father and grandfather.[24]

During the occupation period immediately after the war ended, Brant meticulously compiled a scrapbook dedicated to his then-infant son, Philip. The front page of the scrapbook was inscribed "To Philip Delano Brant Jr.: This book is dedicated to little boys who ask, 'Daddy, what did you do in the war?'" The scrapbook included priceless maps, handwritten narratives, original messages, orders, and photographs of Brant's wartime experiences from March 1945 until occupation duty. The Brant family graciously entrusted this precious scrapbook to me for more than five years while I wrote this book. Without this remarkable primary resource, many details of the initial battle with the Nord Division on 1 April 1945 would have been lost to history forever. I am forever indebted to the Brant family for sharing this valuable resource with me.[25]

Capt. Thomas W. Alvey, the officer who took command of Lieutenant Colonel Brant's Company F a day before the battle north of Rodenbach, also opted to remain in the Army. After a long career that included multiple command and staff assignments, Alvey eventually retired as an infantry lieutenant colonel. Lt. Col. Paul G. Guthrie, the 3rd Battalion commander, made a career of the Army and, after a series of normal staff and other assignments, retired in the rank of lieutenant colonel.[26]

First Lieutenant W. P. Sims, commander of Company M in Guthrie's 3rd Battalion, was promoted to captain just before hostilities ended; after the war he became a tireless champion of his regiment's and company's wartime histories.

A 1942 Texas A&M graduate with a degree in Petroleum Engineering and Geology, "Pete" Sims became a petroleum engineer in California after leaving the Army. Soon after retiring in 1979, he tracked down nearly every former member of his company and developed long-standing relationships with many of them, including mortar ammunition bearer Pfc. Edward G. Rimple and Pvt. William L. Asay, who became ill on seeing the carnage wrought by the artillery barrage on Hill 267. At Sims's urging Rimple produced for me a hand-drawn map of the 3rd Battalion's assault on Hill 267 near Glauberg. I had this map in hand when I visited the battlefield in the spring of 2000. Rimple's memory amazed me; the sketch matched the terrain perfectly and allowed me to pinpoint the precise location where the 3rd Battalion's GIs began their assault on the hill.[27]

Pete Sims continued to gather historical data throughout the years from his fellow veterans and from the National Archives. He painstakingly retraced each detail of his company's actions in the war and ultimately wrote a precise, day-by-day account of Company M entitled "Blue Mike" (Blue was the 14th Regiment's call sign, and Mike was the Army's phonetic term for the letter M, thus resulting in a complete call sign of Blue Mike). Pete is in his late eighties today and has been a tireless supporter of my work and a great friend.[28]

Like the other two regiments, many officers in the 66th Infantry Regiment opted for postwar Army careers. Col. Augustus J. Regnier, the regimental commander, eventually retired in the 1950s as a colonel and settled in Cranston, Rhode Island. Regnier, a 1927 West Point graduate, actually served as an enlisted man in the Navy during World War I. After the war, he had a choice between attending West Point or the U.S. Naval Academy. He quickly chose West Point since he became seasick every time he even looked at the ocean. He later served on the U.S. Army Advisory Group to Greece from 1948 to 1949 and commanded the Area Service Unit at Camp Roberts, California, in 1952, prior to his retirement. Augustus J. Regnier, a recipient of two Silver Stars and the Bronze Star, died on 27 July 1981 at the age of eighty-one.[29]

Regnier's most-gifted battalion commander, Lt. Col. Bryce F. Denno, eventually retired from the Army as a colonel and settled in Coronado, California. Denno, a 1940 West Point graduate and recipient of the Distinguished Service Cross, remained greatly impressed by Company K's assault on Leisenwald and lobbied tirelessly to have the company awarded a Presidential Unit Citation. The effort fell through because, in Denno's estimation, the action had been too "short-lived." An active participant in the 71st Division Association, Bryce F. Denno died on 1 November 2000—but not before providing me with an invaluable first-person account of the action at Leisenwald.[30]

Some officers in the 66th Regiment left active duty shortly after the war only to have the Army recall them for the Korean War. Lt. Roy J. Long, the mortar platoon leader in Company H of Lieutenant Colonel Eikel's 2nd Battalion, stayed in Germany on occupation duty a year after the war ended. The Army recalled Long to active duty in 1951 and sent him to Korea where he served with the 1st Cavalry and 3rd Infantry divisions, earning a second Bronze Star. He eventually settled in Omaha, Nebraska, where he retired in 1984 after thirty-six years as a public-school teacher and athletic coach.[31]

A member of Long's 2nd Battalion, Pfc. Thomas C. Tomich, took advantage of the generous GI Bill and returned to school in California. Tomich, the wireman and messenger for Company G, earned undergraduate and graduate degrees from the University of California's College of Agriculture. He spent the next several decades involved in fruit growing and packing before retiring to tend his own little orchard in Orangevale, California. He took the time in his retirement to write down his wartime experiences, which he privately published with the title *GI's [sic] Forever*.[32]

Members of the other divisional units had equally prosperous postwar careers. Lt. Edward W. Samuell Jr., the 1st Platoon leader in Captain Johnson's 71st Cavalry Reconnaissance Troop, retired from the Army as a colonel in 1971 after twenty-six years of active service. He then went to work for the City of Dallas as a security director and data processor before fully retiring in 1986. He remained in close contact through the years with his platoon sergeant, the late S/Sgt. L. B. "Whitey" Rhatican, who had retired to Sayreville, New Jersey.[33]

Another member of the 71st Reconnaissance Troop, T/4 Mason "Mickey" Dorsey of the 3rd Platoon, went on to become an active member of the division's association. Dorsey, leader of the M8 armored car nicknamed "The Four Rebels," survived a *panzerfaust* round that struck his vehicle in the town of Bönstadt. Like thousands of his fellow World War II veterans, Dorsey took advantage of the GI Bill and graduated from Clemson College in 1949. He went to work for Lubromation, Inc., in 1960 and retired to South Carolina in 1995. Dorsey became a mainstay of the many 71st Division reunions and always brought his collection of war souvenirs and photographs to each event.[34]

A Red Circle artilleryman who enjoyed a highly distinguished postwar career was 1/Lt. Douglas Kinnard, the executive officer for Battery B, 608th Field Artillery Battalion. Kinnard, the officer who took *SS-Oberführer* Goebel's remaining horse-drawn artillery pieces under direct artillery fire, was a West Point graduate of the D-Day class of 6 June 1944. Kinnard enjoyed a highly successful twenty-six-year Army career that included combat in Korea and two tours in Vietnam before retiring as a brigadier general. He went on to earn a doctorate from Princeton, after which he served as the U.S. Army's only civilian Chief of Military History. In 1994 President Bill Clinton appointed Brigadier General Kinnard as a Commissioner on the American Battle Monuments Commission. As the author of seven books (including the excellent autobiography *From the Paterson Station: The Way We Were*), Brigadier General Kinnard remains active in retirement in the Washington, DC, area.[35]

The all-Black tank battalion that supported the division throughout the fighting in the Büdingen forest, the 761st, eventually received a Presidential Unit Citation from President Jimmy Carter in 1978 for "extraordinary heroism in action." Lt. Col. Paul L. Bates, a 1931 graduate of Western Maryland College and All-American football star who entered the Army as a first lieutenant in 1941, had assumed command of the battalion in January 1943. At a time when segregation and racial tensions flourished in the Army, the 761st's tankers loved their White commander, whom they saw as fair and unprejudiced. Bates's stock rose immensely with his men when he refused a promotion to full colonel so he could remain in command of what he knew to be the best tank battalion in the Army. Bates even refused to court-martial one of his Black officers, Jackie Robinson, soon to be a baseball great, for refusing to move to the rear of a bus at Camp Hood in Texas. Bates lobbied tirelessly after the war to get his Black tankers the recognition that racial prejudice had denied them during the war years. The result of his efforts was the Presidential Unit Citation bestowed on the 761st by President Carter. Kareem Abdul-Jabbar, in his 2004 book *Brothers in Arms: The Epic Story of the 761st Tank Battalion, WWII's Forgotten Heroes*, described Bates as "fundamentally decent, honest, modest, and compassionate. He saw and treated the men in the battalion with a simple, direct humanity, and they responded in kind." Bates retired from the Army in 1963 and died of cancer in February 1995 at the age of eighty-six in Dunedin, Florida.[36]

Nearly all the Red Circle men and the GIs from the division's attached units went on to have fulfilling lives and successful careers. Most men saw the GI Bill as a gateway to a better life and seized the opportunity for higher education—opportunities that before the war would have been beyond the financial reach of many. Their chosen professions included medical doctors, machinists, teachers, planners, politicians, city managers, clergymen, corporate executives, aerospace engineers, coaches, and so on. The 71st Division's men were truly a representative slice of what Tom Brokaw ultimately termed the "Greatest Generation." They contributed to America's growth and prosperity like no other generation, and they sacrificed more than any other generation has since that time.

The Red Diamond men of the 5th Infantry Division who played a key supporting role in the destruction of the 6th SS-Gebirgs Division also reflected a similar level of postwar achievement in and out of the Army. Maj. Gen. S. LeRoy Irwin, the division commander and 1915 West Point classmate of Lt. Gen. Omar N. Bradley, took over the helm of XII Corps from Major General Eddy less than three weeks before the war ended. Irwin later served as assistant chief of staff, Army Intelligence, in 1948 before assuming command of all U.S. Army forces in Austria as a lieutenant general. He died in 1956 at the age of sixty-three and was buried at Arlington National Cemetery with full military honors.[37]

Col. A. Worrell Roffe, the commander of the only Red Diamond regiment to participate in the battle, relinquished command of the 2nd Infantry two weeks after the Nord Division's destruction. Col. Walter R. Graham assumed command on 26 April 1945.

Roffe's 3rd Battalion commander, Lt. Col. Robert E. Connor, remained in the Army for a long career that included a tour in Vietnam. Connor, the commander of the first Red Diamond battalion to engage the 6th SS-Gebirgs Division, received a reserve commission in 1939 after graduating from the University of Cincinnati, Ohio. He returned to the United States after the war and attended Command and General Staff College at Fort Leavenworth, Kansas, before moving to Fort Benning, Georgia, as a tactics instructor. As a brigadier general, Connor deployed to Vietnam and served as the Assistant Division Commander, 4th Infantry Division. He retired from the Army soon thereafter and settled in Libertyville, Illinois.[38]

The other 5th Infantry Division unit that had the most contact with the Nord Division was Capt. Donald E. Robinson's 5th Cavalry Reconnaissance Troop. Prior to the battle with the 6th SS-Gebirgs Division, Robinson had become a "hometown hero" of sorts for leading a daring rescue of fifty-eight captured Allied pilots. A Detroit native and graduate of Michigan State College, Robinson was called to active duty in August 1941 and deployed overseas in April 1942. At twenty-nine he was one of the oldest captains in command in the Red Diamond Division. His storied rescue mission on 29 March 1945 resulted in a ten-page spread in *Life* magazine and numerous newspaper articles (a war correspondent had accompanied Robinson's troop). Robinson, a true hometown hero, returned to his native state of Michigan after leaving the Army.[39]

The few Nord men who managed to escape the net cast by the 71st and 5th Infantry divisions faded into the chaotic fabric of a dying Third Reich and either attempted to return to their hometowns and await Armageddon or join other units and keep fighting. Few of these Nord men retained the will to fight but often found themselves impressed into other units and sent into the lines once more against the Americans or the Russians.

The only unit of the 6th SS-Gebirgs Division that remained intact after 4 April 1945 was the division's Ersatz und Ausbildungs Abteilung—in effect, the division's replacement and training battalion. All division-sized (and in some cases brigade-sized) units in the Heer and Waffen-SS had a training and replacement battalion somewhere in Germany that recruited and trained men for their specific organization and then sent these replacements forward on a continuous basis.

The Nord Division's training battalion was located in Leoben, Austria (approximately 243 kilometers southwest of Vienna), and was staffed mostly with *Volksdeutsche* officers and noncommissioned officers from the 7th SS-Freiwilligen (Volunteer)-Gebirgs Division "Prinz Eugen," another Waffen-SS mountain division routinely employed in the Balkans in Yugoslavia. The training battalion had previously been stationed at Hallein about twenty kilometers south of Salzburg, Austria, before moving to Leoben sometime in late 1944 or early 1945. On 26 March 1945 word of the Nord Division's plight—withdrawing under extreme pressure from the oncoming Americans—reached the battalion. Only days earlier the battalion had dispatched nearly five hundred minimally trained replacements to the division. The remaining trainees received immediate orders for active service. The recruits, lacking weapons and rations, loaded onto trucks and headed to Karlsruhe to locate the 6th SS-Gebirgs Division, which was actually moving north and east of Frankfurt at that time. The recruits' orders were to link up with—and join—SS-(Gebirgs) Reconnaissance Battalion 6. However, the SS men were unable to locate any elements of the Nord Division.[40]

On foot and still lacking weapons, the battalion marched eastward past Heilbronn and beyond. They traded their cigarettes and what little rations they scrounged for weapons from German soldiers fleeing west toward the oncoming Americans. Capture by the Americans was clearly preferable to capture by the Russians.

On or about 7 April, the SS recruits had their first clash with the Americans and, in the words of one recruit, played a sort of "cowboys and Indians game carried out in deadly earnest" for the next ten days or so. Around 19 April the battalion received word that they were to be sent to Prague. The SS recruits ultimately found themselves near the Danube River defending against the Americans in the first days of May before facing, like their parent Nord Division, destruction and dissolution. The survivors either fled westward away from the advancing Russians or returned to duty in other units. The unnamed recruit who likened his skirmishes with the Americans to a Wild West adventure managed to reach Munich where he was posted to a hastily created 38th SS-Panzergrenadier Division "Nibelungen" located in Ingolstadt. This organization comprised SS officer cadets from Bad Tolz and never reached more than regimental strength. The SS recruit never located this new unit. The chaos of a dying Germany in the first days of May 1945 overwhelmed everything. The result was inevitable.[41]

SS-Panzergrenadier Battalion 506, detached from the Nord Division along with SS-Gebirgsjäger Regiment 12 in mid-March 1945, continued to fight on as a separate entity until mid-April before dissolving into the turmoil. The battalion commander, *SS-Hauptsturmführer* Karl von Zydowitz, was killed on 16 March, so *SS-Obersturmführer* Hans Bauer took command. While the Nord Division was being destroyed in the Büdingen forest, the 506th was operating forty kilometers south of Gelnhausen with the 416th Infanterie Division. Bauer's superb leadership of the battalion in the war's final days earned him the Knight's Cross of the Iron Cross, the sixth and final such award bestowed on a member of the 6th SS-Gebirgs Division Nord.[42]

When the war in Europe ended on 8 May 1945, all German formations officially dissolved except for a few holdout organizations here and there. The remaining Nord men who escaped to fight now resolved to surrender, turn in their weapons, and return home to rebuild their towns, cities, and lives. These Nord men ultimately helped rebuild a shattered Germany from the ashes. But few in Germany would likely have called them a "greatest generation." Instead, former members of the Waffen-SS had earned the scorn of their compatriots for their organization's close association with Hitler's catastrophic Third Reich. Even though the men of the Nord Division had served well as soldiers, they found themselves concealing their wartime pasts in order to blend back into German society and become productive members of their country's reconstruction effort. Yet the bonds formed among these men as comrades in arms would never dissolve, and they would still gather for many years to come at *treffens* (reunions).

The precise circumstances of *SS-Gruppenführer* Karl Brenner's capture by the Allies remains a mystery, but he likely pressed eastward after the Büdingen forest debacle and joined another German unit until war's end or was captured before 8 May 1945. At some point Brenner fell into captivity and, for the next two years, participated in the U.S. Army's efforts to capture the German perspective of the war. Under the auspices of the Foreign Military Studies Branch, Historical Division, U.S. Army Europe, Brenner produced several manuscripts that recounted the 6th SS-Gebirgs Division's exploits from the time he assumed command in September 1944 until the division dissolved on 3 April 1945. Brenner submitted his last manuscript, MS# B-715, for the period of 19 March to 3 April 1945 on 20 November 1947. With his historical duties complete, the American forces released him from captivity. He settled in Karlsruhe (about 120 kilometers south of his birthplace, Mannheim) and died there on 14 February 1954 at the age of fifty-eight.[43]

The commander of SS-Gebirgsjäger Regiment 11, *SS-Standartenführer* Helmuth Raithel, recovered from the severe injuries he sustained in Leisenwald and enjoyed a long postwar career in agriculture. His ventures in agriculture led him to South Africa, where he spent a great deal of his time before retiring. He returned to Germany and studied history at the University of Munich, earning a doctorate. Despite his advanced years, Raithel continued to be an avid mountaineer and routinely climbed the Alps well into his seventies. He remained a good comrade to his fellow Nord men and met with them often at various *treffens* throughout the years. While returning from one of these reunions at the Semmering on 12 September 1990, he suffered a tragic car accident that took his life. Helmuth Raithel was eighty-two years old.[44]

Raithel's fellow regimental commander, *SS-Standartenführer* Franz Schreiber, was captured in late March or early April 1945 with the remnants of his SS-Gebirgsjäger Regiment 12. Separated from the Nord Division in mid-March, the regiment's mountain troopers fought on until the American tidal wave of men and materiel finally overwhelmed them. Schreiber, after release from captivity, became an ardent supporter and chair of the *Traditions-Verband* (Tradition Association) of the 6th SS-Gebirgs Division Nord. Despite the fact that the Finns had turned on the Germans in September 1944, Schreiber still felt a strong kinship with the Finnish people.

On 15 July 1959 Schreiber and a delegation of Nord veterans returned to Kuusamo, Finland. He still had in his possession the sketch that indicated where the people of Kuusamo could find the two church bells buried by his SS men for safekeeping from the Russians. In September 1944 Schreiber knew the two bells in the Kuusamo church (the larger one a gift from the Swedish king in 1698 and the smaller one a gift to the parish dating from 1721) meant a great deal to the local populace, and he also knew the Russians would not be able to resist looting these treasures. In fact, when the Red Army troops entered Kuusamo, they burned the church to the ground. But fifteen years later, Schreiber and his comrades returned to help the local populace recover their hidden treasures. With the aid of the sketch, Schreiber located the two bells buried near the new church, which the people had built near the site of the one burned by the Russians. A team of workers began digging and discovered the two bells—undisturbed after fifteen years in the ground. After a thorough cleaning, the grateful townspeople mounted the two bells in the steeple of the new church. For Franz Schreiber, this event brought closure to a long chapter in his life and the life of the Nord Division.[45]

In 1969 Schreiber published the definitive history of the 6th SS-Gebirgs Division entitled *Kampf Unter Dem Nordlicht* (Fighting Under the Northern Lights). Alfred Steurich, *SS-Standartenführer* Raithel's adjutant, assisted Schreiber in this endeavor. An impressive and scholarly work published only in German, the book still stands as the best, most thorough history of the division; it proved extremely useful to me in writing this book. Franz Schreiber, one of six Knight's Cross recipients in the Nord Division, died six years later in Hamburg on 26 February 1976 at the age of seventy-one.[46]

Two other former officers of the Nord Division, Alfred Steurich and Wolf Zoepf, contributed greatly to perpetuating the history of the division and its combat exploits. *SS-Hauptsturmführer* Steurich joined the division in June 1941 as a lieutenant and, after a year as the ordnance officer in SS-Infanterie Regiment 7, became the regimental adjutant in February 1942. He left this position to command the 14th Company in SS-Gebirgsjäger Regiment 11 before returning to his adjutant's billet. After *SS-Hauptsturmführer* Degen's death on 16 March 1945, Steurich assumed temporary command of the 1st Battalion and led that unit during the fighting around Leisenwald and Waldensburg. After the war, he became a teacher and school principal in Dortmund. He was very active in the Nord Division's *Traditions-Verband* and served as an honorary board member. He helped to propagate the division's history by publishing an excellent photographic record of the 6th SS entitled *Gebirgsjäger im Bild: 6. SS-Gebirgsdivision* Nord *1940–1945*. Steurich later became chair of the *Traditions-Verband* following Franz Schreiber's death. He remained close with his last regimental commander, Helmuth Raithel, in the years following the war and eulogized his friend at Raithel's interment in October 1990. Steurich died three years later in 1993.[47]

Steurich's friend, Wolf Zoepf, was also an active member of the *Traditions-Verband* who later wrote a definitive work on SS-Gebirgsjäger Regiment 12's actions at Wingen-sur-Moder. *SS-Untersturmführer* Zoepf was a Latvian expatriate of German ethnicity whose family left Riga just before the Soviet occupation in 1939. As adjutant to *SS-Hauptsturmführer* Kurt Kreuzinger, commander of the 3rd Battalion, SS-Gebirgsjäger Regiment 12, Zoepf fell into American hands during the withdrawal from Wingen. A retired *Diplom-Ingenieur* (civil engineer), Zoepf crafted a detailed account of his last battle at Wingen-sur-Moder. In 2001 Aberjona Press published Zoepf's *Seven Days in January: With the 6th SS Mountain Division in Operation* Nordwind, an exquisite, well-researched, and balanced analysis of the battle from both the American and German perspectives. Unfortunately, Wolf Zoepf never lived to see his book in print. He passed away just three weeks after finishing the manuscript on 8 January 1999.[48]

Other members of the Nord Division who survived the cauldrons of Waldensberg and Leisenwald went on to lead either ordinary or extraordinary lives in postwar Germany. *SS-Sturmmann* Egon Krüger, the messenger for the 3rd Battalion, SS-Gebirgsjäger Regiment 11, walked into the darkness on the night Company K, 66th Infantry, assaulted Leisenwald, and never looked back. With an aching bullet wound to his shoulder, Krüger trekked through the woods for two days. At one point he encountered a long column of American troops and vehicles moving on the road to his front and hid in the bushes nearby. When the column passed an hour later, Krüger continued south where he stumbled across four other Nord men. Together, the five men entered Gelnhausen and crossed the Kinzig River south of town. As they traversed the icy water, Krüger fell on the far bank and broke his leg. As his comrades helped him onto a nearby road, several GIs approached and told them to raise their hands high.

Krüger received good medical treatment at the hands of his captors. The Americans soon delivered him to Worms and, later, to Marseilles, France, and Prisoner-of-War Camp 404. The GIs separated Krüger from the other prisoners since he was a member of the Waffen-SS and sent him nearby to Compound 21. In November 1945 the Americans transported him to a small town near Stuttgart as a war crimes suspect, much to Krüger's surprise. The Americans only interrogated him once—obviously realizing that Krüger was no war criminal. They sent him to Dachau in August 1946 and released him from there eight months later in March 1947.

Krüger faced a dilemma. His family farm was in what was then Soviet-occupied East Germany. How could he return home to the farm that had been in his family for years? He traveled to West Berlin and stayed with some relatives. He contacted his mother, who crossed into the Allied-occupied zone of Berlin and told Krüger that the Soviets were no longer detaining members of the populace. His father was very old, and his brother had died at Stalingrad. Krüger was the only one left to run the family farm. So a reluctant Egon Krüger entered East Germany and experienced, in his words, "pure Bolshevism." Because he had lived through the Soviet collectivization of farms and agriculture throughout the postwar years, Krüger believed that the luck that had preserved him during the war had now escaped him.

Krüger spent nearly fifty years operating his family farm behind the Iron Curtain, and traveled to the former West Germany for heart surgery in Würzburg in 1994. He never married, and his parents had long ago passed away. After the fall of the Berlin Wall and the reunification of Germany, Krüger rekindled his friendship with his former comrades of the 6th SS-Gebirgs Division and began attending reunions in the mid-1990s. When I met and interviewed Egon Krüger at the Nord reunion in Bad Windsheim, Germany, in September 1999, I was amazed at his remarkable memory and grasp of events long since passed. He spoke in a type of English learned from reading American Western pulp magazines in the 1930s. He ultimately wrote down his adventures for me in his own cryptic form of English; these letters, and one he had sent to an American veteran, Reuel Long, proved invaluable to me in writing this book. Johann Friedrich Egon Krüger died on 6 June 2003, in Eisenhüttenstadt, Germany—at peace and free of the Soviet yoke he despised.[49]

SS-Unterscharführer Georg Stöwe, the communications chief of the Nord Division's intelligence section, escaped the 2nd Battalion, 5th Infantry's assault in the Büdingen forest on 3 April with *SS-Gruppenführer* Brenner's group. Eventually, the one hundred or so men split into smaller groups. Stöwe remained with the group led by the division staff officer for supply (the *Ib*), who instructed the men to break up into clusters of ten and head for Bamberg. Stöwe remained in the *Ib*'s group.

As the sun set on 3 April, the group approached a crossroads. The officer ordered Stöwe to reconnoiter the intersection and check for American troops. While Stöwe was away from the group on reconnaissance, a local villager appeared and told the *Ib* of a better route. Without waiting for Stöwe, the officer led the group along the new route. When Stöwe returned from his scouting mission, he found no one. Alone and confused Stöwe pressed on toward Bamberg in the pouring rain. He eventually arrived in Lauenburg on the Elbe River at the home of his only relatives who lived outside Berlin (his parents were dead). The date was 8 May 1945. He had evaded capture by the Americans.

The Berlin-born son of a bricklayer, Stöwe quickly secured a bricklaying job with a construction firm. While working in a forest near Lüneburg, he encountered a former draft board officer from Pommerania, who promptly discharged him from the Wehrmacht by making the appropriate entries in Stöwe's SS *Soldbuch*. (Stöwe continued to carry this book on his person for some time after the war.) On 1 February 1948 a small architectural firm hired Stöwe and put him in charge of the building construction department. He married in the spring of 1949 and remained in Lauenburg as a school-trained architectural engineer, building more than 1,500 homes over the years. Stöwe retired on 1 October 1982, and he and his wife, Hildegard, spent their retired years traveling. Thinking his family's property in Berlin was lost forever to the war and the Soviets, Stöwe was surprised when, in 1991, he recovered his family home and land at Schildow just outside Berlin.[50]

SS-Rottenführer Walter Becker and his jeep-mounted comrades from the 3rd Company, SS-Gebirgs Nachrichten Battalion 6, who had escaped the 2nd Squadron, 2nd Cavalry Group's ambush near Wittgenborn, managed to find the German lines. Becker and his group eventually reached the Kinzig River west of Wächtersbach. They crossed the river and drove into the town unmolested. The jeep, driven by Becker's friend, Gerd Weber, then raced through the next town, Bad Orb, undetected by numerous GIs who busied themselves hammering and welding the myriad American vehicles lining the town's streets. Thankful that the GIs ignored their jeep (some of Becker's friends were also wearing American helmets and parts of U.S. uniforms), Becker, Weber, and his friends sped through the American maintenance unit and eventually reached Schweinfurt. While in Schweinfurt, Becker was posted to the hastily formed 38th SS-Panzergrenadier Division "Nibelungen." On reporting to the division (the division never exceeded regimental strength), Becker encountered two other Nord men who had escaped the fighting at Waldensberg and Leisenwald, *SS-Unterscharführer* Ossi Moser and another man from his radio company, Herbert Teuerkauf. All three men compared notes about their escape from the Büdingen forest on Easter weekend. Becker eventually surrendered near Ruhpolding on 8 May 1945 and spent a year in an American POW camp, which the GIs later turned over to French troops. The French soldiers put Becker to work in various French quarries until his release in November 1948. Walter Becker settled in Dortmund, where he labored as a metalworker in a coal mine. He remains there today in retirement.[51]

SS-Rottenführer Eberhard Hilger, the antitank man from SS-Gebirgs Panzerjäger Abteilung 6 who drove off with a captured American M5 General Stuart light tank in early March 1945, was one of many other Nord men who also survived the division's destruction. A modest man, Hilger settled in Weiler, Germany, and ran a small village grocery store for many years. He lives there today in retirement. In his later years Hilger traced and archived the gravesites of all Nord men in Finland, France, and Germany. In the spring of 2000 he sent me a snapshot of himself at a museum posing proudly—with a broad grin—next to an American M5 General Stuart tank.[52]

One of the few SS men to survive the massive artillery bombardment on Hill 267 near Glaubing, *SS-Rottenführer* Karl Müller eventually fell into American captivity as he wandered alone through the Büdingen forest. Müller felt fortunate to have survived the war after being wounded three times. After spending two years as a prisoner, Müller was released and eventually became the regional director for an insurance company, a position he held for twenty-three years before retiring in Darmstadt. He regretted that during those years he could not openly associate with his former SS comrades due to his firm's affiliation with the German Labor Union.[53]

Not all survivors of the Nord Division managed to stay with the division until the final days at Leisenwald and Waldensburg. *SS-Sturmmann* Jochen Seeliger, the leader of a machine-gun squad in the 3rd Battalion, SS-Gebirgsjäger Regiment 11, became a prisoner of the 94th Infantry Division near the village of Lampaden on 7 March 1945. Seeliger was sent to a POW camp in France where, due to his English-language skills, he served as an interpreter and later as a clerk for an American lawyer. Although disgusted by the Nazi atrocities that surfaced during the war-crimes trials in 1945 and 1946 and the general condemnation of his Waffen-SS brethren, Seeliger still took an interest in the constitutional aspects of the proceedings.[54]

After the war Seeliger earned a doctorate of law and enjoyed a highly successful career as a corporate and international lawyer in Essen, Germany. He was an active member of the Nord Division's *Traditions-Verband* following his retirement in Essen, Germany, and helped to memorialize and perpetuate the memory of his division. Seeliger and a delegation of Nord veterans traveled to Finland and the Russian Republic of Karelia on several occasions in the mid- and late 1990s to convince Russian officials to safeguard the Nord Division's gravesites that had remained after the division withdrew in September 1944. Soon after the Soviet Union collapsed in the early 1990s, unpaid and underfed Russian soldiers stationed along the Finnish–Russian border began engaging in a gruesome enterprise. Desperate for money and aware that a collector's market for SS items existed, the Russian soldiers began digging up the graves of German SS soldiers. They collected the skulls of dead SS men and matched them to the portion of the identity disc interred with the remains. The soldiers would then sell these skull-and-identity-tag sets to collectors to earn money to sustain their families. The veterans' visits to the gravesites and talks with the Russian authorities helped put an end to this macabre practice.

After his retirement Seeliger became the editor of the association's publication, *Nord-Ruf* (North Call). Seeliger also wrote and published—in English—a magnificent, insightful account of his wartime experiences that immediately went into multiple printings and translations. Sadly, no German text of this work exists because memoirs of Waffen-SS veterans are unwelcome in Germany. Unfortunately for Seeliger and his comrades, the passing of time and the thinning ranks of Nord veterans compelled the association's members to dissolve the *Traditions-Verband* in November 2002. The organization had officially disbanded by the end of 2004.[55]

As a close friend Dr. Jochen Seeliger proved instrumental to my research for this book. As my link to the Nord veterans, he lobbied his comrades tirelessly on my behalf for information about the final battles at Waldensburg and Leisenwald in April 1945. He and his beautiful wife, Margret, hosted me and my family at his home in Essen, Germany, on several occasions. Jochen also sponsored my attendance at two Nord reunions in Bad Windsheim in 1997 and 1999. Brilliant, erudite, and a true gentleman, Jochen Seeliger gave of his time freely to translate documents for me and answer my numerous questions about the Nord Division. I could not have written this book without him, and I am forever in his debt.

❖

The real victims in any war are the civilians. For the people of Leisenwald, the last days of the chaotic war in Europe brought death and destruction to their little country village. Ushered from their homes on the night of 2 April 1945 by the Americans and sent eastward to Streitberg for their safety, the citizens of Leisenwald experienced the fear and uncertainty that came with becoming refugees in their own country. They depended on the hospitality and kindness of their neighbors in Streitberg, who readily offered their fellow compatriots what meager accommodations were available in that town.

Throughout the night of 2 and 3 April, many of Leisenwald's citizens stood on the outskirts of Streitberg and watched as the numerous fires blazing in their hometown slowly burned out in the distance. Among the few who witnessed this heart-breaking spectacle was Leisenwald resident Johannes Kaltenschnee. Since a few GIs remained in Streitberg with the civilians, Kaltenschnee and some other men approached the soldiers and asked to return to Leisenwald to look after the animals. The GIs denied their request for safety reasons.

Late in the afternoon of 3 April, Kaltenschnee and a small group of men ventured forth from Streitberg and returned to their devastated town. On entering Leisenwald, the men gasped. Buildings still smoldered as GIs from the 66th Infantry Regiment hustled and bustled throughout the town, obviously packing up for their continued drive to the east. Jeeps and other American vehicles sped back and forth along Leisenwald's debris-strewn streets. Livestock and horses, freed by the battle from their stables, roamed throughout the town. The ruins of burned farm buildings emitted a strong smell of charred animal flesh. Many animals had not been able to escape their stalls before the burning buildings collapsed on top of them.

Kaltenschnee split off from the group and went to his own house, which remained surprisingly undamaged by the fighting. He entered his barn to check on his animals and, to his surprise, stumbled on a small detachment of fully uniformed Nord men. The SS men had given up fighting and were desperately trying to avoid capture. They asked Kaltenschnee for some civilian clothes, but he balked. The Americans, he believed, might punish him if they caught him aiding the SS troops. The Nord men then crept from the barn and disappeared.

To the south Kaltenschnee could still hear American artillery rounds exploding in the forest near Waldensberg. The Americans, he surmised, must have located the SS men who withdrew from Leisenwald. As the artillery fire increased, Kaltenschnee and the other men who accompanied him to the town decided to return to their families in Streitberg. They quickly made their way across the open countryside, taking cover several times when the artillery fire to the south intensified.

At 0200 Kaltenschnee heard a knock at the door of the house where a Streitberg family had billeted him and his family. Expecting to find Americans asking for a place to sleep, Kaltenschnee was shocked to see seven fully armed Nord men standing in the doorway. They pushed past him and entered the house.[56]

One of the SS soldiers asked, "Are the Americans around?"

"Not in the house, but they're everywhere else," answered a nervous Kaltenschnee. He then asked the seven men to be careful and not venture into the street for fear that an American guard might discover them.

"The guard we'll shoot up," the man snapped rudely.

"You kill the guard," blurted Kaltenschnee, "and the Americans will raze the whole place to the ground like they did with our village, Leisenwald."[57]

After a few tense moments, Kaltenschnee convinced the Nord men to leave. He breathed easier after they had disappeared into the night. Rumors suggested that the Americans would shoot any armed SS man hiding in the nearby towns and then burn down the house where the soldier was discovered. This rumor (based largely on Major General Eddy's orders) prompted a Streitberg farmer to hand over to the GIs several Nord men hiding in his barn.

The next day, Wednesday 4 April, a column of men (Kaltenschnee included) departed for Leisenwald to begin the long process of rebuilding their town. They left their wives and children safely behind in Streitberg. The men boarded up broken windows and cleared the debris from the streets and surrounding fields. The Americans had already abandoned the town except for a few vehicles and ambulances passing through every now and then.

The men took stock of the damage. Seven civilians had died in the fighting—a miraculously low number given the intensity of the battle. The bodies of dead Nord men littered the streets; the GIs had long since evacuated their dead and wounded. The Americans had converted two homes belonging to the Kling and Schmidt families into field hospitals, but the GIs evacuated the wounded to Frankfurt before the end of the day.

The major damage to the town included the total destruction of four farms and the partial destruction of three others. The schoolhouse lost its tower and suffered considerable damage. The bell and clock, purchased in 1924, were no more. Most other buildings and homes in Leisenwald had suffered some measure of damage either from ordnance or from fire. The parish church, the town parsonage, and the mayor's office all had burned to the ground. Leisenwald's documents and historical files were reduced to ashes. GIs, SS men, or local residents had taken advantage of the chaos to loot some of the homes and shops.

The people of Leisenwald, along with families from neighboring towns like Streitberg, quickly organized relief efforts to provide shelter and clothing to the homeless. The people collected bread, potatoes, and fruit—and even seeds to begin planting their crops anew. The men lacked the material to repair the roofs and buildings, and quickly realized that the restoration of Leisenwald would be a long-term effort. As the men cleared the cast-offs of war from their beloved Leisenwald, they silently cursed their own soldiers—men of the Waffen-SS—for carrying on the fight for such a lost cause. If the Nord men had simply conceded inevitable defeat of Germany, Leisenwald and many lives would have been spared.

On 6 April the townspeople of Leisenwald buried the dead under the town pastor's supervision. Only a week had passed since Good Friday. They buried the civilians first in single plots followed by a mass-grave burial of the thirty-eight dead Nord men recovered from the town and its environs. When the townspeople sorted through the various pay books (*Soldbucher*) and identity documents found on the few Nord men whose bodies still carried such items, they were amazed to see an assortment of non-German-born men who had volunteered for service in the Waffen-SS. The documents revealed birthplaces such as Austria, Hungary, Italy, Russia, and Yugoslavia. For instance, they were surprised to read that one dead Nord man, Klaus Sacharow, had been born in Moscow. He was probably an interpreter in the intelligence section from the division's days in Finland.[58]

After the mail and travel services had resumed, the town began receiving inquiries from the families of fallen Nord men. Family members of the SS men whom the townspeople could identify arrived and either exhumed their loved one for reburial at home or simply stood over the mass grave and prayed. The war had exacted a heavy toll on Leisenwald, but not as heavy a price as the one paid by the neighboring village to the south, Waldensberg.

Waldensberg had suffered terribly during the fighting between the Nord men and the 2nd Battalion, 66th Infantry. Nearly 70 percent of the village had burned to ground. Six civilians died (two of whom were children), and at least fifty farm animals perished. Like Leisenwald, the village church, parsonage, and mayor's office were gone. The town's documents and files were also reduced to ashes. Sadly, looting had also occurred.[59]

Bürgermeister Wilhelm Schmidt and his group of twenty-five or thirty civilians remained huddled in the hay-filled hunting lodge located deep within the Büdingen forest throughout the night of 2 April. Drenched by a night of cold, pouring rain and without food, Schmidt resolved to return to Waldensberg in the morning for provisions.

Schmidt crept through the woods until he reached the forest's edge. In the distance he saw Waldensberg surrounded by a number of SS troops—stragglers—heading for the surrounding forest. He climbed a spruce tree and, from that vantage point, witnessed a number of the houses—and the village church—still in flames. He descended the tree and returned to the group of civilians in the woods.

Schmidt and several men decided at 1200 to return to Waldensberg on 3 April to see what they could learn. Carrying a white flag on a stick, he led the group onto the field outside town. About ten GIs from the 2nd Battalion, 66th Infantry, approached Schmidt's group and led them into the town. The stunned civilians walked past numerous Sherman tanks idling in the streets. Dead German and American troops were scattered everywhere. At the entrance to the village, they saw twenty bodies stacked like cordwood.

The GIs brought Schmidt and the civilians to a company command post. An officer emerged and ordered the men to leave Waldensberg. The GIs then escorted Schmidt and his party to another group of civilians camping in the open on the eastern side of town, the same group that thirty-three-year-old Johanna Jende and her family had joined. At sunset, a GI approached the civilians and led them south along the road to the Weiherhof. When they arrived, the GI directed Schmidt and his group to stay in a hayloft, but the Americans provided them with little to eat. Johanna Jende was somewhat relieved when she was finally able to eat something—no matter how small the portion.[60]

At the Weiherhof, the nearby forest ranger's house became a field hospital. The daughter of *Förster* Leo tried to help the many wounded Nord men who crowded every room of the house. Two German nurses tended the wounded, and the young girl did her best to comfort the men. One SS man entrusted her with a carved wooden stick from Karelia and a watch. He told the young forest master's daughter that he would retrieve the items after the war, but he never returned.[61]

When the Americans arrived at the forest master's house to investigate, they walked among the German wounded and searched for uninjured, able-bodied Nord men. When *Förster* Leo appeared in his forest ranger's uniform, the GIs did not know what to make of him. The Red Circle men could not distinguish between a German Army uniform, a Waffen-SS uniform, a police uniform, or a forest ranger's uniform. The GIs pushed Leo against the wall with his arms raised. Leo's wife acted quickly. She rushed into the basement and returned with an American medical officer, who had been treating wounded civilians and soldiers. The Nord men had apparently captured this medical officer during the ambush on the field hospital near Assenheim, and the man had somehow remained in captivity during the battle. The medical officer had busied himself helping the wounded brought to the Weiherhof area. The GIs were so surprised by the medical officer's appearance that they forgot about *Förster* Leo, who promptly ducked into the house and out of sight.⁶²

After a restless, cold night spent in the hayloft, *Bürgermeister* Schmidt and his party awoke on 4 April and received a written pass from the Americans that allowed them to return to Waldensberg with a small cart to find food. A guard accompanied the men into the village. The carcasses of burned cows and horses, trapped inside stables that had burned to the ground, filled the air with a strong, pungent stench. Small fires burned here and there.

The men first went to the Wilhelm family's cellar and fetched as much bread as possible. Next, the butcher, Karl Schmidt, told Schmidt and the others that he had buried his meat behind the Hirtenhaus, a community hut where the Americans had stored much of their canned meat. When the group approached the hut, they found the structure on fire. With the butcher's meat out of reach, the men settled for twenty cans of American meat, which they promptly loaded onto their cart. The GI accompanying the men shrugged his approval.

The men returned to the group of civilians huddling in the few undamaged buildings and barns at the Weiherhof and distributed the food. When they departed the village, they did not see a single civilian in the town. They noticed a few strangers—Polish women who were displaced persons—moving about freely. The GIs seemingly afforded these displaced persons special rights they did not extend to the German populace.

Bürgermeister Schmidt and the residents eventually returned to their town to rebuild, bury the dead, and press on with their lives. They occupied the few remaining undamaged houses and lived together in these dwellings until they could breathe life back into their beautiful, rural village. Like their neighbors in Leisenwald, they resented the German resistance that resulted in the destruction of their town. If the SS troops had only recognized that the war was lost, Waldensberg would have remained untouched by war.⁶³

Frau Willi Schmidt, the wife of the town's pfarrer, entered the ruins of the Waldensberg church, the one-time focal point of the town's activities. She surveyed the damage with great dismay. As she approached the altar, she looked up at what remained of the church's once-beautiful and colorful stained-glass window. The only fragment that remained displayed the right arm of Jesus Christ, raised as if he were blessing the people. A resident of Waldensberg who immigrated to the United States before the war had donated the window to the church. The irony of American artillery destroying a precious gift from a former Waldensberg resident–turned-American was not lost on Frau Schmidt.

In the coming days, the parish members would visit the damaged window and look on the right arm of Jesus as both a sign of admonition and as a light in the darkness.[64]

Throughout the years that followed, the people of a rebuilt and reinvigorated Waldensberg would commemorate the April 1945 battle between the 6th SS-Gebirgs-Division Nord and the 71st Infantry Division. At the entrance to the newly rebuilt church, local officials erected a small monument—a brass placard affixed to a large stone—that reads, "In memory of the fallen of both world wars and to the civilian fallen of 2 April 1945." Local festivals always include a cautionary tale to the upcoming generations about the horror and suffering of war. Town-sponsored publications that espouse the sights and delights of this rural German town invariably include a section that highlights the Easter battle that razed Waldensberg. In 1999, the 300th anniversary of Waldensberg, the townspeople published a two hundred–page booklet entitled "300 Years of Waldensberg" that commemorated the town's history. A strong theme running throughout the booklet was the tragedy of 2 April 1945 that befell Waldensberg. Oral histories committed to paper from survivors of the battle such as eighty-seven-year-old Johanna Jende received great prominence in the booklet. From the ruins of their town, the people of Waldensberg had found the strength to rebuild, celebrate, and forgive—but they would never forget.[65]

While the people of Waldensberg rebuilt their town, the gruesome task of collecting the dead around the Weiherhof, Waldensberg, and the road to Wittgenborn fell to Herr Brückner, the Weiherhof hut's caretaker. The corridor of the Weiherhof's main building had been filled with wounded, and Frau Brückner had done her best to comfort and care for the wounded Nord men. The Red Circle men eventually evacuated the wounded Germans and left only the dead behind. The GIs allegedly told the civilians not to bury the dead SS troops as a warning to the local populace. The potential repercussions for the civilians of harboring Nord men who might have stripped off their uniforms and blended into the populace were great. Despite such an order, *Bürgermeister* Schmidt still told Brückner to gather the dead, load them onto a horse carriage, and transport them to the future site of the Waldensberg war cemetery.[66]

The task of gathering the dead proved awful and heart wrenching. Brückner scoured the area for bodies and dutifully loaded them onto his horse-drawn cart. He found two corpses near a farm at the Weiherhof; both Nord men appeared to have been shot in the head. Brückner began to notice other gunshot wounds in the necks and heads of other dead German troops.[67]

With help from some other men, Brückner gathered the bodies as quickly as possible. Many had been robbed, their pockets turned inside out. Several Nord men were missing their boots. Brückner searched each body for anything that might reveal the person's identity. Unfortunately, many of the men were missing their *Soldbucher*, identity discs, and uniform insignia. Some bodies were even missing fingers that had been lopped off to steal the silver SS rings worn by many Nord men.

Many *Soldbucher*, papers, and other documents were strewn along the road leading into Waldensberg, but Brückner and his helpers had little luck matching the items to the bodies. The most disturbing discovery for Brückner occurred near the anglers' hut next to the lake. Brückner and his men located the body of seventeen-year-old Luftwaffenhelfer (air force helper) Josef Schüler. Young Schüler belonged to the group of children born in 1928—the last group the Wehrmacht drafted into service. At some point Schüler had attached himself to the Nord Division and participated directly in the heavy fighting around Leisenwald. Seriously wounded near the Weiherhof, Schüler dragged himself to cover next to the hut and died alone.[68]

On 15 April 1945 *Pfarrer* Schmidt of Waldensberg presided over the interment of eighty-two bodies recovered by Brückner and his associates. Before the Americans allowed Schmidt to carry out the funerals, they thoroughly vetted his background to ensure that he was not a Nazi. Schmidt and the townspeople buried the dead in a new war cemetery near the Weiherhof due to a lack of space in the Waldensberg cemetery.[69]

The townspeople marked each individual grave with a cross. Nearly half of the crosses read "Unknown, 2 April 1945." In the coming months and years, the residents of Waldensberg and their descendants cared lovingly for the graves (despite their earlier admonitions to the SS troops for continuing to fight) and later upgraded the markers with headstones. Yet a mystery surrounded the men buried at the Weiherhof. Nearly fifty bodies exhibited gunshot wounds to the head. Had the Americans done such a thing? Did the SS men shoot their own troops for possibly refusing to take up arms? No one really knew. A few eyewitnesses claimed to have witnessed a massacre, but nothing more came of it. Everyone had had a bellyful of war and wanted to put those days behind them. The mystery would lie dormant for sixteen years.[70]

In 1952 former German Army *Oberleutnant* Heinz Heuer visited the towns of Leisenwald and Waldensberg in search of his wife's brother, whom Heuer learned had died during the final battle with the 6th SS-Gebirgs Division. Heuer's brother-in-law, an Army *obergefreiter*, was one of the few bodies the townspeople of Leisenwald and Waldensberg could identify. The man was not buried in the mass grave with his other comrades but was interred at the nearby Wittgenborn cemetery. Ironically, Heuer's brother-in-law had served with the Nord Division in Finland and Norway before leaving the Waffen-SS and joining the Heer. The man had been part of a destroyed army *kampfgruppe* fighting near the Nord Division somewhere east of the Rhine River, so the young *obergefreiter* attached himself to his old SS division and died with his former comrades in their final battle.[71]

Heuer, decorated with the Knight's Cross of the Iron Cross on 22 April 1945 during the final battle of Berlin, had become a police investigator after the war. Wearing his police uniform, Heuer questioned the people of Leisenwald and Waldensberg and learned that his brother-in-law had been shot in the back of the neck. According to some villagers (among them *Förster* Leo), Heuer's brother-in-law had been one of eighty or so men holed up inside a barn who refused to surrender to the Americans. Finally, the Nord men and other German troops from the Heer and Luftwaffe had emerged with hands held high. The Americans, apparently in a fit of pique, ordered the men to form two lines and then shot the Germans dead—all at one time. The villagers claimed that many of the American perpetrators were Black soldiers.[72]

An incensed Heuer immediately filed charges against persons unknown, but nothing came of the matter. The fledgling German government that had emerged after the Third Reich did not want to antagonize the American authorities with such an investigation.[73]

Nearly ten years passed before the issue of a massacre at Leisenwald and Waldensberg surfaced again. Without warning the Volksbund Deutscher Kriegsgräberfürsorge (German War Graves Commission) arrived in Leisenwald in 1961 with a team and began exhuming the dead Nord men from the local cemeteries. The commission intended to move the graves to the war cemetery in Schlüchtern.

The team exhumed thirty-four skeletons. Of these, twenty-three had clearly been shot in the head. The average ages of the men ranged between twenty-five and thirty-five years. The team labeled each unnamed corpse (only one body was identified) from U-223 to U-256, followed by a detailed description of the head wound. The revelation that a massacre had possibly occurred based on eyewitness accounts and the physical evidence available prompted the commission to dig deeper into the mystery. The German officials were more likely to press the issue in 1961 than in 1952. Heinz Heuer even returned to the scene and attempted to invigorate the investigatory effort.

The September 1962 issue of the German weekly newspaper *Deutsche Wochenzeitung* ran a story entitled *"Todesursache Kopfschuss"* (Cause of Death: Shot in the Head). The article listed the number of dead by the letter and number combination assigned them by the commission followed by a description of the type of head wound. The article's author explained how the German War Graves Commission was looking into the matter by issuing lists to veterans and asking if they could identify the dead. In an obviously anti-American spin, the correspondent stated, "Such a number of fatal shots in the head are inconsistent with normal combat practice. In Bavaria many cases of single and mass murders of helpless German prisoners by American troops have been ascertained." The article failed to provide details of these alleged crimes, charges that probably seemed ludicrous to many within and without Germany, given the Third Reich's genocide campaign against the Jews and other "undesirables." The article concluded with a question that no one could answer with any certainty: "What really happened at Leisenwald ?"[74]

What happened at Leisenwald was really a microscopic look at a larger event—the death of the German armed forces and the country's political infrastructure. The last few weeks of combat in Western Europe seemed to burn brightest—by all contrary thinking—just before the Third Reich's flame went out once and for all. For the 6th SS-Gebirgs Division Nord and the people of Leisenwald and Waldensberg, Easter 1945 heralded the end of their war. For these SS troops and their fellow citizens in the surrounding countryside, Armageddon had come five weeks early: Germany's armed forces would soon surrender, and the war would end for them on 8 May 1945.

The fighting continued to be brutal and violent until the bitter end. Perhaps Germany's principal adversary in the west, America's GIs, had opted to give no quarter to those Germans who refused to recognize the war's obvious outcome. No one wanted to be the last soldier to die at the end of a story whose conclusion already had been written. Did the Red Circle men of the 71st Infantry Division perpetrate a massacre? Did the Nord men turn on each other? We may never know—especially since the massacre scenarios outlined by the local villagers do not seem plausible. Someone or some group of people certainly shot several German soldiers in the head. Perhaps their loss can signal to the world once again—in a timeless message—that war is brutal, war is total, and war is unforgiving. Let us all hope that such harsh lessons will never be forgotten.

APPENDIX A

Table of Comparative Ranks

The following table presents a comparison between the rank structure of the U.S. Army, the Heer (German Army), and the Waffen-SS. This book uses the specific rank of the individual when available. However, when referring to a Waffen-SS or German Army soldier, we use the rank in German to avoid confusion. In some cases, these ranks are not in English because some have no American Army equivalent. In other cases, these ranks are only approximations to their counterparts. All Waffen-SS ranks began with the letters SS (for example, SS-Gruppenführer*). All abbreviations are based on official or common usage by the U.S. and German armed forces in World War II.*[1]

U.S. ARMY	HEER	WAFFEN-SS
General of the Army	*Generalfeldmarschall*	*Reichsführer SS*[2]
General (4)[3] (Gen.)	*Generaloberst*	*Oberstgruppenführer*
Lieutenant General (3) (Lt. Gen.)	*General der Infanterie, Artillerie, etc.*	*Obergruppenführer*
Major General (2) (Maj. Gen.)	*Generalleutnant*	*Gruppenführer*
Brigadier General (1) (Brig. Gen.)	*Generalmajor*	*Brigadeführer*
No equivalent	*No equivalent*	*Oberführer*
Colonel (Col.)	*Oberst*	*Standartenführer*

TABLE OF COMPARATIVE RANKS

U.S. ARMY	HEER	WAFFEN-SS
Lieutenant Colonel (Lt. Col.)	*Oberstleutnant*	*Obersturmbannführer*
Major (Maj.)	*Major*	*Sturmbannführer*
Captain (Capt.)	*Hauptmann*	*Hauptsturmführer*
1st Lieutenant (1/Lt.)	*Oberleutnant*	*Obersturmführer*
2nd Lieutenant (2/Lt.)	*Leutnant*	*Untersturmführer*
Master Sergeant (M/Sgt.)	*Stabsfeldwebel*	*Sturmscharführer*
1st Sergeant (1/Sgt.)	*No equivalent*	*No equivalent*
Technical Sergeant (T/Sgt.)	*Oberfeldwebel*	*Hauptscharführer*
Staff Sergeant (S/Sgt.) or Technician 3rd grade (T/3)[4]	*Feldwebel*	*Oberscharführer*
Sergeant (Sgt.) or Technician 4th grade (T/4)[4]	*Unterfeldwebel*	*Scharführer*
Corporal (Cpl.) or Technician 5th grade (T/5)[4]	*Unteroffizier*	*Unterscharführer*
Private First Class (Pfc.)	*Gefreiter / Obergefreiter*[5]	*Rottenführer*
Private (Pvt.)	*Schütze / Oberschütze*	*Oberschütze / Sturmmann*

APPENDIX B

Glossary of Terms and Equipment

The following is a basic list of terms and equipment, both American and German, intended to supplement the text. Where possible, detailed information is given on all terms or weapons systems mentioned. Only relevant data are listed and are not all inclusive.[1]

abteilung: German term for a detachment, but most often used to describe a unit of battalion size.

akjas: Boat-like snow sleds used by German mountain troops in Finland and elsewhere along the Arctic Circle to pull equipment and supplies such as machine guns and ammunition.

armee: German field army.

Armee Oberkommando: AOK; Army High Command.

bazooka (M9): U.S. hand-held, 2.36-inch antitank weapon. Reusable and effective, the bazooka saw significant service throughout the war.

bergstaffel: Mountain echelon of the supply trains for a mountain-troop unit.

blitzkrieg: "Lightning war"; Allies' term for German combined-arms tactics.

bürgermeister: German mayor.

festung: Fortress.

flak: German acronym for an anti-aircraft weapon (*flieger*, or *flugzeug, abwehrkanone*).

förster: Forest ranger.

freikorps: Free corps.

freiwilligen: Volunteer.

funker: Radio operator.

G-1: Personnel staff officer (division level and above).

G-2: Intelligence staff officer (division level and above).

G-3: Operations staff officer (division level and above).

G-4: Logistics staff officer (division level and above).
gasthaus: Local inn.
gebirgs: Mountain.
gebirgsjäger: Mountain troop.
gebirgskorps: Mountain corps.
gestapo: Acronym for the German Secret State Police, or Geheime Staatspolizei.
GI: U.S. soldier in World War II. GI stands for "government issue," or (ironically) "government instrument."
Heer: German Army.
heeresgruppe: Army group.
I&R: Intelligence and Reconnaissance.
Infanteriegeschütz: Infantry gun.
K98k Mauser: Standard German 7.92-mm, bolt-action service rifle used throughout the war, with a maximum effective range of approximately eight hundred meters.
kampfgruppe(n): battle group(s).
kaserne: German military installation or garrison.
kavallerie: Cavalry.
kompanie: Company.
korps: Corps.
korpsgruppe: Corps group.
korpstagesbefehl: Corps order of the day.
Kriegsmarine: German Navy.
kübelwagen: German version of a jeep.
lager: Camp.
landrat: District administrator.
Luftwaffe: German Air Force.
M1: Standard U.S.-issue .30-caliber, the "Garand" was a self-loading service rifle used throughout the war.
M1 81-mm mortar: Standard U.S. crew–served mortar commonly found in the Heavy Weapons Company of an infantry battalion.
M1 carbine: This .30-caliber light rifle used a magazine and could fire in the semiautomatic mode.
M1918 (Browning) (BAR): Browning Automatic Rifle. Intended as a light assault machine gun, the BAR never really lived up to its expectations. Too heavy to be a rifle, the BAR fell between the two. On average, the BAR could fire 500 rounds per minute (RPM).

M1928A1 Thompson submachine gun: A .45-caliber automatic weapon that could use a detachable drum (up to one hundred rounds) or box (up to thirty rounds) magazine. In 1942 the Army modified the gun to a simple blowback mechanism and designated it the M1 (with a later modification to M1A1).

M2 .50-caliber machine gun: A heavy, belt-fed machine gun used either in the ground mode or mounted on tanks or jeeps. It had a maximum effective range of approximately 1,000 to 1,200 meters, and fired from 500 to 800 RPM.

M2 60-mm mortar: Standard U.S. infantry company light mortar.

M24 Chaffee light tank: Last of the American light tanks with a 76-mm main gun.

M3 submachine gun: .45-caliber, automatic-only machine gun with a maximum range of one hundred meters. This magazine-fed "ugly duckling" of American weapons had a cyclic rate of 350 to 540 RPM and was a favorite of tank crews due to its small size and short-range firepower.

M4 Sherman tank: American medium tank, mainstay of the U.S. Armored Force. Various models existed with either a 75-mm or 76-mm main gun and a .30-caliber machine gun.

M5 General Stuart light tank: American light tank outfitted with a 37-mm main gun and a .30-caliber machine gun.

M8 Greyhound armored car: The best of the American armored cars. These six-wheeled reconnaissance vehicles entered service in 1943 and were armed with a 37-mm main gun.

MG42: German belt-fed 7.92-mm light machine gun with a cyclic rate of 1,200 RPM; effective and reliable in the field. The MG42's forerunner was the MG34, which also saw service until the end of the war.

motti: Finnish envelopment tactic adopted by the German troops serving in Finland.

MP40: German 9-mm submachine gun. Produced early in the war, the "Schmeisser" was a favorite weapon among the German ranks, significantly enhancing the German infantryman's firepower prior to the advent of the Sturmgewehr (StG) 44.

MSR: Main supply route.

nachrichten: Word for communication or news normally associated with signal personnel in the German armed forces.

Nationalsozialistische Deutsche Arbeiterpartei: NSDAP; National Socialist German Workers' or Nazi Party.

nebelwerfer: German 10- or 25-cm multibarreled rocket launchers, towed or self-propelled, that fired smoke and high-explosive projectiles.
oberkommando: High command.
Oberkommando der Wehrmacht: OKW; Armed Forces High Command.
panzer: Tank.
panzerfaust: German hand-held disposable antitank weapon developed in the middle stages of the war; plural form *panzerfäuste*.
panzerjäger: Antitank.
pfarrer: Pastor.
pionier: Heer or Waffen-SS combat engineer.
polizei: Police.
reichsautobahn: Improved highways built by the Germans during the interwar years; often credited as a brainchild of Adolf Hitler.
S-1: Personnel staff officer (regimental level and below).
S-2: Intelligence staff officer (regimental level and below).
S-3: Operations staff officer (regimental level and below).
S-4: Logistics staff officer (regimental level and below).
sanitäter: Medic. The abbreviated version used by troops in the field was *sani*.
schloss: Castle.
schützen: Rifle.
SCR: Set, complete, radio.
SCR-300: Standard U.S. Army wireless field radio of limited range and capability.
SCR-506-AFII: AM medium-range radio set with four crystal-controlled frequencies for both wave and voice, with a range of more than 240 kilometers.
SCR-508-AFIII: Eighty-crystal (any ten frequencies preset) FM radio transmitter and two receivers with voice-only capability.
Siegfried Line: Nickname for the fortifications and "dragon's teeth" that lined the German border in the west.
Soldbuch : Pay book that doubled as an identity document for German soldiers in all services. The plural form is *Soldbucher*.
sturmgeschütz: Assault gun.
Sturmgewehr (StG) 44: A late-war, stamped-metal, semi- and fully automatic assault rifle intended to improve the firepower of the average German infantryman. With a 7.92-mm round, the StG 44 could fire 500 RPM and had a maximum effective range of six hundred meters for single shots and three hundred meters on automatic.

talstaffel: Valley section of the German supply echelon. It provided supplies up to the units through the supply train's mountain echelon, the Bergstaffel.

Volksdeutsche: Ethnic Germans from southeast Europe or former German provinces of the Austro-Hungarian Empire.

Volksgrenadier : Heer infantry soldier in a Volksgrenadier division.

Volkssturm: German People's Army; Hitler's last-ditch effort to scratch up manpower to defend Germany by drafting into service teenage boys and older men; special armband, distinguished them as combatants since uniforms were not always available.

Waffen-SS: The SS (Schutzstaffel, or guard echelon) was an offshoot of the Nazi SA (Sturm Abteilung), or Brown Shirts. Hitler intended the SS to be his special bodyguard troops, but he wanted them involved in the war to demonstrate, in his mind, their superior combat prowess—all part of his agenda to prove Germany's Aryan superiority. As a result, the SS generally split into the Allgemeine (or General) SS (of black uniform fame) and the Waffen (or Armed) SS.

Wehrmacht: German Armed Forces.

wirbelwind: Whirlwind. A four-barreled, 2-cm antiaircraft weapons systems fixed to an armored chassis.

APPENDIX C

Select Order of Battle

The following is a select order of battle based solely on German and American units (principally the 6th SS-Gebirgs Division and the 71st Infantry Division) that participated in the fighting. Major commands such as army and corps headquarters are included to add perspective to each organization. Where known, names of commanders, key staff members, and special platoon leaders follow that particular unit's designation. In some cases, the person named may not have been in command at the precise time of the battle with the Nord Division. Authorized and actual strengths, if known, follow specific unit designations.[1]

German

The following German order of battle captures the army group, army, and corps assignments of the 6th SS-Gebirgs Division Nord from the division's arrival on the Western Front until the division's final battle with the 71st Infantry Division. As a general rule, and in keeping with German practice for the time, the numerical designation of regiments and separate battalion-sized organizations appears at the end (such as SS-Gebirgsjäger Regiment 11) while the numerical designations of armies, corps, divisions, and companies appear at the beginning (such as 7th Armee, and so on).

Oberbefehlshaber West (OB West: *Generalfeldmarschall* Gerd von Rundstedt (replaced by Luftwaffe *Generalfeldmarschall* Albert Kesselring on or about 13 March 1945)

Heeresgruppe G: *Generaloberst* Johannes Blaskowitz (replaced by SS-*Obergruppenführer* Paul Hausser in January 1945)

- 7th Armee: *General der Infanterie* Hans Felber
- 1st Armee: *General der Infanterie* Hans von Obstfelder
    - LXXXIX Korps: *General der Infanterie* Gustav Hoehne

6th SS-Gebirgs Division "Nord" (authorized strength as of 1943: 21,851)
- Division Commander: *SS-Gruppenführer* Karl-Heinrich Brenner
- Stab der Division (Division Staff)

SS-Gebirgsjäger Regiment 11 "Reinhard Heydrich": *SS-Standartenführer* Helmuth Raithel
- 1st Battalion: *SS-Hauptsturmführer* Günther Degen (killed in action on 13 March 1945 and later replaced by *SS-Hauptsturmführer* Alfred Steurich)
- 2nd Battalion: *SS-Hauptsturmführer* Adolf Braun
- 3rd Battalion: *SS-Sturmbannführer* Paul Schneider (wounded in action in early January 1945 and replaced by *SS-Hauptsturmführer* Walter Tank, who was captured near Frankfurt in late March 1945)

SS-Gebirgsjäger Regiment 12 "Michael Gaissmair": *SS-Standartenführer* Franz Schreiber
- 1st Battalion: *SS-Hauptsturmführer* Alois Burgstaller (promoted to *SS-Sturmbannführer* on 30 January 1945)
- 2nd Battalion: *SS-Hauptsturmführer* Hellmuth Netrwal
- 3rd Battalion: *SS-Hauptsturmführer* Kurt Kreuzinger (killed in action on 16 March 1945 and replaced by *SS-Obersturmführer* Hans-Heinrich Wodarg)

SS-Gebirgs Artillerie Regiment 6: *SS-Oberführer* Johann-Georg Goebel
- SS-Panzergrenadier Battalion 506 (formerly SS-Schützen Battalion 6 [motorized]: *SS-Hauptsturmführer* Karl von Zydowitz (killed in action on 16 March 1945 and replaced by *SS-Obersturmführer* Hans Bauer up to 5 April 1945)
- SS-(Gebirgs) Panzerjäger (Antitank) Abteilung 6: *SS-Sturmbannführer* Walter Nestler
- 6th SS-Sturmgeschütze (Assault Gun) Batterie: *SS-Hauptsturmführer* Helmut Albert

- SS-Flak (Antiaircraft) Abteilung 6: *SS-Sturmbannführer* Friedrich Hengstmann
- SS-(Gebirgs) Nachrichten (Signals) Abteilung 6: *SS-Hauptsturmführer* Helmut Letz
- SS-(Gebirgs) Aufklärungs (Reconnaissance) Abteilung 6: *SS-Hauptsturmführer* Gottlieb Renz (killed in action on 3 January 1945)
- SS-(Gebirgs) Pionier (Engineer) Battalion 6: *SS-Hauptsturmführer* Alfred Pedersen
- SS-Sanitäts (Medical) Battalion 6: *SS-Obersturmbannführer* Dr. Hugo-Heinz Schmick
- 6th SS-Bekleidungs-Instandsetzungs (Clothing Maintenance) Company
- 6th SS-Veterinär (Veterinarian) Company
- 6th SS-(Gebirgs) Kriegsberichter Zug (War Correspondent Platoon): *SS-Untersturmführer* Jobst Gösling
- 6th SS-Feldgendarmerie Trupp (Field Police Troop): *SS-Obersturmführer* Adolf Wurz

Kampfgruppe Weilburg (28 March until dissolving and blending into the Nord Division during the fighting in the Büdingen forest)

Assorted stragglers and liberated prisoners from the Heer and Luftwaffe

American

The following American order of battle captures the army and corps assignments of the 71st Infantry Division from the division's arrival in France until their final battle with the 6th SS-Gebirgs Division Nord. The dates that follow in parentheses are the 71st Infantry Division's date of assignment to that particular organization.

Fifteenth United States Army: Lt. Gen. Leonard T. Gerow (8 February 1945–9 March 1945)

Seventh United States Army: Lt. Gen. Alexander M. Patch (10 March 1945)

- XV Corps: Maj. Gen. Wade H. Haislip (10 March 1945)
    - 3rd Infantry Division
    - 45th Infantry Division
    - 71st Infantry Division
    - 100th Infantry Division
    - 6th Armored Division
- XXI Corps: Maj. Gen. Frank W. Milburn (21 March 1945)
- VI Corps: Maj. Gen. Edward H. Brooks (25 March 1945)

Third United States Army: Lt. Gen. George S. Patton Jr. (29 March 1945)
- XX Corps: Maj. Gen. Walton H. Walker (29 March 1945)
- XII Corps: Maj. Gen. Manton S. Eddy (31 March 1945)
    - Chief of Staff: Brig. Gen. Ralph J. Canine

71st Infantry Division (authorized strength according to Table of Organization 7 dated June 1944: 14,253)
- Division Commander: Maj. Gen. Willard G. Wyman
- Assistant Division Commander: Brig. Gen. Onslow S. Rolfe
- Division Artillery Commander: Brig. Gen. Frank A. Henning
- Chief of Staff: Col. Oscar R. Johnston
- G-1: Maj. George W. Loveless (or Lt. Col. Morton P. Brooks)
- G-2: Lt. Col. Kenneth W. Foster
- G-3: Lt. Col. Norman H. Lankenau
- G-4: Lt. Col. Clifton D. Blackford
- Division Headquarters Commandant: Maj. John B. Strahan
- Division Headquarters Company: Capt. George H. Rogge
- Division Band
- Division Military Police Platoon
- 71st Cavalry Reconnaissance Troop: Capt. Bernard C. Johnson
- 564th Field Artillery Battalion: Lt. Col. Donald A. Henderson
- 571st Signal Company: Capt. Arthur W. Reese
- 371st Medical Battalion (headquarters only): Maj. Ralph E. Hockenberry (or Lt. Col. Castlelow)
- 271st Engineer Combat Battalion (headquarters only): Maj. Orin R. Eddy
- 771st Ordnance Company (Light Maintenance) : 1/Lt. Oliver H. Davis
- 251st Quartermaster Company: 1/Lt. John Q. Staples

5th Infantry Regiment (Combat Team) (authorized strength according to Table of Organization 7-11 dated 26 February 1944: 3,257)
- Regimental Commander: Col. Sidney C. Wooten
- Regimental Executive Officer: Maj. Fred M. Pokorney
- S-1: Capt. A. D. Boggs
- S-2: Maj. Walter Reese
- S-3: Maj. Irving Heymont
- S-4: Maj. William T. Neel
- Headquarters Company: Capt. Edward T. Davis
- Cannon Company: Capt. William B. Daggett
- Anti-Tank Company: Capt. Joseph T. Frye Jr.
- Service Company: Capt. Spencer B. Glascock
- Intelligence and Reconnaissance Platoon: 1/Lt. Robert B. Emrick
- 607th Field Artillery Battalion: Maj Clarence W. Clapsaddle
- Company A, 271st Engineer Combat Battalion
- Company A, 371st Medical Battalion
- Company A, 761st Tank Battalion
- Company B, 635th Tank Destroyer Battalion: Captain Wikoff

1st Battalion, 5th Infantry: Lt. Col. Ned B. Broyles (authorized strength according to Table of Organization 7-15 dated 26 February 1944: 871. This figure applies to all U.S. battalions mentioned below.)
- Company A: Capt. William V. Zandri
- Company B: Capt. Jack L. Simms
- Company C: Capt. William C. Hartman
- Company D: Capt. John D. Rees

2nd Battalion, 5th Infantry: Lt. Col. Charles M. Gettys
- Company E: Capt. Frederick L. Zebley
- Company F: Capt. John J. Greer Jr.
- Company G: Capt. Herbert B. Neal
- Company H: Capt. Charles J. Traylor

3rd Battalion, 5th Infantry: Maj. Isaac B. Robertson Jr.
- Company I: Capt. Leonard M. Horrender
- Company K: Capt. Horace S. Berry
- Company L: Capt. David M. Buie
- Company M: Capt. John W. Williams

14th Infantry Regiment (Combat Team) (authorized strength according to Table of Organization 7-11 dated 26 February 1944: 3,257)
- Regimental Commander: Col. Carl E. Lundquist (replaced Col. Donald Beeler on 19 March 1945)
- Regimental Executive Officer: Lt. Col. Bryan S. Halter
- S-1: Capt. Milo G. Karsner
- S-2: Capt. Spencer P. Edwards
- S-3: Capt. Jack Borden
- S-4: Maj. Jewel T. Crowe
- Headquarters Company: Capt. Thomas W. Alvey (later assumed command of Company F, 2nd Battalion, on 31 March 1945) / Capt. William R. Swope
- Cannon Company: Capt. Walter J. Segda
- Anti-Tank Company: 1/Lt. Clifford W. Howell
- Service Company: Capt. Tillman J. Johnson
- Intelligence and Reconnaissance Platoon: 1/Lt. Nat R. Freeman
- 608th Field Artillery Battalion: Lt. Col. Clay O. Collier
- Company B, 271st Engineer Combat Battalion
- Company B, 371st Medical Battalion
- Company B, 761st Tank Battalion: Captain Long
- Company C, 635th Tank Destroyer Battalion: Capt. Harold L. Pellegrino

1st Battalion, 14th Infantry: Maj. Samuel E. Hubbard
- Company A: 1/Lt. Wallace E. Felldin
- Company B: Capt. Lloyd W. Engelland
- Company C: Capt. William V. Johnson
- Company D: Capt. Charles O. Schobel Jr.

2nd Battalion, 14th Infantry: Lt. Col. Philip D. Brant
- Company E: Capt. Harry T. Goldman Jr.
- Company F: Capt. William R. (Harold) Swope (changed command with Capt. Alvey on 31 March 1945)
- Company G: Capt. Andrew J. Bass
- Company H: Capt. Harold Brewer

3rd Battalion, 14th Infantry: Lt. Col. Paul G. Guthrie
- Company I: 1/Lt. Caleb H. Paul
- Company K: Capt. Tommy L. Long
- Company L: Capt. Milo D. Krichbaum
- Company M: 1/Lt. W. P. Sims

66th Infantry Regiment (Combat Team) (authorized strength according to Table of Organization 7-11 dated 26 February 1944: 3,257)
- Regimental Commander: Col. Augustus J. Regnier
- Regimental Executive Officer: Lt. Col. Lewis S. Sorley
- S-1: 2/Lt. Harry K. Bjornberg
- S-2: Maj. Harry J. Rainey
- S-3: Maj. William J. Merrill
- S-4: Capt. William F. Harrison
- Headquarters Company
- Cannon Company
- Antitank Company
- Service Company
- Intelligence and Reconnaissance Platoon: Lt. C. R. M. Sheppard
- 609th Field Artillery Battalion: Maj. Donn L. Smith
- Company C, 271st Engineer Combat Battalion
- Company C, 371st Medical Battalion
- Company C, 761st Tank Battalion
- Company A, 635th Tank Destroyer Battalion: Capt. Leland H. Williams

1st Battalion, 66th Infantry: Lt. Col. Everett S. Thomas Jr.
- Company A
- Company B
- Company C: Capt. Joseph E. Dixon
- Company D

2nd Battalion, 66th Infantry: Lt. Col. Gaston B. Eikel
- Company E: Captain MacArthur
- Company F: Capt. John L. Sullivan
- Company G: Capt. Fred J. Kratz
- Company H: Captain Charleton

3rd Battalion, 66th Infantry: Lt. Col. Bryce F. Denno
- Company I: 1/Lt. Frederick L. Tyler
- Company K: Capt. Freddie W. Grambling
- Company L: Capt. Everett W. Gray
- Company M: Lt. (later Capt.) Horace B. Ellison

Attached units (with date attached as applicable):
- 81st Chemical Mortar Battalion
- 530th Antiaircraft Artillery (Automatic Weapons) Battalion
- 635th Tank Destroyer Battalion (headquarters only): Lt. Col. Wint Smith (Attached to the division on 15 March 1945)
- 761st Tank Battalion (headquarters only): Lt. Col. Paul L. Bates (The 761st replaced the 749th Tank Battalion on 28 March 1945, and the tank companies were attached to the combat teams effective 29 March 1945.)

5th Infantry Division (assigned to XX Corps)
- Division Commander: Maj. Gen. S. LeRoy Irwin
- Assistant Division Commander: Brig. Gen. Alan D. Warnock
- Division Artillery Commander: Brig. Gen. Harnold C. Vanderveer
- Chief of Staff: Col. Paul O. Franson
- G-3: Lt. Col. Randolph C. Dickens
- 5th Cavalry Reconnaissance Troop: Capt. Donald E. Robinson

2nd Infantry Regiment: Col. A. Worrell Roffe
- 1st Battalion: Lt. Col. William H. Blakefield
- 2nd Battalion: Maj. Beryl J. Pace
- 3rd Battalion: Lt. Col. Robert E. Connor

10th Infantry Regiment: Col. Robert P. Bell
- 11th Infantry Regiment: Col. Paul J. Black

2nd Cavalry Group (assigned to XII Corps)
- Group Commander: Col. Charles H. Reed
- 2nd Cavalry Squadron: Lt. Col. Walter J. Easton
    - Executive Officer: Maj. Eben R. Wyles
- 42nd Cavalry Squadron: Lt. Col. William A. Hill

Notes

The following is a list of source notes and other specific references that form the basis of the information presented in the book. Documenting all of these sources has been a difficult task. I began researching this battle in 1985, and after more than twenty-five years much of the information I pieced together seems almost second nature to me. I gathered most of this information over a sixteen-year period before I actually put pen to paper. The following is my best attempt to capture all source material for this book, and I believe these notes are quite thorough. Gerald F. McMahon, the 71st Infantry Division Association's historian and a veteran of the division, provided me with many details in countless interviews from 2001 until 2006. Since I am unable to identify exact dates for each bit of information he provided me, I have omitted dates when citing McMahon as an interview source.

Preface

1. These headlines appeared on the front pages of the following newspapers: *The Stars and Stripes*, Liege edition, Vol. I, no. 67, Tuesday, 27 March 1945; *New York Herald Tribune*, Late City Edition, Vol. CIV, no. 35,932, Monday, 2 April 1945; and the *Evening Bulletin*, 98th Year, no. 296, Philadelphia, Saturday, 24 March 1945.
2. *SS-Sturmbannführer* Friedrich Hengstmann appears as a member of the 6th SS-Gebirgs Division Nord in the 1 October 1944 version of the *Dienstaltersliste der Schutzstaffel der NSDAP (SS-Obersturmbannführer und SS-Sturmbannführer)* (Service List of the SS of the NSDAP). He is listed as a recipient of the Iron Cross, First Class, with a Nazi Party number of 3,444,974 and an SS number of 269,889. Hengstmann's birth date is given as 31 October 1901, with his date of promotion to *SS-Sturmbannführer* as 30 January 1942. Hengstmann commanded the division's antiaircraft battalion during the battle. As far as I could determine, he was not a part of the massacre that allegedly occurred at the end of the battle—even though his son, Günter, seemed to suggest to me that he had been part of it.

Chapter 1. The Birth of the Nord Division

1. The two sources that provided much of the early history of the 6th SS-Gebirgs Division Nord were Franz Schreiber's *Kampf Unter Dem Nordlicht: Die Geschichte der 6. SS-Gebirgs-Division Nord* (Osnabrück, Germany: Munin Verlag GMBH, 1969); and Wolf Zoepf's *Seven Days in January* (Bedford, PA: Aberjona Press, 2001). I am grateful to Wolf Zoepf's widow, the late Ruth Zoepf, for permitting me to rely extensively on certain parts of her husband's work for this chapter and for other portions of my book. Roland Kaltenegger, *Mountain Troops of the Waffen-SS, 1941–1945* (Atglen, PA: Schiffer Publishing, 1995), 36–37.
2. *SS-Brigadeführer* Demelhuber, letter to *General der Kavallerie* Feige, 24 June 1941, translated in Kaltenegger, *Mountain Troops of the Waffen-SS*, 125.
3. Roger James Bender and Hugh Page Taylor, *Uniforms, Organization, and History of the Waffen-SS*, Vol. 2 (San Jose, CA: R. James Bender Publishing, 1986), 151; Jochen Seeliger, PhD, email to author, 12 April 2002.
4. Zoepf, *Seven Days in January*, 28.
5. Fritz Ulrich, former commander of the 14th Company, SS-Infanterie Regiment 6, letter to Jochen Seeliger, May 2002.
6. Bender and Taylor, *Uniforms, Organization, and History of the Waffen-SS*, Vol. 2, 151; Jochen Seeliger, "Legion of the North: A Waffen-SS Soldier in World War II" (unpublished manuscript; dated about 1947), 79.
7. Zoepf, *Seven Days in January*, 32. An organization chart for SS-Gebirgs Division Nord (3 October 1942) shows that the total strength of the division was set at 20,075 for officers and men combined, plus 3,240 horses and mules.
8. Seeliger, "Legion of the North," 83–86.
9. Dienstalterliste der Schutzstaffel der NSDAP (SS-Obersturmbannführer und SS-Sturmbannführer), Stand vom 1, Oktober 1944 (Berlin) (hereafter Dienstalterliste Oktober 1944), 22; Jochen Seeliger, email to author, 12 April 2002.
10. Keith E. Bonn, *With Fire and Zeal: The 276th Infantry Regiment in World War II* (Hampton, VA: Aegis Consulting Group, 1998), 31.
11. Bender and Taylor, *Uniforms, Organization, and History of the Waffen-SS*, Vol. 2, 151; Jost W. Schneider, *Verleihung Genehmigt: Their Honor Was Loyalty! Eine Bild- und Dokumentargeschichte der Ritterkreuzträger der Waffen-SS und Polizei 1940–1945* (San Jose, CA: R. James Bender Publishing, 1977), 201. Krüger committed suicide in May 1945 in Austria rather than become a prisoner of either the United States or the Soviet Union.
12. Schneider, *Verleihung Genehmigt*, 303.
13. Schreiber, *Kampf Unter Dem Nordlicht*, 271; Seeliger, "Legion of the North," 151–152.

14. Bender and Taylor, *Uniforms, Organization, and History of the Waffen-SS*, Vol. 2, 152; Schneider, *Verleihung Genehmigt*, 201; Dienstalterliste der Schutzstaffel der NSDAP *(SS-Oberst-Gruppenführer—SS-Standartenführer)*, Stand vom 9. November 1944, 30 (hereafter Dienstalterliste, 9. November 1944). Krüger received the Knight's Cross on 30 September 1944.
15. Alfred Steurich, *Zum Gedenken SS-Standartenführer a. D. Helmuth Raithel, Nordruf: Traditionsverband 6. Geb. Div. Nord Ehem. Waffen-SS e.V.* (Brief Nr. 35, 9. Jahrgang, Dezember 1990), trans. Jochen Seeliger (hereafter Steurich, *Zum Gedenken SS-Standartenführer a. D. Helmuth Raithel, Nordruf*), 7; Dienstalterliste, 9. November 1944, 15; Dienstalterliste Oktober 1944, 98.
16. SS personnel file, Karl-Heinrich Brenner, National Archives, Microfilm Roll Number A3343, SSO-104 (hereafter SS personnel file, Brenner), *personalanlagen* (personal background information).
17. Ibid.; Keith E. Bonn, *When the Odds Were Even* (Novato, CA: Presidio Press, 1994), 192, suggests that Brenner was not a "fanatical National Socialist." Brenner's record strongly suggests a personal desire to benefit professionally from a closer relationship with the Nazi hierarchy, however.
18. SS personnel file, Brenner, *personalanlagen*.
19. Bender and Taylor, *Uniforms, Organization, and History of the Waffen-SS*, Vol. 2, 118–120, 152; Dienstalterliste, 9. November 1944, 13; geocities.com, additional details about Brenner, http://www.geocities.com/~orion47/SS-POLIZEI/SS-Gruf_A-G. html; SS personnel file, Brenner, *personalanlagen, lebenslauf* (personal summary).
20. MS# B-476, *General der Waffen-SS und Polizei*, Karl Brenner, "The 6. SS-Mountain Division Nord and Its Part in Operation Nordwind Northern-Alsace, 1 January to 25 January 1945 (March 1947)," 2 (hereafter Brenner, MS# B-476).
21. Dienstalterliste, 9. November 1944, 101; discussion, 20 June 2003 between Werner Adam, 14th Company, 12. SS-Gebirgsjäger Regiment, and Jochen Seeliger; Steurich, *Zum Gedenken SS-Standartenführer a. D. Helmuth Raithel, Nordruf*, 7; Seeliger, "Legion of the North," 187.
22. Günther Degen's Knight's Cross recommendation states that the encirclement occurred on 17 September, which is inconsistent with other accounts. SS personnel file, Günther Degen, National Archives, Microfilm Roll Number A3343, SSO-139 (hereafter SS personnel file, Degen), *lebenslauf*.
23. Seeliger, "Legion of the North," 187–189; SS personnel file, Degen, *lebenslauf*.
24. John R. Angolia and Adolf Schlicht, *Uniforms and Traditions of the German Army, 1933–1945*, Vol. 3 (San Jose, CA: R. James Bender Publishing Company, 1987), 496; Seeliger, "Legion of the North," 187–189; SS personnel file, Degen, *lebenslauf*; Johann-Georg Goebel, National Archives, Microfilm Roll Number A3343, SSO-017A (hereafter SS personnel, Goebel), "German Cross in Gold citation" and other documents.

25. Zoepf, *Seven Days in January*, 44; Seeliger, "Legion of the North," 190–191; Schreiber, *Kampf Unter Dem Nordlicht*, 435–437.
26. SS personnel file, Franz Schreiber, National Archives, Microfilm Roll Number A3343, SSO-100B (hereafter SS personnel file, Schreiber), *lebenslauf*, and other documents.
27. Seeliger, "Legion of the North," 187.
28. Ibid., 225; Zoepf, *Seven Days in January*, 51.
29. Steurich, *Zum Gedenken SS-Standartenführer a. D. Helmuth Raithel, Nordruf*, 7; Dienstalterliste, 9. November 1944, 98; Schneider, *Verleihung Genehmigt*, 58.
30. Seeliger, "Legion of the North," 214–215.
31. Ibid., 210–216.
32. Werner Adam, *Leben und Überleben: Erinnerungen eines Kriegsfreiwilligen* (Germany: Books on Demand GmbH, 2000), 204–211. Adam still has the dog tag with a perfectly round bullet hole in its lower right-hand side.
33. *Korpstagesbefehl An die 6. SS-Geb. Division Nord, 6.11.44* (SS personnel file, Brenner). The spellings of the place names are from the original document and are, in some cases, incorrect. The translation is by Jochen Seeliger.
34. Seeliger, "Legion of the North," 222.
35. SS personnel file, Kurt Kreuzinger, National Archives, Microfilm Roll Number A3343, SSO-214A (hereafter SS personnel file, Kreuzinger).
36. Brenner, MS# B-476, 2.
37. Edmund C. Arnold, *The Trailblazers: The Story of the 70th Infantry Division* (Richmond, VA: 70th Infantry Division Association, 1989), 79, quotes the Army War College as reporting, "There was some scorched earth as the 6th [SS-Gebirgs Division] retreated but there were no atrocities against the populace."
38. Brenner, MS# B-476, 3.
39. Strangely, Schreiber was not promoted to *SS-Oberführer* at this point although he had been recommended for the promotion. A letter from the SS Main Office in Berlin (SS-Führungshauptamt IIa) 9 November 1944 states that the *Reichsführer-SS* (Heinrich Himmler) had "postponed" the promotion because he (Himmler) believed the promotion to be "premature." The letter does not give Himmler's reasoning. SS personnel file, Schreiber.
40. Brenner, MS# B-476, 3–4.
41. Fred Clinger, Arthur Johnston, and Vincent Masel, *The History of the 71st Infantry Division* (Augsburg, Germany: 71st Division Public Relations Office, 1946), 1. Clinger and colleagues provided most of the information on the division's training and deployment history. See also "Biography of General Willard Gordon Wyman," *The Red Circle News*, 7, no. 1, Spring 1993, 3–4 (hereafter "Biography of Wyman"); Douglas Kinnard, *From the Paterson Station: The Way We Were* (Bloomington, IN: Xlibris Corporation, 2000), 204; David L. Ichelson (M.D.), "I Was There" (unpublished manuscript, n.d., written over a twenty-year period), 61–65.

Chapter 2. Operation Nordwind and Beyond

1. Brenner, MS# B-476, 4. The source that provided many of the details regarding the move to the Western Front by the 6th SS-Gebirgs Division Nord was Zoepf's *Seven Days in January*. See also Arnold, *The Trailblazers*, 61.
2. Wolf Zoepf's work (*Seven Days in January*) and Franz Schreiber's work (*Kampf Unter Dem Nordlicht*) are the principal sources for the Wingen-sur-Moder battle from the German perspective. Wolf Zoepf's work (*Seven Days in January*) is the most definitive primary source currently available about the small-unit actions of Kampfgruppe Wingen. Readers interested in a more detailed account of the battle should seek out his excellent *Seven Days in January* (Bedford, PA: Aberjona Press, 2001).
3. Stephen M. Rusiecki, *The Key to the Bulge: The Battle for Losheimergraben* (Westport, CT: Praeger Publishers, 1996), 1–5.
4. Charles B. MacDonald, *The Last Offensive* (Washington, DC: Department of the Army, Chief of Military History, 1984), 6–7; Bonn, *When the Odds Were Even*, and Zoepf, *Seven Days in January*, served as the principal sources for information on the German planning of Operation Nordwind.
5. Arnold, *The Trailblazers*, 62; Bonn, *With Fire and Zeal*, 22.
6. Zoepf, *Seven Days in January*, 67.
7. Ibid., 78.
8. John Frayn Turner and Robert Jackson, *Destination Berchtesgaden: Saga of the US 7th Army* (New York: Charles Scribner's Sons, 1975), 108–109.
9. Arnold, *The Trailblazers*, 113–115.
10. SS personnel file, Alois Burgstaller, National Archives, Microfilm Roll Number A3343, SSO-122 (hereafter SS personnel file, Burgstaller).
11. Bonn, *With Fire and Zeal*, 39, states that the SS signal troops became prisoners of the 3rd Battalion, 275th Infantry. See also Zoepf, *Seven Days in January*, 102–103.
12. Bonn, *With Fire and Zeal*, 29.
13. Ibid., 30.
14. Zoepf, *Seven Days in January*, 142, 148; Arnold, *The Trailblazers*, 117–118; Bonn, *With Fire and Zeal*, 35.
15. Arnold, *The Trailblazers*, 119.
16. Ibid., 118; Bonn, *With Fire and Zeal*, 36.
17. Zoepf, *Seven Days in January*, 161; Wallace R. Cheves, Lt. Col., Infantry, ed., "Snow Ridges and Pillboxes: A True History of the 274th Infantry Regiment of the 70th Division in World War II" (privately published, 1946), 52.
18. Arnold, *The Trailblazers*, 120.
19. Zoepf, *Seven Days in January*, 186.

20. Zoepf, *Seven Days in January*, 191; Cheves, "Snow Ridges and Pillboxes," 56; Arnold, *The Trailblazers*, 122. Much of the information concerning the actions of Lieutenant Colonel Cheves's 2nd Battalion, 274th Infantry Regiment, comes from Cheves, "Snow Ridges and Pillboxes." Cheves was the supervising editor and compiler of that book.
21. Cheves, "Snow Ridges and Pillboxes," 56–59.
22. Zoepf, *Seven Days in January*, 203; Arnold, *The Trailblazers*, 125; Bonn, *With Fire and Zeal*, 42; Allyn Vannoy, "Into the Maelstrom," *World War II Magazine*, 19, no. 2 (May 2004), 39; Cheves, "Snow Ridges and Pillboxes," 64.
23. Arnold, *The Trailblazers*, 126; Cheves, "Snow Ridges and Pillboxes," 64.
24. Zoepf, *Seven Days in January*, 208.
25. Ibid., 217–218.
26. Arnold, *The Trailblazers*, 126; Vannoy, "Into the Maelstrom," 39; Cheves, "Snow Ridges and Pillboxes," 65.
27. Cheves, "Snow Ridges and Pillboxes," 78–79.
28. Ibid., 239–241.
29. Ibid., 251–252.
30. Ibid., 260–262.
31. Zoepf, *Seven Days in January*, 275.
32. Cheves, "Snow Ridges and Pillboxes," 83–86; Arnold, *The Trailblazers*, 130–131; Bonn, *With Fire and Zeal*, 45.
33. Dienstalterlistic 9. November 1944, 47; SS personnel file, Helmuth Raithel, National Archives, Microfilm Roll Number SSO-0058 (hereafter SS personnel file, Raithel), *personalangaben*; Jochen Seeliger, conversation with author, 25 January 1997, based on an earlier discussion he had with Raithel; John Toland, *Adolf Hitler*, Vol. I (New York: Doubleday and Company, 1976), 178–179.
34. Steurich, *Zum Gedenken SS-Standartenführer a. D. Helmuth Raithel, Nordruf Gedenken SS-Standartenführer*, 6; Helmuth Raithel, *NORDRUF: Traditionsverband 6. Geb. Div. NORD Ehem. Waffen-SS e.V.* (Brief Nr. 35, 9. Jahrgang, Dezember 1990) (trans. Jochen Seeliger), 6; SS personnel file, Raithel, *dienstlaufbahn*.
35. James Lucas, *Hitler's Mountain Troops: Fighting at the Extremes* (London: Cassell Military Classics, 1999), 201; Steurich, *Zum Gedenken SS-Standartenführer a. D. Helmuth Raithel, Nordruf*, 6; SS personnel file, Raithel, *dienstlaufbahn*.
36. Seeliger, conversation with the author, 25 January 1997; Steurich, *Zum Gedenken SS-Standartenführer a. D. Helmuth Raithel, Nordruf*, 6; SS personnel file, Raithel, *dienstlaufbahn*. Raithel's first day as a member of the Waffen-SS was 1 December 1943.
37. Raithel was recommended for the Knight's Cross of the Iron Cross on 11 June 1944 for his leadership and courage while commanding Gebirgsjäger Regiment 28; however, he never received the award. A copy of the award recommendation is in SS personnel file, Raithel.

38. Steurich, *Zum Gedenken SS-Standartenführer a. D. Helmuth Raithel*, *Nordruf*, 6.
39. SS personnel file, Kreuzinger, "Recommendation for the German Cross in Gold."
40. Lucas, *Hitler's Mountain Troops*, 166; Schneider, *Verleihung Genehmigt*, 44.
41. Brenner, MS# B-476, 9.
42. Ibid., 5.
43. Lt. Col. Leo V. Bishop, *The Fighting Forty-Fifth: The Combat Report of an Infantry Division* (Baton Rouge, LA: Army and Navy Publishing Company, 1946), 136; Lucas, *Hitler's Mountain Troops*, 166.
44. Brenner, MS# B-476, 9–10.
45. Ibid., 10.
46. Steurich, *Zum Gedenken SS-Standartenführer a. D. Helmuth Raithel*, *Nordruf*, 7; Bishop, *The Fighting Forty-Fifth*, 139; Brenner, MS# B-476, 11.
47. Bishop, *The Fighting Forty-Fifth*, 139.
48. Seeliger, "Legion of the North," 243–244; Bishop, *The Fighting Forty-Fifth*, 142.
49. Seeliger, "Legion of the North," 244–245.
50. Bishop, *The Fighting Forty-Fifth*, 144, 146.
51. Brenner, MS# B-476, 11, quoted in Bishop, *The Fighting Forty-Fifth*, 138–139; Lucas, *Hitler's Mountain Troops*, 166–167; Seeliger, "Legion of the North," 248; Krüger, letter to U.S. veteran Reuel Long (n.d.). Lt. Col. (Ret.) Hugh Foster (U.S. Army) is currently writing an in-depth analysis of SS-Gebirgsjäger Regiment 11's actions at Reipertswiller. Also Turner and Jackson, *Destination Berchtesgaden*, 114; extract from the *Seventh United States Army Report of Operations in France and Germany 1944–1945*, Vols. I–III (Nashville, TN: Battery Press, 1988), 585–590 on the 70th Infantry Division's Web site, http://www.trailblazersww2.org/seventh_bitche.htm.
52. Brenner, MS# B-476, 12–13.
53. SS personnel file, Kreuzinger, "Recommendation for the German Cross in Gold."
54. Brenner, MS# B-476, 12–13.
55. MS# B-586, "6th SS Mountain Division Nord in Defense [*sic*] Engagements in North Alsace from 26 January to 1 March 1945," Karl Brenner (June 1947), 1 (hereafter Brenner, MS# B-586).
56. Lucas, *Hitler's Mountain Troops*, 167; Turner and Jackson, *Destination Berchtesgaden*, 122; Brenner, MS# B-586, 1.
57. Ibid., 2.
58. Ibid., 3–4.
59. Ibid., 4.
60. Ibid., 4–5.
61. Ibid., 5; MS# B-693, 6th SS Mountain Division (1–19 March 1945), Karl Brenner, Historical Division Headquarters, United States Army, Europe, 1 (hereafter Brenner, MS# B-693).

62. Lucas, *Hitler's Mountain Troops*, 167–168.
63. Gerald F. McMahon, *The Siegfried and Beyond* (Cleveland, OH: The 71st Infantry Division Association), 102; Michael A. Bass, *The Story of the Century* (New York: Century Association, 100th Infantry Division, 1946), 123.

Chapter 3. The Saar-Palatinate Falls

1. Brenner, MS# B-693, 1–2.
2. Seeliger, "Legion of the North," 259; and Lt. Laurence G. Byrnes, ed., *History of the 94th Infantry Division in World War II* (Washington, DC: Infantry Journal Press, 1948), 371, recall the attack date and time to have been 6 March at 0400. Nathan N. Prefer, *Patton's Ghost Corps: Cracking The Siegfried Line* (Novato, CA: Presidio Press, 1998), 191–192, states that the attack began at 0100 on 6 March. However, the Third U.S. Army, "After Action Report," 1 August 1944–9 May 1945, Vol. I, The Operations (hereafter called Third Army AAR), supports Brenner's attack date of 7 March. See also Charles M. Province, *Patton's Third Army: A Chronology of the Third Army Advance, August, 1944 to May 1945* (New York: Hippocrene Books, 1992), 201.
3. Byrnes, *History of the 94th Infantry Division*, 372; William A. Foley Jr., *Visions from a Foxhole: A Rifleman in Patton's Ghost Corps* (New York: Presidio Press / Ballantine Books, 2003), 145; Prefer, *Patton's Ghost Corps*, 191–192. Prefer's work, 154–155, 163–180, outlines the bitter struggle between the Nord men and the 94th Infantry Division in and around Schömerich. The account is an excellent representation of the detailed events that transpired there. However, Foley's account has the 6th SS-Gebirgs Division's attack beginning on 6 March instead of 7 March, which conflicts with Brenner's version and the Third Army AAR. In this case I believe Brenner and the Third Army AAR to be correct. Byrnes, *History of the 94th Infantry Division*, 368–398, provides an excellent, broad-based account of the fighting between the 94th Infantry Division's GIs and the 6th SS-Gebirgs Division along the Lampaden ridge area.
4. Brenner, MS# B-693, 3; Byrnes, *History of the 94th Infantry Division*, 378.
5. Seeliger, "Legion of the North," 259–264.
6. Byrnes, *History of the 94th Infantry Division*, 395–397.
7. Brenner, MS# B-693, 4; Byrnes, *History of the 94th Infantry Division*, 395–397.
8. MacDonald, *The Last Offensive*, 213–217.
9. Ibid., 236; Turner and Jackson, *Destination Berchtesgaden*, 133; *Seventh United States Army Report of Operations*, 693–694;.
10. MacDonald, *The Last Offensive*, 236–237; *Seventh United States Army Report of Operations*, 695.

11. MacDonald, *The Last Offensive*, 237–238.
12. Ibid., 238–241.
13. Ibid., 241–242; Brenner, MS# B-693, 4–5.
14. Brenner, MS#B-693, 4–5.
15. MacDonald, *The Last Offensive*, 243–244.
16. Ibid., 244–245.
17. Brenner, MS# B-693, 5; Franz Schreiber, *Kampf Unter dem Nordlicht*, 364.
18. MacDonald, *The Last Offensive*, 245–247.
19. "Abwehrkampf im Rhein-Mosel-Dreieck, März 1945," 50th Anniversary Memorial Publication published by the *Traditionsverband der ehem. 6. SS-Geb. Div. Nord e.V.*, 10–11 and 13–14 (selected portions trans. Jochen Seeliger).
20. MacDonald, *The Last Offensive*, 247.
21. Ibid., 247–248; Brenner, MS# B-693, 6.
22. MacDonald, *The Last Offensive*, 248–250.
23. SS personnel file, Goebel, *lebenslauf* (n.d.) and *lebenslauf* (27 November 1942).
24. Brenner, MS# B-693, 6–7; MacDonald, *The Last Offensive*, 250. On Das Ritterkreuz Web site (www.das-ritterkreuz.de/rktest2.php4?wert1=967), the date of Degen's death is erroneously listed as 13 March 1945. See also Matthias Thömmes, *"Die Amis kommen!" Die Eroberung des Saar-Hunsrück-Raumes durch die Amerikaner 1944 / 45* (Aachen, Germany: Helios, 2001), 80–81.
25. Krüger, letter to Long, n.d.; Egon Krüger, interview with the author, 25 September 1999.
26. MacDonald, *The Last Offensive*, 250–251.
27. Ibid., 252–253; Turner and Jackson, *Destination Berchtesgaden*, 136; *Seventh United States Army Report of Operations*, 699.
28. Gerald F. McMahon, interview with the author, n.d.; MacDonald, *The Last Offensive*, 254; *Seventh United States Army Report of Operations*, 707–708.
29. MacDonald, *The Last Offensive*, 255–256.
30. McMahon, interview with the author, n.d.; 71st Infantry Division, "After Action Report," March 1945, 1–2; 71st Infantry Division Record of Events; Clinger et al., *The History of the 71st Infantry Division*, 49. *Seventh United States Army Report of Operations*, 698, states that the announcement to assign the 71st Infantry Division to the Seventh Army came on 2 March 1945. *Seventh United States Army Report of Operations*, 704.
31. 71st Infantry Division Actions Against Enemy, Reports After, March 1945.
32. Clinger et al., *The History of the 71st Infantry Division*, 1. Clinger and colleagues provided most of the information on the division's training and deployment history; the other two divisions were the 89th Light Division (Truck) and the 10th Light Division (Pack, Alpine). Kent Roberts Greenfield, Robert R. Palmer, and Bell I. Wiley, *The*

Organization of Ground Combat Troops (Washington, DC: Department of the Army, Historical Division, 1947), 342–349. Greenfield and colleagues explain the reasoning behind the concept of the light division. Shelby L. Stanton, *World War II Order of Battle* (New York: Galahad Book, 1991), 12.

33. "Unit History Report," 71st Infantry Division, 17 March 1945; "Fact Sheet on the 71st Infantry Division," The Information Section, Analysis Branch, Headquarters, Army Ground Forces (Washington, DC, 1 March 1947), 1.

34. Clinger et al., *The History of the 71st Infantry Division*, 23. The 21 January 1944 Table of Organization for a Light Regiment (Truck) actually called for 1,979 men, which was almost one hundred men fewer than the 71st Division's light regiments. The authorized strength for a June 1943 Infantry Regiment by Table of Organization 7-11 was 3,087. The number increased one year later. See Stanton, *World War II Order of Battle*, 11, 15; "Action Against Enemy, Reports After, Report for March 1945" (71st Infantry Division, 21 April 1945; hereafter called 71st Infantry Division AAR March 1945), 1; McMahon, *The Siegfried and Beyond*, 2; Maj. Maynard L. Diamond et al., *The 89th Infantry Division 1942–1945* (Washington, DC: Infantry Journal Press, 1947), 47.

35. Scrapbook developed by Lt. Col. Philip D. Brant after the war (hereafter called Brant Scrapbook), 2; Thomas C. Tomich, "G.I.'s [sic] Forever" (privately published), 5.

36. Historical Data on Ground Divisions (71st Infantry Division, 18 June 1945), 5; McMahon, *The Siegfried and Beyond*, 28, 31; Stanton, *World War II Order of Battle*, 15.

37. "Biography of Wyman," 3–4; McMahon, *The Siegfried and Beyond*, 39; Kinnard, *From the Paterson Station*, 204. Kinnard, 202, explains that the GIs of the 71st Infantry Division, as members of a former mule-pack division, had to keep their trousers bloused inside their leggings to keep them clean when dealing with the animals. As a result, blousing had become a part of the division's culture.

38. Charles F. Platz, letter to the author, 28 August 2001; Ichelson, "I Was There," 61–65, 73; 71st Infantry Division Record of Events, 28 January 1945–31 March 1945; Tomich, "G.I.'s [sic] Forever," 25, 28; McMahon, *The Siegfried and Beyond*, 52, 54, 79; Kinnard, *From the Paterson Station*, 210; 2/Lt. Joseph Edinger, Company H, 2nd Battalion, 5th Infantry Regiment, "Diary," entry for 6 February 1945; Gerald F. McMahon, *Farthest East: A History of the 71st Infantry Division—From the Rocky Mountains to the Central Alps* (LeRoy, NY: Yaderman Books, 1986), 15; Gerald F. McMahon, interview with the author, n.d.

39. Bass, *The Story of the Century*, 123.

40. McMahon, *The Siegfried and Beyond*, 102.

41. 71st Infantry Division AAR March 1945, 1–2, 4; 71st Infantry Division Record of Events; Clinger et al., *The History of the 71st Infantry Division*, 49; McMahon, *The Siegfried and Beyond*, 111. On page 8 of his scrapbook, Lt. Col. Philip D. Brant, the

commander of the 2nd Battalion, 14th Infantry, explained that Colonel Beeler had suffered from a "bad cold" ever since the division landed in France.

42. 71st Infantry Division AAR March 1945, 1–2, 4; 71st Infantry Division Record of Events; Clinger et al., *The History of the 71st Infantry Division*, 49.
43. MacDonald, *The Last Offensive*, 256–257.
44. Ibid., 257; Turner and Jackson, *Destination Berchtesgaden*, 142.
45. Original copy in the author's collection, trans. Jochen Seeliger.
46. Jochen Seeliger, letter to the author relating information from Egon Krüger, 5 June 1997.
47. MS# B-715, 6th SS Mountain Division (19 March–April 1945), Karl Brenner, Historical Division Headquarters, United States Army, Europe, 7–8 (hereafter Brenner, MS# B-715).
48. Krüger, letter to Long, n.d.; Krüger, interview with the author, 25 September 1999.
49. Brenner, MS# B-715, 3–4.
50. Ibid., 1–3; Krüger, letter to Long, n.d.
51. Brenner, MS# B-715, 1–3.
52. Ibid., 2; *General der Infanterie* Gustav Hoehne, a.D., MS# B-584, LXXXIX Corps (18–28 March 1945), Gustav Hoehne, Historical Division Headquarters, United States Army, Europe (17 June 1947) (hereafter Hoehne, MS# B-584), 1; I. V. Hogg, Introduction, in *German Order of Battle 1944* (London: Greenhill Book, 1994, K-12).
53. Brenner, MS# B-715, 4–5; Schreiber, *Kampf Unter Dem Nordlicht*, 364.
54. Lucas, *Hitler's Mountain Troops*, 169.
55. MacDonald, *The Last Offensive*, 257–258; *Seventh United States Army Report of Operations*, 720.
56. MacDonald, *The Last Offensive*, 258–259.
57. Third Army AAR, 310–311; MacDonald, *The Last Offensive*, 259–261.
58. *Seventh United States Army Report of Operations*, 721 and 737; MacDonald, *The Last Offensive*, 260–263.
59. Third Army AAR, 311–321; MacDonald, *The Last Offensive*, 263–264.
60. McMahon, *The Siegfried and Beyond*, 152; Gerald F. McMahon, interview with the author, n.d.; Turner and Jackson, *Destination Berchtesgaden*, 145. *Seventh United States Army Report of Operations*, 726, states that the XXI Corps assumed command of the 71st Infantry Division on 22 March 1945.
61. Historical Summary of the 66th Infantry Regiment, 5, states that the regiment bagged 481 prisoners (National Archives RG 407, Entry 427, Box 11415).
62. 71st Infantry Division AAR March 1945, 1–2 and 5–7; 71st Infantry Division Record of Events; Clinger et al., *The History of the 71st Infantry Division*, 52; McMahon, *The Siegfried and Beyond*, 176.

63. Major Thomas A. Rafferty, "Operations of the 2nd Battalion, 5th Infantry (71st Infantry Division) in the Attack on Germersheim, Germany, 24 March 1945 (Central Europe Campaign)" (Personal Experience of a Battalion S3), unpublished monograph (Advanced Infantry Officers Course, 1949–1950), U.S. Army Infantry School, Fort Benning, Georgia, 8; 71st Infantry Division AAR March 1945, 1–2, 6, and 7; 71st Infantry Division Record of Events; McMahon, *The Siegfried and Beyond*, 186; Third Army AAR, 314.
64. 71st Infantry Division AAR March 1945, 1–2, 6, and 7; 71st Infantry Division Record of Events; Clinger et al., *The History of the 71st Infantry Division*, 54.
65. 71st Infantry Division AAR March 1945, 1–2, 6, and 7; 71st Infantry Division Record of Events; Clinger et al., *The History of the 71st Infantry Division*, 54; McMahon, *The Siegfried and Beyond*, 188–190. For details about Company L's battle in Lingenfeld, Gerald F. McMahon, author of *The Siegfried and Beyond*, relied on an unpublished manuscript written by Harvey Cohen and Bob Arthurs entitled *Whiskey Blue Love*, which stands for the regiment-battalion-company call signs, in that order; Dean P. Joy, *Sixty Days in Combat: An Infantryman's Memoir of World War II in Europe* (New York: Ballantine Books / Presidio Press, 2004)136–137; Rafferty, "Operations of the 2nd Battalion, 5th Infantry (71st Infantry Division)," 14; Irving Heymont, "As I Remember . . . ," 2nd ed. (privately published, 1992), 81–82; 1st Battle Group, 5th Infantry, History of the Fifth United States Infantry, 2nd ed., n.p., June 1962, 46–47.
66. McMahon, *The Siegfried and Beyond*, 190–192.
67. Rafferty, "Operations of the 2nd Battalion, 5th Infantry (71st Infantry Division)," 9–21; Gerald F. McMahon, *Riding Point for Patton: The Combat Trail of the 5th Infantry, 71st Division, XX Corps, Third Army in the European Theater during World War II* (LeRoy, NY: Yaderman Books, 1987), 14, mentions that U.S. artillery destroyed many of the German tanks used singly or in pairs for counterattack purposes; Edinger, "Diary," entry for 24 March 1945; Joy, *Sixty Days in Combat*, 32.
68. Rafferty, "Operations of the 2nd Battalion, 5th Infantry (71st Infantry Division)," 21; History, 5th Infantry Regiment, March 1945, National Archives RG 407, Entry 427, Box 11408 (hereafter 5th Infantry Regiment, Box 11408, March 1945); McMahon, *The Siegfried and Beyond*, 194.
69. Maj. Thomas A. Rafferty ("Operations of the 2nd Battalion, 5th Infantry [71st Infantry Division]," 21) states that the 2nd Battalion men heard explosions near the river at around 1530 and assumed that the Germans had destroyed the bridges at that time; McMahon, *Farthest East*, 43, further explains that the Germans destroyed two smaller bridges in the area at the same time.
70. MacDonald, *The Last Offensive*, 264; 71st Infantry Division AAR March 1945, 1–2, 6, and 7; 71st Infantry Division Record of Events; Clinger et al., *The History of the 71st Infantry Division*, 54.

71. Third Army AAR, 311, concurs with this estimate.
72. MacDonald, *The Last Offensive*, 264–265; Turner and Jackson, *Destination Berchtesgaden*, 148–149; *Seventh United States Army Report of Operations*, 735.

Chapter 4. Convergence

1. MacDonald, *The Last Offensive*, 266; Third Army AAR, 312.
2. MacDonald, *The Last Offensive*, 266–268; Third Army AAR, 313.
3. Hoehne, MS# B-584, 1; MacDonald, *The Last Offensive*, 268–269.
4. Ibid., 269–273.
5. Ibid., 273–274; Third Army AAR, 313.
6. MacDonald, *The Last Offensive*, 274–275; Hoehne, MS# B-584, 3–4.
7. Brenner, MS# B-715, 5; Third Army AAR, Vol. 1, 315
8. Ibid., 316; MacDonald, *The Last Offensive*, 275–276, 279–280.
9. Ibid., 280–284; Richard Baron, Maj. Abe Baum, and Richard Goldhurst, *Raid: The Untold Story of Patton's Secret Mission* (New York: Berkley, March 1984). I have essentially summarized the book in one paragraph.
10. MacDonald, *The Last Offensive*, 284–285; XV Corps Field Order Number 23 issued at 2400 on 24–25 March 1945 initiated planning for the attack but without an established D-Day or H-Hour; Seventh Army Operations Instruction Number 111 issued on 25 March set the actual attack date and time as 26 March at 0230. See *Seventh United States Army Report of Operations*, 747.
11. MacDonald, *The Last Offensive*, 286.
12. *Seventh United States Army Report of Operations*, 748, 750, and 752; MacDonald, *The Last Offensive*, 287–289.
13. *Seventh United States Army Report of Operations*, 748 and 757; Third Army AAR, 314.
14. 71st Infantry Division AAR March 1945, 1–2, 7; Scrapbook developed by Lt. Col. Philip D. Brant after the war, 18; Unit History—14th Infantry Regiment, Month of March 1945, 6.
15. Third Army AAR, 317.
16. Ibid., 292–293.
17. MacDonald, *The Last Offensive*, 293; Third Army AAR, 322.
18. Ibid., 348–350; Brenner, MS# B-715, 5; Hoehne, MS# B-584, 6; Schreiber, *Kampf Unter Dem Nordlicht*, 365.
19. Brenner, MS# B-715, 6–7.
20. MacDonald, *The Last Offensive*, 348–350; Brenner, MS# B-715, 6–7; Hoehne, MS# B-584, 6–8; Schreiber, *Kampf Unter Dem Nordlicht*, 366–367; Krüger, letter to Long, n.d.

21. MacDonald, *The Last Offensive*, 348–350; Brenner, MS# B-715, 6–7; Hoehne, MS# B-584, 6–8; Schreiber, *Kampf Unter Dem Nordlicht*, 366–367.
22. Written account by Georg Stöwe, 25 March 1988; Georg Stöwe, interview with the author, 4 October 1997; Brenner, MS# B-715, 7; Schreiber, *Kampf Unter Dem Nordlicht*, 366.
23. Krüger, letter to Long, n.d.
24. Ibid.; Krüger, interview, 25 September 1999.
25. Walter Becker, "Decline and Fall of the 6. SS-Mount. Div. Nord as I Have Seen It," n.d., and trans. Jochen Seeliger.
26. 71st Infantry Division, G-2 Periodic Report, No. 21, Annex C, 3 April 1945.
27. Brenner, MS# B-715, 7–8; Schreiber, *Kampf Unter Dem Nordlicht*, 367.
28. Eberhard Hilger, letter to the author, 30 June 2000.
29. Brenner, MS# B-715, 8.
30. 71st Infantry Division AAR March 1945, 3; 71st Infantry Division Record of Events; Headquarters, 71st Infantry Division, G-3 Periodic Report Number 14, 29 March 1945, National Archives RG 407, Entry 427, Box 11397; Historical Summary of the 66th Infantry Regiment, 6, RG 407, Entry 427, Box 11415.
31. Third Army AAR, 322; 71st Infantry Division AAR March 1945, 3; 71st Infantry Division Record of Events.
32. Third Army AAR, 323-25; AAR March 1945, 2–3; Headquarters, 71st Infantry Division, G-3 Periodic Report Number 15, 31 March 1945, National Archives RG 407, Entry 427, Box 11397; 71st Infantry Division Record of Events; Clinger et al., *The History of the 71st Infantry Division*, 55; McMahon, *The Siegfried and Beyond*, 211, 214; McMahon, *Farthest East*, 45.
33. MacDonald, *The Last Offensive*, 338–341; Third Army AAR, 323.

Chapter 5. Nord Falls Behind, 31 March 1945

1. MacDonald, *The Last Offensive*, 373.
2. Ibid.; Third Army AAR, Vol. I, The Operations, 323–324.
3. MacDonald, *The Last Offensive*, 379.
4. Ibid., 373–375.
5. Ibid., 374; *Third U.S. Army Report of Operations*, 323–325.
6. MacDonald, *The Last Offensive*, 376; *Third U.S. Army Report of Operations*, 322, 325, 337.
7. Brenner, MS# B-715, 8–9; written account by Georg Stöwe (n.d.) trans. Jochen Seeliger in August–September 1995.

8. Unpublished account by Georg Stöwe (n.d.), trans. Jochen Seeliger in August–September 1995; Brenner, MS# B-715, 9; Stanton, *World War II Order of Battle*, 144.
9. Brenner, MS# B-715, 9.
10. 71st Infantry Division, G-3 Journal, 31 March 1945, Entry 31, National Archives RG 407, Entry 427, Box 11398 (hereafter 71st Infantry Division, G-3 Journal, 31 March 1945); 71st Infantry Division Record of Events, 30–31 March 1945; G-3 Periodic Report, 71st Infantry Division, 31 March 1945, RG 407, Entry 427, Box 11397 (hereafter G-3 Periodic Report, 71st Infantry Division, 31 March 1945).
11. 71st Infantry Division, G-3 Journal, 31 March 1945, Entries 46 and 49.
12. Quoted in Flint Whitlock, "The Battle for Easy Red & Fox Green," *WWII History D-Day!* 60th Anniversary Special Issue, 1, no. 1 (Summer 2004), 54. Colonel Taylor commanded the 16th Infantry Regiment, which was organized as a Regimental Combat Team for D-Day.
13. 71st Infantry Division, G-3 Journal, 31 March 1945, Entry 40.
14. Ibid., Entry 27.
15. Ibid., Entry 23; Kareem Abdul-Jabbar and Anthony Walton, *Brothers in Arms: The Epic Story of the 761st Tank Battalion, WWII's Forgotten Heroes* (New York: Broadway Books, 2004), 29.
16. G-3 Periodic Report, 71st Infantry Division, 31 March 1945, erroneously lists the M36 as a 90-mm M3.
17. 5th Infantry Regiment Unit Journal, 33–34, National Archives RG 407, Entry 427, Box 11408 (hereafter 5th Infantry Regiment Unit Journal); 71st Infantry Division, G-3 Journal, 31 March 1945, Entry 53; AAR March 1945, 7.
18. Register of Graduates and Former Cadets, United States Military Academy, West Point, New York, 1995, Class of 1895 Centennial Edition, 229; Col. (Ret.) Irving Heymont, interview with author, 30 July 2003; Lewington Ponder, unpublished and untitled personal accounts of World War II, 56.
19. Ibid., 56–57.
20. 5th Infantry Regiment Unit Journal; 71st Infantry Division, G-3 Journal, 31 March 1945, Entry 53.
21. G-3 Periodic Report, 71st Infantry Division, 31 March 1945; 14th Infantry Regiment, Unit Report No. 17, 30 March 1945.
22. 14th Infantry Regiment Operations Instruction Number 7, 31 March 1945, National Archives RG 407, Entry 427, Box 11412 (hereafter 14th Infantry Regiment Operations Instruction Number 7, 31 March 1945); Brant Scrapbook, 22.
23. 14th Infantry Regiment Operations Instruction Number 7, 31 March 1945; 71st Infantry Division, G-3 Journal, 31 March 1945, Entry 22, 35, 36, and 95; W. P. Sims, "Blue Mike: The Story of Company M, 14th Infantry in World War II" (privately published), 94–97.

24. Brant Scrapbook, 23.
25. AAR March 1945, 7; 66th Infantry Regiment S-3 Periodic Report No. 16, 30 March 1945, National Archives RG 407, Entry 427, Box 11415; 71st Infantry Division, G-3 Periodic Report Number 15, 31 March 1945, National Archives RG 407, Entry 427, Box 11397; 1st Battalion, 66th Infantry Regiment S-1 Journal, Entry 4, 30/0001 March 1945–31/0001 March 1945, National Archives RG 407, Entry 427, Box 11415; 71st Infantry Division, G-3 Journal, 31 March 1945, Entry 29.
26. 66th Infantry Regiment S-3 Journal, 31/0001 March 1945 to 1/0800 April 1945, National Archives RG 407, Entry 427, Box 14415 (hereafter 66th Infantry Regiment S-3 Journal, 31 March to 1 April 1945), Entry 6; 71st Infantry Division Field Order Number 12, 31 March 1945, National Archives RG 407, Entry 427, Box 11399; 71st Infantry Division, G-3 Journal, 31 March 1945 (hereafter 71st Infantry Division Field Order Number 12, 31 March 1945), Entry 43.
27. Col. (Ret.) Bryce F. Denno, letter to the author, 19 February 1995.
28. Col. (Ret.) Edward W. Samuell Jr., "History of the 1st Platoon, 71st Cavalry Reconnaissance Troop," Chapter III, Operations in Hessen (unpublished, n.d.).
29. Col. (Ret.) Edward W. Samuell Jr., letter to the author, 28 March 1995; George Forty, *U.S. Army Handbook 1939–1945* (Gloucestershire, UK: Alan Sutton Publishing, 1995), 113–117, 124–127.
30. Samuell, letter to the author, 28 March 1995.
31. 71st Infantry Division Field Order Number 12, 31 March 1945.
32. 71st Infantry Division, G-3 Journal, 31 March 1945, Entry 105, outlines a discussion at 2106 between Colonel Wooten and Lieutenant Colonel Lankenau concerning coordination of the foot and motor movements over the bridges across the Main River. Lankenau gives different times for the movement; the foot element would depart at 0830 (time probable: it is difficult to read in the original document) and 1200 for the motorized element; 71st Infantry Division Field Order Number 12, 31 March 1945.
33. 71st Infantry Division, G-3 Journal, 31 March 1945, Entry 109; First Lieutenant Ponder actually retrieved the order from division headquarters at 2143 that night; 71st Infantry Division Field Order Number 12, 31 March 1945; 66th Infantry Regiment S-3 Journal, 31 March to 1 April 1945, Entry 10.
34. Major A. L. Lambert and Captain G. B. Layton, *The Ghosts of Patton's Third Army: A History of the Second U.S. Cavalry* (Munich, Germany: Kunstanstalten GmbH [Bisher F. Bruckmann], (n.d.), 29, 268.
35. Ibid., 44; Stanton, *World War II Order of Battle*, 23.
36. Lambert and Layton, *The Ghosts of Patton's Third Army*, 267–268.
37. Ibid., 269.
38. Ibid., 269–270.

39. 71st Infantry Division, G-3 Journal, 31 March 1945, Entry 96, reports the 2nd Cavalry Group's command post as located at a Niederhasslau, but no such location exists on any map of the Gelnhausen area. I lived in the area from 1983 to 1987 and know of no such place. The soldier keeping the journal must have meant Altenhasslau; Entries 66, 96, 101, and 112.
40. German Culture: Religion in Germany, http://www.germanculture.com.ua/library/facts/bl_religion.htm.
41. 5th Infantry Division After Action Against the Enemy Report, 1–31 March 1945, 2 April 1945; Fifth Division Historical Section, *The Fifth Infantry Division in the ETO* (Nashville, TN: Battery Press, 1981; originally published in 1945; original text lacked page numbers).
42. 5th Infantry Division, G-3 Journal, 31 March 1945, National Archives RG 407, Entry 427, Box 6809.
43. 5th Cavalry Reconnaissance Troop in Combat, After-Action Report extract provided to the author by Donald E. Robinson on 24 January 1996 (hereafter 5th Cavalry AAR); *Diamond Dust*, published daily by the 5th Infantry Division, Vol. IX, No. 31, 31 March 1945; newspaper clipping entitled "Capt. Robinson Leads Infantrymen in Rescue of 58 Captured Allied Airmen: Go 10 Miles Ahead of Troops into Enemy Territory to Effect Liberation" also provided to the author by Donald E. Robinson on 24 January 1996.
44. 5th Cavalry AAR.
45. 5th Infantry Division, G-3 Journal, 31 March 1945, National Archives RG 407, Entry 427, Box 6809.
46. Edinger, "Diary," Special Data entry after 31 March 1945; two small paragraphs (edited) from the middle of this entry.

Chapter 6. The First Day: Assenheim and Altenstadt, 1 April 1945

1. 71st Infantry Division G-2 Periodic Report Number 21, Annex C, 3 April 1945.
2. Brenner, MS# B-715, 10; 71st Infantry Division G-2 Periodic Report Number 21, Annex C, 3 April 1945.
3. Brenner, MS# B-715, 4.
4. *Diamond Dust*, Vol. IX, No. 31, Saturday, 31 March 1945.
5. The story of the events surrounding Krüger's exploits come from Krüger, letter to Long, n.d.
6. Brenner, MS# B-715, 9; Schreiber, *Kampf Unter Dem Nordlicht*, 368.
7. Becker, "Decline and Fall of the 6. SS-Mount. Div. Nord."

8. *Diamond Dust*, Vol. X, No. 3, Tuesday, 3 April 1945; 71st Infantry Division G-2 Periodic Report Number 20, Annex C, 2 April 1945.
9. Ibid.
10. Third Army AAR, Vol. II, Staff Section Reports, Medical Section, Part 17, 54; Lt. Col. George Dyer, *XII Corps: Spearhead of Patton's Third Army* (The XII Corps History Association; privately published, 1947), 394; Capt. Kenneth A. Koyen, *The Fourth Armored Division: From the Beach to Bavaria* (Munich, Germany: Herder Druck, 1946), 113.
11. Ibid., 394.
12. Dyer, *XII Corps*, 394, 398. The names of the other nurses captured are Theo Allen, 1/Lt. Mildred E. Barnett, 1/Lt. Lillian G. Clark, 1/Lt. Lola M. Dickenson, Rosalou Freeland, Lula G. Harward, and 1/Lt. Marie C. Janes. Cosma, Barnett, Clark, Dickenson, and Janes all received Bronze Stars for meritorious service in July 1945. Their names appeared in a "Headquarters, 4th Armored Division, General Order Number 126," 26 July 1945, which suggests that these nurses (each a first lieutenant) might have been assigned to the 4th Armored Division but detailed to the 16th Field Hospital at the time of their capture.
13. Dyer, *XII Corps*, 398. I adapted the dialogue from First Lieutenant Cosma's account of her capture, quoted in Dyer.
14. 71st Infantry Division, G-2 Periodic Report No. 20, Annex C, 2 April 1945; Lewis Sorley, "Personality: Creighton Abrams and Harold Cohen Forged a Lasting Friendship as Comrades during the March Across Europe," *World War II Magazine* 11, no. 4 (November 1996), 72; Baron et al., *Raid*, 20, 267; Koyen, *The Fourth Armored Division*, 113.
15. *Diamond Dust*, Vol. X, No. 3, Tuesday, 3 April 1945.
16. 5th Infantry Division, G-3 Journal, 1 April 1945, National Archives RG 407, Entry 427, Box 6810 (hereafter 5th Infantry Division, G-3 Journal, 1 April 1945); *Diamond Dust*, Vol. X, No. 3, Tuesday, 3 April 1945.
17. Rick Atkinson, *An Army at Dawn: The War in North Africa, 1942–1943* (New York: Henry Holt and Company, 2002), 385.
18. 2nd Infantry Regiment Unit Journal from 1 April 1945 to 30 April 1945, Entry 1, National Archives RG 407, Entry 427, Box 6866 (hereafter 2nd Infantry Regiment Unit Journal 1 April 1945–30 April 1945); 5th Infantry Division, G-3 Journal, 1 April 1945; 5th Cavalry Reconnaissance Troop in Combat, After-Action Report extract provided to the author by Donald E. Robinson on 24 January 1996.
19. 71st Infantry Division, G-3 Journal, 1 April 1945, Entry 15; Dyer, *XII Corps*, 388–394.
20. U.S. Air Force Museum Web site http://www.wpafb.af.mil/museum/air_power/ap2.htm.

21. Dyer, *XII Corps*, 392.
22. 71st Infantry Division, G-3 Journal, 1 April 1945, Entry 15.
23. Ibid., Entries 15, 20.
24. Ibid., Entries 21, 49.
25. Ibid., Entry 21; Samuell, "History of the 1st Platoon"; 71st Infantry Division G-2 Periodic Report, Number 19, 01600 April 1945.
26. 5th Infantry Regiment Unit Journal.
27. 71st Infantry Division, G-3 Journal, 1 April 1945, Entries 36, 43, 45, 46.
28. Ibid., Entry 45; Stanley P. Hirshson, *General Patton: A Soldier's Life* (New York: Harper Collins Publishers, 2002), 624.
29. 71st Infantry Division, G-3 Journal, 1 April 1945, Entries 45, 46.
30. Ibid., Entries 42, 57, 68; 71st Infantry Division, G-3 Periodic Report, Number 16, 11200A April 1945, National Archives RG 407, Entry 427, Box 11397.
31. Brenner, MS# B-715, 9.
32. *SS-Unterscharführer* Georg Stöwe (n.d.), sent to and translated by Jochen Seeliger; Seeliger forwarded the translated report to the author on 4 September 1995.
33. 71st Infantry Division, G-3 Journal, 1 April 1945, Entry 73.
34. Ibid., Entries 74, 76.
35. Dayna Spear Williams (Ed.), *71st Infantry Division: The Red Circle Division* (Paducah, KY: Turner Publishing Company, 2001), 22–23; McMahon, *The Siegfried and Beyond*, 240–242.
36. Williams, *71st Infantry Division*, 23.
37. Ibid., 22–23; McMahon, *The Siegfried and Beyond*, 240–242.
38. 71st Infantry Division, G-3 Journal, 1 April 1945, Entry 82.
39. L. B. Rhatican, telephone conversation with author, 12 March 1995.
40. Samuell, "History of the 1st Platoon."
41. 71st Infantry Division, G-3 Journal, 1 April 1945, Entry 80; Samuell, "History of the 1st Platoon."
42. 71st Infantry Division, G-3 Journal, 1 April 1945, Entries 88, 90.
43. Ibid., Entry 90.
44. Brant Scrapbook, 23; 71st Infantry Division, G-3 Journal, 1 April 1945, Entry 83.
45. Ibid., Entry 67; Brant Scrapbook, 23.
46. 5th Infantry Division, G-3 Journal, 1 April 1945.
47. General George S. Patton Jr., *War As I Knew It* (New York: Bantam Books, 1981), 397; 5th Infantry Division, G-3 Journal, 1 April 1945.
48. 5th Infantry Division, G-3 Journal, 1 April 1945. The language is as quoted directly from the journal from the time entries between 1120 and 1135 on page 4. However, I have written out all abbreviations and added some punctuation as necessary; I indicated major changes to the quoted text using brackets.

49. Brig. Gen. (Ret.) Robert E. Connor, letter to the author, 6 January 1996; Headquarters, 50th Field Artillery Battalion Record of Events, 1 April 1945; Col. (Ret.) J. W. Christy, letter to the author, 22 February 1996; 2nd Infantry Regimental Unit Journal, 1 January 1945–31 December 1945, entry for 1 April 1945, National Archives RG 407, Entry 427, Box 6866; 2nd Infantry Regimental Unit Journal File, Daily Operations Report, Operations for Period 311800A March 1945 to 011800A April 1945, 1 April, National Archives RG 407, Entry 427, Box 6872.
50. 5th Infantry Division, G-3 Journal, 1 April 1945.
51. Brenner, MS # B-715, 10.
52. 71st Infantry Division, G-2 Periodic Report No. 20, Annex C, 2 April 1945.
53. Brenner, MS # B-715, 10.
54. The events surrounding Krüger's exploits come from Krüger, letter to Long, n.d.
55. 71st Infantry Division, G-3 Periodic Report No. 16, 11200A April 1945, National Archives RG 407, Entry 427, Box 11397; 66th Infantry Regiment S-3 Journal, 10/0800 April 1945 to 20/0800 April 1945, Entry 1, National Archives RG 407, Entry 427, Box 11415.
56. 71st Infantry Division, G-3 Journal, 1 April 1945, Entries 94, 110, 112.
57. Ibid., Entries 95, 100, 109, 118; History, 5th Infantry Regiment Box 11408, March 1945.
58. Ibid., Entries 102, 105.
59. Ibid., Entries 119, 120.
60. Brant Scrapbook, 23.
61. Ibid., 22; Chaplain (Capt.) John J. Fahy, letter to Robert V. Reno's widow, 24 July 1945; Cpl. Robert V. Reno, letter to his mother, 31 March 1945; Mrs. R. Brigitt Reno Caito, the as-yet-unborn daughter of Robert V. Reno at the time of the battle, graciously supplied me with copies of the Reno and Fahy letters.
62. Brant Scrapbook, 22.
63. Lt. Col. (Ret.) Thomas W. Alvey, letter to the author, 25 February 1995.
64. Brant Scrapbook, 23.
65. Col. Carl E. Lundquist, combat interview by 1/Lt. Hollis Alpert (n.d.), 1–2, National Archives RG 407, Entry 427, Box 24049.
66. Brant Scrapbook, 23.
67. Samuell, "History of the 1st Platoon"; 71st Infantry Division, G-3 Journal, 1 April 1945, Entry 131.
68. Samuell, "History of the 1st Platoon."
69. Ibid.; Dorsey's account in Williams, *71st Infantry Division*, 22, spells Kieslewski's name "Kiesiluski." A caption on one of Dorsey's photographs shows the spelling as Kieslewski, which is mostly likely the correct version and the one I have chosen to use.

70. Lundquist, combat interview.
71. Ibid.; Brant Scrapbook, 23.
72. Lundquist, combat interview.
73. Ibid.; Brant Scrapbook, 23.
74. Lundquist, combat interview.
75. Brant Scrapbook, 23.
76. Ibid., 23–24.
77. Ibid., 24.
78. Lundquist, combat interview.
79. Brant Scrapbook, 24. Lundquist, combat interview, states that Brant's task force encountered enemy resistance in Rodenbach and had to fight through it before reaching the ridgeline north of town. Brant's version is most likely correct. Brant accounts for the shooting that occurred in the town as a "reconnaissance by fire" tactic used by the tank crews.
80. Brant Scrapbook, 24.
81. Sgt. John F. Cecula, letter to Mrs. Ruth Reno Middleton (mother of Cpl. Robert V. Reno), 15 July 1945.
82. Col. (Ret.) Ray K. Mortensen, telephone conversation with author, 8 May 2002; responses to a questionnaire provided to Col. (Ret.) Ray K. Mortensen by the author.
83. Brant Scrapbook, 24.
84. Frank J. Hagney, letter to Mrs. Ruth Reno Middleton (mother of Cpl. Robert V. Reno), 14 August 1948; responses to a questionnaire provided to Col. (Ret.) Ray K. Mortensen by the author.
85. Cecula, letter to Mrs. Middleton, 15 July 1945; Sgt. Edward Reinsmith, letter to Mrs. Ruth Reno Middleton (mother of Cpl. Robert V. Reno), 17 July 1945.
86. Field Manual 21-11, *First Aid for Soldiers*, War Department, U.S. Government Printing Office, 7 April 1943, 110–111. Each soldier carried a packet of these tablets. When wounded, soldiers were to ingest eight to twelve of these tablets followed by large amounts of water in order to prevent infection in the wounds; responses to a questionnaire provided to Col. (Ret.) Ray K. Mortensen by the author; "14th Officer Gets Third DSC Awarded 71st," *Right of the Line*, 14th Infantry Regimental Newsletter, Vol. 1, No. 4, 28 July 1945.
87. Brant Scrapbook, 24.
88. Letters to Mrs. Ruth Reno Middleton from Sgt. John F. Cecula (15 July 1945), Sgt. Edward Reinsmith (17 July 1945), Capt. (Chaplain) John J. Fahy (24 July 1945), Col. Carl E. Lundquist (28 May 1948), and Frank J. Hagney (14 August 1948).
89. Brant Scrapbook, 24.
90. Alvey, letter to the author, 25 February 1995.

91. Brant Scrapbook, 24.
92. McMahon, *The Siegfried and Beyond*, 239–240.
93. Alvey, letter to the author, 25 February 1995.
94. Brant Scrapbook, 24; Abdul-Jabbar and Walton, *Brothers in Arms*, 231.
95. Alvey, letter to the author, 25 February 1995; McMahon, *The Siegfried and Beyond*, 240.
96. Alvey, letter to the author, 25 February 1995; Unit History, 14th Infantry Regiment, Month of April 1945.
97. McMahon, *The Siegfried and Beyond*, 240.
98. Alvey, letter to the author, 25 February 1995.
99. Brant Scrapbook, 25.
100. Ibid., 24.
101. Ibid., 24a. Information from this incident exists in the form of two handwritten messages (both numbered 43) attached to the back of page 24, Brant Scrapbook. The messages do not explain if the SS men did or did not receive the plasma. I drew my conclusion from the fact that American troops throughout the war generally did not accede to such demands—even under a white flag. American troops generally recognized the notion of safe passage and therefore presumably allowed the SS men, who were probably medics, to depart. Also, no further evidence exists that Captain Swiggert was released at this time, so he may have returned to the Nord Division with the SS men. The first message clearly identifies the German troops as hailing from the "6 MTN SS DIV."
102. 2nd Infantry Regiment Unit Journal 1 April 1945–30 April 1945, Entries 5, 7, 8, 9, National Archives RG 407, Entry 427, Box 6866.
103. Connor, letter to the author, 6 January 1996.
104. Message Number 2, 1 April 1945, from 5th Infantry Division Headquarters to 10th Infantry Regiment.
105. 5th Infantry Division, G-3 Journal, 1 April 1945.
106. Thomas A. Butler Jr., Weapons Platoon runner, Company I, 3rd Battalion, 2nd Infantry Regiment, 37, unpublished draft memoirs. Butler does not give Roberts's rank, but the soldier's position in the platoon, as described by Butler, suggests that the man was a private or a private first class.
107. 5th Infantry Division, G-3 Journal, 1 April 1945.
108. Brant Scrapbook, 24–25; Appendix No. 1, Narrative Excerpts from Unit Journal, Incidents, 635th Tank Destroyer Battalion (Towed), April 1945, Entry 3, as reproduced in Gerald F. McMahon, *Anti-Tank: The Combat Service of the 635th TD Battalion, 14 March 1945–11 May 1945*, 22.
109. 5th Infantry Division, G-3 Journal, 1 April 1945.

110. Brenner, MS# B-715, 11; Headquarters, 50th Field Artillery Battalion Record of Events, 1 April 1945; 5th Infantry Division, G-3 Journal, 1 April 1945.
111. Brant Scrapbook, 25.
112. 14th Infantry Regiment S-1 Journal, 1 April 1945, National Archives RG 407, Entry 427, Box 11411 (hereafter 14th Infantry Regiment, 1 April 1945), Entries 20, 33, 34; Lundquist, combat interview, 3, National Archives RG 407, Entry 427, Box 24049; Brant Scrapbook, 25.
113. Brant Scrapbook, 25.
114. 66th Infantry Regiment S-3 Journal, 10/800 April 1945 to 20/800 April 1945, Entry 5, National Archives RG 407, Entry 427, Box 11415.
115. 71st Infantry Division, G-3 Journal, 1 April 1945, Entries 126, 127.
116. Ibid., Entries 147, 156.
117. Ibid., Entry 148.
118. Ibid., Entries 154, 112.
119. Ibid., Entry 114.
120. 5th Infantry Division, G-3 Journal, 1 April 1945.
121. Ibid.; 71st Infantry Division, G-3 Journal, 1 April 1945, Entry 131.
122. 71st Infantry Division, G-3 Journal, 1 April 1945, Entries 132, 135; 5th Infantry Division, G-3 Journal, 1 April 1945; 5th Infantry Regiment Unit Journal.
123. 71st Infantry Division, G-3 Journal, 1 April 1945, Entries 132, 135.
124. Historical Summary, 66th Infantry Regiment, 10 March 1945 to 10 April 1945, p. 3, National Archives RG 407, Entry 427, Box 11415; 71st Infantry Division, G-3 Journal, 1 April 1945, Entries 133, 135.
125. Ibid., Entry 119.
126. 14th Infantry Regiment, 1 April 1945, Box 11411, Entry 33.
127. 71st Infantry Division G-2 Periodic Report Number 19, 011600 April 1945.
128. 14th Infantry Regiment Unit Report Number 19, 1 April 1945; Sims, "Blue Mike," 100.
129. 14th Infantry Regiment, 1 April 1945, Box 11411, Entry 19.
130. Sims, "Blue Mike," 100.
131. 14th Infantry Regiment, 1 April 1945, Box 11411, Entry 21; 14th Infantry Regiment Operations Instruction Number 9, Overlay of Assembly Areas, 1 April 1945; Kinnard, *From the Paterson Station*, 205.
132. 14th Infantry Regiment Unit Report Number 19, 1 April 1945.
133. 2nd Infantry Regiment, Operations for Period 311800A March 1945 to 011800A April 1945, 1 April 1945, National Archives RG 407, Entry 427, Box 6872; Regimental Unit Journal, 2nd Infantry Regiment, 1 January 1945–31 December 1945, Entry for 1 April 1945, National Archives RG 407, Entry 427, Box 6866; Connor, letter to the author, 6 January 1996.

134. 5th Infantry Division, G-3 Journal, 1 April 1945; 2nd Infantry Regiment Unit Journal 1 April 1945–30 April 1945, Entries 13, 14, National Archives RG 407, Entry 427, Box 6866.
135. 5th Infantry Division, G-3 Journal, 1 April 1945.
136. 5th Infantry Division, G-3 Journal, 1 April 1945; 2nd Infantry Regiment Unit Journal 1 April 1945–30 April 1945, Entry 15.
137. 5th Infantry Division, G-3 Journal, 1 April 1945; 5th Cavalry Reconnaissance Troop unit record, entry for 2 April 1945.
138. Lambert and Layton, *The Ghosts of Patton's Third Army*, 272.
139. Ibid., 272–273.
140. Ibid., 272.
141. Ibid., 273.
142. Schreiber, *Kampf Unter Dem Nordlicht*, 370.
143. Sims, "Blue Mike," 101; Karl Müller, letter to Jochen Seeliger, 8 January 2003.
144. Brenner, MS# B-715, 11.
145. Patton, *War As I Knew It*, 266–267. On page 266, Patton incorrectly identified the 6th SS-Gebirgs Division as the 2nd Mountain (*Gebirgs*) Division, which had been in the same general areas as the 6th SS during the Saar-Palatinate campaign. MacDonald points out the same error in footnote 12 on page 350 of *The Last Offensive*.
146. Patton, *War As I Knew It*, 266–267.
147. Ibid., 267.
148. Ibid. In 1996, a graduate student named Mack O'Quinn was writing his master's thesis on the German and Hungarian armed forces' treatment of prisoners of Jewish, African, and Asian Pacific heritage. O'Quinn heard about my research into the battle and shared two letters with me from members of the 5th Infantry Division. These letters to O'Quinn were in response to queries he made through the 5th Infantry Division Association based on an alleged atrocity perpetrated by the 6th SS-Gebirgs Division outlined in a book by David A. Foy entitled *For You The War Is Over: American Prisoners of War in Nazi Germany* (New York: Stein and Day, 1984). I located Foy's original 1981 University of Arkansas doctoral dissertation on which he based his book and discovered on pages 226–227 his discussion of the incident. Foy simply mentions that German troops massacred some Black soldiers and then footnotes a 4 April 1945 article from the London *Times* that provides more details. After finding a copy of the London *Times* article, O'Quinn investigated the incident further and contacted Lt. Col. (Ret.) George Bachman and Albert Gregory, two former members of the 5th Infantry Division who fought in the area during the battle. (I don't know why O'Quinn focused only on veterans of the 5th Infantry Division and not veterans of the 71st Infantry Division.) Bachman was a member of Battery C, 21st Field Artillery Battalion, which

was the 5th Division's 155-mm general support artillery battalion. Bachman explains in his letter (22 February 1996) that his battery moved to firing positions in Assenheim at the place where the SS troopers had attacked the 620th Ordnance Company a few days earlier. Bachman's personal assessment of the debris-strewn scene suggests that the SS men caught the 620th's troops by surprise because the Black GIs had not posted guards. The battery found two survivors from the company still hiding in the woods. Bachman stated that he observed no evidence of an atrocity. By contrast, 1/Sgt. Albert Gregory of Company H, 2nd Battalion, 2nd Infantry, describes in a letter to O'Quinn dated 24 February 1996 that his company moved through the same location a day or two after the attack and saw the 620th's damaged vehicles, some of which had apparently been forced off the road. At that time, Gregory recalled, he heard that the SS men had shot some of the Black soldiers in the head. On 8 April 1996 I spoke by telephone with Cpl. Ira King, a forward observer in Bachman's Battery C, 21st Field Artillery, who claimed to have seen the bodies of dead Black soldiers "executed" in their tents and the dead bodies of doctors at the nearby field hospital site. Corporal King's account contradicts Bachman's assessment markedly. The relevance of this information supports the fact that, at some point, a rumor about an alleged massacre of Black troops, doctors, and nurses ultimately found its way to Lieutenant General Patton at Third Army headquarters after originating at the individual soldier level based on some hasty, uninformed assessments of the battle scene by GIs who did not understand what they were seeing. The accounts of both Bachman and Gregory, and many other such inconsistent claims (such as Corporal King's and *SS-Sturmmann* Krüger's versions) encountered by me while researching this book, suggest that the rumor began within a few hours of the attack based upon a confused combination of first- and second hand accounts of an extremely chaotic situation. An investigation into how and why the rumor began is not within the scope of this book but does have some relevance to the overall situation.

Chapter 7. The Second Day: Waldensberg, 2 April 1945

1. Brenner, MS# B-715, 11.
2. Becker, "Decline and Fall of the 6. SS-Mount. Div. Nord."
3. Johannes Kaltenschnee, "How the War in Its Final Stages Still Became Fatal for the Inhabitants of Leisenwald and Waldensberg," *Sammlung Geschichte Wächtersbach*, August 2001 (this article is part of a chronicle of the Leisenwald school written between 1950 and 1965; Jochen Seeliger translated the article), 1.
4. Lambert and Layton, *The Ghosts of Patton's Third Army*, 273.
5. Ibid., 273–276.

6. Landrat Heinrich Kress, "Easter 1945: Waldensberg Razed to the Ground," *Zwischen Vogelsberg und Spessart, Heimatjahrbuch des Kreises Gelnhausen*, 1964 (trans. Jochen Seeliger), 33.
7. Brenner, MS# B-715, 12. These flak units often directly supported Heer units on the ground from the ubiquitous Allied aircraft and often became prisoners when the Allies captured German Army combat troops.
8. Lambert and Layton, *The Ghosts of Patton's Third Army*, 273–276.
9. Becker, "Decline and Fall of the 6. SS-Mount. Div. Nord."
10. Lambert and Layton, *The Ghosts of Patton's Third Army*, 273–276.
11. Kress, "Easter 1945," 33.
12. 71st Infantry Division, G-3 Journal, 2 April 1945, Entry 8.
13. Ibid., Entry 23.
14. Ibid., Entries 20, 32; Third Army Report of Operations, Medical Section, Part 17, 54.
15. 71st Infantry Division, G-3 Journal, 2 April 1945, Entries 25, 27, 29, 33.
16. Ibid., Entry 33; *Red Circle News*, Vol. 18, No. 2, June 2004, 6.
17. 71st Infantry Division, G-3 Journal, 2 April 1945, Entry 39.
18. Ibid., Entry 40.
19. Ibid., Entry 41.
20. Kaltenschnee, "How the War in Its Final Stages Still Became Fatal," 1.
21. Brenner, MS# B-715, 11.
22. History of the 66th Infantry Regiment, 9, National Archives RG 407, Entry 427, Box 11415.
23. S-3 Journal, 66th Infantry Regiment, 020800B April 1945 to 030800B April 1945, Entry 4, National Archives RG 407, Entry 427, Box 11415; 71st Infantry Division, G-3 Journal, 2 April, Entry 54.
24. 14th Infantry Regiment, Unit Report No. 20, 0001 2 April 1945 to 2400 2 April 1945, National Archives RG 407, Entry 427, Box 11412.
25. 14th Infantry Regiment, S-1 Journal, 0001 2 April 1945 to 2400 2 April 1945, National Archives RG 407, Entry 427, Box 11411 (hereafter 14th Infantry Regiment, 0001 2 April 1945 to 2400 2 April 1945, Box 11411), Entry 2; Lundquist, combat interview, 4, National Archives RG 407, Entry 427, Box 24049.
26. 14th Infantry Regiment, 0001 2 April 1945 to 2400 2 April 1945, Box 11411, Entry 7.
27. Ibid., Entries 5, 9; 71st Infantry Division, G-3 Journal, 2 April 1945, Entry 49.
28. Lundquist, combat interview.
29. Ibid.; 14th Infantry Regiment, 0001 2 April 1945 to 2400 2 April 1945, Box 11411, Entry 12.
30. Ibid., Entries 10, 11; Brant Scrapbook, 26.
31. 14th Infantry Regiment, 0001 2 April 1945 to 2400 2 April 1945, Box 11411, Entry 12.

32. Ibid., Entry 13.
33. Ibid., Entries 15, 18; 71st Infantry Division, G-3 Journal, 2 April 1945, Entry 57.
34. 71st Infantry Division, G-3 Journal, 2 April 1945, Entry 45.
35. Ibid., Entries 45, 49, 51; G-3 Journal, 5th Infantry Division, 2 April 1945, p. 2, National Archives RG 407, Entry 427, Box 6810.
36. Lambert and Layton, *The Ghosts of Patton's Third Army*, 277. Lambert and Layton state that a Major Steinmetz led this relief column, but no Major Steinmetz appears on the group's officer roster. The 2nd Squadron S-4 was 1/Lt. Roland T. Steinmetz, who was undoubtedly caught up in the fighting at Waldensberg with the rear echelon troops. The only field-grade officer in the area at the time who could have led the 2nd Squadron's relief column was Major Wyles. Lambert seemingly erred in this case and simply confused the names. Coincidentally, a 2/Lt. John F. Steinmetz was the 81-mm mortar platoon leader in Company M, 66th Infantry, and later participated in the attack to seize Leisenwald.
37. Lambert and Layton, *The Ghosts of Patton's Third Army*, 277.
38. Ibid., 277–278.
39. McMahon, *The Siegfried and Beyond*, 261–262; History of the 66th Infantry Regiment, 9, National Archives RG 407, Entry 427, Box 11415.
40. McMahon, *The Siegfried and Beyond*, 261.
41. Ibid., 262.
42. Lambert and Layton, *The Ghosts of Patton's Third Army*, 276–277.
43. History of the 66th Infantry Regiment, 9, National Archives RG 407, Entry 427, Box 11415.
44. Ibid.; Roy J. Long, letter to the author, 4 May 1995; McMahon, *The Siegfried and Beyond*, 260.
45. Ibid., 260.
46. Ibid., 261.
47. History of the 66th Infantry Regiment, 9, National Archives RG 407, Entry 427, Box 11415.
48. Kress, "Easter 1945," 33.
49. Roy J. Long, letter to the author, 24 June 1995.
50. Long, letter, 4 May 1995; McMahon, *The Siegfried and Beyond*, 265.
51. History of the 66th Infantry Regiment, 9–10, National Archives RG 407, Entry 427, Box 11415; McMahon, *The Siegfried and Beyond*, 261.
52. Ibid., 262.
53. Ibid., 262–263.
54. Ibid., 263.
55. Ibid., 257.

56. History of the 66th Infantry Regiment, 9, National Archives RG 407, Entry 427, Box 11415; McMahon, *The Siegfried and Beyond*, 258.
57. Tomich, "G.I.'s [*sic*] Forever," 47.
58. Kress, "Easter 1945," 33.
59. Brenner, MS# B-715, 12.
60. Lambert and Layton, *The Ghosts of Patton's Third Army*, 278.
61. History of the 66th Infantry Regiment, 10, National Archives RG 407, Entry 427, Box 11415.
62. 71st Infantry Division, G-3 Journal, 2 April 1945, Entry 92.
63. Ibid., Entry 59; Lambert and Layton, *The Ghosts of Patton's Third Army*, 273; McMahon, *The Siegfried and Beyond*, 229; MacDonald, *The Last Offensive*, 378; Carl Condon, *The 635th Tank Destroyer Battalion in Europe in World War II*, available on the Museum of the Kansas National Guard Web Site at http://skyways.lib.ks.us/museums/kng/635TDB.html (viewed on 10 January 2001), 74.
64. 71st Infantry Division, G-3 Journal, 2 April 1945, Entries 60, 61; 5th Infantry Unit Journal, 2 April 1945, 34, National Archives RG 407, Entry 427, Box 11408 (hereafter 5th Infantry Unit Journal, 2 April 1945).
65. 71st Infantry Division, G-3 Journal, 2 April 1945, Entry 63; 5th Infantry Unit Journal, 2 April 1945, 34, National Archives RG 407, Entry 427, Box 11408.
66. 71st Infantry Division, G-3 Journal, 2 April 1945, Entry 65.
67. Ibid., Entries 66, 68.
68. Ibid., Entries 78, 80.
69. Ibid., Entry 80; 5th Infantry Unit Journal, 2 April 1945, 34–35.
70. 71st Infantry Division, G-3 Journal, 2 April 1945, Entries 89, 96; G-3 Periodic Report No. 17, 21200B April 1945, 71st Infantry Division, National Archives RG 407, Entry 427, Box 11397; 5th Infantry Unit Journal, 2 April 1945, 35, National Archives RG 407, Entry 427, Box 11408; Clinger et al., *The History of the 71st Infantry Division*, 57.
71. Kinnard, *From the Paterson Station*, 198.
72. Ibid., 198.
73. Ibid., 227.
74. Ibid., 227–228.
75. Ibid. 228; Karl Müller, letters to Jochen Seeliger, 8 January 2003, 12 January 2003.
76. Kinnard, *From the Paterson Station*, 228.
77. Brant Scrapbook, 26.
78. 2nd Infantry Regiment Unit Journal 1 April 1945–30 April 1945, Entry 23.
79. Brant Scrapbook, 26; 14th Infantry Regiment, 2 April 1945, Box 11411, Entry 24.
80. Brant Scrapbook, 26.
81. Sims, "Blue Mike," 101; W. P. Sims, letter to the author, 9 April 1995.

82. Sims, letter to the author, 9 April 1995; excerpts from Unit Journal, Incidents, 635th Tank Destroyer Battalion, Appendix No. 1, April 1945, 6 May 1945, 2 (reprinted in Gerald F. McMahon, *Anti-Tank*).
83. Edward G. Rimple, letter to the author, 9 April 1995. Rimple also provided me with a sketch of the battalion's attack position that outlined the precise locations of companies, tanks, mortars, and howitzers; Sims, letter to the author, 9 April 1995.
84. Sims, "Blue Mike," 101; Müller, letter to Seeliger, 8 January 2003.
85. Ibid.
86. Sims, "Blue Mike," 101.
87. Excerpts from Unit Journal, Incidents, 635th Tank Destroyer Battalion, Appendix No. 1, April 1945, 6 May 1945, 2 (reprinted in McMahon, *Anti-Tank*).
88. Rimple, letter to the author, 9 April 1995.
89. Sims, "Blue Mike," 101.
90. Müller, letter to Seeliger, 8 January 2003.
91. Sims, "Blue Mike," 101.
92. Ibid.; William L. Asay, letter to the author, 18 April 1995; W. P. Sims, interview with author, 25 August 2001.
93. Asay, letter to the author, 18 April 1995; Sims, "Blue Mike," 102; Sims, interview, 25 August 2001.
94. Sims, "Blue Mike," 101; Edward G. Rimple, letter to the author, 9 April 1995. Rimple also provided me with a sketch of the battalion's attack position that specified the location of the dugout where the Red Circle men captured the four SS troops.
95. Sims, "Blue Mike," 101.
96. 14th Infantry Regiment, Unit Report No. 20, 2 April 1945, National Archives RG 407, Entry 427, Box 11412; 71st Infantry Division, G-3 Journal, 2 April 1945, Entries 88, 90.
97. 66th Infantry Regiment S-3 Journal, 2 April 1945, Entry 16, National Archives RG 407, Box 11415 (hereafter 66th Infantry Regiment S-3 Journal, 2 April 1945), Entry 427; 71st Infantry Division, G-3 Journal, 2 April 1945, Entry 92.
98. 66th Infantry Regiment S-3 Journal, 2 April 1945, Entry 21.
99. Ibid., Entries 17, 40; 71st Infantry Division, G-3 Journal, 2 April 1945, Entry 86.
100. 66th Infantry Regiment S-3 Journal, 2 April 1945, Entry 30; Baron et al., *Raid*, 267.
101. Ibid., 267; Tomich, "G.I.s Forever," 47.
102. 71st Infantry Division, G-3 Journal, 2 April 1945, Entries 98, 112; 71st Division After Action Report, 21 June 1945 (hereafter 71st AAR March 1945), 3; Koyen, *The Fourth Armored Division*, 113.
103. Annex C to G-2 Periodic Report Number 20, 71st Infantry Division, 2 April 1945.
104. Long, letter to the author, 24 June 1995.

105. McMahon, *The Siegfried and Beyond*, 266.
106. Tomich, "G.I.'s [*sic*] Forever," 47; McMahon, *The Siegfried and Beyond*, 263.
107. Tomich, "G.I.'s [*sic*] Forever," 47; Long, letter to the author, 4 May 1995. Long believed the SS man to be an officer, but Tomich's account does not specify the German soldier's rank. The History of Headquarters Company, 2nd Battalion, 66th Infantry (unknown author), identifies Berthelot as the Headquarters Company executive officer, a post he may have assumed later in April or in May.
108. Tomich, "G.I.'s [*sic*] Forever," 47; Long, letter to the author, 4 May 1995.
109. Long, letter to the author, 24 June 1995; G-2 Periodic Report Number 20, 71st Infantry Division, 2 April 1945.
110. 66th Infantry Regiment S-3 Journal, 2 April 1945, Entries 38, 41, 42.
111. G-3 Journal, 5th Infantry Division, 2 April 1945, 1 and 3, National Archives RG 407, Entry 427, Box 6810; 5th Cavalry Reconnaissance Troop unit journal, entry for 2 April 1945.
112. G-3 Journal, 5th Infantry Division, 2 April 1945, 2.
113. G-3 Journal, 5th Infantry Division, 2 April 1945, 2 and 3; Headquarters, 50th Field Artillery Battalion Record of Events, 1 April 1945.
114. 2nd Infantry Regiment Unit Journal 1 April 1945–30 April 1945, Entry 20; G-3 Journal, 5th Infantry Division, 2 April 1945, 3.
115. G-3 Journal, 5th Infantry Division, 2 April 1945, 2; 2nd Infantry Regiment Unit Journal 1 April 1945–30 April 1945, Entry 23.
116. G-3 Journal, 5th Infantry Division, 2 April 1945, 2.
117. Headquarters, 2nd Infantry Regiment, After Action Report, 2 May 1945, 3, National Archives RG 407, Entry 427, Box 6664. The 2nd Infantry Regiment's Unit Journal lists the command post as opening at 1345 (Entry 27), which seems too late given the emphasis Colonel Roffe placed on getting his regiment forward as quickly as possible; Headquarters, 50th Field Artillery Battalion Record of Events, 1 April 1945; Headquarters, 2nd Infantry Regiment, Operations for Period 011800A April 1945 to 021800A April 1945, National Archives RG 407, Entry 427, Box 6872.
118. G-3 Journal, 5th Infantry Division, 2 April 1945, 3; 5th Division Record of Events, entry for 2 April 1945.
119. Ibid., 4.
120. 71st Infantry Division, G-3 Journal, Entry 86, 2 April 1945; 66th Infantry Regiment S-3 Journal, 2 April 1945, Entry 18, Entry 427; Denno, letter to the author, 19 February 1995.
121. Denno, letter to the author, 19 February 1995; 66th Infantry Regiment Unit History (two versions), 11 and 2, National Archives RG 407, Entry 427, Box 11415; FM 17-15, Assault Gun Section and Platoon, 8 September 1944, 1–4.

122. Denno, letter to the author, 19 February 1995.
123. 66th Infantry Regiment S-3 Journal, 2 April 1945, Entry 25.
124. Ibid., Entry 32; 71st Infantry Division, G-3 Journal, 2 April 1945, Entries 117, 121.
125. 71st Infantry Division, G-3 Journal, 2 April 1945, Entries 125, 126, 133.
126. 71st Infantry Division, G-3 Journal, 2 April 1945, Entry 125.
127. Brant Scrapbook, 26.
128. Sims, "Blue Mike," 103; 14th Infantry Regiment, 2 April 1945, Box 11411, Entries 50, 53.
129. 14th Infantry Regiment, 2 April 1945, Box 11411, Entry 52.
130. Sims, "Blue Mike," 103.
131. 71st Infantry Division, G-3 Journal, 2 April 1945, Entry 116.
132. 71st Infantry Division, G-3 Journal, 2 April 1945, Entry 141; 5th Infantry Unit Journal, 2 April 1945, p. 35, National Archives RG 407, Entry 427, Box 11408.
133. 71st Infantry Division, G-3 Journal, 2 April 1945, Entries 128, 131; 5th Infantry Unit Journal, 2 April 1945, 35, National Archives RG 407, Entry 427, Box 11408.
134. 71st Infantry Division, G-3 Journal, 2 April 1945, Entry 131.
135. Ibid., Entries 134, 145; 5th Infantry Unit Journal, 2 April 1945, 35, National Archives RG 407, Entry 427, Box 11408.

Chapter 8. The Second Day: Leisenwald, 2 April 1945

1. Brenner, MS# B-715, 12.
2. 66th Infantry Regiment Unit History, 11, National Archives RG 407, Entry 427, Box 11415.
3. Denno, letter to the author, 19 February 1995.
4. Col. (Ret.) Bryce F. Denno, letter to the author, 6 May 1995. The regimental command post passed various reports to the 3rd Battalion command post about the status of the 2nd Battalion in Waldensberg, but whether the information reached Lieutenant Colonel Denno in whole or in part is unclear (66th Infantry Regiment S-3 Journal, 02/0800 April 1945–03/0800 April 1945, Entries 37, 42, National Archives RG 407, Entry 427, Box 11415).
5. Denno, letter to the author, 19 February 1995; "My Combat Autobiography" by Pfc. Leo A. Sims, *Red Circle News*, Vol. 18, No. 1, January 2004, 9.
6. 66th Infantry Regiment Unit History, 11, National Archives RG 407, Entry 427, Box 11415; McMahon, *The Siegfried and Beyond*, 249.
7. 66th Infantry Regiment Unit History, 12, National Archives RG 407, Entry 427, Box 11415; McMahon, *The Siegfried and Beyond*, 247–248. In a letter to the author dated

19 February 1995, Col. (Ret.) Denno stated that he thought the resistance faced by Companies I and L was not as severe as mentioned in the 66th Infantry Regiment's Unit History on page 12. Despite the level of resistance, the two companies spent the better part of the afternoon seizing and then clearing the woods of all German resistance.

8. 5th Cavalry Reconnaissance Troop unit journal, entry for 2 April 1945; Donald E. Robinson, letter to the author, 24 January 1996.
9. 5th Cavalry Reconnaissance Troop unit journal, entry for 2 April 1945.
10. Jan Surmondt, *Tanks & Armoured Vehicles of WWII* (Cobham, Surrey, TAJ Books, 2004), 198 and 209.
11. 5th Cavalry Reconnaissance Troop unit journal, entry for 2 April 1945.
12. G-3 Journal, 5th Infantry Division, 2 April 1945, 4, National Archives RG 407, Entry 427, Box 6810.
13. Ibid., 5; 2nd Infantry Regiment Unit Journal 1 April 1945–30 April 1945, Entry 28.
14. G-3 Journal, 5th Infantry Division, 2 April 1945, p. 5.
15. 71st Infantry Division, G-3 Journal, 2 April, Entry 155.
16. Frankfurt Büdingen Web site http://www.roadstoruins.com/budingen.html (viewed 3 August 2000).
17. James M. Paul (M.D.), letter to the author, 25 April 1995.
18. 71st Infantry Division, G-3 Journal, 2 April, Entry 163.
19. 5th Infantry Regiment Unit Journal.
20. 71st Infantry Division, G-3 Journal, 2 April, Entries 155, 177.
21. Ibid., Entry 173.
22. Ibid., Entry 184.
23. Abdul-Jabbar and Walton, *Brothers in Arms*, 232.
24. 71st Infantry Division, G-3 Journal, 2 April, Entry 184.
25. Jende's account was part of a local Gelnhausen historian's compilation of events in the area during the war. The account was an unpublished document I obtained while stationed there. Renate Knox, the German spouse of one of my infantry platoon's noncommissioned officers, expertly translated the document into English for me.
26. Tomich, "G.I's [sic] Forever," 47.
27. Ibid., 47; 71st Infantry Division, G-3 Journal, 2 April, Entry 159.
28. Tomich, "G.I's [sic] Forever," 47.
29. This account appeared in Tomich's unpublished manuscript "G.I's [sic] Forever" based on what Fisher and Parsley told Tomich after the incident. No further corroborating evidence exists to support such a horrific tale, but the fact that the German woman specified that an SS captain shot her daughter is troublesome. She would have had to understand the rather complex Waffen-SS rank system to make such a distinction,

which seems improbable for a woman hailing from a remote village in central Germany. SS-Gebirgsjäger Regiment 11 had few officers in the grade of *SS-Hauptsturmführer* remaining in the battle group. Among those was the 1st Battalion commander, Alfred Steurich, who was not known for such extreme behavior and most likely would not have performed such an act. I am always careful to include these types of incidents because of the weighty nature of such charges. However, Tomich is a very reliable source, so he likely recorded accurately the details of what he was told although some details may be missing. I include the event only as a cautionary tale that might further explain the emotional tension and strain inherent in high-intensity combat operations.

30. 66th Infantry Regiment Unit History, 10, National Archives RG 407, Entry 427, Box 11415.
31. Brant Scrapbook, 27; 71st Infantry Division, G-3 Journal, 2 April 1945, Entry 157.
32. Brant Scrapbook, 27; FM 21-11, April 7, 1943, 9.
33. Brant Scrapbook, 27; 14th Infantry Regiment, 2 April 1945, Box 11411, Entry 427.
34. Brant Scrapbook, 27; 14th Infantry Regiment, 2 April 1945, Box 11411, Entry 28.
35. 14th Infantry Regiment, 2 April 1945, Box 11411, Entry 28.
36. 71st Infantry Division, G-3 Journal, 2 April 1945, Entry 94.
37. Ibid., Entry 124.
38. 71st Infantry Division, G-3 Journal, 2 April 1945, Entry 137.
39. Samuell, "History of the 1st Platoon."
40. G-3 Journal, 5th Infantry Division, 7, 2 April 1945.
41. 2nd Infantry Regiment Regimental Unit Journal, 1 January 1945–31 December 1945, Entry for 3 April 1945, National Archives RG 407, Entry 427, Box 6866.
42. G-3 Journal, 5th Infantry Division, 6; 2nd Infantry Regiment, After Action Report, 2 May 1945, 3, National Archives RG 407, Entry 427, Box 6664.
43. Samuell, "History of the 1st Platoon." Samuell's account does not specify that the town they observed the 1st Battalion, 2nd Infantry Regiment, attacking was Merkenfritz. Samuell only identifies it as a town south of Gedern; since Merkenfritz was the battalion's stopping point for the day, I believe that Samuell was describing Merkenfritz.
44. Samuell, "History of the 1st Platoon."
45. 5th Cavalry Reconnaissance Troop unit journal, entry for 2 April 1945.
46. 5th Cavalry Reconnaissance Troop (Mecz), After Action Report, 1–30 April 1945, 2 May 1945, National Archives RG 407, Entry 427, Box 6844.
47. 5th Cavalry Reconnaissance Troop unit journal, entry for 2 April 1945.
48. 5th Infantry Division, G-3 Journal, 2 April 1945, 6.
49. 66th Infantry Regiment Unit History, p. 12, National Archives RG 407, Entry 427, Box 11415.
50. Denno, letter to the author, 19 February 1995.

51. Brenner, MS# B-715, 12.
52. Denno, letter to the author, 19 February 1995.
53. "My Combat Autobiography" by Pfc. Leo A. Sims, *Red Circle News*, Vol. 18, No. 1, January 2004, 9.
54. "Letter to Leo T. Kissell from Alec C. Burton," *Red Circle News*, Vol. 18, No. 1, January 2004, 6; Alec C. Burton, telephone conversation, 22 February 2005; Alec C. Burton, letter to the author, 3 March 2004.
55. "Letter to Leo T. Kissell," 6.
56. Denno, letter to the author, 19 February 1995. Included in Denno's letter was a recommended citation Denno submitted for Company K to receive a Presidential Unit Citation for the taking of Leisenwald. This citation provides many of the details about the battle outlined here. The citation was never approved because, Denno believed, the event was quickly forgotten in the series of battles that took place soon after Leisenwald.
57. Pfc. Leo A. Sims, "My Combat Autobiography," *Red Circle News*, Vol. 18, No. 1, January 2004, 9.
58. 66th Infantry Regiment Unit History, 12, National Archives RG 407, Entry 427, Box 11415; Kaltenschnee, "How the War in Its Final Stages Still Became Fatal," 1.
59. Denno, letter to the author, 19 February 1995.
60. Kaltenschnee, "How the War in Its Final Stages Still Became Fatal," 1.
61. Denno, letter to the author, 19 February 1995; 66th Infantry Regiment Unit History, 12, National Archives RG 407, Entry 427, Box 11415.
62. 66th Infantry Regiment Unit History, 12, National Archives RG 407, Entry 427, Box 11415.
63. 71st Infantry Division, G-3 Journal, 2 April 1945, Entry 157.
64. Ibid., Entry 195. This entry expressed Major General Wyman's continued concern about receiving timely, accurate information from the units in contact while fully recognizing the technical limitations of the unit's radios and other problems. The lack of reporting was clearly causing many leaders like Wyman and Regnier to make decisions in the absence of complete or accurate information.
65. 71st Infantry Division, G-3 Journal, 2 April 1945, Entries 148, 154.
66. Ibid., Entries 135, 161.
67. MacDonald, *The Last Offensive*, 378.
68. 71st Infantry Division, G-3 Journal, 2 April 1945, Entry 175; S-3 Journal, 66th Infantry Regiment, Entries 28, 29, National Archives RG 407, Entry 427, Box 11415.
69. 71st Infantry Division, G-3 Journal, 2 April 1945, Entries 150, 183.
70. The events surrounding Krüger's exploits come from Krüger, letter to Long. Additional information comes from Krüger, interview, 25 September 1999.
71. Brenner, MS# B-715, 12; Schreiber, *Kampf Unter Dem Nordlicht*, 371.

72. Brenner, MS# B-715, 12. The events surrounding Krüger's exploits come from Krüger, letter to Long. Additional information comes from Krüger, interview, 25 September 1999.
73. The events surrounding Krüger's exploits come from Krüger, letter to Long. Additional information comes from Krüger, interview, 25 September 1999; written account of Georg Stöwe's wartime experiences (n.d.) (trans. Jochen Seeliger).
74. Written account of Georg Stöwe's wartime experiences (n.d.) (trans. Jochen Seeliger). In separate documents, Stöwe spells his interpreter's name differently, such as Gartenfeld. When I interviewed Georg Stöwe on 4 October 1997, he used the name "Gladenfeld," which is the most consistent use of the name and probably the accurate version. Although Gladenfeld was a senior sergeant in the Heer, Stöwe still commanded the intelligence communications section—presumably because he was a member of the Waffen-SS and Gladenfeld was not.
75. Written account of Georg Stöwe's wartime experiences (n.d.) (trans. Jochen Seeliger); Georg Stöwe, interview with the author, 4 October 1997.
76. Steurich, *Zum Gedenken SS-Standartenführer a. D. Helmuth Raithel*, *Nordruf*, 6.
77. Brenner, MS# B-715, 12.
78. Written account of Georg Stöwe's wartime experiences (n.d.) (trans. Jochen Seeliger).
79. The events surrounding Krüger's exploits come from Krüger, letter to Long. Additional information comes from Krüger, interview, 25 September 1999.
80. Denno, letter to the author, 19 February 1995.
81. "Letter to Leo T. Kissell," 6.
82. 66th Infantry Regiment Unit History, 12–13, National Archives RG 407, Entry 427, Box 11415; McMahon, *The Siegfried and Beyond*, 249.
83. Ibid., 249–250.
84. 66th Infantry Regiment Unit History, 12–13, National Archives RG 407, Entry 427, Box 11415.
85. Ibid., 12.
86. 66th Infantry Regiment Unit History (second version), 1–2, National Archives RG 407, Entry 427, Box 11415.
87. Kaltenschnee, "How the War in Its Final Stages Still Became Fatal," 1.
88. 66th Infantry Regiment Unit History, 13–14, National Archives RG 407, Entry 427, Box 11415.
89. Sims, "Blue Mike," 102; 14th Infantry Regiment, 2 April 1945, Box 11411, Entry 58.
90. 14th Infantry Regiment, 2 April 1945, Box 11411, Entries 58–60; Sims, "Blue Mike," 102; 71st Infantry Division, G-3 Journal, 2 April 1945, Entries 197, 208.
91. Brant Scrapbook, 27; 14th Infantry Regiment, 2 April 1945, Box 11411, Entry 40.
92. Sims, "Blue Mike," 102–103.

93. Ibid., 102.
94. 71st Infantry Division, G-3 Journal, 2 April 1945, Entry 195.
95. Ibid., Entry 214; 14th Infantry Regiment, 2 April 1945, Box 11411, Entry 2; 5th Infantry Regiment Unit Journal.
96. 71st Infantry Division, G-3 Journal, 2 April 1945, Entry 195.
97. Ibid., Entries 195, 204, 208.
98. Ibid., Entry 219; 14th Infantry Regiment, 2 April 1945, Box 11411, Entry 17; 71st AAR March 1945, 2.
99. 71st Infantry Division, G-3 Journal, 2 April 1945, Entry 215.
100. Brenner, MS# B-715, 13. Brenner states that he thinks he left behind two hundred American prisoners, but Lieutenant Colonel Denno reports the liberation of thirty American prisoners. Denno's figure is probably the accurate one since Brenner suffered from communications problems within his own division until departing Leisenwald. Also, Brenner had opted earlier to release most of his prisoners to facilitate the rapid movement of his division south to Gelnhausen.
101. Steurich, *Zum Gedenken SS-Standartenführer a. D. Helmuth Raithel, Nordruf*, 6.
102. Brenner, MS# B-715, 13.
103. Denno, letter to the author, 19 February 1995; 66th Infantry Regiment Unit History, 1–2, National Archives RG 407, Entry 427, Box 11415.
104. McMahon, *The Siegfried and Beyond*, 253–254; Denno, letter to the author, 19 February 1995; 66th Infantry Regiment Unit History, 1–2, National Archives RG 407, Entry 427, Box 11415.
105. 71st Infantry Division, G-3 Journal, 2 April 1945, Entry 217.

Chapter 9. The Third Day: Dissolution, 3 April 1945

1. Brenner, MS# B-715, 13; written account of Georg Stöwe's wartime experiences (n.d.) (trans. Jochen Seeliger); Stöwe, interview, 4 October 1997.
2. Brenner, MS# B-715, 13; Stöwe, interview, 4 October 1997.
3. Written account of Georg Stöwe's wartime experiences (n.d.) (trans. Jochen Seeliger).
4. Brenner, MS# B-715, 13; 5th Infantry Regiment Unit Journal.
5. 71st Infantry Division, G-3 Journal, 2 April 1945, Entry 215, National Archives RG 407, Box 11398; Brant Scrapbook, 27. The original message is taped inside the scrapbook.
6. Ibid., 27. Brant's actual handwritten operations order of the attack on 3 April is attached to the page.
7. 71st Infantry Division, G-3 Journal, 3 April 1945, Entry 4, National Archives RG 407, Entry 427, Box 11398.

8. Ibid., Entries 5, 7; 5th Infantry Regiment S-1 Journal, 3 April 1945, Entry 2, National Archives RG 407, Entry 427, Box 11411 (hereafter 5th Infantry Regiment Box 11411, 3 April 1945).
9. 71st Infantry Division, G-3 Journal, 3 April 1945, Entries 13, 20, 22, 24, 25, 27; Lambert and Layton, *The Ghosts of Patton's Third Army*, 280.
10. 71st Infantry Division, G-3 Journal, 3 April 1945, Entries 11, 16, 18.
11. 2nd Infantry Regiment, Operations for Period 021800A APR 45 to 031800A APR 45, 3 April, National Archives RG 407, Entry 427, Box 6872; 2nd Infantry Regiment After-Action Report, 2 May 1945, 3–4, National Archives RG 407, Entry 427, Box 6664.
12. 2nd Infantry Regimental Unit Journal, 1 January 1945–31 December 1945, Entry for 3 April 1945, National Archives RG 407, Entry 427, Box 6866.
13. Ponder, unpublished and untitled, 96–98.
14. Ibid., 266.
15. Ibid., 252–253; Denno, letter to the author, 19 February 1995.
16. McMahon, *The Siegfried and Beyond*, 252–253.
17. Ibid., 266–268.
18. Brant Scrapbook, 27 and 28; 14th Infantry Regiment S-1 Journal, 3 April 1945, Entry 8, National Archives RG 407, Entry 427, Box 11411 (hereafter 14th Infantry Regiment S-1 Journal, 3 April 1945).
19. Brant Scrapbook, 27 and 28.
20. 5th Infantry Regiment Unit Journal; 71st Infantry Division, G-3 Journal, 3 April 1945, Entry 40; McMahon, *The Siegfried and Beyond*, 271.
21. Joy, *Sixty Days in Combat*, 170–171; 5th Infantry Regiment Unit Journal.
22. 5th Infantry Regiment Unit Journal; 71st Infantry Division, G-3 Journal, 3 April 1945, Entry 36.
23. 5th Infantry Regiment Unit Journal; 71st Infantry Division, G-3 Journal, 3 April 1945, Entry 36.
24. 5th Infantry Regiment Unit Journal; 71st Infantry Division, G-3 Journal, 3 April 1945, Entries 31, 40.
25. 5th Infantry Regiment Unit Journal; 71st Infantry Division, G-3 Journal, 3 April 1945, Entry 34.
26. Written account of Georg Stöwe's wartime experiences (n.d.) (trans. Jochen Seeliger); Stöwe, interview, 4 October 1997.
27. Brenner, MS# B-715, 13.
28. Joy, *Sixty Days in Combat*, 170–171.
29. Written account of Georg Stöwe's wartime experiences (n.d.) (trans. Jochen Seeliger); Stöwe, interview, 4 October 1997; Joy, *Sixty Days in Combat*, 171–172; Edinger, "Diary," entry for 3 April 1945; Schreiber, *Kampf Unter Dem Nordlicht*, 372.

30. Joy, *Sixty Days in Combat*, 172.
31. Written account of Georg Stöwe's wartime experiences (n.d.) (trans. Jochen Seeliger); Stöwe, interview, 4 October 1997.
32. Brenner, MS# B-715, 13.
33. Written account of Georg Stöwe's wartime experiences (n.d.) (trans. Jochen Seeliger); Stöwe, interview, 4 October 1997.
34. Joy, *Sixty Days in Combat*, 172; Platz, letter to the author, 28 August 2001.
35. Joy, *Sixty Days in Combat*, 172.
36. Ibid., 172–173; 5th Infantry Regiment Unit Journal.
37. Joy, *Sixty Days in Combat*, 173.
38. Ibid., 174; 5th Infantry Regiment Unit Journal; 14th Infantry Regiment S-1 Journal, 3 April 1945, Entry 19.
39. Brant Scrapbook, 28; 14th Infantry Regiment Unit Report No. 21, 3 April 1945, National Archives RG 407, Entry 427, Box 11412.
40. Brant Scrapbook, 28; 5th Cavalry Reconnaissance Troop in Combat Unit Diary, entry for 3 April 1945.
41. Brant Scrapbook, 28. The actual teletype message received by Brant's command post is attached to page 28 of the scrapbook. Also 14th Infantry Regiment S-1 Journal, 3 April 1945, Entry 19; Sims, "Blue Mike," 104.
42. Joy, *Sixty Days in Combat*, 175–181.
43. 71st Infantry Division, G-3 Journal, 3 April 1945, Entries 75, 1 (second set of Entries from Büdingen command post location); 5th Infantry Regiment Unit Journal.
44. 71st Infantry Division, G-3 Journal, 3 April 1945, Entries 73, 2, 18 (last two from second set of Entries in Büdingen); Lambert and Layton, *The Ghosts of Patton's Third Army*, 280.
45. 71st Infantry Division, G-3 Journal, 3 April 1945, Entry 5 (second set of Entries from Büdingen); 5th Infantry Regiment Unit Journal.
46. Ibid.; S-3 Journal, 66th Infantry Regiment, 3 April 1945, Entry 3, National Archives RG 407, Entry 427, Box 11415.
47. 71st Infantry Division, G-3 Journal, 3 April 1945, Entries 2, 5 (second set of Entries from Büdingen); 5th Infantry Regiment Unit Journal; McMahon, *The Siegfried and Beyond*, 275.
48. Ponder, unpublished and untitled, 98.
49. Sims, "Blue Mike," 105–106.
50. Ponder, unpublished and untitled, 98–100; Lewington S. Ponder, letter to the author, 18 April 1995.
51. Ichelson, "I Was There," 126.
52. Ibid., 128. Entry for 3 April 1945 from the combat diary of 1/Lt. (Dr.) James M. Paul sent to the author with an accompanying letter from Paul on 25 April 1995. Paul and

his men later discovered the two dead SS men on the road leading out of Büdingen. On searching the dead men's belongings, one of Paul's men found a package of American Swift brand bacon.

53. Ichelson, "I Was There," 128.
54. Ibid., 128–129; 1/Lt. (Dr.) James M. Paul, combat diary, entry for 3 April 1945 sent to the author with accompanying letter from Paul, 25 April 1995.
55. Ichelson, "I Was There," 129.
56. Brant Scrapbook, 29; 14th Infantry Regiment Situation Report No. 15, 31400B April 1945, National Archives RG 407, Entry 427, Box 11412.
57. 14th Infantry Regiment S-1 Journal, 3 April 1945, Entry 27; 14th Infantry Regiment Unit Report Number 21, 3 April 1945, National Archives RG 407, Entry 427, Box 11412; 14th Infantry Regiment S-1 Journal, 3 April 1945, Entries 13, 14.
58. 14th Infantry Regiment S-1 Journal, 3 April 1945, Entries 21, 29, 30.
59. Ibid., Entry 18; Brant Scrapbook, 29.
60. Brant Scrapbook, 29.
61. 71st Infantry Division, G-3 Journal, 3 April 1945, Entry 50; Clinger et al., *The History of the 71st Infantry Division*, 57; History of the Fifth United States Infantry, 48; 71st Infantry Division G-2 Periodic Report No. 21, 3 April 1945, Annex B; 14th Infantry Regiment Unit Report No. 21, 3 April 1945, National Archives RG 407, Entry 427, Box 11412; 66th Infantry Regiment S-3 Periodic Report, 3 April 1945, National Archives RG 407, Entry 427, Box 11415.
62. 71st Infantry Division, G-3 Journal, 3 April 1945, Entries 22, 36, 43 (second set of entries from Büdingen).
63. Ibid., Entries 38, 39; 71st Infantry Division Operations Instruction Number 7, 3 April 1945, National Archives RG 407, Entry 427, Box 11399; 66th Infantry Regiment Operations Instruction No. 9, 3 April 1945, National Archives RG 407, Entry 427, Box 11415. In a letter to the author from Col. (Ret.) Irving Heymont, the former regimental S-3 of the 5th Infantry Regiment, 30 August 1994, explained that Eddy's order also resulted in the detention of many German policemen, firemen, and railroad workers who all wore uniforms the GIs could not identify or distinguish from a German soldier's uniform or, for that matter, from a Waffen-SS soldier's uniform.
64. Brant Scrapbook, 24 (the actual leaflet is included in the scrapbook).
65. 71st Infantry Division, G-3 Journal, 3 April 1945, Entries 16, 23 (second set of entries from Büdingen).
66. 71st Infantry Division, G-3 Periodic Report, 30800-40800 April 1945, 4 April 1945, National Archives RG 407, Entry 427, Box 11397; *Third U.S. Army Report of Operations*, 3 April, 340; Action Against Enemy, Reports After / After Action Reports, 635th Tank Destroyer Battalion, dated 6 May 1945, Appendix No. 1, entry for 3 April 1945.

67. 71st Infantry Division Operations Instruction Number 7, 3 April 1945, National Archives RG 407, Entry 427, Box 11399.
68. 5th Infantry Division, G-3 Journal, 3 April 1945, 3, National Archives RG 407, Entry 427, Box 6810; The transcribed text for the conversation between Eddy and Irwin appears verbatim in the entry for the time 1940; Headquarters, 2nd Infantry Regiment, After Action Report, 2 May 1945, 4, National Archives RG 407, Entry 427, Box 6664; 2nd Infantry Regiment Regimental Unit Journal, 1 January 1945–31 December 1945, Entry for 3 April 1945, National Archives RG 407, Entry 427, Box 6866.
69. AAR March 1945, 3.
70. 2nd Infantry Regiment Regimental Unit Journal, 1 January 1945–31 December 1945, Entry for 3 April 1945, National Archives RG 407, Entry 427, Box 6866.
71. 5th Infantry Division, G-3 Journal, 4 April 1945, Entry for 0855.

Chapter 10. Completing the Record

1. 5th Infantry Division, G-3 Journal, 4 April 1945, 1, National Archives RG 407, Entry 427, Box 6810.
2. Dyer, *XII Corps*, 398; Third Army AAR, Vol. I, The Operations, 340–341; 5th Infantry Division, G-3 Journal, 4 April 1945, 1, National Archives RG 407, Entry 427, Box 6810.
3. Patton Jr., *War As I Knew It*, 268–269; Third Army AAR, Vol. I, The Operations, pp. 340–341; MacDonald, *The Last Offensive*, 379.
4. *London Times*, 4 April 1945; page and volume number are unavailable since I quoted this article from a photocopy of the page provided to me by Mack C. O'Quinn Jr.
5. Clinger et al., *The History of the 71st Infantry Division*, 96–97, 231–232, and passim; MacDonald, *The Last Offensive*, 379; McMahon, *The Siegfried and Beyond*, 441, 485; Historical Data on Ground Divisions, 2. Rendulic later revealed that German intelligence had thought the 71st Division to be motorized because the Red Circle men moved so rapidly from one location to another.
6. Clinger et al., *The History of the 71st Infantry Division*, 92–93; McMahon, *The Siegfried and Beyond*, 469–475.
7. Hirshson, *General Patton*, 630; Dyer, *XII Corps*, frontispiece.
8. Clinger et al., *The History of the 71st Infantry Division*, 58; "Destruction of 6th SS Hailed by Gen. Eddy," *Red Circle News*, Vol. 1, No. 1, Saturday, 28 July 1945, 5; Eddy held a press conference on returning to the U.S. in which he singled out the 71st Division for its successful operation against the 6th SS-Gebirgs Division.
9. Headquarters, 71st Infantry Division, General Orders Number 20, 9 May 1945.

10. Stanton, *World War II Order of Battle*, 141–142; "Fact Sheet on the 71st Infantry Division," 1 March 1947; *Red Circle News*, Vol. 7, No. 1, Spring 1993, p. 4; "Gen. Wyman Leaves 71st for U.S.," *The Right of the Line*, Vol. 1, No. 7, 18 August 1945.
11. *Red Circle News*, Vol. 7, No. 1, Spring 1993, 4; *71st Infantry Division: The Red Circle Division*, 87; Maj. Gen. (Ret.) Albert H. Smith Jr., letter to the author, 25 May 2003.
12. *Red Circle News*, Vol. 18, No. 1. January 2004, 18.
13. Clinger et al., *The History of the 71st Infantry Division*, 9; Maj. Irving Heymont, letter to Mrs. Joan Heymont, 5 April 1945. Colonel (Ret.) Heymont provided the author with a copy of the V-Mail letter in a letter dated 9 November 1994.
14. Col. (Ret.) Irving Heymont, interview with the author, 30 July 2003; *71st Infantry Division: The Red Circle Division*, 68.
15. Telephone conversation with Gerald F. McMahon on 8 December 2005; Register of Graduates and Former Cadets, United States Military Academy, West Point, New York, 1995, Class of 1895 Centennial Edition, 258; Charles F. Platz, *The Stories of the Men of H Company, 2nd Battalion, 5th Infantry Regiment, 71st Infantry Division, 1944–1945, United States–France–Germany–Austria* (privately published), 276–278.
16. Ponder, letter to the author, 14 April 1995.
17. Author's interviews with David L. Ichelson (M.D.) August 2001, September 2004; David L. Ichelson (M.D.), letter to the author, 1 May 1995; James M. Paul (M.D.), letter to the author, 25 April 1995; *71st Infantry Division: The Red Circle Division*, 69.
18. Dean P. Joy, telephone conversation, 24 September 2005.
19. Register of Graduates and Former Cadets, United States Military Academy, West Point, New York, 1995, Class of 1895 Centennial Edition, 218.
20. Col. Carl E. Lundquist, letter to Mrs. Warren Middleton, 28 May 1948 (copy provided to the author by Reno's daughter, R. Brigitt Reno Caito).
21. Register of Graduates and Former Cadets, United States Military Academy, West Point, New York, 1995, Class of 1895 Centennial Edition, 218.
22. *Right of the Line*, Vol. 1, No. 4, 28 July 1945.
23. 71st Infantry Division, General Orders Number 15, 28 April 1945.
24. Register of Graduates and Former Cadets, United States Military Academy, West Point, New York, 1995, Class of 1895 Centennial Edition, 264. Additional information provided by Philip D. Brant Jr.
25. Several interviews of author with Philip D. Brant Jr.; Brant Scrapbook, frontispiece.
26. Alvey, letter to the author, 25 February 1995; W. P. Sims, letter to the author, 29 December 2005.
27. Sims, interview, 25 August 2001; Edward G. Rimple, letter to the author, 9 April 1995; William L. Asay, letter to the author, 18 April 1995; Sims, letter to the author, 29 December 2005.

28. Sims, interview, 25 August 2001.
29. C. R. M. Sheppard, letter to Gerald F. McMahon, 29 August 1992; register of Graduates and Former Cadets, United States Military Academy, West Point, New York, 1995, Class of 1895 Centennial Edition, 208.
30. Denno, letter to the author, 19 February 1995; Historical Data on Ground Divisions, 4.
31. Long, letter to the author, 4 May 1995; *71st Infantry Division: The Red Circle Division*, 72.
32. Thomas C. Tomich, letter to the author, 13 April 1995.
33. Col. (Ret.) Edward W. Samuell Jr., letter to the author, 27 February 1995; *71st Infantry Division: The Red Circle Division*, 81.
34. Multiple interviews by author with Mason "Mickey" Dorsey in September 2004; *71st Infantry Division: The Red Circle Division*, 62.
35. *71st Infantry Division: The Red Circle Division*, 88–89.
36. "Paul Bates, Head of Black Tank Unit, Dead at 86," *New York Times*, Obituary, 25 February 1995; Abdul-Jabbar and Walton, *Brothers in Arms*, 29, 53–58.
37. Hirshson, *General Patton*, 630; Arlington National Cemetery Web Site, http://www.arlingtoncemetery.net/slirwin.htm.
38. Brig. Gen. (Ret.) Robert E. Connor, letter to the author, 2 February 1996.
39. Robinson, letter to the author, 24 January 1996; Robinson enclosed in his letter a photocopy of a wartime newspaper article that outlined the details of his rescue mission, but the name of the newspaper or its exact date were not indicated; 5th Cavalry Reconnaissance Troop in Combat Daily Journal, Entry for 29 March 1945; *Diamond Dust*, Vol. IX, No. 31, 31 March 1945, 2.
40. Lucas, *Hitler's Mountain Troops*, 170–172; Bender and Taylor, *Uniforms, Organization, and History of the Waffen-SS*, Vol. 3, 8–16; Jochen Seeliger, letter to the author, 7 February 2006; Brenner, MS# B-715, 1–3.
41. Lucas, *Hitler's Mountain Troops*, 170–172; Samuel W. Mitcham Jr., *Hitler's Legions: The German Army Order of Battle, World War II* (New York: Stein and Day, 1985), 471.
42. Schreiber, *Kampf Unter Dem Nordlicht*, 364, 372–374, 385; Mitcham, *Hitler's Legions*, 269. The other five Knight's Cross recipients were Gottlieb Renz, Friedrich-Wilhelm Krüger, Günther Degen, Franz Schreiber, and Karl Brenner.
43. Schneider, *Verleihung Genehmigt*, 44; SS personnel file, Brenner.
44. SS personnel file, Raithel; Alfred Steurich, *Nord-Ruf,* Obituary for Helmuth Raithel, Brief Nr. 35, 9. Jahrgang, December 1990; Seeliger, interview, 25 January 1997.
45. Schreiber, *Kampf Unter Dem Nordlicht*, 435–437; Seeliger, letter to the author, 7 February 2006.
46. Schreiber, *Kampf Unter Dem Nordlicht*, 435–437; Zoepf, *Seven Days in January*, 44; Seeliger, letter to the author, 7 February 2006.

47. *Nord-Ruf,* Brief Nr. 35, 9. Jahrgang, December 1990, 13; Seeliger, letter to the author, 7 February 2006.
48. Zoepf, *Seven Days in January,* 276.
49. Krüger, interview, 25 September 1999; Krüger, letter to Long; Jochen Seeliger, email, 24 July 2003.
50. Written account of Georg Stöwe's wartime experiences (n.d.) (trans. Jochen Seeliger); Stöwe, interview, 4 October 1997.
51. Becker, "Decline and Fall of the 6. SS-Mount. Div. Nord"; Seeliger, letter to the author, 7 February 2006.
52. Eberhard Hilger, letter to the author, 30 June 2000; Eberhard Hilger, telephone conversation, June 2000; Jochen Seeliger, letter to the author, 23 March 2000; Seeliger, letter to the author, 7 February 2006.
53. Karl Müller, letter to Jochen Seeliger, 12 January 2003.
54. Jochen Seeliger, letter to the author, 13 August 1995.
55. Jochen Seeliger, email, 4 January 2006; multiple interviews by author with Jochen Seeliger in the mid-to late 1990s.
56. Kaltenschnee, "How the War in Its Final Stages Still Became Fatal," 1.
57. Ibid., 6.
58. Ibid., 1; Kaltenschnee, "How the War in Its Final Stages Still Became Fatal," 6.
59. Ibid., 1.
60. Kress, "Easter 1945," 33. Jende's unpublished account was part of a local Gelnhausen historian's compilation of events in the area during the war; "300 Jahre Waldensberg, 1699–1999: Geschichte Gegenwart," Druckerei Leis GmbH, Spielberg, 1999, 67.
61. This account was part of the same local Gelnhausen historian's compilation of events mentioned in note 60.
62. *Förster* Leo's account was part of the same compilation of events mentioned in note 60.
63. Kress, "Easter 1945," 33.
64. Frau Schmidt's account was part of the same compilation mentioned in note 60.
65. Kress, "Easter 1945," 33; "300 Jahre Waldensberg," 67–70.
66. Herr Brückner's account was part of the same compilation mentioned in note 60.
67. Ibid.; Kaltenschnee, "How the War in Its Final Stages Still Became Fatal," 6.
68. Ibid., 6.
69. This account was part of the same compilation of events mentioned in note 60; Kaltenschnee, "How the War in Its Final Stages Still Became Fatal," 6.
70. See note 66.
71. Jochen Seeliger, letter to the author, 23 August 1995.
72. Jochen Seeliger, letters to the author, 23 August 1995, 13 September 1995; *Die Träger des Ritterkreuzes des Eisernen Kreuzes 1939–1945,* http://www.das-ritterkreuz.de/, accessed on 4 January 2006; memorandum from the *Traditionsverband der ehem. 6. SS-Gebirgsdivision* Nord *e.V.,* 19 March 1997.

73. Seeliger, letter to the author, 23 August 1995.
74. "Todesursache Kopfschuss," *Deutsche Wochenzeitung*, September 1962, trans. Jochen Seeliger.

Appendix A. Table of Comparative Ranks

1. Andrew Mollo, *The Armed Forces of World War II* (New York: Military Press, 1987), 239; Danny S. Parker, *Battle of the Bulge: Hitler's Ardennes Offensive, 1944–1945* (Philadelphia: Combined Books, 1991), 315.
2. *Reichsführer SS* is not really an equivalent grade for a German field marshal. Heinrich Himmler was the only member of the Third Reich to hold this rank, which was a political appointment. Toward the end of the war, Hitler gave Himmler a field command, which arguably made the rank of *Reichsführer SS* into a military grade equivalent to a field marshal.
3. Indicates number of stars.
4. These three ranks have equivalent technician grades indicated by a "T" beneath the chevrons. Soldiers holding these grades had no command authority. These ranks have no German equivalents.
5. The Germans have varying grades of privates and corporals. The grades indicated are the most common, but the Germans also had different grades based on time in service. In addition, the basic private grade depends on the soldier's branch of service. The example shown is for a basic infantry private, a *Schütze*. Other possibilities include *Grenadier* for a *Panzergrenadier* (mechanized infantry), *Kanonier* for an artilleryman, and so on.

Appendix B. Glossary of Terms and Equipment

1. The primary sources for this information are Angolia and Schlicht (*Uniforms and Traditions of the German Army*, Vol. 3, 1987), Forty (*U.S. Army Handbook*, 1995), and Hogg and Weeks (*Military Small Arms of the 20th Century*, 1985).

Appendix C. Select Order of Battle

1. Principal sources for these data are 71st Infantry Division After-Action Reports and unit rosters, Stanton (*World War II Order of Battle*, 1991), Bender and Taylor (*Uniforms, Organization, and History of the Waffen-SS*, 1986), Zoepf (*Seven Days in January*, 2001), Moore's *Führerliste*, testimony from surviving veterans, and so on.

Selected Bibliography

Books

1st Battle Group, 5th Infantry. *History of the Fifth United States Infantry*, 2nd ed., n.p., June 1962.
Abdul-Jabbar, Kareem, and Anthony Walton. *Brothers in Arms: The Epic Story of the 761st Tank Battalion, WWII's Forgotten Heroes*. New York: Broadway Books, 2004.
Adam, Werner. *Leben und Überleben: Erinnerungen eines Kriegsfreiwilligen*. Germany: Books on Demand GmbH, 2000.
Allen, Col. Robert S. *Lucky Forward: The History of General George Patton's Third U.S. Army*. New York: McFadden Books, 1965.
Angolia, John R. (Lt. Col., Ret.). *On the Field of Honor: A History of the Knight's Cross Bearers*, Vol. 1. San Jose, CA: R. James Bender Publishing Company, 1979.
———. *Uniforms and Traditions of the German Army, 1933–1945*, Vol. 2. San Jose, CA: R. James Bender Publishing Company, 1986.
Angolia, John R. (Lt. Col., Ret.), and Adolf Schlicht. *Uniforms and Traditions of the German Army, 1933–1945*, Vol. 3. San Jose, CA: R. James Bender Publishing Company, 1987.
Arnold, Edmund C. *The Trailblazers: The Story of the 70th Infantry Division*. Richmond. VA: 70th Infantry Division Association, 1989.
Atkinson, Rick. *An Army at Dawn: The War in North Africa, 1942–1943*. New York: Henry Holt and Company, 2002.
Baron, Richard, Maj. Abe Baum, and Richard Goldhurst. *Raid: The Untold Story of Patton's Secret Mission*. New York: Berkley, March 1984.
Bass, Michael A. *The Story of the Century*. New York: Century Association, 100th Infantry Division, 1946.
Bellanger, Yves J. *U.S. Army Infantry Divisions 1943–45*, Vol. 1—*Organization, Doctrine and Equipment*. West Midlands, UK: Helion and Company, 2002.
Bender, Roger James, and Hugh Page Taylor. *Uniforms, Organization, and History of the Waffen-SS*, Vol. 1. San Jose, CA: R. James Bender Publishing Company, 1969.

_____. *Uniforms, Organization,* and *History of the* Waffen-SS, Vol. 2. San Jose, CA: R. James Bender Publishing Company, 1986.

_____. *Uniforms, Organization, and History of the* Waffen-SS, Vol. 3. San Jose, CA: R. James Bender Publishing Company, 1986.

Bishop, Lt. Col. Leo V. *The Fighting Forty-Fifth: The Combat Report of an Infantry Division.* Baton Rouge, LA: Army and Navy Publishing Company, 1946.

Bonn, Keith E. *When the Odds Were Even.* Novato, CA: Presidio Press, 1994.

_____. *With Fire and Zeal: The 276th Infantry Regiment in World War II.* Hampton, VA: Aegis Consulting Group, 1998.

Byrnes, Lieutenant Laurence G., ed. *History of the 94th Infantry Division in World War II.* Washington, DC: Infantry Journal Press, 1948.

Clinger, Fred, Arthur Johnston, and Vincent Masel. *The History of the 71st Infantry Division.* Augsburg, Germany: 71st Division Public Relations Office, 1946.

Condon, Carl. *The 635th Tank Destroyer Battalion in Europe in World War II.* Museum of the Kansas National Guard, accessed 10 January 2001, at http://skyways.lib.ks.us/museums/kng/635TDB.html.

Diamond, Major Maynard L,. et al. *The 89th Infantry Division 1942–1945.* Washington, DC: Infantry Journal Press, 1947.

Fifth Division Historical Section. *The Fifth Infantry Division in the ETO.* Nashville, TN: Battery Press, 1981 (originally published 1945).

Foley, William A., Jr. *Visions from a Foxhole: A Rifleman in Patton's Ghost Corps.* New York: Presidio Press / Ballantine Books, 2003.

Forty, George. *U.S. Army Handbook 1939–1945.* Gloucestershire, UK: Alan Sutton Publishing, 1995.

Greenfield, Kent Roberts, Robert R. Palmer, and Bell I. Wiley. *The Organization of Ground Combat Troops.* Washington, DC: Department of the Army, Historical Division, 1947.

Hirshson, Stanley P. *General Patton: A Soldier's Life.* New York: Harper Collins Publishers, 2002.

Hogg, Ian V. Introduction. In *German Order of Battle 1944.* London: Greenhill Book, 1994.

Hogg, Ian V., and John Weeks. *Military Small Arms of the 20th Century.* Northfield, IL: DBI Books, 1985.

Höhne, Heinz. *The Order of the Death's Head: The Story of Hitler's S.S.* New York: Ballantine Books, 1986.

Johnson, Aaron L. *Hitler's Military Headquarters: Organization, Structures, Security, and Personnel.* San Jose, CA: R. James Bender Publishing Company, 1999.

Joy, Dean P. *Sixty Days in Combat: An Infantryman's Memoir of World War II in Europe.* New York: Ballantine Books / Presidio Press, 2004.

Kaltenegger, Roland. *Mountain Troops of the Waffen-SS, 1941–1945.* Atglen, PA: Schiffer Publishing, 1995.

Kinnard, Douglas. *From the Paterson Station: The Way We Were.* Bloomington, IN: Xlibris Corporation, 2000.

Koyen, Capt. Kenneth A. *The Fourth Armored Division: From the Beach to Bavaria.* Munich, Germany: Herder Druck, 1946.

Lambert, Maj. A. L., and Capt. G. B. Layton. *The Ghosts of Patton's Third Army: A History of the Second U.S. Cavalry.* Munich, Germany: Kunstanstalten GmbH (Bisher F. Bruckmann), n.d.

Lucas, James. *Hitler's Mountain Troops: Fighting at the Extremes.* London: Cassell Military Classics, 1999.

MacDonald, Charles B. *The Last Offensive.* Washington, DC: Department of the Army, Chief of Military History, 1984.

McMahon, Gerald F. *Farthest East: A History of the 71st Infantry Division—From the Rocky Mountains to the Central Alps.* LeRoy, NY: Yaderman Books, 1986.

_____. *Riding Point for Patton: The Combat Trail of the 5th Infantry, 71st Division, XX Corps, Third Army in the European Theater during World War II.* LeRoy, NY: Yaderman Books, 1987.

_____. *The Siegfried and Beyond.* Cleveland, OH: The 71st Infantry Division Association, n.d.

Mitcham, Samuel W., Jr. *Hitler's Legions: The German Army Order of Battle, World War II.* New York: Stein and Day, 1985.

Mollo, Andrew. *The Armed Forces of World War II.* New York: Military Press, 1987.

Parker, Danny S. *Battle of the Bulge: Hitler's Ardennes Offensive, 1944–1945.* Philadelphia: Combined Books, 1991.

Patton, General George S., Jr. *War As I Knew It.* New York: Bantam Books, 1981.

Prefer, Nathan N. *Patton's Ghost Corps: Cracking the Siegfried Line.* Novato, CA: Presidio Press, 1998.

Province, Charles M. *Patton's Third Army: A Chronology of the Third Army Advance, August, 1944 to May 1945.* New York: Hippocrene Books, 1992.

Rusiecki, Stephen M. *The Key to the Bulge: The Battle for Losheimergraben.* Westport, CT: Praeger Publishers, 1996.

Sasser, Charles W. *Patton's Panther: The African-American 761st Tank Battalion in World War II.* New York: Pocket Books, 2004.

Schneider, Jost W. *Verleihung Genehmigt: Their Honor Was Loyalty! Eine Bild- und Dokumentargeschichte der Ritterkreuzträger der Waffen-SS und Polizei 1940–1945.* San Jose, CA: R. James Bender Publishing, 1977.

Schreiber, Franz. 1969. *Kampf Unter Dem Nordlicht: Die Geschichte der 6. SS-Gebirgs-Division Nord.* Osnabrück, Germany: Munin Verlag GMBH.

Stanton, Shelby L. *World War II Order of Battle.* New York: Galahad Books, 1991.

Surmondt, Jan. *Tanks & Armoured Vehicles of WWII.* Cobham, Surrey, UK: TAJ Books, 2004.

Thömmes, Matthias. *"Die Amis kommen!" Die Eroberung des Saar-Hunsrück-Raumes durch die Amerikaner 1944/45.* Aachen, Germany: Helios, 2001.

Toland, John. *Adolf Hitler.* Vol. I. New York: Doubleday and Company, 1976.

Turner, John Frayn, and Robert Jackson. *Destination Berchtesgaden: Saga of the US 7th Army.* New York: Charles Scribner's Sons, 1975.

Whiting, Charles. *The Other Battle of the Bulge.* Chelsea, MI: Scarborough House, 1990.

Williams, Dayna Spear, ed. *71st Infantry Division: The Red Circle Division.* Paducah, KY: Turner Publishing Company, 2001.

Williams, Mary H. (compiler). *Chronology 1941–1945.* Washington, DC: Department of the Army, Chief of Military History, 1960.

Zoepf, Wolf. *Seven Days in January: With the 6th SS-Mountain Division in Operation Nordwind.* Bedford, PA: Aberjona Press, 2001.

Unpublished or Privately Published Manuscripts and Monographs

70th Infantry Division History at http://www.trailblazersww2.org/division_history.htm.

"300 Jahre Waldensberg, 1699–1999: Geschichte Gegenwart." Druckerei Leis GmbH, Spielberg, 1999. Privately published.

"Abwehrkampf im Rhein-Mosel-Dreieck, März 1945," 50th Anniversary Memorial Publication published by the Traditionsverband der ehem. 6. SS-Geb. Div. Nord e.V.

Becker, Walter. "Decline and Fall of the 6. SS-Mount. Div. Nord as I Have Seen It." Unpublished monograph.

Brant, Lt. Col. Philip D. Scrapbook of the 2nd Battalion, 14th Infantry. While performing occupation duty in Neu Ulm immediately after the cessation of hostilities in Germany in 1945, Lieutenant Colonel Brant wrote and compiled a scrapbook of his battalion's combat exploits. In addition to Lieutenant Colonel Brant's handwritten narrative, the scrapbook contains hand-drawn maps, copies of operations orders, map overlays, portions of original combat maps, message traffic, and photographs. Lieutenant Colonel Brant dated the scrapbook October 1945.

Cheves, Wallace R., Lt. Colonel, Infantry, ed. *Snow Ridges and Pillboxes: A True History of the 274th Infantry Regiment of the 70th Division in World War II, 1946.* Privately published.

Dyer, Lt. Col. George *XII Corps: Spearhead of Patton's Third Army,* The XII Corps History Association, 1947. Privately published.

Heymont, Irving. "As I Remember . . . ," 2nd ed., 1992. Privately published.

Ichelson, David L., M.D., "I Was There." Unpublished manuscript.

McMahon, Gerald F. Introduction to "Anti-Tank: The Combat Service of the 635th TD Battalion, 14 March–11 May 1945," n.d. Privately published.

_____. "On Guard: The Fourteenth Infantry Regiment in Bavaria 1945–6," n.d. Privately published.

Platz, Charles F. "The Stories of the Men of H Company, 2nd Battalion, 5th Infantry Regiment, 71st Infantry Division, 1944-1945, United States—France—Germany—Austria," n.d. Privately published.

Ponder, Lewington. Unpublished Personal Accounts of World War II, n.d. Untitled.

Rafferty, Major Thomas A. "Operations of the 2nd Battalion, 5th Infantry (71st Infantry Division) in the Attack on Germersheim, Germany, 24 March 1945 (Central Europe Campaign)" (Personal Experience of a Battalion S3). Unpublished monograph (Advanced Infantry Officers Course, 1949–1950). U.S. Army Infantry School, Fort Benning, GA, n.d.

Samuell, Edward W., Jr., Col. (Ret.). "History of the 1st Platoon, 71st Cavalry Reconnaissance Troop, Chapter III, Operations in Hessen," n.d. Unpublished.

Second Infantry Regiment, Fifth Infantry Division Baton Rouge, LA: Army and Navy Publishing Company, 1946. (Privately published. Author located a copy in the National Archives, Records Group 407, Entry 427, Box 6863.)

Seeliger, Dr. Jochen. "Legion of the North: A Waffen-SS Soldier in World War II," n.d. Unpublished manuscript.

Sims, W. P. "Blue Mike: The Story of Company M, 14th Infantry in World War II," n.d. Privately published.

Sitz, Sergeant Donald H. *History of Company "C", Fifth Infantry, World War II*, n.d. Privately published.

Tomich, Thomas C., "GI's [sic] Forever," n.d. Privately published.

Magazines, Newspapers, and Similar Publications

"5th Infantry Spends Day on MT Program Tests." *The Shield*, Fifth Regiment United States Infantry, Vol. II, no. 11 (20 October 1944).

"14th Officer Gets Third DSC Awarded 71st." *Right of the Line*, 14th Infantry Regimental Newsletter, Vol. 1, no. 4 (28 July 1945).

"Biography of General Willard Gordon Wyman." *The Red Circle News,* 7, no. 1 (Spring 1993), 3–4.

"History of the Cemetery Weiherhof near Wittgenborn, 1945–1962." *Sammlung Geschichte Wächtersbach* (January 1999), 6. This article is a printed version of a lecture given by an unknown speaker.

Kaltenschnee, Johannes. "How the War in Its Final Stages Still Became Fatal for the Inhabitants of Leisenwald and Waldensberg." *Sammlung Geschichte Wächtersbach* (August 2001). (This article is part of a chronicle of the Leisenwald school written between 1950 and 1965; trans. Dr. Jochen Seeliger.)

Kress, *Landrat* Heinrich. "Easter 1945: Waldensberg Razed to the Ground." *Zwischen Vogelsberg und Spessart, Heimatjahrbuch des Kreises Gelnhausen* (1964; trans. Dr. Jochen Seeliger).
Moore, John P. *Führerliste der Waffen-SS*. Accessed 2 February 2008 from http://www.geocities.com/~orion47/JohnMoore.html.
Register of Graduates and Former Cadets. United States Military Academy, West Point, New York, 1995, Class of 1895 Centennial Edition.
Sorley, Lewis. "Personality: Creighton Abrams and Harold Cohen Forged a Lasting Friendship as Comrades during the March Across Europe." *World War II Magazine* 11, no. 4 (November 1996), 68–72.
Steurich, Alfred. *Zum Gedenken SS-Standartenführer a. D. Helmuth Raithel, Nordruf:* Traditionsverband 6. Geb. Div. Nord Ehem. Waffen-SS e.V., Brief Nr. 35, 9. Jahrgang (Dezember 1990; trans. Dr. Jochen Seeliger), 5–9.
Whitlock, Flint. "The Battle for Easy Red & Fox Green." *WWII History D-Day!* 60th Anniversary Special Issue 1, no. 1 (Summer 2004), 46–55.
Vannoy, Allyn. "Into the Maelstrom." *World War II Magazine*, 19, no. 2 (May 2004), 35–40, 77–80.

After Action and Official Reports

2nd Infantry Regiment Unit Journal, 31 March 1945, National Archives, Records Group 407, Entry 427, Box 6872.
2nd Infantry Regiment Unit Journal, 1 to 4 April 1945, National Archives, Records Group 407, Entry 427, Boxes 6866 and 6872.
2nd Infantry Regimental Unit Journal, 1 January 1945 to 31 December 1945 (entries for 29 March to 4 April 1945), National Archives, Records Group 407, Entry 427, Box 6866.
5th Division Record of Events, 12 July 1944–1 May 1945.
5th Infantry Regiment Unit Journal, 29 March to 4 April 1945, National Archives, Records Group 407, Entry 427, Box 11408.
5th Infantry Division Situation Report Number 163, 1 April 1945, National Archives, Records Group 407, Entry 427, Box 6810.
5th Infantry Regiment, S-3 Periodic Report Number 18, 30 March 1945, National Archives, Records Group 407, Entry 427, Box 11408.
14th Infantry Regiment Units Report Numbers 17 (30 March 1945), 19 (1 April 1945), 20 (2 April 1945), 21 (3 April 1945), and 22 (4 April 1945), National Archives, Records Group 407, Entry 427, Box 11412.
14th Infantry Regiment Operations Instructions 7 (31 March 1945), 8 (1 April 1945), 9 (1 April 1945), 11 (3 April 1945), 12 (3 April 1945), and 14 (4 April 1945), National Archives, Records Group 407, Entry 427, Box 11412.

14th Infantry Regiment Situation Reports 9 through 18 (2 April 1945 to 4 April 1945), National Archives, Records Group 407, Entry 427, Box 11412.

14th Infantry Regiment, 71st Infantry Division, Interview, Col. Carl E. Lundquist and 1/Lt. Charles W. Cookson, Engagement with 6th SS Mtn Div; Capture of Bayreuth; Final drive into Austria, 26 May 1945, National Archives, Records Group 407, Entry 427, Box 24049.

66th Infantry Regiment Operations Instructions 9 (3 April 1945) and 10 (4 April 1945), National Archives, Records Group 407, Entry 427, Box 11415.

66th Infantry Regiment S-3 Periodic Reports 16 (30 March 1945), 17 (1 April 1945), 18 (2 April 1945), 19 (3 April 1945), and 20 (4 April 1945), National Archives, Records Group 407, Entry 427, Box 11415.

66th Infantry Regiment Situation Reports Numbers 1 (31 March 1945), 7 (2 April 1945), and 8 (2 April 1945), National Archives, Records Group 407, Entry 427, Box 11415.

71st Infantry Division Record of Events, 28 January 1945–31 March 1945.

71st Infantry Division Field Orders 11 (30 March 1945) and 12 (31 March 1945), National Archives, Records Group 407, Entry 427, Box 11399.

71st Infantry Division Operations Instructions 7 (3 April 1945) and 8 (4 April 1945), National Archives, Records Group 407, Entry 427, Box 11399.

Admission and Disposition Report, Collecting Station B, 371st Medical Battalion, 3 April 1945, National Archives, Records Group 407, Entry 427, Box 11412.

After Action Against the Enemy Report, 5th Infantry Division, 2 April 1945, National Archives, Records Group 407, Entry 427, Box 24024.

After Action Against the Enemy Reports, Report for March 1945, 71st Infantry Division, 21 April 1945.

After Action Report, 2nd Infantry Regiment, 2 May 1945, National Archives, Records Group 407, Entry 427, Box 6664.

After Action Report, 5th Cavalry Reconnaissance Troop (MECZ), 9 April 1945, National Archives, Records Group 407, Entry 427, Box 6844.

After Action Report, Office of G-3, 71st Infantry Division, 10 May 1945.

After Action Report, Third U.S. Army, 1 August 1944–9 May 1945, Vol. I, The Operations.

Brenner, Karl, *General der Waffen-SS und Polizei*. MS# B-476, "The 6. SS-Mountain Division 'North' and Its Part in Operation Northwind Northern-Alsace, 1 January to 25 January 1945," March 1947.

———. MS# B-586, 6th SS Mountain Division Nord in Defense [*sic*] Engagements in North Alsace from 26 January to 1 March 1945, June 1947.

———. MS# B-693, 6th SS Mountain Division (1–19 Mar 1945), Historical Division Headquarters, United States Army, Europe.

———. MS# B-715, 6th SS Mountain Division (19 March–April 1945), Historical Division

Department of the Army Pamphlet Number 20-292, Historical Study: Warfare in the Far North, October 1951 (written by *General der Infanterie* Dr. Waldemar Erfurth while in U.S. captivity in 1947).

Dienstalterliste der Schutzstaffel der NSDAP (SS-Oberst-Gruppenführer—SS-Standartenführer), Stand vom 9. November 1944, Berlin 1944.

Dienstalterliste der Schutzstaffel der NSDAP (SS-Obersturmbannführer und SS-Sturmbannführer), Stand vom 1. Oktober 1944, Berlin 1944.

"Fact Sheet on the 71st Infantry Division." The Information Section, Analysis Branch, Headquarters, Army Ground Forces, Washington 25, D.C., 1 March 1947.

G-3 Journal, 5th Infantry Division, 31 March 1945, National Archives, Records Group 407, Entry 427, Box 6809.

G-3 Journal, 5th Infantry Division, 1 to 4 April 1945, National Archives, Records Group 407, Entry 427, Box 6810.

G-3 Journal, 71st Infantry Division, 31 March to 3 April 1945, National Archives, Records Group 407, Entry 427, Box 11398.

G-3 Periodic Reports, 71st Infantry Division, Numbers 13 through 17 (27 March to 2 April 1945) and 19 (4 April 1945), National Archives, Records Group 407, Entry 427, Box 11397.

General Orders 6 (29 March 1945) and 7 (6 April 1945), Fifth Infantry Regiment, National Archives, Records Group 407, Entry 427, Box 11408.

Historical Data on Ground Divisions, 71st Infantry Division, 18 June 1945. Author's collection.

Historical Summary, 66th Infantry Regiment, 12 April 1945, National Archives, Records Group 407, Entry 427, Box 11415.

History, 5th Infantry Regiment, March and April 1945, National Archives, Records Group 407, Entry 427, Box 11408.

History, 66th Infantry Regiment (n.d.), National Archives, Records Group 407, Entry 427, Box 11415.

History, Headquarters Company, 2nd Battalion, 66th Infantry Regiment, 71st Infantry Division (n.d.)

Hoehne, Gustave, *General der Infanterie a.D.* MS# B-584, LXXXIX Corps (18–28 Mar 1945), Historical Division Headquarters, United States Army, Europe, 17 June 1947.

Message Traffic, 5th Infantry Division, 1 April 1945 (four messages: 011045A / 6, two labeled 011435A / 12, and 011545A / 14), National Archives, Records Group 407, Entry 427, Box 6810.

Organizational History of the 71st Division Artillery 1945, Headquarters, 71st Division Artillery, 1–10 May 1945.

Headquarters, United States Army, Europe.

Seventh United States Army Report of Operations in France and Germany 1944–1945, Vols. I–III. Heidelberg, Germany: Aloys Gräf (Heidelberg Gutenberg Printing Company), May 1946.

S-1 Journal, 14th Infantry Regiment, 1 to 4 April 1945, National Archives, Records Group 407, Entry 427, Box 11411.

S-1 Journal, 66th Infantry Regiment, 30 March 1945 to 3 April 1945, National Archives, Records Group 407, Entry 427, Box 11415.

S-3 Journal, 66th Infantry Regiment, 31 March 1945 to 4 April 1945, National Archives, Records Group 407, Entry 427, Box 11415.

SS personnel files on microfilm (A3343) at the National Archives in College Park, Maryland for the following Waffen-SS officers: Brenner (Roll SSO-104), Raithel (Roll SSO-0058), Degen (Roll SSO-139), Schreiber (Roll SSO-100B), Goebel (SSO-017A), Kreuzinger (SSO-214A), and Burgstaller (Roll SSO-122).

Troop History, 5th Cavalry Reconnaissance Troop (MECZ), 5th Infantry Division, 1 July 1944 to 31 December 1945, National Archives, Records Group 407, Entry 427, Box 6844.

Unit History (First Indorsement) [*sic*], 2nd Infantry Regiment, National Archives, Records Group 407, Entry 427, Box 6863.

Unit History Report, 71st Infantry Division, 17 March 1945.

Official Government Publications

Field Manual 17-25. *Assault Gun Section and Platoon*, War Department: U.S. Government Printing Office, 8 September 1944.

Field Manual 21-11. *First Aid for Soldiers*. War Department: U.S. Government Printing Office, 7 April 1943.

Correspondence

Letters or completed questionnaires from Werner Adam, Thomas W. Alvey, Franklin C. Anderson, Henry C. Armstrong, William L. Asay, James A. Behney, Edgar Best, Fred Blahosky, Alec C. Burton, Roberta (Brigitt) Reno Caito, Col. (Ret.) J. W. Christy, Brig. Gen. (Ret.) Robert E. Connor, Olvis W. Day, Col. (Ret.) Bryce F. Denno, John E. Dier, Mason "Mickey" Dorsey, Robert Funke, Col. (Ret.) Philip Grant, John W. Guinee Jr., Col. (Ret.) Irving Heymont, Eberhard Hilger, Dr. David Ichelson, Karl R. Johnson, Dean P. Joy, Egon Krüger, Roy J. Long, Mrs. Tommy L. Long, Gerald F. McMahon, Col. (Ret.) Ray K. Mortensen, Mack C. O'Quinn Jr., Dr. James M. Paul , Charles F. Platz , Col. (Ret.) Lewington S. Ponder, Mel Posner, Joseph G. Rahie, Ed Rimple, Donald E. Robinson, Col. (Ret.) Robert C. Russell, Col. (Ret.) Edward Samuell, Dr. Jochen Seeliger, W. P. Sims, Brig. Gen. (Ret.) Frederick A. Smith. Jr., Georg Stöwe, and Thomas C. Tomich.

Interviews

Author's interviews and / or telephone conversations with Werner Adam, Fred Blahosky, Philip D. Brant Jr., Alec C. Burton, John E. Dier, Mason "Mickey" Dorsey, Earl Flanagan, Robert Funke, Col. (Ret.) Irving Heymont, Eberhard Hilger, Dr. David Ichelson, Dean P. Joy, Ira King, Brig. Gen. (Ret.) Douglas Kinnard, Egon Krüger, Mrs. Tommy L. Long, Gerald F. McMahon, Col. (Ret.) Ray K. Mortensen, Charles F. Platz, Mel Posner, L. B. Rhatican, Col. (Ret.) Edward Samuell, Dr. Jochen Seeliger, W. P. Sims, Georg Stöwe, and Johann Wagner.

Maps

Essen-Mannheim, Germany, 1st ed., Sheet 4, 1:500,000, Geographical Section, General Staff No. 4478, Published by War Office, 1944.

Joint Operations Graphic. NM 32-4 (Köln) and NM 32-5 (Frankfurt am Main), 1:250,000, Militärgeographisches Amt, 1984.

Travel Atlas, Kartographisches Institut König, Frankfurt am Main (n.d.).

Various current and wartime 1:50,000 scale maps (legend data not available).

Index

A

Abbott, Bob, 291
Abdul-Jabbar, Kareem, 336
Abrams, Creighton, 113
Adam, Werner, 18
African-American tank battalion, 89, 97, 101, 336. *See also* U.S. 761st Tank Battalion
African-Americans, German reaction to, 112–14, 247
Altenhasslau action, 103, 166
Altenstadt action, 166; American tank force in, 142–45; German demand for plasma, 151; initial contact in, 140–41; lack of division coordination in, 153; prisoners taken in, 149; sighting of Nord Division in, 144–45
Altenstadt command post, 157, 253
Alvey, Thomas W., 135–36, 147, 149, 150, 209, 249, 250, 252, 294, 303, 315, 316, 333
antipartisan warfare, 11
Ardennes Offensive, 19–20, 24
Armee Oberkommando Norwegen, 3, 4, 5, 6
Army nurses, 113–14, 153
Army Specialized Training Program (ASTP), 62

Arrington, Lowell, 147
Asay, William L., 214, 334
Ashforth, Lewis W., 273
Assenheim action: American communication in, 118; American coordination of efforts in, 128–30, 159; American reconnaissance in, 123; capture of American ordnance company and field hospital, 112–15; German assembly in, 126–27, 130–31; German strength in, 116, 120; Main River crossing prior to, 133–34

B

Bad Nauheim-Frankfurt *reichautobahn*, 109, 110, 117
Bad Orb prisoner of war compound, 166, 204
Bailey (sergeant), 305
Bangs, James E., 239
Bärenklau, Walter, 173, 176
Barstow (lieutenant), 147
Bass, Andrew J., 136, 154, 209, 249, 252, 294
Bates, Paul L., 97, 101, 133, 336
Battle of the Bulge, 19–20
Bauer, Hans, 339

Bauer, Kurt, 271
Baum, Abraham, 80
Becker, Walter, 87, 110, 173, 176, 344–45
Beeler, Donald, 65
Beer Hall *putsch,* 38
Bell, Robert P., 152
Bellanca, Mike, 178, 179
Berg, Ludwig von, 70
Berg, Sidney, 175, 177, 179, 180
Berthelot, Richard J., 220
Bielita, Josef, 271
Bindsachen action, 315
Blackford, Clifton D., 121, 160
Blakefield, William H., 224, 255, 256, 257, 288
Blaskowitz, Johannes, 25, 37, 40, 90
Bleichenbach action, 250–53
blood transfusion, 314
"Blue Mike" (Sims), 334
Boggs (captain), 313
Böhme, Franz, 7
Bönstadt action, 123–26, 135
Boone, Irving A., 148, 150
Borden (captain), 162, 189, 190, 191, 316
Bradley, Omar, 24, 51, 77, 78, 82, 90, 91, 170, 324
Brant, Philip, Jr., 333
Brant, Philip D., 82, 99, 127, 133, 134, 135, 136, 137, 140, 141, 142–45, 150, 151, 154, 155, 156–57, 182, 189, 192, 209, 215, 222, 229, 230, 242, 249, 250, 251, 252, 253, 276, 285, 286, 294, 295, 302, 303, 315, 316, 332–33
Brenner, Karl-Heinrich, 10–11, 17, 20, 21, 43, 46, 48, 52, 53, 57, 67, 68, 70, 79, 83, 84, 85, 87, 88, 93, 94, 104, 109, 116, 122, 130, 137, 155, 156, 168, 169, 172, 185, 187, 202, 218, 234, 235, 261, 266, 271, 272, 280, 284, 299, 302, 303, 304, 320, 324, 339–40
Brewer, Hank, 136, 150, 249, 315
Bridges, Rodney, 175, 178, 179, 180
British 21st Army Group, 51
Brooks, Edward H., 27
Brooks, Paul H., 179
Brothers in Arms: The Epic Story of the 761st Tank Battalion, WWII's Forgotten Heroes (Abdul-Jabbar), 336
Broyles (lieutenant colonel), 232, 245, 297, 311, 312, 330
Brückner (caretaker), 352
Büches action, 206, 232
Büches advance command post, 244, 245
Büdingen, town of, 244–45
Büdingen command post, 297
Büdingen forest: assembly of American troops in, 97–100; assembly of German troops in, 106–7, 169, 224–25; as defensive line, 94; 5th Division's disposition in, 288–89; 5th Division's operations in, 243; 5th Infantry Regiment push into, 232; 14th Infantry Regiment's disposition in, 276–77; Nord Division's advance to, 93, 131–32, 284–85; 71st Division's disposition in, 278–80; Task Force X in, 160–61
Büdingen forest action: American commitment of forces to, 184–85; American coordination issues in, 287–88; American planning for, 162, 285–89; American step-off in, 294–97; artillery coordination in, 163; casualties in, 317; German defeat in, 317–18, 322; German escape ruse in, 285–86, 308; guerrilla activities

following, reports of, 318–20; initial conflict in, 298–302; liaison officers in, 289–90, 310–13; mopping-up action following, 318–20, 325; Nord Division stragglers in, 307; Nord Division strength in, 298; prisoners of war in, 300–301, 317; publicity concerning, 325–26; search for Brenner in, 303–4, 320–21, 323–25, 339–40; 71st Infantry Division command and control in, 307–8, 317–20; 71st Infantry Division's maneuvers prior to, 104; surrender protocol in, 277–78; treatment of wounded in, 313–15; Wyman's instructions for, 206

Burgstaller, Alois, 26, 28, 29, 30, 31, 34, 35, 36, 37
Burns, Delno, 123, 124
Burns, Foster C., 113
Burton, Alec C., 263–64

C

Calbach action, 233
Calhoun, William R., 129, 224
Calloway (captain), 104, 166
Camp Old Gold, 64
Canine, Ralph J., 118, 128, 129
Cannon (private first class), 220
"Cause of Death: Shot in the Head" (*Deutsche Wochenzeitung*), 355
Cecula, John F., 144, 145
Chamberlain, Rex, 274
Charleton (captain), 196, 215, 219
Cheves, Wallace R., 32, 33, 34, 37
Cohen, Harold, 113, 131, 132, 217, 218
Collier, Clay O., 162, 189, 190, 191, 208, 209
Colmar Pocket, 25

company designations, 20–21
concentration camps, 327
Connor, Robert E., 129, 130, 151, 152, 153, 154, 156, 163, 164, 209, 222, 223, 242, 288, 337
Cook, James, 219
Cooley, Harold T., 180
coordination issues, between U.S. forces, 153, 191, 192–93, 222, 229, 230, 242, 244, 278, 323–25
Cosma, Helen R., 113, 153
Cree, Morton, 295, 304

D

daylight savings time, 161, 172
Debes, Lothar, 8, 9
Degen, Günther, 14, 17, 58, 88
Demelhuber, Karl-Maria, 2, 4
Denno, Bryce F., 100, 216, 220, 225, 226, 227, 235, 236, 237, 239, 247, 261, 262, 263, 264, 265, 266, 273, 275, 283, 292, 334
Denslow, Melvin, 200
desertions, 167–68
Devers, Jacob, 24, 50, 51
Dickens, Randolph C., 106, 117, 128, 129, 163, 165, 221, 224
Dietl, Eduard, 3
Donohue, John E., 178
Dorsey, Mason, 123, 124, 125, 335
Dwyer, Godfrey V., 175, 177, 178, 179
Dyer, George, 119

E

Easter Sunday celebration, 105
Easton, Walter J., 103, 166, 307
Eddy, Manton S., 55, 89, 91, 92, 93, 96, 118, 119, 121, 152, 157, 165, 168, 170,

183, 221, 243, 254, 268, 278, 307, 317,
318, 319, 320, 327
Edinger, Joseph, 107
Edwards, Spencer P., 189
Ehlers (major), 27
Eidengesäss action, 103
Eikel, Gaston B., 100, 160, 183, 184, 188,
189, 193, 194, 195, 196, 200, 203, 215,
217, 218, 220, 236, 247, 267, 292, 293
Eiland, Marvin, 124
Eisenhower, Dwight D., 25, 51, 57, 71–72,
81, 90, 324
Ellison, Horace B., 227, 228, 238, 262, 263
Emde, Kendall W., 273
Erbstadt action, 151–53

F

Fahy, John J., 135
Feige, Hans, 2
Felber, Hans, 56, 60, 66, 72, 77, 80, 83
Ferrizzi, Joseph V., 178
Fighting Under the Northern Lights
 (Schreiber), 341
Final Solution, 327
Finland: Nord Division withdrawal from,
 12–19; in Operation Barbarossa, 3;
 Russian invasion of, 2; secret negotiations with Russia, 12; threats to
 Germany's alliance with, 9
Finnish Front, 3
Finnish III Corps, 3, 4, 7
Finnish-German Agreement, 2
Finnish-Soviet armistice, 16
Fisher, Laverne G., 248
Foley, William A., Jr., 47
Fonde (major), 113
Foreign Military Studies Branch,
 Historical Division, U.S. Army
 Europe, 340

Förster Leo, 350–51, 354
Foster, Kenneth W., 100, 161, 182, 217,
 308
"Four Rebels" armored car crew, 123–25
Frankfurt action, 105–6
Franz, Charles A., 178
fraternization, 319
Frederick, Robert T., 27, 30
Freeman, Nat R., 136, 140, 141
Friedly, Harold H., 179
*From the Paterson Station: The Way We
 Were* (Kinnard), 336
funkers (radiomen), 87, 93–94, 187, 272

G

G-2 Periodic Report Number 20, 218
Gaissmair, Michael, 9
Gardner, Dwight, 177
Gay, Hobart R., 121
*Gebirgsjäger im Bild: 6. SS-Gebirgsdivision
 Nord 1940-1945* (Steurich), 341
Gelnhaar action, 240–41, 252
Gelnhausen action: American movement
 toward, 104–5, 133–34; Brenner's
 plan to reinforce, 109, 131, 169; Nord
 Division's mission to join, 131–32,
 137, 172
Gelnhausen occupation, 101
Geneva Convention, 132, 218
German Army Group B, 25, 78, 84, 92
German Army Group G, 51, 52, 54, 84, 92
German Army Group H, 90
German Army Group South, 327
German battle groups. *See* Kampfgruppe
 entries
German 11th Panzer Division, 82
German 15th Armee, 83
German 1st Armee, 37, 51, 52, 53, 65, 72,
 73, 76, 81

German 559th Volksgrenadier Division, 44, 53, 56
German 4th Schwere (Heavy) Company, 55
German Front collapse, 84–85
German Grenadier Ersatz Battalions, 218
German labor camp, 250
German LXXX Korps, 53, 56, 72
German LXXXII Korps, 44, 72, 92
German LXXXIX Korps, 52, 54, 56, 57, 60, 65, 66, 78, 79, 83, 84, 92
German LXXXV Korps, 60, 82, 92
German 19th Armee, 51, 53
German Nord Division: advance to Büdingen forest, 93, 169, 284–85; atrocities ascribed to, 171, 248, 325–26; capture of ordnance company and field hospital by, 112–15, 118–19, 120, 122; capture of Waldensberg by, 180; company designations, 20–21; desertions from, 167–68; division strength, 7, 128, 131, 161, 167, 189, 217–18, 223, 234, 262, 284, 298; ethnicity of replacement troops, 5, 43; Finnish withdrawal of, 12–19; inexperience prior to Operation Barbarossa, 2; march discipline of, 131–32, 137; members' post-war activities, 339–46; news reports concerning, 325–26; orders to disband, 271; origins of, 1; propaganda efforts against, 67; reorganization as mountain division, 6–7; Rhine crossing by Americans and, 79, 83; in Saar defense, 52–53, 56, 66, 70; in Salla wilderness engagement, 4; as threat to XII Corps' command post, 268–69; in Trier-Niederzerf Road action, 46–49; on Western Front, 19–20, 24, 26

German Nord Division training battalion, 338–39
German Nord Division veterans' association, 340, 341, 345, 346
German Nord Division's horse-drawn column. *See* Kampfgruppe Goebel
German Nord Division's motorized column. *See* Kampfgruppe Raithel
German 159th Infanterie Division, 52, 53, 55, 78
German Panzer Division Hermann Göring, 227
German 2nd SS-Gebirgs Division, 44
German 7th Armee, 51, 52, 53, 54, 56, 65, 72, 76, 77, 80, 81, 92
German 7th SS-Freiwilligen (Volunteer)-Gebirgs Division "Prinz Eugen," 338–39
German 16th Volksgrenadier Division, 65
German 6th SS-Gebirgs Division Nord. *See* German Nord Division
German SS-Gebirgs Artillerie Regiment 6, 169
German SS-Gebirgs Nachrichten Battalion 6, 173
German SS-Gebirgs Panzerjäger Battalion 6, 270
German SS-Gebirgs Pioneer Battalion 6, 167
German SS-Gebirgs Reconnaissance Battalion 6, 53, 55, 57, 58, 87, 94, 338
German SS-Gebirgsjäger Regiment 11, 7, 9, 12, 14, 17, 23, 39, 42, 43, 46, 47, 48, 56, 57, 59, 68, 70, 79, 84, 85, 108, 167, 216, 225, 234
German SS-Gebirgsjäger Regiment 12, 7, 9, 12, 14, 17–18, 23, 28, 39, 40, 41, 43, 46, 47, 48, 53, 54, 57, 71, 339, 340

German SS-Infanterie Regiment 6, 3, 4
German SS-Infanterie Regiment 7, 3, 4, 5
German SS-Infanterie Regiment 9, 1, 4
German SS-og Polit Company, 8
German SS-Panzergrenadier Battalion 506, 28, 32, 33, 35, 41, 54, 339
German SS-Ski Battalion "Norge," 8, 40
German 10th Panzer Division, 117
German 38th SS-Panzergrenadier Division "Nibelungen," 339, 344
German 361st Volksgrenadier Division, 28, 30, 32, 33
German 25th Panzergrenadier Division, 25, 27, 34
German 21st Panzer Division, 25, 27, 34
German 256th Volksgrenadier Division, 41, 44
German 276th Infanterie Division, 52, 53, 70
German War Graves Commission, 354, 355
German XC Korps, 41, 44, 73
German XIII Korps, 53, 56, 66, 72, 81
German XIII SS Korps, 60, 73
German XIX Gebirgskorps, 12
German XVIII Gebirgskorps, 7
German XXXVI Korps, 3, 4, 12
Germersheim Bridge action, 73–76
Gerow, Leonard T., 90
Gettys, Charles M., 75, 160, 232, 295, 296, 297, 301, 302, 305, 308, 330–31
GI Bill, 336
GI's Forever (Tomich), 335
Gladenfeld, Martin, 271
Glauberg action, 206–9
Gliessner, Joe, 208
Goebel, Johann-Georg, 53, 57–58, 59, 68, 70, 85, 87, 94, 108, 131, 208, 224, 225, 241, 258, 259, 260, 321, 324. *See also* Kampfgruppe Goebel
Goldman, Harry T., 135, 137, 144, 146, 154, 209, 229, 230, 249, 250, 252, 294, 303
Gongeware, Gilbert, 220
Goodspeed (sergeant), 212
Gorry, George, 118, 119
Gossum, Felix, 147
Graham, Walter R., 337
Grambling, Freddie W., 239, 262, 263, 264, 265, 267, 272, 273, 274, 281, 282, 283
grave robbing, 345–46
Gray, Everett W., 237, 239, 261
Greatest Generation, 336–37
Gunskirchen Lager concentration camp, 327
Guthrie, Paul G., 99, 157, 161, 162, 182, 189, 209, 210, 214, 215, 231, 249, 277, 286, 316, 333
Guzzo (private), 309

H

Hagney, Frank J., 142, 144, 145, 146, 154, 332
Hahm, Walter, 46, 47, 48, 72, 92
Haislip, Wade H., 81, 82
Halter, Bryan S., 204
Hammelburg Raid, 80
Harmon, Chester, 196
Harrison, Henry A., 203
Harsla, Marion E., 175, 176, 180
Hausser, Paul, 51, 52, 53, 56, 66
heavy company, 20–21
Heegheim command post, 162
Hefner, Bill, 89
Heldenbergen action, 159, 163

Henning, Frank, 102, 120, 133, 191
Herms, Paul, 8
Herren, Thomas, 28, 33
Herrmann, Richard, 1
Heuer, Heinz, 353, 354
Heydrich, Reinhard, 8, 12, 326
Heymont, Irving, 97, 98, 246, 312, 330
Hilger, Eberhard, 88, 345
Hill, William A., 103, 166
Hill, Winston C., 180
Hill 267 action, 168; American artillery barrage in, 212; American plan of attack in, 209–11; artillery coordination in, 222; German artillery in, 224–25; German forces in, 207–8, 211–12; German sniper fire in, 212–13, 231; initial confrontation in, 206–9; mop-up in, 214–15; prisoners of war and, 211–12
Hitler, Adolf, 24, 25, 38, 53
Hochbaum, Friedrich, 9
Höchst occupation, 166
Hodges, Courtney H., 91
Hoehne, Gustav, 52, 53, 56, 60, 65, 68, 70, 83, 84, 85, 92
Howard (sergeant), 199
Hubbard, Samuel E., 99, 162, 215, 276
Hurt (major), 246

Ichelson, David L., 313–15, 331
Idstein action, 84
"Ike" jacket, 312, 313
Inciarrano, Jack, 248–49
Irwin, S. LeRoy, 77, 105, 117, 128, 129, 152, 156, 163, 165, 192, 221, 223, 242, 243, 244, 288, 320, 324, 327, 337

J

Jagoda, Stanley, 206
Jende, Johanna, 247, 350, 352
Jensen, Walter, 9
Johnson, Bernard C., 100, 121, 123, 125, 126, 127, 133, 138, 139, 158, 192, 253, 254, 279
Johnston, Oscar R., 120, 205
Joy, Dean P., 299, 300–301, 304, 305–7, 331

K

Kaczor, Joseph, 118, 119
Kainhaus (standartenoberjunker), 85, 86
Kaiserslautern Gap, 50, 51
Kaltenschnee, Johannes, 186–87, 275, 347–48
Kaminsky, George, 226
Kampf Unter Dem Nordlicht (Schreiber), 341
Kampfgruppe Goebel, 108, 109, 131, 132, 141, 144, 146, 147, 148, 149, 155, 165, 167, 168, 169, 187, 190, 205, 208, 210, 222, 224, 234, 240, 252, 257, 258–60, 261, 289, 302–3
Kampfgruppe Koblenz, 52, 60
Kampfgruppe Raithel, 108, 109, 131, 132, 137, 155, 156, 167, 175, 185, 187, 205
Kampfgruppe Schack, 3
Kampfgruppe Schreiber, 5
Kampfgruppe Stämmle, 33
Kampfgruppe Weilburg, 87–88, 95, 108
Kampfgruppe Wingen, 26, 28, 30, 33, 35, 36, 37
Karelian Isthmus, 2
Kasson, William N., 273
Kefenrod action, 258–60
Kennerly, Samuel E., 289–90, 310–13

Kesselring, Albert, 53–54, 60, 66, 79, 83, 84
Kieslewski, Brunislaus, 139
Kinnard, Douglas, 206–9, 210, 335–36
Kleinheisterkamp, Mathias, 7
Knapp (private first class), 263–64
Kniess (general der infanterie), 82, 83
Koblenz action, 60
Korpsgruppe von Gottberg, 11
Kraatz (lieutenant), 193
Kratz, Fred J., 196, 201, 215
Kress, Heinrich, 174
Kreuzinger, Kurt, 19, 24, 26, 34, 39, 342
Krichbaum, Milo D., 161, 277
Krüger, Egon, 68, 84, 132; in capture of ordnance company and field hospital, 111–13, 114–16; in Leisenwald action, 269–72; as messenger, 59–60; in Niederselters action, 85–87; postwar activities of, 342–43; reaction to African-American soldiers, 109–10
Krüger, Friedrich-Wilhelm, 9, 10
Kuusamo church bells, 14–15, 340–41

L

labor camps, 250
Lafargue, Lloyd A., 99, 154
Landrum, Eugene M., 62
Langendiebach command post, 157, 162
Langenselbold command post, 158
Langenselbold-Hailer-Gelnhausen line, 99
Lankenau, Norman H., 96, 99, 101, 102, 121, 123, 126, 127, 134, 158, 160, 182, 204, 205, 206, 229, 233, 246, 254, 268, 269, 278, 285, 287, 307, 318, 319
Lapp, K.W., 9
Lauterbach command post, 118, 221, 268–69, 279

Leisenwald action, 287; American Morse code transmissions during, 271; American preparation for, 262–64; artillery barrage in, 264–65; casualties in, 274–75, 283; civilians in, 275, 346–49; communications issues in, 278; German evacuation in, 272, 280; German preparation for, 234–35, 261–62; house-to-house fighting in, 265–66, 273–75; inaccurate reports concerning, 267–68; mopping-up action in, 292–93
Leisenwald massacre, 354–55
Leisenwald occupation, 186, 234
Lentz, John M., 118
liaison officers, 191, 192–93, 204, 222, 242, 289–90, 307
Lieber, Albert C., Jr., 243–44
Limburg action, 83–84
Limburg-Kirberg road defense, 84
Lingenfeld action, 74–75, 82
Lombard, Gustav, 10
Long, Perry J., 180
Long, Reuel, 343
Long, Roy J., 196, 198, 219, 220, 248, 335
Long, Tommy L., 161, 210, 316
Long (captain), 136, 137, 155, 156, 316
Lundquist, Carl E., 65, 74, 82, 98, 127, 135, 136, 140–41, 147, 156–57, 158, 159, 162, 189, 190, 192, 206, 209, 210, 215, 230, 242, 243, 253, 276, 285, 303, 315, 316, 331–32

M

M9 bazooka rounds, 101
Maack, Berthold, 10
MacArthur (captain), 188, 195, 198, 203, 215, 292

Main River bridgehead, 103
Main River crossing, 91, 101, 133–34
Mainz River bridgehead, 82
Mannerheim, Carl Gustav, 3
Marx (private), 219
massacre rumors, 325–26, 353–55
Mathews, Henry B., 238
Mathis, Jim, 124, 125
Mayfield, John W., 175, 177, 178, 180
Me262 jet, 231
Meiningen action, 326
Merkenfritz action, 256–57
Merrill, William J., 184, 229, 268, 308
Metcalfe, Arthur, 147
Middleton, Mrs. Warren, 332
Middleton, Troy H., 56, 78, 79, 91
military intelligence, 161; on German escape ruse, 285–86, 308
Montgomery, Bernard L., 51, 77
Morgan, A.C., 32, 33
Mortensen, Ray K., 144, 146
Moser, Ossi, 344
motti encirclement technique, 4, 5
"MS# B-715" (Brenner), 340
Müller, Karl, 208, 212, 213, 345
Muonio action, 16–18
Murmansk rail line, 3, 5
musical-chairs ruse, 256–57

N

Nagel, Elizabeth, 201
Neal (captain), 295, 301, 304, 305, 311
Nemeth (lieutenant), 112, 217, 218
Nestler, Walter, 270
Neu Isenburg assembly area, 95, 97
Nieder-Rodenbach occupation, 134
Niederselters action, 86–87
Normandy invasion, 21, 63, 96

Norwegian volunteers, in Nord Division, 8, 40

O

Oberbefehlshaber, 25
Oberkommando der Wehrmacht, 6, 9, 12, 20, 34
Ober-Mockstadt action, 229–30
Obstfelder, Hans von, 25, 83, 92
Ogden (staff sergeant), 199
Omaha Beach, 63, 96
Operation Barbarossa: Finnish role in, 2; German withdrawal plan in, 12; Russian counteroffensive in, 6, 8–10; Salla wilderness engagement in, 3–4
Operation Birke, 12, 14, 16–19
Operation Husky, 63, 227
Operation Nordwind: American inactivity following, 44; assault on Wingen-sur-Moder in, 30–32; failure of, 36, 37, 41; Kampfgruppe Wingen's mission in, 28; operational pause in, 34; planning of, 24–26; withdrawal from Wingen-sur-Moder, 34–35, 36
Operation Undertone, 51
Operation Wacht am Rhein, 20, 24–25, 51
Operations Instruction Number Nine, 189
Operations Instruction Number Seven, 319
Oppenheim Bridge action, 79–80
Orona, Jerry, 273
Orseske, George, 207

P

Pace, Beryl J., 223, 255, 288
Page, Glenn T., 179
panzerfaust, 26
Patch, Alexander, 24, 27, 51, 60, 81

Patton, George S., Jr., 25, 50, 51, 52, 54, 56, 57, 72, 77, 78, 80, 82, 89, 91, 113, 170, 239, 324–25, 327
Paul, Caleb H., 99, 161, 210
Paul, James M., 245, 313, 315, 331
Pellingen action, 47–48
Peterson (sergeant), 194
Pfaffenheck action, 56
Pfeiffer, John, 201
Philippi, Alfred, 29, 32, 34
plasma transfusion, 314
Plösch (sturmscharführer), 169, 208, 211, 212
Ponder, Lewington, 98, 102, 204, 289–90, 310–13, 331
Prekker, Willard E., 211, 214
prisoners of war: American, 42, 80, 106, 166, 204, 211–12, 253, 270, 280, 282; American nurses, 113–14; German, 99, 149, 161, 313–15, 327; German, in Waldensberg, 174–75, 179, 181–82, 202, 216, 234; German abandonment of, 172–73; German records concerning, 326; German treatment of, 132, 217–18; Germans disguised as, 285–86; interrogation of, 161
propaganda leaflets, 67, 319
psychological warfare assets, 136, 157

R
Rädeke, Ernst, 10, 14, 17
radio ranges, 101
Raithel, Helmuth, 38–39, 47, 49, 56, 57, 58, 70, 71, 85, 87, 94, 108, 110, 131, 169, 172, 185, 215, 216, 234, 261, 262, 271, 280, 301, 304, 320, 340, 341. *See also* Kampfgruppe Raithel
Rangell, Johann Wilhelm, 3
Ranstadt railroad line, 164
Ravolzhausen action, 204
Red Circle Division, 22, 62, 65. *See also* U.S. 71st Infantry Division
Red Diamond Division. *See* U.S. 5th Infantry Division
Reed, Charles H., 102, 103, 104, 166, 193, 243, 307, 319
Regnier, Augustus J., 65, 74, 99, 100, 121, 133, 160, 183, 184, 216, 220, 225, 226, 228, 267, 269, 278, 287, 288, 334
Reinsmith, Edward, 145
Reipertswiller action, 41–42
Rendulic, Lothar, 327
Reno, Robert V., 135, 144, 145, 146, 332
Renz, Gottlieb, 9
Rhatican, L.B., 125–26, 138, 139, 335
Rhine gorge action, 78–79
Rhine River crossing, 77, 78–79, 81, 83; by 71st Infantry Division, 88–89, 92–93; 71st Infantry Division in feint mission, 82
Rimple, Edward G., 211, 334
Roberts (private), 153
Robertson (major), 233, 244, 295, 297
Robinson, Donald E., 106, 116, 117, 127, 165, 182, 221, 225, 239, 240, 241, 256, 258, 259, 260, 337
Robinson, Jackie, 336
Rodenbach action, 141, 161
Roffe, A. Worrell, 117, 129, 130, 152, 163, 164, 209, 221, 223, 224, 241, 242, 288, 289, 337
Rohan, Johnny, 299, 300–301, 305, 306
Rolfe, Onslow, 61, 64, 134, 159, 192, 329
Roots, William E., 178–79
Ruhr industrial region, 77, 90, 324, 325
Rundstedt, Gerd von, 25, 51, 53

INDEX

Russian 5th Guards Airborne Division, 327
Russo-Finnish Winter War, 1–2

S

Saar-Palatinate area: as American objective, 49–50; bridgeheads as objectives in, 51–52, 57; casualties in, 76; German inability to defend, 66; German withdrawal from, 72; Germersheim Bridge action in, 73–76; industrial capacity of, 50; Lingenfeld action in, 74–75
Sacharow, Klaus, 349
Salla Wilderness action, 3–4
Samuell, Edward W., Jr., 100, 133, 138, 139, 215, 254, 256, 257, 335
Scheu, Karl-Hans, 55
Schmidt, Willi, 351
Schmidt, Karl, 351
Schmidt, Wilhelm, 174, 181, 199, 201, 275, 349–50
Schneider, Paul, 41
Schömerich action, 47
Schreiber, Franz, 5, 14, 15–16, 18, 21, 26, 28, 34, 38, 40, 47, 53, 54, 71, 340–41
Schröder, Herbert, 271, 299
Schüler, Josef, 353
Schütze, Bruno, 29
Seeliger, Jochen, 47–48, 345–46
Selters action, 158–59
Seven Days in January: With the 6th SS Mountain Division in Operation Nordwind (Zoepf), 342
Sicily landing, 227
Siegfried Line, 50, 51, 53, 54, 73
Sims, Leo A., 264, 277
Sims, W.P., 99, 161, 210, 211, 213, 214, 310, 333–34

Sixty Days in Combat: An Infantryman's Memoir of World War II in Europe (Joy), 331
Smith, E.E., 154, 251
Smith, Wint, 97
Snyder (colonel), 106, 128
Soviet-Finnish armistice, 16
Soviet Union. *See* Operation Barbarossa
Sowers, Ben, 178
Sparks, Felix L., 42
Spencer, Obediah, 227, 228, 293
Spragins, Robert L., 61, 62, 269
Staden action, 167
Stammheim action, 138–40, 141, 167
Stammheim command post, 224, 242
Standfield, Walter E., 136, 154
Stehley, William A., 194
Steinmetz, John F., 238, 263, 264
Sterling, Norman, 240, 259
Steurich, Alfred, 108, 167, 185, 216, 220, 234, 341
Stockheim action, 158–59
Stöwe, Georg, 93, 94, 187, 261, 271, 272, 284, 285, 299, 343–44
Sullivan, John L., 195, 200, 215, 291
supply train organization, 6
surrender protocol, 277–78
Swiggert, W.B., 151
Swope, William R., 135

T

Tank, Walter, 58–59, 68, 88
Tarbell (lieutenant), 201
Task Force Baum, 80
Task Force Herren, 28
Task Force Hudelson, 27
Task Force X, 182, 184; in action against roadblock, 187–89, 193; mission briefing, 189–90; standup of, 160–61;

in Waldensberg action, 193–94, 196–202, 215–17, 218
Taylor, George A., 96
Teuerkauf, Herbert, 344
Thala action, 117
Thode, Harry W., 211, 213, 277
Thomas, Everett C., 268, 288
"Todesursache Kopfschuss" *(Deutsche Wochenzeitung)*, 355
Tomich, Thomas C., 201, 219, 247, 292, 335
Tornio-Muonio road, 17–18
Traditions-Verband (Tradition Association), 340, 341, 345, 346
Trier-Niederzerf Road action, 46–49
Tripp, John, 196, 197, 219, 292–93
Tuhkalla-Suvanto action, 12, 14
Tyler, Frederick, L., 237, 239, 261

U

Ulmbach command post, 166
U.S. 80th Infantry Division, 54, 82, 83, 268
U.S. 803rd Tank Destroyer Battalion (U.S.), 117, 163, 240
U.S. 89th Infantry Division, 57, 65, 78, 79
U.S. 87th Infantry Division, 57, 60, 78, 79
U.S. 11th Armored Division, 56, 57, 65, 72, 92, 93, 105, 133, 268
U.S. 11th Infantry Regiment, 78
U.S. Fifteenth Army, 90
U.S. 5th Cavalry Reconnaissance Troop (mechanized), 106, 116, 117, 120, 165, 168, 182, 221, 225, 230, 239, 240–41, 252, 256, 258–59, 302
U.S. 5th Infantry Division, 77, 78, 80, 89, 92, 95, 105, 116, 123, 127, 151, 152, 158, 165, 184, 191, 192, 221, 223, 243, 249, 255, 324–25, 337

U.S. 5th Infantry Regiment, 65, 74, 75, 97, 102, 120, 121, 133, 157, 159, 160, 205, 229, 232, 233, 278; in Büdingen forest action, 295–97, 298–302, 304–7, 308, 309, 319; 1st Battalion, 224, 255–56, 279, 297, 311, 312; 2nd Battalion, 160, 223–24, 246, 286, 295, 298–302, 302, 304–7, 308; 3rd Battalion, 245, 286, 295, 296–97, 297, 309, 313
U.S. 50th Field Artillery Battalion, 129, 152, 156, 160, 222, 224, 229
U.S. First Army, 82, 90, 91, 171, 324, 325
U.S. 1st Infantry Division, 63, 96, 227
U.S. 45th Infantry Division, 27, 41–42, 60, 81
U.S. 44th Infantry Division, 269
U.S. 42nd Cavalry Squadron, 103, 166, 193, 203
U.S. 42nd Infantry Division, 65, 73
U.S. 14th Armored Division, 73
U.S. 14th Infantry Regiment, 65, 74, 82, 98, 120, 127, 129, 135, 159, 160, 161; in Büdingen forest action, 294–95, 302–4, 315–16; 1st Battalion, 162, 215, 276, 279; 2nd Battalion, 127, 133, 134, 135, 136, 142, 144–46, 147, 148, 149, 150, 154, 182, 190, 192, 209–11, 215, 229, 230, 242, 249, 250, 276–77, 285–86, 294, 295–97, 302, 315–16; 3rd Battalion, 158, 161, 190, 192, 209, 210, 211, 214, 249, 277, 286, 302
U.S. 4th Armored Division, 56, 57, 65, 66, 72, 77, 78, 79, 80, 91, 92, 164, 223, 231
U.S. Intelligence and Reconnaissance Platoon, 14th Infantry Regiment, 136, 140, 205
U.S. 90th Infantry Division, 56, 78, 92
U.S. 94th Infantry Division, 46, 47, 54

U.S. 9th Armored Division, 84, 85
U.S. 9th Infantry Division, 117, 253
U.S. Ninth Army, 90, 171, 324, 325
U.S. 180th Infantry Regiment, 31–32, 33, 35, 37
U.S. 157th Infantry Regiment, 42
U.S. 179th Infantry Regiment, 35, 37
U.S. 106th Cavalry Group, 103
U.S. 106th Evacuation Hospital, 113
U.S. 100th Infantry Division, 41, 60, 64, 65, 74, 89
U.S. 103rd Infantry Division, 89
U.S. 136th Quartermaster Truck Company, 113
U.S. 2nd Cavalry Group, 93, 102–3, 104, 131, 166, 193, 236, 237, 248, 263, 269, 282, 307, 311, 312, 319
U.S. 2nd Cavalry Squadron, 103, 166, 287
U.S. 2nd Infantry Regiment, 117, 123, 129, 151, 159, 223, 242; 1st Battalion, 288; 2nd Battalion, 255, 288; 3rd Battalion, 129, 154, 157, 163, 222, 242, 255
U.S. 749th Tank Battalion, 74, 89
U.S. 761st Tank Battalion, 89, 97, 98–99, 101, 120, 121, 133, 136, 142–45, 150, 160, 183, 200, 211, 228, 247, 249, 251, 286, 293, 316, 336
U.S. 737th Tank Battalion, 152, 165, 221, 224, 240, 255
U.S. Seventh Army, 24, 25, 27, 51, 52, 54, 60, 64, 81, 92, 93
U.S. 70th Infantry Division, 27–28
U.S. 71st Cavalry Reconnaissance Troop, 120, 123, 127, 128, 130, 133, 138, 152, 153, 158, 192, 215, 253–54, 256, 279, 319; elements of, 100–101
U.S. 71st Division Artillery, 156, 270

U.S. 71st Infantry Division, 22, 45, 60, 133; Büdingen forest action command and control, 307–8, 317–20; Büdingen forest action planning, 182, 285–89; combined-arms assets of, 97; communication assets of, 101; coordination and communications issues, 153, 191, 192–93, 222, 229, 230, 242, 244, 278, 323–25; early missions of, 64–65; in Germersheim Bridge action, 73–76; inactivation of, 329; origin of, 61; post-Büdingen forest operations of, 325–27; post-war activities of members of, 329–37; praise for actions of, 327–29; Rhine crossing by, 88–89, 92–93; in river-crossing feint mission, 82; training of, 64; transfer to Third Army, 89; in XII Corps' flank protection, 101, 120, 157, 226, 269
U.S. 71st Light Division, 61–62
U.S. 76th Infantry Division, 106
U.S. 608th Field Artillery Battalion, 158, 162, 190, 206
U.S. 609th Artillery Battalion, 133
U.S. 635th Tank Destroyer Battalion (towed), 97, 154, 212, 245
U.S. 620th Ordnance Company, 112–13, 118, 120, 122, 126, 141, 171, 326
U.S. 16th Field Hospital, 113–15, 116, 118–19, 120, 122, 151, 153, 164, 171, 326
U.S. 6th Armored Division, 80, 91
U.S. 6th Army Group, 50, 51, 90
U.S. 6th Cavalry Group, 79
U.S. 66th Infantry Regiment, 62, 65, 74, 75, 89, 98, 99, 101, 120, 121, 133, 157, 158, 159, 160, 204, 278; in Büdingen forest action, 304, 308–9, 319; 1st

Battalion, 268, 269, 288; ranger platoon, 226, 228; 2nd Battalion, 160, 183, 236, 246, 267, 287, 291, 304, 308–9, 319; Task Force X, 183, 184, 187–89, 189–90, 193, 196–202, 215–17, 218; 3rd Battalion, 235, 237, 238, 239, 261, 263, 275, 278, 281–82, 287, 288, 292, 319

U.S. task forces. *See* Task Force entries

U.S. 10th Armored Division, 54–55, 57, 65, 73

U.S. 10th Armored Infantry Battalion, 113

U.S. 10th Infantry Regiment, 107, 152, 165

U.S. Third Army, 25, 50, 51, 52, 54, 72, 81, 82, 83, 89, 91, 92, 170, 171, 324

U.S. 3rd Infantry Division, 60, 81

U.S. 13th Armored Division, 224, 324, 325

U.S. 36th Infantry Division, 60

U.S. 347th Infantry Regiment, 58

U.S. 314th Infantry Regiment, 35

U.S. 328th Infantry Regiment, 287, 319

U.S. 12th Armored Division, 65, 72, 73, 74, 75, 81

U.S. 12th Army Group, 51, 82, 90, 91, 325

U.S. 21st Field Artillery Battalion, 222

U.S. 26th Infantry Division, 54, 92, 103, 105, 268, 287, 319

U.S. 276th Infantry Regiment, 32–33

U.S. 271st Engineer Battalion, 245, 278

U.S. VI Corps, 60, 73, 81, 82

U.S. VIII Corps, 52, 78, 79, 83, 84, 91

U.S. XII Corps, 52, 54, 55, 72, 77, 89, 91, 92, 96, 101, 103, 113, 120, 123, 128, 133, 157, 158, 170, 174, 221, 242, 268, 279, 287, 324

U.S. XII Corps Artillery, 156

U.S. XV Corps, 60, 61, 64, 81, 82, 96, 269

U.S. XX Corps, 52, 54, 57, 65, 72, 82, 91, 92, 106, 116, 118, 128, 324

U.S. XXI Corps, 60, 73, 81, 82

Usingen action, 95, 106–7

Utrup, Edward R., 309, 310

V

Vanderveer, Harnold C., 222

Veldhuis, Frank, 178

Vincent (private), 306

Volksbund Deutscher Kriegsgräberfürsorge, 354, 355

W

Waffen-SS divisions: 1943 reorganization program for, 8; American propaganda concerning, 319; competency of, 159, 168; fighting spirit of, 171

Wagner, John H., Jr., 195, 200

Wagner, Karl, 275

Waldensberg action, 167, 234, 287; American advance guard arrival in, 174–75; American casualties in, 246; burial of dead following, 352–55; civilians in, 198, 199, 201–2, 247, 349–55; commemoration of, 352; German advance column in, 175; German counterattack in, 220–21; German mission in, 202; German prisoners of war and, 174–75, 179, 181–82, 202, 234; initial contact in, 177–80; mopping-up action in, 291–92; Nord Division capture of town in, 180, 196; Nord Division delay caused by, 185; roadblock impact in, 176, 177, 185–86, 312; sniper fire in, 198; Task Force X in, 193–94, 196–202, 215–17, 218

Waldensberg massacre, 353–55

Walker, Walton H., 54, 82, 91, 128
Wallan (sergeant), 239
Walsensberg-Wittgenborn roadblock action, 187–89, 193, 312
Warnock, Alan D., 222, 223, 242
Waters, John K., 80, 113
Weber, Gerd, 173, 176, 344
Weiherhof action, 310–11, 350–51
Weilburg officer-candidate school, 87–88
"Werewolf" groups, 271
White, Arthur A., 329
Whitehead, Don, 96
Wicker, Coy, 276
Wickstadt action, 138
Wiesbaden officer candidate school, 78
Williams, Carl R., 124
Wingen-sur-Moder action, 26, 27, 28, 30–37
Wirtheim occupation, 166
Wojciechowski, Walter S., 174, 175
Wolferborn action, 283
Wommer, Karl-Heinz, 271
Wooten, Sidney C., 65, 74, 97–98, 134, 160, 184, 185, 204, 206, 229, 232, 233, 244, 245, 278, 297, 302, 303, 307, 309, 311, 312, 330
Wyles, Eben R., 176, 177, 186, 193, 203, 312
Wyman, Willard G., 22, 45, 61, 63–64, 75, 89, 95, 96, 98, 101, 104, 120, 121, 122, 127, 134, 157, 158, 159, 160, 162, 166, 182, 183, 184, 185, 192, 204, 205, 206, 218, 243, 254, 268, 269, 276, 278, 287, 297, 307, 317, 319, 320, 323, 324, 326, 327–28, 329

Z

Zarimba (corporal), 305, 306
Zinswiller action, 42–43
Zoepf, Wolf, 24, 26, 341, 342
Zydowitz, Karl von, 339

About the Author

Lt. Col. (Ret.) Stephen M. Rusiecki is Dean of Academics and Deputy Commandant of the U.S. Army Inspector General School at Fort Belvoir, Virginia. He is also the author of a book on the Battle for Losheimergraben.

The Naval Institute Press is the book-publishing arm of the U.S. Naval Institute, a private, nonprofit, membership society for sea service professionals and others who share an interest in naval and maritime affairs. Established in 1873 at the U.S. Naval Academy in Annapolis, Maryland, where its offices remain today, the Naval Institute has members worldwide.

Members of the Naval Institute support the education programs of the society and receive the influential monthly magazine *Proceedings* or the colorful bimonthly magazine *Naval History* and discounts on fine nautical prints and on ship and aircraft photos. They also have access to the transcripts of the Institute's Oral History Program and get discounted admission to any of the Institute-sponsored seminars offered around the country.

The Naval Institute's book-publishing program, begun in 1898 with basic guides to naval practices, has broadened its scope to include books of more general interest. Now the Naval Institute Press publishes about seventy titles each year, ranging from how-to books on boating and navigation to battle histories, biographies, ship and aircraft guides, and novels. Institute members receive significant discounts on the Press's more than eight hundred books in print.

Full-time students are eligible for special half-price membership rates. Life memberships are also available.

For a free catalog describing Naval Institute Press books currently available, and for further information about joining the U.S. Naval Institute, please write to:

> Member Services
> **U.S. Naval Institute**
> 291 Wood Road
> Annapolis, MD 21402-5034
> Telephone: (800) 233-8764
> Fax: (410) 571-1703
> Web address: www.usni.org

www.ingramcontent.com/pod-product-compliance
Lightning Source LLC
Chambersburg PA
CBHW060348080526
44583CB00012B/214